Software Process Improvement

Software Process Improvement

Edited by Robin B. Hunter and Richard H. Thayer
Foreword by Mark C. Paulk

Original contributions by

Victoria Hailey	Sandra G. McGill
Robin B. Hunter	Terence P. Rout
Capers Jones	Sandy Shrum
Mike Konrad	Marty Sanders
Herb Krasner	Richard H. Thayer

IEEE
COMPUTER
SOCIETY

http://computer.org

Los Alamitos, California

Washington • Brussels • Tokyo

Library of Congress Cataloging-in-Publication Data

Software process improvement / edited by Robin B. Hunter
and Richard H. Thayer ; foreword by Mark C. Paulk.
p. cm.
Includes bibliographical references.
ISBN 0-7695-0999-1
1. Computer software--Development. I. Hunter, Robin, 1938- II.
Thayer, Richard H.
QA76.76.D47 S6634 2001
005.1--dc21

2001005212

IEEE Computer Society Press Order Number BP00999
Library of Congress Number 2001005212
ISBN 0-7695-0999-1

Additional copies may be ordered from:

IEEE Computer Society	IEEE Service Center	IEEE Computer Society
Customer Service Center	445 Hoes Lane	Asia/Pacific Office
10662 Los Vaqueros Circle	P.O. Box 1331	Watanabe Building
P.O. Box 3014	Piscataway, NJ 08855-1331	1-4-2 Minami-Aoyama
Los Alamitos, CA 90720-1314	Tel: +1-732-981-0060	Minato-ku, Tokyo 107-0062
Tel: +1-714-821-8380	Fax: +1-732-981-9667	JAPAN
Fax: +1-714-821-4641	http://shop.ieee.org/store/	Tel: +81-3-3408-3118
http://computer.org/	customer-service@ieee.org	Fax: +81-3-3408-3553
csbooks@computer.org		tokyo.ofc@computer.org

Publisher: Angela Burgess
Group Managing Editor, CS Press: Deborah Plummer
Advertising/Promotions: Tom Fink
Production Editor: Anne Jacobs
Printed in the United States of America

IEEE
COMPUTER
SOCIETY

Software Process Improvement
Table of Contents

Chapter 4: Software Process Improvement: How To Do It

Chapter 5: Developments Following from the SW-CMM

Chapter 6: Software Product Evaluation

Chapter 7: ISO 9000 Series and TickIT

Chapter 8: The SPICE Project

Chapter 9: Experiences of Software Process Assessment

Chapter 10: Software Process Improvement for Small Organizations

Chapter 11 Benefits of Software Process Improvement

Chapter 12: Software Process

Appendix

Contributors of Original Papers

Mr. Jon K. Digerness (illustrator)
North Coast Graphics
7418 Kanai Avenue
Citrus Heights, California 95621
USA
j.digerness@juno.com

Ms. Victoria A. Hailey, CMC
The Victoria Hailey Group Corporation
P.O. Box 334
Thornhill, Ontario L3T 4A2
Canada
vah@vhg.com

Dr. Robin B. Hunter
Department of Computer and Information
Sciences
University of Strathclyde
Richmond Street
Glasgow G1 1XH
United Kingdom
rbh@cis.strath.ac.uk

Mr. Capers Jones
Software Productivity Research, Inc.
6 Lincoln Knoll
Burlington, Massachusetts
USA
capers@spr.com

Dr. Mike Konrad
Software Engineering Institute
Carnegie Mellon University
Pittsburgh, Pennsylvania 15213-3890
USA
mdk@sei.cmu.edu

Dr. Herb Krasner
Krasner Consulting
1901 Ringtail Ridge
Austin, Texas 78746
USA
hkrasner@cs.utexas.edu

Ms. Sandra G. McGill
Lockheed Martin Corporation
Space Systems Company
Missiles and Space Operations
1111 Lockheed Martin Way
B153, O/L7-27
Sunnyvale, California 94089
USA
sandy.mcgill@lmco.com

Mr. Mark C. Paulk
Software Engineering Institute
Carnegie Mellon University
Pittsburgh, Pennsylvania 15213
USA
mcp@sei.cmu.edu

Mr. Terence P. Rout
Software Quality Institute
Griffith University
Faculty of Information and
Communication Technology
School of Computing and Information
Technology
Nathan, Brisbane 4111
Queensland, Australia
T.Rout@sqi.gu.edu.au

Ms. Sandy Shrum
Software Engineering Institute
Carnegie Mellon University
Pittsburgh, Pennsylvania 15213-3890
USA
sshrum@sei.cmu.edu

Ms. Marty Sanders
Sanders Enterprises
Turravagaun, Dromineer
Nenagh, County Tipperary
Ireland
martys@iol.ie

Dr. Richard H. Thayer
Software Management Consultants
Carmichael, California 95608
USA
r.thayer@computer. org

Foreword

Mark C. Paulk
Software Engineering Institute
Carnegie Mellon University
Pittsburgh, Pennsylvania

Anyone familiar with computers is aware, frequently painfully so, of the "software crisis." Our ability to build software-intensive systems is orders of magnitude greater today than it was five decades ago, but our appetite for software has grown even faster, and the software industry is still evolving from a craft into an engineering discipline. Historically, the result has been the chronic software crisis: Software is (almost) always released later than expected, more expensive than planned, and has less functionality than hoped.

The importance of high-quality software products cannot be overemphasized. Recent U.K. court decisions foreshadow a potential for legal action by dissatisfied customers: The concept that software should be sold free of major bugs and should work as intended, like other commercial goods, may be a major paradigm shift for many software developers!

Is there any hope that we will ever overcome the software crisis? Many different strategies have been tried: structured programming, joint application development, rapid prototyping, CASE tools, object-oriented everything, and so forth. During the last decade, the software process movement has moved to the forefront of our attempts to slay the software dragon. Software process has both proponents and detractors. While many see the value of continually examining and improving the way we do our work, others are concerned with the potential for abuses that process models and standards can engender.

During the last decade, the data on the increasing ability of mature software organizations to deliver high-quality software products on budget and on schedule indicate that the proponents of software process are right—at least for that part of the software community that has adopted a systematic approach to software process improvement. There is also evidence that some organizations have installed bureaucratic, inflexible processes that are counterproductive in terms of cost, schedule, quality, and predictability. There are both good and bad ways of pursuing process improvement.

At this writing, it is fair to say that only a minority of software organizations has chosen to pursue systematic improvement. The crux of the problem is that disciplined software engineering is easy to describe but devilishly hard to do. To remain competitive, however, software organizations are challenged to build more functionality faster, more cheaply, and to higher standards. It is impossible to address such wide-ranging goals without systematically changing the way we work.

Much of the problem lies in the fact that "changing the way we do things around here" requires behavioral change across the board. True software process improvement requires that management, especially executives, take an active role in process improvement. It also requires that the workers in the trenches participate in defining and implementing usable and effective processes. This means a diversion from the "real work" of shipping product. If software process improvement is considered a "silver bullet" rather than an investment in the future, then it will wind up being another "flavor of the month" fad, and its potential will never be realized.

Improvement also implies facing a sometimes unpleasant reality. Some of the pain of the software crisis is caused by human nature. In response to the question "Why does software cost so much?", Jerry Weinberg replies "Compared to what?" Tom DeMarco suggests that this assertion is a negotiating position; people complain because they know we work harder when they complain. In one survey, most of the responding professional software managers reported that their estimates were dismal, but they were not on the whole dissatisfied with the estimating process! All too many software professionals would agree with DeMarco, but many software managers and customers are vitally interested in understanding how to manage software projects more effectively.

Customers and managers who use schedule pressure and overtime as motivational tools have to deal with the resulting quality trade-off. If they are interested in truly managing software projects, they have available a number of approaches for systematically improving the process for developing and maintaining software. The results of successfully applying these approaches give us hope that the software crisis is finally coming to an end.

In spite of the fact that only a fraction of the software organizations in the world are doing systematic process improvement, it is heartening that the number is growing rapidly, as evidenced by the number of people attending the annual Software Engineering Process Group (SEPG) Conference, the increasing number of national SEPG conferences around the world, and the growth in software process improvement networks (SPINs), where software professionals can discuss their problems and successes. It is also encouraging that the number of high-maturity organizations is growing rapidly, and that increasing numbers of organizations are reporting their successes in using measurement and statistical control techniques.

Perhaps the best-known approaches to software process improvement are the International Organization for Standardization's ISO 9001 standard for quality management systems, the Software Engineering Institute's (SEI's) Capability Maturity Model$^{®}$ for Software, and the proposed ISO/IEC 15504 (frequently referred to as SPICE) standard for software process assessment. These approaches, among others, apply total quality management principles to the software process. In addition to these organizationally based approaches, the SEI's Personal Software Process^{SM} and Team Software Process^{SM} are applying process rigor to the individual practitioner and the team.

Having led the development of the Software CMM, I have a biased view of the various approaches to software process improvement. While I believe that the Software CMM is the best foundation for software process improvement, any systematic approach to improvement can help an organization succeed. Regardless of the approach chosen, process improvement is becoming essential to survival in today's highly competitive world.

To survive, much less thrive, modern organizations must continually improve all aspects of their business. Improvement in software-intensive products and services is crucial—and difficult. The challenge is to implement good software engineering and management practices in the high-pressure environments that software organizations face. A disciplined and systematic approach to software process and quality improvement, such as these models and standards support, is necessary to survive and thrive.

Process improvement is not, however, sufficient for success. Issues such as

- Building the right product—one that customers want to buy;

$^{®}$ Capability Maturity Model and CMM are registered with the U.S. Patent and Trademark Office.
^{SM} Personal Software Process, PSP, Team Software Process, and TSP are service marks of Carnegie Mellon University.

- Selecting, hiring, and retaining competent staff; and

- Overcoming organizational barriers (for example, between systems engineering and the software staff)

are also fundamental to success. An effective software process improvement program should be aligned with other organizational initiatives, perhaps under a total quality management or Six Sigma umbrella, to address the totality of business issues that are related to process improvement.

Regardless of the approach selected, the process of building a competitive advantage should focus on improvement, not on achieving a score, whether the score is a maturity level, a certificate, or a process profile. This collection of articles should help the reader understand the trade-offs and issues associated with effective software process improvement.

Preface

The purpose of this tutorial is to provide within one volume a significant and useful proportion of the accumulated expertise on Software Process Improvement (SPI). Software Process Improvement has been practised for almost twenty years now, but received a considerable boost around 1987 when the Software Engineering Institute (SEI) in Pittsburgh first launched its Capability Maturity Model, now known as the Capability Maturity Model for Software, or the SW-CMM, in its shortened form.

The SW-CMM has been extremely influential in the area. Not only has it developed considerably over the years, but it also has spawned other related, but sometimes competing, methods of software process improvement such as TRILLIUM, BOOTSTRAP, and ISO/IEC 15504/SPICE. Software Process Improvement is of course based on Software Process Assessment (SPA), and this tutorial charts the development of SPA and SPI from 1987 until the start of the millennium, and beyond.

This tutorial is a collection of new and prepublished papers concerned with SPA and SPI. The prepublished papers have been chosen for their tutorial nature, in that they introduce each topic and explain its ramifications in a way that is interesting and informative to the reader. Where we have not been able to find a suitable prepublished paper in an area we consider essential, we have commissioned a new paper of a tutorial nature from a leading international expert in the field.

The effect has been to provide a broad coverage of SPI that should be valuable to readers in the following groups:
- Software managers who wish to learn about the benefits of, and the requirements, for SPI
- Software process staff who require to understand the mechanisms of SPA and SPI
- Software developers who are affected by SPI and require to understand how it involves them
- College level students who wish to understand the various methods of SPA and SPI and to be able to compare their relative benefits and limitations

We think the following features will be particularly useful to these readers:
- The emphasis on international standards, especially ISO 9000, ISO/IEC 9126 and ISO/IEC 15504, but also ISO/IEC 12207 and ISO/IEC 14598
- The chapter on software product evaluation, a topic not covered much in the literature, but complimentary to SPA
- The chapter on SPI for small organizations that collects together a useful body of experience in this area
- The practical information in Chapter 4 entitled Software Process Improvement: How to Do It.
- The chapter on ISO 9000 and TickIT that provides an alternative approach to SPA to that provided by CMM type models, and includes up to date developments on the ISO 9000 series.
- The original paper in Chapter 5 by Mike Konrad and Sandy Shrum giving the latest information on the CMM Integration (CMMI) project

This is a particularly apt time to produce a tutorial on SPI, as there are strong signs of convergence between the alternative approaches to the topic. This can be seen at three levels.
- Convergence between ISO/IEC 12207 and ISO/IEC 15504: the process dimension of 15504 is already very close to 12207, and in the 15504 standard now emerging it seems likely that a range of models including 12207 will be acceptable as the process dimension

- Convergence between CMMI and ISO/IEC 15504: CMMI is more broadly based than the SW-CMM and has a continuous as well as discrete view, which makes it more similar to 15504 than the SW-CMM was
- Convergence between ISO 9000 series and ISO/IEC 15504 through the new improvement based approach seen in the emerging standards of the ISO 9000 series

For all these reasons this seems a good time to publish a tutorial providing a comprehensive coverage of software process improvement.

Chapter One of the tutorial introduces the topics of SPA and SPI. In particular, the "big three" methods of SPA and SPI, SW-CMM, ISO 9000 and ISO/IEC 15504/SPICE are introduced and their relative benefits and future directions are discussed. Other methods are also discussed and a web site showing the plethora of approaches to SPA and SPI is referenced.

Chapter Two describes the development of the SW-CMM (formerly just the CMM) from its release by the SEI in 1987 until the development of its latest version, version 1.1. Chapter Three is concerned with other approaches to software process assessment, some (but not all) of which were inspired by the SW-CMM. Chapter Four contains practical advice on how to manage SPI, including an extended version of a prepublished paper on how to manage the software process statistically. Chapter Five is concerned with developments from the SW-CMM, including Humphrey's PSP (Personal Software Process) and TSP (Team Software Process) as well as an original paper on the CMMI (CMM integration) project.

Chapter Six is on software product evaluation and Chapter Seven is on the ISO 9000 series applied to software and the UK scheme TickIT. Chapter Eight is about the SPICE project, set up to support the production of the emerging international standard for software process assessment and improvement, ISO/IEC 15504. Chapter Nine is concerned with experiences of SPA, including experiences gained by follow up investigations by the SEI, experiences from the SPICE trials, the results of reliability studies performed in the context of the SPICE trials, and some European experiences of software process improvement.

Chapter Ten of the tutorial addresses the issues of SPI for small companies (those with less than 50 IT personnel) in the context of each of the "big three" methods of SPA and SPI, while Chapter Eleven describes the benefits of SPI, both qualitative and quantitative, including Return on Investment (ROI) issues.

Chapter Twelve provides a more general look at the software process, including process programming and process modeling. It takes a critical look at software process work up to now, and the issues that need to be concentrated on in the future.

The preface and the chapter introductions are each illustrated by a cartoon by Jon K. Digerness. The theme of the cartoons is food and drink and their preparation, and the cartoons follow the fortunes of three trainee chefs in a variety of circumstances. This theme was chosen as a metaphor for the software production process which itself cannot be readily pictured.

The glossary contains the meanings of a large number of technical terms used in SPA and SPI. In most cases the definitions are taken from international standards.

Software Process Improvement has been a rapidly developing area but one that now shows clear signs of maturity. While the area will continue to develop, many of the papers in this tutorial will be seen in the future as describing important steps in its growth to maturity.

It has been a great pleasure to put this tutorial together. The editors would like to express their appreciation to those authors who have allowed their papers to be reprinted in it, and to those authors who have willingly gone to so much trouble to provide original papers. More specific acknowledgements appear below.

Acknowledgements

Our sincere thanks go to Jon K. Digerness for the excellent cartoons that provide some light relief to what hopefully is not too dull a text, to Mildred C Thayer for her work on the Glossary and to Anne Jacobs and her colleagues of the IEEE Computer Society Press for their painstaking work in preparing the text for the press.

Robin B. Hunter
Richard H. Thayer

November 2000

Chapter 1

Software Process Assessment

1. Introduction to Chapter

The production of high quality software on time and within budget has largely eluded the software industry world-wide for several decades now. What became known as the "software crisis"—a term coined in the late sixties—has refused to go away. As software has become more pervasive, as well as becoming larger and more complex, so the opportunities for software 'disasters' caused by faulty or overdue software have become much greater, more than offsetting any improvements to software development and maintenance methods. Consideration of software development and maintenance as an engineering discipline, and control of the processes involved, however, have helped to alleviate the situation and offer hope for the future.

When the term "software engineering" was introduced in 1969 [7], it was hailed as identifying an approach to software production that would lead to an engineering-type process for developing (and maintaining) software. Since then, significant contributions to the development of software engineering been made, including

1

- the use of structured analysis and design,

- the introduction of the object-oriented approach to software development,

- the application of software measurement.

While the benefits of the engineering approach have been real and significant, software "disasters" continue to occur and , according to Curtis [2], 25 percent of software projects still do not reach fruition, many projects are up to 40 percent over budget, and project schedules are only met about half of the time.

The emphasis on the engineering aspects of software development and maintenance can lead to an overemphasis on the use of methods and tools to produce software products, whereas it is now being realized that people and process issues also have to be addressed if quality products are to be produced. People issues arise in software development and maintenance due to the fact that they are largely human-based activities. Support for the tedious, and some of the error prone, parts of the process can, and should be, supported by tools where appropriate. However the creative parts of the process, including the design, are largely performed by people and, inevitably, the quality of the software product depends on the abilities of, and the care taken by, the people involved in its production and maintenence.

The process approach to software development and maintenance attempts to model all significant aspects of software development and maintenance. The ultimate aim of this approach is to produce software in a controlled way that will be on time, within budget, and of appropriate quality. The process approach is not so much concerned with the use of particular methods or tools but more with using a well-defined and controlled process that may be supported by appropriate methods and tools.

According to Humphrey [4], the software process is defined as

The set of activities, methods, and practices that are used in the production and evolution of software.

At the heart of the process approach to software development and maintenance/evolution is the concept of Software Process Assessment (SPA), which is concerned with assessing a software process against a process standard or framework. Such a standard or framework would normally incorporate a number of achievement levels of increasing sophistication. For example, the Capability Maturity Model for Software (SW-CMM) developed by the Software Engineering Institute (SEI) in Pittsburgh has five levels of achievement.

Software Process Assessment can be used for a number of purposes, the two principal ones being

- *Capability Determination* (CD), used by software procurers to determine the capability of potential contractors;

- *Software Process Improvement* (SPI), used by software producers to improve their software processes in line with their business aims.

In addition, the results of process assessments are sometimes used to represent the state of the practice in software development, though this should only be done with care, as the sample used for this purpose is rarely representative of the industry as a whole.

While the original purpose of SPA was primarily capability determination, it is now used extensively for SPI and it is with SPI that this tutorial is principally concerned. However, process improvement depends on process assessment, and much of this tutorial will also be concerned with SPA.

The notions of process assessment and process improvement are not unique to software but have been developed from more general notions, including:

- Shewart's [8] Plan-Do-Check-Act cycle for quality improvement, developed in the 1930's;

- Juran's [6] four steps to quality improvement:

  - Collect defect data

  - Develop a theory

  - Test the theory

  - Implement corrective actions;

- Deming's [3] approach to continuous improvement.

2. Description of Articles

The first paper in this chapter introduces and summarizes the main approaches to software process improvement. It is by Mark Paulk and is entitled "Models and Standards for Software Process Assessment and Improvement". In it Paulk introduces and describes the "big three" methods for assessing software products:

- ISO 9000 – Quality Management Systems (see Chapter 7);

- SW-CMM (The Capability Maturity Model for Software) (see Chapter 2);

- ISO/IEC 15504/SPICE (see Chapter 8).

For each of these methods, he provides an overview, describes the method and its context, identifies its strengths and weaknesses, and discusses its future. In addition, the paper covers more briefly some other methods of process assessment such as Bootstrap (see Chapter 3), SDCE (Software Development and Capability Evaluation) [1], TRILLIUM (see Chapter 3), and Software Productivity Research (see Capers Jones [5] and Chapter 3).

In the conclusions to the paper, Paulk suggests that an organization will normally choose to use one of the "big three" methods of process assessment, based on the environment in which the organization operates. For example, large US companies will tend to use the SW-CMM, while multinational companies may tend to use ISO/IEC 15504/SPICE since it is an emerging international standard specific to software assessment. The international series of standards ISO 9000 was pioneered for use with software in the United Kingdom. The series tends to be used most (at least in its software context) in Europe, as well as in certain other countries such as Japan and India.

The Paulk paper also contains a large number of references to published work in the area as well as references to websites where more information concerning the various software assessment methods may be found. More details of many of them can also be found in later chapters of this volume, and in the references associated with these chapters.

The second paper in the chapter is frequently referenced. It is entitled "The Frameworks Quagmire" and is by Sarah Sheard. The author categorizes the various frameworks by the purpose served, which may be one or more of

- Standards and Guidelines
- Process Improvement Models and Internal Appraisal Methods
- Contractor Selection Vehicles
- Quality Awards
- Software Engineering Life Cycle Models
- System Engineering Models

Each of the purposes is described in detail and the characteristics of seven of the frameworks are outlined. While the author sees signs of consolidation of the current frameworks as an encouraging trend, she also draws attention the complexity of the current situation in one of the figures in the paper.

The author gives a reference to a clickable version of the quagmire available on the internet, itself a valuable source of information on the various schemes and frameworks for software quality. The actual website where the "quagmire'" is shown has been updated since the illustration shown in the paper was created and is well worth consulting.

References

[1] P. Babel; "Software Development Capability Evaluation: An Integrated System and Software Approach", *Crosstalk*, volume 10, 1997, pp. 3-7.

[2] B. Curtis; "Building a Cost Benefit Case for Software Process Improvement," Tutorial at 7th Software Engineering Process Group Conference, Boston, 1995.

[3] W. E. Deming; *Out of Crisis*, Cambridge University Press, 1982.

[4] W. S. Humphrey; *Managing the Software Process*, Addison Wesley, 1989, p. 249

[5] C. Jones; *Software Quality: Analysis and Guidelines for Success*, International Thomson Press, 1997.

[6] J. M. Juran; "Product Quality—A Prescription for the West"; *Management Review*, June 1981.

[7] P. Naur, B. Randell (eds); *Software Engineering: A Report on a Conference Sponsored by the NATO Science Committee*, NATO, 1969.

[8] W. Shewart; *Economic Control of Quality of the Manufactured Product*, Van Nostrand, 1981.

Models and Standards for Software Process Assessment and Improvement

Mark C. Paulk

Software Engineering Institute
Carnegie Mellon University
Pittsburgh, PA 15213-3890
Tel: +1 (412) 268-5794
Fax: +1 (412) 268-5758
Internet: mcp@sei.cmu.edu

Abstract

The "software crisis" has inspired a number of efforts by software suppliers and customers to improve the state-of-the-practice in building software. This chapter provides an overview of models and standards underlying the three best-known approaches to software process improvement: the ISO 9001 standard for quality management systems, the Software Engineering Institute's Capability Maturity Model® for Software, and the proposed ISO/IEC 15504 standard for software process assessment. Other approaches are also briefly discussed, including the SEI's Personal Software Process[SM] and Team Software Process[SM].

Keywords: Capability Maturity Model for Software, CMM®, IDEAL[SM], ISO 9000-3, ISO 9001, ISO/IEC 12207, ISO/IEC 15504, software process assessment, software process improvement, Personal Software Process[SM], PSP[SM], SPICE, Team Software Process[SM], TickIT, TSP[SM].

"Software Process Appraisal and Improvement: Models and Standards" by Mark C. Paulk from *Advances in Computers: The Engineering of Large Systems*, Volume 46, edited by Marvin Zelkowitz, copyright ©1998 by Academic Press, reprinted by permission of the publisher. All rights of reproduction in any form reserved.

Outline

1. Introduction

2. ISO 9000 – Quality Management Systems

    2.1 An Overview of ISO 9001

    2.2 Placing ISO 9001 in Context

    2.3 ISO 9000 Certification

    2.4 Strengths and Weaknesses of ISO 9000

    2.5 The Future of ISO 9000

3. The Capability Maturity Model for Software

    3.1 An Overview of the Software CMM

    3.2 Placing the Software CMM in Context

    3.3 CMM-Based Appraisals

    3.4 Strengths and Weaknesses of the Software CMM

    3.5 The Future of the Software CMM

4. ISO 15504 – An International Standard for Software Process Assessment

    4.1 An Overview of ISO 15504

    4.2 An Overview of the ISO 15504-2 Reference Model

    4.3 Strengths and Weaknesses of ISO 15504

    4.4 The Future of ISO 15504

5. Other Models and Standards

6. Conclusions

References

1. Introduction

The size, complexity, and power of software-intensive systems have exploded since the beginning of the Information Age, and software has become a core competency that is critical to high technology companies. Computers are now an integral part of our day-to-day lives. We use them, even if we don't realize it, when we drive a car, withdraw money from an automated teller machine, or telephone a friend.

At the same time, anyone familiar with computers is also familiar, frequently painfully so, with the "software crisis" [Gibbs94]. Our ability to build software-intensive systems is orders of magnitude greater today than it was five decades ago, but our appetite for software has grown even faster, and the software industry is still evolving from a craft to an engineering discipline [Shaw90]. Historically, the result has been the chronic software crisis: software is (almost) always later than expected, more expensive than planned, and with less functionality than hoped. There is hope, however, that we have turned the corner on the software crisis.

Why do we have a chronic software crisis? Partially it is because the software discipline is still maturing, but some of the pain is caused by human nature. In response to the question "Why does software cost so much?", Weinberg replies "Compared to what?" and DeMarco points out that the question is based on the assertion that software is too pricey [DeMarco95]. DeMarco suggests that this assertion is a negotiating position; people complain because they know we work harder when they complain. In one survey, most of the responding professional software managers reported that their estimates were dismal, but they weren't on the whole dissatisfied with the estimating process [Lederer92]!

All too many software professionals would agree with DeMarco, but many software managers and customers are vitally interested in understanding how to manage software projects more effectively. Can we plan and manage software projects effectively? While some have argued not, the evidence is that we can – within the bounds of the business paradigm that is chosen.

The business paradigm is crucial because for significant software projects we rarely understand all the requirements at the beginning of the software project. The waterfall software life cycle model, which assumes that the requirements are frozen at the beginning of the software project, has largely been superseded by evolutionary or incremental life cycles. Software project management thus emphasizes managing risks and controlling change.

Customers and managers who use schedule pressure and overtime as motivational tools have to deal with the resulting quality tradeoff. Customers and managers who are interested in truly managing software projects – and facing up to a sometimes unpleasant reality – have available a number of approaches for systematically improving the process for developing and maintaining software. The results of successfully applying these approaches give us hope that the software crisis is finally coming to an end. A growing number of software organizations credit their increasing ability to achieve functionality, quality, schedule, and budget goals to systematic improvement of their software processes.

Perhaps the best-known approaches to software process improvement are the International Organization for Standardization's ISO 9001 standard for quality management systems, the

Software Engineering Institute's Capability Maturity Model for Software (CMM or Software CMM), and the proposed ISO/IEC 15504 standard for software process assessment. These approaches, among others, apply Total Quality Management (TQM) principles to the software process.

ISO 9000 is a suite of standards dealing with quality management systems that can be used for external quality assurance purposes. ISO 9001, which addresses quality assurance in design, development, production, installation, and servicing, is the standard of specific interest to the software community, but it is much broader in scope than just software; software-specific guidance is provided in ISO 9000-3. Although the scope of ISO 9001 is broader than software, its application can be of value to software organizations [Stelzer96], and ISO 9001 certification is required to do business in many markets.

The Capability Maturity Model for Software [Paulk95a] describes the process capability of software organizations and provides a roadmap for software process improvement. Developed at the request of the U.S. Department of Defense to help identify the capability of software contractors [Humphrey87, Byrnes96, Besselman93], its use for improving the software process has spread far beyond the DoD community. The Software CMM is arguably the best known and most widely used model for software process appraisal and improvement today. The author of this chapter is the product manager for the Software CMM, so there may be some bias in this discussion.

Many models and standards for software process improvement have been developed. This proliferation led to the development of ISO/IEC 15504, a suite of standards for software process assessment [Dorling93]. Popularly known as SPICE (Software Process Improvement and Capability dEtermination), ISO/IEC 15504 is currently under development and may change significantly before its final release. ISO/IEC 15504 will provide a framework for harmonizing different approaches to assessing and improving the software process.

The importance of high-quality software products cannot be overemphasized. Recent UK court decisions and proposed changes to the U.S. Uniform Commercial Code foreshadow a potential for legal action by dissatisfied customers: "UK Court of Appeal judges have ruled for the first time that software should be sold free of major bugs and should work as intended, like other commercial goods... attempts by software vendors to exclude or limit liability for product performance will be judged in terms of the Unfair Contract Terms Act (1977)." [UK-Court96] Fortunately the increasing maturity of the software field encourages us to think this goal may now be within our grasp.

2. ISO 9000 – Quality Management Systems

Established by the International Organization for Standardization (ISO), the ISO 9000 series of standards is a set of documents dealing with quality management systems that can be used for external quality assurance purposes. They specify quality system requirements for use where a contract between two parties requires the demonstration of a supplier's capability to design and supply a product. The two parties could be an external client and a supplier, or both could be internal, e.g., marketing and engineering groups in a company.

There are several standards and guidelines in the ISO 9000 series. ISO 9001 is the standard that is pertinent to software development and maintenance. It is for use when conformance to specified requirements is to be assured by the supplier during several stages, which may include design, development, production, installation, and servicing. ISO 9001 addresses the minimum criteria for an acceptable quality system[1] within a broad scope: hardware, software, processed materials, and services.

ISO 9000-3 provides guidelines for the application of ISO 9001 to the development, supply, and maintenance of software. A British program called TickIT [TickIT, Lloyd's94] provides additional information and training for using ISO 9001 and ISO 9000-3 in the software arena.

2.1 An Overview of ISO 9001

The fundamental premise of ISO 9001 is that every important process should be documented and every deliverable should have its quality checked through a quality control activity. This is sometimes expressed as "Say what you do; do what you say." ISO 9001 requires documentation that contains instructions or guidance on what should be done or how it should be done.

ISO 9001 has only 20 clauses, expressed in less than five pages, which are summarized in Table 1.

Table 1. The Clauses in ISO 9001.

ISO 9001 Clause	ISO 9001 requires that
4.1. Management Responsibility	The quality policy is defined, documented, understood, implemented, and maintained; responsibilities and authorities for all personnel specifying, achieving, and monitoring quality are defined; and in-house verification resources are defined, trained, and funded. A designated manager ensures that the quality program is implemented and maintained.
4.2. Quality System	A documented quality system, including procedures and instructions, is established. ISO 9000-3 characterizes this quality system as an integrated process throughout the entire life-cycle.
4.3. Contract Review	Contracts are reviewed to determine whether the requirements are adequately defined, agree with the bid, and can be implemented.
4.4. Design Control	Procedures to control and verify the design are established. This includes planning design and development activities; defining organizational and technical interfaces; identifying inputs and outputs; reviewing, verifying, and validating the design; and controlling design changes. ISO 9000-3 elaborates this clause with clauses on the purchaser's requirements specification (5.3), development planning (5.4), quality planning (5.5), design and implementation (5.6), testing and validation (5.7), and configuration management (6.1).

---

[1] This statement is somewhat controversial. Some members of the standards community maintain that if you read ISO 9001 with insight, it does address continuous process improvement.

ISO 9001 Clause	ISO 9001 requires that
4.5. Document and Data Control	Distribution and modification of documents and data is controlled.
4.6. Purchasing	Purchased products conform to their specified requirements. This includes the evaluation of potential subcontractors and verification of purchased products.
4.7. Control of Customer-Supplied Product	Any customer-supplied material is verified, controlled, and maintained. ISO 9000-3 discusses this clause in the context of included software product (6.8), including commercial-off-the-shelf software.
4.8. Product Identification and Traceability	The product is identified and traceable during all stages of production, delivery, and installation.
4.9. Process Control	Production processes are defined and planned. This includes carrying out production under controlled conditions, according to documented instructions. When the results of a process cannot be fully verified after the fact, the process is continuously monitored and controlled. ISO 9000-3 clauses include design and implementation (5.6); rules, practices, and conventions (6.5); and tools and techniques (6.6).
4.10. Inspection and Testing	Incoming materials are inspected or verified before use and in-process inspection and testing is performed. Final inspection and testing are performed prior to release of finished product. Records of inspection and test are kept.
4.11. Control of Inspection, Measuring, and Test Equipment	Equipment used to demonstrate conformance are controlled, calibrated, and maintained. Test hardware or software are checked to prove they are capable of verifying the acceptability of a product before use and rechecked at prescribed intervals. ISO 9000-3 clarifies this clause with clauses on testing and validation (5.7); rules, practices, and conventions (6.5); and tools and techniques (6.6).
4.12. Inspection and Test Status	The status of inspections and tests is maintained for items as they progress through various processing steps.
4.13. Control of Nonconforming Product	Nonconforming product is controlled to prevent inadvertent use or installation. ISO 9000-3 maps this concept to clauses on design and implementation (5.6); testing and validation (5.7); replication, delivery, and installation (5.9); and configuration management (6.1).

ISO 9001 Clause	ISO 9001 requires that
4.14. Corrective and Preventive Action	The causes of nonconforming product are identified. Corrective action is directed toward eliminating the causes of actual nonconformities. Preventive action is directed toward eliminating the causes of potential nonconformities. ISO 9000-3 quotes this clause verbatim, with no elaboration, from the 1987 release of ISO 9001.
4.15. Handling, Storage, Packaging, Preservation, and Delivery	Procedures for handling, storage, packaging, preservation, and delivery are established and maintained. ISO 9000-3 maps this to clauses on acceptance (5.8) and replication, delivery, and installation (5.9)
4.16. Control of Quality Records	Quality records are collected, maintained, and dispositioned.
4.17. Internal Quality Audits	Audits are planned and performed. The results of audits are communicated to management, and any deficiencies found are corrected.
4.18. Training	Training needs are identified and training is provided, since selected tasks may require qualified personnel. Records of training are maintained.
4.19. Servicing	Servicing activities are performed as specified. ISO 9000-3 addresses this clause as maintenance (5.10).
4.20. Statistical Techniques	Statistical techniques are identified and used to verify the acceptability of process capability and product characteristics. ISO 9000-3 simply characterizes this clause as measurement (6.4).

2.2 Placing ISO 9001 in Context

ISO 9001 may be the minimal criteria for a quality management system, but it also provides a foundation that other parts of the ISO 9000 series elaborate. In particular, ISO 9004-1 describes a basic set of elements by which quality management systems can be developed and implemented.

Shaughnessy points out three themes that run through the ISO 9000 series: quality, capability, and evidence [Shaughnessy94]. Quality means satisfying both stated and implied needs. Capability is based on statistical understanding. Evidence is required that quality is being managed and outcomes are reliable and predictable. If these three are addressed, then an organization is well on its way to continual process improvement.

2.3 ISO 9000 Certification

Although originally intended for two-party contractual purposes, the most common use of ISO 9001 today is for third-party certification. The precise meaning of the terms "certification," "registration," and "accreditation" vary in different countries [Sanders94], and technically the term "certification" should be reserved for the verification of conformance of products to standards. In the U.S. "registrars" assess organizations against ISO 9001 (or one of the other ISO 9000 standards) and "register" that the organization has passed the audit – that it has an acceptable quality management system according to the requirements of the standard, and a "certificate of registration" is issued. "Accreditation" refers to the process for ensuring that the registrar is reputable and objective.

There is currently no international "certification," "registration," or "accreditation" body, although ISO has published criteria for the accreditation of registration bodies. National bodies around the world have established accreditation bodies with their own certification or registration schemes. Many of these accreditation bodies have agreed to mutual recognition of their ISO 9000 certificates, but mutual recognition is currently established by pair-wise agreements.

2.4 Strengths and Weaknesses of ISO 9000

Many companies share a belief that ISO 9000 is an inadequate standard in today's highly competitive world. Motorola, for example, has criticized ISO 9000 as being expensive and of limited value [Buetow94]:

> "Motorola will make its purchases based on excellence in product and service, not on compliance to a system of standards... ISO 9000 certification has no direct connection to a product or service... ISO 9000 represents the old paradigm of an internal, overlay, quality program implying that quality costs money."

The piece-wise nature of certification and the mutual recognition needed between national bodies has led to criticism that ISO 9001 certification is being used by some countries for restraint of trade. Requirements for ISO 9001 certification according to restrictive criteria, e.g., by a local registrar, can be an effective market barrier.

In addition to these general complaints, ISO 9001 has been criticized by the software industry for being written from a manufacturing perspective and not providing adequate guidance in the software world. ISO 9000-3, which provides the official guidance for applying ISO 9001 to software, is considered inadequate by many [Matsubara94, Harauz94]. Even the architecture of ISO 9000-3 does not reflect that of ISO 9001; there are many-to-many relationships between the clauses in the standard and those in the guide.

The British TickIT program was established to ensure that ISO 9001 auditors are knowledgeable about software engineering and management and have been trained in how to interpret ISO 9001 for the software domain. Sector-specific schemes such as TickIT have their detractors, however. A similar effort to TickIT was proposed for the U.S. called Software Quality System Registration (SQSR). After much debate, SQSR was killed, as was a similar effort in Japan. There are at least two opposition camps to sector-specific guides. The first argues that "if you can audit, you can audit anything." The second argues that the added cost of sector-specific certification far outweighs the benefits; especially if the value of the baseline standard is considered questionable.

12

Studies have shown that ISO 9001 can be used in successfully improving the software process [Stelzer96]. One surprising result, however, was the observation that only two of the ten critical success factors were explicit requirements of ISO 9001. Success depends on whether the spirit or the letter of the standard is followed.

2.5 The Future of ISO 9000

ISO 9001 was released in 1987, revised in 1994, and a major revision is planned for 2000 [Marquardt91, West00]. Major changes planned include:

- removing the manufacturing bias
- restructuring the standard logically as linked processes
- simplifying the expression and increase user friendliness
- emphasizing effectiveness of the quality management system
- expanding customer interface requirements
- linking to ISO 9004-1

ISO 9000:2000 will consist of four primary standards:
- ISO 9000: Quality management systems - Concepts and vocabulary
- ISO 9001: Quality management systems - Requirements
- ISO 9004: Quality management systems - Guidelines
- ISO 19011: Guidelines on Quality and Environmental Auditing

The new ISO 9001 will have four major clauses on management responsibility, resource management, process management, and measurement, analysis, and improvement. Management responsibility will address policy, objectives, planning, quality management system, and management review. Resource management will deal with human resources, information, and facilities. Process management will cover customer satisfaction, design, purchasing, and production. Measurement, analysis, and improvement will address audit, process control, and continual improvement.

The new ISO 9004 will focus on quality management principles, including customer focus, leadership, involvement of people, process approach, system approach to management, continual improvement, factual approach to decision making, and mutually beneficial supplier relationships.

Although a number of issues are still being discussed at this writing, the consensus on ISO 9000:2000 appears to be that it is a significantly improved standard. A new version of ISO 9000-3, the software guide for interpreting ISO 9001, is also planned and will reflect the new architecture of ISO 9001. Some have argued against another release of ISO 9000-3, however, as part of a general campaign against sector-specific guides. At this writing a ballot is in process on moving responsibility for ISO 9000-3 from TC 176, the technical committee responsible for quality management systems, to ISO/IEC JTC1/SC7, the subcommittee on software engineering standards.

13

For further information on ISO, see the World Wide Web page
http://www.iso.ch/

3. The Capability Maturity Model for Software

The Capability Maturity Model for Software [Paulk95a] describes the principles and practices underlying software process maturity and is intended to help software organizations improve the maturity of their software processes in terms of an evolutionary path from ad hoc, chaotic processes to mature, disciplined software processes. The current release is Version 1.1.

The success of the Software CMM has led to the development of other capability maturity models that deal with systems engineering [Bate95], people issues [Curtis95], and software acquisition [Ferguson96].

3.1 An Overview of the Software CMM

The Software CMM is organized into the five maturity levels described in Table 2.

Table 2. The Maturity Levels in the Software CMM.

Software CMM Maturity Level	Description of Software CMM Maturity Levels
1) Initial	The software process is characterized as ad hoc, and occasionally even chaotic. Few processes are defined, and success depends on individual effort and heroics.
2) Repeatable	Basic project management processes are established to track cost, schedule, and functionality. The necessary process discipline is in place to repeat earlier successes on projects with similar applications.
3) Defined	The software process for both management and engineering activities is documented, standardized, and integrated into a set of standard software processes for the organization. Projects use a defined software process that is tailored from the organization's standard software processes.
4) Managed	Detailed measures of the software process and product quality are collected. Both the software process and products are quantitatively understood and controlled.
5) Optimizing	Continuous process improvement is enabled by quantitative feedback from the process and from piloting innovative ideas and technologies.

Except for Level 1, each maturity level is decomposed into several key process areas that indicate the areas an organization should focus on to improve its software process.

14

The key process areas at Level 2 focus on the software project's concerns related to establishing basic project management controls.

- Requirements Management: establish a common understanding between the customer and the software project of the customer's requirements that will be addressed by the software project. This agreement with the customer is the basis for planning and managing the software project.

- Software Project Planning: establish reasonable plans for performing the software engineering and for managing the software project. These plans are the necessary foundation for managing the software project.

- Software Project Tracking & Oversight: establish adequate visibility into actual progress so that management can take effective actions when the software project's performance deviates significantly from the software plans.

- Software Subcontract Management: select qualified software subcontractors and manage them effectively.

- Software Quality Assurance: provide management with appropriate visibility into the process being used by the software project and of the products being built.

- Software Configuration Management: establish and maintain the integrity of the products of the software project throughout the project's software life cycle.

The key process areas at Level 3 address both project and organizational issues, as the organization establishes an infrastructure that institutionalizes effective software engineering and management processes across all projects.

- Organization Process Focus: establish the organizational responsibility for software process activities that improve the organization's overall software process capability.

- Organization Process Definition: develop and maintain a usable set of software process assets that improve process performance across the projects and provide a basis for defining meaningful data for quantitative process management. These assets provide a stable foundation that can be institutionalized via mechanisms such as training.

- Training Program: develop the skills and knowledge of individuals so they can perform their roles effectively and efficiently. Training is an organizational responsibility, but the software projects should identify their needed skills and provide the necessary training when the project's needs are unique.

- Integrated Software Management: integrate the software engineering and management activities into a coherent, defined software process that is tailored from the organization's standard software process and related process assets. This tailoring is based on the business environment and technical needs of the project.

- Software Product Engineering: consistently perform a well-defined engineering process that integrates all the software engineering activities to produce correct, consistent software products effectively and efficiently. Software Product Engineering describes the technical activities of the project, for instance requirements analysis, design, code, and test.

- Intergroup Coordination: establish a means for the software engineering group to participate actively with the other engineering groups so the project is better able to satisfy the customer's needs effectively and efficiently.

- Peer Reviews: remove defects from the software work products early and efficiently. An important corollary effect is to develop a better understanding of the software work products and of the defects that can be prevented. The peer review is an important and effective engineering method that can be implemented via inspections, structured walkthroughs, or a number of other collegial review methods.

The key process areas at Level 4 focus on establishing a quantitative understanding of both the software process and the software work products being built.

- Quantitative Process Management: control process performance of the software project quantitatively. Software process performance represents the actual results achieved from following a software process. The focus is on identifying special causes of variation within a measurably stable process and correcting, as appropriate, the circumstances that drove the transient variation to occur.

- Software Quality Management: develop a quantitative understanding of the quality of the project's software products and achieve specific quality goals.

The key process areas at Level 5 cover the issues that both the organization and the projects must address to implement continuous and measurable software process improvement.

- Defect Prevention: identify the causes of defects and prevent them from recurring. The software project analyzes defects, identifies their causes, and changes its defined software process.

- Technology Change Management: identify beneficial new technologies (such as tools, methods, and processes) and transfer them into the organization in an orderly manner. The focus of Technology Change Management is on performing innovation efficiently in an ever-changing world.

- Process Change Management: continually improve the software processes used in the organization with the intent of improving software quality, increasing productivity, and decreasing the cycle time for product development.

Each key process area is described in terms of the key practices that contribute to satisfying its goals and that are allocated to the common features. The key practices describe the specific infrastructure and activities that contribute most to the effective implementation and institutionalization of the key process area.

The Software CMM is approximately 500 pages long and is now available as a book: **The Capability Maturity Model: Guidelines for Improving the Software Process** [Paulk95a].

3.2 Placing the Software CMM in Context

Although most discussions of the SEI's software process improvement work focus on the Software CMM, the model is part of a comprehensive approach – the IDEAL approach – to software process improvement [McFeeley96]. IDEAL consists of five phases:

I *Initiating.* Laying the groundwork for a successful improvement effort.

D *Diagnosing.* Determining where you are relative to where you want to be.

16

E *Establishing*. Planning the specifics of how you will reach your destination.

A *Acting*. Doing the work according to the plan.

L *Learning*. Learning from the experience and improving your ability to adopt new technologies in the future.

The Initiating phase is perhaps the most significant difference between IDEAL and most other improvement models. Giving explicit and thorough attention to the activities of this phase is critical to the success of an improvement effort. While attending to the issues of the Initiating phase will not guarantee success by itself, skipping or neglecting this phase will almost certainly lead to reduced effectiveness or failure. The business reasons for undertaking the effort are clearly articulated. The effort's contributions to business goals and objectives are identified, as are its relationships with the organization's other work. The support of critical managers is secured, and resources are allocated on an order-of-magnitude basis. Finally, an infrastructure for managing implementation details is put in place.

The Diagnosing phase builds upon the Initiating phase to develop a more complete understanding of the improvement work that needs to be done. During the Diagnosing phase two characterizations of the organization are developed: one as it is at present and the second as it is intended to be after implementing the improvement. These organizational states are used to develop an approach to achieving improved business practice.

The purpose of the Establishing phase is to develop a detailed plan for doing the work. Priorities are set that reflect not only the recommendations made during the Diagnosing phase, but also the organization's broader operations and the constraints of its operating environment. An approach is then developed that honors and factors in the priorities. Finally, specific actions, milestones, deliverables, and responsibilities are incorporated into an action plan.

The activities of the Acting phase help an organization implement the work that has been so carefully conceptualized and planned in the previous three phases. These activities will typically consume much more calendar time and many more resources than all of the other phases combined. If the work of the first three phases has been done conscientiously, the likelihood of success during the Acting phase is greatly improved.

The Learning phase (formerly named the Leveraging phase) completes the improvement cycle. One of the concerns of the IDEAL approach is continuously improving the ability to implement change. In the Learning phase, the entire IDEAL experience is reviewed to determine what was accomplished, whether the effort accomplished the intended goals, and how the organization can implement change more effectively and/or efficiently in the future.

3.3 CMM-Based Appraisals

CMM-based appraisals come in two major classes: assessments performed for internal process improvement and evaluations performed by a customer. All CMM-based appraisal methods should satisfy requirements documented in the CMM Appraisal Framework [Masters95].

A *software process assessment* is an appraisal by a trained team of software professionals to determine the state of an organization's current software process, to determine the high-priority software process-related issues facing an organization, and to obtain the organizational support for software process improvement. There are various degrees of formality in the assessment method chosen; the most rigorous is the CMM-Based Appraisal for Internal Process Improvement (CBA IPI) [Dunaway96].

In contrast, a *software capability evaluation* (SCE) is an appraisal by a trained team of professionals to identify contractors who are qualified to perform the software work or to monitor the state of the software process used on an existing software effort [Byrnes96, Besselman93]. The use of the CMM in evaluations has inspired government contractors, particularly for the Department of Defense, to establish software process improvement programs based on the CMM to remain competitive.

In a similar vein, a number of companies have chosen to use the Software CMM to encourage software process improvement and build stronger customer-supplier relationships with their suppliers of software-intensive systems. Perhaps the best known of these is Boeing's Advanced Quality System for Software [D1-9001]. Boeing is increasingly reliant on the integrity of supplier software quality systems; D1-9001 requires that Boeing suppliers commit to process and product improvement based on the Software CMM. Boeing visualizes its suppliers using the Software CMM to reach a level of capability in which reliable processes and world-class product quality goals are institutionalized. Boeing policy is to work with suppliers to measure and continuously improve software processes and products. Suppliers are expected to commit to improvement and go through several stages, beginning with establishing a process improvement commitment.

3.4 Strengths and Weaknesses of the Software CMM

Several papers have been published criticizing the CMM [Bach94, Jones95], particularly its application in SCEs [Bollinger91, Saiedian95, O'Connell00]. Criticisms of the Software CMM include:

- The Software CMM does not address all of the critical factors for successful software projects, including non-software disciplines such as systems engineering and marketing; hiring, developing, and retaining a competent software staff; strategic business planning; and so forth.

- The Software CMM is a large and complex document that is difficult to understand.

- The Software CMM is primarily addressed at large organizations performing contractual work.

- Maturity levels are gross measures of process capability, oversimplifying a complex set of issues.

- Key process areas are static and do not provide an evolutionary view of processes, which would be of value to the individuals responsible for implementing, controlling, and improving a specific process.

- It may be difficult for the non-expert to tailor or extend the Software CMM.

- Appraisals, especially software capability evaluations, are frequently performed by untrained and unqualified appraisers, leading to inconsistency and unreliability in appraisal results.

- Appraisals frequently do not result in action to address the problems identified, thus failing to achieve the objective of software process improvement.

There are counter-arguments to these criticisms [Curtis94, Humphrey91]:

- The Software CMM is deliberately focused on the software process, and other factors should be addressed as part of a larger program, such as a TQM initiative. Other CMMs can aid organizations dealing with these issues [Konrad96, Bate95, Curtis95, Ferguson96].

- The Software CMM is structured hierarchically. The normative component is fairly short: 18 key process areas and 52 goals. The practices are informative components that help CMM users interpret what is intended. The guidance in the key practices and subpractices is a significant help in understanding what a key practice or goal means.

- The Software CMM explicitly describes organizational capability in terms of the maturity levels.

- The Software CMM focuses organizations on the "vital few" issues in process improvement. It identifies improvement priorities that are generally true for any (software) organization.

- Training is available for assessors and evaluators from both the SEI and authorized distribution partners.

- The SEI recommends that software process maturity be a consideration in choosing software suppliers rather than a maturity level being a requirement for competing.

- Use of the Software CMM by the government and companies in selecting and monitoring software suppliers has inspired many suppliers to tackle software process improvement.

- The Software CMM has been reviewed by thousands of software professionals as it has evolved [Paulk95b].

- There is a large body of CMM users who interact through local software process improvement networks (SPINs) and annual Software Engineering Process Group conferences in both the U.S. and Europe.

- The Software CMM has become the de facto standard for software process improvement around the world and spanning application domains.

Using the Software CMM correctly requires professional judgment [Paulk96a, Paulk97]. The software process may be repeatable, but it is not a deterministic, repetitive process. Software engineering is a human-centered, design-intensive process that requires both discipline and creativity. Although the Software CMM provides a significant amount of guidance for making judgments on the software process, it is not a rigid set of objective requirements.

3.5 The Future of the Software CMM: CMM Integration

The SEI had originally planned to release version 2 of the Software CMM in 1997. That release was halted, however, at the direction of the SEI's sponsor, the Office of the Under Secretary of Defense for Acquisition and Technology, in favor of work on the CMM Integration (CMMI) effort. Software CMM v2 Draft C was the last version before work was halted and is available online at

http://www.sei.cmu.edu/cmm/draft-c/c.html

The version 2 archives are available at

http://www.sei.cmu.edu/cmm/cmm-v2/cmm.v2.html.

CMMI will address software, systems engineering, and integrated product and process development issues and includes Software CMM v2C as one of its source documents, as well as EIA 731, the Systems Engineering Capability Model, and the Integrated Product Development CMM. The first version of the CMMI model and method are planned for release in the summer of 2000. Current information on CMMI is available at

http://www.sei.cmu.edu/cmm/cmms/cmms.integration.html

Software CMM v1.1 and CMMI v1 will both be supported for a three-year overlapping window after CMMI v1 is released.

4. ISO/IEC 15504 – An International Standard for Software Process Assessment

The International Organization for Standardization (ISO) is developing a suite of standards on software process assessment: ISO/IEC 15504. This work, frequently referred to as SPICE – Software Process Improvement and Capability dEtermination, was inspired by the numerous efforts on software process around the world [ImproveIT]. The ISO/IEC 15504 set of documents are currently published as type 2 technical reports; they are not yet an international standard.

ISO/IEC 15504 focuses on software process issues but is also concerned with people, technology, management practices, customer support and quality, as well as software development and maintenance practices. Organizations will be able to use this standard in many ways:

- in capability determination mode, to help a purchasing organization determine the capability of a potential software supplier against a recognized international standard;

- in process improvement mode, to help a software organization improve its own software development and maintenance processes; and

- in self-assessment mode, to help an organization determine its ability to implement a new software project.

The requirements for ISO/IEC 15504 [ISO-N944R] are that the process assessment standard shall:

A. encourage predictable quality products

B. encourage optimum productivity

C. promote a repeatable software process

D. provide guidance for improving software processes aligned to business goals, including starting point and target

E. support process capability determination for risk identification and analysis within an organization

F. support process capability determination for risk identification and analysis within a two-party contractual situation

G. be capable of being employed reliably and consistently

H. be simple to use and understand

I. be culturally independent

J. not presume specific organizational structures, management philosophies, software life cycle models, software technologies, or software development methods

K. recognize different application domains, business needs, and sizes of organizations

L. for each process, define baseline practices which are appropriate across all application domains, business needs, and sizes of organization. The baseline practices should be extensible to allow for industry or business variants.

M. define standard requirements for the development of industry or business variants of the baseline practices

N. be applicable at the project and organizational levels with connectivity between the two

O. focus on process, but also address people and application of technology

P. be objective

Q. be quantitative wherever possible

R. support output as process profiles which allow views at different levels of detail. The profiling method should support comparisons against other similar entities or industry "norms."

S. require that agreement is reached over ownership and confidentiality of assessment results prior to assessment

T. define the initial and ongoing qualification of assessors

U. be supportive of and consistent with other ISO JTC1/SC7 standards and projects

V. be supportive of, and consistent with, the ISO 9000 series of standards.

W. be subject to continuous improvement through periodic reviews to maintain consistency with current good practice

4.1 An Overview of ISO/IEC 15504

ISO/IEC 15504 is intended to harmonize the many different approaches to software process assessment. It provides a framework for the assessment of software processes. This framework can be used by organizations involved in planning, managing, monitoring, controlling, and improving the acquisition, supply, development, operation, evolution and support of software. ISO/IEC 15504 consists of nine parts, described in Table 3, under the general title *Software Process Assessment.*

Table 3. The Components of ISO/IEC 15504.

ISO/IEC 15504 Part	ISO/IEC 15504 Part Description
Part 1 : *Concepts and introductory guide*	Describes how the parts of the suite fit together, and provides guidance for their selection and use.
Part 2 : *A reference model for processes and process capability*	Defines a two dimensional reference model for describing the outcomes of process assessment. The reference model defines a set of processes, defined in terms of their purpose, and a framework for evaluating the capability of the processes through assessment of process attributes structured into capability levels.
Part 3 : *Performing an assessment*	Defines the requirements for performing an assessment in such a way that the outcomes will be repeatable, reliable and consistent.
Part 4 : *Guide to performing assessments*	Provides guidance on performing software process assessments and interpreting the requirements of Part 3 for different assessment contexts.
Part 5 : *An assessment model and indicator guidance*	Provides an exemplar model for performing process assessments that is based upon and directly compatible with the reference model in Part 2.
Part 6 : *Guide to competency of assessors*	Describes the competence, education, training and experience of assessors that are relevant to conducting process assessments.
Part 7 : *Guide for use in process improvement*	Describes how to define the inputs to and use the results of an assessment for the purposes of process improvement.
Part 8 : *Guide for use in determining supplier process capability*	Describes how to define the inputs to and use the results of an assessment for the purpose of process capability determination. The guidance is applicable either for use within an organization to determine its own capability, or by a acquirer to determine the capability of a (potential) supplier.
Part 9 : *Vocabulary*	A consolidated vocabulary of all terms specifically defined for the purposes of ISO/IEC 15504.

The approach to process assessment defined in ISO/IEC 15504 is designed to provide a basis for a common approach to describing the results of process assessment, allowing for some degree of comparison of assessments based upon different but compatible models and methods.

22

Process assessment has two principal contexts for its use, as shown in Figure 1.

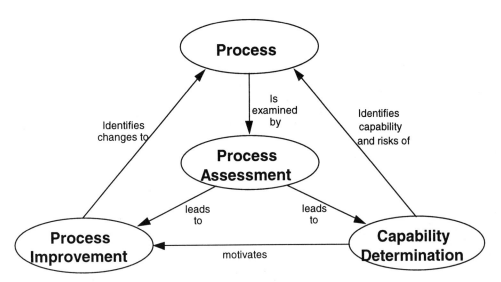

Figure 1. The context for software process assessment

Within a process improvement context, process assessment provides the means of characterizing the current practice within an organizational unit in terms of the capability of the selected processes. Analysis of the results in the light of the organization's business needs identifies strengths, weakness and risks inherent in the processes. This, in turn, leads to the ability to determine whether the processes are effective in achieving their goals, and to identify significant causes of poor quality, or overruns in time or cost. These provide the drivers for prioritizing improvements to processes.

Process capability determination is concerned with analyzing the proposed capability of selected processes against a target process capability profile in order to identify the risks involved in undertaking a project using the selected processes. The proposed capability may be based on the results of relevant previous process assessments, or may be based on an assessment carried out for the purpose of establishing the proposed capability.

4.2 An Overview of the ISO/IEC 15504-2 Reference Model

Part 2 of ISO/IEC 15504 defines a reference model of processes and process capability which forms the basis for any model to be used for the purposes of process assessment. The reference model documents the set of universal software engineering processes that are fundamental to good software engineering and that cover best practice activities. It describes processes that an organization may perform to acquire, supply, develop, operate, evolve and support software and the process attributes that characterize the capability of those processes. The purpose of the reference model is to provide a common basis for different models and methods for software process assessment, ensuring that results of assessments can be reported in a common context.

The reference model architecture is two dimensional. The process dimension is characterized by process purpose statements, which are the essential measurable objectives of a process.

The Part 2 processes are shown in Figure 2. They are related, but not identical, to the processes described in ISO/IEC 12207, which is the ISO standard for software life cycle processes.

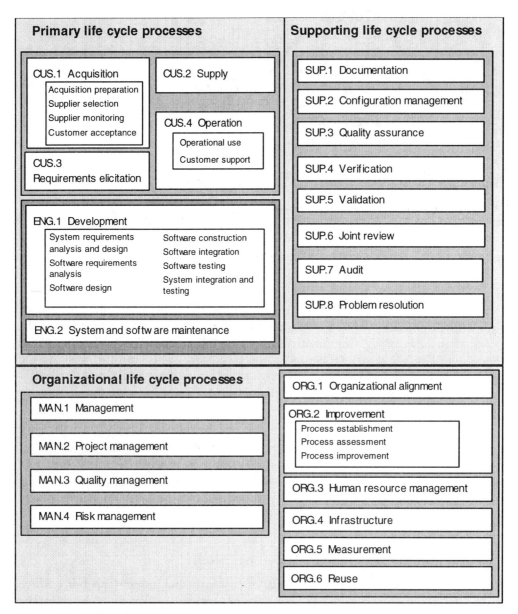

Figure 2. ISO/IEC 15504-2 Processes.

The *process capability dimension* is characterized by a series of process attributes, applicable to any process, which represent measurable characteristics necessary to manage a process and improve its capability to perform. Each process attribute describes an aspect of the overall capability of managing and improving the effectiveness of a process in achieving its purpose and contributing to the business goals of the organization. There are nine process attributes, which are grouped into capability levels, one at capability level 1 and two each at levels 2-5. Capability levels constitute a rational way of progressing through improvement of the capability of any process. The underlying principles are similar to the Software CMM maturity levels, although targeted to the process rather than the organization. The six capability levels are described in Table 4.

Table 4. The Capability Levels in ISO/IEC 15504-2.

Capability Level	ISO/IEC 15504-2 Capability Level Description
Level 0 *Incomplete*	There is general failure to attain the purpose of the process. There are little or no easily identifiable work products or outputs of the process.
Level 1 *Performed*	The purpose of the process is generally achieved. The achievement may not be rigorously planned and tracked. There are identifiable work products for the process, and these testify to the achievement of the purpose.
Level 2 *Managed*	The process delivers work products according to specified procedures and is planned and tracked. Work products conform to specified standards and requirements.
Level 3 *Established*	The process is performed and managed using a defined process based upon good software engineering principles. Individual implementations of the process use approved, tailored versions of standard, documented processes to achieve the process outcomes.
Level 4 *Predictable*	The defined process is performed consistently in practice within defined control limits, to achieve its defined process goals.
Level 5 *Optimizing*	Performance of the process is optimized to meet current and future business needs, and the process achieves repeatability in meeting its defined business goals.

The process attributes are defined in ISO/IEC 15504-2 and elaborated in ISO/IEC 15504-5 by process indicators, called generic practices in earlier drafts of the evolving standard.

A capability level is further characterized by a set of attribute(s) that work together to provide a major enhancement in the capability to perform a process, as listed in Table 5. Process attributes are features of a process that can be evaluated on a scale of achievement, providing a measure of the capability of the process. They are rating components of ISO/IEC 15504-2. They are applicable to all processes. Each process attribute describes a facet of the overall capability of managing and improving the effectiveness of a process in achieving its purpose and contributing to the business goals of the organization.

Table 5. ISO/IEC 15504 Process Attributes.

ISO/IEC 15504-2 Capability Level	ISO/IEC 15504-2 Process Attributes
Level 0: Incomplete process	
Level 1: Performed process	PA 1.1 Process performance
Level 2: Managed process	PA 2.1 Performance management
	PA 2.2 Work product management
Level 3: Established process	PA 3.1 Process definition
	PA 3.2 Process resource
Level 4: Predictable process	PA 4.1 Measurement
	PA 4.2 Process control
Level 5: Optimizing process	PA 5.1 Process change
	PA 5.2 Continuous improvement

4.3 Strengths and Weaknesses of ISO/IEC 15504

It is intended that the international standard on software process assessment will:

- provide a public, shared model for process assessment;
- lead to a common understanding of the use of process assessment for process improvement and capability evaluation;
- facilitate capability determination in procurement;
- be controlled and regularly reviewed in the light of experience of use;
- be changed only by international consensus; and
- encourage harmonization of existing schemes.

In particular, the reference model fully describes the evolution of processes from ad hoc to continuously improving, and adding processes and integrating with other models is relatively simple. Its weaknesses, however, include difficulty in interpretation and the possibility that less critical process issues can drown out the "vital few" when there are clashes over improvement priorities.

Another concern is incompatibility with the flagship software engineering standard on "Software Life Cycle Processes," ISO/IEC 12207. It establishes a common framework for software life-cycle processes. It contains processes, activities, and tasks that are to be applied during the acquisition of a system that contains software, a stand-alone software product, and software service and during the supply, development, operation, and maintenance of software products. Although each baseline of ISO/IEC 15504-2 has converged toward ISO/IEC 12207, significant differences – for arguably good reasons – remain. It is likely that feedback from the ISO/IEC 15504 developers may result in changes to ISO/IEC 12207 in its next revision that support convergence from both directions.

Based on the Phase 1 trials, the length of time to rate processes completely and rigorously is on the order of 10 hours per process instance, which implies a process assessment lasting over 300 hours [Woodman96]. An assessment of each process in ISO/IEC 15504-2 against each generic practice or each process attribute provides a thorough, but perhaps overly detailed, process profile. Some appraisal methods focus on the "vital few" issues for the improvement effort, but the criteria for identifying the vital few may vary in different assessment approaches. One of the strengths of the SPICE effort, however, is the trials program and the emphasis on gaining empirical evidence to base decisions on how the standard should evolve [Emam96, Marshall96].

Although it is agreed that ISO/IEC 15504 should not be used in any scheme for certification or registration of process capability, there is a danger that the standard will be used for certification. The topic comes up repeatedly, and there are differences within the international community regarding whether certification should be encouraged or discouraged. Most members of the SPICE project oppose certification, but ISO cannot prevent certification mechanisms being established by the user community, as occurred for ISO 9001.

There is also a concern that ISO/IEC 15504 will inappropriately replace existing assessment approaches, although the SPICE goal is to harmonize existing approaches rather than replace them. If any ISO/IEC 15504-conformant model and method can generate comparable process profiles, then a useful framework will have been developed for navigating the quagmire of process assessment models and standards. If, on the other hand, ISO/IEC 15504 becomes a competing model and method for software process assessment and improvement, perhaps required by some customers and markets, it will further confuse an already turbulent environment. In such a case, ISO/IEC 15504 will have the advantage of being an international standard, but it will be competing with a number of already well-established approaches.

4.4 Relating ISO/IEC 15504-2 to the Software CMM

The Software CMM is sometimes characterized as a staged model because it describes organizational capability in terms of maturity levels that represent evolutionary stages of capability, and the ISO/IEC 15504 model is sometimes, perhaps less accurately, described as a continuous model. The ISO/IEC 15504 model describes the terrain of software process maturity from the perspective of the individual process, where the Software CMM provides a roadmap for organizational improvement.

A staged model can be described as:
- an *organization-focused* model, since its target is the organization's process capability,
- a *descriptive* model, because it describes organizations at different levels of achieved capability,
- a *prescriptive* or normative model, since it prescribes how an organization should improve its processes.

A staged architecture focuses on software process improvement and, in the case of the Software CMM, provides 500 pages of mostly informative material on software processes that has been prioritized by being in key process areas. The rating components, i.e., the key process areas and goals, are a comparatively small part of the document; there are 18 key process areas and 52 goals.

The term *continuous* is not a strictly accurate description since the ISO/IEC 15504 architecture is also based on (capability) levels. Other descriptive terms that could be used include:

- a *process-focused* model, since its target is process capability,
- a *terrain* model, from the analogy to a description of the software process terrain, and
- a *reference* model, since its primary use is in assessment as the reference for rating processes.

One of the objectives of ISO/IEC 15504 is to create a way of measuring process capability, while avoiding a specific approach to improvement such as the SEI's maturity levels, so that the many different kinds of assessment, model, and their results, can be meaningfully compared to one another. The approach selected is to measure the implementation and institutionalization of specific processes; a process measure rather than an organization measure. Maturity levels can be viewed as sets of process profiles using this approach [Paulk95c, Paulk96b]. This addresses one of the deficiencies in the staged approach: lower maturity key process areas evolve with the organization's maturity. For example, there are organizational standards and required training for Software Configuration Management in a maturity level 3 organization, even though this is not explicitly stated in the Software CMM.

Both the staged and continuous perspectives have value, and they are conceptually compatible, but there is a fundamental philosophical difference between the two architectures. This philosophical difference implies strengths and weaknesses for both architectures, as described in Table 6.

Table 6. Comparing Staged and Continuous Architectures.

Characteristic	Staged Architecture (Software CMM)	Continuous Architecture (ISO/IEC 15504)
Vital few	Attention is focused on the "vital few" issues in process improvement that are generally true for any organization.	Less important process issues can drown out the "vital few" issues when there are clashes over improvement priorities.

Characteristic	Staged Architecture (Software CMM)	Continuous Architecture (ISO/IEC 15504)
Organization capability	Organizational capability is explicitly described in terms of maturity levels.	Organizational capability is implicit; it can be intuitively understood by looking at the organizational processes, the process attributes, and their dependencies.
Process evolution	Key process areas are a snapshot of the evolving process.	The evolution of processes from ad hoc to continuously improving is "fully" described.
Guidance	Extensive guidance in the key practices and subpractices provides significant help in understanding what a key practice or goal means, although it is typically oriented towards the practices of large organizations and projects in a contracting environment.	Abstract processes and process attributes can be difficult to interpret. No particular organizational improvement path is prescribed.
Extendibility	It may be difficult for the non-expert to extend the CMM principles to new disciplines or focus areas.	Adding processes and integrating with other models is a relatively straightforward definition, with the application of the capability dimension for rating the processes.

Some processes are "invisible" in a staged model, until the point that focusing on their improvement becomes critical to organizational maturity. Engineering processes, for example, are not a focus of maturity level 2, so they "suddenly appear" at level 3. Level 1 organizations perform engineering processes, but they are not represented in the Software CMM until level 3. This is intrinsic to the way the maturity levels are defined: the critical problems for level 1 organizations are managerial, not technical, so the improvement focus is not on the engineering processes at level 2.

This focus on the "vital few" processes at each maturity level for building organizational capability becomes a challenge when layering a staged model on top of a continuous architecture.

For example, should every process described in the continuous model be placed under quantitative or statistical control if the organization is to be characterized as level 4 or higher? The staged model lets the decision of what processes should be quantitatively or statistically controlled be driven by business objectives. No rule, other than "all processes," has been articulated yet for aggregating process capability levels to achieve an organizational maturity level when using a continuous model. Should all processes be standardized? Under statistical control? Optimal?

This is both a strength and a weakness of the layering approach to integrating staged and continuous models. It highlights standardizing and tailoring (capability level 3) as issues for level 2 key process areas in a maturity level 3 organization, but flexibility in applying these principles to all (versus critical) processes is desirable from a business objective perspective. Conversely, the improvement priorities in the staged model describe an "80% solution" to effective process improvement; organizations have unique improvement needs driven by their business needs and environment.

Key process areas are not processes. A process changes over time and hopefully matures. A process is dynamic. A key process area is a static description of essential attributes (i.e., key practices) of a process when that process is fully realized, and it does not tell how the process is performed.

The CMM Integration effort is dealing with these two improvement architectures by explicitly supporting both perspectives. This is intended to support conforming with ISO/IEC 15504 requirements and to allow CMMI users to select the architectural perspective they find most useful.

4.5 The Future of ISO/IEC 15504

ISO/IEC 15504 continues to evolve as the type 2 technical reports are trialled, but its potential is significant. Significant changes may be expected as current concerns are addressed [Kitson97, Paulk95e]. Current plans are that ISO/IEC 15504 will be revised and released as an international standard in 2002.

For further information on ISO/IEC 15504, see the World Wide Web page
  http://www-sqi.cit.gu.edu.au/spice/

5. Other Models and Standards

While the three approaches to software process appraisal and improvement described in this chapter may be the best known, there are many others that the reader should be aware of, such as Bootstrap, SDCE, SPR, and Trillium.

Bootstrap was developed by an ESPRIT project [Kuvaja94, Haase94]. It extended the SEI's work with features based on guidelines from ISO 9000 and European Space Agency process model standards. The extensions were made to fit the methodology into the European context, and to attain more detailed capability profiles in addition to maturity levels, separately for both organizations and projects. Although the Bootstrap approach was formed by extending the Software CMM with new and reshaped features, it is still possible to distinguish maturity levels that are equivalent to the SEI model. For further information on Bootstrap, see the World Wide Web page

http://www.etnoteam.it/bootstrap/institut.html

Software Development Capability Evaluation (SDCE) is a method to evaluate the capability and capacity of organizations proposing to develop software-intensive defense systems [Babel97, SDCE], developed for the U.S. Air Force. SDCE not only addresses software engineering capability, but also the systems engineering and related development disciplines integral to the successful development of a software-intensive defense system. It is based on the Software Development Capability/Capacity Review (SDCCR) method [SDCCR], developed by the U.S. Air Force Aeronautical Systems Center, and the SEI's SCE method. The SDCE method's primary objective is to reduce development risk by selecting contractors who are capable of successfully developing embedded software to meet program life cycle requirements. For further information on SDCE, see the World Wide Web page

http://www.afmc.wpafb.af.mil/pdl/afmc/63afmc.htm

Trillium is a telecommunications product development and support capability model developed by Bell Canada, Northern Telecom and Bell-Northern Research [Trillium]. It is used to assess the product development and support capability of prospective and existing suppliers of telecommunications or information technology-based products. Trillium can also be used as a reference benchmark in an internal capability improvement program. Trillium is based on the Software CMM, but it also addresses ISO 9001, Bellcore standards, and the relevant parts of the Malcolm Baldrige National Quality Award criteria. For further information on Trillium, see the World Wide Web page

http://ricis.cl.uh.edu/process_maturity/trillium/

Capers Jones' SPR (Software Productivity Research) method includes software quality and productivity research data on productivity, quality, schedules, costs, and other quantifiable factors. SPR assessments rate organizations on a five level scale against industry norms using this data [Jones96, Jones97]. For further information on SPR, see the World Wide Web page

http://www.spr.com/homepage.htm

Many other models and standards for process appraisal and improvement are available, but this chapter provides an overview of the most prominent ones.

6. Conclusions

The three approaches to software process appraisal and improvement discussed in this chapter provide useful information from somewhat different perspectives. To survive, much less thrive, modern organizations must continually improve all aspects of their business. Improvement in software-intensive products and services is crucial – and difficult.

There are many sources for best practices in the software industry [Brown96, Maguire94, McConnell96]. The challenge is to implement good software engineering and management practices in the high-pressure environment software organizations face. A disciplined and systematic approach to software process and quality improvement, such as these models and standards support, is necessary to survive and thrive.

The relative merits of these three approaches depend to large degree on the business environment of the organization. Companies doing business with customers or in markets where ISO 9001 certification is required will naturally use ISO 9001. Companies doing business with the U.S. government, in particular the Department of Defense, will be motivated to use the Software CMM. Multinational companies or companies that have to deal with multiple approaches are likely to be interested in ISO/IEC 15504, but since it is still under development, it is difficult to make definitive statements about its intrinsic merits or problems at this time.

The ISO 9000 series has the intrinsic advantage of being a well-recognized and widely used international standard. It is a short document, so interpretation of the standard can be an issue. This is much less of a problem with the Software CMM, which provides detailed guidance and is widely used in the software world. An extensive infrastructure has developed to support both ISO 9000 and the Software CMM. For organizations that must deal with both ISO 9000 and the Software CMM, a frequent recommendation is to begin with ISO 9001 certification and continue the process improvement journey using the Software CMM.

Regardless of the approach selected, building competitive advantage should be focused on improvement, not on achieving a score, whether the score is a maturity level, a certificate, or a process profile.

References

Babel97	Philip Babel, "Software Development Capability Evaluation: An Integrated Systems and Software Approach," Crosstalk: The Journal of Defense Software Engineering, Vol. 10, No. 4, April 1997, pp. 3-7.
Bach94	James Bach, "The Immaturity of the CMM," American Programmer, Vol. 7, No. 9, September 1994, pp. 13-18.
Bate95	Roger Bate, et al, "A Systems Engineering Capability Maturity Model, Version 1.1," Software Engineering Institute, CMU/SEI-95-MM-003, November 1995.
Besselman93	Joseph J. Besselman, Paul Byrnes, Cathy J. Lin, Mark C. Paulk, and Rajesh Puranik, "Software Capability Evaluations: Experiences from the Field," SEI Technical Review '93, 1993.
Bollinger91	T. Bollinger and C. McGowan, "A Critical Look at Software Capability Evaluations," IEEE Software, Vol. 8, No. 4, July 1991, pp. 25-41.
Brown96	Norm Brown, "Industrial-Strength Management Strategies,"" IEEE Software, Vol. 13, No. 4, July 1996, pp. 94-103.
Buetow94	Richard C. Buetow, "A Statement from Motorola Regarding ISO 9000," American Programmer, Vol. 7, No. 2, February 1994, pp. 7-8.

Byrnes96   Paul Byrnes and Mike Phillips, "Software Capability Evaluation Version 3.0 Method Description," Software Engineering Institute, Carnegie Mellon University, CMU/SEI-96-TR-002, DTIC Number ADA309160, 1996.

Curtis94   Bill Curtis, "A Mature View of the CMM," American Programmer, Vol. 7, No. 9, September 1994, pp. 19-28.

Curtis95   Bill Curtis, William E. Hefley, and Sally Miller, "People Capability Maturity Model," Software Engineering Institute, CMU/SEI-95-MM-02, September 1995.

D1-9001   "Advanced Quality System for Software Development and Maintenance: D1-9001," The Boeing Company, Seattle, WA, October 1994.

DeMarco95   Tom DeMarco, *Why Does Software Cost So Much?*, Dorset House, New York, NY, 1995.

Dorling93   Alec Dorling, "Software Process Improvement and Capability dEtermination," Software Quality Journal, Vol. 2, No. 4, December 1993, pp. 209-224.

Dunaway96   Donna K. Dunaway and Steve M. Masters, "CMM-Based Appraisal for Internal Process Improvement (CBA IPI): Method Description," Software Engineering Institute, Carnegie Mellon University, CMU/SEI-96-TR-007, DTIC Number ADA307934, 1996.

Emam96   Khaled El Emam and Dennis R. Goldenson, "Some Initial Results from the International SPICE Trials," Software Process Newsletter, IEEE Computer Society Technical Council on Software Engineering, No. 6, Spring 1996, pp. 1-5.

Ferguson96   J. Ferguson, J. Cooper, et al., "Software Acquisition Capability Maturity Model (SA-CMM) Version 1.01," Software Engineering Institute, Carnegie Mellon University, CMU/SEI-96-TR-020, December 1996.

Gibbs94   W. Wayt Gibbs, "Software's Chronic Crisis," Scientific American, September 1994, pp. 86-95.

Haase94   Volkmar Haase, Gunter Koch, Hans J. Kugler, and Paul Decrinis, "Bootstrap: Fine-Tuning Process Assessment," IEEE Software, Vol. 11, No. 4, July 1994, pp. 25-35.

Harauz94   John Harauz, "ISO Standards for Software Engineering," Standards Engineering, July/August 1994, pp. 4-6.

Humphrey87   Watts S. Humphrey and W. L. Sweet, "A Method for Assessing the Software Engineering Capability of Contractors," Software Engineering Institute, Carnegie Mellon University, CMU/SEI-87-TR-23, DTIC Number ADA187320, September 1987.

Humphrey91	Watts S. Humphrey and Bill Curtis, "Comments on 'A Critical Look'," IEEE Software, Vol. 8, No. 4, July 1991, pp. 42-46.
ImproveIT	Alec Dorling, Peter Simms, and Harry Barker, "ImproveIT," UK Ministry of Defense, June 1991.
ISO-N944R	"Study Report: The Need and Requirements for a Software Process Assessment Standard," ISO/IEC JTC1/SC7, Document N944R, Issue 2.0, 11 June 1992.
Jones95	Capers Jones, "The SEI's CMM—Flawed?," Software Development, Vol. 3, No. 3, March 1995, pp. 41-48.
Jones96	Capers Jones, *Patterns of Software System Failure and Success*, Intl Thomson Computer Pr, ISBN 1850328048, 1996.
Jones97	Capers Jones, *Software Quality: Analysis and Guidelines for Success*, Intl Thomson Computer Pr, ISBN 1850328676, 1997.
Kitson97	David H. Kitson, "An Emerging International Standard for Software Process Assessment," *Proceedings of the Third IEEE International Software Engineering Standards Symposium and Forum*, Walnut Creek, CA, 1-6 June 1997, pp. 83-90.
Konrad95	Michael D. Konrad, Mark C. Paulk, and Allan W. Graydon, "An Overview of SPICE's Model for Process Management," *Proceedings of the Fifth International Conference on Software Quality*, Austin, TX, 23-26 October 1995, pp. 291-301.
Konrad96	M. Konrad, M.B. Chrissis, J. Ferguson, S. Garcia, B. Hefley, D. Kitson, and M. Paulk, "Capability Maturity Modeling at the SEI," Software Process: Improvement and Practice, Vol. 2, Issue 1, March 1996, pp. 21-34.
Kuvaja94	Pasi Kuvaja, Jouni Simila, et al, *Software Process Assessment & Improvement: The BOOTSTRAP Approach*, Blackwell Business, Oxford, United Kingdom, 1994.
Lederer92	Albert L. Lederer and Jayesh Prasad, "Nine Management Guidelines for Better Cost Estimating," Communications of the ACM, Vol. 35, No. 2, February 1992, pp. 51-59.
Lloyd's94	"Lloyd's Register TickIT Auditors' Course, Issue 1.4," Lloyd's Register, March 1994.
Mackie93	C.A. Mackie and P.G. Rigby, "Practical Experience in Assessing the Health of the Software Process," Software Quality Journal, Vol. 2, No. 4, December 1993, pp. 265-276.
Maguire94	Steve Maguire, *Debugging the Development Process*, Microsoft Press, Redmond, WA, 1994.

Marquardt91	Donald Marquardt, et al., "Vision 2000: The Strategy for the ISO 9000 Series Standards in the '90s," ASQC Quality Progress, Vol. 24, No. 5, May 1991, pp. 25-31.
Marshall96	Peter Marshall, Fiona Maclennan, and Mary Tobin, "Analysis of Observation and Problem Reports from Phase One of the SPICE Trials," Software Process Newsletter, IEEE Computer Society Technical Council on Software Engineering, No. 6, Spring 1996, pp. 10-12.
Masters95	Steve Masters and Carol Bothwell, "CMM Appraisal Framework, Version 1.0," Software Engineering Institute, Carnegie Mellon University, CMU/SEI-95-TR-001, February 1995.
Matsubara94	Tomoo Matsubara, "Does ISO 9000 Really Help Improve Software Quality?" American Programmer, Vol. 7, No. 2, February 1994, pp. 38-45.
McConnell96	Steve McConnell, *Rapid Development: Taming Wild Software Schedules*, Microsoft Press, Redmond, WA, 1996.
McFeeley96	Bob McFeeley, "IDEAL: A User's Guide for Software Process Improvement," Software Engineering Institute, CMU/SEI-96-HB-001, February 1996.
O'Connell00	Emilie O'Connell and Hossein Saiedian, "Can You Trust Software Capability Evaluations?" IEEE Computer, Vol. 33, No. 2, February 2000, pp. 28-35.
Paulk94	Mark C. Paulk and Michael D. Konrad, "An Overview of ISO's SPICE Project," American Programmer, Vol. 7, No. 2, February 1994, pp. 16-20.
Paulk95a	Carnegie Mellon University, Software Engineering Institute (Principal Contributors and Editors: Mark C. Paulk, Charles V. Weber, Bill Curtis, and Mary Beth Chrissis), *The Capability Maturity Model: Guidelines for Improving the Software Process*, Addison-Wesley Publishing Company, Reading, MA, 1995.
Paulk95b	Mark C. Paulk, "The Evolution of the SEI's Capability Maturity Model for Software," Software Process: Improvement and Practice, Vol. 1, Pilot Issue, Spring 1995, pp. 3-15.
Paulk95c	Mark C. Paulk, Michael D. Konrad, and Suzanne M. Garcia, "CMM Versus SPICE Architectures," IEEE Computer Society Technical Council on Software Engineering, Software Process Newsletter, No. 3, Spring 1995, pp. 7-11.
Paulk95d	Mark C. Paulk, "How ISO 9001 Compares With the CMM," IEEE Software, Vol. 12, No. 1, January 1995, pp. 74-83.
Paulk95e	Mark C. Paulk, "A Perspective on the Issues Facing SPICE," *Proceedings of the Fifth International Conference on Software Quality*, Austin, TX, 23-26 October 1995, pp. 415-424.

Paulk96a

Mark C. Paulk, "Effective CMM-Based Process Improvement," *Proceedings of the 6th International Conference on Software Quality*, Ottawa, Canada, 28-31 October 1996, pp. 226-237.

Paulk96b

Mark C. Paulk, "Process Improvement and Organizational Capability: Generalizing the CMM," *Proceedings of the ASQC's 50th Annual Quality Congress and Exposition*, Chicago, IL, 13-15 May 1996, pp. 92-97.

Paulk97

Mark C. Paulk, "Software Process Proverbs," Crosstalk: The Journal of Defense Software Engineering, Vol. 10, No. 1, January 1997, pp. 4-7.

Paulk99

Mark C. Paulk, "Analyzing the Conceptual Relationship Between ISO/IEC 15504 (Software Process Assessment) and the Capability Maturity Model for Software," *Proceedings of the Ninth International Conference on Software Quality*, Cambridge, MA, 4-6 Oct 1999, pp. 293-303.

Saiedian95

Hossein Saiedian and Richard Kuzara, "SEI Capability Maturity Model's Impact on Contractors," IEEE Computer, Vol. 28, No. 1, January 1995, pp. 16-26.

Sanders94

Joc Sanders and Eugene Curran, *Software Quality: A Framework for Success in Software Development and Support,* Addison-Wesley, Reading, MA, 1994.

SDCCR

"Software Development Capability/Capacity Review," U.S. Air Force, ASD Pamphlet 800-5, 10 September 1987.

SDCE

"Acquisition -- Software Development Capability Evaluation," U.S. Air Force, AFMC Pamphlet 63-103, Volumes 1 and 2, June 15, 1994.

Shaughnessy94

R.N. Shaughnessy, "ISO 9000 Current Status & Future Challenges," Straight Talk About ISO 9000 Conference, ASQC and ANSI, Los Angeles, CA, 27-28 October 1994.

Shaw90

Mary Shaw, "Prospects for an Engineering Discipline of Software," IEEE Software, Vol. 7, No. 6, November 1990, pp. 15-24.

SPICE-2

"Software Process Assessment Part 2: A Model for Process Management," International Organization for Standardization, ISO/IEC JTC1/SC7/WG10 Working Draft, July 1995.

Stelzer96

D. Stelzer, W. Mellis, and G. Herzwurm, "Software Process Improvement via ISO 9000? Results of Two Surveys Among European Software Houses," Software Process: Improvement and Practice, Vol. 2, Issue 3, September 1996, pp. 197-210.

TickIT

"TickIT: A Guide to Software Quality Management System Construction and Certification Using EN29001, Issue 2.0," UK Department of Trade and Industry and the British Computer Society, 28 February 1992.

Trillium   "Trillium: Model for Telecom Product Development and Support Process Capability" Release 3.0, Bell Canada, December 1994.

UK-Court96   "UK judges: Software must be sold bug-free," IEEE Computer, Vol. 29, No. 10, October 1996, pg. 16.

West00   Jack West, Charles A. Cianfrani, and Joseph J. Tsiakals, "A Breeze or a Breakthrough? Conforming to ISO 9000:2000," ASQ Quality Progress, Vol. 33, No. 3, March 2000, pp. 41-44.

Woodman96   Ian Woodman and Robin Hunter, "Analysis of Assessment Data from Phase One of the SPICE Trials," Software Process Newsletter, IEEE Computer Society Technical Council on Software Engineering, No. 6, Spring 1996, pp. 5-9.

The Frameworks Quagmire

Sarah A. Sheard
Software Productivity Consortium

Organizations that wish to remain competitive often want to comply with all possible contractor evaluation criteria, process models, and quality standards, but the rapidly evolving field requires they dedicate enormous amounts of resources to keep up. This article describes the categories of compliance frameworks and the characteristics of seven important ones: the Capability Maturity Model (CMM[SM]), Systems Engineering (SE)-CMM, Integrated Product Development (IPD)-CMM, International Organization for Standardization (ISO) 9000, Software Development Capability Evaluation (SDCE), MIL-STD-498, and Trillium. It also discusses trends and recommendations to deal with the "frameworks quagmire."

More and more often, software and system developers are discovering that their ability to win and perform on contracts is as subject to investigation of their processes as it is of their products' quality, cost, or effectiveness. The number of frameworks against which their processes are evaluated continues to increase, as Figure 1 illustrates.

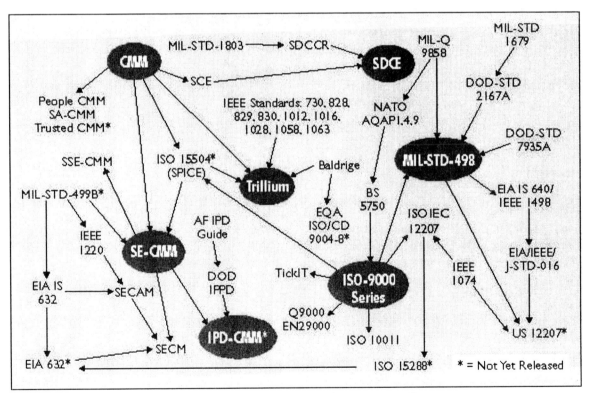

Figure 1. *The "frameworks quagmire."*

In the late 1980s, the CMM for software was created to help software developers mature their software development processes to better meet contractual requirements. Recently, the engineering community presented two capability models—SE-CMM and the Systems Engineering Capability Assessment Model (SECAM)—for companies to use to improve their systems engineering processes.

Meanwhile, the international community developed several different groups of process improvement and quality standards—ISO 9000, ISO 15501, or Software Process Improvement Capability dEtermination (SPICE), and military-developed methods, such as the SDCE—to evaluate bidders during source selection.

Even now, new standards appear regularly. Asterisks in Figure 1 indicate frameworks that have not yet been publicly released. Omitted from this chart are efforts, such as the Testing Maturity Model [1], that were not driven by large standards-setting or professional groups. The amount of available frameworks is, at best, confusing.

It is evident that organizations need help to determine which standards and other frameworks are most beneficial. As a consortium of member companies, the Software Productivity Consortium has studied the compliance frameworks relevant to companies that build software-intensive systems. This article highlights some of the main points of a consortium course on compliance frameworks, including framework types, characteristics, trends, and recommendations.

A Multitude of Frameworks

From Figure 1, it is evident that developers may need to consider a daunting number of frameworks. The field truly is a quagmire in which process improvement efforts can bog down if an organization is not careful.

The arrows in Figure 1 show the usage of one framework in the development of another. For example, the SE-CMM of Enterprise Process Improvement Collaboration (EPIC)[1] was developed from the CMM[2], ISO SPICE, MIL-STD-499B (draft), and the Institute of Electrical and Electronics Engineers standard for systems engineering (IEEE 1220). The SE-CMM was later used to create the IPD-CMM, the Security Systems Engineering (SSE)-CMM [2], and a merged systems engineering capability model (SECM) currently under development and facilitated by the Electronics Industries Association (EIA).

Types of Compliance Frameworks

The first step toward making sense of the quagmire is to categorize the frameworks by purpose. One or more of the following six categories apply to most of the frameworks:

- Standards and guidelines.
- Process Improvement Models and Internal Appraisal Methods.
- Contractor Selection Vehicles
- Quality Awards.
- Software Engineering Lifecycle Models.
- Systems Engineering Models.

Standards and Guidelines

Standards and guidelines establish what must be done in a contractual situation. Most can be tailored as desired by both parties and may be used as recommendations of good practices in general. Guidelines may interpret associated standards or collect practices not intended to be specified in a contract.

Standards include

- U.S. military standards, such as MIL-STD-498 (software development and documentation), and guidelines, such as the Air Force guidelines for integrated product development.
- Commercial standards, such as EIA Interim Standard (IS) 632, for the systems engineering process.
- International standards, such as the ISO 9000 series for quality systems (which includes guidelines as well as standards).

Process Improvement Models and Internal Appraisal Methods

In general, these frameworks define characteristics of good processes but do not prescribe how they should be enacted. The purpose of process improvement models is to establish a road map by which a route can be drawn from "where we are today" to "where we want to be." To determine "where we are today," an organization performs an appraisal, sometimes with the aid of an outsider with specific expertise in the model. These models include

- CMM relatives, including the CMM, the SE-CMM, IPD-CMM, People (P)-CMM, and others.
- SECAM.
- The Trillium model, for telecommunications.

Contractor-Selection Vehicles

These frameworks specify the examination of an organization's processes by an outsider, either a second party (the potential acquirer) or a third party (usually hired by the potential acquirer). The result is a detailed comparison of competitors' strengths and weaknesses that will minimize procurement risk to the acquiring agency. Two methods in use are

- Software Capability Evaluation (SCE) (associated with the CMM).
- SDCE, from the U.S. Air Force.

Quality Awards

In 1987, the U.S. government established an award program, the Malcolm Baldrige National Quality Award [3], to improve American businesses' focus on quality and customer satisfaction. Subsequently, Europe established an award with extremely similar criteria and selection methods; recently, ISO has begun a draft standard with identical categories to the Baldrige's seven categories. Quality awards include

- Malcolm Baldrige National Quality Award.
- European Quality Award.
- ISO/CD 9004-8, draft standard on quality management principles.

Software Engineering Lifecycle Models

MIL-STD-498 was developed from Department of Defense (DOD)-STD-2167A (for software development), DOD-STD-7935A (for documentation), and MIL-Q-9858 (for quality). Approved after the official date of "no more military standards" in 1993, this standard was intended to be an interim standard until commercial standards replaced it after about two years. ISO/IEC 12207 is an international standard in the same area, and MIL-STD-498 is being adapted (in several steps) to add ISO/IEC 12207-type requirements on acquirers, maintainers, and operators—parties not mentioned in MIL-STD-498. Lifecycle models include

- MIL-STD-498.
- EIA/IEEE J-STD-016 (J-STD-016).
- ISO/IEC 12207.
- U.S. 12207 (IEEE/EIA 12207).

Systems Engineering Models

The SE-CMM was developed in 1994 by half- and full-time authors working on the model for a year. Funding was provided by the authors' companies as a provision of their participation in EPIC, then called the Industrial Collaboration. The model was completed within one year and revised, along with an accompanying appraisal method, within the next 18 months. At the same time, an International Council on Systems Engineering (INCOSE) working group developed the SECAM from several systems engineering assessment models used internally by companies in the aerospace and defense industry.

One primary difference between the SE-CMM and the SECAM is that the former was first developed as a model and the latter as an assessment method, with systems engineering standards (from the EIA and IEEE) that served as the model. They also differ in that the SE-CMM confines its scope to process characteristics, whereas the SECAM includes nonprocess characteristics, such as work quality and systems engineering team experience. Finally, the SE-CMM considers all practices "base practices"—performance in an informal manner would earn the organization a Level 1 rating in the process area—but the SECAM allows some practices to be required only of higher-capability organizations so that Level 1 organizations need not perform them at all. In the SECM merger effort being facilitated by the EIA, these differences have been resolved and the models are being merged. Initial public release is scheduled for mid-1997.

ISO 15288 is an effort to create an international system lifecycle standard, initiated by the group who created the ISO software lifecycle standard, ISO/IEC 12207, and augmented by people with systems engineering expertise. Release is scheduled for 2001. Systems engineering models include

- MIL-STD-499B (Systems Engineering).
- SE-CMM.
- SECAM.
- IEEE 1220.
- EIA IS 632 and EIA 632.
- ISO 15288.

Characteristics of Seven Frameworks

Table 1 compares characteristics of the seven important frameworks represented in Figure 1. Brief notes about the frameworks follow.

Framework	Scope	Purpose	Length, pages	Major Focus	Notes
CMM	Software developing organization	PI (Process Improvement)	500	SW Process	Staged architecture provides "Triptik" (after the AAA map with exact roads, stops, and times highlighted) for improvement.
SE-CMM	Organization developing systems	PI	250	SE Process	Continuous architecture provides map of terrain.
IPD-CMM	Enterprise	PI	220	Process	Staged-continuous architecture provides map plus "Triptik."
ISO 9000	Product producing organization	Trade	16	Quality Process	Registration certifies a minimum quality system compliance.
SDCE	Bidding organization	Contractor selection	600	Process, Capacity, Technology	Evaluates risks to acquirer for each bid and reduces risks with winning contractor.
Software Lifecycle Standards	Software developing organization	Contract compliance	60-200	Management Process	Standards are evolving to include role of acquirer and others, as well as supplier.
Trillium	Enterprise	PI	130	Process	Combines requirements from CMM, ISO, Baldridge, and software quality standards.

Table 1. *Characteristics of seven frameworks.*

CMM

The CMM "nucleus" includes the CMM, the P-CMM, the Software Acquisition (SA)-CMM, and the Trusted (T)-CMM. The CMM, P-CMM, and T-CMM address the software development organization within an enterprise. The SA-CMM applies to an acquisition agency. In contrast, the SE-CMM addresses the organization-building systems, which will be larger than the software development organization if the systems include hardware and software. The IPD-CMM addresses the product development enterprise, including such groups as marketing, manufacturing, and business management, as well as the development organizations.

SE-CMM

Frameworks centered on the SE-CMM nucleus all involve systems engineering. The systems engineering standards' definition for systems engineering includes most of the 12 systems engineering roles described in a previous article of mine [4]. IEEE 1220 primarily takes a technical management view, whereas EIA IS 632 leans more toward requirements development and system design. The latter two are now apparently being consolidated into the anticipated EIA 632.

IPD-CMM

EPIC, the creator of the SE-CMM, is also creating the IPD-CMM. The authors used the Air Force IPD guide and the DoD guide to Integrated Product and Process Development (DOD IPPD) as input and visited organizations that practice IPD well to verify principles and practices.

One goal of the IPD-CMM is to establish a framework into which other CMMs can fit. Its architecture is a hybrid of the staged and continuous models. Implementation of the integration depends, in part, on the existence of minimal "plug-and-play" models in specific domains. These models would be combined with the basic product development, integration, or supporting processes already covered by the IPD-CMM to form a model that is appropriate for the specific organization that uses it.

Because the IPD-CMM model is considered highly complex and because questions have arisen concerning the support the IPD-CMM gives to organizations that wish to implement IPD, EPIC is, at press time, reconsidering its imminent release.

ISO 9000

ISO 9000 registration was intended to facilitate trade rather than process improvement, yet the quest for registration often has the same effect on the organization as the quest for a CMM level (generally Level 2 or Level 3): the organization's processes are documented, and discipline is tightened to ensure that documented processes are followed. Although, in theory, ISO addresses only "quality-impacting" processes, that definition is broad enough that virtually all the CMM and SE-CMM processes fall under the ISO 9000 umbrella.

TickIT, described by roughly 75 pages, was developed by the British Standards Institute. TickIT provides detailed ISO 9000 guidance for software development. TickIT registration generally is optional, except in the United Kingdom. The ISO 10011 series of standards specifies requirements and training for ISO 9000 auditors.

SDCE

The SDCE evolved from the Air Force's Software Development Critical Capacity Review and from the SCE, which is an assessment method associated with the CMM. To CMM-type questions, the SDCE adds several areas of focus, including systems engineering and technology (such as artificial intelligence). The SDCE's technology areas, in particular, may not apply on all procurements, and more than half of the questions may be deleted to tailor the SDCE for any one procurement.

Software Lifecycle Standards

These standards specify lifecycles, including reviews that approve moving from one phase to the next. These standards provide processes, in contrast to CMMs, which provide requirements that good processes will meet.

Initial modification of MIL-STD-498 to become more commercial proceeded under the numbers EIA IS 640 and IEEE 1498. These numbers were retired before the standard was released, and the standard was given a J series number (J-STD-016), meaning a joint standard between the two organizations. The current name for the expected commercial version is U.S. 12207, but IEEE 12207 and IEEE/EIA 12207 are also quoted.

Trillium

The Trillium model, created by Bell Canada, combines requirements from the ISO 9000 series, the CMM, and the Malcolm Baldrige criteria, with software quality standards from the IEEE. Two conditions prevent the model from being adopted as is: in some cases, goals of the frameworks are used rather than their detailed requirements, and the model includes process information that is unique to the telecommunications field.

However, the model serves as proof that the requirements of several of the popular frameworks can be combined, and it provides a template for additional efforts in this area.

Frameworks Trends

To those who follow the field of compliance frameworks, four trends are now evident:

- Evolution.
- Proliferation.
- Integration and Coordination.
- Consolidation.

Evolution

Current models are being improved and adapted to better meet stakeholder needs. Professional standards and the CMMs have comment-logging and solution-approval processes and are often updated on a predetermined schedule. This is a positive trend: the models need to be improved, and improvements can include better integration with other models. However, any changes will be read, understood, and responded to by those who have used the old model. Because there are approximately 5,000 organizations with investment in the CMM and over 10,000 with investment in the ISO 9000 series, the inertia against change may be considerable.

Proliferation

More models are being developed on a continual basis. The T-CMM and SSE-CMM are examples of recent additions. This proliferation is both good news and bad news. It is good in that new models tend to capture wisdom and best practices because developers have been seeking "best practices" for years.

But the implementation of best practices in a real organization is at least as hard as the assembly of hard lessons from the groups who have learned them. A person who deposits a new 300-page model on a process engineer's desk is not likely to walk away feeling appropriately appreciated. Time must be devoted to read the new models and to understand changes to existing models as they emerge. If a new model is not seamlessly and obviously integratable with current frameworks, half a staff-year can easily be consumed in the determination of what, if anything, a new model suggests should be done differently.

Integration and Coordination

As mentioned above, the IPD-CMM provides a framework for future integration of CMMs. In addition, the Software Engineering Institute (SEI) sponsors the CMM integration effort, which may impose (on CMM revisions) requirements that will make model integration easier for users. The SEI also coordinates with other model makers, notably ISO 9000 (to the degree that they keep up with them and publish comparisons between the models) and ISO SPICE. Furthermore, as various frameworks evolve, authors read other frameworks and incorporate the best features. It is reasonable to expect fewer differences in the next cycle of models.

Consolidation

Retirement of multiple models as they are consolidated into a single new model is a highly positive trend. This appears to be happening with software lifecycle standards and, to a smaller extent, systems engineering standards and models.

Figure 2 shows an idealized picture of what the quagmire might look like if similar frameworks are consolidated. Each line would indicate a defined interface with a defined purpose. Frameworks listed together would be consolidated. Even more consolidation may occur with the CMMs and the SECM.

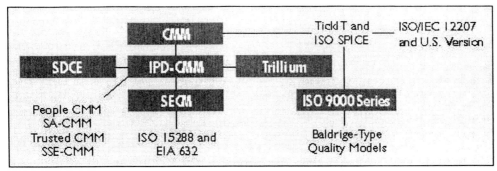

Figure 2. *A better frameworks quagmire.*

Recommendations for Creators of Frameworks

It is clear that those who write standards, process models, and contractor selection vehicles need to understand the predicament of software developers. Although there certainly is a need for well-crafted collections of best practices, creators of frameworks must take note of the frameworks that already exist and must tailor their additions to fit into some of them. How should organizations integrate compliance with a new model and compliance with other frameworks?

Recommendations for Software Developers

Cost competitiveness and time-to-market are the dominant factors that will keep companies alive, not to mention profitable, in the 1990s and beyond. But to define and implement process changes costs significant money—how can this be efficient?

The key lies in the adoption of only a few, high-leverage frameworks. In addition to the CMM (which most have already adopted), the Software Productivity Consortium's member companies are generally considering the SE-CMM, ISO 9000, and the SDCE (when they bid on Air Force contracts). Many members already have contracts that require compliance with MIL-STD-498 or its predecessors, so they look to the future, when MIL-STD-498 will be merged with ISO/IEC 12207. Members also look to the IPD-CMM to provide a needed integration framework.

It is recommended that developers delay implementation of most of the other frameworks. Some will disappear from lack of support. Others, which may prove long-lived, can be adopted after better integration methods have been made available.

Conclusions

Companies should focus on the identification of a small set of high-value frameworks to adopt. Those that already work with the CMM may add the SE-CMM and the IPD-CMM to help broaden their process improvement effort, and may delay the adoption of other CMMs until methods to integrate CMMs are better defined.

Other frameworks worth investigation are the ISO 9000 series of standards, the SDCE (if the bid is for Air Force contracts), Trillium (particularly for telecommunications companies), and the IPD-CMM.

Organizations with frameworks questions or problems in this area should consider joining with other industrial, academic, and government institutions in order to leverage their efforts to navigate the frameworks quagmire.

About the Author: Sarah A. Sheard has 17 years experience in systems engineering. She worked as a satellite engineer at Hughes Aircraft Space and Communications Group and in software systems at the Federal Systems group of IBM and Loral. Currently, she coordinates systems engineering efforts at the Software Productivity Consortium in Herndon, Va., where she also develops technical products and consults and teaches in systems engineering, process improvement, and integrated product teams. She received a master's degree in chemistry from the California Institute of Technology in 1979.

Software Productivity Consortium
2214 Rock Hill Road
Herndon, VA 20170-4214
Voice: 703-742-7106
Fax: 703-742-7200
E-mail: sheard@software.org

References

1. Burnstein, Ilene, Taratip Suwannasart, and C. R. Carlson, "Developing a Testing Maturity Model," Parts I and II, *Crosstalk*, STSC, Hill Air Force Base, Utah, August and September 1996.
2. Hefner, Rick, David Hsiao, and Warren Monroe, "Experience with the Security Systems Engineering CMM," *Proceedings of INCOSE*, 1996.
3. National Institute of Standards and Technology, Malcolm Baldrige National Quality Award.
4. Sheard, Sarah, "Twelve Systems Engineering Roles," *Proceedings of INCOSE*, 1996. Available from http://www.vtcorp.com/wma-incose/library.htm.

Notes

1. EPIC is a collaboration of industry, government, and academic institutions.
2. The acronym CMM, when used alone, refers to the CMM for software.

Other Resources

The Software Productivity Consortium maintains a "clickable" version of Figure 1 on its Web site at http://www.software.org/quagmire/ . This site provides current descriptions of all frameworks shown, including relationships to other frameworks and links to sources for the frameworks.

1. **CMM** - Paulk, M. C., B. Curtis, M. B. Chrissis, and C. V. Weber, *Capability Maturity Model for Software*, Version 1.1, Software Engineering Institute, CMU/SEI-93-TR-24, February 1993.
2. **DOD IPPD** - *DoD Guide to Integrated Product and Process Development*, Feb. 5, 1996, OUSD(A&T)/DTSE&E; ATTN: Mr. Mark D. Schaeffer, 3110 Defense Pentagon, Washington, DC 20301.
3. **EIA IS 632** - Electronics Industry Association, *EIA IS 632, Draft for Technical Committee Review, Systems Engineering*, Sept. 20, 1994.
4. **IEEE 1220** - IEEE Computer Society, *IEEE Trial-Use Standard for Application and Management of the Systems Engineering Process*, IEEE-STD-1220-1994, New York, Feb. 28, 1995.
5. **ISO 9000** - International Organization for Standardization, *ISO 9000 International Standards for Quality Management*. Switzerland, 1991.
6. **ISO 15288** - Lake, Dr. Jerome G., "ISO Standard 15288, System Life Cycle Processes," *INSIGHT*, Spring 1997.
7. **ISO/IEC 12207** - *Information technology - Software life cycle processes*, International Organization for

Standardization and International Electrotechnical Commission, ISO/IEC 12207:1995 (E), Aug. 1, 1995.

8. **IPD-CMM** - Software Engineering Institute and EPIC, *An Integrated Product Development Capability Maturity Model*, Carnegie Mellon University, Version 0.9, Oct. 28, 1996.

9. **J-STD-016** - Electronics Industry Association, *EIA/ IEEE/J-STD-016, Standard for Information Technology - Software Life Cycle Processes - Software Development - Acquirer-Supplier Agreement*, Feb. 6, 1996.

10. **P-CMM** - Curtis, Bill, William E. Hefley, and Sally Miller, "People Capability Maturity Model," Software Engineering Institute, CMU/SEI-95-MM-02, September 1995.

11. **SA-CMM** - *Software Acquisition Capability Maturity Model.*

12. **SDCE** - Software Development Capability Evaluation.

13. **SECAM** - INCOSE Capability Assessment Working Group, *Systems Engineering Capability Assessment Model*, Version 1.50, June 1996.

14. **SE-CMM** - EPIC, *A Systems Engineering Capability Maturity Model*, Version 1.1.

15. **SPICE** - International Organization for Standardization, *SPICE: Software Process Improvement Capability dEtermination.*

16. **Trillium** - Bell Canada, Northern Telecom, and Bell-Northern Research. *The Trillium Model.*

CMM and Capability Maturity Model are service marks of Carnegie Mellon University.

Chapter 2

The Capability Maturity Model for Software

1. Introduction to Chapter

The Capability Maturity Model for Software (SW-CMM) was developed in the mid 1980s by the Software Engineering Institute's (SEI's) Software Process Program led by Watts Humphrey. The SEI had been set up in 1984 with the mission

To provide leadership in advancing the state-of-the-practice of software engineering to improve the quality of systems that depend on software.

The Software Process Program was not the only significant program undertaken by the federally funded SEI in its early days. Other programs included:

- Ada-Based Software Engineering Program

- Software Engineering Computing Environment Program

- Training and Transition Methods Program

- Education Program

However, the Process Program was to become the program by which the SEI would become best known. To develop it, Watts Humphrey built on some ideas that had originated at IBM [5]. They are described in his book *Managing the Software Process* [3], in which he provides six basic principles for process change:

- Major changes to the software process must start at the top;

- Ultimately, everyone must be involved;

- Effective change requires a goal and a knowledge of the current process;

- Change is continuous;

- Software process changes will not be retained without conscious effort and periodic reinforcement;

- Software process improvement requires investment.

The SW-CMM (then known simply as the CMM) was launched at the SEI's Affiliates Symposium held in Pittsburgh in June 1987 and was received with great interest, especially by the potential government contractors who attended the symposium.

The first public version of the SW-CMM was based on two questionnaires, a maturity questionnaire and a technology questionnaire. The maturity questionnaire was concerned with the maturity of the software process (principally, how well it was defined and controlled), whereas the technology questionnaire was concerned with the extent to which advanced technology was used in the process. The result of a process assessment depended on the answers to the questions in both questionnaires and was two-dimensional, with low maturity, low technology processes being represented on the bottom left of a two-dimensional grid and high maturity, high technology processes on the top right of the grid. It was also suggested that an organization might progress from the bottom left position of the grid to the top right position of the grid in a period of around five years, though this rate of progress would now be considered rather ambitious.

As far as the route that an organization might take to go from the bottom left to the top right of the grid was concerned, it was strongly suggested that priority should be given to maturing the process in the first instance, followed by increasing the level of technology to support the maturer aspects of the process. At the time, this was seen as radical thinking in a context where many software producers were trying to buy their way out of trouble by investing in the latest technology.

Later versions of the SW-CMM were one- (rather than two-) dimensional, the emphasis now being on maturity rather than technology. However, the original two-dimensional scheme is still reflected in the diagonal layout of the five capability levels defined in the SW-CMM.

Later versions of the SW-CMM were also much less dependent on questionnaires, which were seen to be rather arbitrary, and more based on a conceptual model in the context of which information about the process could be sought.

Originally known simply as the CMM, the model became known as the SW-CMM in the light of various other CMMs that have appeared over the last few years, including

- People CMM (P-CMM),

- Systems Engineering CMM (SE-CMM),

- Software Acquisition CMM (SA-CMM),

- Integrated Product Development CMM (IPD-CMM).

The best source for references on each of the above models is the frameworks quagmire website [6] referred to in Chapter 1.

The latest (and final) version of SW-CMM is version 1.1. This will be succeeded by a new model (see introduction to Chapter 5) formed by integrating the Software CMM, the Integrated Product Development CMM, and the Systems Engineering CMM. The papers in this chapter are arranged chronologically and reflect the development of the SW-CMM through its various phases.

2. Description of Articles

The first paper is a copy of Chapter 1 of Watts Humphrey's definitive text "Managing the Software Process." In it, Humphrey introduces the idea of a Software Process Framework based on Deming's work on statistical process control [2]. He also introduces the idea of Software Process Improvement based on the use of the five Process Maturity Levels—*Initial, Repeatable, Defined, Managed, Optimizing*—and explains the significance of each of the levels.

The book continues with chapters on the principles of process change, the practicalities of conducting reliable assessments, and the requirements and significance of each of the Maturity Levels from 2 to 4.

The second paper, entitled "Software Process Improvement at Hughes Aircraft," is also by Watts Humphrey, with Terry Snyder and Ronald Willis of the Hughes Aircraft Corporation. It is taken from a 1991 issue of *IEEE Software* in which all of the main papers are devoted to the SW-CMM.

The Humphrey, Snyder, and Willis paper describes the successful experience of the Hughes Aircraft Corporation in using the SW-CMM as a basis for their software process improvement program, which allowed Hughes' Software Engineering Division to progress from level 2 to level 3 of the SW-CMM in two years. At the end of the first assessment in 1988, a five-point action plan was determined. The five points were

- to form a software engineering process group,

- to implement quantitative process management,

- to fill gaps in the training program,

- to standardize an effective review process,

- to move toward a software engineering discipline.

On the completion of a second assessment two years later, Hughes was found to be clearly at level 3 with many level 4 and level 5 activities in place. In addition, further findings and recommendations were made so that Hughes could continue to improve its process. The paper concludes by summarizing the lessons learned from the improvement exercise.

The same issue of *IEEE Software* also included an important paper by Terry Bollinger and Clement McGowan [1] that is not included in this tutorial. It is entitled "A Critical Look at Software Capability Evaluations" and is rather critical of the SW-CMM, reflecting the views of some in the software industry at the time. The main point made is that the SW-CMM *at the time* was really only a set of questions and lacked an underlying conceptual model.

These criticisms were taken very seriously by the SEI and resulted in the development of Version 1.1 of the SW-CMM. This new version is described in "Capability Maturity Model, version 1.1," the third paper in this chapter, by Mark Paulk, Bill Curtis, Mary Beth Chrissis, and Charles Weber, as well as in the textbook by the same authors [4].

Version 1.1 of the maturity model has key process areas associated with each maturity level. For example, at level 2 (Repeatable) two of the key process areas are

- Requirements Management
- Software Configuration Management

while at level 5 (Optimising) two of the key process areas are

- Defect prevention
- Process change management.

It is these key process areas only that are assessed at each level of the SW-CMM. In addition, Version 1.1 identifies *key practices* which should be in place at each level, and these key practices suggest *activities* that should take place and *infrastructure* that should be present. Assessors should then be principally concerned with whether the activities take place and whether the infrastructure is present, rather than seeking the answers to predefined questions. In this way the SEI countered many of the criticisms that had been made of earlier versions of the SW-CMM.

3. References

[1] T. Bollinger, C. McGowan; *IEEE Software,* vol. 8, no. 4, 1991.

[2] W. E. Deming; *Out of Crisis,* Cambridge University Press, 1982.

[3] W. Humphrey; *Managing the Software Process*, Addison Wesley, 1989.

[4] M. C. Paulk, C. V. Weber, B. Curtis, M. B. Chrissis; *The Capability Maturity Model: Guidelines for Improving the Software Process,* Addison Wesley, 1995.

[5] R. Radice, J. Harding, P. Munnis, R. Phillips; "A Programming Case Study", *IBM Systems Journal,* volume 24, number 2, pp. 91-101, 1985.

[6] Sheard S, "The Frameworks Quagmire"

http://www.software.org/quagmire/

A Software Maturity Framework

Watts S. Humphrey

In launching an improvement program, we should first consider the characteristics of a truly effective software process. Fundamentally, it must be predictable. That is, cost estimates and schedule commitments must be met with reasonable consistency, and the resulting products should generally meet users' functional and quality expectations.

The software process is the set of tools, methods, and practices we use to produce a software product. The objectives of software process management are to produce products according to plan while simultaneously improving the organization's capability to produce better products. The basic principles are those of statistical process control, which have been used successfully in many fields. A process is said to be stable or under statistical control if its future performance is predictable within established statistical limits. [4]

When a process is under statistical control, repeating the work in roughly the same way will produce roughly the same result. To obtain consistently better results, it is thus necessary to improve the process. If the process is not under statistical control, sustained progress is not possible until it is.

Dr. W. E. Deming, in his work with the Japanese after World War II, applied the concepts of statistical process control to many of their industries.[4] While there are important differences, these concepts are just as applicable to software as they are to producing consumer goods like cameras, television sets, or automobiles.

The basic principle behind statistical control is measurement. As Lord Kelvin said a century ago: "When you can measure what you are speaking about, and express it in numbers, you know something about it; but when you cannot measure it, when you cannot express it in numbers, your knowledge is of a meager and unsatisfactory kind; it may be the beginning of knowledge, but you have scarcely in your thoughts advanced to the stage of science. "[5]

There are several factors to consider in measuring the programming process .First, one cannot just start to use numbers to control things. The numbers must properly represent the process being controlled, and they must be sufficiently well defined and verified to provide a reliable basis for action. While process measurements are essential for orderly improvement, careful planning and preparation are required or the results are likely to be disappointing.

The second point is equally important: The mere act of measuring human processes changes them. Since people's fears and motivations are involved, the results must be viewed in a different light from data on natural phenomena. It is thus essential to limit the measurements to those with a predefined use. Measurements are both expensive and disruptive; overzealous measuring can degrade the process we are trying to improve.

1.1 Software Process Improvement

An important first step in addressing software problems is to treat the entire software task as a process that can be controlled, measured, and improved. For this purpose we define a process as that set of tasks that, when properly performed, produces the desired result. Clearly, a fully effective software process must consider the relationships of all the required tasks, the tools and methods used, and the skill, training, and motivation of the people involved.

To improve their software capabilities, organizations must take six steps:

1. Understand the current status of their development process or processes.
2. Develop a vision of the desired process.
3. Establish a list of required process improvement actions in order of priority.
4. Produce a plan to accomplish the required actions.
5. Commit the resources to execute the plan.
6. Start over at step 1.

To improve an organization, it is helpful to have a clear picture of the ultimate goal and some way to gauge progress along the way. The framework used here for this purpose roughly parallels the quality maturity structure defined by Crosby. [3] It addresses the six improvement steps by characterizing the software process into one of five maturity levels. By establishing their organization's position in this maturity Structure, software professionals and their managers can more readily identify areas where improvement actions will be most fruitful.

1.2 Process Maturity Levels

The five levels of process maturity are discussed further in the balance of this chapter, They are as shown in Fig. 1.1 and have the following general characteristics:

1. *Initial*   Until the process is under statistical control, orderly progress in process improvement is not possible. While there are many degrees of statistical control, the first step is to achieve rudimentary predictability of schedules and costs.
2. *Repeatable*   The organization has achieved a stable process with a repeatable level of statistical control by initiating rigorous project management of commitments, costs, schedules, and changes.
3. *Defined*   The organization has defined the process as a basis for consistent implementation and better understanding. At this point advanced technology can usefully be introduced.
4. *Managed*   The organization has initiated comprehensive process measurements and analysis. This is when the most significant quality improvements begin.
5. *Optimizing*   The organization now has a foundation for continuing improvement and optimization of the process .

These levels have been selected because they:

- Reasonably represent the actual historical phases of evolutionary improvement of real software organizations
- Represent a measure of improvement that is reasonable to achieve from the prior level
- Suggest interim improvement goals and progress measures
- Make obvious a set of immediate improvement priorities, once an organization' s status in this framework is known

While there are many other elements to these maturity level transitions, the primary objective is to achieve a controlled and measured process as the foundation for continuing improvement.

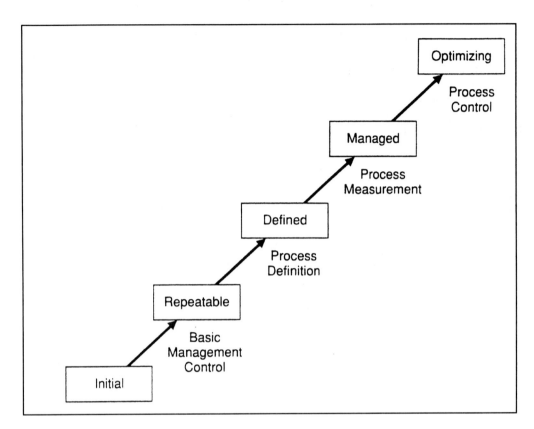

Figure 1.1
Process Maturity Levels

This process maturity structure is intended for use with an assessment methodology and a management system. [7, 8, 9, 12] Assessment helps an organization identify its specific maturity status, and the management system establishes a structure for implementing the priority improvement actions. Once its position in this maturity structure is defined, the organization can concentrate on those items that will help it advance to the next level.

When, for example, a software organization does not have an effective project-planning system, it may be difficult or even impossible to introduce advanced methods and technology. Poor project planning generally leads to unrealistic schedules, inadequate resources, and frequent crises. In such circumstances, new methods are usually ignored and priority is given to coding and testing.

1.2.1 The Initial Process (Level 1)

The Initial Process Level could properly be called ad hoc, and it is often even chaotic. At this stage the organization typically operates without formalized procedures, cost estimates, and project plans. Tools are neither well integrated with the process nor uniformly applied. Change control is lax, and there is little senior management exposure or understanding of the problems and issues. Since many problems are deferred or even forgotten, software installation and maintenance often present serious problems.

While organizations at this level may have formal procedures for planning and tracking their work, there is no management mechanism to ensure that they are used. The best test is to observe how such an organization behaves in a crisis. If it abandons established procedures and essentially reverts to coding and testing, it is likely to be at the Initial Process Level. After all, if the techniques and methods are appropriate, then they should be used in a crisis; if they are not appropriate in a crisis, they should not be used at all.

One key reason why organizations behave in this fashion is that they have not experienced the benefits of a mature process and thus do not understand the consequences of their chaotic behavior. Because many effective software actions (such as design and code inspections or test data analysis) do not appear directly to support shipping the product, they seem expendable.

It is much like driving an automobile. Few drivers with any experience will continue driving for very long when the engine warning light comes on, regardless of their rush. Similarly, most drivers starting on a new journey will, regardless of their hurry , pause to consult a map. They have learned the difference between speed and progress.

In software, coding and testing seem like progress, but they are often only wheel spinning. While they must be done, there is always the danger of going in the wrong direction. Without a sound plan and a thoughtful analysis of the problems, there is no way to know.

Organizations at the Initial Process Level can improve their performance by instituting basic project controls. The most important are project management, management oversight, quality assurance, and change control.

The fundamental role of a *project management* system is to ensure effective control of commitments. This requires adequate preparation, clear responsibility, a public declaration, and a dedication to performance. [8]

For software, project management starts with an understanding of the job's magnitude. In any but the simplest projects, a plan must then be developed to determine the best schedule and the anticipated resources required. In the absence of such an orderly plan, no commitment can be better than an educated guess.

A suitably disciplined software development organization must have *senior management oversight*. This includes review and approval of all major development plans prior to their official commitment.

Also, a quarterly review should be conducted of facility-wide process compliance, installed quality performance, schedule tracking, cost trends, computing service, and quality and productivity goals by project. The lack of such reviews typically results in uneven and generally inadequate implementation of the process as well as frequent overcommitments and cost surprises.

A *quality assurance* group is charged with assuring management that software work is done the way it is supposed to be done. To be effective, the assurance organization must have an independent reporting line to senior management and sufficient resources to monitor performance of all key planning, implementation, and verification activities. This generally requires an organization of about 3 percent to 6 percent the size of the software organization.

Change control for software is fundamental to business and financial control as well as to technical stability. To develop quality software on a predictable schedule, requirements must be established and maintained with reasonable stability throughout the development cycle. While requirements changes are often needed, historical evidence demonstrates that many can be deferred and incorporated later. Design and code changes must be made to correct problems found in development and test, but these must be carefully introduced. If changes are not controlled, then orderly design, implementation, and test is impossible and no quality plan can be effective.

1.2.2 The Repeatable Process (Level 2)

The Repeatable Process has one important strength that the Initial Process does not: It provides control over the way the organization establishes its plans and commitments. This control provides such an improvement over the Initial Process Level that the people in the organization tend to believe they have mastered the software problem. They have achieved a degree of statistical control through learning to make and meet their estimates and plans. This strength, however, stems from their prior experience at doing similar work. Organizations at the Repeatable Process Level thus face major risks when they are presented with new challenges.

Examples of the changes that represent the highest risk at this level are the following:

- *Unless they are introduced with great care, new tools and methods will affect the process, thus destroying the relevance of the intuitive historical base on which the organization relies.* Without a defined process framework in which to address these risks, it is even possible for a new technology to do more harm than good.

- *When the organization must develop a new kind of product, it is entering new territory.* For example, a software group that has experience developing compilers will likely have design, scheduling, and estimating problems when assigned to write a real-time control program. Similarly, a group that has developed small self -contained programs will not understand the interface and integration issues involved in large-scale projects. These changes again destroy the relevance of the intuitive historical basis for the organization's process.

- *Major organizational changes can also be highly disruptive.* At the Repeatable Process Level, a new manager has no orderly basis for understanding the organization's operation, and new team members must learn the ropes through word of mouth.

The key actions required to advance from the Repeatable to the next stage, the Defined Process, are to establish a process group, establish a development process architecture, and introduce a family of software engineering methods and technologies.

Establish a process group. A process group is a technical resource that focuses exclusively on improving the software process. In software organizations at early maturity levels, all the people are generally devoted to product work. Until some people are given full-time assignments to work on the process, little orderly progress can be made in improving it.

The responsibilities of process groups include defining the development process, identifying technology needs and opportunities, advising the projects, and conducting quarterly management reviews of process status and performance. While there is no published data at this point, my experience indicates that the process group should be about 1 to 3 percent the size of the software organization. Because of the need for a nucleus of skills, groups smaller than about four professionals are unlikely to be fully effective. Small organizations that lack the experience base to form a process group should address these issues by using specially formed committees of experienced professionals or by retaining consultants.

A frequent question concerns the relative responsibilities of process groups and quality assurance. While this is discussed in more detail in Chapters 8 and 14, the assurance group is focused on enforcing the current process, while the process group is directed at improving it. In a sense, they are almost opposites: assurance covers audit and compliance, and the process group deals with support and change.

Establish a software development process architecture, or development life cycle, that describes the technical and management activities required for proper execution of the development process. [11] This process must be attuned to the specific needs of the organization, and it will vary depending on the size and importance of the project as well as the technical nature of the work itself. The architecture is a structural decomposition of the development cycle into tasks, each of which has a defined set of prerequisites, functional descriptions, verification procedures, and task completion specifications. The decomposition continues until each defined task is performed by an individual or single management unit.

If they are not already in place, *introduce a family of software engineering methods and technologies*. These include design and code inspections, formal design methods, library control systems, and comprehensive testing methods. Prototyping should also be considered, together with the adoption of modem implementation languages.

1.2.3 The Defined Process (Level 3)

With the Defined Process, the organization has achieved the foundation for major and continuing progress. For example, the software teams, when faced with a .crisis, will likely continue to use the process that has been defined. The foundation has now been established for examining the process and deciding how to improve it.

As powerful as the Defined Process is, it is still only qualitative: there is little data to indicate how much is accomplished or how effective the process is. There is considerable debate about the value of software process measurements and the best ones to use. This uncertainty generally stems from a lack of process definition and the consequent confusion about the specific items to be measured. With a Defined Process, we can focus the measurements on specific tasks. The process architecture is thus an essential prerequisite to effective measurement.

The key steps required to advance from the Defined Process to the next level are:

1. Establish a minimum basic set of process measurements to identify the quality and cost parameters of each process step. The objective is to quantify the relative costs and benefits of each major process activity, such as the cost and yield of error detection and correction methods.
2. Establish a process database and the resources to manage and maintain it. Cost and yield data should be maintained centrally to guard against loss, to make it available for all projects, and to facilitate process quality and productivity analysis.
3. Provide sufficient process resources to gather and maintain this process data and to advise project members on its use. Assign skilled professionals to monitor the quality of the data before entry in the database and to provide guidance on analysis methods and interpretation.
4. Assess the relative quality of each product and inform management where quality targets are not being met. An independent quality assurance group should assess the quality actions of each project and track its progress against its quality plan. When this progress is compared with the historical experience on similar projects, an informed assessment can generally be made.

1.2.4 The Managed Process (Level 4)

In advancing from the Initial Process through the Repeatable and Defined Processes to the Managed Process, software organizations should expect to make substantial quality improvements. The greatest potential problem with the Managed Process is the cost of gathering data. There are an enormous number of potentially valuable measures of the software process, but such data is expensive to gather and to maintain.

Approach data gathering with care, therefore, and precisely define each piece of data in advance. Productivity data is essentially meaningless unless explicitly defined. For example, the simple measure of lines of source code per expended development month can vary by 100 times or more, depending on the interpretation of the parameters.[6] The code count could include only new and changed code or all shipped instructions. For modified programs, this can cause variations of a factor of 10. Similarly, noncomment nonblank lines, executable instructions, or equivalent assembler instructions can be counted with variations of up to 7 times.[14] Management, test, documentation, and support personnel mayor may not be counted when calculating labor months expended. Again, the variations can run at least as high as a factor of 7. [16]

When different groups gather data but do not use identical definitions, the results are not comparable, even if it makes sense to compare them. The tendency with such data is to use it to compare several groups and to criticize those with the lowest ranking. This is an unfortunate misapplication of process data. It is rare that two projects are comparable by any simple measures. The variations in task complexity caused by different product types can exceed five to one.[6] Similarly, the cost per line of code of small modifications is often two to three times that for new programs.[6] The degree of requirements change can make an enormous difference, as can the design status of the base program in the case of enhancements.

Process data must not be used to compare projects or individuals. Its purpose is to illuminate the product being developed and to provide an informed basis for improving the process. When such data is used by management to evaluate individuals or teams, the reliability of the data itself will deteriorate. The Fifth Amendment of the U .S. Constitution is based on sound principles— few people can be counted on to provide reliable data on their own performance.

The two fundamental requirements for advancing from the Managed Process to the next level are:

1. Support automatic gathering of process data. All data is subject to error and omission, some data cannot be gathered by hand, and the accuracy of manually gathered data is often poor.
2. Use process data both to analyze and to modify the process to prevent problems and improve efficiency.

1.2.5 The Optimizing Process (Level 5)

In varying degrees, process optimization goes on at all levels of process maturity. With the step from the Managed to the Optimizing Process, however, there is a paradigm shift. Up to this point software development managers have largely focused on their products and will typically gather and analyze only data that directly relates to product improvement. In the Optimizing Process, the data is available to tune the process itself. With a little experience, management will soon see that process optimization can produce major quality and productivity benefits.

For example, many types of errors can be identified and fixed far more economically by design or code inspections than by testing. Unfortunately, there is only limited published data available on the costs of finding and fixing defects. [1, 13] However, from experience, I have developed a useful rule of thumb: It takes about 1 to 4 working hours to find and fix a bug through inspections and about 15 to 20 working hours to find and fix a bug in function or system test. To the extent that organizations find that these numbers apply to their situations, they should consider placing less reliance on testing as their primary way to find and fix bugs.

However, some kinds of errors are either uneconomical to detect or almost impossible to find except by machine. Examples are errors involving spelling and syntax, interfaces, performance, human factors, and error recovery .It would be unwise to eliminate testing completely since it provides a useful check against human frailties.

The data that is available with the Optimizing Process gives us a new perspective on testing. For most projects, a little analysis shows that there are two distinct activities involved: the removal of defects and the assessment of program quality. To reduce the cost of removing defects, inspections should be emphasized, together with any other cost-effective techniques. The role of functional and system testing should then be changed to one of gathering quality data on the programs. This involves studying each bug to see if it is an isolated problem or if it indicates design problems that require more comprehensive analysis.

With the Optimizing Process, the organization has the means to identify the weakest elements of the process and to fix them. At this point in process improvement, data is available to justify the application of technology to various critical tasks, and numerical evidence is available on the effectiveness with which the process has been applied to any given product. We should then no longer need reams of paper to describe what is happening since simple yield curves and statistical plots could provide clear and concise indicators. It would then be possible to assure the process and hence have confidence in the quality of the resulting products.

1.3 People in the Optimizing Process

Clearly, any software process is dependent on the quality of the people who implement it. There are never enough good people, and even when you have them there is a limit to what they can accomplish. When they are already working 50 to 60 hours a week, it is hard to see how they could handle the vastly greater challenges of the future.

The Optimizing Process enhances the talents of quality people in several ways. It helps managers understand where help is needed and how best to provide people with the support they require. It lets the professionals communicate in concise, quantitative terms. This facilitates the transfer of knowledge and minimizes the likelihood of wasting time on problems that have already been solved. It provides a framework for the professionals to understand their work performance and to see how to improve it. This results in a highly professional environment and substantial productivity benefits, and it avoids the enormous amount of effort that is generally expended in fixing and patching other people's mistakes.

The Optimizing Process provides a disciplined environment for professional work. Process discipline must be handled with care, however, for it can easily become regimentation. The difference between a disciplined environment and a regimented one is that discipline controls the environment and methods to specific standards, while regimentation defines the actual conduct of the work.

Discipline is required in large software projects to ensure, for example, that the many people involved use the same conventions, don't damage each others' products, and properly synchronize their work. Discipline thus enables creativity by freeing the most talented software professionals from the many crises that others have created. A disciplined process, then, empowers the intellect, while regimentation supplants it.

1.4 The Need for the Optimizing Process

There are many examples of disasters caused by software problems, ranging from expensive missile aborts to enormous financial losses. [2, 10, 15] As the computerization of our society continues, the public risks due to poor-quality code will become untenable. Not only are our systems being used in increasingly sensitive applications, but they are also becoming much larger and more complex.

While questions can appropriately be raised about the size and complexity of current systems, these are human creations, and they will, alas, continue to be produced by humans beings (with all their failings and creative talents) .While many of the currently promising technologies will undoubtedly help, there is an enormous backlog of needed function that will inevitably translate into vast amounts of code .

Unless we dramatically improve our error rates, this greater volume of code will mean increased risk of error. At the same time, the complexity of our systems is increasing, which will make the systems progressively more difficult to test. In combination these trends expose us to greater risks of damaging errors as we attempt to use software in increasingly critical applications. These risks will thus continue to increase as we become more efficient at producing volumes of new code.

As well as being a management issue, quality is an economic one. It is always possible to do more reviews or to run more tests, but it costs both time and money to do so. It is only with the Optimizing Process that the data is available to understand the costs and benefits of such work. The Optimizing Process provides the foundation for significant advances in software quality and simultaneous improvements in productivity.

There is little data on how long it takes for software organizations to advance through the maturity levels toward the Optimizing Process. Based on my experience, transitions from Level I to Level 2 or from Level 2 to Level 3 take from one to three years, even with a dedicated management commitment to process improvement. To date, I have observed only a few software teams at level 4 or 5, and no complete organizations. People could reasonably argue that this limited anecdotal evidence is hardly proof of the benefits of these process levels. They would of course be right. On the other hand, this framework has essentially fueled four centuries of scientific and engineering development. These concepts have been proven in physics, engineering, and manufacturing, and I have yet to see evidence that they won't work for software as well. While I cannot expect all readers to blindly share this conviction, I do assert that there is little alternative. Rather than continuing to struggle with their current immature processes, this framework at least offers software organizations an improvement path. I assert that it will work. If you find it doesn't precisely fit your needs, make some changes, try it out, and if it works, publish your findings so we can all learn and improve.

There is an urgent need for better and more effective software organizations. To meet this need, software managers and professionals must establish the goal of moving to the Optimizing Process.

1.5 Summary

The improvement of software development organizations follows six steps:

1. Understand the current status of the development process.
2. Develop a vision of the desired process.
3. Establish a list of required process improvement actions in order of priority.
4. Produce a plan to accomplish the required actions.

61

5. Commit the resources to execute the plan.

6. Start over at step 1.

A maturity structure addresses these six steps by characterizing a software process into one of five maturity levels. These levels are:

1. *Initial* — Until the process is under statistical control, no orderly progress in process improvement is possible.

2. *Repeatable* — The organization has achieved a stable process with a repeatable level of statistical control by initiating rigorous project management of commitments, costs, schedules, and changes.

3. *Defined* — The organization has defined the process. This helps ensure consistent implementation and provides a basis for a better understanding of the process.

4. *Managed* — The organization has initiated comprehensive process measurements and analyses beyond those of cost and schedule performance.

5. *Optimizing* — The organization now has a foundation for continuing improvement and optimization of the process.

The Optimizing Process helps people to be effective in several ways:

- It helps managers understand where help is needed and how best to provide the people with the support they require.

- It lets the professionals communicate in concise, quantitative terms.

- It provides the framework for the professionals to understand their work performance and to see how to improve it.

References

1. Basili, v. R., and R. W. Selby. "Comparing the effectiveness of software testing strategies," *IEEE Transactions on Software Engineering*, vol. SE-13, no.12, December 1987.

2. Boming, A. "Computer system reliability and nuclear war," *Communications of the ACM*, vol. 30, no 2, February 1987.

3. Crosby, P. B. *Quality Is Free*. New York: McGraw-Hill, 1979.

4. Deming, W. E. *Quality, Productivity, and Competitive Position*. Cambridge, MA: Massachusetts Institute of Technology Center for Advanced Engineering Study, 1982.

5. Dunham, J. R., and E. Kruesi. "The measurement task area," *IEEE Computer*, vol. 16, no.11, November 1983.

6. Flaherty, M. J. "Programming process measurement system for System/370," *IBM Systems Journal*, vol. 24, no.2, 1985.

7. Humphrey, W. S. "The IBM large-systems software development process: objectives and direction, " *IBM Systems Journal*, vol. 24, no. 2, 1985.

8. Humphrey, W. S. *Managing for Innovation—Leading Technical People*. Englewood Cliffs, NJ: Prentice-Hall, 1987.

9. Humphrey, W. S., and D. H. Kitson. "Preliminary Report on Conducting SEI-Assisted Assessments of Software Engineering Capability," *SEI Technical Report* SEI-87-TR-16, July, 1987.

10. Myers, G. J. *Software Reliability—-Principles and Practices*. New York: Wiley, 1976.

11. Radice, R. A., N. K. Roth, A. C. O'Hara, Jr., and W. A. Ciarfella. "A programming process architecture," *IBM Systems Journal*, vol. 24, no. 2, 1985.

12. Radice, R. S., J. T. Harding, P. E. Munnis, and R. W. Phillips. "A programming process study," *IBM Systems Journal*, vol. 24, no.2, 1985.

13. Shooman, M. L., and M. I. Bolsky. "Types, distribution and test and correction times for programming errors," *Proceedings of the 1975 International Conference of Reliable Software*. New York: IEEE, 1975, pp. 347-357.

14. Shooman, M. L. *Software Engineering: Design, Reliability, and Management*. New York: McGraw-Hill, 1983.

15. The New York Times. "Making sure the computers keep running." February 8, 1987.

16. Wolverton, R. W. "The cost of developing large-scale software," *IEEE Transactions on Computers*, June 1974.

Software Process Improvement at Hughes Aircraft

WATTS S. HUMPHREY, *Software Engineering Institute*
TERRY R. SNYDER *and* RONALD R. WILLIS, *Hughes Aircraft*

◆ *In just two years, Hughes' Software Engineering Division progressed from level 2 to level 3. Here's how they did it, how much it cost, and what they gained.*

In 1987 and 1990, the Software Engineering Institute conducted process assessements of the Software Engineering Division of Hughes Aircraft in Fullerton, Calif. The first assessment found Hughes' SED to be a level 2 organization, based on the SEI's process-maturity scale of 1 to 5, where 1 is worst and 5 is best.[1]

This first assessment identified the strengths and weaknesses of the SED, and the SEI made recommendations for process improvement. Hughes then established and implemented an action plan in accordance with these recommendations. The second assessment found the SED to be a strong level 3 organization.

The assessment itself cost Hughes about $45,000, and the subsequent two-year program of improvements cost about $400,000. Hughes found that the investment improved working condi-tions, employee morale, and the performance of the SED as measured in project schedule and cost. Hughes estimates the resulting annual savings to be about $2 million.

In this article, we outline the assessment method used, the findings and recommendations from the initial assessment, the actions taken by Hughes, the lessons learned, and the resulting business and product consequences.

We write this article in the broad interest of software-process improvement, particularly its costs and benefits. Because its assessments are confidential, the SEI cannot publicize costs and benefits until it has amassed a large body of data. So, during the second assessment in 1990, Watts Humphrey and Terry Snyder agreed to write an article – Humphrey to provide material on the assessment process and Hughes to provide material on results and benefits.

Background. The SED is one division in Hughes' Ground Systems Group. Although it is the largest dedicated software organization in the Ground Systems Group and provides contract support for many other divisions, there are other (project-related) software organizations in the group.

The SED, formed in 1978, primarily works on US Defense Dept. contracts. It employs about 500 professionals. Of these, 41 percent have 10 to 20 years experience in software and 12 percent have 20 or more years experience. The assessments described here examined only the work of the SED in Fullerton; the findings and recommendations are pertinent only to that organization. However, Hughes has capitalized on this experience to launch a broader process-improvement effort.

At the time of the 1990 assessment, the SEI had conducted 14 assessments and observed 18 self-assessments. As a result, it had gained a great deal of experience on effective methods for identifying the actual state of practice in software organizations. It is thus our opinion that the overall effect of misunderstandings and errors on these assessments was modest.

ASSESSMENT PROCESS

A process assessment helps an organization characterize the current state of its software process and provides findings and recommendations to facilitate improvement. The box on pp. 14-15 explains the SEI's process-improvement paradigm, its supporting process-maturity structure, and the principles of process assessment.

Hughes assessments. The two Hughes assessments were conducted by teams of SEI and Hughes software professionals. In both assessments, all the team members

were experienced software developers. The 1987 assessment was conducted by a team of seven: one from Hughes and six from the SEI. The 1990 assessment team included nine professionals: four from Hughes and five from the SEI. Two of the authors, Watts Humphrey and Ronald Willis, were members of both teams.

The SED team members prepared a list of candidate projects for review by the entire assessment team during training. The entire team then selected projects that it felt reasonably represented the development phases, typical project sizes and applications, and the major organization units. Six projects were reviewed in the 1987 assessment and five in 1990. Only one project was included in both assessments.

Before the assessment, the Hughes SED manager, Terry Snyder, and the SEI's process-program director, Watts Humphrey, signed confidential agreements covering the ground rules for the assessments. The key points in these agreements were:

♦ The SEI and the assessment team members were to keep the assessment results confidential. Hughes could use the assessment results in any way it chose.

♦ The SED manager agreed to participate in the opening and closing assessment meetings.

♦ In addition to the regular team members, the SED manager agreed that Hughes would provide needed support to handle the assessment arrangements and to lead the work on the follow-up action plan.

♦ The SED manager also committed Hughes to developing and implementing appropriate action plans in response to the assessment recommendations. If Hughes deemed that action was not appropriate, it was to explain its reasons to the assessment team.

After the SEI agreed to consider conducting an assessment:

♦ A commitment meeting was held with the SEI and the SED manager and his staff to agree on conducting the assessment and to establish a schedule.

♦ For both assessments, Hughes and the SEI selected the assessment team members, and the SEI trained them in its assessment method. These two-day training programs were held at the SEI, where the entire assessment team was familiarized with the assessment process and prepared for the on-site period.

♦ The on-site assessment was conducted.

♦ A detailed, written report of the assessment findings and recommendations was prepared and a briefing on the recommendations was delivered to the SED management team and all the assessment participants. In both assessments, the SED manager invited senior corporate executives to attend the briefing. Because he did not know the findings in advance, this involved some risk. However, the added understanding provided by these briefings contributed materially to the launching of a Hughes corporate-wide process-improvement initiative modeled on the SED's work.

♦ The SED developed and implemented an action plan based on these recommendations.

Maturity levels. In 1987, the assessments focused on the responses to the level 2 and level 3 questions: Because the assessment period is intentionally limited to four days, we decided to devote our attention to those areas most pertinent to the organization's perceived maturity level. This was possible because the SEI assessment process uses the questionnaire to help focus on the most informative interview topics.

In the 1990 assessment, the team briefly reviewed the level 2 responses and then interviewed the project representatives on the questions at levels 3, 4, and 5. In areas where the project responses differed or where the response pattern was atypical, the team requested more information. Because these discussions were on Tuesday afternoon and the additional ma-

> A process assessment helps an organization characterize the current state of its software process and provides findings and recommendations to facilitate improvement.

terials were needed by Thursday morning, the representatives were told to bring only available working materials and not to prepare anything special.

As a consequence, we believe the team determined an organizational maturity level with a fair degree of accuracy in both the 1987 and 1990 assessments. There is, of course, the possibility that some questions were not discussed in sufficient detail to identify all misunderstandings or errors.

1987 ASSESSMENT

The first SEI assessment of six Hughes projects was conducted November 9-12, 1987. The final report, including recommendations, was presented in January 1988.

Recommendations. The assessment team made seven recommendations.

Quantitative process management. The assessment team found that the professionals working on the assessed projects gathered a significant amount of data on many aspects of the process. While this was important in moving the organization toward a managed software process (level 4), much of the long-term potential value of this data was lost because it was kept in multiple, disparate databases. Furthermore, the lack of a central location for this data made it difficult for project managers and professionals to know what data was available, what data should be gathered, and how it could most effectively be used for product and process improvement.

The team recommended that the SED establish the goal of achieving quantitative process management. To establish the foundation for statistical process management, this goal should include:

◆ Establishing a centralized database to include current and future data on cost estimates, cost experience, error data, and schedule performance. Additional process data should be included as it is gathered.

◆ Establishing uniform data definitions across projects.

◆ Augmenting the process definitions to include those key measures and analyses required at each major project milestone,

together with appropriate responsibilities.

◆ Providing the resources needed and the responsibility assignments required for gathering, validating, entering, accessing, and supporting the projects in analyzing this data.

Process group. The team recommended that the SED establish a technical group to be the focal point for process improvement. This group's initial tasks would be to lead the development of action plans for accomplishing the assessment team's recommendations, to lead, coordinate, and track the implementation of the action plans, and to establish the centralized process database.

Requirements. The team found that the SED generally was not involved in early system definition. Whenever software considerations were not integrated into systems engineering early in the system-definition phase, the software specifications often were ambiguous, inconsistent, untestable, and subject to frequent last-minute changes. Because in general the quality of a software product cannot exceed the quality of its requirements, the team perceived this as a critical problem.

The team recommended that the SED be involved in the specification development for all new Hughes software-intensive projects. It also suggested that systems-engineering groups attend applicable software-engineering courses.

Quality assurance. Although the existing software quality-assurance organization at Hughes performed several necessary functions, it suffered from widely different views of its usefulness and could not fully contribute to the software-development process because it was understaffed and its personnel were not adequately trained.

To strengthen the role of SQA, the

team recommended a training program that would include software-engineering principles, Hughes standard procedures, phases of the life cycle, and the functions of SQA personnel. It was also recommended that the value added by SQA be clarified for program management so it could better understand the need to allocate resources to it.

Training. The team found that Hughes had a comprehensive, company-sponsored software-engineering training program. However, the team also found that certain training categories were either not available or not being used adequately. Key examples were training for assistant project managers, review leaders, and requirements specification.

The team recommended that Hughes review its software-training requirements. The review was to conclude with plans for restructuring the current training programs, providing new subjects, creating a training priority structure, and using new training methods as appropriate. It was also recommended that Hughes consider a required training program.

Review process. Although Hughes had made provision for technical reviews during the development process, they were not performed uniformly across all projects. So the team recommended that Hughes reassess its current review practices and determine how to assure a consistent and uniform review practice at appropriate points in the software-development process. The objective was to improve product quality, reduce reliance on testing, and improve overall project predictability and productivity.

Working relationship. During the assessment, the working relationship with the Defense Dept.'s Defense Contract Adminstrative Services department was often

> In general the quality of a software product cannot exceed the quality of its requirements, so the team recommended the SED be involved in specification development.

SEI PROCESS ASSESSMENT PROCEDURES

To make orderly improvement, development and maintenance organizations should view their process as one that can be controlled, measured, and improved. This requires that they follow a traditional quality-improvement program such as that described by W. Edwards Deming.[1]

For software, this involves the following six steps:

1. Understand the current status of their process.

2. Develop a vision of the desired process.

3. Establish a list of required process-improvement actions in priority order.

4. Produce a plan to accomplish these actions.

5. Commit the resources and execute the plan.

6. Start over at step 1.

The SEI has developed a framework to characterize the software process across five maturity levels. By establishing their organization's position in this framework, software professionals and their managers can readily identify areas where improvement actions will be most fruitful.

Many software organizations have found that this framework provides an orderly set of process improvement goals and a helpful yardstick for tracking progress. Some acquisition groups in the US Defense Dept. are also using this maturity framework and an associated SEI evaluation method called the Software Capability Evaluation to help select software contractors.

Maturity framework. Figure A shows the SEI's software process-maturity framework. The SEI derived this empirical model from the collective experiences of many software managers and practitioners. The five maturity levels

♦ reasonably represent the historical phases of evolutionary improvement of actual software organizations,

♦ represent a measure of improvement that is reasonable to achieve from the prior level,

♦ suggest interim improvement goals and progress measures, and

♦ make obvious a set of immediate improvement priorities once an organization's status in the framework is known.

While there are many aspects to these transitions from one maturity level to another, the overall objective is to achieve a controlled and measured process as the foundation for continuous improvement.

Assessment. The process-maturity framework is intended to be used with an assessment method. A process assessment is a review of an organization's software process done by a trained team of software professionals. Its purpose is to determine the state of the organiza-tion, to identify the highest priority process issues, and to facilitate improvement actions.

The assessment process facilitates improvement by involving the managers and professionals in identifying the most critical software problems and helping them agree on the actions required to address these problems.[2] The basic objectives of an assessment are to

♦ learn how the organization works,

♦ identify its major problems, and

♦ enroll its opinion leaders in the change process.[3]

In SEI assessments, five or six projects are typically selected as representative samples of the organization's software process. The guiding principle for selecting projects is that they represent the mainstream software business for the organization.

On-site period. The on-site assessment period is an intense

Level	Characteristics	Key challenges	Result
5 **Optimizing**	• Improvement fed back into process • Data gathering is automated and used to identify weakest process elements • Numerical evidence used to justify application of technology to critical tasks • Rigorous defect–cause analysis and detect prevention	• Still human-intensive process • Maintain organization at optimizing level	Productivity & quality
4 **Managed**	(Quantitative) • Measured process • Minimum set of quality and productivity measurements established • Process database established with resources to analyze its data and maintain it	• Changing technology • Problem analysis • Problem prevention	
3 **Defined**	(Qualitative) • Process defined and institutionalized • Software Engineering Process Group established to lead process improvement	• Process measurement • Process analysis • Quantitative quality plans	
2 **Repeatable**	(Intuitive) • Process dependent on individuals • Established basic project controls • Strength in doing similar work, but faces major risk when presented with new challenges • Lacks orderly framework for improvement	• Training • Technical practices (reviews, testing) • Process focus (standards, process groups)	
1 **Initial**	(Ad hoc/chaotic process) • No formal procedures, cost estimates, project plans • No management mechanism to ensure procedures are followed, tools not well integrated, and change control is lax • Senior management does not understand key issues	• Project management • Project planning • Configuration management • Software quality assurance	Risk

Figure A. *The SEI process-maturity framework.*

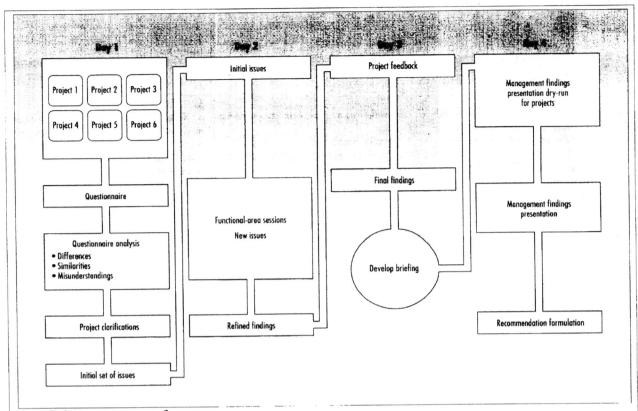

Figure B. *On-site assessment process flow.*

four "half-days" : The team members are involved for more than half of each 24 hours, generally starting at 7:30 a.m. and not concluding until 10:00 or 11:00 p.m. No one has time to perform normal duties during this phase.

While this is a potentially stressful activity, the extensive training prepares the team members to make a highly productive effort and to build the cohesion and team spirit required to achieve consensus on the complex issues encountered. The dedication and enthusiasm of the assessment team also significantly contributes to their credibility to the organization and to acceptance of the findings.

Figure B shows the flow of the on-site activities during SEI process assessments. Each on-site assessment starts with a presentation to the manager, staff, and all the assessment participants. This

meeting covers the assessment ground rules, assessment principles, and the schedule.

The assessment team then meets in closed session to review the questionnaire responses in preparation for the first round of discussions with project leaders. Project managers and functional experts are interviewed to clearly determine the key issues behind their responses to an SEI questionnaire.[4]

Next, a private discussion is held with each project leader to clarify any issues identified by the assessment team during its review of project responses and to request explanatory materials, if appropriate.

Next, a full day is devoted to discussions with software practitioners from selected technical areas such as requirements and high-level design, and code and unit test. Typically, about six professionals are selected from across

the organization for each functional area. These functional area representatives are selected with the following criteria:

♦ Be considered an expert in the technical area by his or her peers.

♦ Be assigned to, and working on, one or more mainstream projects at the site (not necessarily a project included in the assessment).

♦ Be considered an opinion leader in the organization.

A second round of individual project leader meetings is then held to review the supporting materials, resolve remaining issues, and review the preliminary assessment findings. On the last day, a findings briefing is presented to senior management and all the assessment participants.

The final assessment activity is the preparation and presentation of a written report

and recommendations to the site manager and staff. The recommendations highlight the assessment team's view of the highest priority items for immediate action. Following the assessment, the organization prepares and implements an action plan. In accordance with the agreement, the SEI reviews and comments on these plans.

REFERENCES

1. W.E. Deming, *Out of the Crisis*, MIT Center Advanced Eng. Study, Cambridge, Mass., 1982.
2. R.A. Radice et al., "A Programming Process Study," *IBM Systems J.*, No. 2, 1985, pp. 91-101.
3. D.H. Kitson and W.S. Humphrey, "The Role of Assessment in Software Process Improvement," Tech. Report CMU/SEI-89-TR-3, Software Eng. Inst., Carnegie Mellon Univ., Pittsburgh, 1989.
4. W.S Humphrey and W. Sweet, "A Method for Assessing the Software Engineering Capability of Contractors," Tech. Report CMU/SEI-87-TR-23, Software Eng. Inst., Carnegie Mellon Univ., Pittsburgh, 1987.

identified as ineffective or counterproductive. It was thus recommended that the SED work to improve this relationship.

Actions taken. Within two months of the January 1988 recommendations briefing, Hughes developed an action plan to implement the recommended improvements. As predetermined, the assessment site coordinator was the primary author for the action plan, although many people contributed to the decision and approval process.

Because implementation of the proposed actions was estimated to require a 2-percent increase in division overhead rate, it took three more months (until June 1988) to get the action plan and required funding approved by Ground Systems Group management. In so doing, top management became committed to the improvement program.

For the most part, the 1988 action plan was implemented on schedule and under budget. It took 18 months and was completed just one month before the 1990 reassessment.

Action plan. The 1988 action plan began with a one-page summary of the assessment life cycle and the projects assessed. It then listed the goals and put the action plan in the context of a Ground Systems

---

3.1 FORM SOFTWARE ENGINEERING PROCESS GROUP

3.1.1 Summary of the SEI Findings. Decentralization of the software organization into geographically isolated projects and even into separate product line divisions has impaired progress in software-technology development. Such decentralization has already affected quality-indicator data collection leading to multiple, disparate databases.

3.1.2 Requirements. The following are necessary attributes of the desired solution.

a. An organizational entity, the software-engineering process group (SEPG), exists and has the following attributes:
- serves as the focal point for software process improvement
- leader has technical credibility and influence
- staff is experienced
- initial staff size is three people
- eventual staff size is 2 percent to 3 percent of software developers
- staff is rotated every 2 to 3 years

b. The SEPG performs the following functions:
- lead development and implementation of the SEI action plan
- define/improve technical and management software practices
- lead definition of standards for software processes/products
- establish and maintain the software-process database
- initiate the definition, collection, analysis of process data
- facilitate periodic assessment of software-engineering process
- identify and promote the organization's technology needs
- establish requirements and plans for training
- research, develop, and transfer new technology
- define requirements for process automation (i.e. tools)
- facilitate periodic management reviews on state of practice

3.1.3 Responsibilities.

Manager, Software Engineering Division, forms SEPG and assigns SEPG leader, approves SEPG charter, provides funding for SEPG activities, and periodically reviews SEPG progress. Leader, Software Engineering Process Group, develops SEPG charter, develops and implements plans to accomplish 3.1.2, and recruits and selects full-time technical staff for the SEPG.

3.2 IMPLEMENT QUANTITATIVE PROCESS MANAGEMENT

3.2.1 Summary of the SEI Findings. Although data on projects is collected, it is kept in multiple, unrelated databases. The lack of a central focal point for data makes it difficult to know what data is available, what data should be gathered, and how it can be most effectively used for product and process improvement.

3.2.2. Requirements. The following are necessary attributes of the desired solution:

a. A centralized database exists that has the following attributes:
- standardized data definitions across all projects
- fed by all projects
- sufficient data element types to statistically manage the software-development process

b. Software process and product standards exist that specify when and what data to collect to be able to statistically manage the software-development process.

c. Software process and product standards exist that specify analyses to be performed at each project milestone, together with appropriate responsibilities, to be able to statistically manage the software-development process.

d. An organization exists (SEPG) that provides the following services:
- gathers, validates, and enters data into the database
- controls access to the database
- supports projects in analyzing the data

e. Formal means exist to enforce these requirements.

3.2.3. Responsibilities.

Leader, Software Engineering Process Group, assigns responsibility for 3.2.2a through 3.2.2.d, ensures implementation of 3.2.2.e.

3.3 FILLS GAPS IN TRAINING PROGRAM

3.3.1 Summary of the SEI Findings. Although there is clear evidence of commitment to training, there are unfilled gaps in certain areas, opportunities for more effective training, and not enough required training (as opposed to optional training).

3.3.2 Requirements. The following are necessary attributes of the desired solution:

a. A report based on review of current training needs and training effectiveness exists and is used to modernize the existing training program. The report contains the following:

Figure 1. *Section 3 of Hughes SED 1988 action plan. The action plan lists tasks as process-requirements specifications in the context of the Ground Systems Group.*

Group organizational improvement strategy.

The plan then detailed five improvement tasks, written as process-requirement specifications:

- Form a software-engineering process group.
- Implement quantitative process management.
- Fill in the gaps in training.
- Standardize an effective review process.
- Move toward a software-engineering discipline.

Figure 1 shows a part of the plan's wording. As the figure shows, the plan specified testable conditions for each task that, if met, would satisfy the recommended process improvements. The plan also avoided specifying solutions, to allow implementation flexibility.

Two of the SEI's recommendations were not included in the action plan because they involved organizations not under SED control. The first, to strengthen SQA, dealt with a function that was in another division of Hughes. Although the SED was striving to regain a centralized SQA function that would be under its control, it had not yet achieved that reorganization and therefore could not guarantee the outcome. (Later, the SED did achieve a centralized SQA organization.)

- recommended restructuring of current training program
- unfilled gaps in training curriculum
- training priorities
- recommended changes to existing training methods

b. A training curriculum exists that contains all training that is currently defined plus the following additional training subjects:

- associate program manager (APM)
- review leader (for internal reviews)
- use of engineering techniques in software development
- understanding and using software practices and procedures
- how to write good software-requirements
- how to test at the software-requirements level
- how to test at the unit level
- software quality assurance
- practical guide to the use of performance analysis

c. A directive exists that specifies training requirements in terms of specific subjects versus job position and that these training requirements be considered in annual performance evaluations.

3.3.3 Responsibilities.

Leader, Software Engineering Process Group, leads the effort to accomplish 3.3.2.a, 3.3.2.b, and 3.3.2.c.

Manager, Software Engineering Division, approves and enforces the training practice developed as a result of 3.3.2.c.

3.4 STANDARDIZE AN EFFECTIVE REVIEW PROCESS

3.4.1 Summary of the SEI Findings. While Hughes does include provision for reviews during the development process, reviews do not appear to be uniformly performed across projects.

3.4.2 Requirements. The following are necessary attributes of the desired solution:

a. Review standards exist as part of the directive system. They include the following:

- overall review practice (i.e., what reviews, when, who is responsible)
- specific criteria to be used in each review
- procedures for conducting reviews

- required data collection and reporting from reviews

b. Required training curriculum includes review-leader training.

3.4.3 Responsibilities.

Leader, Software Engineering Process Group, leads the effort to accomplish 3.4.2.a and 3.4.2.b.

Manager, Software Engineering Division, approves and enforces the standards developed as a result of 3.4.2.b.

3.5 MOVE TOWARD SOFTWARE-ENGINEERING DISCIPLINE

3.5.1 Summary of the SEI Findings. Software engineering is not uniformly treated as an engineering discipline. There are several aspects to this problem, including lack of early software involvement in systems definition, lack of the use of experimentation (i.e., prototyping) as an engineering tool, and skipping software-development steps when schedule pressures increase. On several of the projects studied, software engineering is appropriately addressing these systems-engineering concerns, and software engineering is treated as an engineering discipline; however, on other projects, this was found not to be the case.

3.5.2 Requirements. The following are necessary attributes of the desired solution:

a. Software-development plans for all new projects include an approved budget and task for software-engineering participation in system design and software-requirements specification.

b. System engineers are invited and attend appropriate software-engineering training classes.

c. All required software-development steps are carried out, regardless of schedule pressure.

3.5.3 Responsibilities.

Software Associate Program Managers (APMs) implement 3.5.2.a and 3.5.2.c.

Manager, Software Engineering Division, ensures 3.5.2.a and 3.5.2.c. Leader, Software Engineering Process Group, leads the effort to accomplish 3.5.2.b.

The second recommendation not included, to improve relations with Defense Contract Administrative Services, again dealt with an organization over which the SED had no control. To negotiate an effective interface with the DCAS was not something Hughes could guarantee, so it was excluded from the action plan. (However, an effective interface was later negotiated.)

The action plan then estimated the labor for implementation to be 100 man-months over 18 months, divided into six major functions:

- ♦ process-group leader: 8 percent,
- ♦ process definition: 6 percent,
- ♦ technology development: 28 percent,
- ♦ quantitative-process management: 41 percent,
- ♦ training: 16 percent, and
- ♦ review-process standardization: 1 percent.

Budget cuts later reduced the 100 man-months of labor to 78. Not included in these estimates were other direct charges for such things as computers, office space, and training facilities, and the existence of certain services such as training and central computer facilities.

Process group. In June 1988, the idea of an SEPG was relatively new at the SEI. Although the concept was well-understood, the implementation was assumed to require that certain roles be organized into a separate function focused on process-technology improvement.

At first, Hughes didn't understand the process-group concept very well, so it tried to implement this SEI approach literally. Also, Hughes' experience with centralizing technology improvement was that, over time, walls of miscommunication developed, leading to just the opposite of technology transfer.

However, on further examination, it was found that the SED, a high level 2 organization with significant progress toward level 3, already had formal roles in place for many process-group functions. All but three functions (action-plan implementation, technology transfer, and development of a required training policy) were either in place or being formed independently of the action plan. Hughes just didn't call it a process group.

To implement the action plan, Hughes issued a bulletin that created the process group, named the existing major functions, and named the person responsible for each function. The bulletin was enlightening to those who understood both what already existed and the SEI's concept of a process group because it made the concept tangible.

The process group, however, was not yet complete. Three key additions brought it all together as an effective focus for process improvement:

- ♦ Technology steering committee. Although the technology steering committee already existed, Hughes did not fully understand its role as a process-group driving function. Given the newly established functions and responsibilities, the process group did not have one person as a leader but instead was directed by the technology steering committee. Thus, it became the committee's job to develop technology road maps, assess current technology, evaluate the overall direction, and make general technology-policy decisions.

- ♦ Technology management. Hughes' practices and procedures addressed people management, project management, resource management, and management of other *things*, but not management of *technology*. One of the first improvements was to formalize the management of technology, as with any other corporate resource. This was done through brainstorming and consensus decision making. The plans were recorded as a new practice, technology management.

- ♦ Technology transfer. A new job function, head of technology transfer, was created and staffed with a full-time person. It was soon clear that the establishment of this function was the most profound action in the entire improvement process. It is not clear if the very positive effect of this action was due to the person's abilities, the existence of the function, or just the timing — but without a doubt this function had more effect than any other single improvement.

Among other things, the head of technology transfer coordinated self-assessments, developed a questionnaire glossary, became the local expert in the SEI maturity questionnaire, became a member of the Software Productivity Consortium's technology-transfer advisory group, developed an SPC technology-transfer plan, briefed senior management on the state of process maturity, maintained a database of technology used on each project and an awareness of what technology each project needed, facilitated technology transfer among projects, ran a special-interest group on process improvement, supported the corporate-wide technology-transfer program, and served on the practices and procedures change-review board, the training policy committee, and the technology steering committee.

Two other additions to the process group that were very helpful were a training committee to periodically review training requirements and their effectiveness and a special-interest group on process improvement. These groups met as needed to find and fix process problems.

Quantitative process management. Before the 1988 action plan, the SED collected "quality indicators" in response to a company-wide push for total quality management. These indicators were error or defect counts, categorized into types, shown in bar graphs with descending importance, and used in postanalyses to isolate where improvement was needed. Each project collected its own data in its own format.

> The action plan estimated the labor for implementation to be 100 man-months over 18 months. Budget cuts later reduced the 100 man-months of labor to 78.

The new approach called for senior management to be briefed every month on the health of each project. To do this, information was collected from each project and compiled into a report that included the project's accomplishments, problems, program trouble reports, quality indicators, scope changes, resource needs, and lessons learned. Also presented were plots of actual versus planned values over time to show the project's schedule, milestones, rate chart, earned value, financial/labor status, and target-system resource use.

The SED implemented a new, division-wide quantitative process-management function and selected one person to be its champion. It standardized the data collected and the reports produced with it, centralized its error-and-defect database, and established a technology center for process-data analysis.

This effort firmly ingrained error-and-defect data collection and analysis into the Hughes culture. It provided the capability required for level 3 maturity and serves as a foundation for future improvement. But time and budget constraints caused it to fall short of achieving all the goals. Some capabilities not achieved are

♦ collecting historical data to support predictions,

♦ projecting analyses within the context of division-wide data,

♦ automating data collection and reporting, and

♦ optimizing data collection based on business needs.

Training gaps. The SED also implemented an organizational policy for required training. Although a policy for required training was not achievable the first time it was tried in 1985, by 1988 the time was right to make it work. (Hughes made training a job requirement, not a promotion requirement, thus solving the equal-employment-opportunity problem that stalled the 1985 effort.)

The company's thrust in continuous measurable improvement and total quality management, combined with the SED manager's personal belief in training resulted in a new policy that required training for all software engineers in the divi-

sion. To support the new requirement, the SED implemented a training-records database that recorded the training status of each employee yearly, at about the time of performance appraisals, and it established a training committee to periodically review training requirements and effectiveness.

Before the 1988 action plan, the SED's internal formal training classes included 17 on modern programming practices, 51 on programming languages and CASE tools, and three on job-specific topics. Enrollment was first-come, first-served. Although training was encouraged and well attended, it was not required.

Although the action plan suggested specific additions to the training program, the SED surveyed its employees to establish what new training was needed. Based on that survey, it added classes on project management, internal reviews, requirements writing, requirements- and unit-level testing, and quality assurance. All these courses had been developed and conducted several times by the 1990 reassessment.

The training programs were open to all engineering functions. Attendance was advertised to and encouraged for all engineers. As of November 1989, 20 percent (174) of the attendees at the training classes were from organizations outside the SED.

Standardized reviews. Before the 1988 action plan, Hughes had established an overall technical-review practice, review criteria, review reporting, data-collection procedures, and the requirement to have a quality-evaluation plan for each project.

Despite these practices, the assessment revealed that the review process was inconsistent. The 1988 action plan included a standard procedure for conducting reviews as well as the training of review leaders in how to conduct reviews. Both were

> The SED implemented a new, division-wide quantitative process-management function and selected one person to be its champion.

completed in 1989.

Software-engineering discipline. The 1988 action plan required that software engineers be involved in the system-engineering process, that system engineers become more involved with software, and that software engineers use traditional engineering techniques such as prototypes and experimentation.

The SED could not require that the system-engineering organization implement these changes because system engineering was not under its control.

Instead, the plan required that the SED participate in the system-engineering process, with the realization that some system-engineering organizations might be reluctant to accept its help. In those cases where software engineers were involved with system design, considerably fewer problems occurred and better products resulted.

1990 REASSESSMENT

Early in 1989, Hughes asked the SEI to conduct a second assessment of the SED. The SEI's resources are limited and it can conduct only a few assessments per year, but the opportunity to evaluate a major software organization at two points in its process-improvement program interested the SEI greatly.

The findings and recommendations from the second assessment indicated that substantial improvements had been implemented. From level 2 in 1987, Hughes had progressed to being a strong level 3, with many activities in place to take it to level 4 and 5.

Improvements included the formation of a process group, key training actions, and a comprehensive technical review process. The assessment concluded that Hughes had achieved a strong position of

Question		1987 assessment	1990 assessment	Average response (from *State of the Practice*)
Level 2				
2.1.4	Is a formal procedure used to make estimates of software size?	50	100	33
2.2.2	Are profiles of software size maintained for each software configuration item over time?	83	100	36
Level 3				
1.1.7	Is there a software-engineering process group or function?	50	100	69
1.2.3	Is there a required software-engineering training program for software developers?	50	100	44
1.2.5	Is a formal training program required for design- and code-review leaders?	0	100	12
2.4.13	Is a mechanism used for controlling changes to the software design?	50	100	100
2.4.19	Is a mechanism used for verifying that the samples examined by software quality assurance are truly representative of the work performed?	33	100	69
2.4.21	Is there a mechanism for assuring the adequacy of regression testing?	33	80	23

software-process leadership and had established the foundation for continuing process improvement.

The assessment team also found that the professional staff was committed to high-quality software work and that it demonstrated disciplined adherence to the established process.

Findings. The SEI made five basic findings in the second assessment:

♦ The SED's role in the Ground Systems Group. The software-engineering process was constrained by lead program managers' misunderstandings of software issues.

♦ Requirements specifications. The SED had become involved in specifying software requirements for some, but not all, projects.

♦ Process data. The SED had made substantial progress in gathering data, but the progress still required solidification. For example, it needed more assistance for data application and analysis. (Although data analysis at the project level was maturing, division-wide data analysis was limited.)

♦ Process automation. The SED had improved its CASE technologies, but the team found that improvement in six areas would reduce the drudgery and labor of recurring tasks: unit-test procedure generation, execution and analysis of regression tests, path-coverage analysis, CASE-tool evaluation, tool expertise, and tool- and method-effectiveness evaluation.

♦ Training. Training was identified as an organizational strength. However, the team found that additional training was needed to help the projects effectively use the process data being gathered.

Recommendations. The team made six recommendations.

Process awareness. Enhance the awareness and understanding of the software process within lead divisions and Ground Systems Group management.

Process automation. Establish a project-oriented mechanism to assess tool needs and effectiveness, develop or acquire automation support where needs assessment justi-

fies its use, provide ongoing information on CASE availability and capabilities, and make tools expertise available to the projects.

Process-data analysis. Expand the process-data analysis technology to include error projection, train employees to analyze project-specific process data, develop a division-wide context for interpreting project-specific data, and ensure that process data is not used to evaluate individuals.

Data-collection/-analysis use. Optimize process data collection and analysis to best benefit product and business results.

Requirements process. Continue efforts to increase participation in the software-requirements process, update SED bidding practice to require SED input and participation in requirements generation, and increase the skill level of software engineers in writing requirements.

Quality assurance. Ensure adequate SQA support for SED software efforts. In particular, it should ensure that Ground Systems Group SQA practices are consistently applied on all efforts in which the SED is responsible for the software and that the level of SQA effort is sufficient to support each project's needs.

ASSESSMENT COMPARISON

The SEI has compiled data on all the assessments it has conducted in its *State of the Software Engineering Practice*. [2] Tables 1 and 2 detail the two Hughes assessment results compared with the state-of-the-practice data for level 2 and level 3 questions. (Because there was insufficient data on level 4 and 5 questions at the time of the state-of-the-practice report, we cannot include this comparison.)

To provide a valid comparison between the two SED assessments, we used the same SEI questionnaire in both assessments. In 1987, the SED met the level 2 criteria in all important aspects. As Table 1 shows, of the six projects assessed, there were only four negative answers to two of the 12 key level 2 questions. In other words, of 72 answers, 68 were yes. In 1987, the SED could not answer yes to many key level 3 questions, as Table 1 also shows. Table 2 shows the more interesting

changes in the key level 4 questions between the two assessments.

We drew several conclusions from these results. First, in 1987 there was not agreement among projects on some organization-wide questions. For example, in Table 1 questions 1.1.7, 1.2.3, and 1.2.5 concern the total organization, not individual projects. In all cases, these responses should have been 0 percent. Similarly, in Table 2, questions 1.3.4, 2.3.1, 2.3.8, and 2.4.2 relate to the entire organization. Here, the numbers should have been 0 percent for the first three and 100 percent for 2.4.2.

Second, the analysis and error-projection activities asked about in the level 4 questions typically are difficult and require extensive training and support. Because the intent is to focus attention on the key error causes, to build understanding of these critical factors, and gradually to establish the means to control them, considerable data analysis and experience is required before proficiency can be expected.

LESSONS LEARNED

Hughes learned 11 important lessons from the SED process-improvement ef-

fort, listed here in order of importance.

Management commitment. The path to improvement requires investment, risk, time, and the pain of cultural change. Delegation is not strong enough to overcome these roadblocks. Commitment is. Process improvement should be tied to the salary or promotion criteria of senior management.

Pride is the most important result. Improvements are one-time achievements, but pride feeds on itself and leads to continuous measurable improvement. When the whole organization buys into the improvement and sees the results unfold, it gains a team esprit de corps and from that, pride. Hughes' people pulled together to improve the entire organization's software process and they all share in the success.

Increases in maturity decrease risk. Another important benefit (and goal) of process maturation is decreased risk of missing cost and schedule estimates. The two concepts of risk and process maturity are closely coupled. As an organization matures, its performance in meeting planned costs and schedules improves.

TABLE 2
COMPARISON OF RESPONSES TO LEVEL 4 QUESTIONS
(PERCENTAGE OF POSITIVE RESPONSES)

Question		1987 assessment	1990 assessment
1.3.4	Is a mechanism used for managing and supporting the introduction of new technologies?	16	100
2.2.5	Are design errors projected and compared to actuals?	16	20
2.2.6	Are code and test errors projected and compared to actuals?	16	20
2.2.14	Is test coverage measured and recorded for each phase of functional testing?	83	100
2.3.1	Has a managed and controlled process database been established for process metrics data across all projects?	50	100
2.3.2	Are the review data gathered during design reviews analyzed?	16	100
2.3.3	Is the error data from code reviews and tests analyzed to determine the likely distribution and characteristics of the errors remaining in the product?	16	20
2.3.4	Are analyses of errors conducted to determine their process-related causes?	83	100
2.3.8	Is review efficiency analyzed for each project?	50	100
2.4.2	Is a mechanism used for periodically assessing the software-engineering process and implementing indicated improvements?	83	100

The indicator the SED uses for cost risk, and the indicator for which there is historical data available, is a cost-performance index, which is calculated as CPI = BCWP/ACWP, where BCWP is the budgeted cost of work performed and ACWP is the actual cost of work performed.

The CPI has shown a steady improvement, from 0.94 in July 1987 to 0.97 in March 1990. In other words, in July 1987 the SED averaged about 6 percent actual costs over budgeted costs; in March 1990 it had reduced this average to 3 percent. This 50-percent reduction nets Hughes about $2 million annually. These values are averages for all SED projects at the time.

When considering all the direct labor, support, overhead, travel, and equipment costs for the assessment and improvement costs, these first-year benefits are five times the total improvement expenditures.

Assuming that the Hughes maturity is at least maintained, these financial benefits should continue to accrue. Furthermore, the improved contract performance makes Hughes' estimates of software cost more credible during contract negotiations.

The benefits are worth the effort and expense. When the improvement effort was begun in 1988, Hughes was not sure what the benefits would be, other than achieving the next higher level on the process-maturity model. However, Hughes received a handsome return on its investment: The quality of work life has improved, and the company's image has benefited from the improved performance.

The SED has experienced very few crises at the Ground Systems Group facility since applying a mature process to each project. Although volatile requirements continue to be a persistent engineering problem, the effect of shifting requirements on cost and schedule is under con-

trol and reliably predictable.

A less quantifiable result of process maturity is the quality of work life. Hughes SED has seen fewer overtime hours, fewer gut-wrenching problems to deal with each day, and a more stable work environment. Even in the volatile aerospace industry in California, software-professional turnover has been held below 10 percent.

Software technology center is key. A software technology center works most effectively when most of the development, project management, administration, technology development, training, and marketing are housed in one organization.

The size and focus of such a central organization makes it possible to afford, for example, an SEPG that focuses on technology improvement, a full-time person in charge of technology transfer, an organization-wide data-collection and -analysis service, independent software research and development, and a CASE center. All these are important contributors to improving process maturity.

A coherent culture exists at level 3. A coherent organizational culture results from the cumulative effect of a long-lived organization with a common purpose, environment, education, and experience base. You can quickly sense the nature of an organization's culture when you hear people speaking in the same technical language, sharing common practices and procedures, and referring to organizational goals as their own.

At level 3, Hughes found that the common culture helped foster an esprit de corps that reinforced team performance. In fact, Hughes concluded it needed to achieve a common process across the organization, to establish an organization-wide training program, and to enable buy-in of organizational goals. Although it is difficult to precisely phrase a question to determine if an organization does or does

not have such a positive culture, an assessment team can agree whether or not team members experienced it during an assessment.

A focal point is essential. Disintegrated, asynchronous improvement is not only inefficient but also ineffective for solving organization-wide problems. Although there is still the need for cell-level improvement teams, there must also be an organizational focal point to plan, coordinate (integrate), and implement organization-wide process improvements. The SEI calls this focal point an SEPG. Hughes calls it the technology steering committee, others might call it an engineering council. Whatever the name, there must be a focal point.

Technology transfer is essential. The establishment of a technology-transfer function was judged the most profound of the actions taken.

Software-process expertise is essential. In 1987, the SEI questionnaire and a few SEI professionals were all the expert help there was. Now there is a growing literature on software process, a draft capability maturity model, and an improved draft questionnaire. Many SEI people are experts in software process, and even more people in industry have become experts in software process.[1]

To understand and use the available knowledge, process-improvement teams must become process experts and they must be able to interpret the assessment questionnaire in the context of the organization. For example, the SED wrestled over the ambiguity of the phrase "first-line managers" in the questionnaire. In the Hughes organization, "manager" is used only for the third promotion level and above in the line-management hierarchy, but this isn't what the SEI meant. After discussions with the SEI over the meaning of the phrase, Hughes concluded that it meant the first supervisory position for software engineers, a position Hughes called group head.

Because group heads did not sign off on schedules and cost estimates, Hughes

> Hughes SED has seen fewer overtime hours, fewer gut-wrenching problems to deal with each day, and a more stable work environment.

considered changing their practices to require the heads to do so. However, Hughes found that some software projects have eight people, while others might include an entire lab of 250 people with several sections and many groups. It thus did not always seem appropriate to have group heads approve schedules and cost estimates.

Hughes finally concluded that "first-line manager" in the Hughes culture meant associate project manager, the person who is in charge of software development on a project (no matter what level), and the one who negotiates and approves schedules and cost estimates with the program manager, documenting those agreements in a work authorization and delegation document. Hughes SED thus translated the question "Do software first-line managers sign off on their schedules and cost estimates?" as "Do associate project managers approve work authorization and delegation documents?"

An action plan is necessary. An action plan based on process-maturity assessment recommendations will not necessarily move an organization to the next stage of maturity. Assessment recommendations come from a brainstorming and consensus-building team process that, because of the nature of the process and the time limitations, can address only the top priority recommendations (about 10 out of 36 in the last assessment). Furthermore, action plans tend to not include many people-oriented changes (such as getting people to buy in on changes) that are needed for progress.

The only ones questioning the value of level 2 are those who have not achieved it. To an organization that has achieved it, level 2 capabilities seem obvious and indispensable. It is simply a natural, responsible way of conducting business.

When compared with those of the general population of SEI-assessed organizations, it is clear that the 1987 Hughes improvement efforts started from a very strong base. Based on the SEI data, the Hughes process in 1987 was in approximately the 90th percentile of all organizations studied.[2]

It is also clear that given sufficient management emphasis and competent, skilled, and dedicated professionals, significant improvement in software process is possible. Improvements like those made at Hughes' SED can significantly help a software organization's overall business performance. The SEI assessment of Hughes' SED formed the bases for a sustained improvement effort.

Finally, improvement is reinforcing. As each improvement level is reached, the benefits are demonstrated and the opportunities for further improvement become clear. ◆

ACKNOWLEDGMENTS

We thank Ken Dymond, Larry Druffel, George Pandelious, Jeff Perdue, and Jim Rozum for their helpful review comments. We very much appreciate Dorothy Josephson's support in preparing the manuscript and the able editorial assistance of Linda Pesante and Marie Elm. The comments and suggestions of Carl Chang and the anonymous referees were also a great help in converting our manuscript into a finished article.

This work was sponsored by the US Defense Dept.

REFERENCES

1. W.S. Humphrey, *Managing the Software Process*, Addison-Wesley, Reading, Mass., 1989.
2. W.S. Humphrey, D.H. Kitson, and T.C. Kasse, "The State of Software-Engineering Practice: A Preliminary Report," Tech. Report CMU/SEI-89-TR-1, Software Eng. Inst., Carnegie Mellon Univ., Pittsburgh, 1989.

Watts S. Humphrey, a reseach scientist at the Software Engineering Institute, founded its software-process program, which helps establish advanced software-engineering processes, metrics, methods, and quality programs for the US government and its contractors. He is the author of three books and holds five US patents.

Humphrey received a BS in physics from the University of Chicago, an MS in physics from Illinois Institute of Technology, and an MBA from the University of Chicago. He is an IEEE fellow, a member of ACM, and a member of the board of examiners for the Malcolm Baldrige National Quality Award.

Terry R. Snyder is manager of Hughes Aircraft's Ground Systems Group. He has more than 30 years experience managing and programming large-scale, real-time systems. The Ground Systems Group develops air defense and air traffic control systems, communication systems, ground and shipboard radar, shipboard electronic systems, and military displays.

Snyder received a BS in math from Penn State and is a graduate of UCLA's Executive Management Program. He serves on Software Productivity Consortium's board of directors, is a member of the Aerospace Industries Association's embedded software committee, and serves on the University of California at Irvine's Computer Science Dept's. advisory board.

Ronald R. Willis is a member of the technical staff of Hughes Aircraft's Ground Systems Group, where he is a chief scientist in the Software Engineering Division. He has coauthored a book, written many technical articles, and has developed systems for discrete-event simulation, graphical modeling and simulation analysis, and software quality engineering.

Willis received a BS in mathematics from California State University at Long Beach and an MS in computer science from the University of Southern California. He is a member of ACM.

Address questions about this article to Humphrey at Software Engineering Institute, Carnegie Mellon University, Pittsburgh, PA 15213; Internet watts@sei.cmu.edu.

Capability Maturity Model, Version 1.1

MARK C. PAULK, BILL CURTIS, and MARY BETH CHRISSIS
Software Engineering Institute
CHARLES V. WEBER, *IBM Federal Systems Company*

◆ *The new version has more consistent wording and should be easier to use. It is based on more than six years of experience with software-process improvement and the contributions of hundreds of reviewers.*

After two decades of unfulfilled promises about productivity and quality gains from applying new software methodologies and technologies, developers are realizing that their fundamental problem is their inability to manage the software process. In many organizations, projects are often excessively late and over budget, and the benefits of better methods and tools cannot be realized in the maelstrom of an undisciplined, chaotic project.

In November 1986, the Software Engineering Institute, with assistance from Mitre Corp., began developing a process-maturity framework that would help developers improve their software process. In September 1987, the SEI released a brief description of the process-maturity framework[1] which was later expanded in Watts Humphrey's book, *Managing the Software Process.*[2]

The SEI also developed two methods — software-process assessment and software-capability evaluation — and a maturity questionnaire[3] to appraise software-process maturity.

After four years of experience with the process-maturity framework and the preliminary version of the maturity questionnaire, the SEI evolved the maturity framework into the Capability Maturity Model.

The CMM presents sets of recommended practices in a number of key process areas that have been shown to enhance software-development and maintenance capability. The CMM is based on knowledge acquired from software-process assessments and extensive feedback from both industry and government.

The CMM guides developers on how to gain control of their development and maintenance processes and how to evolve toward a culture of software-engineering and management excellence. It was designed to help developers select process-improvement strategies by determining their current process maturity and identifying the most critical issues to improving their software quality and process.

By focusing on a limited set of activities and working aggressively to achieve them, a developer can steadily improve the organization-wide software process to enable continuous and lasting gains in capability.

The initial release of the CMM, version 1.0, was reviewed and used by the software community during 1991 and 1992. A workshop, held in April 1992, on CMM 1.0 was attended by about 200 software professionals. The current version of the CMM[4] is the result of the feedback from that workshop and ongoing feedback from the software community. In this article, we summarize the technical report that describes version 1.1; the box below summarizes the changes made.

IMMATURITY VERSUS MATURITY

Setting sensible goals for process improvement requires an understanding of the difference between immature and mature software organizations.

Immaturity. In an immature organization, software processes are generally improvised by practitioners and their managers during a project. Even if a software process has been specified, it is not rigorously followed or enforced.

The immature software organization is reactionary — its managers are usually focused on solving immediate crises (better known as fire fighting). Schedules and budgets are routinely exceeded because they are not based on realistic estimates. When hard deadlines are imposed, product functionality and quality are often compromised to meet a schedule.

An immature organization has no objective way to judge product quality or solve product or process problems. Therefore, product quality is difficult to predict. Activities intended to enhance quality, such as reviews and testing, are often curtailed or eliminated when projects fall behind schedule.

Maturity. A mature organization possesses an organization-wide ability to manage development and maintenance. Managers can accurately communicate the software process to staff and new employees, and work activities are carried out according to the planned process.

The mandated processes are usable and consistent with the way the work actually gets done. These defined processes are updated when necessary, with improvements developed through controlled pilot tests and cost-benefit analyses. Roles and responsibilities are clear within a project and across an organization. In a mature organization, managers

---

SUMMARY OF DIFFERENCES BETWEEN CMM VERSION 1.0 AND VERSION 1.1

Most of the changes we made to CMM version 1.0 were done to improve the consistency of the key-practices structure, clarify concepts, and provide consistent wording. We made no changes to the high-level maturity framework. We also added an index and expanded and refined the glossary to provide additional clarification for terms.

We are working on a technical report that summarizes the changes and will include detailed traceability tables, summaries of the change for each key process area, and the document-design criteria. This is a summary of that draft document.

General changes. The names of some key process areas have changed, but the content of most areas remains the same.

We rewrote all the goals, to emphasize process end states rather than results, and to remove subjective words like "effective." The goals now serve as an integrating framework for rating key process areas: Each key practice maps to one or more goals, and each goal and its associated practices can be considered a subprocess area. Satisfying all the goals satisfies the key process area.

We also eliminated redundant practices and expanded cross-referencing significantly. When appropriate, we cross-reference directly to key practices rather than to the entire area.

Language changes. We developed and used wording templates to add consistency and to help users understand when we are and aren't talking about similar concepts — wording differences are now purposeful.

We expanded the overview section of the key practices that apply to groups and roles, to better explain these concepts. Conversely, we removed the conceptual organization chart, to emphasize that each organization should map the CMM roles to their own organization.

The wording template for policies changed from "the organization follows a written policy for X" to "the project follows a written organizational policy for X." This reflects the emphasis in many key process areas on project activities. It does imply that organizational policies are required, even at level 2, where the scope of the policy was ambiguous before. We made this change to reflect the CMM's emphasis on organizational improvement.

When both organizational and project activities are expected, the language in version 1.1 explicitly identifies the entity intended to be the performer.

When appropriate, we substituted the term "software work product" for "software product." These definitions are now generally consistent with IEEE usage, which defines a software work product to include both nondeliverable and deliverable products and a software product to include deliverables only.

We carefully considered the use of the wording "reviews and approves" or "reviews and agrees to;" only when the

monitor the quality of products and the process that produced them. There is an objective, quantitative basis for judging product quality and analyzing problems with the product and process. Schedules and budgets are based on historical performance and are realistic; expected results for cost, schedule, functionality, and quality are usually achieved.

In general, a disciplined process is consistently followed because all the participants understand the value of doing so, and an infrastructure exists to support the process.

FUNDAMENTAL CONCEPTS

A software process is a set of activities, methods, practices, and transformations that people use to develop and maintain software and associated products (project plans, design documents, code, test cases, user manuals, and so on). As an organization matures, the software process becomes better defined and more consistently implemented throughout the organization.

◆ *Software-process capability* describes the range of expected results that can be achieved by following a software process. An organization's software-process capability is one way to predict the most likely outcome of the next software project it undertakes.

◆ *Software-process performance* represents the actual results achieved by following a software process. Process performance focuses on achieved results; process capability focuses on expected results.

◆ *Software-process maturity* is the extent to which a specific process is explicitly defined, managed, measured, controlled, and effective. Maturity implies a potential for growth in capability and indicates both the richness of an organization's software process and the consistency with which it is applied in projects throughout the organization.

As a software organization gains in maturity, it institutionalizes its software process via policies, standards, and organizational structures. Institutionalization

entails building an infrastructure and a corporate culture that supports the methods, practices, and procedures of the business so that they endure after those who originally defined them have gone.

Five maturity levels. Continuous process improvement is based on many small, evolutionary steps rather than revolutionary innovations. The staged structure of the CMM is based on principles of product quality espoused by Walter Shewart, W. Edwards Deming, Joseph Juran, and Philip Crosby.

The CMM provides a framework for organizing these evolutionary steps into five *maturity levels*, shown in Figure 1, that lay successive foundations for continuous process improvement. The levels define an ordinal scale for measuring process maturity and evaluating process capability. The levels also help an organization prioritize its improvement efforts.

Each maturity level comprises a set of process goals that, when satisfied, stabilize an important component of a software

---

agreement aspect was appropriate did we retain that wording. Otherwise, we used only "reviews," usually when the software-engineering group would not be expected to have the authority to approve the item.

We replaced the phrase "This procedure/policy requires that:" to "This procedure/policy typically specifies that:" to remove the implication that what follows is a checklist. Key practices describe the normal behavior expected in an organization; they are not intended to be a requirements specification for the process.

To reduce confusion about the terms "process," "activity," and "task," we used "task" when we meant to describe a defined unit of work with known entry and exit criteria,

and "activity" only when a more general term was appropriate.

Level 2 changes. In general, at this level we replaced the word "process" with "activity" or "procedure." In version 1.1, we reserve "process" for higher levels, in the context of an organization's standard or a project's defined process.

◆ *Requirements Management*: Here we tried to sharpen the focus on requirements management as seen from a software-engineering perspective, while recognizing that the development and revision of requirements typically is not the responsibility of the software-engineering group.

◆ *Software Project Planning*: We added a verification practice to address senior manage-

ment's involvement in planning activities.

◆ *Software Project Tracking and Oversight*: Many of the changes in this area are intended to clarify who does what, emphasizing the software-engineering group's responsibilities.

◆ *Software Subcontract Management*: This area addresses the role of strategic business alliances in subcontracting. The focus of the practices is on a principal-subordinate, not an equal, relationship.

◆ *Software quality assurance*: We added ability 1 ("a group that is responsible for coordinating and implementing SQA for the project ... exists or is established") in the document-design criteria.

◆ *Software Configuration Management*: We replaced the

hierarchy of configuration item, configuration component, and configuration unit with the phrase "configuration item/unit." This change reflects the ongoing evolution of the terminology in the standards world and maximizes flexibility.

Level 3 changes. We made the interrelationships among the Organization Process Focus, Organization Process Definition, and Integrated Software Management key process areas more explicit through cross-referencing.

◆ *Organization Process Focus*: This area covers the creation of the organization's standard process and related process assets.

◆ *Organization Process Definition*: This area describes the assets created above, which are

81

process. Achieving each level of maturity establishes a different component in a software process, resulting in an increase in the process capability of an organization. The labeled arrows in Figure 1 indicate the type of process capability being institutionalized by an organization at each step of the maturity framework.

Behavioral characterization. Maturity levels 2 through 5 can be characterized through the activities performed by an organization to establish or improve its software process, by activities performed on each project, and by the resulting process capability across projects. We include a behavioral characterization of level 1 to establish a base of comparison for process improvements at higher maturity levels.

♦ *Level 1: Initial.* At the Initial level, an organization typically does not provide a stable environment for developing and maintaining software. Such organizations frequently have difficulty making commitments that the staff can meet with an orderly engineering process, resulting in a

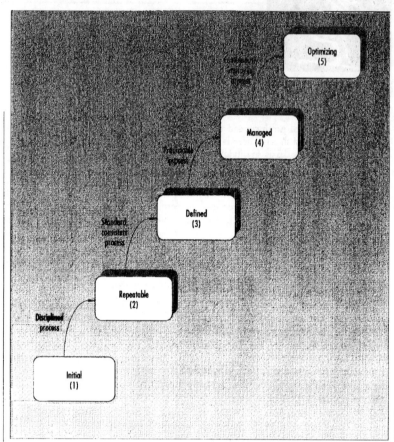

Figure 1. Maturity framework with five levels, each one the foundation for the next.

tailored by the projects to create a defined process in Integrated Software Management. We deleted activity 1, which described the process assets that must be developed and maintained as inappropriately prescriptive.

♦ *Training Program:* The 1992 CMM Workshop proposed refocusing this key process area to Skills Building, which was drafted but very controversial. This was resolved by recognizing explicitly that training vehicles other than formal classroom training may be an appropriate way to implement this key process area.

♦ *Integrated Software Management:* We removed redundancies with Software Project Planning and Software Project Tracking and Oversight.

♦ *Software Product Engineer-*

ing: We added ability 3 to address the concept of orientation and cross-training in disciplines other than an individual's main assignment.

♦ *Intergroup Coordination:* We changed the terminology about groups throughout, eliminating the term "project groups" in favor of "software-engineering group," "(other) engineering groups," "software-related groups," and "(other) affected groups," to clarify the interrelationships intended.

♦ *Peer Reviews:* We changed the specific data on the conduct and results of peer reviews in activity 3 to examples and dropped the organizational database.

Level 4 changes. We changed the names of both level 4 key process areas: Quality Manage-

ment became Software Quality Management and Process Measurement and Analysis became Quantitative Process Management.

♦ *Quantitative Process Management:* We added commitment 1, which addresses policy implementation by the project. This key process area involves significant activities by both projects and the organization, although the majority of activities are project-focused.

♦ Software Quality Management: Activities 6 through 10 in version 1.0 were folded into activity 3 in version 1.1. These key practices described software-quality goals. Having them be key practices overemphasized their importance in relation to overall goal setting and measurement.

Level 5 changes. We changed the name of Technology Innovation to Technology Change Management and made the integration between Technology Change Management and Process Change Management more explicit, through cross-references.

♦ *Defect Prevention:* We made several wording changes throughout this key process area to differentiate between organization and project.

♦ *Technology Change Management:* We deleted subpractices for activity 7 because they were redundant to the subpractices of activity 5 in Process Change Management.

♦ *Process Change Management:* We moved ability 1, on establishing a software process improvement program, to become activity 1.

series of crises. During a crisis, projects typically abandon planned procedures and revert to coding and testing.

Success depends entirely on having an exceptional manager and a seasoned and effective development team. Occasionally, capable and forceful software managers can withstand the pressures to take shortcuts, but when they leave the project their stabilizing influence leaves with them. Even a strong engineering process cannot overcome the instability created by the absence of sound management practices. (Selecting, hiring, developing, and retaining competent people are significant issues for organizations at all levels of maturity, but they are largely outside the scope of the CMM.)

EVEN A STRONG PROCESS CANNOT OVERCOME UNSOUND MANAGEMENT.

In spite of this ad hoc, even chaotic, process, level 1 organizations frequently develop products that work, even though they may be over budget and behind schedule. Success in level 1 organizations depends on the competence and heroics of the people in an organization and cannot be repeated unless the same competent individuals are assigned to the next project. Thus, at level 1, capability is a characteristic of individuals, not organizations.

♦ *Level 2: Repeatable.* At the Repeatable level, policies for managing a software project and procedures to implement those policies are established. The planning and managment of new projects is based on experience with similar projects. Process capability is enhanced by imposing basic process-management discipline project by project.

Projects in level 2 organizations have installed basic management controls. Realistic project commitments are based on the results observed on previous projects and on the requirements of the current project. Project managers track costs, schedules, and functionality and identify problems in meeting commitments when they arise.

Software requirements and the work products developed to satisfy them are baselined, and their integrity is controlled. Project standards are defined, and the organization ensures they are faithfully followed. The project team works with their subcontractors, if any, to establish a customer-supplier relationship.

Processes may differ among projects in a level 2 organization. To achieve level 2, an organization must have policies that help project managers establish appropriate management processes.

The process capability of level 2 organizations can be summarized as disciplined because project planning and tracking are stable and earlier successes can be repeated.

♦ *Level 3: Defined.* At the Defined level, a typical process for developing and maintaining software across the organization is documented, including both software-engineering and management processes, and these processes are integrated into a coherent whole. The CMM calls this an organization's *standard* software process.

Processes established at level 3 are used (and changed, as appropriate) to help managers and staff perform more effectively. An organization exploits effective software-engineering practices when standardizing its processes.

A group — like a software-engineering process group[5] — is responsible for an organization's process activities. An organization-wide training program ensures that the staff and managers have the knowledge and skills they require.

Project teams tailor an organization's standard software process to develop their own *defined* process, which takes into account the project's unique characteristics. A defined process contains a coherent, integrated set of well-defined software-engineering and management processes.

A well-defined process includes readiness criteria, inputs, standards and procedures for performing the work, verification mechanisms (such as peer reviews), outputs, and completion criteria. Because the process is well-defined, management has good insight into technical progress on all projects.

The software-process capability of level 3 organizations can be summarized as standard and consistent because both software engineering and management activities are stable and repeatable. Within product lines, cost, schedule, and functionality are under control and quality is tracked. This process capability is based on a common, organization-wide understanding of the activities, roles, and responsibilities in a defined process.

♦ *Level 4: Managed.* At the Managed level, an organization sets quantitative quality goals for both products and processes and instruments processes with well-defined and consistent measurements. Productivity and quality are measured for important process activities across all projects as part of an organizational measurement program. Software products are of predictably high quality.

An organization-wide process database is used to collect and analyze the data available from a project's defined processes. These measurements establish the quantitative foundation for evaluating a project's processes and products. Projects control their products and processes by narrowing the variation in their performance to fall within acceptable quantitative boundaries. Meaningful variations in process performance can be distinguished from random variation (noise), particularly within established product lines. The risks involved in moving up the learning curve of a new application domain are known and carefully managed.

The software-process capability of level 4 organizations can be summarized as being quantifiable and predictable because the process is measured and operates within measurable limits. This level of capability lets an organization predict trends in process and product quality within the quantitative bounds of these limits. Because the process is both stable and measured, when some exceptional circumstance occurs, an organization can identify and address the *special* cause of the variation. When the known limits of the process are exceeded, managers take action to correct the situation.

♦ *Level 5: Optimizing.* At the Optimizing level, the entire organization is focused on continuous process improvement. The organization has the means to identify weaknesses and strengthen the process proactively, with the goal of preventing defects. Data on process effectiveness is used to perform cost-benefit analyses of new technologies and propose changes to the process. Innovations that exploit the best software-engineering practices are identified and transferred throughout an organization.

Project teams in level 5 organizations analyze defects to determine their causes, evaluate the process to prevent known types of defects from recurring, and disseminate lessons learned to other projects.

Every system has chronic waste, in the form of rework, due to random variation in the tasks to be performed. At level 5, waste is unacceptable; organized efforts to remove waste result in changing the system by changing the *common* causes of inefficiency. Reducing waste happens at all the maturity levels, but it is the focus of level 5.

The software-process capability of level 5 organizations can be summarized as continuously improving because level 5 organizations are continuously striving to improve the range of their process capability, thereby improving the process performance of their projects. Improvement occurs both by incremental advancements in the existing process and by innovations in technologies and methods. Technology and process improvements are planned and managed as ordinary business activities.

Predicting performance. An organization's process maturity helps predict a project's ability to meet its goals. Projects in level 1 organizations experience wide variations in achieving cost, schedule, functionality, and quality targets.

As Figure 2 illustrates, we can expect three improvements in meeting targeted goals as an organization's process matures. These expectations are based on the quantitative results process improvement has achieved in other industries, and they are consistent with the initial case study results reported.[7-10]

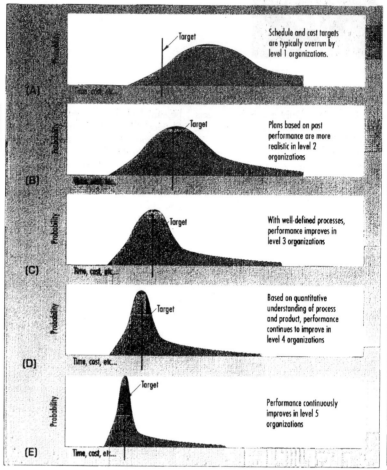

Figure 2. Expected improvements in meeting goals (time, cost, etc.) as a process matures. (A) The curve in level 1 organizations is to the right of the target line because schedules and budgets are largely not met, and it covers a broad area because performance cannot be predicted; (B) more mature organizations can deliver projects of similar size and application in a smaller range and closer to the target; (C) still more mature organizations not only deliver more projects on target, but displace the target line horizontally, indicating shorter development time or reduced cost; (D) performance continues to improve because the process is adjusted based on quanitative data; and (E) reduced rework and improved predictability are key to further improvement.

First, as maturity increases, the difference between targeted results and actual results decreases across projects. For example, level 1 organizations often miss their originally scheduled delivery dates by a wide margin. In Figure 2a, this is illustrated by how much of the area under the curve lies to the right of the target line. More mature organizations should be able to meet targeted dates with increased accuracy.

Second, as maturity increases, the variability of actual results around targeted results decreases. For example, in level 1 organizations, delivery dates for projects of similar size are unpredictable and vary widely. Similar projects in a more mature organization, however, will be delivered within a smaller range. In Figure 2b, this is illustrated by how much of the area under the curve is concentrated near the target line.

Third, as an organization matures, costs decrease, development time shortens, and productivity and quality increase. In a level 1 organization, development time can be quite long because of rework. In contrast, more mature organizations have increased process efficiency and reduced rework, shortening development time. In Figure 2c, this is illustrated by the horizontal displacement of the target line from the origin.

Improved prediction rests on the assumption that reducing noise, often in the form of rework, improves predictability. Unprecedented systems complicate the picture, because new technologies and applications lower process capability by in-

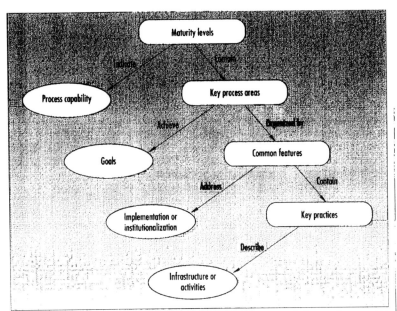

Figure 3. Each maturity level is composed of key process areas, which are composed of common features, which in turn specify key practices.

creasing variability.

Nevertheless, the management and engineering practices characteristic of more mature organizations help identify and address problems in unprecedented systems earlier in development than would be possible in less mature organizations. In some cases, a mature process means that "failed" projects are identified early, so investment in a lost cause is minimized.

The documented case studies of software-process improvement indicate that they result in significant improvements in both quality and productivity. The return on investment seems to be in the 5:1 to 8:1 range for successful process-improvement efforts.

Skipping levels. Trying to skip maturity levels is counterproductive because each level is a necessary foundation from which to achieve the next level. Organizations can institute specific process improvements at any time, even before they are prepared to advance to the level at which the practice is recommended. However, developers should understand that the stability of these improvements is at greater risk because they do not rest on a complete foundation. Processes without a proper foundation fail at the very time they are needed most — under stress — and provide no basis for future improvement.

For example, a well-defined level 3 process can be placed at great risk if man-

agement makes a poorly planned schedule commitment or fails to control changes to the baselined requirements. Similarly, many developers have collected the detailed data that is characteristic of level 4, only to find they cannot interpret it because their process is inconsistent.

At the same time, process improvement should focus on the needs of an organization in the context of its business environment. Higher level practices may address a project's or an organization's immediate needs. For example, one of the recommended steps to move from level 1 to level 2 is to establish a software-engineering process group, which is an attribute of level 3 organizations. So, while such a group is not a necessary characteristic of a level 2 organization, it can be useful in achieving level 2.

CMM OPERATIONAL DEFINITION

The CMM framework represents a path of improvements to increased software-process capability. The operational elaboration of the CMM is designed to support the many ways it will be used, four of which are

♦ Assessment teams will use it to identify strengths and weaknesses in an organization.

♦ Evaluation teams will use it to identify the risks of selecting among contractors and to monitor contracts.

♦ Upper management will use it to understand the activities necessary to launch a process-improvement program in their organization.

♦ Technical staff and process-improvement groups will use it as a guide to help them define and improve their organization's process.

Because these uses are diverse, the CMM must be decomposed in sufficient detail so that actual recommendations can be derived from it. This decomposition indicates the key processes and their structure that characterize software-process maturity and software-process capability.

Internal structure. The CMM decomposes each maturity level into constituent parts, with the exception of level 1. As Figure 3 shows, each level is composed of several *key process areas*. Each key process area is organized into five sections called *common features*. The common features specify *key practices*, which, when collectively addressed, accomplish the goals of the key process area.

Key process areas. Key process areas indicate where an organization should focus to improve its software process. They identify the issues that must be addressed to achieve a maturity level, as Figure 4 illustrates.

Each key process area identifies a cluster of related activities that, when performed collectively, achieve a set of goals considered important for enhancing process capability. The path to achieving these goals may differ across projects, depending on the application domain or environment. Nevertheless, all the goals of a key process area must be achieved for an organization to satisfy it.

The use of the adjective "key" implies that there are process areas (and processes) that are not key to achieving a maturity level. The CMM does not describe in detail all the process areas involved with developing and maintaining software, only those that have been identified as key determiners of process capability.

Key process areas may be viewed as requirements for achieving a maturity level: To achieve a maturity level, the key process areas for that level must be satisfied. (Level 1 has no key process areas.)

The specific practices to be executed in each key process area will evolve as an organization achieves higher levels. For example, many of the project-estimating capabilities described in the project planning key process area at level 2 must evolve to handle the additional project data available at level 3.

Level 2. The key process areas at level 2 focus on establishing basic project-management controls.

♦ *Requirements Management* means establishing a common understanding between a customer and a project team of the customer's requirements. This agreement is the basis for planning and managing a project.

♦ *Software Project Planning* means establishing reasonable plans for engineering and managing a project. These plans are the foundation project management.

♦ *Software Project Tracking and Oversight* means to establish adequate visibility into actual progress so that management can take effective action when a project's performance deviates significantly from the plans.

♦ *Software Subcontract Management* means to select qualified subcontractors and manage them effectively.

♦ *Software Quality Assurance* means to provide management with appropriate visibility into the process being used and the products being built.

♦ *Software Configuration Management* means to establish and maintain the integrity of a project's products throughout its life cycle.

Level 3. The key process areas at level 3 address both project and organizational issues, as an organization establishes an infrastructure that institutionalizes effective software-engineering and management processes across all projects.

♦ *Organization Process Focus* means to establish an organizational responsibility for activities that improve an organization's overall software-process capability.

♦ *Organization Process Definition* means to develop and maintain a usable set of

process assets that improve processes across projects and provide a basis for defining meaningful data for quantitative process management. These assets are a foundation that can be institutionalized through mechanisms like training.

♦ *Training Program* means to develop the skills and knowledge of individuals so that they can be effective and efficient. Training is an organizational responsibility, but projects should identify necessary skills and provide training when their needs are unique.

♦ *Integrated Software Management* means to integrate software-engineering and management activities into a coherent, defined process that is tailored from an organization's standard software process and related process assets. Tailoring is based on the business environment and technical needs of a project.

♦ *Software Product Engineering* means to consistently perform a well-defined process that integrates all technical activities — requirements analysis, design,

code, and test, among others — to produce correct, consistent software products effectively and efficiently.

♦ *Intergroup Coordination* means to establish a way for a software-engineering group to participate actively with other engineering groups so that a project team can better satisfy the customer's needs.

♦ *Peer Reviews* means to remove defects from work products early and efficiently. An important corollary effect is to develop a better understanding of the work products and preventable defects. Peer review is an important and effective method that can be implemented through inspections or structured walkthroughs, for example.

Level 4. The key process areas at level 4 focus on establishing a quantitative understanding of both the software process and the software work products being built.

♦ *Quantitative Process Management* means to control a project's process performance quantitatively. A project's pro-

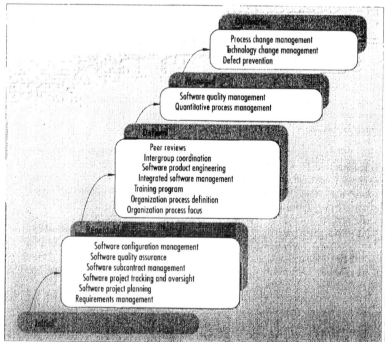

Figure 4. *Key process areas identify goals that must be met to achieve a maturity level. The path to achieving these goals may differ across projects.*

cess performance comprises the actual results achieved from following a software process. The focus is on identifying special causes of variation within a measurably stable process and correcting, as appropriate, the circumstances that created them.

♦ *Software Quality Management* means to develop a quantitative understanding of the quality of a project's products to achieve specific quality goals.

Level 5. The key process areas at level 5 focus on issues that both organizations and projects must address to implement continuous and measurable process improvement.

♦ *Defect Prevention* means to identify the causes of defects and prevent them from recurring by analyzing them and changing the defined process.

♦ *Technology Change Management* means to identify beneficial new technologies (such as tools, methods, and processes) and transfer them into an organization in an orderly manner. The focus here is on efficient innovation in an ever-changing world.

♦ *Process Change Management* means to continually improve an organization's processes with the intent of improving quality, increasing productivity, and decreasing development time.

Goals. Goals, which summarize key practices, are used to determine if an organization or project has effectively implemented a key process area. The goals signify the scope, boundaries, and intent of each key process area.

Common features. For convenience, the practices that describe the key process areas are organized by common features. The common features are attributes that indicate whether the implementation and institutionalization of a key process area is effective, repeatable, and lasting.

The five common features are

♦ *Commitment to perform*, which de-

scribes the actions an organization must take to ensure its process is established and enduring. This typically involves establishing organizational policies and obtaining senior-management sponsorship.

♦ *Ability to perform*, which describes the preconditions in a project or organization to implement the process competently. This typically involves resources, organizational structures, and training.

♦ *Activities performed*, which describes the roles and procedures necessary to implement a key process area. This typically involves establishing plans and procedures, performing the work, tracking it, and taking corrective actions as necessary.

♦ *Measurement and analysis*, which describes the need to measure the process and analyze the measurements. This typically involves obtaining sample measurements that could determine the status and effectiveness of activities performed.

♦ *Verifying implementation*, which describes the steps to ensure that the activities are performed in compliance with the standard process. This typically involves reviews and audits by management and quality assurance.

Activities performed describes what must be implemented to establish a process capability; the others, taken as a whole, are the basis by which an organization can institutionalize activities performed.

Key practices. Each key process area is described in terms of key practices that contribute to satisfying its goals. Key practices describe the infrastructure and activities that contribute most to the effective implementation and institutionalization of the key process area.

Each key practice consists of a single sentence, often followed by a more detailed description, which may include examples and elaboration. These key practices, also called top-level key practices, state the fundamental policies, proce-

> ## KEY PRACTICES DESCRIBE WHAT TO DO, BUT THEY DO NOT MANDATE HOW TO DO IT.

dures, and activities for the key process area. The components of the detailed description are frequently referred to as subpractices.

The key practices describe *what* to do, but they do not mandate *how* to do it. Alternative practices may also accomplish the goals of the key process area. The key practices should be interpreted rationally, to judge if the goals of the key process area are effectively, although perhaps differently, achieved. The key practices are contained in a separate report, along with guidance on their interpretation.[6]

FUTURE DIRECTIONS

Achieving higher levels of software-process maturity is incremental and requires a long-term commitment to continuous process improvement. Software organizations may take 10 years or more to build the foundation for, and a culture oriented toward, continuous process improvement. Although a decade-long process improvement program is foreign to most US companies, this level of effort is required to produce mature software organizations.

The CMM is not a silver bullet and does not address all the issues important for successful projects. For example, it does not currently address expertise in particular application domains, advocate specific software technologies, or suggest how to select, hire, motivate, and retain competent people -- although these issues are crucial to a project's success.

During the next few years, the CMM will continue to undergo extensive testing through use in software-process assessments, software-capability evaluations, and process-improvement programs. CMM-based products and training materials will be developed and revised as appropriate. The CMM is a living document that will be improved, but the SEI anticipates that CMM version 1.1 will remain the baseline until at least 1996. This provides an appropriate and realistic balance between the need for stability and the goal of continuous improvement. A book on the CMM is in progress for the SEI series published by Addison-Wesley.

The SEI is also working with the International Standards Organization in its efforts to build international standards for software-process assessment, improvement, and capability evaluation. This effort will integrate concepts from many process-improvement methods. The development of the ISO standards (and the contributions of other methods) will influence CMM version 2.0, even as the SEI's process work will influence the activities of the ISO.

The CMM represents a common-sense-engineering approach to software-process improvement. The maturity levels, key process areas, common features, and key practices have been extensively discussed and reviewed within the software community. While the CMM is not perfect, it does represent a broad consensus of the software community and is a useful tool for guiding software-process-improvement efforts.

The CMM provides a conceptual structure for improving the management and development of software products in a disciplined and consistent way. It does not guarantee that software products will be successfully built or that all problems in software engineering will be adequately resolved. However, current reports from CMM-based improvement programs indicate that it can improve the likelihood with which a software organization can achieve its cost, quality, and productivity goals.[7-10]

The CMM identifies practices for a mature software process and provides examples of the state of the practice (and in some cases, the state of the art), but it is not meant to be either exhaustive or dictatorial. The CMM identifies the characteristics of an effective software process, but the mature organization addresses all issues essential to a successful project, including people and technology, as well as process. ◆

ACKNOWLEDGMENTS

The CMM was produced by a dedicated group of people who spent many hours discussing the model and its features and then documenting it. Contributors, other than ourselves, include Edward Averill, Judy Bamberger, Joe Besselman, Marilyn Bush, Anita Carleton, Marty Carlson, Susan Dart, Betty Deimel, Lionel Deimel, Peter Feiler, Julia Gale, Suzie Garcia, Jim Hart, Ron Higuera, Watts Humphrey, Purvis Jackson, Tim Kasse, Richard Kauffold, David Kitson, Mike Konrad, Peter Malpass, Mark Manduke, Steve Masters, Mary Merrill, Judah Mogilensky, Warren Moseley, Jim Over, George Pandelios, Bob Park, Jeff Perdue, Dick Phillips, Mike Rissman, Jim Rozum, Jane Siegel, Christer von Schantz, Cynthia Wise, and Jim Withey.

We appreciate the administrative help from Todd Bowman, Dorothy Josephson, Debbie Punjack, Carolyn Tady, Marcia Theoret, Andy Tsounos, and David White and the editorial assistance from Suzanne Couturiaux and Bill Pollak.

Special thanks go to the members of the CMM Correspondence Group, who contributed their time and effort to reviewing drafts of the CMM and providing insightful comments and recommendations, and to the members of the CMM Advisory Board, who helped guide us. The current members of the Advisory Board are Constance Ahara, Kelley Butler, Bill Curtis, Conrad Czaplicki, Raymond Dion, Judah Mogilensky, Martin Owens, Mark Paulk, Sue Stetak, Charles Weber, and Ron Willis. Former members who worked with us on CMM 1.0 include Harry Carl, Jim Hess, Jerry Pixton, and Jim Withey.

This work was sponsored by the US Department of Defense.

REFERENCES

1. W.S. Humphrey, "Characterizing the Software Process: A Maturity Framework," Tech. Report CMU/SEI-87-TR-11, ADA182895, Software Eng. Institute, Pittsburgh, June 1987; also in *IEEE Software*, Mar. 1988, pp. 73-79.
2. W.S. Humphrey, *Managing the Software Process*, Addison-Wesley, Reading, Mass., 1989.
3. W.S. Humphrey and W.L. Sweet, "A Method for Assessing the Software Engineering Capability of Contractors," Tech. Report CMU/SEI-87-TR-23, ADA187320, Software Eng. Institute, Pittsburgh, 1987.
4. M.C. Paulk et al., "Capability Maturity Model for Software, Version 1.1," Tech. Report CMU/SEI-93-TR-24, Software Eng. Institute, 1993.
5. P. Fowler and S. Rifkin, "Software Engineering Process Group Guide," Tech. Report CMU/SEI-90-TR-24, ADA235784, Software Eng. Institute, Pittsburgh, 1990.
6. M.C. Paulk et al., "Key Practices of the Capability Maturity Model, Version 1.1," Tech. Report CMU/SEI-93-TR-25, Software Eng. Institute, Pittsburgh, 1993.
7. R. Dion, "Elements of a Process-Improvement Program," *IEEE Software*, July 1992, pp. 83-85.
8. W.S. Humphrey, T.R. Snyder, and R.R. Willis, "Software Process Improvement at Hughes Aircraft," *IEEE Software*, July 1991, pp. 11-23.
9. W.H. Lipke and K.L. Butler, "Software Process Improvement: A Success Story," *Crosstalk*, Nov. 1992, pp. 29-31.
10. D.H. Kitson and S. Masters, "An Analysis of SEI Software Process Assessment Results: 1987-1991," Tech. Report CMU/SEI-92-TR-24, Software Eng. Institute, Pittsburgh, 1992.

Mark C. Paulk, a member of the technical staff at the Software Engineering Institute, is the project leader for the Capability Maturity Model project, which develops products for software-process determination and improvement.

Paulk received a BS in mathematics from the University of Alabama, Huntsville, and an MS in computer science from Vanderbilt University. He is a senior member of the IEEE and a member of the American Society for Quality Control.

Mary Beth Chrissis, a member of the SEI technical staff, has been involved in the initial development and revision of the CMM. She is interested in developing methods and tools that will help organizations improve their software processes.

Chrissis received a BS in technical writing from Carnegie Mellon University and has pursued postgraduate studies in computer science at Johns Hopkins University.

Bill Curtis is the former director of the software-process program at the SEI, where he continues to work on developing a human-resource maturity model. He is also a founding faculty member of the Software Quality Institute at the University of Texas at Austin, and works with organizations to increase their software-development capability.

Curtis serves on the editorial boards of several technical journals and edits *IEEE Software's* Interface department. He is a member of the IEEE, ACM, American Psychological Association, Human Factors Association, and American Association of Artificial Intelligence.

Charles V. Weber is a member of the system-development-process group at IBM Federal Systems Co., Boulder, Colorado. As an SEI resident affiliate, he was the primary author of the practices of CMM version 1.0; he contributed significantly to version 1.1.

Weber received a BS in mathematics from the University of Minnesota in Minneapolis. He chairs the SEI's CMM Advisory Board.

For information about the CMM, training, and performing process assessments and capability evaluations, contact SEI Customer Relations, Software Eng. Institute, Carnegie Mellon University, Pittsburgh, PA 15213-3890; Internet: customer-relations@sei.cmu.edu.

Chapter 3

Other Approaches to Software Process Assessment

1. Introduction to Chapter

While the SW-CMM was the first process assessment method to be widely used and is still by far the best known model in use, there are a number of other assessment models in use that are important in particular application domains, in particular regions of the world, or for particular types of software. In this chapter we outline some of these alternative models and present some papers that describe the models in more detail.

The alternatives to the SW-CMM that will be described fall into two categories:

- models that have been clearly influenced by the SW-CMM but differ from it in certain aspects, because of the type of software for which they have been developed or for the geographical region in which they are expected to be used;

- models that have been developed independently from the SW-CMM.

Models that have been clearly influenced by the SW-CMM include

- BOOTSTRAP, developed for use within Europe,

- TRILLIUM, developed for use by the telecom industry,

- the Software Technology Diagnostic [1], developed for use by "small" software development organizations in Scotland.

The BOOTSTRAP model was originally developed as a European ESPRIT project. BOOTSTRAP is clearly based on the SW-CMM, with additional features added in order to adapt it to the European environment. These features included aspects of the ISO 9000 approach to process assessment (see chapter 7) and of the European Space Agency's (ESA) process model standard (PSS-05-0 [5]).

The phases of a BOOTSTRAP assessment are similar to those of a SW-CMM assessment. They are:

- Preparation,

- Assessment,

- Action plan derivation.

Since the end of the ESPRIT project that originally developed it, the BOOTSTRAP model has been in the care of the BOOTSTRAP Institute, an independent body set up by the BOOTSTRAP partners. The model is under continual development and has now been brought in line with ISO/IEC 12207-1995[2] (Software Lifecycle Processes) and ISO/IEC 15504[3] (see also Chapter 8 of this tutorial).

Note: ISO/IEC 12207 has been replaced in the U.S. by IEEE/EIA Standard 12207-IEEE/EIA 12207 is packaged in three parts. The three parts are, briefly, as follows:

- IEEE/EIA 12207.0, 1996: Standard for Information Technology Software Life Cycle Processes.—This contains ISO/IEC 12207 in its original form plus six additional annexes (E through J): Basic Concepts; Compliance; Life Cycle Process Objectives; Life Cycle Data Objectives; Relationships; and Errata.

- IEEE/EIA P12207.1-1997: Guide for ISO/IEC 12207 Life Cycle Data. This provides additional guidance on recording life cycle data.

- IEEE/EIA P12207.2-1997, Guide for ISO/IEC 12207 Lifecycle Processes Implementation Considerations. This provides additions, alternatives, and clarifications to the ISO/IEC 12207's life cycle processes as derived from U.S. practices.

TRILLIUM was developed around 1991 by a partnership of Bell Canada, Northern Telecom, and Bell Northern Research. It was clearly inspired by the SEI's SW-CMM and can be used as a customer-focused benchmark for one of two purposes:

- Assessment of a supplier's development process;

- Internal process improvement.

TRILLIUM, unlike the SW-CMM, has a clear product focus, where the product is defined to be the software that is delivered to the customer including, in the case of embedded software, the system of which the software is a part. TRILLIUM emphasizes roadmaps that lead from one level to another, as distinct from the key process areas emphasized in the SW-CMM.

The development of the Software Technology Diagnostic (STD) was originally sponsored by the Scottish Development Agency, a UK government body concerned with economic development in Scotland. It has been extensively used by Compita, a private company based near Edinburgh in Scotland. The STD was developed soon after the SW-CMM, and was aimed at small organizations with around 5-40 staff, in the main. The STD was intended as a process assessment tool to be used as part of a performance improvement program that could be conducted speedily, but without major disruption to the organization being assessed. A key feature of the STD was the collection of business data so that assessments could be analyzed in the context of the organization's business needs.

Two well known approaches to process assessment that have not been based on the SW-CMM are those used by

- the Software Engineering Laboratory

- Software Productivity Research

The Software Engineering Laboratory (SEL) is a consortium composed of the University of Maryland, NASA's Goddard Space Flight Center, and the Computer Sciences Corporation. The SEL has long been committed to empirical research in software engineering and to software process improvement.

The SEL's approach to software process improvement is heavily project-based and is concerned with collecting data from ongoing projects (each viewed as an experiment) in order to assess the effectiveness of the software process used, and to identify process improvements to be applied to the processes used in ongoing and subsequent projects. The SEL approach for process assessment/improvement is sometimes referred to as a "bottom-up" approach, as distinct from the SEI's top-down approach. Needless to say, each approach has its advocates.

The Software Productivity Research (SPR) organization, a wholly owned subsidiary of Artemis Management Systems founded in 1984 by Capers Jones and based in Burlington Massachusetts, has collected a vast amount of data concerning the processes used by their clients.

While both the SW-CMM and SPR use a five-point scale in order to assess processes, the scales are different in two respects:

- The scales go in the opposite direction. For the SPR scale, level 1 is the desirable end, whereas for the SW-CMM scale, level 5 is the desirable end.

- The distribution of process assessment results is quite different. The distribution on the SPR scale is approximately symmetrical about the center (i.e., it is bell-shaped), whereas the distribution on the SW-CMM scale is distinctly skewed towards the less desirable end.

The SPR scale is the older one, since it was first published by Capers Jones in 1986 [4], before the SEI scale was published.

2. Description of Articles

There are five papers included in this chapter, two concerned with CMM-type assessment models and three with other types of assessment models. In the first of these papers, "BOOTSTRAP 3.0 – A SPICE Conformant Software Process Assessment Methodology," Pasi Kujava describes the background and history of the BOOTSTRAP assessment method and the formation of the BOOTSTRAP Institute. BOOTSTRAP version 3.0 is described as being conformant with the international standards ISO/IEC 15504 (SPICE) (described in Chapter 8) and ISO/IEC 12207. The Kujava paper describes the assessment method used by BOOTSTRAP and its three dimensions: process, capability, and technology support.

The process dimension is known as the BOOTSTRAP process model, and is heavily influenced by ISO/IEC 15504, ISO/IEC 12207, the SW-CMM, and the ISO 9000 series, as well as by European Space Agency standards. The capability dimension is (at least at its highest level) identical to that defined in the ISO/IEC 15504. The technology support dimension is concerned with the adoption of tools to strengthen process capability. The paper describes how the BOOTSTRAP method is used for process improvement and how the method has been used in two European projects.

The second paper, by Francois Coallier, is about TRILLIUM. In , "TRILLIUM: A Model for the Assessment of Telecom Product Development and Support Capability," Coallier describes the main features of TRILLIUM, including its relationship to the SW-CMM. TRILLIUM has five levels, like t.1e SW-CMM, although levels 2, 3, and 4 are a little higher than the corresponding levels of the SW-CMM and are more standards-related. In fact, TRILLIUM specifies relevant IEEE standards for each of these levels. A diagram shows how capabilities, roadmaps, and practices in the TRILLIUM model are related, and each of these notions is carefully described.

The third paper in this chapter is by David N. Card and is entitled "Sorting Out Six Sigma and the CMM." In it the author compares the two approaches (Six Sigma and the SW-CMM) towards software process improvement. Certain organizations such as Motorola and General Electric tend to use the Six Sigma approach, whereas other organizations such as Lockheed Martin and Telecordia tend to use the Capability Maturity Model.

The Six Sigma approach is basically data driven and concentrates on moving business product or service attributes to within the range of customer specifications, and dramatically shrinking process variation. The SW-CMM, on the other hand, is more concerned with practices than with results, and provides roadmaps from one level to the next higher level by focusing on the key process areas that need to be improved in order to progress. Where the two approaches come together is at level 4 of the SW-CMM, where the emphasis is on gaining statistical control of the software process. The Six Sigma approach seems most relevant to levels 4 and 5 of the SW-CMM and, as the paper points out, it may not be worth applying Six Sigma techniques to an organization that has not at least reached level 3 of the SW-CMM. Statistical control of the software process is further discussed in Chapter 4.

The fourth paper is about the SEL's approach to software process improvement and is by Victor Basili, Marvin Zelkowitz, Frank McGarry, Jerry Page, Sharon Waligora, and Rose Pajerski. In "SEL's Software Process Improvement Program," they describe the SEL's twenty-year-old program and summarize its impact in terms of software products and processes, both of which have substantially changed over the period. Error rates have declined sharply, there has been a dramatic increase in reuse levels, and the use of measurement has greatly increased. The cost of these improvements is about 11% of the software budget. Benefits of process improvement are further discussed in Chapter 11.

In the fifth paper in this chapter, "Measuring Software Process Improvement," Capers Jones describes six stages of software process improvement from software process improvement and baseline through to focus on industry leadership. He uses figures from a very large number of organizations from which his organization has collected data to provide approximate answers to the following questions.

- What does it cost to achieve software excellence?

- How long does it take to achieve excellence?

- What kind of value will result from achieving software excellence?

- What kinds of quality, schedule and productivity levels can be achieved?

The paper concludes by emphasising the positive benefits of using function point metrics rather than the more old fashioned lines of code metrics when investigating these issues.

References

[1] M. Craigmyle, I. Fletcher; "Improving IT Effectiveness through Software Process Assessment," *Software Quality Journal,* vol.2, pp. 257-264, 1993.

[2] ISO/IEC 12207, *Information Technology: Software Lifecycle Processes*, 1995.

[3] ISO/IEC TR 15504, parts 1-9, *Information Technology — Software Process Assessment,* 1998.

[4]C. Jones, *Programming Productivity*, 1986.

[5] PSS-05-0 *ESA Software Engineering Standards*, European Space Agency, 1991.

BOOTSTRAP 3.0—A SPICE[1] Conformant Software Process Assessment Methodology

PASI KUVAJA   pasi.kuvaja@oulu.fi

Department of Information Processing Sciences, INFOTECH Research Group, University of Oulu, Oulu, Finland

Abstract. BOOTSTRAP methodology was initially developed in an ESPRIT project together with European industry. After February 1993, the methodology has been managed and further developed by a European Economic Interest Group, called BOOTSTRAP Institute. BOOTSTRAP methodology version 3.0 was released in September 1997. It is compliant with the ISO/IEC software engineering standard number 15504, the emerging standard on software process assessment. The core of the methodology consists of an assessment model and method. The assessment model of the methodology version 3.0 was updated to align with the ISO 12207 life-cycle and 15504 reference model requirements. In addition to the Process and Capability dimensions, it contains a Technology dimension. The Process dimension contains 33 different processes organised in six clusters: Organisation, Life Cycle Dependent, Management, Support, Customer-Supplier, and Process Related. The Capability dimension consists of six levels, each level consisting of one or more process attributes, adopted from ISO 15504. An assessment is conducted at SPU and project levels. The BOOTSTRAP Institute organises and co-ordinates assessor training and registration scheme. BOOTSTRAP methodology is being used in two European projects: SPAM and PROFES.

Keywords: Software process, assessment, improvement, capability, technology support, assessment methodology, process model, assessment model, capability level, CMM, BOOTSTRAP, ESPRIT, SPICE, ISO 9001, SPAM, PROFES, ISO 15504

1. Introduction

This paper introduces the latest version of the BOOTSTRAP software process assessment and improvement methodology. It describes the evolution of the BOOTSTRAP methodology as part of an ESPRIT project[2] and the formation of the BOOTSTRAP Institute. Sections 4 and 5 describe the objectives and the main features of the methodology respectively. Finally, a brief description of the use of the methodology in on-going ESPRIT projects, SPAM[3] and PROFES,[4] is provided.

2. Background

A European consortium partially funded by the European Commission within the ESPRIT program initially developed the BOOTSTRAP methodology. This project lasted from 1990 to 1992. The initial goal of the project was to fertilise the ground for good software engineering practices in Europe and to analyse the awareness of the European software industry in this area. The main outcome of the project was

"A Spice Conformant Software Process Assessment" by Pasi Kuvaja from *Software Quality Journal*, Volume 8, no. 1 1999, Kluwer Academic Publishers, pp. 7-19. Reprinted by permission of the publisher.

the BOOTSTRAP methodology version 2.22,[5] but the project also predated the European Systems and Software Initiative (ESSI), a technology transfer program proposed by the Commission of the European Communities.

The American experiences inspired the project to develop a kernel of a process assessment methodology based on the initial version of the Capability Maturity Model (CMM) called "A method for assessing the software engineering capability of contractors" (Humphrey and Sweet 1997) and developed by the Software Engineering Institute (SEI) at Carnegie Mellon University. As at the time of the project, in Europe ISO 9000 standards (ISO 9001 1989; ISO 9000-3 1991) were becoming the main reference also for the software industry; these standards were taken as major starting point to be integrated with the CMM approach. The newly developed approach was piloted during the initial development project, at Bosch GmbH Laboratories in Germany and it soon proved to be very helpful in establishing the basis for effective process improvement. Furthermore, the goal to provide a preliminary evaluation of the European awareness in software engineering provided the starting point for a database of assessment data. A more detailed explanation about the background and the previous versions of the BOOTSTRAP methodology is found in Kuvaja and Bicego (1993) and Kuvaja et al. (1994).

After the completion of the ESPRIT project, some of the participating partners, decided to exploit its results by establishing an international organisation to professionally carry on the development and use of the methodology. This organisation is the BOOTSTRAP Institute.

3. BOOTSTRAP Institute

The BOOTSTRAP Institute was founded in March 1994 as a European Economic Interest Group (EEIG), a non-profit organisation legally established under the European law.

The objectives of the BOOTSTRAP Institute are to:

- Continuously improve the BOOTSTRAP methodology for the assessment and improvement of software process quality (also taking into account the relevant ISO standards and other international initiatives in the field including the proper packaging of the methodology and related training material);
- Promote the BOOTSTRAP methodology;
- License the BOOTSTRAP methodology to third parties;
- Administer the database containing results of the assessments carried out by BOOTSTRAP licensees;
- Run courses for training and accreditation of BOOTSTRAP assessors;
- Certify the assessed organisations.

Within its objective of continuously enhancing the BOOTSTRAP methodology, the BOOTSTRAP Institute has developed a new release of the BOOTSTRAP methodology (Release 3.0). This is to ensure full conformance to the emerging ISO standard for software process assessment and improvement, better known as

SPICE (ISO 15504), and to align to ISO 12207 "Information Technology—Software Life Cycle Processes."

4. Objectives of the methodology

Software process assessment has its origin in the TQM movement, and derives from the basic premise that quality of manufactured products is largely determined by the quality of the processes which produce them (Deming 1982). In SPICE project software process assessment is understood as the disciplined examination of the processes used by an organisation against a set of criteria to determine the capability of those processes to perform within quality, cost and schedule goals. The aim is further to characterise current practise, identifying strengths and weaknesses and the ability of the process to control or avoid significant causes of poor quality, cost and schedule performance (see Kuvaja et al., 1995).

The software process assessment can be used either for software process improvement or capability determination. Sometimes the motive is both the improvement and the capability determination. In software process improvement assessment is used for determining current status of the processes in order to improve them or to evaluate their suitability for a particular set of requirements. In capability determination process assessment is used for determining the suitability of potential supplier's processes for a particular contract or specific requirements. In the BOOTSTRAP methodology the starting point is to use the methodology for software process improvement.

In process improvement the first question to be answered with assessment results is: "Where are we?" or "How well we are performing?" The resulting capability profiles show where in the capability scale each process of the company is placed (see Figure 4 in subsequent section 5.3). The overall maturity of the organisation additionally characterises the general performance of the company. The second question to be answered is: "Where is the rest of the world?" or "How well we are performing in comparison with our competitors?" This requires that the assessment approach produces comparable results and provides benchmarking data against which the company specific results can be compared. In BOOTSTRAP methodology the BOOTSTRAP data base stores results from all assessments performed and provides a continuously updating benchmarking data.

In the light of the viewpoints presented above the objectives of the BOOTSTRAP methodology are to:

- provide support to the evaluation of process capability against a set of recognised software engineering best practices;
- include internationally recognised software engineering standards as sources for identification of best practices;
- support the evaluation of how the reference standards have been implemented in the assessed organisation;
- assure the evaluation is reliable and repeatable;
- identify strengths and weaknesses in the organisation's processes;

- provide benchmarking data for assessment results comparison;
- provide results that form a suitable and reliable basis for improvement planning;
- plan improvement actions that support achievement of the organisation's goals;
- help increasing process effectiveness while implementing standard requirements in the organisation.

5. Overview of the methodology

The main features of the BOOTSTRAP methodology include:

- the assessment method,
- the underlying process model,
- the capability levels for evaluation,
- scoring, rating and result presentation principles, and
- process improvement guidelines.

5.1. The assessment method

The BOOTSTRAP assessment is performed in three main phases:

- *The Preparation Phase*, where context information is collected and the forthcoming steps are planned. This phase starts focusing on the organisation specific needs and objectives, which drive both the assessment as well as the improvement phase. Organisation needs and goals drive definition of the assessment scope, including processes where the assessment might need to be focused, organisational units involved, documentation to be used, and key people to be interviewed. This phase includes an initial briefing to the organisation staff, with the purpose of increasing management commitment and creating awareness of issues related to the assessment and improvement.
- *The Execution Phase*, where information about the organisation's processes are collected by performing interviews of key personnel and evaluating available documents as planned in the Preparation phase. The information is collected at organisation level as well as at project level. Qualified assessors conduct interviews. Interviewees are always requested to support their statements with evidence. A preliminary presentation of assessment results completes the Execution phase. This is a review session aimed at correcting any misunderstanding that may have taken place while collecting information.
- *The Improvement Planning Phase*, where assessment results are used to identify suggested improvement areas and priorities. The consolidated assessment results and improvement recommendations are presented to the assessed organisation to get agreement and raise commitment for the subsequent improvement activities. The final output is an assessment report.

THE ASSESSMENT PROCESS

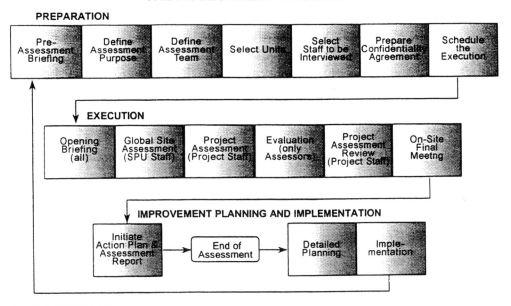

Figure 1. BOOTSTRAP assessment process.

The three stages along with all the sub-stages of the assessment process are shown in Figure 1.

5.2. *The process model*

The BOOTSTRAP assessment model contains process dimension, capability dimension and technology support dimension. The process dimension is called the BOOTSTRAP process model. The BOOTSTRAP process model integrates requirements from several internationally recognised standards like ISO 9001 (1989), ISO 9000-3 (1991), ISO 12207 (1995), ISO 15504 (1993), ESA PSS-05-0 (1991) and the CMM (Humphrey 1989; Paulk et al. 1993a, b) as shown in Figure 2. The

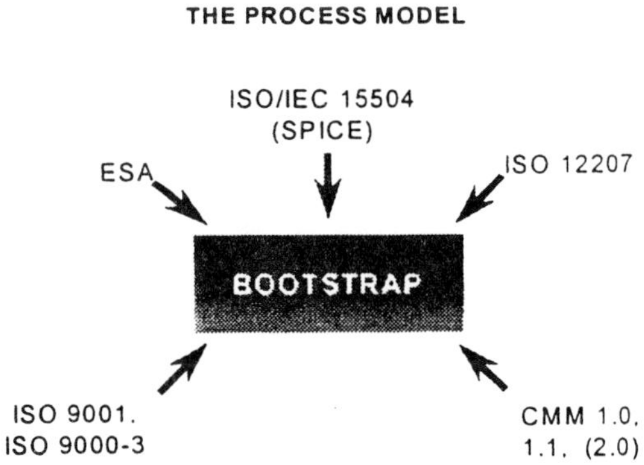

THE PROCESS MODEL

ISO/IEC 15504
(SPICE)

ESA   ISO 12207

BOOTSTRAP

ISO 9001.   CMM 1.0.
ISO 9000-3   1.1. (2.0)

Figure 2. Integration of requirements of the international standards.

BOOTSTRAP process model contains cross references to the requirements of these standards, thus allowing evaluation of the assessed organisation against the selected reference standard, while evaluating process capability. The resulting model is fully compatible with the requirements of the emerging international standard for software process assessment known ISO 15504 (1998), being developed as part of the SPICE project (Paulk and Konrad 1994) as it covers all the processes defined and applies the capability dimension as such.

Within the above mentioned standards the following ones play a particular role:

- ISO 9001 provides the organisational focus, particularly with regards to the quality system and organisation wide procedures;
- ISO 12207 provides a recognised framework for software processes;
- ISO 15504 provides the framework for process and capability definition;
- CMM has been one of the main references for the initial version of the BOOTSTRAP methodology and is intended to be used as a reference for further evolution of the methodology.

The processes in the BOOTSTRAP process model together with the technology support dimension form a tree structure (see Figure 3). Technology support is also addressed in the BOOTSTRAP assessment. Technology assessment aims at evaluating the extent to which the process capability is strengthened with adoption of suitable tools for each process.

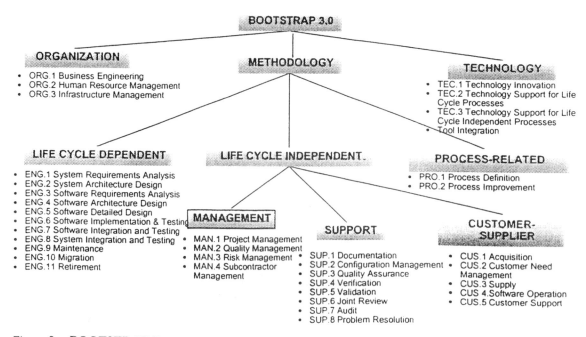

Figure 3. BOOTSTRAP Process tree.

5.3. The capability levels

During a BOOTSTRAP assessment, the processes of the target organisation are evaluated to determine each process capability. Process capability is the ability of each process to achieve its goals in the context of the assessed organisation. Process capability evaluation is performed based on the BOOTSTRAP assessment model, which includes description of the processes and capability levels.

Process capability is measured based on the following capability levels (aligned with ISO 15504 requirements):

- *Level 0: Incomplete Process*—the process fails to achieve its purpose as it is incompletely implemented;
- *Level 1: Performed Process*—a set of practices is performed that allow the process to achieve its purpose;
- *Level 2: Managed Process*—the process delivers work products of acceptable quality within defined time-scale and resources;
- *Level 3: Established Process*—the process is performed based on a recognised organisational process definition;
- *Level 4: Predictable Process*—the established process is performed using defined quantitative control limits;
- *Level 5:—Optimising Process*—changes to the definition, management and performance of the process are identified and performed in a controlled way to continuously improve process performance.

When presenting the assessment results each capability levels are divided into quartiles in order to get more precise capability values and to facilitate monitoring the improvement progress. The capability levels apply to each process, resulting in a potential improvement path from Level 0 to Level 5, as shown in Figure 4.

5.4. Scoring, rating and result presentation

Assessment results are the basis for process improvement planning. Effective process improvement can take place only if assessment data are reliable and provide a fair representation of the assessed organisation's capability. Reliability and repeatability are obtained by:

- ensuring that assessors have the required software engineering background and use the same approach (this is guaranteed by the BOOTSTRAP assessor accreditation scheme), and
- applying precise scoring and rating rules.

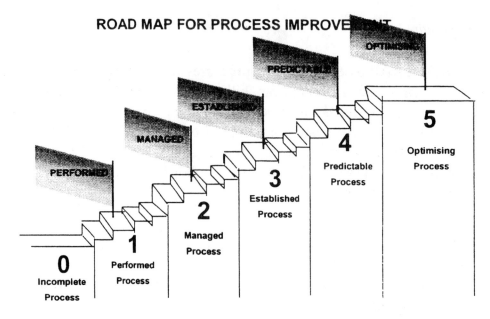

ROAD MAP FOR PROCESS IMPROVEMENT

5
Optimising
Process

4
Predictable
Process

3
Established
Process

2
Managed
Process

1
Performed
Process

0
Incomplete
Process

Each process can be improved from level 0 to level 5. Each organisation identifies
improvement targets and priorities driven by its own needs and goals.

Figure 4.   Improvement road map.

Each practice is evaluated based on a four-point scale (Kuvaja et al. 1994, 1995). The capability level is then counted in two ways:

- by applying the BOOTSTRAP algorithm showing quartiles within each level;
- by applying the SPICE rules for deriving the capability level rating (where the overall results depend largely on the assessor's evaluation).

Final assessment results are presented as capability profiles of each process assessed (see Figure 5). These output profiles are specific to the BOOTSTRAP methodology.

The capability profile is produced at two levels:

- the SPU[6] level, and
- the project level.

The SPU level profile shows the capability of organisational processes and reflects the management's point of view. The project level profile shows the process capability of the individual projects. At least two projects must be assessed to perform a complete BOOTSTRAP assessment. It is also possible to focus the assessment on a subset of processes, particularly to validate the results of improvement efforts. SPU results are not a mere integration of project profiles but show a distinct set of findings. Comparison between SPU and project profiles provides invaluable information to support improvement planning. The overall maturity of the assessed organisation can be shown also as a maturity tree showing capability for each hierarchical level of the BOOTSTRAP process structure.

Process Capability profile

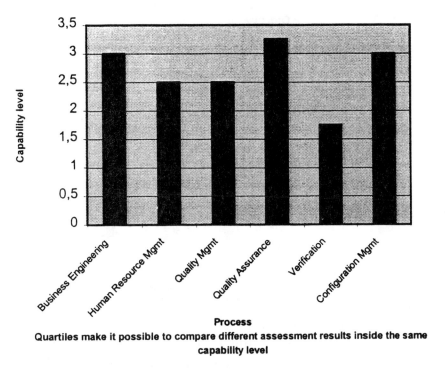

Process

Quartiles make it possible to compare different assessment results inside the same capability level

Figure 5. Capability profile of each process assessed.

In addition to capability profiles, the BOOTSTRAP assessors collect information about the current practices, problems and needs as perceived both by practitioners and managers. This information is structured and presented together with the capability results. In specific the findings are of use in improvement planning.

5.5. Process improvement guidelines

A common issue when implementing software-engineering standards in an organisation is how to tailor the standard's requirements to the organisation's needs and goals. Sometimes standard requirements seem to negatively affect achievement of the organisation's goals, in that they mandate rules that might reduce flexibility and timely answers to external stimuli. It is difficult to find a unique way to implement software engineering standards and to identify a common improvement path suitable to all kinds of organisations.

The BOOTSTRAP methodology considers organisation needs and goals, capability profile of its processes, and industry benchmarks as the main drivers for process improvement as shown in Figure 6. The BOOTSTRAP process model, aligned to ISO 15504 (ISO 9004-4 1993; SPICE 1993; ISO 15504 1998), provides an improvement path for each process, but does not provide any suggestions on how to prioritise process improvement. Defining priorities is up to each organisation. The BOOTSTRAP methodology provides guidelines to identify which processes highly

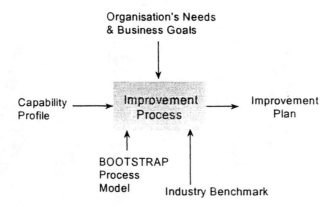

Figure 6. BOOTSTRAP improvement principles.

affect achievement of the organisation goals; then improvement priorities are assigned to each process. Processes with low capability but high impact on the organisation's goals are prioritised the highest.

As part of the improvement plan mitigation actions are identified to account for the risks, should the identified improvement actions fail to achieve their purpose. Typical risks include insufficient management commitment, insufficient resources, and barriers to accept change.

6. BOOTSTRAP methodology in use in European projects

The BOOTSTRAP methodology is currently being used in two projects in Europe, namely PROFES and SPAM.

6.1. PROFES

An ESPRIT project called "PROFES" (PROduct Focused improvement of Embedded Software processes) started in January 1997 with the aim of developing a customer oriented product driven improvement approach for embedded systems (Bicego 1997). The intention is to link the product characteristics directly to the process characteristics and enable a continuous product improvement. This is being done by integrating SPICE conformant (in this case BOOTSTRAP) approach with the most recent Goal Question Metric (GQM) methodology and process modelling. One of the deliverables of the project will be an enhanced version of BOOTSTRAP methodology validated in three industrial application experiments.

The project is in its first phase. Already, experiments carried in three industrial partners show that product viewpoint needs more visibility in software process assessments. The viewpoint is only indirectly addressed in while assessing relationship of customer with its supplier. The enhanced version of the BOOTSTRAP methodology will be verified in the second phase of the project beginning in April 1998.

6.2. *SPAM*

The primary objective of SPAM (Software Portability Assessment Methodology) is to develop a methodology for assessing software portability.

SPAM's underlying philosophy is that adequate solutions to software portability cannot be obtained unless both process and software aspects are considered (as with many other aspects of software quality). Therefore the objective of the SPAM methodology is to provide a comprehensive and repeatable approach for assessing how portable a software product is and how geared towards portability is the development process that produced it. This is achieved by taking into account four main aspects: the development process, the usage of the programming language, Application Programming Interfaces conformance and actual platform dependencies.

The process model for portability assessment is based on BOOTSTRAP 3.0 and includes the process model itself, the process indicators for portability, and guidelines to conduct process assessment for portability.

7. Conclusions

BOOTSTRAP methodology was developed as part of an ESPRIT project especially by taking the European industry requirements into account. This brought ISO 9001 conformance into BOOTSTRAP. Another clear advantage was to show the capabilities of single processes as capability profiles and with quartile precision. It is being further developed by the BOOTSTRAP Institute by enhancing especially the risk management features and assessment process into the methodology. BOOTSTRAP Assessor training and acreditation has produced about 300 trained BOOTSTRAP Assessors mainly into Europe. To date there are also about 50 registered BOOTSTRAP Lead Assessors.

The methodology includes a process model, an assessment process, a mechanism to score the process and present the results, and guidelines on process improvement. The current version of the BOOTSTRAP Methodology is conformant with the emerging ISO/IEC software engineering standard number 15504 on software process assessment and improvement.

The BOOTSTRAP methodology is being used in two European projects—PROFES and SPAM. In PROFES, the methodology is being integrated with the GQM approach to produce an improvement methodology for embedded systems. In SPAM, the process model for portability assessment is based on the BOOTSTRAP methodology. The new findings of the projects will lead to a more sophisticated new version of the BOOTSTRAP methodology in the near future. Specifically special assessment in the embedded systems area and product improvement focused assessments are already now quite obvious directions.

Acknowledgment

This paper was written in an ongoing Esprit project PROFES, and is regarded as a PROFES related paper. All the members of the BOOTSTRAP Institute methodology development team have contributed to this research during the BOOTSTRAP version 3.0 development. We are especially grateful to Adriana Bicego, Etnoteam S.p.A, Milan, Italy and Munish Khurana, Southampton Institute, Southampton, UK for their contributions to the early versions of this work.

Notes

1. Software Process Improvement and Capability dEtermination—SPICE, an international project set by ISO JTC1, Technical Committee 7 (Software engineering) Working Group 10 (Software process assessment) to develop initial working draft material for the becoming standard ISO 15504 "Information technology—Software process assessment."
2. An ESPRIT Project No. 5441, BOOTSTRAP, funded by the European Commission during 1990–1992.
3. An ESPRIT Project No. 22356, SPAM (Software Portability Assessment Methodology), funded by the European Commission during 1997–1999.
4. An ESPRIT Project No. 23239, PROFES (PROduct Focused improvement of Embedded Software processes), funded by the European Commission during 1997–1999.
5. The version of the methodology is described in Kuvaja, et al. (1994).
6. Software Producing Unit.

References

Bicego, A., Koskinen, E., Kuvaja, P., Oivo, M., Rodenbach, E., Ruhe, G., and Van Latum, F. 1997. PROFES: Announcing the marriage between process assessment and measurement (poster). Int. Conf. Software Eng., ICSE'97, Boston.

Deming, W. E. 1982. *Out of Crisis*, Cambridge, MA, MIT Center for Advanced Engineering Study.

ESA, Software Engineering Standards. 1991. ESA PSS-05-0. Issue 2, Paris, ESA Board for Software Standardisation and Control, European Space Agency, February.

Humphrey, W. S. 1989. *Managing the Software Process*, Reading, MA, Addison-Wesley.

Humphrey, W. S., and Sweet, W. L. 1987. A method for assessing the software engineering capability of contractors, SEI Technical Report, SEI-87-TR-23, Pittsburgh, Software Engineering Institute, September.

ISO 9001. 1989. Quality Systems. Model for Quality Assurance in Design/Development, Production, Installation and Servicing, Geneva, ISO.

ISO 9000-3. 1991. Quality Management and Quality Assurance Standards. International Standard. Part 3: Guidelines for the Application of ISO 9001 to the Development, Supply and Maintenance of Software, Geneva, ISO.

ISO 9004-4. 1993. Quality Management and Quality System Elements, International Standard. Part 4: Guidelines for Quality Improvement, Geneva, ISO.

ISO 12207, ISO/IEC 12207. 1995. International Standard: Information Technology—Software Life Cycle Processes, 1st ed., 1995-08-01, Geneva, ISO.

ISO 15504, ISO/IEC TR 15504-2: 1998 (E). 1998. Information Technology—Software Process Assessment—Part 2: A Reference Model for Processes and Process Capability, Geneva, ISO.

Kuvaja, P., and Bicego, A. 1993. BOOTSTRAP: Europe's assessment method. *IEEE Software* 10(3):93–95.

Kuvaja, P., Bicego, A., and Dorling, A. 1995. SPICE: The software process assessment model, Proc. ESI-ISCN '95 Conf. Measurement Training Based Process Improvement, September 11–12, Vienna, Austria.

Kuvaja, P., Similä, J., Krzanik, L., Bicego, A., Koch, G., and Saukkonen, S. 1994. *Software Process Assessment and Improvement. The BOOTSTRAP Approach*, Oxford, UK, Blackwell Business.

Paulk, M. C., and Konrad, M. D. 1994. An overview of ISO's SPICE project, *Amer. Programmer* February.

Paulk, M., et al. 1993. Capability Maturity Model for Software, Version 1.1, CMU/SEI-93-TR-24, February.

Paulk, M., et al. 1993. Key Practices of the Capability Maturity Model, Version 1.1, CMU/SEI-93-TR-25, February.

SPICE. 1993. Software process capability determination standard product specification for a software process capability determination standard, Document WG10/N016. ISO/IES JTC1/SC7/WG10.

Pasi Kuvaja is Assistant Professor in Software Engineering at the Department of Information Processing Sciences, University of Oulu, Oulu, Finland. His interests are software quality, software product quality, software process assessment and improvement, embedded systems, value-added services in mobile telecommunication, and software metrics. He is one of the main developers of recent versions of the BOOTSTRAP software assessment and improvement methodology and PROFES—product quality driven software process improvement approach. He has been actively contributing the SPICE project and is co-editor of the ISO/IEC 1504 Part 7—Process Improvement Guide. He is a member of INFOTECH Research Group in the University of Oulu and full member of IEEE Computer Societe Technical Committee on Software Engineering and IFIP WG8.6. He has also served as International Program and Organizing Committee member of many IEEE, IFIP and IFAC Conferences. He has published a couple of books and over 100 articles, and is co-author of the book *Process Assessment and Improvement: The BOOTSTRAP Approach*. He is a speaker at many national and international conferences and seminars.

TRILLIUM: A Model for the Assessment of Telecom Product Development & Support Capability

Francois Coallier

Bell Canada

Since 1982, Bell Canada Corporate Quality Assurance (QA) has been assessing the software product development process of prospective suppliers as a means to minimize the risks involved and ensure both the performance and timely delivery of purchased software systems.

Since April 1991, a new assessment model, subsequently named *TRILLIUM*, has been developed in partnership with Northern Telecom and Bell Northern Research. Inspired by the Software Engineering Institute's (SEI) Capability Maturity Model (CMM), the *TRILLIUM* model aims to benchmark an organization's product development and support capability in a commercial context.

Bell Canada has been using *TRILLIUM* since the Summer of 1991. The model and its application method have been already improved many times based on this experience and feedback from suppliers.

1. Model Purpose

The purpose of this article is to describe the *TRILLIUM* model for Telecom Software Product Development Capability Assessment. It can be used as a customer focused benchmark for either:

- auditing the product development and support capability of a supplier of telecommunications or Management Information Systems (MIS) products, or
- an internal product development and support capability continuous improvement program for organizations developing and supporting telecommunications or Management Information Systems (MIS) products.

In the *TRILLIUM* context, Capability refers to:

The ability of an organization to, in a competitive commercial environment, consistently and predictably deliver and support a product or an enhancement to an existing product:

- *that meets customer expectations,*
- *with minimal defects (none affecting operations or end user services),*
- *for the lowest life-cycle cost, and*
- *in the shortest calendar time.*

Product in the *TRILLIUM* context refers to what the customers receive, use and perceive. For an embedded telecommunications product, this would include: hardware, software, documentation, training, and support services.

The ultimate objective of improvement programs initiated as a result of a *TRILLIUM* assessment is increased customer (and shareholder) satisfaction, rather than rigid conformance to the standards referenced by this document.

A higher capability, in the *TRILLIUM* context, means for customer organizations that:

- the development organization is more responsive to customer and market demands,

- the life-cycle cost of the product(s) is minimized, and
- end-user satisfaction is maximized.

For the development organization, achieving a higher capability can result in:
- lower development and maintenance costs,
- shorter cycle time and development intervals,
- more reliable project risk analysis and effort estimation,
- an increasing ability to meet quantifiable design and quality objectives at all stages of the development process,
- greater ability to plan and achieve committed deliverable content and schedule.

2. Model Scope

The *TRILLIUM* model is a set of practices derived from a benchmarking exercise. The scope of these benchmarks is aimed at all practices that would contribute to an organization's product development and support capability as defined above. The principal sources of benchmarking information are, in decreasing order of importance:
- version 1.1 of the Software Engineering Institute's Capability Maturity Model,
- ISO 9000-3, Malcolm Baldrige examination criteria for 1993, Bellcore's TR-179 & IPQM TA-1315, IEEE Software Engineering standards and IEC 300, and
- professional and technical references.

The *TRILLIUM* model is only a collection of practices that has been organized in a specific way. It is expected that the readers will refer to the sources of information for specifics.

The *TRILLIUM* model covers all aspects of the software development life-cycle, most system and product development and support activities, and a significant number of related marketing activities. It has been designed to be applied to embedded software systems such as telecommunications systems.

Although *TRILLIUM* is aimed at embedded software systems, much of the model can be applied to other segments of the software industry such as Management Information Systems (MIS). A significant percentage of the practices described in the model can be applied directly to hardware development.

3. Model Foundation

The *TRILLIUM* model is based on the CMM. In the *TRILLIUM* context, the product development and support processes are viewed as an integral part of the organization's business processes. The architecture of the *TRILLIUM* model differs significantly from the CMM version 1.1. The most significant differences are:
- a roadmap based concept (instead of key product areas),
- a product perspective (instead of software),
- a wider coverage of capability impacting issues, and
- a strong customer satisfaction focus.

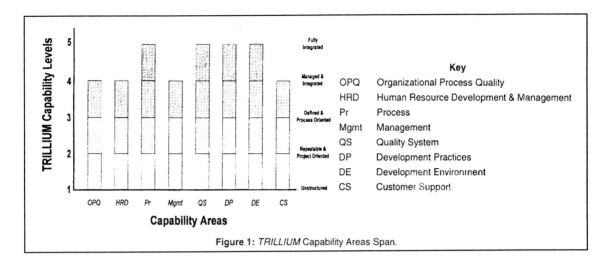

Figure 1: *TRILLIUM* Capability Areas Span.

This version of the *TRILLIUM* model covers most of the CMM 1.1 activities, as well as abilities and most commitments. In addition to the above, this version of the model incorporates the intent of:

- ISO 9001:1987 (and its companion guide ISO 9000-3:1991) standard,
- ISO 8402:1991 standard,
- IEEE Software Engineering Standards Collection, 1993 Edition,
- the IEC 300:1987 standard,
- Bellcore TR-NWT-000179:1993 standard,
- Bellcore FA-NWT-001315 Document, 1993,
- relevant parts of the Malcolm Baldrige National Quality Award Criteria, 1993.

The *TRILLIUM* model incorporates additional practices from the following topics:

- Quality Management
- Business Process Engineering
- Technological Maturity
- Development Environments
- Systems Engineering
- Co-Engineering
- Concurrent Engineering
- Reliability Engineering
- Customer Support/Partnership
- Usability Engineering

4. *TRILLIUM* Architecture

The *TRILLIUM* model is based on the concept of a roadmap. A roadmap is a set of related practices that spans many levels on the *TRILLIUM* scale.

Within a given roadmap, the order of the practices is based on their respective degree of maturity. The most fundamental practices are at a lower level whereas the most advanced ones are located at the higher levels. Practices build upon each other. An organization will mature through the roadmap levels. Lower level practices should be implemented before the higher levels for maximum efficiency and effectiveness.

Roadmaps are organized into *Capability Areas*. Each represents a significant capability for a software development organization. There are 8 *Capability Areas* that can span the 5 *TRILLIUM* Capability Levels. A graphical representation of the span of each Capability Area is shown in Figure 1. Each of the 5 levels can be characterized, in a commercial environment, as shown in Tables 1 and 2.

For the purpose of *TRILLIUM*, note that the IEEE Software Engineering Standards, which are mostly work products (e.g., Software design description, project management plan, etc.) oriented, are to be used as *guidelines* only.

Table 3 relates the Capability Areas, Roadmaps and a list of *TRILLIUM* levels covered by the Roadmaps. The relationship between Capability Areas, Roadmaps and Practices is illustrated in Figure 2. Each Capability Area incorporates one or more Roadmaps. Each Roadmap comprises one or more Practices that span several *TRILLIUM* levels (see Table 3). The complete model has 8 Capability Areas, 28 Roadmaps and 371 Practices.

5. Benchmark Integration

The TRILLIUM model was built by integrating practices as per the following algorithm:

1. Practices are taken from the SEI CMM.

2. A mapping is performed between the CMM practices and ISO 9001 and ISO 9000-3 clauses. CMM practices may be modified to accommodate mapping.

3. From ISO 9001 and ISO 9000-3 clauses that cannot be mapped to CMM practices are extracted, added and integrated.

4. Bellcore standards clauses are mapped to the practices generated by steps 1,2 & 3. Some practices may be adjusted to accommodate mapping.

5. From Bellcore standards clauses that cannot be mapped, practices are extracted, added and integrated.

6. The same process is repeated with relevant portions of the Malcolm Baldrige examination criteria.

7. Practices from IEC 300 are added.

8. Professionals benchmarks are added.

Lvl	Level Name	Risk	Interpretation
1	Unstructured	High	ad-hoc development process
2	Repeatable and Project Oriented	Medium	basic project based process
3	Defined and Process Oriented	Low	state of the art development process
4	Managed and Integrated		generally difficult to achieve now
5	Fully Integrated		technologically challenging

Table 1: *TRILLIUM* Capability Levels.

112

When practices are extracted from the CMM, they go through the following transformation if applicable:

1. The practice is generalized by either removing references to "software", or replacing them by "product and services" or "systems".

2. The practice is generalized by either removing references to "development", or replacing them by "development and support".

3. References to "group" or other specific organizational units are replaced by "function".

4. Allusions to specific documents are replaced by allusion to a process (e.g., "quality plan" by "quality planning") or to "documentation" or "information".

The same type of transformations were applied when extracting practices from other standards.

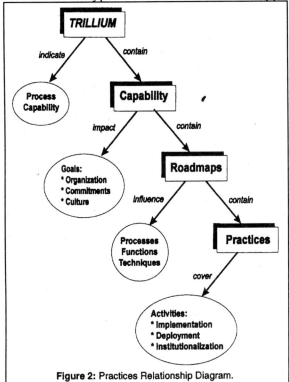

Figure 2: Practices Relationship Diagram.

Assignment to a given level is based on the general guidelines of Table 1:

- Practices that are considered fundamental for the successful conclusion of a development project are assigned to Level 2.

- Practices that are the state of the art and that are fundamental to put in place a development process that can be put under a continuous improvement program are assigned to Level 3.

- Practices that are considered as being presently too challenging in a commercial environment, or where subject matter experts cannot reach a consensus for level 3 assignment are assigned to Level 4.

- Practices that are technologically challenging are assigned to Level 5.

- Professional benchmarks are initially generated through the consensus of subject matter experts. They are subsequently validated in a peer review process.

	Level 1	Level 2	Level 3	Level 4	Level 5
Process	Ad-hoc	Project based	Organization-wide		
Standards	None	IEEE[a] SEI Level 2+ Bellcore TR-NWT-000179 (75%)	IEEE[b] SEI Level 3+ ISO 9001 IEC 300 (system)[d] Bellcore TR-NWT-000179	SEI Level 4+ IEC 300 (software)[c]	SEI Level 5
Process Improvement	None	Unstructured	Deployed	Systematic	

a. Stds. 730, 828, 830, 1016, 1028, 1058.1, 1063
b. Std. 1012
c. future standard
d. as applicable to the hardware component of a system

Table 2: *TRILLIUM* Level/Key Industry Indicators.

6. Capability Profile

To achieve a *TRILLIUM* level, an organization must achieve all practices of that level in each of the 8 Capability Areas that are applicable to the organization that is assessed.

A profile of the Capability Areas is an important measure of a software development organization since it illustrates the relative areas of strength and weakness. Figure 3 shows a sample profile. As can be seen in this profile, it is possible to achieve certain practices at a given level without having completed all the practices at the lower levels (e.g., OPQ and CS in Figure 3).

Achieving Level 3 on the *TRILLIUM* scale means that an organization meets the intent of the following:
- SEI Level 3 key activities,
- ISO 9001 (and the associated ISO 9000-3 Guidelines for Software),
- IEC 300 for system,
- IEEE Standards 730, 828, 1012, 1016, 1028, 1058.1, 1063,
- Bellcore TR-NWT-000179
- the relevant parts of the Malcolm Baldrige National Quality Award Criteria, and
- additional *TRILLIUM* practices not covered by these practices.

The TRILLIUM model does not provide automatic conformance to any standards.

7. Application Principles

The *TRILLIUM* model should always be used in a pragmatic fashion keeping in mind that the bottom-line in all *TRILLIUM* based activities or program is improving customers' (and share-holders') satisfaction. All *TRILLIUM* activities should thus be context driven. This means taking into account factors such as:
- the nature of the product,
- the context in which the product will be used,
- the perception that the customer(s) has of the product (or product line) and its evolution, and
- the pertinent development and support organizations.

114

Capability Area	Roadmap	Level Span
Organizational Processes Quality	Quality Management	2-4
	Business Process Engineering	2-3
Human Resource Development and Management	Human Resource Development and Management	2-4
Process	Process Definition	2-4
	Technology Management	2-4
	Process Improvement & Engineering	2-5
	Measurements	2-4
Management	Project Management	2-4
	Subcontractor Management	2-3
	Customer-Supplier Relationship	2-3
	Requirements Management	2-4
	Estimation	2-3
Quality System	Quality System	2-5
Development Practices	Development Process	2-5
	Development Techniques	2-5
	Internal Documentation	2-4
	Verification & Validation	2-4
	Configuration Management	2-5
	Re-Use	2-5
	Reliability Management	2-4
Development Environment	Development Environment	2-5
Customer Support	Problem Response System	2-3
	Usability Engineering	2-4
	Life-Cycle Cost Modeling	2-3
	User Documentation	2-3
	Customer Engineering	2-3
	User Training	2-3

Table 3: Capability Area/Roadmap Relationship. (Note: there are no level 1 practices)

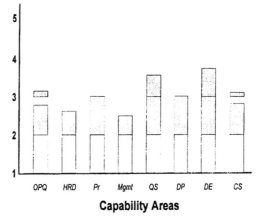

Figure 3: Sample of a *TRILLIUM* Profile.

This implies that the applicability of some practices and their implementation strategy will change as a function of the above factors. The professionalism of the staff and the organization involved in *TRILLIUM* based activities is thus critical.

The leaders of all *TRILLIUM* based activities should be experienced engineering personnel having TickIT lead auditor and SEI CMM self-assessment formal qualifications or equivalent. Malcolm Baldrige assessor and QAI CQA, or equivalent, would also be good assets.

Customers perceive a supplier organization as a black box delivering products and services (e.g., marketing, Sales, Customer Support, Research & Development [hardware, software, system, silicon], Quality Assurance, etc.). *TRILLIUM* based activities should thus, ultimately, make abstractions of internal organizational boundaries in their application.

In a *TRILLIUM* context, internal organizations such as marketing, engineering, customer support, etc. are all contributing to customer (and shareholder) satisfaction. The customer will always perceive more acutely the impact of the weakest contributor. All those organizations should thus, for instance, adhere to a systematic improvement program with common and compatible goals.

8. *TRILLIUM* Activities

The following TRILLIUM based activities can be performed:

- supplier capability assessments,

- participation in supplier capability joint-assessment,
- participation in supplier capability self-assessment, and
- participation in supplier capability continuous improvement programs.

While the first activity does not require that a special relationship exist between a customer and its supplier, the next three require increasing levels of partnership to be really effective.

Supplier Capability Assessment

The objective of this activity is to assess, by way of an auditing exercise using the *TRILLIUM* model as the reference benchmark, the product development and support capability of a supplier. This activity is performed as per recognized auditing practices such as ISO 10011-2, but as per the application principles described earlier.

TRILLIUM supplier capability assessments are performed for:
- assessing the risks associated with the procurement of a given product, and incidentally doing business with its supplier,
- monitoring a quality/capability improvement program as part of its acquisition supplier quality management program.
- To be successful, such an assessment needs:
- an assessor or team of assessors with adequate qualifications, experience and skills,
- a minimum of cooperation from the supplier, and
- adequate preparation.

Supplier Capability Joint-Assessment

A joint-assessment in the *TRILLIUM* context is an assessment with the difference that it is performed by both customer and supplier as a team exercise. This implies that the conclusions and recommendations of a *TRILLIUM* joint-assessment represent a consensus of the joint team.

To be successful, a joint-assessment needs:
- a team of assessors with adequate qualifications, experience, and skills,
- adequate partnering maturity between both organizations, and
- clear and unequivocal buy-in from senior management in both organizations.

A *TRILLIUM* joint-assessment that meets the above criteria will be far more efficient and reliable in getting a comprehensive appraisal of the supplier organization, but will require more resources than the normal assessment.

With skilled personnel, a joint-assessment will be very efficient in appraising a low maturity organization (i.e., 20/80 or Pareto rule).

Supplier Capability Self-Assessment

A *TRILLIUM* capability self-assessment is essentially an SEI self-assessment (as described in SEI-89-TR-7) with the following differences:
- at least one customer representative is on the self-assessment team. This representative is adequately qualified and has an improvement focused attitude,
- customer issues are systematically considered by the self-assessment team throughout all phases of the self-assessment,

- the self-assessment is implemented as per the application principles described earlier, and
- the *TRILLIUM* model is used as the reference benchmark.

Like an SEI self-assessment, a TRILLIUM capability assessment is very demanding resource-wise, but is an efficient initiator of a capability improvement program because of the buy-in it generates in the organization for its findings and recommendations.

Supplier Capability Continuous Improvement Program

A capability Continuous Improvement (CI) program is essentially a Deming PDCA cycle. A *TRILLIUM* capability CI program is a Deming PDCA cycle where:

- at least one customer representative is on the CI program steering and management teams. This representative is adequately qualified and has an improvement focused attitude,
- customer issues are systematically considered by the CI teams throughout all the phases of the CI cycle,
- the *TRILLIUM* model is used as the reference benchmark, and
- the "Check" part of the cycle is always associated with the contribution to customer (and shareholder) satisfaction.

In order to achieve the highest possible capability, development and support organizations must strive to:

- make the continuous improvement philosophy part of the organization culture, and ensure that the proper mechanisms and processes are in place to support and encourage this culture,
- engineer and optimize their processes to meet customer or market requirements and objectives for the specific product or service, and
- continuously optimize the resources available for each development project.

The presence of an efficient capability continuous improvement program in a supplier is, for Bell Canada, a reassuring sign of organizational maturity. Being invited to participate in such a program is a sign, from a supplier quality management perspective, of high maturity in the customer-supplier partnership.

The efficiency of a capability CI program should be measured in terms of:

- contributions to customer (and shareholder) satisfaction improvement, and
- improvements in capability maturity.

9. Future Versions

The next major release of *TRILLIUM* will be version 3.0 in the fall of 1994. This version will essentially be 2.4d with updated traceability tables, further polishing of the practices, further polishing of the Malcolm Baldrige coverage and a re-written introduction. Version 3.0 will be both published in a Bell Canada edition and as an NTL standard.

A Quebec-France cooperative project, titled *CAMELIA*, funded by both the Quebec and French government is aiming at optimizing *TRILLIUM* to the Management Information Systems domain. *CAMELIA* will include the addition to *TRILLIUM* 2.3 of practices in:

- Re-Engineering,
- Business Process Engineering,
- Architectures,
- Data Management,

- Data Centre Management, and
- Maintenance.

Bell Canada plans to publish in the Spring of 1995 version 3.1. This version will include all the new practices that have been developed as part of the *CAMELIA* project. Future plans are to cover hardware development, manufacturing and service capability.

Acknowledgements

TRILLIUM is the result of cooperative work and contribution of many individuals. The author would like to especially thank Neil Gammage, Allan Graydon, Jean-Normand Drouin, Jean Mayrand, John Wilson and Richard McKenzie.

Sorting Out Six Sigma and the CMM

David N. Card

Over the past few years, two approaches to process improvement have gained widespread acceptance. You'll find the Six Sigma approach broadly applied across major corporations such as Motorola and General Electric, while others such as Lockheed Martin and Telecordia have focused on the Capability Maturity Model. Some corporations have adopted both. The purpose of this column is to help sort out the relationship between these two approaches.

What Is Six Sigma?

Six Sigma provides a generic quantitative approach to improvement that applies to any process. The specific measures and analyses employed must be tailored to the domain of processes under study. You'll find Six Sigma commonly described as a philosophy that implies the body of knowledge required to implement it. The curriculum of the Six Sigma Institute's training program provides the best definition of the relevant body of knowledge. Jerome Blakeslee Jr. provides a definition of Six Sigma in his July 1999 *Quality Progress* article, "Implementing the Six Sigma Solution":

> *Basically, it is a high-performance data-driven approach to analyzing the root causes of business problems and solving them. It ties the output of a business directly to marketplace requirements.*
>
> *At the strategic level, the goal of Six Sigma is to align an organization keenly to its marketplace and deliver real improvements (and dollars) to the bottom line. At the operational level, Six Sigma's goal is to move business product or ser-vice attributes within the zone of customer specifications and to dramatically shrink process variation—the cause of defects that negatively affect customers.*

The name, Six Sigma, derives from a statistical measure of a process's capability relative to customer specifications. The Six Sigma notion of capability does not have the same meaning as the definition of capability implied in the title of the CMM. The latter deals with the maturity of practices, not results.

What Is the CMM?

The CMM describes the principal disciplines, or key process areas, that an effective software engineering organization must master. These include basic software engineering and management as well as improvement practices. The implementation of key process areas is organized into five sequential steps or levels. Level 1 does not re-quire mastery of any processes. Levels 2 and 3 require mastery of 13 key processes and focus on defining a software organization's basic technical and management processes. Levels 4 and 5 address controlling and improving those defined processes. Five key process areas make up Levels 4 and 5. In *The Capability Maturity Model: Guidelines for Improving the Software Process* (Addison Wesley, 1994), Mark C. Paulk and his colleagues showed how two of these key process areas largely parallel Six Sigma:

> *Quantitative Process Management involves establishing goals for the performance of the project's defined software process, which is described in the Integrated Software Management*

key process area, taking measurements of the process performance, analyzing those measurements, and making adjustments to maintain process performance within acceptable limits.

Defect Prevention involves analyzing defects that were en-countered in the past and taking specific actions to prevent the occurrence of those types of defects in the future. The defects may have been identified on other projects as well as in earlier stages or tasks of the current project. Defect prevention activities are also one mechanism for spreading lessons learned between projects.

The other Level 4 and 5 key process areas go beyond a Six Sigma pro-gram's usual scope. *Software Quality Management* addresses estimating the output quality of a series of software processes, each of which might be subject to control and improvement. *Technology Management* pro-vides a proactive focus on technology as a means of improvement. *Process Change Management* helps provide coordination for improvement activities across a software organization.

Six Sigma's Weaknesses

Six Sigma evolved from experience in manufacturing. A manufacturing process has inherent visibility. For ex-ample, you can observe the flow of materials, and opportunities for measurement are usually obvious. By contrast, software development is an intellectual process that must be made visible (that is, documented) before you can measure and manage it. Six Sigma doesn't specifically address this situation. The CMM focuses on defining processes through Levels 2 and 3.

Six Sigma relies on trained personnel to find processes that need improvement and act accordingly. Training alone often doesn't change behavior. Important process elements might or might not get attention. The CMM requires a systematic search for and prioritization of improvement opportunities.

Six Sigma doesn't have a formal connection to ISO 9000 or other certification programs for organizations, al-though proposed updates to ISO 9000 incorporate Six Sigma techniques. In the long term, business benefits are what count and Six Sigma stresses them. However, the CMM levels and certification can provide near-term incentives and convenient milestones for checking an implementation's progress.

Six Sigma focuses internally on learning from current process experience. It does not consider, systematically, how externally developed technology might revolutionize or even eliminate a process. The CMM requires a specific technology focus, which can be essential to survival in a dynamic business such as software.

CMM's Weaknesses

The CMM document describes process control in terms of means, standard deviations, special causes, common causes, and so on. However, significant elements of the CMM user community resist the obvious need for statistical methods to achieve Levels 4 and 5. No such ambiguity exists in the Six Sigma approach.

The CMM states that measures and processes should be selected based on their relationship to strategic business plans and goals, but this requirement often gets overlooked. Software engineering process teams often set software goals without considering business goals. Six Sigma stresses the need to link process improvement to business performance.

The CMM does not describe the body of knowledge required to implement it. Many implementations merely restate CMM requirements. Thus, the improvement effort might not incorporate the full range of measurement and analysis techniques that Six Sigma promotes.

Although the Software Engineering Institute certifies CMM assessors, no comparable program exists for CMM implementers. Assessors must be familiar with the CMM, not the underlying body of knowledge—for example, statistical process control. The Six Sigma Institute provides competence certification for relevant subject matter.

Common Elements of Six Sigma and CMM

Both approaches focus on reducing defects as the primary method of improvement. However, Six Sigma provides a relatively broad definition of a defect, and the CMM acknowledges the possibility of focusing on other dimensions for improvement.

Both approaches stress a quantitative, fact-based approach to decision-making that relies heavily on measurement. Successful introduction of measurement often requires cultural changes that neither approach specifically addresses. To some degree, the Six Sigma approach minimizes this by introducing these techniques opportunistically, addressing each process element (using CMM terms) individually.

Both approaches draw from the same toolkit of statistical process control techniques (control charts, pareto charts, cause–effect diagrams, and so on), although Six Sigma might intro-duce more advanced methods such as design of experiments, when appropriate. Unfortunately, the CMM's in-tent to encourage statistical methods sometimes gets lost.

Both Six Sigma and the CMM have drawn broad criticism—but such complaints are largely based on how these concepts have been implemented in specific organizations or promoted within the community, rather than fundamental problems in the approaches. The effective application of statistical techniques to soft-ware engineering has been amply demonstrated (for example, see the *Proceedings of the Software Engineering Process Group Conference*, Soft-ware Engineering Institute, 1999). Nevertheless, no single technique applies in every situation—the analyst needs a toolkit.

The concepts of CMM Levels 4 and 5 and Six Sigma are synergistic. For example, Six Sigma training helps build the skills necessary to address the CMM's Quantitative Process Management and Defect Prevention requirements. The CMM provides a structure that helps ensure the systematic application of Six Sigma techniques. The CMM helps explain how to adapt Six Sigma techniques to software processes.

The situation, however, merits two notes of caution. First, some organizations rated at CMM Level 5 might not have implemented Six Sigma techniques because they opted to instead satisfy CMM requirements with ad hoc analysis methods. You can't assume that a Level 5 rating implies Six Sigma competence. Second, a software engineering organization that has not made significant progress to-ward defining its key process elements (for example, CMM Level 3) should only introduce Six Sigma techniques on a small-scale pilot basis. There are too many examples of large investments in extensive Six Sigma training for personnel working in unstructured environments—investments that led to little return.

Six Sigma offers another path to-ward measurable improvement for CMM Level 3 organizations. Instead of pursuing full CMM Level 4 and 5 maturity, an organization can just address the subset that constitutes Six Sigma—depending on its business needs for CMM certification. Moreover, the Six Sigma toolkit pro-vides the basic technology necessary for continuous improvement beyond the CMM Level 5 certificate.

David N. Card is the chief scientist for quantitative methods at the Software Productivity Consortium; card@software.org.

SEL'S SOFTWARE PROCESS-IMPROVEMENT PROGRAM

In 1993, the IEEE Computer Society and the Software Engineering Institute jointly established the Software Process Achievement Award to recognize outstanding improvement accomplishments. This award is to be given annually if suitable nominations are received by the SEI before November 1 each year. The nominations are reviewed by an award committee of Barry Boehm, Manny Lehman, Bill Riddle, myself, and Vic Basili (who did not participate in this award decision because of his involvement in the Software Engineering Laboratory).

It is particularly fitting that the SEL was selected as the first winner for this award. They started their pioneering work nearly a decade before the Software Engineering Institute was founded, and their work has been both a guide and an inspiration to all of us who have attempted to follow in their footsteps.
— Watts Humphrey

VICTOR BASILI
and MARVIN ZELKOWITZ
University of Maryland

FRANK McGARRY,
JERRY PAGE,
and SHARON WALIGORA
Computer Sciences Corporation

ROSE PAJERSKI
NASA Goddard Space
Flight Center

For nearly 20 years, the Software Engineering Laboratory has worked to understand, assess, and improve software and the software-development process within the production environment of the Flight Dynamics Division of NASA's Goddard Space Flight Center. We have conducted experiments on about 125 FDD projects, applying, measuring, and analyzing numerous software-process changes. As a result, the SEL has adopted and tailored processes — based on FDD goals and experience — to significantly improve software production.

The SEL is a cooperative effort of NASA/Goddard's FDD, the University of Maryland Department of Computer Science, and Computer Sciences Corporation's Flight Dynamics Technology Group. It was established in 1976 with the goal of reducing

♦ the defect rate of delivered software,

♦ the cost of software to support flight projects, and

♦ the average time to produce mission-support software.

Our work has yielded an extensive set of empirical studies that has guided the evolution of standards, management practices, technologies, and training within the organization. The result has been a 75 percent reduction in defects, a 50 percent reduction in cost, and a 25 percent reduction in cycle time. Over time, the goals of SEL have matured. We now strive to:

♦ *Understand* baseline processes and product characteristics, such as cost, reliability, software size, reuse levels, and error classes. By characterizing a production environment, we can gain better insight into the software process and its products.

♦ *Assess* improvements that have been incorporated into development projects. By measuring the impact of available technologies on the software

process, we can determine which technologies are beneficial to the environment and — most importantly — how the technologies should be refined to best match the process with the environment.

♦ *Package and infuse* improvements into the standard SEL process and update and refine standards, handbooks, training materials, and development-support tools.[1-3] By identifying process improvements, we can package the technology so it can be applied in the production environment.

As Figure 1 shows, these goals are pursued in a sequential, iterative process that has been formalized by Basili as the Quality Improvement Paradigm[4] and its use within the SEL formalized as the Experience Factory.[5]

IMPROVING THE PROCESS

We select candidates

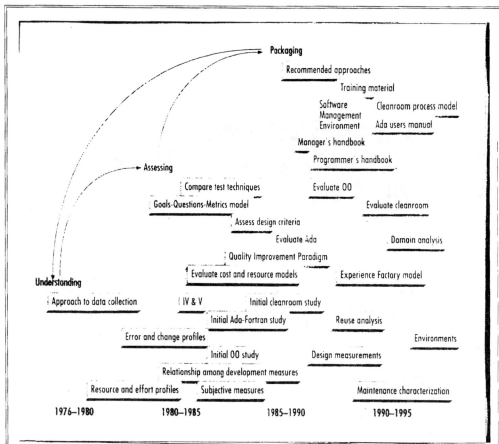

Figure 1. *The SEL goals are pursued in a sequential, iterative fashion. The diagram includes some of the many SEL studies that have been conducted over the years, including those of Cleanroom, Ada, and Fortran.*

for process change on the basis of quantified SEL experiences (such as the most significant causes of errors) and clearly defined goals for the software (such as to decrease error rates). After we select the changes, we provide training and formulate experiment plans. We then apply the new process to one or more production projects and take detailed measurements. We assess a process's success by comparing these measures with the continually evolving baseline. Based upon the results of the analysis, we adopt, discard, or revise the process.

Process improvement applies to individual projects, experiments (the observation of two or three projects), as well as the overall organization (the observation of trends over many years). In

the early years, the SEL emphasized building a clear understanding of the process and products within the environment. This led us to develop models, relations, and general characteristics of the SEL environment. Most of our process changes consisted of studying specific, focused techniques (such as program-description language, structure charts, and reading techniques), but the major enhancement was the infusion of measurement, process-improvement concepts, and the realization of the significance of process in the software culture.

SEL OPERATIONS

The SEL has collected and archived data on more than 125 of its software-

development projects. We use the data to build typical-project profiles against which we compare and evaluate ongoing projects. The SEL provides its managers with tools for monitoring and assessing project status. The FDD typically runs six to 10 projects simultaneously, each of which is considered an experiment within the SEL.

For each project, we collect a basic set of information (such as effort and error data). From there, the data we collect may vary according to the experiment or be modified as changes are made to specific processes (such as the use of Ada). As the information is collected, it is validated and placed in a central database. We then use this data with other information — such

as the subjective lessons learned — to analyze the impact of a specific software process and to measure and feed back results to both ongoing and follow-on projects.

We also use the data to build predictive models and to provide a rationale for refining current software processes. As we analyze the data, we generate papers and reports that reflect the results of numerous studies. We also package the results as standards, policies, training materials, and management tools.

PROCESS AND PRODUCT ANALYSIS

The FDD is responsible for the development and maintenance of flight-dynamics ground-support software for all Goddard flight projects. Typical FDD projects range in size from 100,000 to 300,000 lines of code. Several projects exceed a million lines of code; others are as small as 10,000 lines of code. (At SEL, reused code is not "free"; it is counted as 20 percent of new Fortran code and 30 percent of new Ada code.) The SEL improvement goal is to demonstrate continual improvement of the software process within the FDD environment by carrying out analysis, measurement, and feedback to projects within this environment.

Understanding. Understanding what an organization does and how it operates is fundamental to any attempt to plan, manage, or improve the software process. This is especially true for software-development organizations. The SEL supports this understanding in several ways, including, for example, the study of effort distribution and error-detection rate.

♦ Effort distribution identifies which phases of the life cycle consume which portion of development effort. Figure 2 presents the effort distribution of 11 Fortran projects by life-cycle phase and activity. Understanding these distributions helps us plan new efforts, evaluate new technologies, and assess the similarities and differences within an ongoing project.

♦ Error-detection rate provides the absolute error rate expected in each phase. At SEL, we collected information on software errors and built a model of the expected errors in each life-cycle phase. For 1,000 lines of code, we found about four errors during implementation; two during system test; one during acceptance test; and one-half during operation and maintenance. The trend we derive from this model is that error detection rates fall by 50 percent in each subsequent phase. This pattern seems to be independent of the actual error rates; it is true even in recent projects, in which the overall error rates are declining. We use this model of error rates, as well as other similar types of models, to better predict, manage, and assess change on newly developed projects.

Assessing and refining. We consider each SEL project to be an experiment, in which we study some software method in detail. Generally, the subject of the study is a specific modification to the standard process — a process that obviously comprises numerous software methods.

For example, the Cleanroom software methodology[6] has been applied on four projects within the SEL, three of which have been analyzed thus far. Each project gave us additional insight into the Cleanroom process and helped us refine the method for use in the FDD environment. After training teams in the Cleanroom methodology, we defined a modified set of Cleanroom-specific data to be collected. The teams studied the projects to assess the impact that Cleanroom had on the process, as well as on measures such as productivity and reliability. Figure 3 shows the results of the three analyzed projects.

The Cleanroom experiments required significant changes to the standard SEL development methodology and thus extensive training, preparation, and careful study execution. As in all such experiments, we generated detailed experimentation plans that described the goals, the questions that had to be addressed, and the metrics that had to be collected to answer the questions. Because Cleanroom consists of many specific methods — such as box-structure design, statistical testing, and

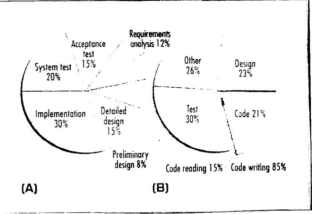

Figure 2. *Effort distribution by (A) life-cycle phase and (B) activity. Phase data counts hours charged to a project during each calendar phase. Activity data counts hours attributed to a particular activity (as reported by the programmer), regardless of when in the life cycle the activity occurred.*

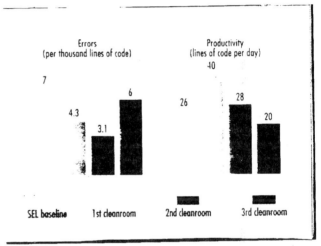

Figure 3. *Results of three completed Cleanroom projects, compared against the SEL baseline.*

rigorous inspections — each particular method had to be analyzed, along with the Cleanroom methodology itself. As a result of these projects, a slightly modified Cleanroom approach was deemed beneficial for smaller SEL projects. Anecdotal evidence from the recently completed fourth Cleanroom project confirms the effectiveness of Cleanroom. The revised Cleanroom-process model was captured in a process handbook for future applications to SEL projects. We have analyzed and applied many other

methodologies in this way.

Packaging. Once we have identified beneficial methods and technologies, we provide feedback for future projects by capturing the process in standards, tools, and training. The SEL has produced a set of standards for its own use that reflect the results of its studies. Such standards must continually evolve to capture modified characteristics of the process (the SEL typically updates its basic standard every five years.) Standards we have pro-

TABLE 1
EARLY SEL BASELINE

Project (number & name)	Reuse (percent)	Mission Cost* (staff months)	Reliability (error/KSLOC)
1. GROAGSS	14	381	4.42
2. COBEAGSS	12	348	5.22
3. GOESAGSS	12	261	5.18
4. UARSAGSS	10	675	2.81
5. GROSIM	18	79	8.91
6. COBSIM	11	39	4.45
7. GOESIM	29	96	1.72
8. UARSTELS	35	80	2.96

*Mission cost = cost of telemetry simulator + cost of AGSS (GRO = projects 1 + 5, COBE = 2 + 6, GOES = 3 + 7, UARS = 4 + 8).

TABLE 2
CURRENT SEL BASELINE

Project (number & name)	Reuse (percent)	Cost* (staff months)	Reliability (error/KSLOC)
1. EUVEAGSS	18	155	1.22
2. SAMPEX	83	77	.76
3. WINDPOLR	18	476	n/a†
4. EUVETELS	96	36	.41
5. SAMPEXTS	95	21	.48
6. POWITS	69	77	2.39
7. TOMSTELS	97	n/a‡	.23
8. FASTELS	92	n/a‡	.69

*Mission cost = cost of telemetry simulator + cost of AGSS (GRO = projects 1 + 5, COBE = 2+6, GOES = 3+7, UARS = 4 + 8).
†Excluded because it used the Cleanroom development methodology, which counts errors differently.
‡Total mission cost for TOMS and FAST cannot be calculated because AGSSs are incomplete (they are not included in the cost baseline).

duced include:

♦ *Manager's Handbook for Software Development*,[1]
♦ *Recommended Approach to Software Development*,[2] and
♦ *The SEL Relations and Models*.[3]

In addition to the evolving development standards, policies, and training material, successful packaging includes generating experi-ment results in the form of post-development analysis, formal papers, and guide-books for applying specific software techniques.

IMPACT OF SEL

Our studies have invol-ved many technologies, ranging from development and management practices to automation aids and technologies that affect the full life cycle. We have col-lected and archived detailed information so we can assess the impact of technologies on both the software process and product.

Product impact. To deter-mine the effect of sustained SEL efforts as measured against our major goals, we routinely compare groups of projects developed at dif-ferent times. Projects are grouped on the basis of size, mission complexity, mission characteristics, lan-guage, and platform. On these characteristic pro-jects, we compared defect rates, cost, schedule, and levels of reuse. The reuse levels were studied carefully with the full expectation that there would be a corre-lation between higher reuse and lower cost and defect rates. These characteristic projects become our "base-lines." Table 1 shows an early baseline — eight pro-jects completed between 1985 and 1989. These pro-jects were all ground-based attitude-determination and -simulation systems ranging in size from 50,000 to 150,000 lines of code that were developed on large IBM mainframes. Each was also a success, meeting mis-sion dates and requirements within acceptable cost. Table 2 shows the current SEL baseline, which com-prises seven similar projects completed between 1990 and 1994.

As the tables show, the early baseline projects had a reliability rate that ranged from 1.7 to 8.9 errors per 1,000 lines of code, with an average rate of 4.5 errors. The current baseline pro-jects had a reliability rate ranging from 0.2 to 2.4 errors per 1,000 lines of code, with an average rate of 1 error. This is about a 75-percent reduction over the eight-year period.

The dramatic increase in our reuse levels — aided by experimentation with tech-niques such as object-ori-ented development and domain-engineering con-cepts — have been a major contributor to improved project cost and quality. Reuse, along with increased productivity, also con-tributed to a significant decrease in project cost. We examined selected missions from the two baselines and found that, although the total lines of code per mis-sion remained relatively equal, the total mission cost decreased significantly. The average mission cost in the early baseline ranged from 357 to 755 staff-months, with an average of 490. The current baseline projects had costs ranging from 98 to 277 staff-months with an average of 210. This is a decrease in average cost per mission of more than 50 percent over the eight-year period. This reduction occurred despite the increased mission complexi-ty, shown in Table 3.

Process impact. The most significant changes in the SEL environment are illus-trated by the standards, training programs, and development approaches incorporated into the FDD

126

TABLE 3
COMPARING INCREASE
IN BASELINE COMPLEXITY

Attribute	Early SEL baseline	Current SEL baseline
Control	Spin stabilized	Three-axis stabilized
Sensors	1	8 to 11
Torques	1	2 to 3
Onboard computer	Analog simple control	Digital control
Telemetry	5	12 to 15
Data rates	2.2 kbs	32 kbs
Accuracy	1 degree	0.02 degree

process. Although specific techniques and methods have had a measurable impact on a class of projects, significant improvement to the software-development process — and an overall change in the environment — has occurred because we have continuously incorporated detailed techniques into higher level organizational processes.

The most significant process attributes that distinguish our current production environment from that of a decade earlier include:

♦ Process change and improvement has been infused as a standard business practice. All standards and training material now contain elements of our continuous-improvement approach to experimentation.

♦ Measurement is now our way of doing business rather than an add-on to development. Measurement is as much a part of our software standards as documentation. It is expected, applied, and effective.

♦ Change is driven by process *and* product. As the process-improvement program matured over the years, our concern for product attributes grew to equal our concern for process attributes. Product goals are always defined before process change is infused. Measures of product are thus as important as those of process (if not more so).

♦ Change is bottom-up. Although process-improvement analysts originally assumed they could work independently of develop-

ers, we have realized over the years that change must be guided by development-project experience. Direct input from developers as well as measures extracted from development activities are key factors in change.

♦ "People-oriented" technologies are emphasized, rather than automation. The most effective process changes are those that leverage the thinking of developers. These include reviews, inspections, Cleanroom techniques, management practices, and independent-testing techniques — all of which are driven by disciplined programmers and managers. Automation techniques have sometimes provided improvement, but people-driven approaches have had farther reaching impacts.

The SEL has invested approximately 11 percent of its total software budget into process-improvement. This expense includes project overhead, as well as overhead for data archiving and processing and process and product analysis. We have maintained detailed records so we can accurately record and report process-improvement costs.

Our investment in process-improvement has brought many benefits. The cost, defect rates, and cycle time of flight-dynamics software have decreased significantly since we started the program. Today, our software developers are building better software

more efficiently — using many techniques and methods considered experimental only a few years ago. Their progress has been facilitated throughout by the SEL focus on defining organizational goals, expanding domain understanding, and judiciously applying new technology, allowing the FDD to maximize the lessons from local experience. ♦

REFERENCES

1. L. Landis et al., "Manager's Handbook for Software Development," Revision 1, Tech. Report SEL-84-101, Software Eng. Laboratory, Greenbelt, Md., 1989.
2. L. Landis et al., "Recommended Approach to Software Development," Revision 3, Tech. Report SEL-81-305, Software Eng. Laboratory, Greenbelt, Md. 1992.
3. W. Decker, R. Hendrick, and J. Valett, "Relationships, Models and Measurement Rules," Tech. Report SEL-91-001, Software Eng. Laboratory, Greenbelt, Md., 1991.
4. V.R. Basili and D.M. Weiss, "A Methodology for Collecting Valid Software Engineering Data," *IEEE Trans. Software Eng.*, Nov. 1984, pp. 728-738.
5. V.R. Basili, "Software Development: A Paradigm for the Future," *Proc. Compsac*, IEEE CS Press, Los Alamitos, Calif., 1989, pp. 471-485.
6. V.R. Basili and S. Green, "Software Process Evolution at the SEL," *IEEE Software*, July 1994, pp. 58-66.

Victor Basili is a professor in the Institute for Advanced Computer Studies and the Computer Science Department at the University of Maryland. He is co-editor-in-chief of the *International Journal on Empirical Software Engineering*.

Marvin Zelkowitz is a professor in the Institute for Advanced Computer Studies and the Computer Science Department at the University of Maryland and has been involved with the SEL since its inception in 1976. His research interests include language design, environments, and formal methods.

Frank McGarry is a senior member of the executive staff at Computer Sciences Corporation. Previously at NASA, he was a founding director of the SEL in 1976.

Jerry Page is the vice president of the System Science Division at Computer Sciences Corporation. Until last year, he managed SEL activities within CSC.

Sharon Waligora has worked for the Computer Science Corporation since 1974 and directs the CSC branch of the SEL, leading efforts in software process improvement, process definition, and measurement activities.

Rose Pajerski has worked for the Goddard Space Flight Center for more than 20 years and directs the GSFC branch of the SEL. Her research interests include testing processes, systems management through measurement, and tailoring approaches for process-improvement programs.

Address questions about this article to Basili at the Department of Computer Science, University of Maryland, 4121 A.V. Williams, College Park, MD 20742; basili@cs.umd.edu.

Measuring Software Process Improvement

Capers Jones, Chief Scientist

Software Productivity Research, Inc.
(an Artemis Company)
6 Lincoln Knoll
Burlington, MA 01803
Capers@spr.com
http://www.spr.com

Abstract

A key aspect of software process improvement work is the need to demonstrate that improvements actually generate tangible benefits in terms of quality, schedules, effort, costs, user satisfaction, or other measurable factors. Unfortunately project-level data measured with the lines-of-code metric is not a good choice. This is because more than half of the work of software development consists of noncoding activities. The most effective method for demonstrating the value of software process improvements utilizes a combination of activity-based costs and function point metrics.

This report summarizes the process improvement strategies of a number of excellent software producers for whom we have performed assessments and baseline studies. Four tangible aspects of software process improvement are examined: (1) What it costs to achieve software excellence; (2) wow long it takes to achieve excellence; (3) what value results from achieving software excellence; and (4) what kinds of quality, schedule, and productivity levels can be achieved as a result of process improvement work?

Measuring Software Process Improvements

Software is an important but troublesome technology. Cost overruns, schedule delays, and poor quality have been endemic within the software industry for more than 50 years. (The author has been studying software overruns for more than 30 years and has collected data on software problems dating back to the 1950s.)

Since the incorporation of the Software Engineering Institute (SEI) in 1984 it has been asserted that companies or projects that use state-of-the-art development processes and advanced tool suites can create software applications faster and with fewer risks of failure than traditional methods.

Some of the assertions and articles are based on theory rather than fact. For software process improvement, comparatively little solid, empirical data has been published on three important topics:

1. What does it cost to improve software processes?
2. How long will it take to see tangible improvements if processes do improve?
3. What kind of value will result from process improvements in terms of:

Better quality?
Better productivity?
Shorter schedules?
Higher user satisfaction?

The author and his colleagues at Software Productivity Research have examined data from more than 10,000 software projects between 1984 and today. Our methodology includes the use of standardized questionnaires for gathering both qualitative and quantitative information. A discussion of this methodology is outside the scope of this article. For information on how the data are collected, refer to the author's books *Applied Software Measurement* (McGraw Hill, 1996) and *Software Assessments, Benchmarks, and Best Practices* (Addison Wesley Longman, 2000).

We have examined software projects at all five levels of the SEI Capability Maturity Model (CMM). We have also examined many projects that do not utilize the SEI CMM. (Refer to Paulk *et al.*, 1995, for a discussion of the CMM.) This work has led us to develop some practical methods for quantifying the results of software process improvement activities. Some of our findings have been published in a number of books that address the economic and quality aspects of software process improvement (Jones, 1994, 1996, 1997, 1998a, 2000).

The author is fortunate to have access to project-level data that comprises more than 10,000 software projects derived from about 750 organizations in the United States, Europe, South America, and the Pacific Rim. More than 350 of these organizations are attempting some form of software process improvement, and more than 250 are moving up on the SEI's CMM.

Significant software process improvements do not occur in random patterns. When the patterns used by companies that are the best overall are examined, we can see that the initial activity is a formal process assessment and a baseline, followed by a six-stage improvement program in a specific order:

Stage 0:   Software Process Assessment, Baseline, and Benchmark

Stage 1:   Focus on Management Technologies

Stage 2:   Focus on Software Processes and Methodologies

Stage 3:   Focus on New Tools and Approaches

Stage 4:   Focus on Infrastructure and Specialization

Stage 5:   Focus on Reusability

Stage 6:   Focus on Industry Leadership

These six stages provide a structure for software improvement strategies. However, each company is different and therefore the specifics of each company's improvement strategy must match its local culture and individual needs. Other authors also discuss various strategies for software process improvement (Grady, 1997).

Six Stages of Software Process Improvement

The six stages along the path to process improvements usually occur in the same sequence from company to company. The sequence is based on practical considerations. For example, software managers have to produce the cost justifications for investments, so they need to be fully aware of the impacts of the latter stages. Unless project management excellence is achieved first, it is not likely that the latter stages will even occur.

Let us consider the assessment and baseline stages, and then examine each of the six improvement stages in turn.

Stage 0: Software Process Assessment and Baseline

The first or 0 stage is numbered so that it is outside the set of six improvement phases. There is a practical reason for this. Neither an assessment nor a baseline, by itself, causes any tangible improvements. Some companies forget this important point and more or less stop doing anything after their initial assessment and baseline.

The starting point of successful software process improvement begins with a formal process assessment and the establishment of a quantitative baseline of current productivity and quality levels.

- The *assessment* is like a medical diagnosis to find all of the strengths and weaknesses associated with software.

- The *baseline* is to provide a firm quantitative basis for productivity, schedules, costs, quality, and user satisfaction in order to judge future rates of improvement.

In addition, many companies may also commission benchmarks in order to judge their performance against similar companies within the same industry, such as banking, insurance, telecommunications, defense, or whatever.

A *benchmark* is a formal comparison of software methods and quantitative results against those of other similar organizations. External benchmarks are often performed by third-party consulting groups such as Compass Group, Gartner Group, the International Function Point Users Group, Meta Group, Howard Rubin Associates, or Software Productivity Research. These companies have large collections of software data from many companies and industries.

Benchmarks are more complex logistically than either assessments or baselines, due to the fact that they involve multiple companies that may be in competition with each other. Therefore it is necessary to ensure that specific company data are kept confidential, unless the companies included give permission to publish their results.

Assessments, baselines, and benchmarks are all valuable and are mutually supporting and synergistic. Assessments alone lack the quantification of initial quality and productivity levels needed to judge improvements later. A quantitative baseline is a necessary prerequisite for serious process improvements, since the cost justifications for the initial investments have to be proven by comparing future results against the initial baseline. External benchmarks against other companies are an optional but useful adjunct to software process improvement tasks. It is likely that the quantitative data will be collected using function point metrics. A short discussion of function point metrics may be useful.

Function point metrics were developed by A. J. Albrecht and colleagues at IBM in the mid-1970s (Albrecht, 1979). The function point metric was placed in the public domain by IBM in 1978, and responsibility for function point counting rules was taken over by a nonprofit organization in 1984. The organization responsible for defining function point counting rules is the International Function Point Users Group (IFPUG). Readers may refer to the IFPUG Web site (http://www.IFPUG.org) for additional information. A new primer on function point analysis was recently published by David Garmus and David Herron, who are officers in the IFPUG organization (Garmus and Herron, 2001).

Function points are derived from the external aspects of software applications. Five external attributes are enumerated: inputs, outputs, inquiries, logical files, and interfaces. Because the counting rules are complex, accurate counting of function points is normally carried out by specialists who have passed a certification exam administered by the IFPUG organization.

Compared to lines-of-code (LOC) metrics, function points offer some significant advantages for baselines and benchmarks. Because coding is only part of the work of building software, LOC metrics have not been useful for measuring the volume of specifications, the contributions of project management, nor the defects found in requirements and design documents. Further, LOC metrics tend to behave erratically from language to language. Indeed for some languages such as Visual Basic, no effective LOC counting rules are available .

Because function point metrics can measure all software activities (requirements, design, coding, testing, documentation, management, etc.), they have become the de facto standard for software baselines and benchmarks. This is not to say that function point metrics have no problems of their own. But for collecting quantitative data from software projects function points offer such significant advantages over LOC metrics that most of the published software benchmark data uses function point metrics. Let us now consider what happens after the assessment, baseline, and benchmark data have been collected.

Stage 1: Focus on Management Technologies

Because software project management is often a weak link on software projects, the first improvement stage concentrates on bringing managers up to speed in critical technologies such as planning, sizing, cost estimating, milestone tracking, quality and productivity measurement, risk analysis, and value analysis.

It is important to begin with managers, because they are the ones who need to calculate the returns on investment that will occur later. They will also have to collect the data to demonstrate progress, so it is folly to even begin unless managers are trained and equipped for their roles. Instruction in function point metrics is also common during the initial stage.

Stage 2: Focus on Software Processes and Methodologies

The second stage concentrates on improved approaches for dealing with requirements, design, development, and quality control. Because tools support processes—rather than the other way around—new development processes need to be selected and deployed before investments in tools occur.

Some of the proven processes deployed in this stage include joint application design (JAD); any of several formal design methods such as Warnier-Orr, Yourdon, Merise, the Unified Modeling Language (UML); or several others. Formal design and code inspections and formal change management procedures are also selected and deployed during this stage.

Stage 3: Focus on New Tools and Approaches

As improved software processes begin to be deployed, it is appropriate to acquire new tools and to explore advanced or new technologies. It is also the time to explore difficult technologies with steep learning curves such as client–server methods and the object-oriented paradigm. Jumping prematurely into client—server projects, or moving too quickly toward object-oriented analysis and design usually results in problems because poorly trained practitioners are seldom successful. The first-time failure rate of new technologies is alarmingly high. Therefore careful selection of new technologies and thorough training of personnel in the selected technologies are necessary prerequisites to successful deployment of new technology.

Some of the kinds of tools acquired during this stage might include configuration control tools, code complexity analysis tools, test case monitors, analysis and design tools, and perhaps advanced language tools for Java or very high level programming languages.

Stage 4: Focus on Infrastructure and Specialization

To reach the top plateau of software excellence, it is necessary to have a top-notch organizational structure as well as excellent tools and methods.

The infrastructure stage deals with organization and specialization and begins to move toward establishment of specialized teams for handling critical activities. We have long known that specialists can outperform generalists in a number of key software tasks. Some of the tasks where specialists excel include testing, maintenance, integration, configuration control, technical writing, and quality assurance. Policies on continuing education are important too during this stage.

In addition to better development processes and better tool suites, industry leaders in software productivity and quality are usually characterized by better organizational structures and more specialists than average companies or laggards.

Stage 5: Focus on Reusability

Reusability has the best return on investment of any software technology, but effective reuse is surprisingly difficult. For a general discussion of software reuse, refer to Jacobsen *et al.* (1997).

If software quality control is not top-notch, then reuse will include errors that cause costs to go up instead of down. Also, reuse includes much more than just code. In fact, an effective software reuse program should include a minimum of six reusable artifacts:

1. Reusable requirements,

2. Reusable designs and specifications,

3. Reusable source code,

4. Reusable user documents,

5. Reusable test plans, and

6. Reusable test cases and test scripts.

If only source code is reused, the return on investment will be marginal. Optimal benefits occur only when reusability spans all major deliverable items.

Stage 6: Focus on Industry Leadership

Organizations that go all the way to the sixth stage are usually the leaders in their respective industries. These organizations are the kind that would be found at level 5 of the SEI CMM. These organizations may be in a position to acquire competitors. They can almost always outperform their competitors in all phases of software development and maintenance work unless the competitors are also at the top.

Industry leadership is a coveted goal that many companies strive to achieve, but few succeed. Among the attributes of industry leadership that are visible to outside consultants such as the author, the following 12 factors stand out as highly visible:

1. Effective project management tool suites,

2. Effective software development tool suites,

3. Effective quality assurance and testing tool suites,

4. Effective software processes and methods,

5. Effective organizational structures,

6. Effective management teams,

7. Effective technical teams with substantial specialization,

8. High morale among the software staff,

9. High user-satisfaction levels as noted by customer surveys,

10. High regard by top corporate management,

11. High regard by industry analysts, and

12. High regard by competitive organizations.

No company examined so far has been excellent in every single attribute of software success, but the leaders are superior in so many attributes that they demonstrate a tangible pride in their accomplishments when visited.

Let us examine the costs, timing, and anticipated results of software process improvement activities as noted among our clients engaged in process improvement activities.

Costs, Schedule, and Value of Process Improvements

Although this article contains general industry data, each company needs to create an individualized plan and budget for their own improvement strategy. Table 1 presents information based on the overall size of companies in terms of software personnel. The cost data in Table 1 are expressed in terms of "cost per capita" or the approximate costs for each employee in software departments. The cost elements include training, consulting fees, capital equipment, software licenses, and improvements in office conditions.

The sizes in Table 1 refer to the software populations, and divide organizations into four rough size domains: less than 100 software personnel, less than 1,000 personnel, less than 10,000 personnel, and more than 10,000, which implies giant software organizations such as IBM, Andersen Consulting, and Electronic Data Systems all of which have more than 50,000 software personnel corporate-wide.

Table 1. Process Improvement Expenses Per Capita

Stage	Meaning	Small < 100 Staff	Medium < 1,000 Staff	Large < 1,0000 Staff	Giant > 10000 Staff	Average
0	Assessment	$100	$125	$150	$250	$156
1	Management	$1,500	$2,500	$3,500	$5,000	$3,125
2	Process	$1,500	$2,500	$3,000	$4,500	$2,875
3	Tools	$3,000	$6,000	$5,000	$10,000	$6,000
4	Infrastructure	$1,000	$1,500	$3,000	$6,500	$3,000
5	Reuse	$500	$2,500	$4,500	$6,000	$3,375
6	Industry leadership	$1,500	$2,000	$3,000	$4,500	$2,750
	Total expenses	$9,100	$17,125	$22,150	$36,750	$21,281

As can be seen from Table 1, software process assessments are fairly inexpensive. But actually improving software processes and tool suites after a software process assessment can be very expensive indeed.

Another important topic is how long it will take to move through each of the stages of the process improvement sequence. Table 2 illustrates the approximate number of calendar months devoted to moving from stage to stage.

Table 2. Process Improvement Stages in Calendar Months

Stage	Meaning	Small < 100 Staff	Medium < 1,000 Staff	Large < 1,0000 Staff	Giant > 10000 Staff	Average
0	Assessment	2.00	2.00	3.00	4.00	2.75
1	Management	3.00	6.00	9.00	12.00	7.50
2	Process	4.00	6.00	9.00	15.00	8.50
3	Tools	4.00	6.00	9.00	12.00	7.75
4	Infrastructure	3.00	4.00	9.00	12.00	7.00
5	Reuse	4.00	6.00	12.00	16.00	9.50
6	Industry leadership	6.00	8.00	9.00	12.00	8.75
	Sum (worst case)	26.00	38.00	60.00	83.00	51.75
	Overlap (best case)	16.90	26.60	43.20	61.42	33.64

Smaller companies can move much more rapidly than large corporations and government agencies. Large companies often have entrenched bureaucracies with many levels of approval. Thus change in large companies is often slow and sometimes *very* slow.

For large companies, process improvement is of necessity a multiyear undertaking. Corporations and government agencies seldom move quickly even if everyone is moving in the same direction. When there is polarization of opinion or political opposition, progress can be very slow or nonexistent.

An important topic is what kind of value or return on investment will occur from software process improvements? Table 3 shows only the approximate improvements for schedules, costs, and quality (here defined as software defect levels). The results are expressed as percentage improvements compared to the initial baseline at the start of the improvement process.

Table 3. Improvements in Software Defect Levels, Productivity, and Schedules

Stage	Meaning	Delivered Defects	Develop. Product.	Develop. Schedule
0	Assessment	0.00%	0.00%	0.00%
1	Management	−10.00%	10.00%	−12.00%
2	Process	−50.00%	30.00%	−17.00%
3	Tools	−10.00%	25.00%	−12.00%
4	Infrastructure	−5.00%	10.00%	−5.00%
5	Reuse	−85.00%	70.00%	−50.00%
6	Industry leadership	−5.00%	50.00%	−5.00%
	Total	−95.00%	365.00%	−75.00%

The best projects in the best companies can deploy software with only about 5 percent of the latent defects seen in similar projects in lagging companies. Productivity rates are higher by more than 300 percent, and schedules are only about one-fourth as long. These are notable differences that can be used to justify investments in software process improvement activities.

As can be seen from this rough analysis, the maximum benefits do not occur until stage 5, when full software reusability programs are implemented. Because reusability has the best return and greatest results, our clients often ask why it is not the first stage?

The reason that software reuse is delayed until stage 5 is that a successful reusability program depends on mastering of software quality. Mastering software quality implies deploying a host of precursor technologies such as formal inspections, formal test plans, formal quality assurance groups, and formal development processes. Unless software quality is at state-of-the-art levels, any attempt to reuse materials can be hazardous. Reusing materials that contain serious errors will result in longer schedules and higher costs than would not having any reusable artifacts at all.

Activity-Based Costs for Measuring Process Improvements

For measuring process improvements over time, gross measures of entire projects are not granular enough to be effective. We have learned that it is necessary to get down to the level of specific activities in order for process improvements to become visible and measurable.

Activity-based costs can highlight the actual activities that benefit from process improvements and can also illustrate activities where no tangible benefits are noted. This kind of analysis is not possible when using only project-level data.

The software benchmarking companies have found that function point metrics are superior to the older LOC metrics for measuring activity-based costs and schedules. As mentioned earlier, the reason for this is that function points can measure noncoding activities such as requirements, design, documentation, and management.

We utilize the function point metrics defined by the IFPUG. The current standard for function points published by the IFPUG organization is Version 4.1, which is used in this article. For a general introduction to the topic of function point analysis, refer to Dreger (1989) or to Garmus and Herron (1995).

Note that while IFPUG function points are the most widely used metric in the United States and Western Europe, other forms of function point metrics are also in use. For example, in the United Kingdom the use of Mark II function points is very common. For a discussion of Mark II function points refer to Symons (1991).

Table 4 illustrates a hypothetical project that is 1,000 function points in size (roughly 125,000 C source statements). The organization producing this application would be a typical civilian organization at level 1 on the five-level SEI CMM scale. Level 1 organizations are not very sophisticated in software development approaches. Thus level 1 organizations often experience missed schedules, cost overruns, and poor quality levels.

Most of the information in Tables 4 and 5 is self-explanatory but four topics may need explanation. The word "burdened" applied to average monthly salaries refers to the additional amounts needed to pay for taxes, medical benefits, office space, and other overhead items. These extra costs are added to basic salary levels when calculating the total costs of building software. Thus, the phrase "Average monthly salary (burdened)" refers to the sum of basic compensation and additional overhead cost items. The word "burden" is a standard accounting term.

The column labeled "Staff" refers to the numbers of workers assigned to major activities such as design, coding, testing, and so forth. Decimal values indicate that some personnel are only working part time on the project.

The values shown under the column labeled "Effort" refer to person-months. In this article, a person-month is assumed to consist of 22 work days, each having an 8-hour duration. Of course, these assumptions vary widely from country to country and company to company.

The values shown under the column labeled "Schedules" refer to normal calendar months. The abbreviation "FP" refers to "function points" and in this article Version 4.1 of the IFPUG function point is the specific metric utilized. The abbreviation "LOC" refers to "lines of code" and means noncommentary source code.

Table 4. Example of Activity-Based Cost Analysis for SEI CMM Level 1

Application class	Systems software
Programming language(s)	C
Size in function points	1,000
Size in lines of code	125,000
Work hours per month	132
Average monthly salary (burdened)	$7,500

Activity	Work Hrs per FP	Staff	Effort (Months)	Schedule (Months)	Costs by Activity	Percent of Costs
Requirements	1.20	2.00	9.09	4.55	$68,182	4%
Design	2.93	3.33	22.22	6.67	$166,667	11%
Design reviews	0.38	4.00	2.86	0.71	$21,429	1%
Coding	7.76	6.67	58.82	8.82	$441,176	29%
Code inspections	0.53	8.00	4.00	0.50	$30,000	2%
Testing	8.25	6.67	62.50	9.38	$468,750	31%
Quality assurance	1.32	1.00	10.00	10.00	$75,000	5%
Documentation	1.10	1.00	8.33	8.33	$62,500	4%
Management	3.57	1.00	27.03	27.03	$202,703	13%
TOTAL	27.04	6.33	204.85	32.35	$1,536,406	100%

FP per month	4.88
LOC per month	610

Cost per FP	$1,536.41
Cost per LOC	$12.29

The most obvious characteristic of level 1 organizations is that testing is both the most expensive activity and the most time consuming. The root cause of this phenomenon is that level 1 organizations usually have excessive defect levels and are deficient in two key quality factors: (1) defect prevention and (2) pretest reviews and inspections.

By contrast, table 5 illustrates exactly the same size and kind of software project. However, Table 5 shows the results that have been noted for somewhat more mature level 3 organizations on the SEI CMM scale. For the level 3 organization, testing has diminished significantly in terms of both timing and costs. This is due to the fact that defect prevention methods have improved and pretest design reviews and code inspections have both been strengthened.

Table 5. Example of Activity-Based Cost Analysis for SEI CMM Level 3

Application class	Systems software
Programming language(s)	C
Size in function points	1,000
	125,000
Size in lines of code	
Work hours per month	132
Average monthly salary (burdened)	$7,500

Activity	Work Hrs per FP	Staff	Effort (Months)	Schedule (Months)	Costs by Activity	Percent of Costs
Requirements	1.06	2.00	8.00	4.00	$60,000	5%
Design	2.64	3.33	20.00	6.00	$150,000	12%
Design reviews	0.88	4.00	6.67	1.67	$50,000	4%
Coding	6.00	6.67	45.45	6.82	$340,909	28%
Code inspections	1.06	8.00	8.00	1.00	$60,000	5%
Testing	3.30	6.67	25.00	3.75	$187,500	15%
Quality assurance	2.20	1.00	16.67	16.67	$125,000	10%
Documentation	1.10	1.00	8.33	8.33	$62,500	5%
Management	3.30	1.00	25.00	25.00	$187,500	15%
TOTAL	21.53	6.33	163.12	25.76	$1,223,409	100%

FP per month	6.13
LOC per month	766
Cost per FP	$1,223.41
Cost per LOC	$9.79

A side-by-side analysis (Table 6) of the costs of the two versions indicates an overall reduction of about 20 percent between the level 1 and level 3 versions, but the activity costs illustrate that most of the savings occur during the testing phase. Indeed, the costs of inspections are higher, rather than lower, for the CMM level 3 version. Also, some costs such as those of "user documentation" are unchanged between the two scenarios. Activity-based cost analysis allows a detailed scrutiny of differences between processes and provides a way to perform rather sophisticated cost and schedule models, an activity that cannot be accomplished with coarser project-level data.

Table 6. Side by Side Comparison of Activity-Based Costs

Application class	Systems software
Programming language(s)	C
Size in function points	1,000
Size in lines of code	125,000
Work hours per month	132
Average monthly salary (burdened)	$7,500

Activity	SEI CMM Level 1	SEI CMM Level 3	Variance in Costs	Variance Percent
Requirements	$68,182	$60,000	–$8,182	–12.00%
Design	$166,667	$150,000	–$16,667	–10.00%
Design reviews	$21,429	$50,000	$28,571	133.33%
Coding	$441,176	$340,909	–$100,267	–22.73%
Code inspections	$30,000	$60,000	$30,000	100.00%
Testing	$468,750	$187,500	–$281,250	–60.00%
Quality assurance	$75,000	$125,000	$50,000	66.67%
Documentation	$62,500	$62,500	$0	0.00%
Management	$202,703	$187,500	–$15,203	–7.50%
TOTAL	$1,536,406	$1,223,409	–$312,997	–20.37%
Cost per FP	$1,536.41	$1,223.41	–$313.00	–20.37%
Cost per LOC	$12.29	$9.79	–$2.50	–20.37%

If we turn now to quality, the results of improving both defect prevention approaches and defect removal approaches in the level 3 example cause a very significant reduction in delivered defects. In turn, the reduced numbers of defects allow shorter and more cost-effective development cycles. When projects run amuck, it often happens that problems escape notice until testing begins. When major defects begin to be found during testing, it is too late to bring the project back under control. The goal is to prevent defects from occurring or eliminate them before testing gets under way.

Table 7 illustrates the differences in defect potentials, defect removal efficiency levels, and delivered defects of the two cases. In Table 7 the column "Potential Defects" refers to all defects that are likely to be encountered from the start of requirements through at least 1 year of customer usage. The column "Removal Efficiency" refers to the percentage of potential defects found before delivery of the software to customers.

The abbreviation "KLOC" refers to thousands of lines of code, where "K" is the standard software abbreviation for thousands. The abbreviation "Funct. Pt." Stands for "function point" and refers to Version 4.1 of the IFPUG function point metric.

Table 7. SEI CMM Level 1 and Level 3 Defect Differences

Level	Potential Defects	Removal Efficiency	Delivered Defects	Defects per Func. Pt.	Defects per KLOC
SEI Lev 1	6150	85.01%	922	0.92	7.38
SEI Lev 3	3500	95.34%	163	0.16	1.30

As can be seen in Table 7, a combination of defect prevention and defect removal can yield significant reductions in delivered defect levels. Because finding and fixing defects is the most costly and time-consuming activity for software, those projects that are successful in preventing defects or removing them via inspections will achieve shorter schedules and higher productivity as well as better quality.

If software process improvement is to become a proven and successful technology, it is important to demonstrate exactly what is being improved, and by how much.

Activity-based cost analysis illustrates that process improvement does not create a homogeneous improvement in every activity equally. Improvements tend to be very significant for key activities such as testing but scarcely visible for other activities such as requirements or user documentation. Indeed, for a number of important activities such as design and code inspections and quality assurance work, the costs will be higher for more mature organizations at level 3 on the CMM than for those at level 1 on the CMM.

Summary and Conclusions

Software process improvement is now a major international research topic and may continue to grow in importance well into the 21st century. However, some software technologies have a shorter lifetime. Unless tangible results can be achieved, interest in process improvement technology will quickly wane.

The data presented here are approximate and have a high margin of error. Further, software projects range in size from less than 100 function points to more than 100,000 function points. The examples used here centered on 1,000 function points, and the data should not be used for significantly larger or smaller projects. Every company should create its own data using its own assessment and baseline studies.

Function point metrics provide useful and interesting insights into the economics of software and into the domain of software process improvement in particular. The older LOC metric is not a good choice for exploring software process improvement for the noncoding phases such as requirements and design phases. Incidentally, for large software projects above 10,000 function points in size, noncoding activities comprise more than 50 percent of the total effort. The activities that can be studied using LOC metrics (primarily coding) may comprise less than 30 percent of the total effort devoted to large systems, as illustrated by the two examples used in this article.

Function point metrics are not perfect, but they are leading to new and useful discoveries that extend beyond those made with the older LOC metrics. Success in exploring the impact of software process improvements is a sign that the function point metric is a useful one. However, the real goal of such studies is to understand the economics of software. Metrics are only tools that lead to understanding, and should be used only until better metrics become available.

References and Readings

Albrecht, A. (1979), "Measuring Application Development Productivity," *Proc. Joint Share/Guide/IBM Application Development Symp.,* Monterey, CA, April, 10 pages.

Dreger, B. (1989), *Function Point Analysis,* Prentice Hall, Upper Saddle River, NJ, ISBN 0-13-332321-8, 185 pages.

Garmus, D., and D. Herron (1995), *Measuring the Software Process: A Practical Guide to Functional Measurement*, Prentice Hall, Upper Saddle River, NJ.

Garmus, D., and D. Herron (2001), *Function Point Analysis*, Addison Wesley Longman, Reading, MA, 2001.

Grady, R.B. (1997), *Successful Process Improvement*, Prentice Hall, Upper Saddle River, NJ, ISBN 0-13-626623-1, 314 pages.

IFPUG Counting Practices Manual, Release 4.1 (1999), International Function Point Users Group, Westerville, OH, April, 85 pages.

Jacobsen, I., M. Griss, and P. Jonsson (1997), *Software Reuse—Architecture, Process, and Organization for Business Success*, Addison Wesley Longman, Reading, MA, ISBN 0-201-92476-5, 500 pages.

Jones, C. (1994), *Assessment and Control of Software Risks*, Prentice Hall, Upper Saddle River, NJ, ISBN 0-13-741406-4, 711 pages.

Jones, C. (1995), *Patterns of Software System Failure and Success*, International Thomson Computer Press, Boston, ISBN 1-850-32804-8, 292 pages.

Jones, C. (1996), *Applied Software Measurement*, 2nd ed., McGraw-Hill, New York, ISBN 0-07-032826-9, 618 pages.

Jones, C. (1997), *Software Quality—Analysis and Guidelines for Success*, International Thomson Computer Press, Boston, ISBN 1-85032-876-6, 492 pages.

Jones, C. (1998a), *Estimating Software Costs*, McGraw Hill, New York, ISBN 0-07-9130941, 725 pages.

Jones, C. (1998b), "Sizing Up Software," *Scientific American,* vol. 279, no. 6, December, pp. 104–111.

Jones, C. (2000), *Software Assessments, Benchmarks, and Best Practices*, Addison Wesley Longman, Reading, MA, ISBN 0-201-48542-7, 657 pages.

Paulk, M., V. Charles, B. Curtis, and M.B. Chrissis (1995), *The Capability Maturity Model—Guidelines for Improving the Software Process*, Addison Wesley, Reading, MA.

Symons, C.R. (1991), *Software Sizing and Estimating—Mk II FPA (Function Point Analysis)*, John Wiley & Sons, Chichester, UK, ISBN 0 471-92985-9, 200 pages.

Chapter 4

Software Process Improvement: How to Do It

1. Introduction to Chapter

We have introduced various models for process assessment and process improvement in previous chapters, but have said little about how to go about process improvement. A later chapter (Chapter 11) will be concerned with the benefits of process improvement. In this chapter, authors who are directly involved in process improvement describe their experiences, including:

- what they found the requirements to be for successful software process improvement,

- how they went about process improvement,

- what they found to work well, and what did not work so well.

The experiences of software process improvement at the Lockheed Martin Corporation and Hewlett Packard are described, as well as that of software process control gained in

connection with the on-board space shuttle software. Based on these accounts, some of the requirements for successful process improvement seem to be:

- engineers need to be convinced of the need for a standard process,

- appropriate training is essential,

- a clearly defined improvement model is required,

- fault and failure analysis is important,

while benefits identified include

- greater ability to respond to changes,

- reduced time spent on the investigation phase of a project,

- higher maturity levels, leading to accelerated spread of proven best practices across an organization.

These findings complement Humphrey's six basic principles of process change described in Chapter 2. The last of these basic principles, namely that *software process improvement requires investment*, requires emphasis. Process improvement is costly but recent studies (see Chapter 11) suggest that the investment is amply repaid.

Textbooks that provide advice on process improvement include Zahran's *Software Process Improvement: Practical Guidelines for Business Success* [4] and *The SPIRE Handbook* by Sanders, et al [2]. Both books provide practical assistance to organizations starting out on process improvement. *The SPIRE Handbook* builds on the experiences of software process improvement case studies in a number of European countries, and is written in the context of the SPICE standard (see Chapter 8). Zahran's book, on the other hand, covers all the main assessment methods including SW-CMM, SPICE, TRILLIUM, ISO 9001, etc.

There are clearly considerable benefits to be gained from sharing software process improvement experiences, and for this reason a number of SPIN (Software Process Improvement Network) groups have been set up throughout the world. These groups exist to allow the sharing of successful and unsuccessful experiences of software process improvement projects. Clearly there is just as much to be gained through learning from others about unsuccessful experiences as from successes. However, human nature being what it is, it is the successful experiences which tend to be publicized more than the unsuccessful ones. Information about SPINs, including where they are located, how to join one, and how to form one, is located at the SEI's web site [1].

2. Description of Articles

The first paper in this chapter is by Sandra McGill of the Lockheed Martin Corporation. It is entitled "Overcoming Resistance to Standard Processes or. Herding Cats." In it, the use of a process implementation workshop to explain the need for, and benefits to be gained from, a standard software process is described. McGill also identifies the goals for a process implementation workshop, and describes the various elements of the one under discussion, principally:

- software process training,

- software risk assessment,

- identification of critical aspects of the implementation program,

- analysis of the gap between the existing and the standard process,

- identification of action items.

The workshops were clearly extremely successful, not least because the author realized the need to introduce some fun into what might have seemed to some a somewhat cheerless activity.

The second paper in this chapter is by Robert Grady of Hewlett-Packard, entitled "Software Failure Analysis for High-Return Process Improvement Decisions." It advocates the use of software failure analysis and root cause analysis to provide criteria for selecting process improvement activities. The author advocates a proactive (as well as a reactive) approach to faults in software. Even more important than eliminating the fault when it is found, the process must be improved so that this type of fault does not occur again. This is particularly appropriate at levels 3 and above of the SW-CMM. The proactive approach to fault elimination depends on having a method of categorizing software defects and the paper describes a method developed by the Hewlett-Packard Software Metrics Council. The author also describes three approaches to failure analysis based on the capability of the organization, and proposes a Software Failure Analysis Maturity Model that parallels the SW-CMM.

The third paper in this chapter is by William Florac, Anita Carleton, and Julie Barnard and is entitled "Statistically Managing the Software Process." In it, the authors address the issues of level 4 of the SW-CMM, where processes must be "quantitatively understood and stabilized" and "sources of individual problems must be understood and eliminated." Both of those issues are addressed using the principles of statistical process control. A similar approach is taken in a paper by E. F. Weller, not included in this tutorial. [3]

This paper also describes how control charts were used to understand and eliminate problems with a software system developed for the space shuttle program through a joint project involving Lockheed Martin and the Software Engineering Institute in Pittsburgh. The project focused on the inspection process and showed the effects on it of common cause variation and assignable cause variation. The raw data collected is successively refined as the reasons for apparent discrepancies in the data are understood. At each stage, italicized commentary elaborates on the particular issues involved. The paper ends by describing the apparent benefits obtained by the project and advocating the wider use of such approaches.

3. References

[1] Software Engineering Institute,
http ://www.sei.cmu.edu /collaborating/spins/spins.html

[2] SPIRE Project Team, *The SPIRE Handbook,* Centre for Software Engineering, Dublin, 1998.

[3] E.F. Weller; "Practical Applications of Statistical Process Control", *IEEE Software,* volume 17 pp. 48-55, May/June 2000.

[4] S. Zahran; *Software Process Improvement: Practical Guidelines for Business Success,* Addison Wesley, 1998.

Overcoming Resistance to Standard Processes or... "Herding Cats"

Sandra G. McGill

Lockheed Martin Corporation
Space Systems Company
Missiles and Space Operations
1111 Lockheed Martin Way
B153, O/L7-27
Sunnyvale, California, 94089
USA
sandy.mcgill@lmco.com

Abstract

One of the most difficult hurdles to process improvement is convincing engineers that a standard process is something that will help them, not hinder them. The LMSSC-MSO Software Engineering Process Group has established a process implementation workshop that helps engineers see the strong correlation between what they are currently doing and what our standard process recommends as "best practices." In addition, it provides some fun along the way.

Introduction

Throughout its history, Lockheed Martin Space Systems Company, Missiles and Space Operations (LMSSC-MSO) has been composed of a collection of widely diverse and nearly autonomous programs. These programs have different types of products, different customers, and different standards. In the past, this has made establishing and enforcing a standard process a monumental task to pursue. An apt analogy is trying to herd cats—it rarely accomplishes much, and it irritates the cats.

Our most difficult process problem has not been the establishment of the process itself, but convincing the staff that implementing the process would be an advantage, not a burden. While dictating that staff use the process is a simple solution, it does not "win their hearts." We wanted to convince them that it was the smart thing to do.

One obstacle was that the perceived size and complexity of the software process can be daunting at first. Our critical task was to get program personnel to look in detail at the individual activities and tasks, rather than the whole, to get a better perspective of its scope. This article provides a brief look at the history of how we developed the process, then describes in detail how we are convincing personnel to willingly adopt it.

LMSSC-MSO Standard Software Process Background and History

When we began our process workshops in 1998, three major software process initiatives were being used by the software industry to model, monitor, and measure software development processes:

1.   Software Engineering Institute (SEI) Capability Maturity Model (SW-CMM)™,

2.   IEEE/EIA Joint-Standard-16: Software Development, and

3.   ISO 9001, the quality program standard, and its software interpretation, ISO 9000-3.

Most of our LMSSC-MSO programs were being required (either by government contracts or by company process commitments) to respond to one or more of the three standards above, causing considerable duplication of work in supporting the various assessment efforts. To ease the confusion, the LMSSC-MSO Software Engineering Process Group (SEPG) took on the commitment to establish an LMSSC-MSO standard software process (SSP) that is compliant with all of the major standards. This, in turn, allowed our programs to focus on compliance with a single unifying standard—the LMSSC-MSO SSP—versus compliance with multiple standards (see Figure 1).

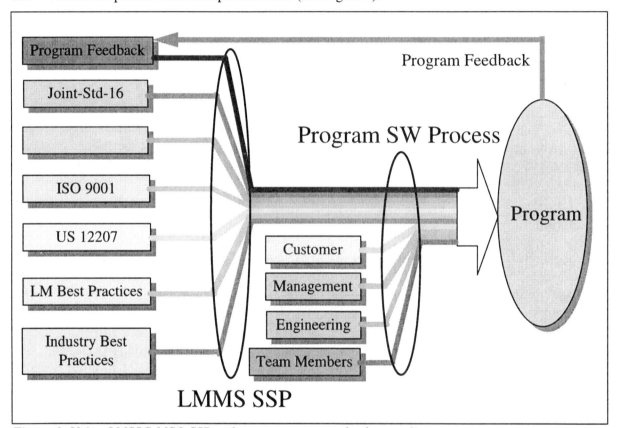

Figure 1. Using LMSSC-MSO SSP to focus program standards compliance.

In creating the SSP, we defined a set of 23 software life cycle activities, based in large part on the 25 activities defined in Joint-Standard-16. The activities are grouped into four domains (Figure 2):

1.   *Software Process Management:* management activities concerned with planning, tracking, measuring, and improving the software life cycle activities and support activities;

2. *Software Product Management:* critical support activities concerned with managing the quality of software products;

3. *Software–System Interface:* interface activities concerned with software's support of system-level activities; and

4. *Software Engineering:* the "typical" software life cycle activities.

Each activity is decomposed into tasks (104 at the top level), which in turn can be further decomposed if the task complexity warrants it. The activities and tasks are supplemented by various process support products, such as guidebooks, templates, standards, and checklists.

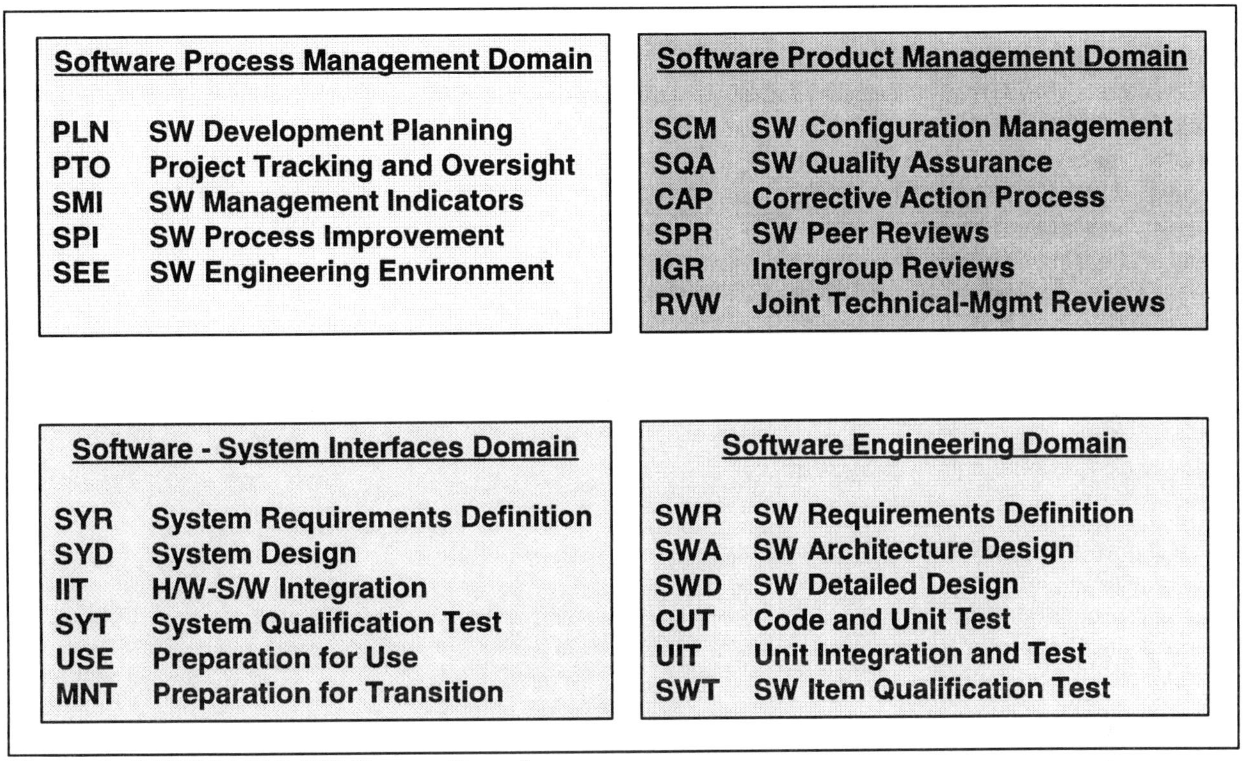

Software Process Management Domain		**Software Product Management Domain**	
PLN	SW Development Planning	SCM	SW Configuration Management
PTO	Project Tracking and Oversight	SQA	SW Quality Assurance
SMI	SW Management Indicators	CAP	Corrective Action Process
SPI	SW Process Improvement	SPR	SW Peer Reviews
SEE	SW Engineering Environment	IGR	Intergroup Reviews
		RVW	Joint Technical-Mgmt Reviews
Software - System Interfaces Domain		**Software Engineering Domain**	
SYR	System Requirements Definition	SWR	SW Requirements Definition
SYD	System Design	SWA	SW Architecture Design
IIT	H/W-S/W Integration	SWD	SW Detailed Design
SYT	System Qualification Test	CUT	Code and Unit Test
USE	Preparation for Use	UIT	Unit Integration and Test
MNT	Preparation for Transition	SWT	SW Item Qualification Test

Figure 2 - LMSSC-MSO SSP Process Domains

We established a Web-based SSP, which allows software personnel to see as much (or as little) detail as is required for each specific task. The LMSSC-MSO SSP has been up and running since January 1997.

Implementing the SSP

During the next year of working with programs to implement the process, we determined that new projects are not generally the problem. The personnel on new projects are more than willing to accept a ready-made process, rather than build one from scratch. The bigger problem has been persuading established programs to adopt the SSP in place of their own familiar processes, the "not-invented-here" syndrome. We needed to establish a quick and easy approach for convincing the engineers (and management also) that the SSP was something that would help them, not hinder them. We also needed to convince them that the SSP was not radically different from what they were currently doing, since it was based on best practices gathered from existing programs across the company.

We finally settled on the approach of using SSP implementation workshops on a program-by-program basis, focusing on the specific needs for each program. We established four primary goals for the workshop:

1. Encourage engineers and management alike to look at the SSP in detail.

2. Show project personnel "what's in it for me."

3. Convince project personnel that moving to the SSP is not a major effort.

4. Have some fun doing it.

The following paragraphs outline the basic steps we go through during the workshops, and how each step helps to meet our workshop goals above.

Step 1: Training

The first step in the workshop is training. We require all workshop participants to take an introductory course that describes why process is important, what major process initiatives are "out there," and how LMSSC-MSO has responded to the initiatives. The training includes an introduction to the structure and content of the SSP and a demonstration of the SSP Web site and how to access it. While this training started us down the path to goal 1 (look at the details), it was not sufficient in itself. It did not force (oops—encourage) them to become familiar with the gory details. That came later. It did help in one other way, though. It offered the "cats" the tempting "catnip" that using the SSP could help them understand and meet LMSSC-MSO process objectives and/or commitments to government customers to achieve CMM compliance or ISO 9001 compliance.

Step 2: Program Software Risk Assessment

The second step in the workshop is software risk assessment for the specific program holding the workshop. The workshop facilitator leads a brainstorming session with the participants to identify the major risks that could impact their specific program. If they have a current risk plan (which they generally do), we use those risk items. If not, we generate an ad hoc list. The intent behind this activity is to address goal 2 ("what's in it for me") by showing staff that the process could help them avoid or mitigate problems that have "bit them in the past." As we tailor the process, we frequently refer back to the list to make sure that we include mitigation approaches in the appropriate place. Offline from the workshop itself, we work with the programs to complete the risk assessment—assessing the risks for probability and impact and establishing risk mitigation approaches and fallback plans.

Step 3: Critical Program Characteristics

The third step is one of the more fascinating ones for me, especially when dealing with existing programs: defining or reviewing critical program characteristics that can impact how the program needs to implement the SSP. We look at key decisions that were made early in the program, such as:

- *Software life cycle*: waterfall, incremental, evolutionary;

- *Software methodologies:* requirements methods, design methods, test methods; and

- *Software team composition:* interfaces with subcontractors, associate contractors, and so on.

This step (especially defining the life cycle) can be helpful in convincing older, established programs of the worth of process (goal 2). Many of the decisions made early in a program's life evolve during the life of the program. What started out as a fairly typical waterfall may have evolved into an iterative approach as requirements and technology changed over the years. This step encourages personnel to think about what their true life cycle is, where the problems are, and (ta-da!) where the process may be able to help them by defining better entry and exit criteria for moving to the next activity.

Step 4: Process Gap Analysis

The fourth step is to perform a gap analysis of the program's existing process against the LMSSC-MSO SSP. We accomplish this by stepping through each of the 104 tasks that make up the 23 activities. As individuals, each participant reads the task description and marks on their copy whether or not they feel the task is currently performed (a) consistently, (b) more often than not, (c) sometimes, or (d) not at all. They then transfer their individual votes to large size posters on the wall. Figure 3 shows a sample gap analysis form. This approach accomplishes two critical things: It prevents people's votes from being swayed by peer pressure and, even more importantly, it gets people up and out of their chairs, moving around and talking. Otherwise, they tend to start napping around the third task.

Task ID: **PLN.2**   Task Title: **Define Software Team and Program Interfaces**
Task Description:
[PLN.2.1 Define Software Team Interfaces] - Software Management defines the responsibilities for each software team role and identifies and defines the lines of communication between each.
[PLN.2.2 Define Program Interfaces] - Software Management defines the reporting mechanism for communicating with the product team, if any, and the Program Office.
[PLN.2.3 Define Subcontractor Interfaces] - Software Management defines the mechanisms for interfacing with subcontractors.

Performed Consistently & Evidence Exists	Performed More Often than Not	Performed Some Times	Not Performed At All	NOT Applicable Needs LMMS SEPG Approval
Use ABOVE Task Description AS-IS		**Modify ABOVE Task Description As Stated:**		
Additional Process Definition Required ☐ Lower Level Task Descript ☐ Standard ☐ Template ☐ Checklist ☐ Procedure ☐ Other _____		**Allow Implementation Variance Between Software Teams** ☐ YES ☐ As Stated: ☐ NO		**Additional Notes:**
Improvement Action:				

Figure 3. Sample gap analysis form.

As a group, we analyze the results, looking both at where the majority vote lies and also at the spread in the votes. If the votes are widely spread across the spectrum between "Performed Consistently" and "Not Performed at All," we discussed what was causing the spread:

- Have people interpreted the task description differently?

- Is the task being performing inconsistently across the teams?

- Do we need standards or procedures to ensure that the task is being done adequately?

If the votes trend toward the low end, we discuss what is preventing the task from being performed:

- Is the task not being planned into the schedule?

- Are people unaware that the task needs to be performed?

- Is the task perceived as "busy work" or non-value-added?

Based on the results of the analysis, we determine the most appropriate approach to close each identified process gap. Do we modify what is currently being performed on the program to match the SSP? This would be a good approach if we were to introduce unacceptable quality risk by *not* adopting this more rigorous process. Do we modify the SSP to match what is currently being performed? This might be a good approach if we were to introduce unacceptable schedule or cost risk by trying to adopt the more rigorous process.

A third approach is to take the middle ground between the two extremes, that is, to modify both the SSP and the existing process to a compromise process. During the gap analysis, we also identify any additional process support products that exist or are needed to flesh out the process. These may include such items as:

- Standards (software design notation, code, document format, etc.),

- Checklists (peer reviews, formal reviews, etc.),

- Procedures (software build, configuration control boards, software discrepancy report submittals, etc.), and

- Templates (metrics reports, review packages, etc.).

Each task is evaluated on a case-by-case basis, ensuring that each task is considered both as a standalone item and as part of the bigger picture of the entire process. In each case, the guiding principle was risk assessment: Which approach minimized the risk for the program cost, schedule, and quality.

In most of the workshops to date, only about 10 percent of the tasks were significantly modified or deleted. Of the remaining 90 percent, workshop participants generally agreed that they were either currently performing the tasks or *should* be if they were not. The 90 percent accepted tasks were either accepted as-is or moderately tailored to match what the program was currently doing. While this may seem like an unusually high correlation between the process and what is being performed on the program, bear in mind that the process itself was based on current best practices from our existing programs.

Generally, the participants are astonished and rather pleased with themselves when they see how closely they match the "best practices" of the SSP. This gap analysis step helps accomplish goal 1 (look at the details) and goal 3 (convince staff it is not a major effort to comply with our SSP).

Step 5: Collect and Assign Action Items

The fifth and last step is to collect all action items, including recommended changes to the SSP, recommended changes to their current process, and new process support products. Either as part of the workshop or in a follow-up meeting, we correlate the action items, prioritize them, and assign them to personnel or working groups to work. If a working group needs to be established, we generate a detailed mission statement to ensure that the working group members understand precisely what specific products they are to produce, how much time to spend per week on the average, and when the final products are due. The program's process engineer works with program engineers and the central Software Engineering Process Group (SEPG) to ensure closure of the actions within a reasonable time span.

Having Fun

So where does goal 4 (have fun) come in? As many places as possible. We make sure donuts, cookies, and other snacks are made available at strategic points in the workshop. We stage the workshops away from the engineers' work environment. We use cartoon stickers for transferring the votes to the wall posters. (You haven't lived until you've seen two senior managers fight over who gets Bugs Bunny!) We have "toys" to play with while participants wait for others to finish. We tell jokes and war stories to help illuminate the problems with the existing process. We take frequent short breaks, rather than infrequent long ones (that way they cannot go back to their desks)—anything to keep the atmosphere light and upbeat, and keep the "cats" going in the same direction.

Bottom Line

By now you're probably saying "Interesting approach, but what's the bottom line?" During the last few years, the workshops have been averaging about 24 hours to complete, with the actual hours ranging from about 12 at a minimum to 30 at the maximum. The actual hours depend on the team size and the amount of discussion that occurs. The closer the existing process is to the SSP, the shorter the workshop.

We recommend breaking the workshop into six 4-hour sessions spread over 2 weeks, rather than try to do them all in a 3-day span. The one workshop that we conducted in 3 days straight resulted in a roomful of people with brains the size of raisins. The activities on the third day went smoothly because no one had the energy to argue, but they weren't nearly as productive or as fun (goal 4). On the other hand, if you spread the sessions out over a month or more, you tend to lose momentum; you spend too much time trying to remember what you did on a similar task 2 weeks ago.

The workshop team sizes range from 3 to 20 people, depending on the number of project software teams represented and on the size of the program. (Program sizes vary from a 4-person R&D team to a major program with 150+ software personnel). The workshop team includes a trained meeting facilitator and engineering personnel who can adequately represent the six software roles in our SSP: software management, software systems engineering, software development, software test, software configuration management, and software quality assurance. The representatives need the program experience to understand the current documented program process (if one exists), but they also need the knowledge of what "really" happens and the authorization to make decisions regarding what will happen in future.

Summary

Overall, feedback from the participants has been extremely favorable, with participants citing the workshops as a relatively quick and informative approach for familiarizing themselves with the details of the SSP and identifying gaps within their program. The LMSSC-MSO SEPG has recognized the workshops as being a key factor in the successful deployment of the SSP on its major programs. LMSSC-MSO has since been assessed as being SEI CMM level 3 compliant, using programs that participated in our workshops and implementing the process improvement plans that resulted from them.

Principal Author Biography

Sandy McGill is currently supporting a major LMSSC-MSO program. Prior to that, she was the LMSSC-MSO engineering assessment lead, with responsibility for assessing all engineering disciplines (systems, software, hardware, etc.) against our internal engineering processes and appropriate external standards, such as the SEI CMMI™. Sandy McGill has also been the lead of the LMSSC-MSO SEPG staff. As a SEPG lead and member for more than 10 years, Sandy contributed to a wide variety of software process-oriented activities, including these tasks:

- Software process consulting for various programs and proposals.

- Internal Capability Maturity Model assessments of LMSSC-MSO software programs.

- Concept design of the "new improved" Web-based LMSSC-MSO standard software process,

- Authoring the *LMSSC-MSO Software Engineering Process Group Guidebook,*

- Authoring the *Standard Software Process Implementation Guidebook* and workshop, and

- Software process training material preparation and presentation.

Before joining the SEPG staff, Sandy spent 12 years in the software "trenches" on various ground and flight software projects. She started as a software developer, moved to software systems engineering and systems engineering, and then became the supervisor of a software requirements and test group. While acting as supervisor for the requirements and test group, she began her involvement in process activities, introducing a new mechanism for relaying requirements changes from systems engineering to software engineering and implementing an improved test documentation approach. Since 1989, she has received 10 LMSSC-MSO special achievement awards for her process-related work, and received the 1994 Lockheed Corporate Award for Individual Software Process Excellence.

Software Failure Analysis for High-Return Process Improvement Decisions

Software failure analysis and root-cause analysis have become valuable tools in enabling organizations to determine the weaknesses in their development processes and decide what changes they need to make and where.

by Robert B. Grady

When I was growing up, my father was fond of using sayings to encourage me to remember important lessons. One of his favorites was "Do you know the difference between a wise man and a fool?" He would then go on to say that a wise man makes a mistake only once. A fool makes the same mistake over and over again.

Applying my father's saying to software defects, it sometimes seems as if there are many "fools" among software developers. However, there aren't. Individually, they learn from their mistakes. What's missing is organizational learning about our software mistakes. I guess that many organizations have earned my dad's "fool" label.

One useful way to evaluate software defects is to transfer process learning from individuals to organizations. It includes not only analyzing software defects but also brainstorming the root causes of those defects and incorporating what we learn into training and process changes so that the defects won't occur again. There are five steps:

1. Extend defect data collection to include root-cause information. Start shifting from reactive responses to defects toward proactive responses.

2. Do failure analysis on representative organization-wide defect data. *Failure analysis is the evaluation of defect patterns to learn process or product weaknesses.*

3. Do root-cause analysis to help decide what changes must be made. *Root-cause analysis is a group reasoning process applied to defect information to develop organizational understanding of the causes of a particular class of defects.*

4. Apply what is learned to train people and to change development and maintenance processes.

5. Evolve failure analysis and root-cause analysis to an effective continuous process improvement process.

How do these steps differ from other popular methods for analyzing processes? One popular method is process assessments, for example, SEI (Software Engineering Institute) process assessments.[1] Most assessments document peoples' answers to subjective questions that are designed around somebody's model of ideal software development practices. If such models are accurate and if peoples' answers reflect reality, the models provide a good picture of an organization's status. Thus, the results may or may not be timely, representative, or motivational.

The combination of failure analysis and root-cause analysis is potentially more valuable than subjective assessments, because it quantifies defect costs for a specific organization. The key point to remember is that software defect data is your most important available management information source for software process improvement decisions. Furthermore, subsequent data will provide a measurable way of seeing results and evaluating how methods can be further adapted when a specific set of changes is done.

Reactive Use of Defect Data (A Common Starting Point)

After initial analysis, everyone reacts to defects either by fixing them or by ignoring them. Customer dissatisfaction is minimized when we react quickly to fix problems that affect a customer's business. This is often done with fast response to issues and by following up with patches or workarounds, when appropriate. Some Hewlett-Packard divisions track the resolution of "hot sites." Fig. 1 shows an example.[2] Such a chart is a valuable way to track responsiveness, but it does little to prevent future defects. Furthermore, hot sites and patch management are very expensive.

Cumulative defects for long-lived software products are also tracked. For example, Fig. 2 shows the incoming service requests or discrepancy reports, the closed service requests or discrepancy reports, and the net progress for one NASA software project.[3] Some HP divisions also track progress like this,[2] although HP's progress measure subtracts incoming defects from closed defects so that positive progress represents a net reduction in defects. NASA appears to do the reverse.

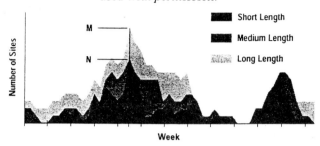

Fig. 1. *Tracking the number of hot sites during any particular week. For example, for the week indicated there were M − N hot sites that had been hot for a long time and N hot sites that had been hot for a short time. © 1992 Prentice-Hall used with permission.*

Fig. 2. *Incoming maintenance requests, closed maintenance requests, and net progress for one NASA project. This figure is reprinted by permission of the publisher from "A Software Metric Set for Program Maintenance Management," by G. Stark, G.L. Kern, and C. Vowell, Journal of Systems and Software, Vol 24, p. 243. © 1994 by Elsevier Science Inc.*

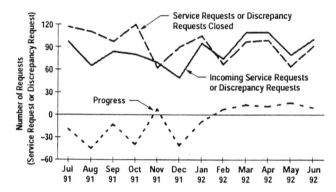

Both the hot site graph and the defect closure progress graph show reactive uses of defect data. In the examples, the respective organizations were using the data to try to improve their immediate customer situations. The alternative is to ignore the data or to react much more slowly.

Ignoring defect data can lead to serious consequences for an organization's business. For example, the division producing one HP software system decided to release its product despite a continuing incoming defect trend during system test. The result was a very costly update shortly after release, a continued steady need for defect repairs, and a product with a bad quality reputation. This is the kind of mistake that can cause an entire product line's downfall. A recent article described how one company learned this lesson the hard way.[4]

Responses should not be limited only to reaction. Besides endangering customer satisfaction and increasing costs, here are some other dangers that could occur if reactive processes aren't complemented with proactive steps to eliminate defect sources:

1. People can get in the habit of emphasizing reactive thinking. This, in turn, suggests that management finds shipping defective products acceptable.

2. Managers get in the habit of primarily rewarding reactive behavior. This further reenforces fixing defects late in development or after release. Late fixes are both costly and disruptive.

3. People place blame too easily in highly reactive environments because of accompanying pressure or stress. This is demoralizing, since the root causes of most defects are poor training, documentation, or processes, not individual incompetence.

Remember that effectively reacting to defects is an important part of successfully producing software products. However, because business conditions change rapidly, many organizations can't seem to find the time to break old habits of using defect data reactively without considering ways of eliminating similar future problems. The elimination of the causes of potential future defects must be included in any successful long-term business strategy.

Failure Analysis (Changing Your Mental Frame of Reference)

The proactive use of defect data to eliminate the root causes of software defects starts with a change in mental frame of reference. The reactive frame generally focuses on single defects and asks "How much do they hurt?" It also considers how important it is to fix particular defects compared with others and asks "When must they be fixed?" The proactive frame asks, "What caused those defects in the first place? Which ones cause the greatest resource drain? How can we avoid them next time?"

Various reports have described successful efforts to analyze defects, their causes, and proposed solutions. But the terminology among them has differed, and the definitions could mean different things to different people. In the fall of 1986, the HP Software Metrics Council addressed the definition of standard categories of defect causes. Our goal was to provide standard defect terminology that different HP projects and labs could use to report, analyze, and focus efforts to eliminate defects and their root causes. Fig. 3 is the model that has evolved from our original definitions.[2]

Fig. 3. Categorization of software defects. © 1992 Prentice-Hall used with permission.

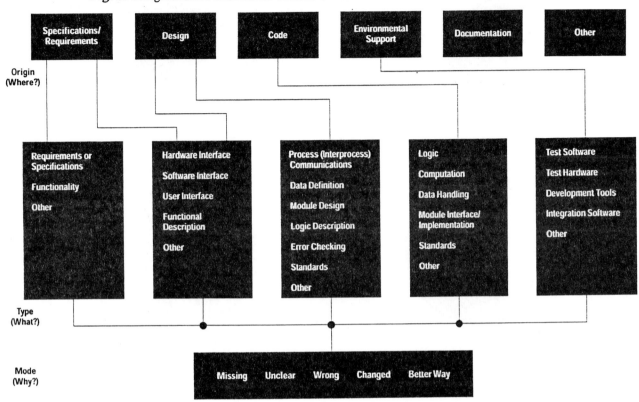

The model is used by selecting one descriptor each from origin, type, and mode for each defect report as it is resolved. For example, a defect might be a design defect in which part of the user interface described in the internal specification was missing. Another defect might be a coding defect in which some logic was wrong.

Fig. 4 gives some idea of how defects vary from one entity to another.[5] The different shadings reflect the origin part of Fig. 3. The pie wedges come from the middle layer of Fig. 3, the defect types. The eight largest sources of defects for different HP divisions are shown in each pie. All four results profile defects found only during system and integration tests.

We can immediately see from Fig. 4 that the sources of defects vary greatly across the organizations. No two pie charts are alike. These differences are not surprising. If everyone developed the same way and experienced the same problems, then we would have fixed those problems by now. Instead, there are many different environments. While many proposed solutions to our problems apply to different situations, they don't necessarily apply equally well to all problems or all environments.

Some of the differences are because of inconsistencies in peoples' use of the origin and type definitions. Because the definitions are just a means to focus process improvement efforts on the costliest rework areas, groups resolve inconsistencies when they define root causes to problems and brainstorm potential fixes. It is the triggering of these discussions that makes the data in Fig. 4 so important. Discussing root causes is a way to instill a process improvement attitude in an organization. Defect data will provide a measurable basis for decisions that must be made. By continuing to track defect data, an organization can also measure how successful its solutions are.

Acting on Causal Data

Collecting defect source data is only the first step. Persuasive as the data might be, improvements won't happen automatically. Both managers and engineers must agree on what the data means and the importance of acting on it. One of the best ways to help ensure that this happens is to tie proposed improvements to stated business goals. This also keeps improvement priorities high enough to help ensure sustained management support.

Besides management support, some first-line managers and engineers affected by a proposed change must be motivated to do something and be assigned responsibility to plan and do the necessary changes. Finally, as for any effective project, there must be a way of monitoring progress and gauging success.

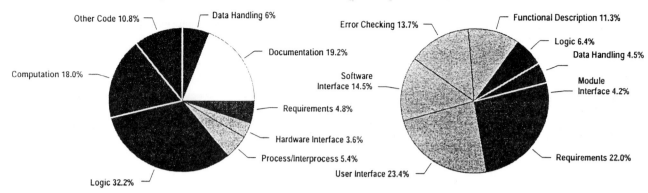

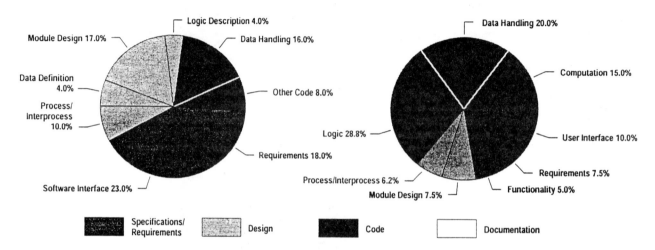

Fig. 4. *Sources of defects found during testing in four HP divisions.*

As a group, software developers now have several decades of software development experience. It is time to break out of our pressure-driven reactive habits and use our accumulated knowledge to drive lasting improvements. Failure analysis changes the way managers and developers look at software defects. This finally opens the way to a proactive frame of reference.

Root-Cause Analysis Processes

There are many possible ways to analyze root-cause data. Any successful way must be sensitive to project pressures and personnel motivation. HP has used several approaches in different organizations. For this discussion, I will label three that seem to evolve naturally from each other as *one-shot root-cause analysis, post-project root-cause analysis,* and *continuous process improvement cycle.* These three approaches include many common steps. Since the first is an introductory process, the most detailed explanation is saved for the post-project root-cause analysis.

One-Shot Root-Cause Analysis

A good starting approach for organizations that have not previously categorized their defect data by root causes is a one-shot root-cause analysis. This approach minimizes the amount of organizational effort invested by using someone from outside the organization to facilitate the process. At HP most divisions have defect tracking systems with complete enough information to extract such data.

The one-shot process has six steps.

1. Introduce a group of engineers and managers to the failure-analysis model (Fig. 3) and the root-cause analysis process. (About one hour.) Make it clear that the goals of the one-shot process are to:

   - Create a rough picture of divisional defect patterns.
   - Identify some potential improvement opportunities.

2. Select 50 to 75 defects from the defect tracking system using a random process. Make sure that the team thinks the defects have enough information to enable them to extract the necessary causal information. (About two hours sometime before the meeting.)

3. Have the people in the group classify one defect per person and discuss the findings as a group. Then have them classify enough defects so that you have about 50 total. Draw a pie chart of the top eight defect types. (About two hours.)

4. Pick two defect types to focus on. Create fishbone diagrams from the combined root causes and additional comments. A fishbone diagram is a brainstorming tool used to combine and organize group thoughts.[2,6] (About half an hour.)

5. Develop some recommendations for improvements. (About half an hour)

6. Present the results and recommendations to management. Make assignments to do initial changes. (About one hour)

Participants in this process have been generally surprised and excited that they could learn so much in a very short time. They have also been uniformly interested in adopting the analysis process permanently. How quickly they have followed through has varied, depending on many business variables such as immediate product commitments, other in-progress changes, or a tight economic climate.

Post-Project Root-Cause Analysis

The major difference between this process and the one-shot process is that organizations that start with the one-shot process have not previously collected causal data. Organizations that already collect failure-analysis data and have an understanding of their past defect patterns analyze their data and act on their results more efficiently. The steps in this approach follow the meeting outline shown in Fig. 5. Note that the times shown in Fig. 5 are intended to force the meeting to keep moving. It is best to schedule a full two hours, since all that time will be needed. The example used here to illustrate this process came from a root-cause analysis meeting done at an HP division shortly after a team at that division released a new product.

Fig. 5. *Root-cause analysis meeting outline.*

Premeeting
- Identify the division's primary business goal.
- Have the division champion and root-cause facilitator analyze data.
- Have the champion send out the meeting announcement and instructions to engineers.
  - Pick two defects from their code that have been chosen from the defect categories.
  - Think of ways to prevent or find defects sooner.

Meeting
- State the meeting's goal (use insights gained from failure analysis data to improve development and support practices).
- Perform issues selection (10 minutes).
- Review the defects brought to the meeting (15 minutes).
- Perform analysis (15 minutes).
- Take a break (10 minutes).
- Brainstorm solutions (10 minutes).
- Test for commitment (10 minutes).
- Plan for change (10 minutes).

Postmeeting
- Have the division champion and root-cause facilitator review meeting process.
- Have the division champion capture software development process baseline data.

Premeeting:

- Identify the organization's primary business goal. This goal is an important input when prioritizing which high-level defect causes should be addressed first. It also helps to frame management presentations to ensure sustained management support. Typical business goals might be framed around maximizing a particular customer group's satisfaction, evolving a product line to some future state, or controlling costs or schedule to get new customers.

- The division champion and root-cause facilitator analyze the data. The champion is a person who promotes a process or improvement activity, removes obstacles, enthusiastically supports implementers and users, and leads through active involvement. The root-cause facilitator is a person who runs the root-cause analysis meeting. The champion and the facilitator need to be skilled at meeting processes and dynamics and be familiar with software development and common defect types. One simple data-analysis approach is to enter the data into an electronic spreadsheet. Draw pie charts of the top eight defect types by quantity and by find and fix effort (either actual or estimated). Fig. 6 shows the system-test data for four projects at one HP division. The shading represents defect origin information, and the pie wedges are defect types. The left pie chart shows the eight most frequently recorded causes of defects. The right pie chart shows the data adjusted to reflect that design and specification defects found during system test cost much more to fix than coding defects do. Since the HP division that provided this data did not collect their defect-fix times, the weighting factors are based on six industry studies summarized in reference 2. The right pie chart in Fig. 6 was prepared by multiplying the left pie chart wedge percentages (or counts) by the appropriate weighting factor and then converting back to 100%.

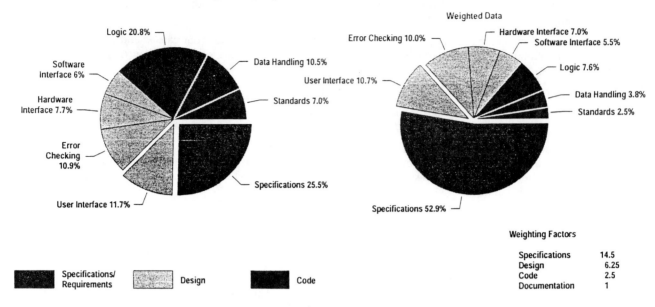

Fig. 6. *Top eight causes of defects for one division.*

Weighting Factors	
Specifications	14.5
Design	6.25
Code	2.5
Documentation	1

- Select two defect types to brainstorm based on the best estimate of the organization's concern or readiness to implement solutions. The two defect types selected for this meeting were user-interface defects and specifications defects. The specifications defect type was picked because it was the largest division category (64 out of 476 defects were classified as specifications defect types for this project team). User-interface defects were picked because they were the largest category (110 defects) that the particular brainstorming team had experienced. Both categories represented significant divisional improvement opportunities.

- Send out instructions to engineers. The organization champion should have each engineer bring hard-copy information on two defects from their code, based on the chosen types. Tell invitees to think back to the most likely root cause for each defect and to propose at least one way to prevent or find each defect sooner.

Meeting:

- State the meeting's goal (use insights gained from failure-analysis data to improve the organization's development and maintenance practices). Present the defect categorization model, show typical patterns for other organizations, and show your organization's pattern. Set a positive tone for the meeting. Remind participants that they will be looking at process flaws, and that they must avoid even joking comments that might belittle the data or solutions discussed.

- Issues selection. Reiterate the reasons for selecting this meeting's particular defect types. Let people make initial comments. Address concerns about potential data inaccuracies (if they come up at this point) by emphasizing the solution-oriented nature of the brainstorming process. Suggest that inaccuracies matter less when combining pie wedges to consider solutions. For example, for the sample division meeting, some engineers had a hard time calling some defects "user interface" as opposed to "specifications." We simply used both labels for such defects during the meeting instead of getting sidetracked on resolving the differences. You want to get people ready to share their defects by discussing a future time (like their next major product release) when they will have done something in their process to eliminate the reasons for the defects.

- Review the defects brought to the meeting. Have engineers read their own defects, root causes, and solutions. The major reason to do this is to get attendees involved in the meeting in a nonthreatening way. Thus, don't criticize those who did not prepare, rather encourage them to contribute in real time. Unlike inspections, root-cause analysis meetings require very little preparation time for attendees. After their first meeting, attendees will realize this, and it will be easier to get them to review their defects before the next meeting.

Get in a creative, brainstorming mood by showing the engineers that all their inputs are right, and begin to form a shared understanding of terminology and definitions, and an acceptable level of ambiguity. This section also gives you some idea whether there is some enthusiasm for any particular defect types. You can use such energy later to motivate action.

The following two examples are from the root-cause meeting held by the example HP division. There were 12 engineers and managers at this meeting.

1. User-interface defect: There was a way to select (data) peaks by hand for another part of the product, but not for the part being analyzed.

   Cause: Features added late; unanticipated use.

160

Proposed way to avoid or detect sooner: Walkthrough or review by people other than the local design team.

2. Specifications defect: Clip function doesn't copy sets of objects.

   Cause: Inherited code, neither code nor error message existed. Highly useful feature, added, liked, but never found its way back into specifications or designs.

   Proposal to avoid or detect sooner: Do written specifications and control creeping features.

- Perform analysis. Create fishbone diagrams[2,6] from combined root causes and additional comments. Use this discussion to bring the group from their individual premeeting biases regarding defects to a group consensus state. A useful technique for grouping the defects is to write the suggested causes on movable pieces of paper. Then have the group silently move the papers into groupings of related areas. If some of the papers move back and forth between two groups, duplicate them. The resulting groupings are called an *affinity diagram*.[7] These are major bones of the fishbone that the group must name. Don't expect the fishbone to be perfect here or even complete. The next session will potentially contribute more. Also, don't get concerned about form. Let the group know that a fishbone is just a means to an end, that it will be cleaned up after the meeting, and that it is likely to change even after that point. The fishbone diagrams in Figs. 7 and 8 are from analyzing the two defect types mentioned above.

- Take a break. This type of meeting takes a lot of energy and focus. It's hard to sustain that for two full hours.

- Brainstorm solutions. Use this time as an orthogonal approach to analyzing the issues at hand. This is also the transition from analysis to action planning for change. Think about what group energy can be turned into solution planning.

Fig. 7. *Fishbone diagram for the causes of user-interface defects.*

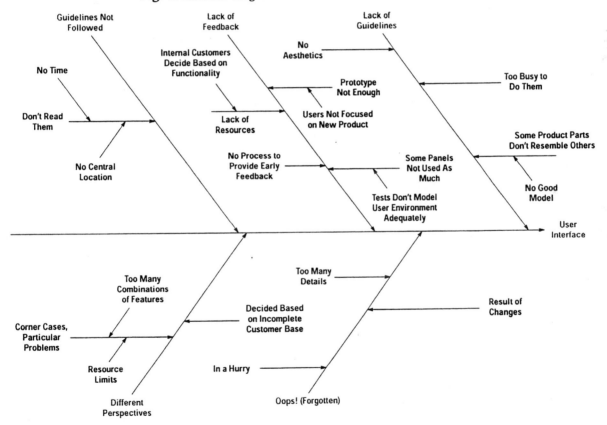

For our sample team, there was a lot of group interest in both defect types. Because a task force already was working on specification defects as a result of the previous root-cause analysis meetings, planning focused on user-interface defects. In the solution list they created, some of the solutions may seem vague. Remember that the brainstorm list is only an intermediate step toward defining action steps. Just be sure that the group understands what it means by the solutions. If members seem to understand the solutions, there is no need to slow down the brainstorming process for more precise definitions. These can be added later.

Fig. 8. *Fishbone diagram for the causes of specifications defects.*

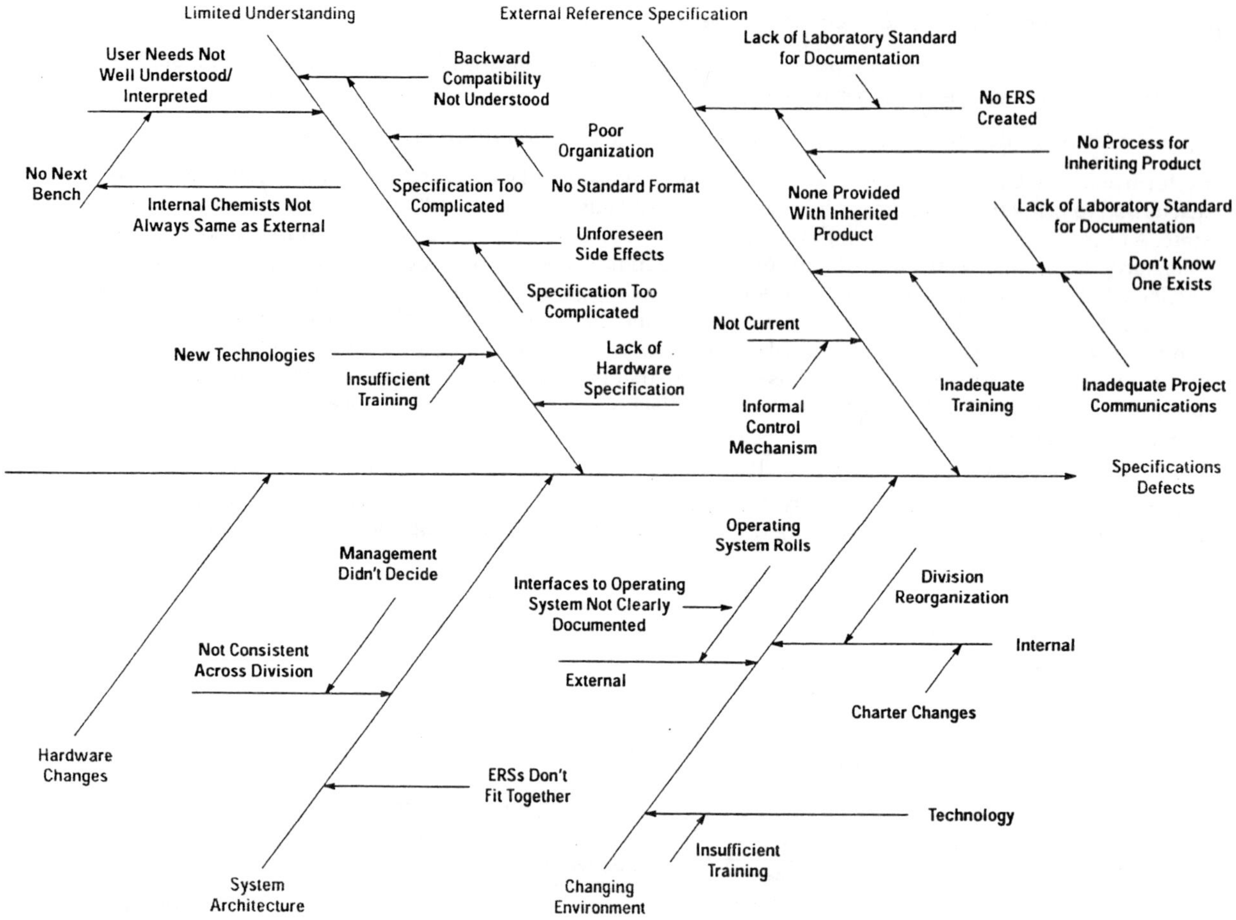

The solution list they created is as follows:

1. Learn from past experience—track user interfaces, particularly when changes occur.

2. When new functionality is thought of or added, always design and specify user-interface implications.

3. Evaluate other applications.

4. Use a checklist when designing panels.

5. Use the Caseworks design tool.

6. Complete an entire feature when you do it.

7. Give a new feature to someone else to use right away.

8. Solicit thoughtful feedback. Create guidelines for feedback and watch users use interfaces.

9. Perform usability walkthroughs and training.

10. Use standard modules (e.g., common dialog boxes).

- Test for commitment. Normally there is no need for this section, but some organizations that are more tightly controlled than others may not feel empowered to implement solutions. In these organizations, solutions should be directed toward doing what the group feels it is empowered to do. When those solutions are successful, they can be more broadly or completely applied. You may need to test to identify the roadblocks to change (e.g., time, schedule, etc.).

Our example HP division seemed very committed. This was reinforced in the next step when several people volunteered to initiate specific changes.

- Plan for change. Discuss which defects can be eliminated with the proposed solution. Create an action plan with responsibilities and dates. A model action plan might contain the following steps:

1. Establish working group 10/8
2. Meet and define outputs 10/15
3. Present objectives and gather inputs 11/1
4. Create a change process and artifacts 12/1
5. Inspect and fix process and artifacts 12/15
6. Celebrate
7. Use and measure results. 2/1

Our example division team decided to create guidelines for user interface designs that addressed many of its fishbone-diagram branches. The division's action plan consisted of the following steps.

1. Patty will create a checklist for designing panels. (First pass by 12/17)

2. The project manager will set expectations that all new functionality will be accompanied by design and specification implications. (Consider using new specification formats.)

3. Art will give the project team a presentation on Caseworks.

4. Follow up the project presentation with a discussion on the use of prototyping.

Remember to end the meeting with a clear understanding of ownership and responsibility. Use standard project-management techniques to plan and schedule follow-up.

Postmeeting:

- Review meeting process. The organization champion and root-cause facilitator review the process and develop changes to meeting format, data collection, analysis, and responsibilities. They should redo the fishbone diagram, being careful not to change it so much that participants no longer feel that it is theirs. Promptly send out meeting notes that include the fishbone diagram, responsibilities and action items, and schedule dates.
- Capture process baseline data. As part of structuring a process improvement project for success, someone (the organization champion) should record a minimum amount of process information before and after the project.[2] It is particularly important to document the basic divisional processes so that when the improvement is done, the group can better understand other influences besides the particular changes that were made. In this example, the team didn't do this step.

Results from Eliminating Defect Root Causes

The team from the example division did their checklist and used it during their next project. It had 30 items to watch out for, based on their previous experience and their defects. Fig. 9 shows an excerpt from their checklist. Over 20 percent of the defects on their previous project had been user-interface defects (though the division-wide average was lower). The results of their changes were impressive.

Fig. 9. A checklist of things to look for while developing dialog boxes.

- •
- •
- •

7. Are fields case sensitive or not? What implications are there?
8. Are abbreviations kept to a minimum?
9. Are there any spelling mistakes on the panel?
10. Does the panel have a title that matches the action of the panel?
11. Is the screen too crowded? For data entry, less than 50 percent of the panel should be writing. Controls should "fill" the panel without cluttering it.
12. Is help available to the user? Is there a help line to aid the user in understanding the field?
13. Has the help writer been updated with information on the new panel?
14. Are the units for edit fields given when appropriate?

- •
- •
- •

- They reduced the percentage of user-interface defects in test for their new year-long project to roughly five percent of their total system test defects.
- Even though the project produced 34 percent more code, they spent 27 percent less time in test.

Of course, other improvement efforts also contributed to their success. But the clear user interface defect reduction showed them that their new guidelines and the attention they paid to their interfaces were major contributors.[8] Finally, the best news is that customers were very pleased with the user interface, and initial product sales were very good.

Fig. 10. *Root-cause analysis process.*

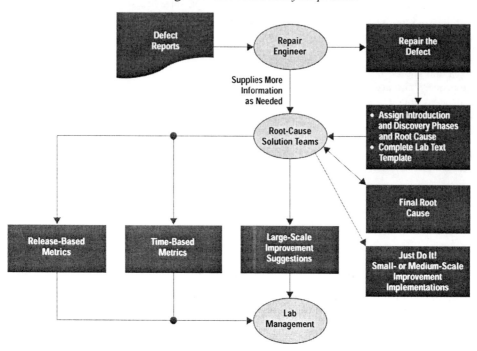

Two other project teams finished their projects recently, and their results were equally impressive. Both projects used new standard divisional specification templates created to eliminate many of the root causes shown in Fig. 8. A cross-project team task force had created two two-page specification templates (one for user-interface-oriented routines, one for software-interface-oriented ones) that they felt would help. Both teams substantially reduced specification defects compared with their previous project levels. While the reason for one team's reduction could possibly be that the project was second-generation, the other project wasn't.

While the action steps discussed here follow those of successful improvement projects at one HP division, they can also be applied in organizations with different defect patterns and business needs. One of the division people who worked with all three project teams summarized their results:

"...We must conclude that the root-cause approach is an effective mechanism to identify and introduce change into our software development process."[9]

Continuous Process Improvement Cycle

Some organizations have felt that root-cause analysis is so beneficial that they now use it to pursue continuous process improvement. It appears to be a natural evolution from post-process root-cause analysis successes. This approach extends the supporting infrastructure and requires an ongoing management commitment.

The first step that an organization generally takes is to widely adopt root-cause information logging by engineers. Causal information is then included as a normal part of the defect-handling process. Analysis is triggered in a variety of ways, often by a product or system release. Sometimes it is triggered by the end of a development phase or a series of inspections. It can also be triggered by an arbitrary time period. Fig. 10 shows how one HP division runs its process. Root-cause solution teams are empowered by management to initiate smaller process improvements.[10] More far-reaching improvements still require lab management approval.

Knowing which defects occur most often in test or later helps to focus improvement efforts. We saw two examples of this in the post-project root-cause analysis discussion. The continuous process improvement cycle encourages examination of similar data throughout the development process. Take the HP division whose test data was shown as the lower-right pie chart in Fig. 4. It also captured data for specifications, design, and code inspections. All this data is shown in Fig. 11. Some caution should be used in interpreting this specific data, since it was not uniformly collected. For example, there may have been a higher percentage of design work products than code work products, but still less than there was code tested. Nevertheless, this figure suggests some interesting questions and reveals possible insights.

The bars above the centerline show counts for different defects that were found in the same phase in which they were created. Tall bars represent good opportunities to reduce these defect sources significantly. For example, the large number of module design defects suggests that a different design technique might be needed to replace or complement existing methods.

The bars below the line show counts for defects found in phases after the ones in which they were created. The later defects are found, the more expensive they are to fix. Therefore, the tall bars are sources of both better prevention and earlier detection opportunities. For example, the requirements, functionality, and functional description defects combine to suggest that designs may be changing because of inadequate early product definition. It might be useful to use prototypes to reduce such changes.

It is clear that this type of data can contribute to more informed management decisions. It also provides a way of evaluating the results of changes with better precision than in the past. The amount of effort required to sustain a continuous process improvement cycle will vary, depending largely on the cost of implementing the changes suggested by analyses. Which changes are chosen for implementation will depend on other business aspects besides the projected costs and benefits. Just remember that the cost to sustain failure-analysis practice and modest improvements is small, and the returns have proven to far outweigh those costs.[2,5,8]

Conclusion

Process improvement projects are started in many ways, for many reasons. In the software field especially, processes are changing and adapting daily, and software products and businesses are also rapidly evolving. One of the most effective ways to both motivate and evaluate the success of net improvements is to look at defect trends and patterns. This paper has shown how software defect data is a powerful management information source. Using it effectively will help achieve an optimal balance between reacting to defect information and proactively taking steps toward preventing future defects. HP divisions have used several successful approaches to handling defect causal data. The three root-cause analysis processes described in this paper are positioned against a suggested five-level maturity model shown in Fig. 12.

Like many other best practices, failure analysis can be applied with increasing levels of maturity that lead to different possible paybacks. HP's experience says that the biggest benefits of driving to higher maturity levels are:

- Increased likelihood of success when implementing process changes, particularly major ones
- Accelerated spread of already-proven best practices
- Increased potential returns because necessary infrastructure components are in place.

Our successful results from three failure-analysis approaches are very encouraging. While the time it takes to progress to higher maturity levels will vary among groups, our experience suggests that failure analysis starts providing returns almost immediately, particularly in visualizing progress.

Ironically, the main limiter to failure-analysis success is that many managers still believe that they can quickly reduce total effort or schedules by 50 percent or more. As a result, they won't invest in more modest process improvements. This prevents them from gaining 50 percent improvements through a series of smaller gains. Because it takes time to get any improvement adopted organization-wide, these managers will continue to be disappointed.

It has not been difficult to initiate use of the Fig. 3 defect model and the root-cause analysis process. The resulting data has led to effective, sometimes rapid, improvements. There are few other available sources of information that are as useful in identifying key process weaknesses specific to an organization. This information will help to drive process improvement decisions and commitment in an organization.

Fig. 11. *A defect profile, an interesting way of analyzing defect data during the continuous process improvement phase.*

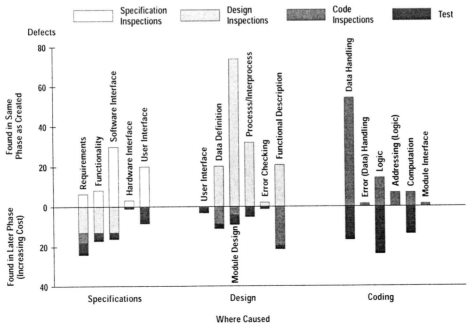

Fig. 12. *A five-level software failure-analysis maturity model.*

Software Failure Analysis Maturity Model

Level 5: Optimizing: Divisional goals set to achieve competitive advantage via specific software capabilities. People given primary responsibilities that include process improvement through root-cause analysis.

Level 4: Managed: Root-cause analysis meetings are a regular part of development process. There may be people responsible for improvements. Not all root-cause analysis meetings result in action items, but management reviews data.

Level 3: Defined: Defect source information uniformly collected, root-cause analysis meetings held, but not as a standard part of process. Data validating subsequent improvements is mostly anecdotal.

Level 2: Emerging: Defect source information collected, but not necessarily uniformly and not necessarily validated. General agreement on what requirements, design, and coding are.

Level 1: Initial/Ad hoc: Defect source information not regularly collected. No recognized divisional defect source patterns. Incomplete R&D process descriptions.

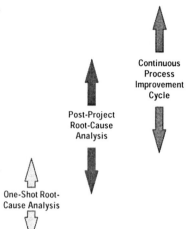

Continuous Process Improvement Cycle

Post-Project Root-Cause Analysis

One-Shot Root-Cause Analysis

Acknowledgments

I'd like to thank Jan Grady, Debbie Caswell, Cate Meyers, Barbara Zimmer, Dell Fields, Tom Van Slack, and Jean MacLeod for their helpful suggestions in the development of this article. Finally, thanks to Brad Yackle, Marc Tischler, and others at HP's Scientific Instrument Division for sharing their failure-analysis results.

References

1. M. Paulk, B. Curtis, M. Chrissis, and C. Weber, "Capability Maturity Model, Version 1.1," *IEEE Software*, July 1993, pp. 18-27.

2. R. Grady, *Practical Software Metrics for Project Management and Process Improvement*, Prentice-Hall, Inc., 1992, pp. 37, 79, 129, 130, 137-157.

3. G. Stark, G., L. Kern, and C. Vowell, "A Software Metric Set for Program Maintenance Management," *Journal of Systems and Software 24*, 1994, pp. 239-249.

4. D. Clark, "Change of Heart at Oracle Corp.," *San Francisco Chronicle*, July 2, 1992, pp. B1 and B4.

5. R. Grady, "Practical Results from Measuring Software Quality," *Proceedings of the ACM*, Vol. 36, no. 11, November 1993, pp. 62-68.

6. K. Ishikawa, *A Guide to Quality Control*, Tokyo: Asian Productivity Organization, 1976.

7. M. Brassard, *The Memory Jogger Plus+*, GOAL/QPC, 1989.

8. R. Grady, , "Successfully Applying Software Metrics," *IEEE Computer*, September 1994, pp. 18-25.

9. M. Tischler, e-mail message, Aug. 10, 1994.

10. D. Blanchard, "Rework Awareness Seminar: Root-Cause Analysis," March 12, 1992.

Statistically Managing the Software Process

William Florac
Software Engineering Institute[1]

Anita Carleton
Software Engineering Institute

Julie Barnard
United Space Alliance

Abstract

The demand for increased efficiency and effectiveness of our software processes places measurement demands on the software engineering community beyond those traditionally practiced. Statistical and process thinking principles lead to the use of statistical process control methods to determine consistency and capability of the many processes used to develop software. This paper presents several arguments and illustrations suggesting that the software community examine the use of control charts to measure the stability and capability of software processes as a basis for control and process improvement. Finally, the results of a technical collaboration between the Software Engineering Institute and the Space Shuttle Onboard Software Project (collaboration established through Lockheed Martin at the time) are discussed where studies were conducted applying statistical process control analysis to inspection activities.

Introduction

Over the past decade, the concepts, methods, and practices associated with process management and continual improvement have gained increased importance in the software community. These concepts, methods, and practices embody a way of thinking, a way of acting, and a way of understanding the data generated by processes that collectively result in improved quality, increased productivity, and competitive products. The acceptance of this "process thinking" approach has motivated many to start measuring software processes that are responsive to questions relating to process performance. In that vein, traditional software measurement and analysis methods of measuring "planned versus actual" are not sufficient for measuring or predicting process performance. So we believe that the time has come to merge the concepts of "process thinking" with "statistical thinking" when measuring software process behavior.

"Process thinking" stems from W. Edwards Deming's [Deming 86] approach to process management and suggests

- focusing on processes to improve quality and productivity

- focusing on fixing processes, not blaming people

---

[1] The Software Engineering Institute is a federally funded research and development center sponsored by the U.S. Department of Defense.

- using data from the process to guide decisions, and

- recognizing that variation is present in all processes and that it is an opportunity for improvement

"Statistical thinking" [Britz 97] embraces three principles:

- All work occurs in a system of interconnected processes.

- Variation exists in all processes.

- Understanding variation is the basis for management by fact and systematic improvement.

If we examine the basis for these "process thinking" and "statistical thinking" concepts, we find that they are founded on the principles of statistical process control. These principles hold that by establishing and sustaining stable levels of variability, processes will yield predictable results. We can then say that the processes are under statistical control. Controlled processes are stable processes, and stable processes enable one to predict results. This in turn enables one to prepare achievable plans, meet cost estimates and scheduling commitments, and deliver required product functionality and quality with acceptable and reasonable consistency. If a controlled process is not capable of meeting customer requirements or other business objectives, this is known in advance. Then, the process must be improved or retargeted or commitments renegotiated.

Additionally, for organizations engaged in Capability Maturity Model$^{®2}$ (CMM)-Based software process improvement, there are measurement implications for advancing through the CMM levels. The Software Process Maturity Framework described in [Paulk 95] asserts that "Processes are quantitatively understood and stabilized" at Level 4 and that the "Sources of individual problems are understood and eliminated." The Capability Maturity Model Integrated (CMMI) Systems/Software Engineering draft volume [CMMI 99] further elaborates on the goals of Maturity Level 4. Goal 2 is to "Statistically manage the subprocesses." One of the supporting activities suggests identifying the subprocesses based on historical stability and capability data. We need to determine—What do terms like "stability," "capability," and "statistically managing the process"– mean and what are the implications for improvement activities?

What is statistical process control (SPC)? SPC is the use of statistical tools and techniques to analyze a process or its outputs to control, manage, and improve the quality of the output or the capability of the process. What is implied by SPC? Operationally, SPC implies the use of seven basic tools [Ishikawa86]:

1. flow charts

2. scatter diagrams

3. histograms

4. Pareto analysis

5. cause-and-effect (fishbone) diagrams

6. run (trend) charts

7. control charts

Note that two of the seven basic SPC tools – flow charts and cause-and-effect diagrams – are not even quantitative, much less statistical. SPC implies the use of control charts, and the focus of this paper will be on the use of control charts in the software process.

---

2 Capability Maturity Model and the CMM are registered in the U.S. Patent and Trademark Office.

Process Performance

When we relate the notions of process and statistical thinking to the operational process level, we realize that a key concern of process management is that of process performance--how is the process performing now (effectiveness, efficiency), and how can it be expected to perform in the future?

First we should be concerned about process performance in terms of compliance – is the process being executed properly, are the personnel trained, are the right tools available, etc. For if the process is not in compliance, we know that there is little chance of satisfactory performance.

If a process is compliant, the next question is–Is the process performance (execution) reasonably consistent over time? Is the effort, cost, elapsed time, delivery, and quality consumed and produced by executing the process consistent? Realizing that variation exists in all processes, is the variation in process performance predictable?

Finally if the process performance is consistent, we ask the question–Is the process performing satisfactorily? Is it meeting the needs of interdependent processes and/or the needs of the customers? Is it effective and efficient?

Historically, software organizations have addressed the question of compliance by conducting assessments, which compare the organizations' software processes against a standard (e.g., the Capability Maturity Model[3]). Such an assessment provides a picture of the process status at a point in time and indicates the organization's capacity to execute various software processes according to the standard's criteria. However, it does not follow that the process is executed consistently or efficiently merely because the assessment results satisfied all the criteria.

The questions of process consistency, effectiveness, and efficiency require measurement of process behavior as it is being executed over some reasonable time period. Other disciplines have addressed this issue by using statistical process control methods, specifically, using Shewhart control charts. They have come to realize that control charts, or more appropriately process behavior charts, provide the basis for making process decisions and predicting process behavior.

Successful use by other disciplines suggests it is time to examine how statistical process control techniques can help to address our software process issues. In so doing, we find that Shewhart's control charts provide a statistical method for distinguishing between variation caused by normal process operation and variation caused by anomalies in the process. Additionally, Shewhart's control charts provide an operational definition for determining process stability and predictability as well as quantitatively establishing process capability to meet criteria for process effectiveness and efficiency.

Process Performance Variation and Stability

The basis for control charts is recognition of two types of variation – common cause variation and assignable cause variation.

Common cause variation is variation in process performance due to normal or inherent interaction among the process components (people, machines, material, environment, and methods). Common cause variation of process performance is characterized by a stable and consistent pattern over time, as illustrated in Figure 1. Variation in process performance due to common cause is thus random, but will

---

3 Capability Maturity Model is a registered in the U.S. Patent and Trademark Office.

vary within predictable bounds. When a process is stable, the random variations that we see all come from a constant system of chance causes. The variation in process performance is predictable, and unexpected results are extremely rare.

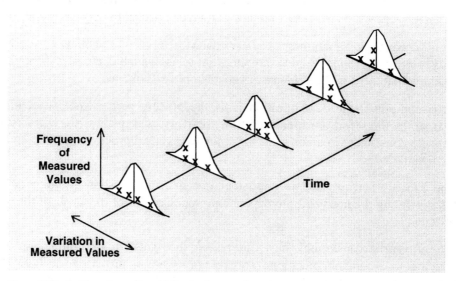

Source: Wheeler, Donald J. & Chambers, David S. *Understanding Statistical Process Control.* Knoxville, Tenn.: SPC Press, 1992.

Figure 1: The Concept of Controlled Variation [Wheeler 92]

The key word in the paragraph above is "predictable." Predictable is synonymous with "in control."

The other type of variation in process performance is due to assignable causes. Assignable cause variation has marked impacts on product characteristics and other measures of process performance.[4] These impacts create significant changes in the patterns of variation. This is illustrated in Figure 2, which we have adapted from Wheeler and Chambers [Wheeler 92]. Assignable cause variations arise from events that are not part of the normal process. They represent sudden or persistent abnormal changes to one or more of the process components. These changes can be in things such as inputs to the process, the environment, the process steps themselves, or the way in which the process steps are executed. Examples of assignable causes of variation include shifts in the quality of raw materials, inadequately trained people, changes to work environments, tool failures, altered methods, failures to follow the process, and so forth.

---

[4]Assignable causes are sometimes called "special causes," a term introduced by W. Edwards Deming.

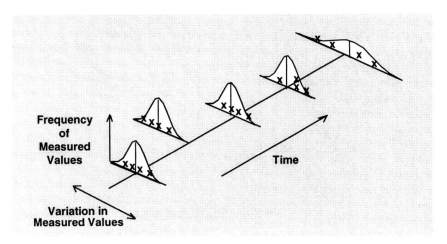

Source: Wheeler, Donald J. & Chambers, David S. *Understanding Statistical Process Control.* Knoxville, Tenn.: SPC Press, 1992.

Figure 2: The Concept of Uncontrolled or Assignable Cause Variation [Wheeler 92]

When all assignable causes have been removed and prevented from recurring in the future so that only a single, constant system of chance causes remains, we have a stable and predictable process.

Stability of a process with respect to any given attribute is determined by measuring the attribute and tracking the results over time. If one or more measurements fall outside the range of chance variation, or if systematic patterns are apparent, the process may not be stable. We must then look for the assignable causes, and remove any that we find, if we want to achieve a stable and predictable state of operation.

When a process is stable, 99+% of process performance variation will fall within 3 sigma of the mean or average of the variation. When the process variation falls outside of the 3-sigma limits, the variation is very likely caused by an anomaly in the process.

When a process is stable, or nearly so, the 3 sigma limits determine the amount of variation that is normal or natural to the process. This is the "voice of the process" or the process telling us what it is capable of doing. This may or may not be satisfactory to the customer; if it is, it is "capable," if it is not, the process must be changed since we know that the remaining variation is due to the process itself.

Using Control Charts

Now let's examine how control charts can be used to investigate process stability and lead to process improvement.

There are a number of different kinds of control charts applicable to software process measurement [Florac 99]. In software environments, measurements often occur only as individual values. For instance, we might report on the number of unresolved problem reports each week. For data as such as these, the individuals and moving range (XmR) charts are used to examine the time-sequenced behavior of process data. For example, Figure 3 shows an XmR control chart for the number of reported but unresolved problems backlogged over the first 30 weeks of system testing. The chart indicates that the problem resolution process is stable, and that it is averaging about 20 backlogged problems (the center line, CL, equals 20.4), with an average change in backlog of 4.35 problems from week to week. The upper control limit (UCL) for backlogged problems is about 32, and the lower control limit (LCL) is about 8. If future backlogs were to exceed these limits or show other forms of nonrandom behavior, it would be likely that the process has become unstable. The causes should then be investigated. If the upper limit is exceeded at any point, this could be a signal that there are problems in the problem-resolution process. Perhaps a particularly thorny defect is consuming resources, causing problems to pile up. If so, corrective action must be taken if the process is to be returned to its original (characteristic) behavior.

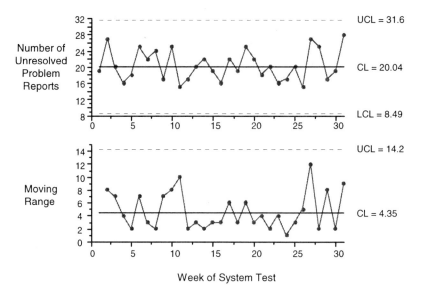

Source: W. Florac and A. Carleton, *Measuring the Software Process: Statistical Process Control for Software Process Improvement*, Addison-Wesley, June 1999.

Figure 3: Control Chart for the Backlog of Unresolved Problems

We must be careful not to misinterpret the limits on the individual observations and moving ranges that are shown in the control chart. These limits are estimates for the limits of the process, based on measurements of the process performance. The process limits together with the center lines represent the "voice of the process."

The performance indicated by the voice of the process is not necessarily the performance that will meet the customer's requirements (the voice of the customer). If the variability and location of the measured results are such that the process, albeit stable, does not meet the customer requirement or specification (e.g., produces too many nonconforming products), the process must be improved. This means reducing the process performance variability, moving the average, or both.

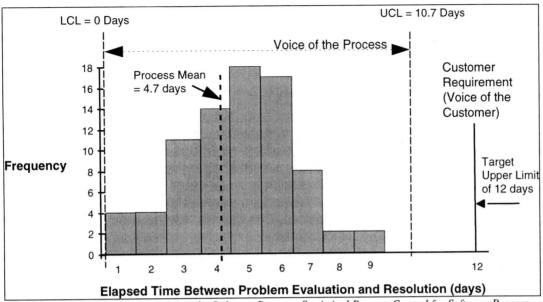

Source: W. Florac and A. Carleton, *Measuring the Software Process: Statistical Process Control for Software Process Improvement*, Addison-Wesley, June 1999.

Figure 4: Frequency Histogram Reflecting Voice of the Process and Voice of the Customer

Process Behavior Measurement and Analysis Factors

Early users of control charts for process analysis and improvement in the software community realize that there are a number of important notions that must be considered to fully appreciate the use of control charts to measure and analyze software processes. For example, the following is a partial list of the factors that come into play when measuring and analyzing process behavior with control charts:

- Selection of appropriate processes

- Identifying and collecting key process attributes for measurement

- The role and use of operational definitions

- Sufficiency of data points (long and short runs)

- Using the correct control charts

- When to recalculate limits

- Aggregation and decomposition of measurement data

- Data homogeneity and rational subgrouping

- Anomalous patterns and assignable causes

- Processes consisting of multiple cause systems

- Taking corrective action to stabilize the process

- Comparison of processes' performance

- Process knowledge and professional judgement

Awareness and attention to these factors and others are critical to successful use of control charts to analyze software processes. Indeed, once the basic control chart structure and calculations are understood, these and other factors become the dominant issues when measuring and analyzing process behavior. Complete discussion of these topics, and others like them, cannot be adequately addressed in a paper of this length, but rather form the core of a number of reference books on statistical process control.[5]

The section that follows illustrates a collaborative activity with the Space Shuttle Onboard Software Project in using statistical process control techniques to further improve inspection process effectiveness. So the reader can obtain a sense of the import of these factors, we have added commentary on the role of several of these measurement and analysis factors.

Collaboration with Onboard Space Shuttle

The Space Shuttle Onboard Software Project consists of six major components that are used to control and support systems, maneuvers, and payloads of the space shuttle vehicle from liftoff to touchdown. Needless to say, software quality is of prime importance. The software is modified to match each space mission as required and is upgraded periodically with new or additional features to meet the expanding function of the space shuttle.

Each of the six major software components has its own development team. Each team is guided by a common system architecture group and a software engineering process group (SEPG). The components are integrated, tested, verified, and released by a separate system evaluation team. Since human life depends on reliable and accurate operation of the shuttle and its components, to say nothing of the tremendous cost of failure, NASA reviews various quality records collected during development and testing to support the Onboard Space Shuttle Software Project's prediction of accuracy and reliability.

The purpose of this part of the joint study was to determine if, by using SPC to analyze selected processes, reliability predictions of the already highly reliable space shuttle software could be reinforced and enhanced earlier in the development cycle. The SEPG team selected the software inspection process as the trial process because it is a well-documented, common process across all six software components, it has been practiced by all personnel since early in the project, and it has proven to be a cost-effective process in terms of producing an exceptionally high quality product. What's more, there already existed a database containing an extensive number of inspection process attribute values covering several years of activity. The existing database allowed the examination of a very large number of inspection-process attributes without having to invoke a data-collection process, and avoided having to wait for weeks or months for access to the data. Thus, the initial task of the joint study team was to review the database contents and select appropriate measures for analysis.

Commentary. This is an example of the process manager or analyst being judicious in selecting processes to measure. The term "software process" refers not just to an organization's overall software process, but to any process or subprocess used by a software project or organization. In fact, a good case

---

[5] See reference list for a short list of such books.

can be made that it is only at subprocess levels that true process management and improvement can take place. Thus, the concept of a software process should be viewed as applying to any identifiable activity that is undertaken to produce or support a software product or service. This includes planning, estimating, designing, coding, testing, inspecting, reviewing, measuring, and controlling, with an emphasis on the subtasks and activities that constitute these undertakings.

Generally this means starting small, selecting key, critical processes. There is evidence that some software organizations quickly grow frustrated with SPC because they start out using it to measure a big process comprising many subprocesses, or even the organization's entire software process. If the process being measured encompasses many other processes, the accumulated variation may appear as common cause variation, and significant signals of process anomalies will not appear. In addition, it may take much longer to collect data to be analyzed if the process cycle is measured in terms of months or years. Selecting a subprocess that is done in every development project with a small number of variables, day in and day out—a test, inspection, or design process—will yield the best results. When it is determined that the process is stable, this is a basis for improving. There is also a basis for measuring a more encompassing process, knowing that its subprocesses are stable.

Selecting Measures

The SEPG team considered consistency of inspection review effort as a key issue of the inspection process. Because the number of inspectors and the size of the inspection package varied with each inspection, it was important to establish whether or not the review effort was consistent from one inspection to the next. Demonstrating that the review effort was consistent (stable) was considered a prerequisite to examining the process performance in terms of escaped errors.

After conferring with the each of the software development teams, the SEPG selected the software inspection process attributes listed in Figure 5 as the initial set of attributes that would usefully quantify the process behavior in terms of review effort. The inspection package material consisted of a requirements description, a listing of modules changed or added, design statements and a source program listing, and the number of modified and new source lines of code (SLOC). The number of new and modified SLOC was chosen to be the key measurement factor to determine the review rate since it highly correlated to the inspection preparation effort.

Release ID
Build ID
Component Name
Date of Inspection
Inspection Type
Number of Inspectors
Inspection Preparation Effort Total
Inspection Package-Modified & New SLOC

Figure 5:   Software Inspection Process Performance Data

The inspection rate for each inspection was expressed as SLOC reviewed per Average Preparation-Hour, where:

- SLOC reviewed = Modified & New SLOC in the Inspection Package

- Average Preparation-Hour per Inspector = Total Inspection Preparation Effort divided by Number of Inspectors.

In effect, this expressed the rate that modified and new SLOC were reviewed by the average inspector.

It became evident, as the study proceeded, that our understanding of what activities constituted an inspection activity, and just what was included in the SLOC count would require clarification. For example, this set of attributes was later amended to include the inspection review time for each inspector for each inspection, so that the stability of each inspector's review effort could be ascertained from inspection to inspection and release to release. Similarly, as the study progressed, the elements that were counted in the SLOC would come under scrutiny and undergo more detailed definition.

Commentary. This demonstrates that the need for operational definitions is fundamental to any measurement activity and is essential when process performance data are analyzed. It is not enough to identify measures. Measures must be defined in such a way as to tell others exactly how each measure is obtained so that they can collect and interpret the values correctly.

The primary issue is not whether a definition for a measure is correct, but that everyone understands, completely, what the measured values represent. Only then can we expect people to collect values consistently and have others interpret and apply the results to reach valid conclusions.

Operational definitions must satisfy two important criteria:

- *Communication. If someone uses the definition as a basis for measuring or describing a measurement result, will others know precisely what has been measured, how it was measured, and what has been included and excluded?*

- *Repeatability. Could others, armed with the definition, repeat the measurements and get essentially the same results?*

These criteria are closely related. In fact, if you can't communicate exactly what was done to collect a set of data, you are in no position to tell someone else how to do it. Far too many organizations propose measurement definitions without first determining what users of the data will need to know about the measured values in order to use them intelligently. In short, when we can communicate clearly what we have measured, we have little trouble creating repeatable rules for collecting future data and have an unambiguous understanding of what the data represents.

Initial Control Chart Plots

The process analyst first grouped the inspection data by release to preserve the homogeneity of the data. This allowed an analysis of process performance consistency of each inspection within a release and allowed comparisons among each of the releases demonstrating stability. The analyst initially used the data from one release to plot the first 30 inspections from all six components, calculating and plotting the SLOC review rate using the XmR control chart seen in Figure 6.

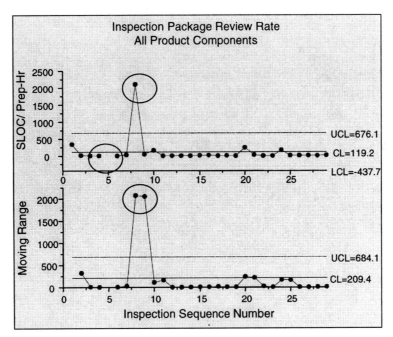

Figure 6: Initial Control Chart of Inspection Package Review Rate (SLOC/Prep-Hr)

Two discrepancies are immediately apparent on the chart. The first is a missing value for inspection number five. The second is the absurdly high value for inspection number eight. Examination of the data revealed that both discrepancies are due to key entry errors by inexperienced personnel, and it was necessary to obtain the correct data from the moderator original records. The long run of data points below the centerline is due to the influence of the erroneous data of inspection eight on the average and does not represent an assignable cause.

Mixtures and Separate Cause Systems

When reviewing the data, the process analyst remembered that the plot included data from all six major components. Since the development and inspection processes for each of the components represents a separate cause system (the set of personnel, skills, resources, products, support systems were not the same across all six components), the process analyst separated the inspection data into six groups—one for each component. The review rate data for each of the components was plotted on a separate chart. The data for component A is plotted in Figure 7.

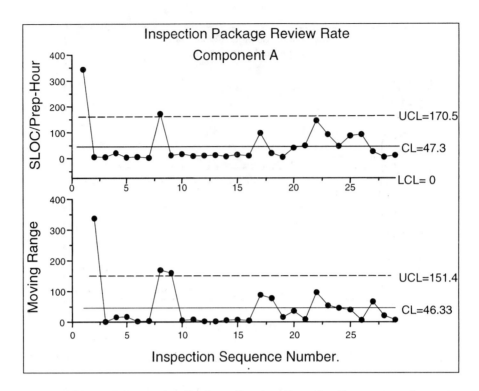

Figure 7:Inspection Package Review Rate for Component A

The control chart in Figure 7 indicates that there are several assignable causes signaled by both the individuals chart and the moving range chart. Closer examination of the inspection data records revealed that the points exceeding the limits were calculated from inspections consisting solely of data lists, tables, and arrays. When questioned about the high review rate indicated by the points beyond the limits, the component A inspectors and developers informed the process analyst that the process for reviewing data lists, tables and the like was not the same as that for inspecting design and program modules due to the use of several verification and validity checking tools.

Since the inspection of data lists, tables, etc. apparently is truly a different process–even though the inspection process description did not recognize this difference–the process analyst removed all the plotted values based on such inspections. The points removed are marked with a "X" in Figure 8. Note that more than just the points beyond the limits have been removed since they too are based on inspection of data lists and tables, even though they appear to be within the control limits. This is consistent with the notion of separation of different cause systems data to simplify and clarify process behavior.

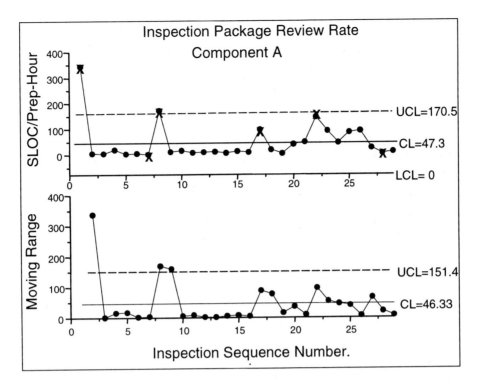

Figure 8:Removal of Values from Separate Cause System

The sequence of points between inspection number nine and inspection number fifteen also indicate a possible assignable cause (eight sequential points on the same side of the centerline). The process analyst decided to defer examining the reason for this until she re-calculated the control chart limits and re-plotted the control chart using the remaining data.

Commentary. Note that in the foregoing activity, the analyst started with data from several releases, decomposed the data to that from one release, decomposed again to that from one component out of six contained in the release, and decomposed again to eliminate data from inspections involving data tables and lists. The rationale for such decomposition is based on the notion of analyzing the variation of a process with a common cause system. A process is defined as "any set of conditions or set of causes that work together to produce a given result."[6] In other words, a process is a system of causes. While not unique to software processes, many defined software processes actually consist of several implicit or "hidden" processes with their own system of causes. When several such processes dominate the overall process, resulting in a mixture of cause systems, control charts will signal their existence by forming anomalous data patterns. The analyst must draw on his or her process knowledge and judgement to identify the nature of the implicit processes, and determine what analysis action is required to isolate cause systems. This requires that the analyst be knowledgeable of the processes' underlying cause systems and aware of changes in the process environment over time.

Finding Trial Limits

The revised control chart, seen in Figure 9, indicates that the inspection process for component A is not stable despite removing erroneous data and eliminating data values pertaining to other cause systems.

---

6 Western Electric Statistical Quality Control Handbook

The process analyst observed that the inspection review rate for the first fifteen inspections was less than 26 SLOC/ Preparation-hour, then jumping to review rates in excess of 26 SLOC/Preparation-hour for the next seven inspections, then returning to a lower rate at the last recorded inspection.

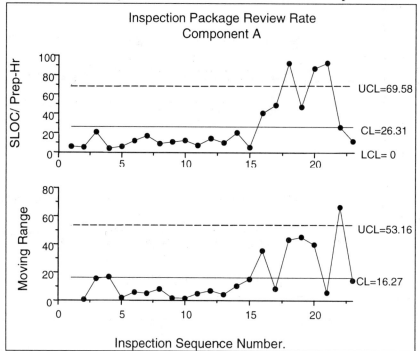

Figure 9:Revised Control Chart for Component A Inspection Review Rate

Noting that this behavior was similar to a mixed pattern or a shift in process pattern, the analyst decided to separate the points into two categories–those with values of less than 26 SLOC/ Preparation-hour and those with values equal to or greater than 26 SLOC/Preparation-hour. She then aligned the inspection package size (modified and new SLOC) with the respective inspection review rates. This is seen in Figure 10.

Review Rate SLOC/PrepHr	Inspection Package SLOC
6.00	6
5.33	4
20.83	15
4.00	4
6.00	3
11.93	24
17.07	14
8.95	17
10.71	15
12.17	20
7.22	7
14.23	51
9.90	17
20.31	22
5.09	14
11.60	58
40.47	86
48.86	86
92.11	75
46.96	90
86.77	188
92.50	185
26.00	130

Figure 10: Inspection Review Rates Compared to Inspection Package Size

The process analyst could see by examining the data that the inspection review rates appeared to significantly increase when the inspection package size was over 60 SLOC. The analyst reasoned if the average preparation time was truly proportional to the size of the inspection package, there would not be changes of this magnitude in the review rate ratio. It appeared to the analyst that something was happening to change the inspection review rate when the inspections package size was larger than 60 SLOC. Discussions with the inspection moderators only verified that the inspection data was accurate and there was nothing unusual about the inspections from their perspective.

Since there didn't appear to be any obvious process non-compliance, the process analyst decided to prepare two control charts showing the inspection review rates—one for inspection packages of less than 60 SLOC and another for inspection packages equal or greater than 60 SLOC. The results are seen in Figures 11 and 12.

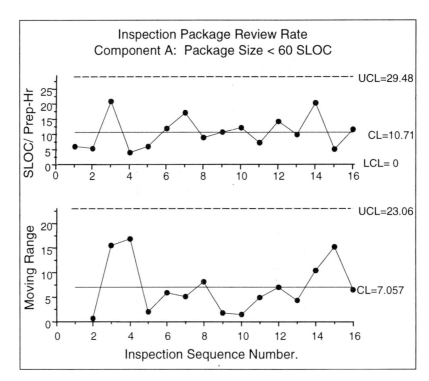

Figure 11: Process Performance for Inspection Packages of < 60 SLOC

Neither control chart shows any assignable causes, but there appears to be two different review rates in operation. The inspection review rate averages about 10.7 SLOC per Preparation-hour when the amount of SLOC to be reviewed is 60 or less, otherwise the review rate jumps to an average of nearly 62 SLOC per Preparation-hour when the number of SLOC in the inspection package is over 60 SLOC. If the next dozen or so inspection review rates followed this same pattern, the process analyst felt that the process behavior charts would be telling her that another "invisible" process was buried in the inspection process, in effect two separate cause systems resulting in a mixed pattern when all the inspection review rates were plotted on the same chart.

Since there were additional inspections to complete for this release, the process analyst decided to plot the future inspection rates on the charts she had just completed, keeping the centerline, upper and lower control limits the same, essentially using them as trial control limits for the inspection process.

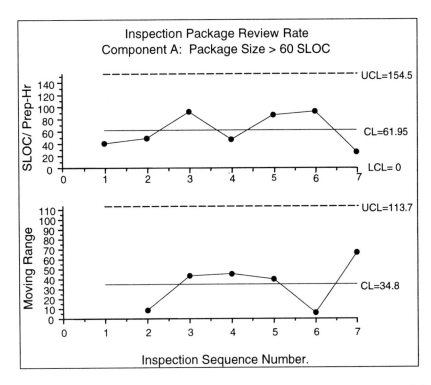

Figure 12: Process Performance for Inspection Packages of > 60 SLOC

Commentary. The data in Figures 11 and 12 illustrate the principle of data homogeneity. When measurement data is collected under essentially the same conditions or from the same system of causes, we obtain homogeneous data. Because of the non-repetitive nature of software product development processes, some believe obtaining homogenous data is not feasible or likely. From the results of the study discussed so far, we can see that homogeneous data emerges when multiple cause systems are separated from the process measurements Whether we are talking about producing widgets or software products, the issue of homogeneity of data is a judgement that must be made by one with extensive knowledge of the process being measured. The unique feature of control charts is their ability to form data into patterns that, when considered statistically, can lead one to information about the process behavior. This includes determining whether or not ones' judgement about homogeneous data sources is correct.

With regard to establishing trial control limits with limited data, it cannot be denied that the control limits computed using limited amounts of data may not represent the process control limits to the same accuracy as if more data were available. However, they do represent the process control limits over the time the process was measured. Several risk possibilities exist. It is possible that the limited data may contain an out-of-control range that will inflate the limits and obscure possible out-of-control values. This cannot be resolved until more data is available. On the other hand, those points that fall outside of the computed limits are more likely to be signals of assignable causes than false alarms. Using the limited data to compute the control limits can alert the analyst to assignable causes in the process. Not using the data to compute the limits results in missing the signal. In this situation, the quality of the limits is not the primary issue. Detection of possible assignable causes, early in the process, is the issue. So if only limited amounts of data are available, calculate the control limits, and when more data becomes available, recalculate the limits.

Testing the Limits

Inspection data collected over the next several weeks was added to the charts. The analyst plotted the inspection rates according to the size of the inspection package, just as she had done previously. An additional twenty-six inspection reports were added, including sixteen with inspection packages of less than 60 SLOC, and ten with inspection packages of 60 or more SLOC.

The control charts with the additional data plotted are shown in Figures 13a and 13b.

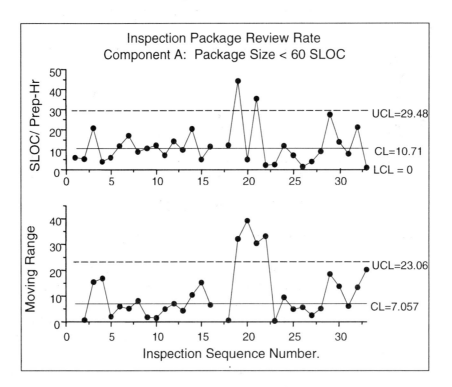

Figure 13a: Control Chart with Additional Observations

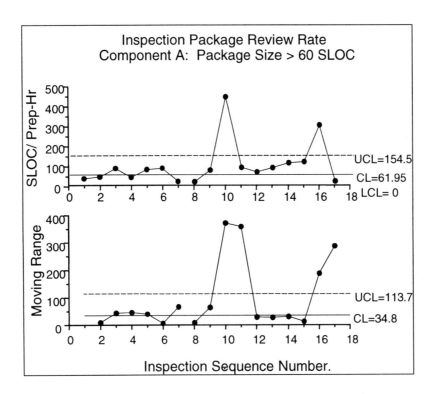

Figure 13b: Control Chart with Additional Observations

Both control charts contain apparent assignable causes. When the process analyst reviewed the inspection measurement data, she did not find any erroneous data, but she did notice that over half of the recent inspections were coded as "re-inspections". When she spoke to the inspection moderators about the significance of this, she learned that sometimes the inspection packages require re-inspection because portions of the design or code did not properly interpret the requirements, or the requirements needed to be re-confirmed because of the design or code complexity. In such cases, the inspection packages were scheduled for re-inspection when the requirements issues were resolved. As a result, the recorded package size (SLOC) did not necessarily represent the size of the material being re-inspected, since the original size was not changed to reflect the size of the material being re-inspected.

Given the information about the re-inspection measurement data, the process analyst decided to remove the re-inspection control chart points since the measurements did not reflect the re-inspection process. (She made a note to see that correct measurements of re-inspection process were instituted.) The points removed from each chart are seen in Figures 14a and 14b.

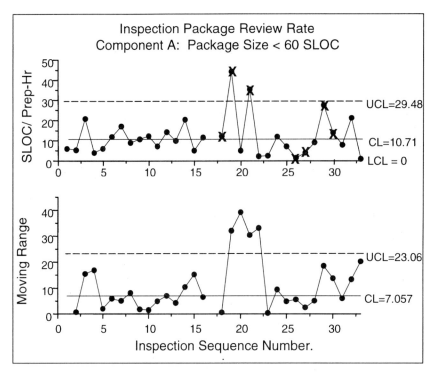

Figure 14a: Process Performance with Re-Inspection Activity Removed

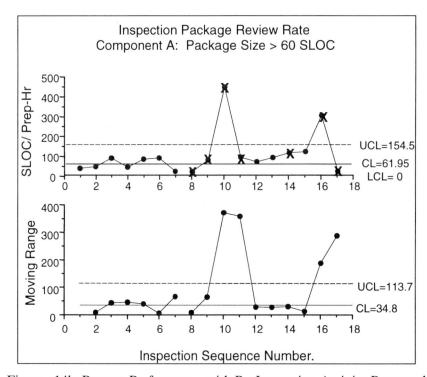

Figure 14b: Process Performance with Re-Inspection Activity Removed

182

Baseline Process Performance

After eliminating the re-inspection data points, the process analyst plotted the remaining data points on the respective charts as shown in Figures 15a and 15b. All the remaining data points fall within the control chart limits and no other anomalous patterns are apparent. The process analyst concluded that while it was premature to consider the processes stable (especially the process for inspection packages over 60 SLOC), the processes did not display any instability either, and therefore she decided to continue using the respective average and limits as the baseline for future analysis of the inspection processes review rate. The process performance would continue to be tracked, the control charts updated with additional process inspection rates, and any assignable causes investigated to determine if changes in the process had taken place.

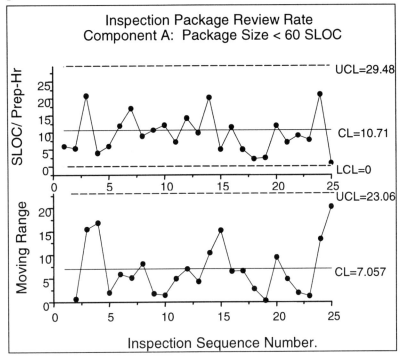

Figure 15a: Process Performance for Inspection Packages < 60 SLOC

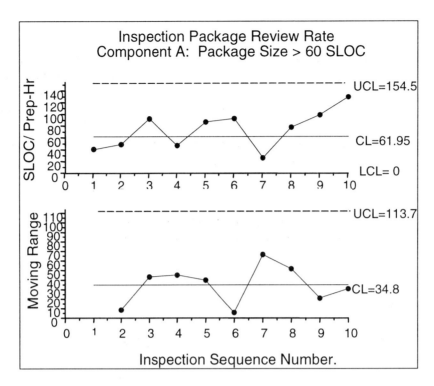

Figure 15b: Process Performance for Inspection Packages > 60 SLOC

Commentary. When first starting to measure a process, there will be a period in which the process behavior signals assignable causes and anomalous patterns. The assignable causes for these signals and patterns must be determined and eliminated. When this is done the control limits are recalculated omitting the assignable cause signals. If the analyst has calculated control limits using limited data, the control limits may be recalculated when additional data become available. When sufficient data has been used to calculate reliable control limits, recalculation with additional data is not necessary unless all of the conditions below are satisfied (Wheeler[7]):

- *The data displays a distinctly different kind of behavior than in the past*

- *The reason for this change in behavior is known*

- *The change in behavior is desirable*

- *It is expected that the new behavior will continue.*

If the first condition is not true, there is no reason for new limits. If any of the remaining conditions are not true, reasons for the assignable cause should be determined.

Wrap Up

At this point, the process analyst reviewed the results of her analysis with the inspection teams, identifying the factors that provided a new and more accurate understanding of the inspection process:

---

[7] *Advanced Topics in Statistical Process Control*, pp 122, Donald J. Wheeler, ©1995, SPC Press ,Inc. Knoxville, Tenn.

1. The existing inspection process contains several undocumented (invisible) subprocesses:

      a. inspection of data modules and tables

      b. re-inspection inspections

      c. design/code inspections

2. The review rate of the design/code inspection process appears to be stable (consistent) when the inspection package is separated into two categories–less than 60 SLOC and greater than or equal to 60 SLOC.

3. Inspection packages of 60 SLOC or more were reviewed on average about 6 times faster than inspection packages with less than 60 SLOC.

The process analyst indicated that she would use the nearly stable inspection review rates as baseline data to investigate the several newly identified issues that could lead to improved process performance. For example, why are the larger packages reviewed so much faster? Is this good or bad? Is there a difference in effectiveness between the inspection package sizes, e.g., does one find more errors or allow fewer escapes? How effective are the data inspections or the re-inspections? Do the other components' inspection processes behave similarly? How do the components compare within a release? How do the components compare from release to release?

In addition, several issues required action:

1. documentation of the processes for re-inspection and data/tables

2. training of key entry personnel, inspectors, and moderators regarding inspection data recording

3. establishment of data collection activity to capture the preparation time of each inspector for each inspection (This is necessary to validate that the assumption the inspection effort is consistent across all inspectors.)

Commentary. Note that no action has been taken to change the process. There remain many related questions to answer and pursue before determining what actions if any are appropriate. At this point, the analyst knows that there are several cause systems at work within the inspection process, all prospective candidates for correction or improvement. Upon reviewing the study results, the software development team responded with enthusiasm and suggestions of other process areas to study for better insight to the process behavior. In the safety critical world of the space shuttle project, gaining control over defect detection and removal processes throughout the life-cycle is critical. Each of the actions discussed earlier was another step towards greater control and predictability in the process.

Some Early Benefits Realized

Many in the software community are now raising questions of the value and benefit of SPC, much the same way that the software community raised issues of return on investment of CMM®-based software process improvement activities. Although many SEPGs are starting to amass this kind of data, we still do not have much of this quantitative return on investment data to report yet. However, we are starting to understand some of the more qualitative aspects of using control charts, or as Don Wheeler characterizes them, "process behavior charts."

Ted Keller [Keller 99], Coordination Manager of the Space Shuttle Onboard Software Project, explained that applying SPC to their software development activities helped them to:

- understand the "reliability" of human processes

- establish bounds on management expectations

- understand patterns and causes of variations, and

- validate measurement analysis used for forecasting and planning

Since software engineering is a human-intensive activity, Keller contends that humans will fail, but the issues are how often and which root causes can be eliminated or minimized. Bounding management expectations entails distinguishing variations due to people problems from variations that are process problems; fixing the wrong problem could be catastrophic. Furthermore, it is critical to recognize what constitutes a genuine signal and cause for reaction in process performance as opposed to what is simply noise in the process execution that should not result in reaction. Understanding patterns and causes of variations enabled the Space Shuttle Onboard Software Project to understand what parameters represented stability and what "stable" meant in this particular environment. And finally, using measurement analysis for forecasting and planning were paramount because repeatability and predictability of processes are key to effective forecasting and planning. In an environment where high safety, reliability, and stringent quality are demanded by the customers and users (NASA's imposed quality requirements are two tenths of an error per KSLOC in delivered product), having access to data and information that could potentially allow decisions about risk and additional corrective actions to be considered even earlier in the lifecycle is essential.

Summary

As organizations seek to improve their software engineering processes, they are turning to quantitative measurement and analysis methods to evaluate how well processes performed in the past and to predict how well they will perform in the future. One approach that is generating great interest is SPC, a discipline that is common in manufacturing and industrial environments, but has only recently received attention as an aid for software engineering.

SPC helps organizations understand processes and then points the way to improving those processes by reducing variation in the process behavior. Reducing process variation leads to high-quality products and services. While SPC includes a collection of tools to help users understand a particular process, chief among them are the Shewhart control charts.

The goal with SPC is to predict process behavior by ensuring that the process is stable, capable, and under control. The control chart is the tool for analyzing the behavior of a process, since it measures process performance over time and provides an operational definition of stability and capability. Applying SPC to software engineering encompasses an understanding of two key concepts:

- **Process stability**: Is the process that we are managing behaving predictably? That is, how do we know whether a process is stable? Examining process performance through the use of process behavior charts will allow us to determine whether a process is stable (within limits) and hence predictable.

- **Process capability**: Is the process capable of delivering products that meet requirements and does the performance of the process meet the business needs of the organization?

Start small and choose key, critical processes. Pick a subprocess that is done in every development with a small number of variables, day in and day out—a test, inspection, or design process. From there, you find important process characteristics to measure and look for consistency in process performance. If you can show that the process is stable, you have a basis for improving.

Effective use of SPC requires detailed understanding of processes and a willingness to pursue exploratory analyses. As with everything else, there is a learning curve. One has to be willing to do research, try things, make mistakes, and learn how to use it. It is not an overnight exercise. Some of the lessons we learned were that:

- Knowledge of the process is fundamental.

- Examining, normalizing, and determining stable process performance variables takes considerable effort.

- Consistency in data collection and reporting is imperative.

- Clarifying and understanding how the data is defined is crucial to knowing what the data represents.

The experimentation and analyses stages are iterative and will require digging deeper and asking related "what if" questions. Examining one chart may lead to asking more questions and decomposing the process further and instigate constructing more charts that result in more questions, etc.

Software organizations are beginning to appreciate the value that control charts add when they are used to provide engineers and managers with quantitative insights into the behavior of their software development processes. In many ways the control chart is a form of instrumentation–like an oscilloscope, or a temperature probe, or a pressure gauge–it provides data to guide decisions and judgements by process-knowledgeable software engineers and managers.

References

Britz 97   Britz, Galen, Emerling, Don, Hare, Lynne, Hoeri, Roger, Shade, Janice, "How to Teach Others to Apply Statistical Thinking." Quality Progress (June 1997): 67-78.

CMMI 99   Capability Maturity Model®-Integrated Systems/Software EngineeringStaged Representation – Volume II, Version 0.2b, (Public Release DRAFT), September 1999.

Deming 86   Deming, W. Edwards, *Out of the Crisis*, MIT Center for Advanced Engineering Study, Cambridge, MA, 1986.

Florac 99   Florac, William A. and Carleton, Anita D., *Measuring the Software Process: Statistical Process Control for Software Process Improvement*, ISBN:0-201-60444-2, Addison-Wesley, Reading, MA, 1999.

Grady 92   Grady, Robert B., *Practical Software Measurement for Project Management and Process Improvement*, ISBN: 0137203845, Prentice Hall, Englewood Cliffs, NJ, May 1992.

Humphrey 89   Humphrey, Watts S., *Managing the Software Process*, ISBN 0-201-18095-2, Addison-Wesley, Reading, MA, 1989.

Ishikawa 86   Ishikawa, Kaoru. Guide to Quality Control, 2d rev. ed. White Plains, N.Y.:UNIPUB— Kraus International Publishers, 1986.

Keller 99   Keller, Ted, "Applying SPC Techniques to Software Development—A Management Approach," 1999 SEPG Conference.

Paulk 95   Paulk, Mark C., Weber, Charles V., Curtis, Bill, Chrissis, Mary Beth, et. al., *The Capability Maturity Model: Guidelines for Improving the Software Process*, ISBN 0-201-54664-7, Addison-Wesley, Reading, MA, 1995.

Paulk 99   Paulk, Mark C., "Practices of High Maturity Organizations", Proceedings of the 1999 Software Engineering Process Group Conference, Atlanta, Georgia, March 1999.

Western 58   Western Electric Co., Inc. *Statistical Quality Control Handbook.* Indianapolis: AT&T Technologies, 1958.

Wheeler 92   Wheeler, Donald J. & Chambers, David S. *Understanding Statistical Process Control*, Knoxville, Tenn.: SPC Press, 1992.

Wheeler 98   Wheeler, Donald J. and Poling, Sheila R., Building Continual Improvement: A Guide for Business, SPC Press, Knoxville, TN, 1998.

Chapter 5

Developments Following from the SW-CMM

Introduction to Chapter

The Capability Maturity Model for Software, or the SW-CMM, led naturally to the development of other maturity models for aspects of software and systems development and for acquisition. We have already looked at BOOTSTRAP and TRILLIUM, which were clearly inspired by the SW-CMM. In this chapter we introduce maturity models that are closely related to the SW-CMM in that they were either developed by Watts Humphrey or developed at the SEI.

Watts Humphrey's major contributions since his development of the SW-CMM at the SEI have been to introduce

- the personal software process (PSP);
- the team software process (TSP).

The PSP is described in Watts Humphrey's book *A Discipline for Software Engineering* [2]. The purpose of the PSP is to improve the effectiveness of software engineers by encouraging them to plan, track, and measure their personal performance as part of the software process.

W. Humphrey, Managing the Software Process, chapter 1, © 1989 Addison Wesley Longman Inc., Reprinted by permission of Addison Wesley Longman.

The approach taken by the PSP is to:

- identify those large-system software methods and practices that can be used by individuals;

- define the subset of these methods and practices that can be applied while developing small programs;

- structure these methods and practices so that they can be gradually introduced;

- provide exercises suitable for practising these methods in an educational setting.

The book goes on to show in detail how this approach can lead to stage by stage improvement of the personal software process. PSP thus provides a type of training (or coaching) that improves the capability of the individual to produce software.

Humphrey's related model, the TSP, focuses on the development of software by teams of people. Again the coaching analogy is relevant, as skill-building, team-building and teamwork are all emphasized. According to Webb and Humphrey's "Using the TSP on the TaskView Project,"[4] teams begin by learning the PSP, after which there is a project launch workshop where team members

- develop team working practices,

- establish goals,

- select roles,

- define processes,

- make plans.

The TSP provides the environment and training to allow team members to work effectively together rather than as an unfocused group of individuals. The TSP is described more fully in Humphrey's "Introduction to the Team Software Process." [3].

A number of maturity models have been developed at the SEI for activities more or less closely associated with software engineering. To avoid confusion, the original CMM is now known as the CMM for Software, or more briefly as the SW-CMM.

Other CMMs developed include:

- SE-CMM (System Engineering CMM)

- IPD–CMM (Integrated Product Development CMM)

- P–CMM (People CMM)

- SA-CMM (Software Acquisition CMM)

While the SEI had plans to produce an updated version of the SW-CMM, to be known as version 2.0 and followed a little later by version 2.1, these plans were abandoned in 1998 in favor of a project known as CMM-Integration (CMMI). The CMMI project is intended to produce a new CMM based on the integration of the SW-CMM, the IPD-CMM and the SE-CMM. The new project is a collaborative effort sponsored by the U.S. Office of the Secretary of Defense/Acquisition and Technology (OSD/A&T) and involving government and industry as well as the SEI.

The project's objective is to develop a product suite that provides industry and government with a set of integrated products to support process and product improvement.

Description of Articles

There are four papers in this chapter, one each about the Personal Software Process and the Team Software Process, and two about CMMs, in particular about the SA-CMM and CMMI.

The first paper is by Watts Humphrey and was one of three papers that appeared in Cross Talk during 1998. The original title was "Three Dimensions of Process Improvement, Part II: The Personal Process," but has been re-titled here simply "The Personal Software Process."

According to Humphrey, the PSP provides the "how" to the SW-CMM's "what" He explains how he improved his own software process in terms of productivity, quality of work and ability to plan; and how from this experience he devised a program that engineers could use to improve their personal processes. In his paper he shows by means of graphs just how effective the process can be.

He identifies three requirements for the effective introduction of PSP:

- training must be by a qualified PSP instructor;
- training must be focused on groups or teams, rather than on individuals;
- strong management support is essential.

The second paper in this chapter is by David Webb and Watts Humphrey, and is entitled "Using the TSP on the TaskView Project." It describes how the TSP was used in connection with a software intensive system project at the Hill Air Base in Utah.

Overall, use of the TSP was found to:

- be popular with engineers,
- improve team spirit,
- be cost effective,
- improve relationships between management and engineers.

Both of the authors acted as leaders and coaches of TaskView teams, which they found to be a rewarding and enlightening experience.

The third paper in this chapter is by Peter Kind of SARCOS and Jack Ferguson of the SEI, and is entitled "The Software Acquisition Maturity Model^{SM}." It describes how a team representing the Department of Defense, various federal agencies, the SEI, and industry developed the SA-CMM.

The SA-CMM can be used both for off-the-shelf acquisition of software as well as for purpose-built software systems. It is also intended for use in connection with the development of both small and large software systems by both small and large organizations.

The SA-CMM is concerned with the buyer's or acquirer's role in the acquisition of software intensive systems. It supports goal setting for senior management involved in acquisition as well as prediction of potential performance. The SA-CMM has five maturity levels corresponding to the five levels of the SW-CMM. This is appropriate since the software developer from whom the system is acquired is likely to be using the SW-CMM. However, the SA-CMM corresponds to the acquirer's view of the development while the SW-CMM corresponds to the developer's view. To an extent, the SA-CMM processes correspond to the CUS process category of the SPICE model.

The fourth paper is by Mike Konrad and Sandy Shrum of the SEI and is entitled "CMM® Integration^{SM} – Enterprise-Wide Process Improvement Using the Next Generation of CMMs®." It describes the stage at which the CMMI project had reached at the time the paper was written. In August 2000 the first integrated model had just been released, and details were available via the CMMI website [1].

The first product was the CMMI-SE/SW, an integrated maturity model for systems and software engineering. The authors present an overview of the model, as well as an outline of future plans for CMM integration. The model has both staged and continuous representations and the differences and relative merits of these two representations are discussed. A feature of this model not present in the SW-CMM is process areas, which are divided into four types:

- process management;
- project management;
- engineering;
- support.

Each type (apart from engineering processes) is further subdivided into both basic and advanced process areas, and the authors show how the processes interact with one another.

References

[1] http://www.sei.cmu.edu/cmmi/

[2] W. S. Humphrey; *A Discipline for Software Engineering*, Addison Wesley, 1995.

[3] W. S. Humphrey; *Introduction to the Team Software Process*, Addison Wesley, 1999.

[4] D. Webb and W.S. Humphrey; "Using the TSP on the TaskView Project" *Cross Talk*, February 1999.

The Personal Software Process

Watts S. Humphrey
Software Engineering Institute

Part I of this article (Crosstalk, February 1998) described the Capability Maturity Model®, why it was developed, and how it can help organizations improve their performance. Part II addresses the Personal Software Process (PSP)^{SM}, which shows engineers how to perform their tasks in an effective and professional way. In the final analysis, to have high-performance software organizations, you must have high-performance software engineers working on high-performance software teams. The objective of the PSP is to show software engineers how to use process principles in their work. Part III of this article (April 1998 issue of Crosstalk) describes the Team Software Process, which shows integrated product teams how to consistently produce quality products under aggressive schedules and for their planned costs.

Moving from "What" to "How"

Although the Capability Maturity Model (CMM) provides a powerful improvement framework, its focus is necessarily on "what" organizations should do and not "how" they should do it. This is a direct result of the CMM's original motivation to support the Department of Defense acquisition community. We knew management should set goals for their software work but we also knew that there were many ways to accomplish these goals. Above all, we knew no one was smart enough to define how to manage all software organizations. We thus kept the CMM focus on goals, with only generalized examples of the practices the goals implied.

As organizations used the CMM, many had trouble applying the CMM principles. In small groups, for example, it is not generally possible to have dedicated process specialists, so every engineer must participate at least part time in process improvement. We kept describing to engineers *what* they ought to do and they kept asking us *how* to do it. Not only did this imply a need for much greater process detail, it also required that we deal more explicitly with the real practices of development engineers. We needed to show them precisely how to apply the CMM process principles.

Because software development is a rich and sophisticated process, we realized a single set of cookbook methods would not be adequate. We thus chose to deal with fundamental process principles and to show engineers how to define, measure, and improve their personal work. The key is to recognize that all engineers are different and that each must know how to tune their practices to produce the most personal benefit.

Changing Engineers' Practices

Improvement requires change, and changing the behavior of software engineers is a nontrivial problem. The reasons for this explain why process improvement is difficult and illustrate the logic for the PSP.

The problems related to improving the personal practices of software engineers have long interested me, so after I had been at the Software Engineering Institute (SEI) for several years, I looked for someone else to lead the CMM work so I could address this issue. I decided to first demonstrate how process improvement principles could be applied to the work of individual engineers. Over the next several years, I wrote 62 small to moderate-sized programs as I developed as close to a Level 5 personal process as I could devise.

The results were amazing. I became more productive, the quality of my work improved sharply, and I could make accurate personal plans. The next step was to demonstrate the effectiveness of these methods for others. I first tried meeting with engineering groups to describe what I had done and to get them to try it. Despite management support, this was a dismal failure. One laboratory manager even told his people that it was more important for them to use these methods than to meet their project schedules. The engineers all said they would do so, but none of them did. The question was why not?

A Question of Conviction

Software engineers develop their personal practices when they first learn to write programs. Since they are given little or no professional guidance on how to do the work, most engineers start off with exceedingly poor personal practices. As they gain experience, some engineers may change and improve their practices, but many do not. In general, however, the highly varied ways in which individual software engineers work are rarely based on a sound analysis of available methods and practices.

Engineers are understandably skeptical about changes to their work habits; although they may be willing to make a few minor changes, they will generally stick fairly closely to what has worked for them in the past until they are convinced a new method will be more effective. This, however, is a chicken-and-egg problem: engineers only believe new methods work after they use them and see the results, but they will not use the methods until they believe they work.

The Personal Software Process

Given all this, how could we possibly convince engineers that a new method would work for them? The only way we could think of to change this behavior was with a major intervention. We had to directly expose the engineers to the new way of working. We thus decided to remove them from their day-to-day environment and put them through a rigorous training course. As shown in Figure 1, the engineers follow prescribed methods, represented as levels PSP0 through PSP3, and write a defined set of 10 programming exercises and five reports [1]. With each exercise, they are gradually introduced to various advanced software engineering methods. By measuring their own performance, the engineers can see the effect of these methods on their work.

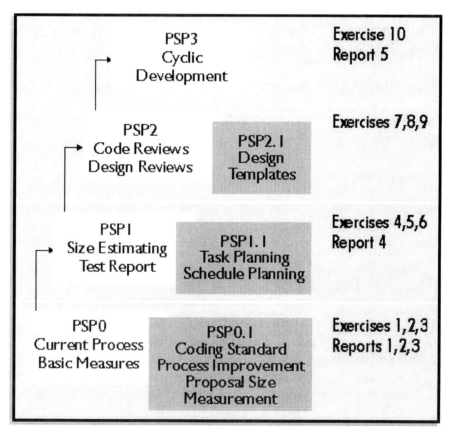

Figure 1. *The PSP process evolution.*

Figures 2 through 5 show some of the benefits engineers experience [2, 3]. Figure 2 shows the average reduction in size-estimating error for nearly 300 engineers who took the PSP course and provided data to the SEI. Their size-estimating error at the beginning of the course is indicated at the left of the chart, and their error at the end of the course is shown at the right. This shows that size-estimating errors averaged 63 percent with PSP0 (the first three programs) and 40 percent for PSP2 and PSP3 (Programs 7, 8, 9, and 10). Note that the PSP introduces a disciplined estimating method (Proxy-Based Estimating) with PSP1 (Program 4) [1].

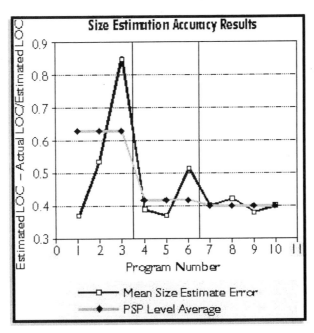

Figure 2. *Size estimation results.*

Similarly, for time estimating, Figure 3 shows an improvement from a 55 percent error to a 27 percent error or a factor of about two. As shown in Figure 4, the improvement in compile and test defects is most dramatic. From PSP0 to PSP3, the engineers' compile and test defects dropped from 110 defects per 1,000 lines of code (KLOC) to 20 defects per KLOC, or over five times. Figure 5 shows that even with their greatly improved planning and quality performance, the engineers' lines of code productivity was more or less constant.

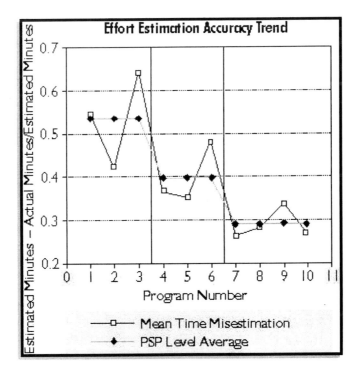

Figure 3. *Effort estimation results.*

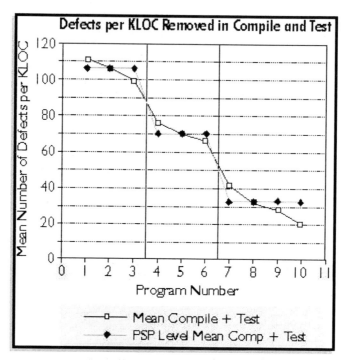

Figure 4. *Quality results.*

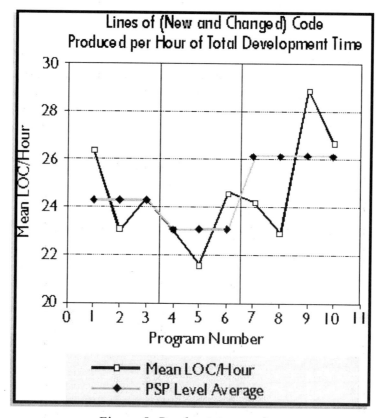

Figure 5. *Productivity results.*

Perhaps the most impressive PSP change is in the way the engineers spend their time. With Program 1, as shown in Figure 6, this group of nearly 300 engineers spent on average less time designing their programs than they did on any other task. They even spent more time compiling than designing. At the end of the course, they spent more time designing than in any other technical activity. We have been trying to get software engineers to do this for years. Until they can experience the benefits of more thorough designs, they will likely continue to concentrate on coding, compiling, and testing.

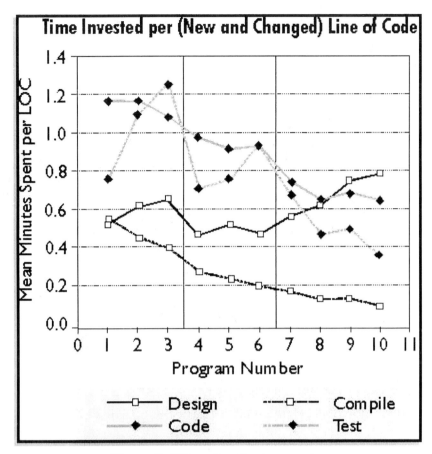

Figure 6. *Effort distribution results.*

Industrial Results with the PSP

A growing number of organizations are using the PSP, such as Baan, Boeing, Motorola, and Teradyne. Data from some early users clearly demonstrate the benefits of PSP training [4]. Figure 7 shows data from a team at Advanced Information Services (AIS) in Peoria, Ill. They were PSP trained in the middle of their project. The three bars on the left of the chart show the engineers' time estimates for the weeks it would take them to develop the first three components. For Component 1, for example, the original estimate was four weeks, but the job took 20 weeks. Their average estimating error was 394 percent. After PSP training, these same engineers completed the remaining six components. As shown on the right, their average estimating error was -10.6 percent. The original estimate for Component 8, for example, was 14 weeks and the work was completed in 14 weeks.

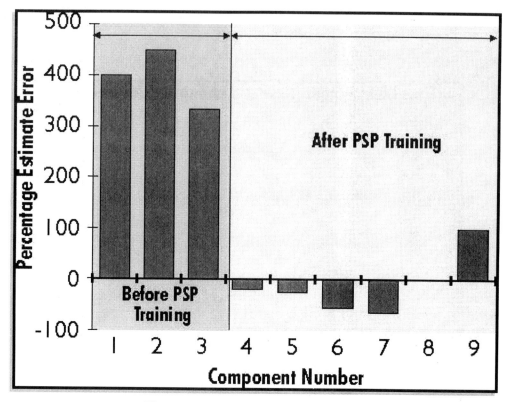

Figure 7. *Schedule estimating error.*

Table 1 shows acceptance test data on products from one group of AIS engineers. Before PSP training, they had a substantial number of acceptance test defects and their products were uniformly late. After PSP training, the next product was nearly on schedule, and it had only one acceptance test defect. Table 2 shows the savings in system testing time for nine PSP projects. At the top of the chart, system test time is shown for several products that were completed before PSP training. At the bottom, system test time is shown for products the same AIS engineers completed after PSP training. Note that A1 and A2 are two parts of the same product, so testing for them was done together in one and one-half months.

Not Using PSP	KLOC	Months Late	Acceptance Test Defects
1	24.6	9	N/A
2	20.8	4	168
3	19.9	3	21
4	13.4	8+	53
5	4.5	8+	25
Using PSP			
1	22.9	1	1

Table 1. *Acceptance test improvement.*

System test time before PSP training		
Project	Size	Test Time
A1	15,800 LOC	1.5 months
C	19 requirements	3 test cycles
D	30 requirements	2 months
H	30 requirements	2 months

System test time after PSP training		
Project	Size	Test Time
A2	11,700 LOC	1.5 months
B	24 requirements	5 days
E	2,300 LOC	2 days
F	1,400 LOC	4 days
G	6,200 LOC	4 days
I	13,300 LOC	2 days

Table 2. *System test time savings.*

Introducing the PSP

Although the PSP can be introduced quickly, it must also be done properly. First, the engineers need to be trained by a qualified PSP instructor. The SEI trains and authorizes PSP instructors and provides limited on-site PSP training. There is also a growing number of SEI-trained PSP instructors who offer commercial PSP training (see http://www.sei.cmu.edu).

The second important step in PSP introduction is to train in groups or teams. When organizations ask for volunteers for PSP training, they get a sparse sprinkling of PSP skills that will generally have no impact on the performance of any project.

Third, effective PSP introduction requires strong management support. This, in turn, requires that management understand the PSP, know how to support their workers once they are trained, and regularly monitor their performance. Without proper management attention, many engineers gradually slip back into their old habits. The problem is that software engineers, like most professionals, find it difficult to consistently do disciplined work when nobody notices or cares. Software engineers need regular coaching and support to sustain high levels of personal performance.

The final issue is that even when a team of engineers are all PSP trained and properly supported, they still have to figure out how to combine their personal processes into an overall team process. We have found this to be a problem even at higher CMM levels. These are the reasons we are developing the Team Software Process (TSP).

Part III of this article, which describes what the TSP is and how it helps teams to work more effectively, will appear in the April 1998 issue of *Crosstalk*. Although the TSP is still in development, early industrial experience demonstrates that it can substantially improve the performance of integrated product teams.

**About the Author: Watts S. Humphrey** is a fellow at the SEI of Carnegie Mellon University, which he joined in 1986. At the SEI, he established the Process Program, led initial development of the CMM, introduced the concepts of Software Process Assessment and Software Capability Evaluation, and most recently, the PSP and TSP. Prior to joining the SEI, he spent 27 years with IBM in various technical executive positions, including management of all IBM commercial software development and director of programming quality and process. He has master's degrees in physics from the Illinois Institute of Technology and in business administration from the University of Chicago.

Software Engineering Institute
Carnegie Mellon University
Pittsburgh, PA 15213
Voice: 412-268-6379
E-mail: watts@sei.cmu.edu

References

1. Humphrey, W.S., *A Discipline for Software Engineering*. Addison-Wesley, Reading, Mass., 1995.
2. Hayes, Will, "The Personal Software Process: An Empirical Study of the Impact of PSP on Individual Engineers," CMU/SEI-97-TR-001.
3. Humphrey, W.S., "Using a Defined and Measured Personal Software Process," *IEEE Software*, May 1996.
4. Ferguson, Pat, Watts S. Humphrey, Soheil Khajenoori, Susan Macke, and Annette Matvya, "Introducing the Personal Software Process: Three Industry Case Studies," *IEEE Computer*, Vol. 30, No. 5, May 1997, pp. 24-31.

The SEI's work is supported by the Department of Defense. Capability Maturity Model and CMM are registered with the U.S. Patent and Trademark Office. Personal Software Process, PSP, Team Software Process, and TSP are service marks of Carnegie Mellon University.

Using the TSP on the TaskView Project

David Webb, *Ogden Air Logistics Center, Software Engineering Division*
Watts S. Humphrey, *Software Engineering Institute*

This article reports the first results of using the Team Software Process (TSP)^{TM} on a software-intensive system project. The TSP was developed by the Software Engineering Institute (SEI) to guide integrated teams in producing quality systems on their planned schedules and for their committed costs. The TaskView team at Hill Air Force Base, Utah used the TSP to deliver the product a month ahead of its originally committed date for nearly the planned costs. Because the engineers' productivity was 123 percent higher than on their prior project, they included substantially more function than originally committed. Testing was completed in one-eighth the normal time, and as of this writing, the customer has reported no acceptance test defects.

THIS ARTICLE DESCRIBES the experiences of a team that used the TSP to produce a software-intensive product for the U.S. Air Force. The Ogden Air Logistics Center, Software Engineering Division, Hill Air Force Base, Utah, has a long history of producing avionics and support software for the Air Force. The division had previously been assessed at a Capability Maturity Model (CMM)® Level 3 and has just recently been assessed at CMM Level 5. TaskView, one of the products they delivered, is a system to help Air Force pilots produce flight plans. Flight planning is labor-intensive and time-consuming; TaskView automates much of this work. It helps mission planners produce accurate flight plans with less labor and in less time than previously possible. The project was completed ahead of its original schedule and within its committed budget. The product is currently in customer acceptance testing with no defects reported to date. This article is the first published report of project results with the TSP.

Following a brief TSP overview, we describe the software organization, the TaskView project, and the team's experiences in introducing and using the TSP. Next, we cover the engineers' reactions to using this process. We conclude with a brief summary of the key findings from the TaskView experience. The

division already had a high-maturity software process, so it had data available from prior work. We can thus compare the performance of the TSP team to previous projects. Although this article presents some of the data, we only show a few of the indicators that are potentially available for TSP projects.

The TSP

Although the concepts and methods for running integrated teams are well known, the specific steps often are not obvious to working engineers and managers. For example, to be effective, teams need precise goals, clearly stated roles, a defined engineering process, and a detailed plan for the work. They need a framework for periodic coordination and structured methods to review and track project risks and issues. Team measures must be defined and recorded, tracking mechanisms developed, and a reporting system established.

Although none of these items is particularly complex or difficult, the specific actions often are not obvious.

Before engineers can work effectively in an integrated team environment, they need to know precisely what to do. If they have not done such work before or do not have a detailed process to guide them, they will generally defer the new or unfamiliar items until they know how to handle them. They then do the tasks they fully understand. As a result, many of the actions required for effective teaming do not get done. Teams can waste a great deal of time trying to establish goals, resolving their working relationships, and figuring out how to do the work.

How the TSP Works

The TSP defines the steps required to build and run software-intensive integrated product development (IPD) teams [1]. First, the engineers are trained precisely how to do quality work, use a defined process, and make and use process measurements. For engineers to use these methods on the job, they must have hands-on training, explanation of the methods, and experience using them

The SEI's work is supported by the Department of Defense.

Figure 1. *How PSP and TSP provide IPD capabilities.*

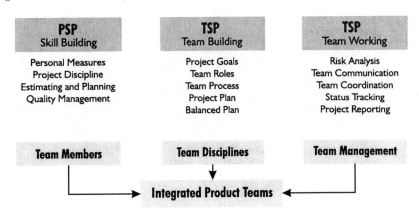

on realistic project-like exercises. This training is provided by an intensive 120-hour course that teaches the Personal Software Process (PSP)[SM] [2,3,4,5]. Figure 1 shows how the PSP training and the TSP process provide the capabilities for integrated teamwork.

After acquiring basic process, planning, and quality management skills, engineers have the prerequisites to use the TSP. Every project then starts with a three-day TSP launch workshop, where engineers develop teamworking practices, establish goals, select roles, define processes, and make plans. A shorter two-day relaunch workshop is then repeated at the start of every major project phase. Because team members work directly on their project during the launch, these three days are part of the job and are not a training exercise.

Finally, the TSP provides the mechanisms to maintain an effective teamworking environment. This is done with structured weekly team meetings and periodic relaunch workshops. The team meeting is much like the football huddle: all members participate, and they focus on precisely what to do next. If the plan is working, they follow it. If it is not, they may decide to change it. The team meeting not only maintains effective team communication but also facilitates precise status tracking, provides a context for team decision making, and supports continuous risk tracking and project reporting. As in football, periodic "huddles" are important; if teams did not huddle, they would do a lot of running around but not win many games.

Figure 2. *The TSP launch process.*

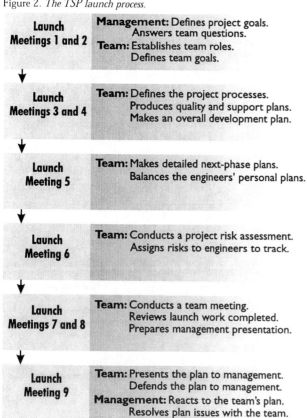

The team relaunch is conducted at every principal project milestone. It serves to help the team evaluate and rebalance the project plan, reassess project risks, integrate new team members, reassign team roles, and re-emphasize the team's goals and charter. At the conclusion of each launch or relaunch, the team reviews its status, plans with management, and resolves any issues and problems.

What the TSP Provides

The TSP process provides a set of forms, scripts, and standards that lead the team through the process steps. Once they are PSP trained, engineers know how to develop and follow a defined process, and they understand how to use the process measures to consistently produce quality products. The PSP can be viewed as a language of process. Until engineers are reasonably fluent in this language, they generally are not able to follow the process and use its measures. PSP training provides the engineers the process fluency they need to use the TSP.

The TSP process also provides the guidance engineers need to work effectively in a team context. As shown in Figure 2, this is done during the three-day team launch. By following the launch process, the team members can quickly determine their own and everyone else's responsibilities, and they can readily track and coordinate their work with their teammates and other teams.

Because the TSP produces a large volume of data, managing and tracking the data can become a burden. The SEI has developed a support tool that helps engineers record and track TSP data. The initial tool support is in Microsoft Excel for Windows 95 and Windows NT. The TSP teams that have used this tool report that it substantially simplifies their data-gathering and reporting tasks. An enhanced tool is under development.

Engineering Support

During the launch and relaunch workshops, the team works as a unit to develop their process, quality, support, and project plans. These detailed plans identify and schedule the work for the next phase to the level of 10 task hours or fewer. Thus, the team members and their management know what tasks are to be done and when they are to be completed. In one example, Dave Webb, the TaskView team leader, needed to temporarily assign one engineer to help another project with a critical problem. By reviewing the detailed task schedule with the engineer, he precisely determined the impact of this reassignment and made workload adjustments to ensure that the project schedule was not affected.

The team as a unit also performs continuous risk management. In the launch and periodic relaunches, members do a complete project risk assessment. All risks are rated for likelihood and impact, and the more important risks are assigned to individual members for tracking. The assigned team members then develop mitigation plans for the immediate priority risks and monitor and report risk status in the weekly team meetings.

Figure 3. *TaskView converts complex ASCII text to tree structures to map routes.*

The TSP process helps working groups develop into cohesive and effective engineering teams. With defined and agreed-to goals and a process and plan to meet these goals, team members are more likely to submerge their personal problems and strive for the common objective. Efficiency is enhanced by the defined process, and communication is maintained by the weekly meetings of all team members. These meetings take less than one hour for teams of about 10 members. Team members review their role activities, planned vs. actual tasks completed, and risk status. Each member reports personal earned-value status, any needed team or management actions, and personal plans for the next period. These weekly meetings permit the team as a whole to periodically rebalance the workload, resolve issues, and make decisions.

TSP Status

The TSP process is being developed by the SEI, and it is currently under test by approximately 10 engineering groups and several dozen teams. Based on the experience to date, four TSP versions have been produced. The TSP has been used with teams as small as two engineers and with groups as large as 17. Some teams have been composed of software professionals, and others have also had hardware, systems, test, or other engineering participants. The project categories include maintenance, new product development, and product enhancement. System types have ranged from components of large commercial data-processing systems to embedded real-time controllers. TSP projects have covered proprietary product development, industrial software contracts, and military development and enhancement work.

Hill Air Force Base

The TaskView project was conducted by the Ogden Air Logistics Center, Technology and Industrial Support Directorate (TI), Software Engineering Division (TIS) at Hill Air Force Base, Utah. The TIS vision statement declares that they will provide "exceptional weapon system software and related hardware solutions and technology adoption expertise to enhance our nation's defense."

TIS is a high-maturity organization with a strong history of software process improvement. In March 1995, TIS was assessed as a CMM Level 3 organization, and the assessment conducted in July 1998 rated them at CMM Level 5. This is the first software organization in the Department of Defense (DoD) to receive this rating, and it is one of the few Level 5 software groups in the world.

The software products produced by TIS include operational flight programs for the F-16 Fighting Falcon aircraft, test program sets for F-16 automated test equipment, mission-planning software for a variety of aircraft, and avionics test-station software. TIS is also the home of the Software Technology Support Center (STSC), which provides technology adoption expertise to the DoD, sponsors the annual Software Technology Conference, and publishes *CROSSTALK*.

During the summer of 1996, TIS introduced the PSP to a small group of software engineers. Although the training was generally well received, use of the PSP in TIS started to decline as soon as the classes were completed. Soon, none of the engineers who had been instructed in PSP techniques was using them on the job. When asked why, the reason was almost unanimous: "PSP is extremely rigorous, and if no one is asking for my data, it's easier to do it the old way."

Although the TIS Software Engineering Process Group (SEPG) believes that PSP training accelerated CMM improvement work, members were concerned that the PSP methods were not being used. They therefore asked the SEI how to get engineers to consistently use PSP practices on the job. Because the TSP was then being designed to address this exact problem, the SEI suggested that TIS become involved in TSP pilot testing. TIS decided to do so, and this project is the result.

The TaskView Project

TIS chose the TaskView project as the TSP pilot. TaskView is a UNIX-based tool that parses an Air Tasking Order (ATO), which is a set of battle instructions for all aircraft involved in a strike, including fighters, bombers, and refuelers. As shown in Figure 3, it describes the flight plans, aircraft armament, and specific mission roles and tasks. Once the battle has been planned, a complex set of computer programs generates an ASCII text file that contains the ATO information. This ATO is then delivered electronically to each of the units participating in the strike.

Currently, the ATO is "broken out" manually— interpreted, sorted, and restructured—by the participating groups, who use hard copies and highlighters to mark their specific instructions. This is a laborious process that can take several hours. Once the information has been identified, the data must then be manually entered into mission-planning software tools for each unit, which provides ample opportunity for further mistakes. The TaskView tool parses the ATO and automatically "breaks out" (sorts and structures) the needed information in a few seconds. Additionally, TaskView can port data directly to mission-planning software tools, which greatly reduce the defects introduced during manual entry.

An initial prototype version of TaskView had been developed by another organization, and the TIS contract was to produce a product from this prototype, enhance it for a new ATO format, and port it from the UNIX environment to a PC Windows NT operating system.

TIS chose the TaskView project as a pilot for the TSP for several reasons:

- The team members were already PSP trained.
- TaskView was a small (under 20,000 lines of code [LOC]), short-duration (eight months) project from which results would be immediately apparent.
- The project manager for TaskView (Dave Webb) was an SEI-certified PSP instructor.

The TaskView project started a month before the introduction of TSP. The team had already been through the planning process required by TIS, and a detailed plan already existed before the first TSP launch. Since the TSP is designed to build on and augment an organization's existing process, the TaskView project could use the TIS Standard Engineering Process and tracking tools. When organizations do not have a fully defined process, the TSP launch process guides the team in defining and developing the needed process elements.

Using the TSP Process

The first TSP launch for the TaskView project was held at the end of February 1998. During the launch, we reviewed TSP concepts with the team and guided them through the project planning and tracking steps. The team spent about two and one-half days in this launch workshop.

Team Goals and Roles

During the project launch, the team members determined and documented the project goals. Some were high level,

such as "delight our customers" and "be an effective pilot project for TSP in the Air Force and the DoD." More specific goals included "provide clean beta versions of TaskView to [the customer]" and "meet or exceed our quality plan." One important goal was to meet the customer's recent request that the TaskView project be delivered one month earlier than the original Sept. 30, 1998 commitment date.

Next, team members chose their personal team roles from among the TSP basic set: Customer Interface Manager, Design Manager, Implementation Manager, Planning Manager, Process Manager, Quality Manager, Support Manager, and Test Manager. Because of the limited size of the team, some members received more than one job. These roles were assigned so that when risks or issues arose, there would be a point of contact already designated and prepared to handle them. As usual, the official team leader had already been designated by management.

Detailed Planning

With the goals and roles determined, the team refined its existing project plan. The previously developed TaskView plan contained about three dozen work breakdown structure elements and tasks. During the TSP launch, the engineers produced a detailed list of more than 180 tasks. Using standard productivity rates, the team next estimated the task hours and the size of each task's product, usually in LOC. They also estimated each engineer's available task hours for each week of the project.

Task hours are hours spent working *only* on the tasks in the task list. Time spent in meetings, on the telephone, using E-mail, or engaged in any other activity that is not defined in the plan is not counted toward TSP task hours. Although these activities are necessary and are definitely work hours, they are not tracked as part of the project earned value. Based on the experiences of other TSP projects, the TaskView team estimated that in an engineer's standard 40-hour workweek, 20 hours would be an aggressive goal for task-related work.

The TSP Earned-Value Tool

TSP tools were then used to turn this top-down plan into an earned-value chart with a projected completion date. On the first run, the team and management were delighted to find that the new completion date projected by the top-down plan matched perfectly with the customer requirement for a one-month schedule acceleration.

Next, the software engineers were each given a copy of the task list and asked to estimate their personal work, using their own line of code and effort data. Such data are a product of the PSP course, which every engineer should complete before starting a TSP project. The TSP tool was then used to combine these individual estimates into a bottom-up estimate, also with earned value and a projected completion date. This estimate did not match the schedule requirements or the top-down estimate completed only a few hours earlier because some engineers were tasked more heavily than others. Because project schedules often slip if only one engineer is overburdened, the TSP launch process includes a workload-balancing step.

After workload balancing, the bottom-up schedule matched the top-down estimate and the customer's need. At this point, all engineers had a personal task and earned-value plan for which they individually had provided the estimates.

Risk Assessment and Mitigation

At the next TSP launch meeting, the TaskView team identified the risks associated with the project. They listed these risks in a brainstorming session, prioritized risk likelihood and impact, and assigned responsibility for mitigation and tracking. For example, the risk that "there will be a day-for-day slip in schedule if we do not receive the necessary header files by 3 March" was given a high likelihood and impact and assigned to the official team leader.

Fourteen risks were identified in this initial launch, of which seven were assigned to the team leader, and the balance were handled by team mem-

Module Number	Estimated New and Changed LOC	Actual New and Changed LOC	Percent Error*
1	1,500	1,656	10.40%
2	1,500	1,350	-10.00%
3	500	418	-16.40%
4	3,000	4,525	50.83%
5	1,000	973	-2.70%
6	500	1,067	113.40%
7	500	0	-100.00%
8	1,100	3,377	207.00%
9	1,500	848	-43.47%
10	500	956	91.20%
11	1,500	1,494	-0.40%
12	9	4	-55.56%
13	500	653	30.60%
14	unused	unused	unused
15	500	965	93.00%
16	1,177	2,973	152.59%
17	819	1131	38.10%
18	3,000	4,386	46.20%
Total	19,105	26,776	40.15%

Table 1. *TaskView estimated vs. actual LOC. *Note that underestimates are positive, and overestimates are negative.*

bers. The team leader also agreed to share responsibility with the engineers to track and mitigate the other management-related risks.

Management Review
The final launch activity was a management review of the team's launch results. Normally, such meetings provide the forum to resolve serious scheduling or resource issues. For TaskView, however, the management review reaffirmed the existing project commitments.

Tracking the Work
After the two-and-one-half-day TSP launch, the team started on the job. Using the PSP, the engineers tracked, in minutes, the time they spent on each task and process phase, recorded the defects found at every phase, and measured the sizes of the products they produced. The data were stored in the engineers' data tracker and in the TSP tracking tools. Thereafter, the team

met weekly to review earned-value status, goals, risks, issues, and action items.

Within the next few weeks, it was evident that the team had a problem. The engineers were not achieving the 20 task hours per week they had planned. Their earned-value data, however, showed them to be on or ahead of schedule. From the data, the team found that there were two offsetting factors: Tasks had generally been overestimated, and it was much harder to achieve 20 task hours per week than had been expected. Even though the schedule impact to date had been minimal, this new understanding helped the team make better plans, and it showed where to focus to improve performance.

The Team Relaunch
In May 1998, we guided the TaskView team in assessing their progress and conducting a relaunch. The relaunch was necessary because the project was moving into its second phase, and the engineers felt a new plan was needed. This new plan would reflect lessons learned from the prior phase, more realistically address task hours, and include new tasks.

Although relaunch workshops normally take two days, this team was able to accomplish it in only one day. During this period, they replanned the project, refined their size and time estimates, adjusted their schedule to reflect 15 weekly task hours per engineer, and reassessed risks. Based on the cost, schedule, risk, and quality data, the overall project was judged to be ahead of plan. Because tasks had been generally accomplished with less effort than originally planned, some functions were completed early, whereas one important function planned for Phase 1 had slipped to Phase 2.

Because of the project's progress, TaskView could either return some money to the customer or add new functionality. The customer interface manager worked with the customer and found that new functionality was more important than cost reduction. Management then agreed to add more tasks and more people to the project. These new functions caused a modest schedule delay, so the customer interface manager reviewed the new functionality and schedule with the customer for approval. Since the planned delivery was still months away, the customer decided to accept the small schedule change in order to get the added functions.

Project Results
To determine the benefits of the TSP, TIS compared the TaskView pilot with similar projects that followed the organization's standard process. The project manager and the software engineers were also asked how the TSP had helped or hindered their personal work. Because TIS projects already routinely meet schedules, commitment performance was not an important factor in the analysis.

Estimating Accuracy
Use of the TSP was found to substantially improve size and effort estimating accuracy. During the first launch, TaskView was estimated to be 14,065 LOC. By the second launch, with the new functions, the total estimated size grew to 19,105

Phase	TIS	TSP
Requirements inspection	X	X
High-level design inspection	X	X
Detailed design personal review		X
Detailed design inspection	X	X
Personal code review		X
Compile	X	X
Code inspection	X	X
Functional test	X	X
Candidate evaluation (CPT&E)	X	X
System test (ERT)	X	X
Operational test and evaluation (acceptance test)	X	X
Operational usage (external)	X	X

Table 2. *TIS and TSP defect-removal process steps.*

LOC. When the TaskView project was completed, the final new and changed LOC for the project was 26,776, an underestimate of 40 percent. When the 9,455 LOC of added function were subtracted, the team's original 14,065 LOC size estimate had an error of 23 percent.

Table 1 shows the size estimates the engineers made during the second TSP launch. Module 7 took no new and changed code because the engineer reused an existing routine. Although some individual estimates were reasonably close, there was considerable variation. By using a sound statistically based method and their personal historical data, however, the engineers were able to make balanced estimates. This meant that, on average, they were as likely to estimate high as low. Because the errors in the individual estimates tended to compensate, the overall estimate was much more accurate than were the individual estimates. Team members believed that their large personal estimating errors were largely due to the lack of historical data for this kind of project. Future project estimates will benefit from the data gathered during this project and should be more accurate.

The TaskView effort estimates were originally made before the introduction of the TSP. At the first launch, the effort was again estimated to determine if the costs were appropriate and if the load was properly balanced among the engineers. By the second launch, it was obvious that effort had been overestimated; the project was able to meet earned-value goals with fewer task hours than had originally been expected. After including the customer-requested new functionality, the final delivery date was only two days later than the accelerated schedule, and the cost error was negligible.

Productivity

The TIS software process database contains the average productivity in LOC per man-hour for this team's prior project, and the average productivity for every project that used the TIS organizational process. Although the exact numbers are proprietary, the TaskView project increased productivity to 16 percent above the TIS average. These particular engineers increased their productivity to 123 percent above their previous project, or more than two times. Data on the relative productivity in LOC per programmer-hour for TaskView, the team's prior project, and the average of all TIS projects are shown in Figure 4. The TIS average is shown as 100 and TaskView as 116.

Productivity figures are impacted by many factors. Because TaskView and the team's prior project involved different languages, application domains, and development environments, the productivity improvement cannot be considered a measure of the TSP. The results do, however, suggest that the TSP improves productivity.

Quality Improvement

As shown in Table 2, the standard TIS process includes inspections (peer reviews) of all work products. The TSP adds a set of personal design and code reviews. One important question was whether the time spent doing these personal reviews was worthwhile. The TIS process typically removes about 13 defects for every thousand lines of code (KLOC) during design and code inspections. The rest must be found in test or by the user. With TSP, the TaskView project increased the yield of early defect removal by more than 60 percent by removing 21 defects per KLOC in both the reviews and the inspections. The benefits of this early attention to quality are apparent from the results of the later test phases.

Assuming the engineering process has rigorous testing criteria, an indicator of product and process quality is the time spent running tests. Generally, the fewer defects there are to be found, the less time is spent in test and the higher is the resulting product quality. The TIS process has three test phases, all with rigorous criteria, that must be completed before the product is passed to an external agency for operational testing: functional test, candidate evaluation, and system test. These phases are then followed by the customer's operational test and evaluation and then by operational usage. Typical TIS projects require 22 percent of the project schedule (in days) to perform the final two TIS test phases. The TaskView project, using TSP, sharply reduced this percentage to 2.7 percent. This is a schedule savings of nearly 20 percent. Only one high-priority defect was found in these last two test phases.

Data from the completed TaskView project show that the defect density at the functional testing phase was close to that normally achieved by other TIS projects only after all engineering testing

Table 3. *TaskView testing time. *Acceptance test is continuing but no defects have been reported to date.*

	TaskView	Project 1	Project 2	Project 3
Program Size – LOC	26,776	67,291	7,955	86,543
CPT&E Test Days	4	22	10	33
ERT (System Test) Days	2	41	13	59
Total Test Days	6	63	23	92
Test Days/KLOC	0.22	0.94	2.89	1.06
System Test Defects/KLOC	0.52	2.21	4.78	2.66
Acceptance Test Defects/KLOC	0*	N/A	1.89	0.07

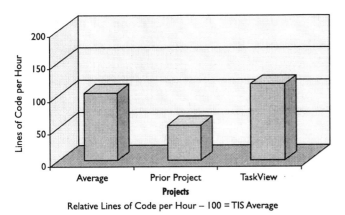

Figure 4. *Relative productivity.*

phases have been completed. In TaskView, to find only one high-priority defect in the TaskView product during system and operational testing is unprecedented for any TIS project.

Because of the improved quality from the TSP process, TaskView testing time was sharply reduced, as shown in Table 3. Here, the test data for the TaskView project are compared with three comparable prior projects. Although one could reduce testing time by running incomplete tests, the fact that the customer has so far reported no defects during acceptance test suggests that this was not the case. By using the TSP, TaskView not only produced a higher-quality product, it also took only one-eighth the testing time normally required for similar projects.

Qualitative Results

A critical question in introducing any new software engineering tool or technology is whether the engineers will use it. If the engineers do not like a tool or method, they will probably not use it, regardless of its effectiveness. To assess this issue, we privately asked all the TSP team members four questions:

- What do you believe are the advantages of the TSP?
- What do you believe are the disadvantages of the TSP?
- What about the TSP would you change?
- What about TSP would you keep the same?

Without knowing their teammates' responses, every team member said the TSP helped them form a closer, more effective team than any they had worked on before and that they would like to continue to use it. One team member said, "The TSP creates more group involvement. Everyone feels like they're more part of a group instead of a cog in a wheel. It forces team coordination to talk about and solve problems—there's no pigeonholing." Another team member said, "This really feels like a tight team. I was on the same team for a year [while working on another project] and didn't know the team members as well as I do now."

Another qualitative advantage expressed by multiple team members was increased effectiveness in project planning and tracking. "TSP gives you better insight into your current state," said one software engineer. "It provides better focus for the software developer on tasks to be done." Another TaskView team member summed up the planning and tracking benefits

of TSP in this way: "Measuring progress helps generate progress."

The principal weakness the TaskView team mentioned was the need for better TSP tool support. Several members said that the tracking and earned-value support needed to be improved, and another suggested more automated data gathering and analysis. Work on TSP tool improvement has already begun at the SEI, and a newer, better version of the planning and tracking tool will soon be available.

The lead software engineer gave perhaps the best testimonial to the qualitative results of the TSP. When asked what he would not change about the TSP, he said, "I've seen a lot of benefits [from the TSP]. I'd like to see us continue to use it."

Conclusions

One of the fears many have about process improvement initiatives like the TSP is that the cost of doing extensive planning, personal reviews, and data gathering will increase the overall cost of the project. It is evident from the TaskView data, however, that the time spent performing these activities is more than made up by improved planning accuracy and reduced test time. As Philip Crosby once noted, "Quality is free." [6]

Perhaps the greatest change with the TSP is in the relationship between management and the engineers. To be most effective, engineers must be motivated and energetic; they need to be creative and concerned about the quality of their products, and they should enjoy their work and be personally committed to its success. This can only be achieved if management trusts the engineers to work effectively and the engineers trust their management to guide and support them.

Although trust is an essential element of effective teamwork, it must rest on more than mere faith. The engineers must follow appropriate methods and consistently strive for quality results. They must report on their progress and rapidly expose risks and problems. Similarly, management must recognize that the engineers generally know more about their detailed work than the managers, and they must rationally debate cost and schedule issues. Management also needs to ensure that the engineers consistently follow disciplined methods and that the teams do not develop interpersonal problems.

The TSP is designed to address these issues and show engineers and managers how to establish an environment in which effective teamwork is normal and natural. Because this will often require substantial attitude changes for the engineers and the managers, to introduce the TSP is a non-trivial step. As the TaskView data show, however, the TSP can produce extraordinary results. ◆

Acknowledgments

Being a leader and a coach for the TaskView team has been a rewarding experience for each of us. It would not, however, have been as rewarding or satisfying without a dedicated and hard-working team. For their support and cooperation, we thank Pattie Adkins, Keith Gregersen, Neil Hilton, Craig Jeske, Ken Raisor, Mark Riter, and Capt. David Tuma. We also enjoyed excellent support from Tresa Butler for configuration management, Pat Cosgriff for SEPG support, and Jim Van Buren of the STSC for PSP consultation.

For quality engineering work, consistent and informed management leadership is essential. For their trust in us and their willingness to support us in pioneering the early use of TSP in practice, we thank Dan Wynn, Robert Deru, Don Thomas, LaMar Nybo, and Eldon Jensen. Lt. Col. Jacob Thorn, the TaskView program manager at Eglin Air Force Base, Fla., also supported our process improvement initiatives. His dedication to quality and informed oversight made the job possible.

We also thank those who reviewed this article. Their comments and suggestions were a great help. Our particular thanks to Rushby Craig, Walter Donohoo, Linda Gates, John Goodenough, and Bill Peterson. Finally, the professional help and guidance of the *CROSSTALK* staff have, as always, been a great help.

About the Authors

David Webb has a bachelor's degree in electrical and computer engineering from Brigham Young University. He has worked for TIS for more than 11 years as a software engineer. Six of those years he spent as an F-16 Operational Flight Program software test engineer and system design engineer, three years as a member of the TIS SEPG, and two years

as a technical program manager for TIS mission-planning software. He has participated in three CMM-Based Appraisals for Internal Process Improvement, including TIS's 1998 Level 5 assessment. He has also been certified by the SEI as a PSP course instructor.

OO-ALC/TISHD
6137 Wardleigh Road
Hill Air Force Base, UT 84056
Voice: 801-775-2916 DSN 775-2916
E-mail: webbda@software.hill.af.mil

Watts S. Humphrey is a fellow at the SEI at Carnegie Mellon University, which he joined in 1986. At the SEI, he established the Process Program, led initial development of the CMM, introduced the concepts of Software Process Assessment and Software Capability Evaluation, and most recently, the PSP and TSP. Prior to joining the SEI, he spent 27 years with IBM in various technical executive positions, including management of all IBM commercial software development and director of programming quality and process. He has a master's degree in physics from the Illinois Institute of Technology and in business administration from the University of Chicago. He is the 1993 recipient of the American Institute of Aeronautics and Astronautics Software Engineering Award and an honorary doctorate in software engineering from Embry Riddle Aeronautical University in 1998. His most recent books include *Managing the Software Process* (1989), *A Discipline for Software Engineering* (1995), *Managing Technical People* (1996), and *Introduction to the Personal Software Process* (1997).

Software Engineering Institute
Carnegie Mellon University
Pittsburgh, PA 15213
Voice: 412-268-6379
E-mail: watts@sei.cmu.edu

References

1. Humphrey, Watts S., "Three Dimensions of Process Improvement, Part III: The Team Process," *CROSSTALK*, Software Technology Support Center, Hill Air Force Base, Utah, April 1998, pp. 14-17.
2. Ferguson, Pat, Watts S. Humphrey, Soheil Khajenoori, Susan Macke, and Annette Matvya, "Introducing the Personal Software Process: Three Industry Case Studies," *IEEE Computer*, May 1997, pp. 24-31.
3. Humphrey, Watts S., *A Discipline for Software Engineering*, Reading, Mass., Addison-Wesley, 1995.
4. Humphrey, Watts S., "Using a Defined and Measured Personal Software Process," *IEEE Software*, May 1996.
5. Humphrey, Watts S., "Three Dimensions of Process Improvement, Part II: The Personal Process," *CROSSTALK*, Software Technology Support Center, Hill Air Force Base, Utah, March 1998, pp. 13-15.
6. Crosby, Philip B., *Quality Is Free: The Art of Making Quality Certain*, McGraw-Hill, New York, 1979.

The Software Acquisition Capability Maturity Model[SM]

Peter A. Kind, *SARCOS*
Jack Ferguson, *Software Engineering Institute*

In a collaborative effort among the Department of Defense (DoD), federal agencies, the Software Engineering Institute (SEI), and industry, a select team of people with acquisition expertise developed, pilot tested, and is now planning the implementation of a Software Acquisition Capability Maturity Model[SM] (SA-CMM) and associated acquisition process improvement support material. The SA-CMM is intended to provide a framework to benchmark and improve the software acquisition process. The SA-CMM's users are those organizations that have responsibilities to acquire products that contain software and also those that provide support to the acquisition of software products, e.g., government program managers (PMs) and program executive officers (PEOs), government software support activities, industry PM and PEO equivalents, and senior executives. This article briefly describes the structure and content of the SA-CMM, compares the roles of the software acquirer and the developer, with emphasis on how the SA-CMM relates to the acquirer's role, and discusses its use to date.

According to a recent report by the Standish Group, *Charting the Seas of Technology: The CHAOS Study,*

- Nearly one-third of information technology (computer and software) projects were canceled before completion.
- Over half of the project budgets exceeded 189 percent of the original estimates.
- The average schedule overrun for projects that were in difficulty was 222 percent.
- On average, the delivered product contained only 61 percent of the originally specified features.

To understand why these results occur, read the following comments of a few managers of software-intensive projects:

"I'd rather have it wrong than have it late." -- *An industry senior software manager*

"The bottom line is schedule. My promotions and raises are based on meeting schedule first and foremost." -- *A government program manager*

"By regularly putting the development process under extreme time pressure, and then accepting poor-quality products, the software user community has shown its true quality standard." -- *DeMarco and Lister (Peopleware, 1987)*

The SEI developed the Capability Maturity Model[SM] for Software (SW-CMM) [1] to address these problems from a software developer's viewpoint. Based on work by Edward Deming [2], J. M. Juran [3, 4], and Philip B. Crosby [5], the SW-CMM describes five levels of organizational software engineering maturity. A primary use of the model is assessments of software engineering processes by software-related industries as a part of a process improvement program.

Industry is now successfully improving their software development processes with the SW-CMM (CMU/SEI-94-TR-13; CMU/SEI-95-TR-009). But as Tom DeMarco and Timothy Lister state, the acquirers or the buyers of software-intensive systems continue to be a large part of the problem. Because of the intimate interaction between buyer and supplier and the perceived immaturity of acquisition organizations, a group of government and industry managers encouraged the SEI to lead development of a CMM for the buyer--the SA-CMM. The SEI responded by forming the Software Acquisition Project with leadership by a steering group composed of government and industry managers.

SA-CMM Steering Group

The SA-CMM Steering Group, which met first in October 1994, has consisted of the following members over the last three years:

SARCOS, Inc.
  Peter Kind, Chairman

U.S. Army
  S. Wayne Sherer

Office of the Secretary of Defense
  Cynthia Rand
  Jim Luciano
  Steve Johnston
  Terry Sellers
  Brenda Zettervall
  Linda Brown

U.S. Navy
  Marshall Potter

U.S. Air Force
  Lt. Col. Dan Romano
  Maj. George Newberry

The MITRE Corporation
  Judy Clapp

Lockheed Martin Corporation
  Joan Weszka

Defense Information Systems Agency (DISA)
  Joanne Arnette
  Donna Leigh
  Mike Falat

Logicon, Inc.
  Marilyn Stewart

Defense Systems Management College (DSMC)
  Lyn Dellinger
  Lt. Col. Jim Craig
  Sherwin Jacobsen

SEI
  Tom Brandt
  Scott Reed
  Jack Ferguson

The steering group birthed the SA-CMM, guided its development, made architecture, structure, and overall design decisions, provided visibility for the SA-CMM to decision makers in their organizations, and directed pilot use of the model for the services and DISA. The members are now planning implementation of the SA-CMM and associated process improvement tools in government and industry.

SA-CMM Development

After initial planning, SA-CMM development began in October 1994 with resources from the Army, Navy, Air Force, DISA, National Oceanic and Atmospheric Administration (NOAA), industry through the National Security Industrial Association, and SEI. Version 1.01 of the SA-CMM was published in December 1996. The authors of the SA-CMM are

  Jack Ferguson, SEI, Project Lead

Jack Cooper, Anchor Software Management, Chief Architect
Mike Falat, DISA
Matt Fisher, U.S. Army
Tony Guido, U.S. Navy
Jordan Matejceck, NOAA
John Marciniak, Kaman Sciences
Bob Webster, U.S. Air Force

To develop the SA-CMM, decisions that concern architecture, scope, e.g., time: beginning and end of "acquisition" in the model and domain: software vs. system acquisition, target audience, and level of detail had to be answered. Decisions were made jointly, with proposals from the authors debated and agreed upon or modified by steering group members. In many cases, comments from reviewers external to the project team led to changes in the model design. Results of these decisions are presented later in sections that describe the design and use of the SA-CMM.

Purpose of the SA-CMM

The SA-CMM describes the acquirer's or the buyer's role in software-intensive system acquisition. Its purpose is to provide a framework to benchmark and improve an organization's software acquisition process. It supports goal setting for senior management and prediction of potential performance.

A capability maturity model, as defined by the SEI, is an organized collection of best practices, termed *Activities* in the model. The best practices are agreed upon by the affected community through peer reviews. The practices are organized in key process areas (KPAs), which are collections of practices with common purposes and goals. To support goal setting and improvement planning, the SA-CMM defines stages (maturity levels) through which software acquisition organizations evolve as they improve their processes. These levels are

Level 1: The Initial Level -- the organization does not have documented processes.

Level 2: The Repeatable Level -- basic acquisition management instills discipline at the project level.

Level 3: The Defined Level -- acquisition organization-wide processes are defined, then tailored for each project.

Level 4: The Quantitative Level -- decisions on processes and products are based on formal quantitative measures.

Level 5: The Optimizing Level -- continual process and acquisition methodology improvements occur based on quantitative feedback and from piloting innovative ideas and technologies.

The model supports institutionalization and continued use of the best practices through Institutionalization Common Features (common to each KPA). The relationship of level, goals, institutionalization common features, and activities is shown in Figure 1.

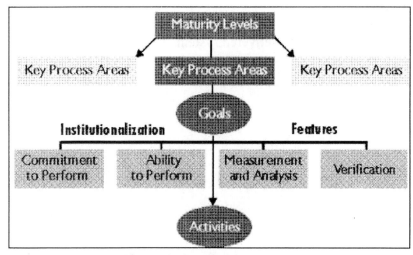

Figure 1. *SA-CMM structure.*

Using the SA-CMM

The SA-CMM is intended to be used by those organizations that acquire or support the acquisition of software products or services, including software-intensive systems, sustainment and upgrade of existing systems, and software-related services. Language in the model is generic such that it applies to both government and industry acquisition activities, regardless of the size of the organization.

"Acquisition" in the model spans the time from germination of a requirement, possibly before formation of an office responsible for the project, through selection of a contractor and prosecution of the software engineering effort, to delivery of the system to the user. Maintenance of a system is viewed as another acquisition, in which all of the facets of the model are again applied, with the maintenance contractor selected and managed in the same manner as an original developer.

Use of the SA-CMM is not limited to situations where software is being acquired under formal contract. It can be used by any organization that acquires software or software-related services. For this usage, the term *contractor* refers to the organization that performs the software engineering effort. The term *project team* refers to the individuals within the acquiring organization who have an assigned software acquisition responsibility, and the term *contract* refers to the agreement between the organizations.

The SA-CMM does not intend to indicate any specific organizational structure or size. In the model, the terms *group, team, office,* and similar terms may indicate situations where the specific implementation may vary from a single employee assigned part time, to several part-time employees assigned from other organizations, to several individuals dedicated full time.

The SA-CMM is intended to also be used for acquisitions that involve commercial-off-the-shelf and nondevelopmental item software. Nothing in the model should inhibit its use in these situations. However, it may be appropriate that some of the areas of the model be tailored to fit the specific instance.

One purpose of the SA-CMM is to increase the visibility of and support for software aspects of major system acquisitions. Because of this, the SA-CMM is limited to software acquisition and should not be viewed as a system acquisition model, although many of the practices contained in the model, such as requirements management and planning for evaluation and lifecycle support, are useful for system acquisition.

The SA-CMM neither contains all practices relevant to software acquisition (hence the term "key process area"), nor should the examples in the model be used as checklists to be applied without understanding the business goals, organization structure, and mission of the affected organization. The SA-CMM is not engraved in stone. It is intended to be applied with intelligence and common sense.

SA-CMM Key Process Areas

The KPAs of the SA-CMM are shown in Figure 2. In line with SEI maturity level definitions, Level 2 KPAs describe basic software acquisition project management, although Level 3 contains both organization process and pro-active acquisition management KPAs. Level 4 focuses on quantitative techniques applied to the acquisition process and the products being acquired, and Level 5 uses these quantitative measures as a basis for continuous improvement. Similar to the SW-CMM, the bar on the right indicates that moving up in maturity level reduces risk and increases quality in the delivered system.

Level	Focus	Key Process Areas	
5 Optimizing	Continuous Process Improvement	Acquisition Innovation Management Continuous Process Implementation	Quality Productivity
4 Quantitative	Quantitative Management	Quantitative Acquisition Management Quantitative Process Management	
3 Defined	Process Standardization	Training Program Acquisition Risk Management Contract Performance Management Project Performance Management Process Definition and Maintenance	
2 Repeatable	Basic Project Management	Transition to Support Evaluation Contract Tracking and Oversight Project Management Requirements Development Management Solicitation Software Acquisition Planning	
1 Initial	Competent People and Heroics		Risk Rework

Figure 2. *SA-CMM key process areas.*

Acquisition vs. Development

The SA-CMM applies to organizations that acquire software-intensive products from software developers who are subject to the SW-CMM. For this reason, the SA-CMM follows the same architecture, design, and language of the SW-CMM. The role of the acquirer, however, while intertwined with the developer, is different. The SA-CMM and the SW-CMM describe these roles. The relationships of the respective CMM KPAs are shown in the following figures:

Figure 3 shows the KPA relationships for Level 2, with SA-CMM KPAs on the left and SW-CMM KPAs on the right. Software Acquisition Planning and Solicitation (Sol) provide Acquisition Plans and Solicitation Requirements that feed into Software Project Planning (SPP). The output of SPP is a proposal that is evaluated in Sol. Requirements are developed in Requirements Development and Management and passed to the developer who manages them via Requirements Management. Although the acquisition organization develops and manages requirements from the beginning of the project, both the acquirer and the developer have roles in the management of changing requirements throughout the development.

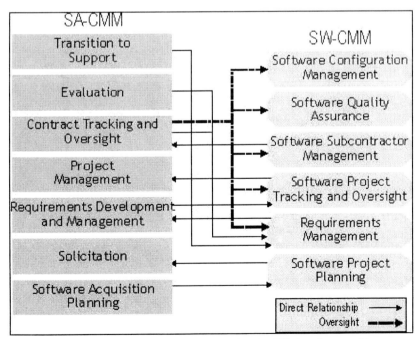

Figure 3. *Level 2 SA-CMM SW-CMM KPA relationships.*

Once the contract period begins, Project Management collects information from Software Project Tracking and Oversight for overall project management, and Contract Tracking and Oversight provides buyer insight into all of the developers' software engineering activities.

Throughout the contract period, Evaluation and Transition to Support provide evaluation and support requirements to the developer (and to the maintainer).

Figure 4 shows the Level 3 relationships. The SA-CMM combines Organizational Process Focus and Definition in Process Definition and Maintenance. Project Performance Management (PPM) takes several of the project-oriented activities from Level 2 KPAs and matures them to Level 3. PPM also receives data from Integrated Software Management (ISM) and contains the coordination and agreement tracking activities that are in Intergroup Coordination.

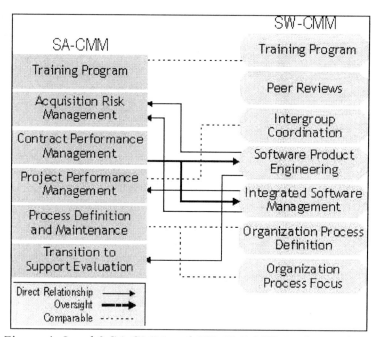

Figure 4. *Level 3 SA-CMM and SW-CMM KPA relationships.*

Contract Performance Management matures Contract Tracking and Oversight, and provides more pro-active management than its Level 2 counterpart. It also provides oversight of relevant contractor activities. Acquisition Risk Management (ARM) includes risk management in both the planning and the software development phases of the acquisition. ARM incorporates data from the contractor's ISM and Software Product Engineering (SPE) KPAs. The SA-CMM Training Program is similar to the same KPA in the SW-CMM except that the required training is specific to acquisition.

It is interesting to note that evaluation and transition requirements do not appear in the SW-CMM until the SPE KPA, thus they provide data to the two Level 2 KPAs. This does not mean that the SA-CMM requires Level 3 developers; rather, project offices may levy evaluation and transition requirements when the SW-CMM does not.

Figure 5 shows KPA relationships for Levels 4 and 5. Quantitative Process Management is similar in both models, with the SA-CMM version being oriented to acquisition processes. Quantitative Acquisition Management provides measurable product goals to Software Quality Management, collects data related to those goals, and provides insight into the developer's quality management program.

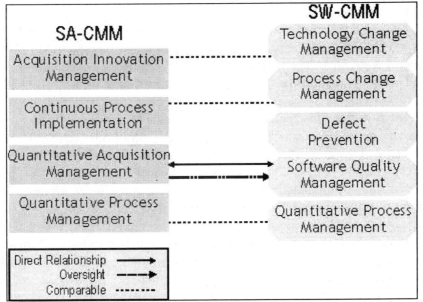

Figure 5. *Level 4-5 SA-CMM SW-CMM KPA relationships.*

At Level 5, Continuous Process Improvement uses the Level 4 measurements to improve the acquisition process, whereas Acquisition Innovation Management is similar to Technology Change Management except it includes innovative acquisition techniques that may or may not require new technologies.

User Experience

Organizations from DoD and other federal agencies have participated in six assessments (for self-improvement) and one evaluation (audit) using the SA-CMM.

The SA-CMM builds on the techniques and success of SW-CMM. Care has been taken to ensure consistency and complementary use. The SA-CMM is designed for use by government and industry and is applicable on large and small projects by small and large companies or agencies. Pilot tests were conducted within DoD and federal services and agencies to validate and refine the model. The SA-CMM is now being institutionalized. It will be maintained by the SEI under DoD sponsorship. Several of the assessed organizations developed process improvement plans based on SA-CMM findings and are now engaged in acquisition process improvement.

Retired Lt. Gen. Peter A. Kind, U.S. Army, is senior vice president and chief information officer of SARCOS Incorporated. SARCOS develops and produces high-technology products in telemedicine, physical linkage to virtual reality, MicroElectrical Mechanical Systems, entertainment and industrial robotics, drug delivery, and precision medical products. He also is chairman of the steering group for the SACMM.

Kind received his bachelor's degree in 1961 from the University of Wisconsin and a master's degree in business administration in 1969 from Harvard University. He is a graduate of the U.S. Marine Corps Communications Officer Course, the U.S. Army Command and Staff College and the U.S. Army War College.

Kind has commanded and directed units that provide communications and information services worldwide, to include the 1st Signal Brigade in Korea; NATO's Central Operating Authority, which supports all alliance nations; the U.S. Army Signal Center and Ft. Gordon, where he trained Army, Air Force, Navy, and Marine students as well as those of 65 other countries; and the U.S. Army Information Systems Command with 37,000 members providing Army and joint information services worldwide. As program executive officer for Command and Control Systems, he managed the development, acquisition, and fielding for six programs and 21 products supporting tactical forces with automation. He served as director of information systems for command, control, computers, and information of the Army in his last assignment.

SARCOS, Incorporated
828 East Edgehill Road
Salt Lake City, UT 84103
Voice: 801-581-0155
E-mail: p.kind@ced.utah.edu

Jack Ferguson is project leader for the SA-CMM at the SEI. In addition to the SA-CMM, he recently wrote a paper that compares commercial practices of software acquisition with current DoD practices. He spent more than 25 years in technical, managerial, and teaching capacities, primarily concerned with the DoD space program. He was mission director and orbital software manager for the CORONA reconnaissance spacecraft. He was also the program manager of the SEI Joint Program Office, where he was instrumental in starting the Software Process Program and led the first DoD Software Capability Evaluation.

Ferguson holds a doctorate in aerospace engineering from the University of Texas at Austin, where he specialized in the use of Kalman filters in satellite orbit determination.

He is a member of the Institute of Electrical and Electronics Engineers, a former member of the SEI Software Process Advisory Board, and is listed in Jane's *Who's Who in Aerospace* and *Who's Who in the World*. Prior to coming to the SEI, he was the visiting professor of astronautics at the U.S. Air Force Academy.

SEI
1155 Kelly Johnson Boulevard, Suite 111
Colorado Springs, CO 80920
Voice: 719-548-4744
Fax: 719-590-7652
E-mail: jfr@sei.cmu.edu

References

1. Paulk, M.C., et al., *Capability Maturity Model for Software*, CMU/SEI-93-TR-24, Carnegie Mellon

University, Software Engineering Institute, Pittsburgh, Pa., 1993.
2. Deming, W. Edward, *Out of the Crisis*, Massachusetts Institute of Technology, Center for Advanced Engineering Study, Cambridge, Mass., 1986.
3. Juran, J.M., *Juran on Planning for Quality*, Free Press, New York, 1988.
4. Juran, J.M., *Juran on Leadership for Quality*, Free Press, New York, 1989.
5. Crosby, Philip B., *Quality is Free: The Art of Making Quality Certain*, McGraw-Hill, New York, 1979.

CMM Integration: Enterprise-Wide Process Improvement Using the Next Generation of CMMs®

Mike Konrad and Sandy Shrum

Since 1998, the CMM Integration[SM] (CMMI[sm])[1] project, a joint industry, government, and Software Engineering Institute (SEI) project, has been developing integrated models, training, and an appraisal method to support enterprise-wide process improvement that helps organizations achieve their business objectives. CMMI products are derived from a common framework that supports systems engineering and software engineering as well as expansion to address other disciplines.

Since 1991, Capability Maturity Models® (CMMs)[2] have been developed for a myriad of disciplines. A CMM describes the characteristics of mature, capable processes and identifies the practices that are crucial to implementing effective processes. Some of the most notable include models for software engineering, systems engineering, software acquisition, human resources and workforce management, integrated product and process development, and security engineering. Many organizations in both industry and government have pursued suborganizational improvement using the CMMs developed prior to the CMMI project to help them achieve their business objectives.

The CMM Integration project's initial efforts are based on these three source models:

1. Capability Maturity Model for Software (SW-CMM), Version 2.0, draft C;

2. Electronic Industries Alliance/Interim Standard (EIA/IS) 731[3]; and

3. Integrated Product Development Capability Maturity Model (IPD-CMM), Version 0.98.

In this article, we provide the rationale for CMMI, an overview of the CMMI models currently available for use (CMMI-SE/SW and CMMI-SE/SW/IPPD, Version 1.02), and future plans for CMM Integration.

The Reason to Integrate CMMs

Many organizations would like to focus their improvement efforts across software engineering, systems engineering, and potentially other disciplines because of the critical roles such disciplines play in product development. Although single-discipline software engineering and systems engineering models have proven useful to many organizations in improving their capability to develop products, the differences in the architecture, content, and approach of these models has made a wider focus difficult. For example:

1. The contents of the SW-CMM and EIA/IS 731 overlap. Both models cover areas such as requirements, project management, and process definition. These models offer different guidance and terminology in their many areas of overlap, but these differences are often not

---

[1] CMM Integration and CMMI are service marks of Carnegie Mellon University.

[2] Capability Maturity Model and CMM are registered in the U.S. Patent and Trademark Office.

[3] EIA/IS 731, Systems Engineering Capability Model, is an evolution of and based, in part, on the Systems Engineering CMM (SE-CMM) model developed in 1994 and revised in 1995.

specific to the practice of software engineering or systems engineering, nor are they significant enough to be necessary.

2. EIA/IS 731 process areas span multiple capability levels rather than being defined within a maturity level structure as in the SW-CMM. This difference is reflected in the different ways in which the two models are structured. Systems engineering models employ a continuous representation. The SW-CMM employs a staged representation.

The difficulties arising from differences such as these are compounded when other disciplines are involved. There is a need to address additional disciplines in a way that leverages existing descriptions of best practices from process management, project management, and support processes.

A Historic Opportunity to Bring Two Engineering Disciplines Together

Historically, systems engineers have been selected from the "hardware disciplines" and have learned to be systems engineers on the job. Their background in or understanding of software development often proves to be anecdotal. Conversely, many software engineers are not skilled in the physical sciences or engineering. Their training typically covers only computer science, with little training in management, engineering, "hardware," or manufacturing. Consequently, these two groups may have little common ground with which to foster discussions on how they may collaboratively work to improve their processes.

A model that integrates software engineering and systems engineering will prove valuable to many organizations. Such a model enables model and appraisal training to be simpler and more effective. Further, an integrated model promotes the transfer of knowledge between multiple disciplines.

An integrated model is valuable even to organizations producing software-only solutions. The systems engineering functions, not typically addressed in other software-only models, are discussed using a familiar terminology and model architecture. The combination of (1) useful information on engineering a product and (2) proven practices for managing processes, results in a well-integrated model for both functions that will facilitate project management and improve the development process—and the resulting products.

Although the initial focus of the CMMI project has been on these two disciplines, the project has developed a framework for incorporating other disciplines , thereby supporting enterprise-wide process improvement.

What Do CMMI Models Look Like?

To provide an overview of the CMMI-SE/SW and CMMI-SE/SW/IPPD Version 1.02 models, it is useful to describe the disciplines covered in these models, the model components of each representation, the five maturity levels, and the process areas covered by these models.

In CMMI models, a *process area* is a cluster of related best practices that, when performed collectively, achieves a set of goals considered important for establishing the capability of an organization in that area.

Disciplines and Environments Covered by the Version 1.02 Models

Currently two disciplines are included in the CMMI models: systems engineering and software engineering. Currently one environment is included in the CMMI models: Integrated Product and Process

Development (IPPD). The CMMI-SE/SW model addresses product development and maintenance that includes both software engineering and systems engineering disciplines. The CMMI-SE/SW/IPPD model addresses product development and maintenance within an IPPD environment.

When integrating the source models from the two disciplines, we found that distinctions between the systems engineering and software engineering material were limited to "amplifications" that were more appropriate to one discipline than the other. Consequently, we chose not to produce separate models (i.e., one for software engineering and another for systems engineering) when the distinction was small within otherwise identical process areas.

Because the differences between these models are few, we suggest you use the full, integrated CMMI-SE/SW or CMMI-SE/SW/IPPD model, even if both disciplines do not take part in or integrate with the development processes of your organization.

The *systems engineering* discipline covers the development of total systems, which may or may not include software. Systems engineers focus on transforming customer needs, expectations, and constraints into product solutions and supporting those product solutions throughout the life of the product.

The *software engineering* discipline covers the development of software systems. Software engineers focus on the development, operation, and maintenance of software.

Staged or Continuous: Which Representation Should Be Chosen?

The Version 1.02 models are available in both staged and continuous representations. There are many valid reasons to select one representation or the other. Perhaps your organization will choose to use the representation with which it is most familiar. The following lists describe some of the possible advantages and disadvantages to selecting each of the two representations.

Staged Representation: If you choose the staged representation for your organization, expect that the model will do the following:

- Provide a proven sequence of improvements, beginning with basic management practices and progressing through a predefined and proven path of successive levels, each serving as a foundation for the next.

- Permit comparisons across and among organizations by using maturity levels.

- Provide an easy migration from the SW-CMM to CMMI.

Continuous Representation: If you choose the continuous representation for your organization, expect that the model will do the following:

- Allow you to select the order of improvement that best meets the organization's business objectives and mitigates the organization's areas of risk.

- Enable comparisons across and among organizations on a process area-by-process area basis or by comparing maturity levels through the use of equivalent staging.

- Provide an easy migration from EIA/IS 731 to CMMI.

- Afford an easy comparison of process improvement to ISO/IEC 15504 (Software Process Improvement and Capability dEtermination, SPICE) because the capability levels are derived, in large part, from ISO/IEC 15504.

Whether used for process improvement or appraisals, both representations are designed to offer essentially equivalent results over time.

What Does the Staged Representation Look Like?

The structure and relationship of components in a CMMI model with a staged representation are illustrated in Figure 1.

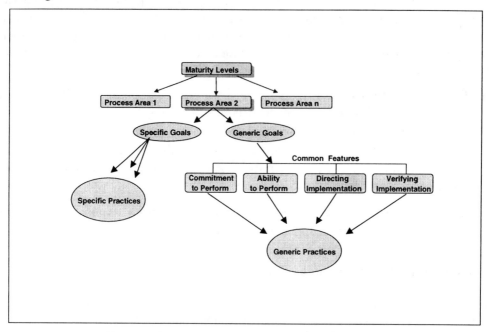

Figure 1. CMMI model components: staged representation.

Maturity levels provide a recommended order for approaching process improvement in stages so that not all process areas are addressed at the same time. Experience has shown that organizations do their best when they focus on a manageable number of process areas that require increasingly sophisticated effort as the organization improves.

A maturity level is a defined evolutionary plateau of process improvement. Each maturity level stabilizes an important part of the organization's processes. Achieving each maturity level results in an increase in the capability of the organization to develop software-intensive products.

Maturity levels organize the process areas. Within the process areas are generic and specific goals as well as generic and specific practices. Specific goals organize specific practices. The common features organize generic practices.

An organization achieves a maturity level by satisfying the specific and generic goals that apply to a predefined set of process areas. As organizations satisfy the generic and specific goals of the set of process areas in a maturity level, they increase their process maturity and reap the benefits of process improvement.

What Does the Continuous Representation Look Like?

The structure and relationship of components in a CMMI model with a continuous representation are illustrated in Figure 2.

222

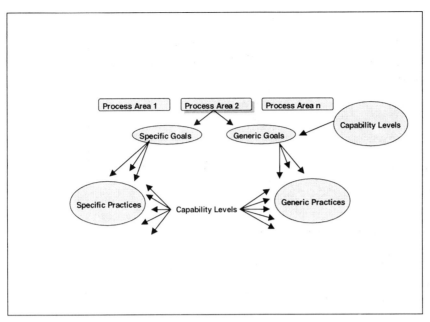

Figure 2. CMMI model components: continuous representation.

Capability levels provide a recommended order for approaching process improvement within each process area. At the same time, the continuous representation allows some flexibility for the order in which the process areas are addressed. These levels enable the organization to track, evaluate, and demonstrate its progress as it improves processes associated with process areas.

Within the process areas are generic and specific goals as well as generic and specific practices. Specific goals organize specific practices. Generic goals organize generic practices. Specific goals and specific practices apply to individual process areas. Generic goals and generic practices apply to multiple process areas.

Capability levels are determined by reviewing the organization's implementation of the specific and generic practices and its satisfaction of the associated goals through that capability level. As an organization satisfies the generic and specific goals for a process area at a particular capability level, it increases its capability to perform the processes associated with the selected process area and reaps the benefits of process improvement.

Maturity Levels versus Capability Levels

The continuous representation uses capability levels, whereas the staged representation uses maturity levels. The main difference between these two types of levels is the representation they belong to and how they are applied.

Capability levels, which belong to a continuous representation, apply to an organization's process improvement achievements for each process area. Each capability level corresponds to a generic goal and a defined set of generic practices.

Maturity levels, which belong to a staged representation, characterize an organization's overall process improvement capability and organizational maturity. Each maturity level comprises a predefined set of process areas and generic goals.

Capability and maturity levels have similar but not identical names, as shown in Table 1.

Table 1. Comparison of Capability Levels and Maturity Levels

Level	Continuous Representation Capability Levels	Staged Representation Maturity Levels
Level 0	Incomplete	N/A
Level 1	Performed	Initial
Level 2	Managed	Managed
Level 3	Defined	Defined
Level 4	Quantitatively Managed	Quantitatively Managed
Level 5	Optimizing	Optimizing

CMMI Process Areas Organized by Maturity Level

The following list of CMMI-SE/SW Version 1.02 process areas is organized by maturity level, which is a presentation more familiar to organizations that use a staged representation, such as SW-CMM Version 1.1. (The same process areas make up the continuous representation in CMMI, which has a structure more like EIA/IS 731. The continuous representation, however, uses the following maturity levels in its equivalent staging, which allows comparisons of the process improvement achieved by different organizations.) There are no process areas at maturity level 1, the Initial maturity level. The process areas at maturity level 2 (Managed) include the following:

- Requirements Management,

- Project Planning,

- Project Monitoring and Control,

- Supplier Agreement Management,

- Measurement and Analysis,

- Process and Product Quality Assurance, and

- Configuration Management .

In the following descriptions, the interactions of the process areas belonging to CMMI-SE/SW are described within the four process area categories.

The process areas at maturity level 3 (Defined) include the following:

- Requirements Development,

- Technical Solution,

- Product Integration,

- Verification,

- Validation,

- Organizational Process Focus,

- Organizational Process Definition,

- Organizational Training,

224

- Integrated Project Management,
- Risk Management, and
- Decision Analysis and Resolution.

The process areas at maturity level 4 (Quantitatively Managed) include the following:

- Organizational Process Performance and
- Quantitative Project Management.

The process areas at maturity level 5 (Optimizing) include the following:

- Organizational Innovation and Deployment and
- Causal Analysis and Resolution.

The process areas and their interrelationships are described next.

Four Categories of CMMI Process Areas

A process area is a group of related practices that are performed collectively to satisfy a set of goals. All CMMI process areas are common to both continuous and staged representations, and can be assigned to four categories:

- Process management processes,
- Project management processes,
- Engineering processes, and
- Support processes.

Process Management Processes

Process management process areas contain the interproject practices related to defining, planning, resourcing, deploying, implementing, monitoring, controlling, verifying, measuring, and improving processes. For ease of illustrating their interrelationships, we present the process management process areas in two groups:

1. The basic process management process areas enable the organization to achieve a basic capability to document and share best practices, process assets, and learning across the organization. The "basic" process management process areas are Organizational Process Focus (OPF), Organizational Process Definition (OPD), and Organizational Training (OT).

2. The advanced process management process areas enable the organization to achieve an advanced capability to meet its quantitative objectives for quality and process performance. The "advanced" process management process areas are Organizational Process Performance (OPP) and Organizational Innovation and Deployment (OID).

Figure 3 provides a bird's-eye view of the interactions among the basic process management process areas. OPF enables the organization to establish and maintain an understanding of its processes and process assets, and to identify, plan, and implement its process improvement activities. OPD enables the organization to establish and maintain a usable set of organizational process assets. OT enables the organization to develop the skills and knowledge of its people so they can perform their roles effectively and efficiently.

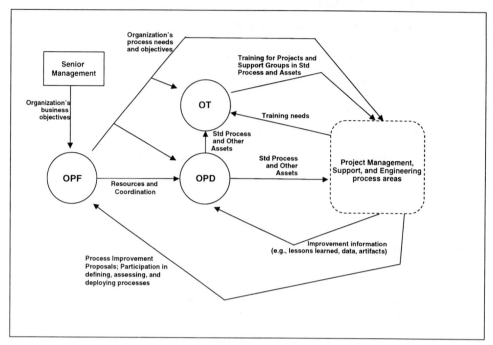

Figure 3. Basic process management process areas.

Figure 4 provides a bird's-eye view of the interactions among the advanced process management process areas. Each of the advanced process management process areas is strongly dependent on the organization's ability to develop and deploy process and supporting assets. The basic process management process areas enable the organization to develop this ability.

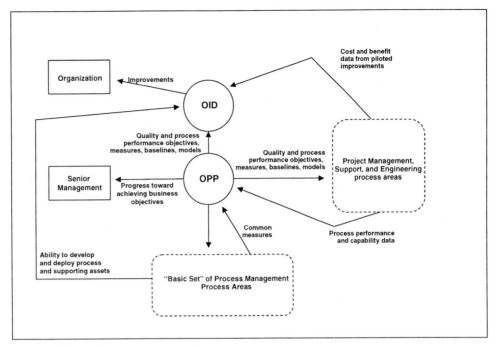

Figure 4. Advanced process management process areas.

OPP enables the organization to establish and maintain a quantitative understanding of the performance of its set of standard processes and to provide the process performance data, baselines, and models to quantitatively manage the its projects. OID enables the organization to select and deploy incremental and innovative improvements that measurably improve its processes and technologies. These improvements support the organization's quality and process performance objectives as derived from the organization's business objectives.

Project Management Processes

Project management process areas cover the project management activities related to planning, monitoring, and controlling the project. For ease of illustrating their interrelationships, we present the project management process areas in two groups:

1. The basic project management process areas address the basic activities related to establishing and maintaining the project plan, establishing and maintaining commitments, monitoring progress against the plan, taking corrective action, and managing supplier agreements. The "basic" project management process areas are Project Planning (PP), Project Monitoring and Control (PMC), and Supplier Agreement Management (SAM).

2. The advanced project management process areas address activities such as establishing a defined process that is tailored from the organization's set of standard processes, coordinating and collaborating with relevant stakeholders, risk management, and quantitatively managing the project's defined process. The "advanced" process management process areas are Integrated Project Management (IPM), Risk Management (RSKM), and Quantitative Project Management (QPM).

Figure 5 provides a bird's-eye view of the interactions among the basic project management process areas and with other process areas.

227

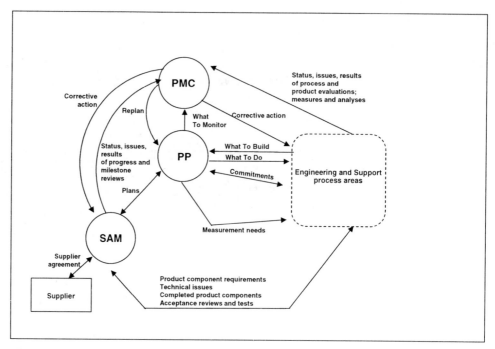

Figure 5. Basic project management process areas.

PP enables the project to establish and maintain plans that define project activities. PMC enables the project to understand its progress so that appropriate corrective actions can be taken when the project's performance deviates significantly from the plan. SAM enables the project to manage the acquisition of products and services from suppliers external to the project for which there exists a formal agreement.

Figure 6 provides a bird's-eye view of the interactions among the advanced project management process areas. Each of the advanced project management process areas is strongly dependent on the ability to plan, monitor, and control the project that is enabled by the basic project management process areas.

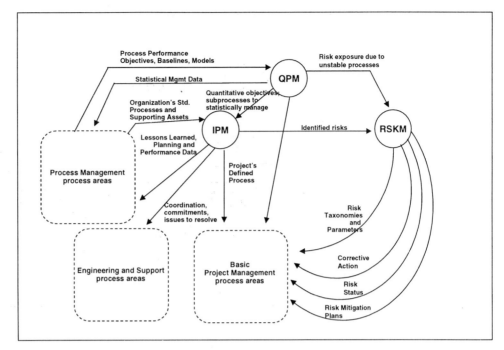

Figure 6. Advanced project management process areas.

IPM enables the project to manage the project and the involve relevant stakeholders according to an integrated and defined process that is tailored from the organization's set of standard processes. RSKM enables the project to identify potential problems before they occur, so that risk-handling activities can be planned and invoked as needed across the life of the project to mitigate adverse impacts on achieving objectives. QPM enables the project to quantitatively manage its defined process to achieve the project's established quality and process performance objectives.

Engineering Processes

The engineering process areas are written in a general engineering terminology so any technical discipline involved in the product development process (for example, software engineering or mechanical engineering) can use them for process improvement. The process management, project management, and support process areas apply to all such disciplines, as well as others.

These engineering process areas apply to the development of any product or service in the engineering development domain (for example, software products, hardware products, services, or product-related processes such as the manufacturing process, training process, and repair process). Also, the engineering process areas apply to each decomposition of a product or product component into one or more product components. Thus, different segments of a very large project can be assessed using the same model.

Figure 7 provides a bird's-eye view of the interactions among all engineering process areas.

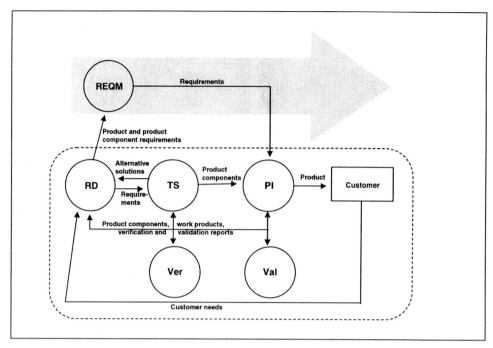

Figure 7. Engineering process areas.

Requirements management (REQM) enables the project to manage changes to the requirements of the product and product components and to identify inconsistencies between the project's plans and work products and the requirements. Requirements development (RD) enables the project to develop customer, product, and product component requirements and produce analyses required for their development and understanding.

Technical solution (TS) enables the project to develop, design, and implement solutions to requirements. Solutions, designs, and implementations encompass products, product components, and product-related processes either singly or in combinations as appropriate. Product integration (PI) enables the project to assemble the product from the product components, to ensure that the product, as integrated, functions properly, and to deliver the product.

Verification (Ver) enables the project to ensure that selected work products meet their specified requirements. Validation (Val) enables the project to demonstrate that a product or product component fulfills its intended use when placed in its intended environment.

Support Processes

The support process areas describe essential processes that are typically used in the context of performing other processes described by the CMMI model and are typically used in the context of performing these other processes. In general, the support process areas are targeted toward the project (except for Process and Product Quality Assurance), but can be applied more generally to the organization. For example, Measurement and Analysis can be applied in tandem with all other process areas to enable organizations to provide useful and accurate information about the processes and work products. While the support process areas have a primary focus on the project, the activities they characterize also apply to organizational functions. For ease of illustrating their interrelationships, we present the support process areas in two groups:

1. The basic support process areas address basic support functions that potentially will be used by processes described in other process areas. Although all support process areas rely on the other process areas in the CMMI model, the basic support process areas can also provide many of the support functions described by the generic practices. The "basic" support process areas are Measurement and Analysis (MA), Process and Product Quality Assurance (PPQA), and Configuration Management (CM).

2. The advanced support process areas address an advanced support capability. Each of these process areas relies on specific inputs or activities described in other process areas. The "advanced" support process areas are Decision Analysis and Resolution (DAR) and Causal Analysis and Resolution (CAR).

Figure 8 provides a bird's-eye view of the basic support process areas' interactions.

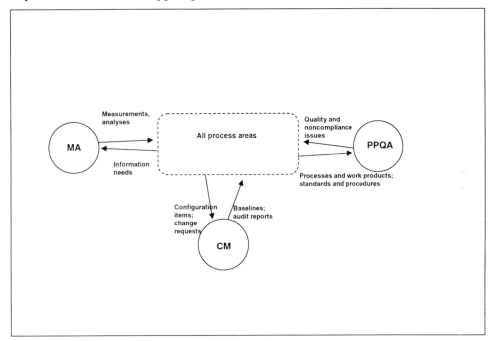

Figure 8. Basic support process areas.

MA enables the project or organization to develop and sustain a measurement capability that is used to support management information needs. PPQA enables the project or organization to provide staff and management with objective insight into the processes and associated work products. CM enables the project or organization to establish and maintain the integrity of work products using configuration identification, configuration control, configuration status accounting, and configuration audits.

Figure 9 provides a bird's-eye view of the advanced support process areas' interactions.

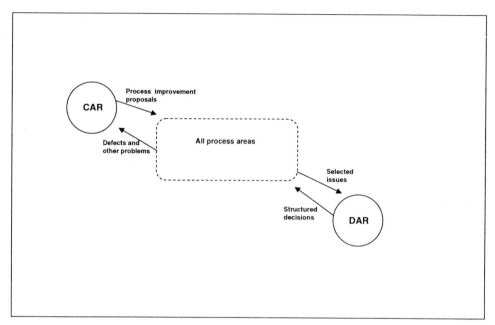

Figure 9. Advanced support process areas.

DAR enables the project or organization to make decisions using a structured approach that evaluates identified alternatives against established criteria. CAR enables the project or organization to identify causes of defects and other problems and to take action to prevent them from occurring in the future.

What Can I Expect from CMMI?

The CMMI Version 1.02 models were released in December 2000, so many enhancements and additions are yet to come. New model extensions will become available that address disciplines beyond software engineering and systems engineering. An updated description of the standard CMMI appraisal method for process improvement will be provided. Additional training classes, reports, and other transition products will continually be provided to inform you about CMM Integration. A demonstration of conformance with ISO/IEC 15504 will be provided. Finally, the CMMI-SE/SW and CMMI-SE/SW/IPPD models (and other components of the CMMI product suite) are scheduled to be updated to Version 1.1 by early 2002.

New Model Extensions

In early 2002, the CMMI project team plans to release CMMI-SE/SW and CMMI-SE/SW/IPPD Version 1.1 for public use. Model extensions that represent additional disciplines or environments will be integrated into the CMMI framework after that release. Ultimately, each extension will be covered in one or more CMMI models (for example, CMMI-SE/SW/IPPD/A will cover acquisition as well as software engineering, systems engineering, and IPPD). These extensions will increase the ability of a CMMI model to fit your organization's unique needs.

The first new extension to become available for use is the acquisition (A) extension.

232

CMMI Appraisal Method

An appraisal method and appraisal materials have been developed to support organizations using the CMMI-SE/SW and CMMI-SE/SW/IPPD Version 1.02 models. A description of the appraisal method and lead assessor program can be found on the SEI Web site (see below).

More Transition Support

Training and an appraisal method for the CMMI-SE/SW and CMMI-SE/SW/IPPD models were developed concurrently with these models to support their broad adoption. Training CMMI models and the appraisal method is now available. Consult the CMMI Web site (see below) for more information on specific training courses, conference reports, articles, and other transition products, including mappings to the CMM for Software Version 1.1, EIA/IS 731, and ISO 15504.

Development of Version 1.1

Development of Version 1.1 of the CMMI-SE/SW and CMMI-SE/SW/IPPD models is underway and will be complete in early 2002. As with Version 1.02, time will be set aside for public review, focus groups, and feedback from actual use. We encourage your participation. Please consult our Web site (see below) for more information.

Conformance with ISO/IEC 15504

Being consistent and compatible with ISO/IEC 15504 is important for CMMI products for a number of reasons. First, conformance provides access to an internationally recognized framework for "translating" appraisal outcomes to a common measurement framework for measuring the capability of an organization to perform processes. Second, any process improvement methods that are consistent and compatible with international standards will meet a common condition of business required in many international markets.

During development of the CMMI Version 1.02 models, maps from CMMI to ISO/IEC 15504 were developed. These will be analyzed and aggregated to develop a demonstration of ISO/IEC 15504 conformance. In addition, results from pilots using the CMMI models and appraisal methods and a to-be-developed translation mechanism will be incorporated into the Software Process Improvement and Capability dEtermination (SPICE) trials.

Where to Go for More Information

The CMMI Web site is continually updated with the latest information about CMMI products and CMMI project activities. Check these pages for the latest information: http://www.sei.cmu.edu/cmmi/.

About the Authors

Mike Konrad is co-leader of the CMMI product development team responsible for revising the CMMI models based on public review, focus groups, and pilot feedback. Mike is a senior member of the technical staff, administrative leader of the CMMI Initiative of the SEI, and has been with the SEI since 1988. Prior to participating in CMMI, Mike contributed to the development of initial versions of both SW-CMM Version 1.0 and the ISO/IEC 15504 technical reports. Before joining the SEI, Mike held a variety of positions in industry and academia. Mike has a PhD and BS in mathematics from Ohio University, Athens, Ohio.

Sandy Shrum is a member of the CMMI product development team and has been a senior writer/editor at the SEI since 1995. Before joining the SEI, she spent 8 years with Legent Corp., where she was a senior information developer and member of the product development team and corporate data center. Sandy has an MA in professional writing from Carnegie Mellon University and a BS in business administration and marketing from Gannon University.

References

CMMI A-Specification, Version 1.4, Software Engineering Institute, Pittsburgh, PA, July 15, 1998, http://www.sei.cmu.edu/cmmi/org-docs/aspec1.4.html.

Integrated Product Development Capability Maturity Model, Version 0.98, Enterprise Process Improvement Collaboration and Software Engineering Institute, Carnegie Mellon University, 1997.

Paulk, M.C., B. Curtis, M.B. Chrissis, and C. V. Weber, *The Capability Maturity Model: Guidelines for Improving the Software Process.,* Reading, MA: Addison-Wesley Publishing Company, 1995.

<no longer available on the Web>

Software Process Improvement and Capability dEtermination Model (SPICE), ISO/IEC 15504, International Organization for Standardization and International Electrotechnical Commission, Geneva, 1998, http://www.esi.es/Projects/SPICE.html.

Systems Engineering Capability Model, EIA/IS-731, Electronic Industries Association, Washington, DC, 1998, http://geia.org/sstc/G47/731dwnld.htm.

Chapter 6

Software Product Evaluation

1. Introduction to Chapter

In this chapter we consider Software Product (rather than Process) Evaluation. In the context of the software product, the term "evaluation" is normally used rather than "assessment." Here we are concerned with assessing the product directly, rather than with assessing the process and then assuming that a good process will necessarily produce a quality product. This approach has the benefit of being more direct, as far as the product is concerned, but is less indicative of the capability of the contractor who produced the product.

First it is necessary to define what we mean by software product quality. This is usually defined by a set of quality factors that a quality product may have, such as functionality, reliability, portability, etc. McCall, et al. defined 11 of these factors in "Factors in Software Quality" [5] and Boehm et al. defined seven in "Characteristics of Software Quality" [1]. Quality models such as those of McCall and Boehm associate a set of criteria with each factor and a set of metrics with each criterion. The metrics are supposed to be directly measurable. As an example, McCall associated the quality factor *maintainability* with the criteria *consistency, simplicity, conciseness, self descriptiveness*, and *modularity*. The criteria were then defined in terms of directly measurable features of the software or, alternatively, by means of checklists.

235

A number of quality models such as those proposed by McCall and Boehm are described in the literature. While individual models provide valuable insight into the issues of software quality, collectively they tend to cause confusion. Not only is there a lack of consistency between them, but the models tend to have too many factors and criteria to offer a readily assimilated view of software quality. As a result, Working Group 6 of ISO/IEC JTC1/SC7 was charged with producing an international standard quality model with a manageable number of independent quality factors. The quality model produced in 1991 defined six quality characteristics (factors), which among them covered all significant aspects of software quality with minimal overlap. They were:

functionality,

reliability,

efficiency,

usability,

maintainability,

portability.

The working group also attempted to define subcharacteristics (criteria) for each characteristic, but these did not become part of the official standard. At the time of writing, a new version of ISO/IEC 9126 is emerging. Its quality model is described in ISO/IEC 9126-1 [2]. ISO/IEC 9126 has moved on considerably since it was first published in 1991. Since then ISO/IEC 14598 [4], which is concerned with software product evaluation has been published, and the new 9126 is not concerned with evaluation as such.

It does, however, describe (in section 6) the quality model, which comprises the six quality characteristics described in the old 9126. In fact it goes further and refines each of these characteristics into a set of subcharacteristics. In the previous version of 9126 the sub-characteristics were merely illustrative.

The other main section of the standard is section 7, which describes a model for quality in use. This model has four attributes—*effectiveness*, *productivity*, *safety* and *satisfaction*—each of which is carefully defined.

Part 1 of the standard explains carefully how 9126 and 14598 relate to each other. Other parts of ISO/IEC 9126 include,

Part 2 : External Metrics.

Part 3: Internal Metrics.

Part 4: Quality in use Metrics.

In Europe, the ESPRIT project SCOPE (Software CertificatiOn Programme for Europe), described in Rae et al.[6], was concerned with software product quality and used industrial case studies to identify, validate and experiment with metrics to measure software quality. Tools were developed to capture, store and analyze metric values within and across case studies. Each of the 9126 quality characteristics was considered and software tools or checklists used to assess it. Some of the SCOPE work was used to produce what were originally guides to 9126, but have now become parts of ISO/IEC 14598 [4].

Of course, there is no unique way of assessing quality factors in terms of metrics. If there were, then there would be little problem in assessing them. As it is, there are two feasible approaches that may be taken for assessing quality factors and criteria in terms of metrics:

- assume a consensus view of the relationship between factors and metrics;

- adopt an instance-by-instance view of the relationship between factors and metrics.

In defining the checklists it used, the SCOPE project adopted the consensus view, based on the opinions of the project members who belonged to the 12 industrial and academic partners involved in the project. The instance-by-instance view, however, allows the assessor to choose the relationships between the factors/criteria and metrics (or checklists) according to their own preference and the needs of the situation. The relative importance of the factors themselves will also vary from one software project to another and may be determined by the assessor.

In this chapter we include some of the key work in the area of software product evaluation. It is worth noting that this area has received much less attention in recent years than software process assessment. This may be partly because it is a much more difficult area in which to make headway. However, its relatively poor predictive power, compared with software process assessment, has also meant that it has not received support from the major procurers of software in the same way as has the software process work.

2. Description of Articles

The first paper in this chapter is James Sanders's clever and amusing editorial entitled "Product, not Process: A Parable," which makes an admirable case for the product approach for assuring software quality. It would be superfluous to add further comment to it.

The second paper in this chapter, entitled "Quality Evaluation of Software Products," is by Jørgen Bøegh. In it, the need for and the benefits to be obtained from software product evaluation are described. The relevant international standards are reviewed, including ISO/IEC 9126 [2], ISO/IEC 12119 on quality requirements and testing (based on the German DIN 66285 Standard) [3], and the emerging ISO/IEC 14598 [4], which is concerned with software product evaluation to be used in conjunction with ISO/IEC 9126.

The author describes the main product evaluation schemes that have been used or are still in use, including the pioneering Gütegemeinschaft Scheme in Germany, the SCOPE method developed by the ESPRIT project, the MicroScope evaluations in Denmark, the Brazilian ASSESPRO scheme which awards prizes to the "best" software produced in Brazil in each of six categories, and the SQUID approach for continual evaluation of software products during development.

The paper concludes by outlining some experience gained using the MicroScope scheme, with which the author is particularly familiar.

The third paper, entitled "IusWare: A Methodology for the Evaluation and Selection of Software Products", is by M. Morisio and A. Tsoukias. It describes a software evaluation methodology that clearly separates the subjective and objective aspects of software measurement. The subjective aspects, which they refer to as "preferences," include the choice of measures to be used in the evaluation, the choice of aggregation methods, etc.

The methodology has two phases:

- design of the evaluation model;
- application of the evaluation model.

The design phase has four parts:

- identification of the purpose of the evaluation, the actors involved in the evaluation, and the resources available for the evaluation;
- identification of the type of evaluation required (e.g., ranking of products);
- definition of a hierarchical set of attributes to be evaluated;
- explanation of how the attribute measures are to be combined in order to perform the type of evaluation already identified.

Once the evaluation model has been designed, it may be applied in a straightforward way. The paper includes a detailed case study that brings out all the features of the methodology.

The fourth paper in this chapter, entitled "A Model for Software Product Quality," is by Geoff Dromey of the Software Quality Institute in Griffith University, Brisbane, Australia. In it, the author proposes a Software Quality Model based on ISO/IEC 9126 with the added quality characteristic of re-usability. Instead of defining subcharacteristics and metrics, the model associates quality-carrying properties of source language features such as variables and expressions, the absence of which lead to quality defects in the software.

The benefits of this approach are two-fold:

- it allows quality to be built into software;
- it allows the systematic detection and classification of defects.

Defects in software arise from violation of quality-carrying attributes associated with one or more structural forms. These defects do not necessarily give rise to losses in functionality or reliability, as far as the software is concerned, though they are liable to lead to problems with one or other of the quality factors and should therefore be avoided.

In order to ensure that the quality properties described in the paper are adhered to, a powerful static analyzer has been implemented by means of which structural defects, defined by rules, may be detected automatically. The tool produces comprehensive reports on C programs; including the values of metrics, such as the number of quality defects per thousand lines of code, the number of defects affecting each of Reliability. Maintainability etc. The responsibility for the production of quality code lies largely with the programmer. However, as the paper points out, some of this responsibility may be shifted to the language designer or implementor since clearly some languages and implementations are more liable to be associated with quality defects than others.

References

[1] B. W. Boehm, J. R. Brown, J. R. Kaspar, et al., *Characteristics of Software Quality,* TRW Series on Software Technology, North Holland, 1978. ;

[2] ISO/FDIS 9126-1, *Information Technology - Software Product Quality – Part 1: Quality Model, ISO/IEC 1999.*

[3] ISO/IEC 12119, *Information Technology - Software packages; Quality Requirements and Testing,* ISO/IEC, 1994.

[4] ISO/IEC 14598, *Information Technology - Software Product Evaluation ,* ISO/IEC 1998.

[5] J. A. McCall, P. K. Richards, G. F. Walters; "Factors in Software Quality", *RADC TR-77-369,*1977 vols. I, II, III, US Rome Air Development Centre Reports NTIS AD/A-049 014, 015, 055, 1977.

[6] A. Rae, P. Robert, H.-L. Hausen; *Software Evaluation for Certification,* McGraw Hill, 1994.

Product, Not Process: A Parable

In the November 1996 issue, I compared software development to home construction—a discipline that combines labor and art, but mostly labor. As a companion to that piece, I wrote a follow-on essay for this issue that compared software development to musical composition—a discipline that is primarily art. I wrote it as a parable that spoke exclusively about music, letting the reader see the "obvious" parallels to software. After I submitted the parable, Jim Sanders, one of our two excellent staff editors, contacted me to say that he had some concerns regarding my essay. We reviewed his comments together and quickly reached the conclusion that, in its original form, my essay was unsalvageable. Jim came to the rescue. Based on the points I had tried to raise, he wrote this wonderful parable. I hope you enjoy it.

—Al Davis

SO ADVANCED WAS HIS DEAFness, Ludwig van Beethoven did not notice his valet until the man tapped him gently on the shoulder. The visitor the valet announced was a neatly dressed gentleman with a satchel under one arm. Beethoven did not recognize him—nor did he care to. It was late in the summer of 1823 and he was deeply immersed in the composition of what would become his ninth symphony.

Before he could snarl a protest at being interrupted, the man crossed the study and slammed his satchel down on Beethoven's desk. "Good day, Herr Beethoven." The words came to him only faintly. The composer saw that the satchel bore the crest of the Austrian baron who was secretly underwriting his work. He must listen to this fool, then. He nodded for the man to continue.

"My employer is concerned about the slow progress of your work. He insists that you finish by the end of the year so that he can stage an exclusive premiere of your symphony at his New Year's Ball."

Did it matter that the process was ugly if the finished product was beautiful?

"But of course." Beethoven knew that if the angels smiled upon him, he might complete the Ninth by next February. March was more likely. Experience had taught him never to disclose such bad news until absolutely necessary.

"But *not* of course." The man dug into his satchel and pulled out a sheaf of crinkled papers. Beethoven realized they were manuscript pages from an earlier draft of the Ninth—pages he'd discarded weeks ago. "You are taking too much time to write your symphony," the man said. "Worse, you are padding it with far too many notes. At this rate you will finish months late and deliver a work so large and ungainly no one will listen to it."

Beethoven glanced at his valet; the man would not meet his eyes. So. His manservant had betrayed him and now the world knew what a tortured struggle each composition was for him. Did it matter that the process of creation was ugly if the finished product was beautiful, even brilliant? Apparently so. Beethoven felt strangely exposed and, for once, had no retort.

His visitor mistook Beethoven's silence for despair and placed a comforting hand on his shoulder. "Don't worry, friend. I have the solution to your problems." He reached into his satchel and withdrew a stack of charts and graphs. "I have studied your compositional procedures and although they may be excusable for a novice, they are unforgivable for a mature composer. I've isolated several practices I think you can improve upon. For example, look here. This section with the long cello solo—very inefficient. The violins could play it much faster, yes?"

The visitor pulled out another chart. "Speaking of violins, why do you use the strings and woodwinds so much, yet neglect the brass? For that matter, why don't you write more *tutti* passages? The musicians get paid as much whether they play or just sit, so it's most economical to have them all play at the same time, don't you think?"

Beethoven gasped, his mouth worked, but no words would come.

"Ah, I see you're a quick-minded fellow, you grasp the implications immediately. You'll be delighted to know that I've volunteered to spend the coming weeks at your side, monitoring your work. Oh, those bloated passages bursting with too many notes, those interminable crescendos, those meandering codas—just think of the inefficiencies we can eliminate. Why, we'll double the number of notes you write per hour!"

Beethoven rocked back in his chair. "No!"

> ## Just think of the inefficiencies we can eliminate. Why, we'll double the number of notes you write per hour!

"Incredible, yes? But don't thank me now, it will only slow us down." The visitor flipped over another chart. "Let's jump right in, shall we? Here—you intro-

duce a theme and then restate it later in the movement. A fairly standard practice and an efficient one that saves you from having to compose a new section entirely. Ah, but here's where you go wrong: you vary the theme too much to make reusing the notes worthwhile. All this breaking passages down and tossing them back and forth between the violins and the oboes...." The visitor paused and drew a finger across his throat. "That's the best solution, don't you think? With this section tightened and more self-contained, we can drop it in here...and here...and cut by almost half the time it will take you to write the entire movement."

Beethoven finally found his voice. "Who *are* you?"

The visitor drew himself to attention. "Herr Nummerich, at your service. I was an officer in the Austrian artillery during the wars against Napoleon."

Beethoven glared at him. "And this somehow makes you an expert on music?" Nummerich nodded emphatically. "Why? Because my tympani remind you of your guns firing?"

"No. Because artillery is all math: the bore and length of the gun barrel, the weight of the shot, the curve of the ball's trajectory and the force of its impact. Music is all math too: the pitch and duration of notes, the intervals between those notes in a scale, the timing between beats in a measure. People think of music as an art, but they're wrong. It's a science, or it could be. Music *wants* to be a science. I feel that. Don't you?"

"No, you cretin. Now get out."

Nummerich made no move to leave. "I must inform you that if you refuse to accept my counsel, my employer will withdraw his support. Immediately."

"Fine. I'll find another patron."

"I doubt it. With all modesty, I confess that my ideas are much *en vogue* with Vienna's nobles. Any one of them would most likely hire first an efficient composer who costs less and produces more."

"I see." Although outwardly calm, Beethoven felt deeply shaken. The thought of spending the rest of his days an impoverished invalid held little appeal. Still, to let this fool cut the heart

from his music and extinguish its fire—it was unbearable. And yet...what of all the charts and numbers that lay spread before him? Beethoven shuddered— maybe *he* was wrong. "Perhaps I have

> ## Music wants to be a science. I feel that. Don't you?

reacted hastily, Herr Nummerich. What else do you propose?"

Nummerich bent over the desk eagerly. "I've run some estimates. My projections indicate that your next symphony will take more than an hour to play. Ach! Mozart and Haydn never wrote such monsters. So first, we reduce the length of your composition by 41.4 percent." Beethoven winced, then nodded.

"Good." Nummerich shuffled through the papers and pulled out a rumpled page from the fourth movement. "We can start with the chorus. A chorus in a symphony? Madness! If listeners want to hear singing they can attend an opera or a chorale."

"But the Ode—"

"Is not part of the requirements. Really, now. Cutting the chorus reduces the composition by nearly 15 percent. Besides, you should leave such wild innovations for upstarts trying to make a name for themselves. You and your patron have a reputation to uphold and listeners to satisfy."

Beethoven would always remember that afternoon as the longest of his life. Months later, when the symphony premiered—on time—Beethoven was appalled by the audience's lukewarm applause and stifled yawns. Yawns? His works had provoked tears, laughter, even outrage, but never this. Herr Nummerich, at his side throughout the performance, asked what he thought of the premiere. "For the first time in my life," Beethoven told him, "I am happy to be deaf." ◆

James Sanders is a staff editor at IEEE Software. *He can be reached at* jsanders@ computer.org.

TOP TEN REASONS WHY SYMPHONIES AND SOFTWARE ARE ALIKE

Al Davis

Of course, it seems ludicrous to apply process metrics to symphonic composition. But I think symphonies and software bear enough similarities to make us question the wisdom of applying process metrics to software.

1. The building blocks for composition are very small.
2. Measures per month (M/mo.) and lines of code per month (LOC/mo.) are both easily tracked and equally meaningless.
3. The process that creates a product is totally unimportant once that product is delivered.
4. The product reveals a great deal about its creator's beliefs and values.
5. As Christopher Alexander observed when explaining his "quality without a name" concept, great products are easily recognized—but describing exactly *why* they are great is difficult.
6. Not surprisingly, then, no absolute rules exist for measuring product quality.
7. User satisfaction completely drives a product's popularity and economic success.
8. The greatest works in the field have tremendous emotional impact and stylistic influence.
9. Both forms permeate our culture.
10. Preconceived requirements do not encompass all user desires. Users can be surprised and delighted by the unexpected; sometimes they learn what they want only after they experience it in a finished product.

TOP TEN REASONS WHY SYMPHONIES ARE NOT LIKE SOFTWARE

James Sanders

I agree with Al that *conceptually* software design and symphonic composition have much in common. But software products, given their nature and use, will inevitably benefit from a system that can codify good practice without hamstringing creativity and innovation.

1. Symphonies are not written by teams.
2. Symphonies are not revised continually in response to end-user requirements.
3. Listeners do not need a consultant to tell them which symphonies to listen to, when, or how.
4. Symphonies do not require maintenance, are never upgraded, and do not become obsolete when technology advances.
5. Symphonies are always platform-independent: the violin parts, for example, can be played by a Stradivarius, a Yamaha, or a synthesizer—the symphony doesn't care.
6. Symphonies are not application-specific. Beethoven never wrote an accounting symphony; Brahms never wrote a word processing symphony; Mozart never even wrote a Java applet.
7. Large corporations do not routinely contract with composers to write symphonies, nor must symphonies ever model a corporation's work processes.
8. Symphonies cannot be critical systems: a symphonic bug (incorrect meter, unintentional disharmony) has never caused death, injury, or business failure.
9. Symphonies—no matter how badly written or played—never crash the orchestra, even when listeners wish they would.
10. Bill Gates has no plans for controlling the direction, structure, and pricing of all symphonies...yet.

ERRATUM

In our January/February '97 issue we neglected to acknowledge that copyright of the Timepoint Architecture example in "Recursive Design of an Application-Independent Architecture," by Sally Schlaer and Stephen J. Mellor, belongs to Project Technology, Inc., 1996.

ANOTHER VIEW

For a different perspective on the relationship between software engineering and musical composition, see "Fugue for MMX," by Jim Blinn in the March/April issue of *IEEE Computer Graphics and Applications*, pp. 88-93.

Quality Evaluation of Software Products

JØRGEN BØEGH
DELTA Software Engineering

Software quality evaluation is the systematic examination of the software's capability to fulfill specified quality requirements. This article discusses the needs for and advantages of software product evaluation. It reviews the relevant international standards, both published and forthcoming.

Practical software evaluation schemes have been introduced in recent years. Some of these schemes are described and their market acceptance is reviewed. Finally, the experiences gained with the MicroScope evaluation scheme based on almost 80 commercial evaluations are presented.

Key words: accreditation, certification, quality characteristics, requirements, standards, testing laboratories

INTRODUCTION

Software use is growing dramatically and so are the number of critical computer systems. Faults in critical systems can lead to serious consequences. Therefore, the quality of these systems' software is important for individuals, companies, and society in general, which leads to a growing demand for quality evaluation of software products.

CRITICAL APPLICATION

Most software quality evaluations are conducted for critical applications. This includes national critical applications such as defense systems, where large software developments are carried out. Here the evaluation effort is often of the same magnitude as the development effort.

Until now, life-critical systems have been the main target for independent third-party quality evaluations. Such systems include traffic-control systems, medical systems, process-control systems, robots, and so on. The evaluation effort for this type of application can be large; public authorities often require independent evaluations of these systems.

Other systems are equally critical. Modern society depends on such software systems as electronic payment systems, public-administration systems, and telephone systems. These have equally high quality requirements and extensive quality evaluations.

Similarly, corporate-critical systems such as production systems, financial systems, and consumer products (including software and customer databases) should be considered systems with high-quality requirements. This type of software, however, is often neglected with respect to quality evaluation. As companies realize the advantages of ensuring the quality of their software, the market for software evaluations should increase substantially.

Market Advantages

Currently most independent quality evaluations are done because they are required by law or public authorities. There are, however, other reasons for demanding software evaluations. In some cases a software company may be asked by an acquirer to accept an independent quality evaluation as part of the development contract. This can actually be an advantage for both parties since disputes about the delivered software can be referred to the evaluation, and therefore, legal actions can be avoided.

Some evaluation schemes are devoted to issuing quality marks or seals. The aim is to give a marketing advantage to good quality software products. A few quality marks have been introduced, but until now, they have not been generally accepted in the market.

Yet another group of evaluation schemes is used for comparing similar software products. Many software magazines apply this approach for benchmarking software packages, but it is also relevant in other circumstances, such as when choosing a software supplier. In any case, a quality seal should have a positive influence on a buying decision.

INTERNATIONAL STANDARDIZATION

It is generally accepted that a professional development process is a prerequisite to achieving quality products. This is the background for process-related standards such as ISO 9000 and ISO/IEC 12207: Software Life-Cycle Processes (ISO/IEC 12207 1995). A good development process alone, however, cannot guarantee a high-quality product. When product quality is important it is also necessary to consider the product itself. The process view and product view should therefore complement each other. This article is mainly concerned with the product view of software quality.

The need for product quality evaluations is reflected in standardization activities. Currently several international standards are either being finalized or revised to fit the present state of the art. The requirements of the standardization work and the most important standards are presented here.

Evaluation Requirements

By definition, quality evaluation is the systematic examination of the extent to which an entity is capable of fulfilling specified requirements. Hence, software product evaluation must follow some strict rules and satisfy some basic requirements, or evaluation results will not be valid. This is especially true for independent third-party evaluation. Requirements for testing laboratories can be found in ISO Guide 25: General Requirements for the Technical Competence of Testing Laboratories (ISO Guide 25 1990). It emphasizes the following requirements for evaluation:

- *Repeatability.* Repeated evaluation of the same product to the same evaluation specification by the same evaluator will give the same result.

- *Reproducibility.* Repeated evaluation of the same product to the same evaluation specification by different evaluators will give the same result.

- *Impartiality.* Evaluation will be free from unfair bias toward achieving any particular result.

- *Objectivity.* The evaluation will be obtained with the minimum of subjective judgment.

These requirements must be fulfilled by any reliable evaluation scheme. In addition, there may be other considerations, such as cost effectiveness of the evaluation, inclusiveness (the evaluation covers all quality characteristics), and indicativeness (when some discrepancies or other problems are found by the evaluation, their causes and required actions are indicated).

ISO/IEC 9126: Quality Characteristics

ISO/IEC 9126 (ISO/IEC 9126 1991) is the relevant standard for defining software quality and is recommended for quality evaluations in most situations. In ISO quality is defined as "the totality of characteristics of an entity that bear on its ability to satisfy stated and implied needs." ISO/IEC 9126 suggests a hierarchical quality model with six quality characteristics and attached subcharacteristics:

- *Functionality.* A set of attributes that bear on the existence of a set of functions and their specified properties. The functions are those that satisfy stated or implied needs.

FIGURE 1 Examples of Product Evaluation Schemes and Related Standards

Evaluation scheme	Area	ISO/IEC 9126	ISO/IEC 14598	ISO/IEC 12119	ISO/IEC 12207
GGS	Germany	X		X	
SCOPE	Europe	X	X		
Microscope	Denmark, Greece, Hungary	X	X		
TÜV Nord	Germany	X		X	
Assespro	Brazil	X	X	X	
Squid	Denmark, Germany, Italy, United Kingdom	X	X		
NF-Logiciel	France	X		X	
Medical software	Ireland	X	X		
Q-Seal	Italy	X			
Product and process	Korea	X	X		X
Product evaluation	The Netherlands	X	X		
Product evaluation	Sweden	X	X		

©1999, ASQ

Subcharacteristics are suitability, accuracy, interoperability, compliance, and security.

- *Reliability.* A set of attributes that bear on the capability of software to maintain its level of performance under stated conditions for a specified time period. Subcharacteristics are maturity, fault tolerance, and recoverability.

- *Usability.* A set of attributes that bear on the effort needed for use and on the individual assessment of such use by a stated or implied set of users. Subcharacteristics are understandability, learnability, and operability.

- *Efficiency.* A set of attributes that bear on the relationship between the software's performance level and the resources used under stated conditions. Subcharacteristics are time behavior and resource behavior.

- *Maintainability.* A set of attributes that bear on the effort needed to make specified modifications. Subcharacteristics are analyzability, changeability, stability, and testability.

- *Portability.* A set of attributes that bear on the ability of software to be transferred from one environment to another. Subcharacteristics are adaptability, installability, conformance, and replaceability.

ISO/IEC 9126 is applicable to most types of software. In some situations, however, it may be better to use another quality model (such as for security evaluations).

ISO/IEC 12119: Quality Requirements and Testing

This standard (ISO/IEC 12119 1994) is based on the German standard DIN 66285 and is applicable to software packages. It establishes a set of quality requirements and provides instructions on how to test software against these requirements. In contrast with ISO/IEC 14598 (ISO/IEC 14598 1998), it only deals with software as offered and delivered; it does not deal with the production process, including development activities and intermediate products such as specifications and source code. ISO/IEC 12119 uses ISO/IEC 9126 as the underlying standard for defining software quality.

ISO/IEC 14598: Software Product Evaluation

ISO is currently preparing a new standard for software product evaluation. It is also intended to be used in conjunction with ISO/IEC 9126. The new standard consists of the following parts:

Part 1: General overview

This part provides an overview of the other parts and explains the relationship between ISO/IEC 14598 and the quality model in ISO/IEC 9126. It defines the technical terms used in the standard, contains general requirements for specification and evaluation of software quality, and clarifies the concepts. Additionally, it provides a framework for evaluating the quality of all types of software products and states the requirements for methods of software product measurement and evaluation.

Part 2: Planning and management

Part 2 provides requirements and guidelines for a support function responsible for the management of software product evaluation and technologies necessary for software product evaluation. The responsibilities of this support function include people motivation and education relevant to the evaluation activities, preparation of suitable evaluation documents, standards, and response to queries on evaluation technologies. The main targets for evaluation support are the software development and system integration projects, which include software acquisition, both at a project and organizational level.

Part 3: Process for developers

This part provides requirements and recommendations for the practical implementation of software product evaluation when the evaluation is conducted in parallel with development and carried out by the developer. The evaluation process described defines the activities needed to analyze evaluation requirements; specify, design, and perform evaluation actions; and conclude the evaluation of any software product. The evaluation process is designed to be used concurrently with the development. It must be synchronized with the software development process and the entities evaluated as they are delivered.

Part 4: Process for acquirers

Part 4 contains requirements, recommendations, and guidelines for the systematic measurement, assessment, and evaluation of software product quality during acquisition of off-the-shelf software products, custom software products, or modifications to existing software products. The evaluation process helps meet the objectives of deciding on the acceptance of a single product or selecting a product. The evaluation process may be tailored to the nature and integrity level of the application. It is also flexible enough to cost-effectively accommodate the wide range of forms and uses of software.

Part 5: Process for evaluators

This part provides requirements and recommendations for the practical implementation of software product evaluation when several parties need to

understand, accept, and trust evaluation results. The process defines the activities needed to analyze evaluation requirements; specify, design, and perform evaluation actions; and conclude the evaluation of any kind of software product. The evaluation process may be used to evaluate already existing products, provided that the needed product components are available, or to evaluate products in development. This part may be used by testing laboratories when providing software product evaluation services.

Part 6: Documentation of evaluation modules

This part describes the structure and content of an evaluation module. An evaluation module is a package of evaluation technology for a specific software quality characteristic or subcharacteristic. The package includes descriptions of evaluation methods and techniques, inputs to be evaluated, data to be measured and collected, and supporting procedures and tools. This part should be used by testing laboratories and research institutes when developing evaluation modules.

In 1997 "Part 5: Process for Evaluators" was approved as an international standard (ISO/IEC 14598-5 1997) and "Part 1: General Overview" is currently in the final-ballot stage. The other parts are expected to become international standards sometime this year.

PRACTICAL EVALUATION SCHEMES

There are a number of practical software quality evaluation schemes, some of which are outlined here. The selection is not exhaustive, but it gives an impression of the trends in the area. Most activities are currently taking place in Europe, but South America and Asia are beginning to appear on the scene. Figure 1 provides an overview of the evaluation schemes and relevant standards discussed.

The Gütegemeinschaft Software Seal

One of the first initiatives to develop a quality seal for software products was the German GGS controlled by the Gütegemeinschaft Software Association (Knorr 1990). The GGS association was founded in the mid-

1980s with the aim of defining quality criteria for software products and organizing a software quality certification scheme. This resulted in the publication of the German standard DIN 66285 in 1990, which defines the quality requirements for a software package and specifies the testing procedure that could lead to a certificate. This standard was adapted for international standardization and published by ISO in 1994 as standard ISO/IEC 12119.

The GGS seal has never been very successful in Germany and has only been awarded to a few software products.

The SCOPE Experiment

The ESPRIT project SCOPE (Software Certification Program in Europe) was the first major international attempt to set up a certification scheme for software product evaluation (Robert and Roan 1990). SCOPE lasted from 1989 to 1993. The project involved 13 companies from eight countries with a total effort of 110 person-years.

The SCOPE project was successful, although it failed to set up a certification scheme. Its main achievement was the development of a framework for software quality evaluation that is now widely accepted and used as a basis for evaluations around the world.

The main results of SCOPE were an evaluation method, a collection of evaluation technologies, and extensive practical experience. Additionally, a thorough review of the legal aspects of evaluation and certification was carried out, including the legal view of software, rights exclusion clauses, criteria for successful claims, common legal defenses, and the implications of the European Communities Directives on product liability (Rae, Robert, and Hausen 1995).

The SCOPE project carried out 30 trial evaluations (Welzel, Hausen, and Bøegh 1993). These case studies were conducted in two phases. In the first phase six evaluations were carried out applying different evaluation procedures and techniques. The results were analyzed and used for planning the second phase. Here all evaluations followed the same procedure, and care was taken to select software products that covered a wide range of applications and software development approaches.

The SCOPE evaluation method was developed as a result of an analysis of the trial evaluations. It was documented in the "Evaluators Guide," which was submitted to ISO for consideration (Bøegh, Hausen, and Welzel 1992). This document has now been adapted and published as ISO/IEC 14598-5: Process for Evaluators.

The concept of evaluation modules was also an important outcome from SCOPE (Bøegh 1995). It was introduced to make it easy and flexible to manage the use of the different evaluation technologies.

MicroScope Evaluations

The MicroScope approach to software evaluation was introduced in Denmark by DELTA Software Engineering in 1991 (Kyster 1995). MicroScope is based on the results of the SCOPE project and follows standards ISO/IEC 9126 and ISO/IEC 14598-5.

The MicroScope evaluations are being used in many situations. The most common purposes are to state the conformance to a specified external standard or regulation and to validate that the level of documentation and safety for a software product is satisfactory.

The evaluations are based on an agreement between a client and DELTA on which quality characteristics of the software product should be considered and evaluation modules should be used. The MicroScope evaluation modules are checklist based. There are 12 modules covering all six characteristics of ISO/IEC 9126. The evaluations are performed at one of four possible levels for each relevant characteristic corresponding to the criticality of the product.

MicroScope emphasizes the evaluation of the workmanship of the software and related documentation (for example, that design descriptions, coding standards, test documentation, and so on comply with the best state of practice in the software industry). Experiences with the MicroScope approach will be discussed more in detail later.

TÜV Nord Evaluations

TÜV Nord in Germany has developed an evaluation method aimed at process control and real-time systems with safety relevance. The evaluation method is based on several standards, including IEC 880, draft IEC 1508/IEC 65A, DIN V VDE 801, and DIN 19250. TÜV Nord received an accreditation by DEKITZ as a software testing laboratory for evaluating software according to these standards. Off-the-shelf software is evaluated based on ISO/IEC 12119. TÜV Nord is accredited as a testing laboratory by the Gütegemeinschaft Software Association.

The mentioned standards are mainly concerned with functionality. TÜV Nord is also elaborating quality profiles based on ISO/IEC 9126 using the TASQUE approach (Anders and Flor 1994). They have been involved in national and European research projects, which have resulted in the adoption of new methods and tools such as CATS (Technischer Fachbericht 1993) and SQUID (Kitchenham et al. 1997a). These tools are used to enhance the evaluation capabilities.

The ASSESPRO Prize

In Brazil the Technological Center for Informatics Foundation (CTI) is in charge of a major effort to provide software product evaluation services to the Brazilian software industry (Tsukumo et al. 1995; Tsukumo et al. 1996; and Tsukumo et al. 1997). They have developed the method MEDE-PROS based on the international standards ISO/IEC 9126, ISO/IEC 12119, and ISO/IEC 14598 drafts.

The checklist-based method has similarities to the MicroScope approach. The checklists are continuously being improved and now include more than 100 questions. The method evaluates the product description, documentation, and programs and data according to ISO/IEC 12119. The main emphasis of MEDE-PROS evaluations are on functionality and usability for software packages.

The evaluation method is applied by the Brazilian Association of Software Houses (ASSESPRO) for awarding the best software product of the year in Brazil. The ASSESPRO prize only includes software packages and is given in six categories:

- Systems for documentation and planning support

- Systems software and systems of support to software development

- Tools for graphic design

- Information and services automation systems

- Engineering, scientific, and industrial automation systems

- Education and entertainment systems

Each year since 1993 between 20 and 50 software packages have been evaluated for the ASSESPRO prize, and considerable statistical material has been collected. Currently the MEDE-PROS evaluation method is also being applied to support a Brazilian software export initiative with the aim of increasing the Brazilian share of the world market.

The SQUID Approach

The SQUID approach to software quality evaluation is slightly different from the others. It is intended for use during software development as described in ISO/IEC 14598-3 (Bøegh and Panfilis 1996). The aim of the SQUID method is to provide support to a software developer. It is an approach to modeling, measuring, and evaluating software quality during the development process. SQUID is supported by a toolset currently under development.

The toolset assists in quality specification, planning, control, and evaluation. More specifically, for quality specification it provides the means to establish targets for the product quality requirements and evaluate their feasibility. Then, the toolset supports the identification of internal software product and process attributes that must be controlled during the development process to fulfill project quality requirements. This is called quality planning and control. Finally, the toolset helps assess the fulfillment of project quality requirements.

Ongoing evaluation of the SQUID approach and toolset is part of the work (Kitchenham et al. 1997b). One experiment is to apply SQUID as a supporting tool for third-party testing laboratories in connection with independent software product evaluations. This study is carried out by TÜV Nord in cooperation with DELTA Software Engineering.

Other Initiatives

Several other attempts to develop quality certification schemes and seals have taken place in different countries during recent years. In 1996 the French national standardization body initiated the development of a software product marking called NF Logiciel (Geyres 1997). This quality mark should be applicable to any type of software product. It is based on ISO/IEC 12119 and requires a product to be composed of product description, user documentation, and program and data. For a software product to obtain a NF Logiciel marking, the claims in user documentation must be able to be verified in the program and data by an independent evaluator. Several trial evaluations were started, but the quality mark has not yet been adopted in France.

In Ireland an evaluation scheme based on the

SCOPE approach and standards ISO/IEC 9126 and ISO/IEC 14598 was established in 1994 (O'Duffy 1997). This scheme was extended to a certification scheme covering products for practice management for general practitioners in Ireland. In 1997 a total of nine software products had received certification.

In Italy an initiative to implement an evaluation scheme for software based on ISO/IEC 9126 called Q-Seal was initiated. It applies a predefined profile based on characteristics, subcharacteristics, and levels. Some case studies were conducted in 1995 and 1996.

In 1996, the National Computerization Agency in Korea started to set up a software product evaluation scheme. It decided from its organization's perspective to concentrate on custom-made software, and it is following an approach to integrate software product evaluation and software process evaluation into a common framework. The process evaluation is based on the software life-cycle processes defined in ISO/IEC 12207: Software Life-Cycle Processes.

In the Netherlands KEMA has recently developed a technique for third-party evaluation of quality characteristic maintainability (Punter 1998). The technique combines the use of quality metrics (such as number of statements, comment frequency, and number of levels) with checklists. KEMA's evaluation procedure complies with ISO/IEC 14598-5.

Finally, the Swedish Association of Software Houses SPI (Föreningen Svensk Programvaruindustri) has prepared an annotated translation of ISO/IEC 14596-5 (Battison et al. 1996) and developed a series of small evaluation modules. A first experimental software product evaluation was successfully completed in 1997.

MicroScope Experiences

MicroScope is an example of a commercially successful software evaluation scheme. Many evaluations have been conducted since its introduction in 1991. The accreditation to the European standard EN 45001 obtained in 1996 confirmed the soundness of the scheme.

Evaluation Procedure

The MicroScope evaluation procedure consists of five activities that are conducted in cooperation with the client of the evaluation. The activities are performed on the basis of data and other information provided by the client or produced by other activities during the evaluation. Figure 2 shows the evaluation process.

Analysis of evaluation requirements

The purpose is to establish the objectives of the evaluation. Such objectives relate to the intended use of the software product and its associated risks. The client of the evaluation must provide an initial version of the evaluation requirements. The evaluator will then assist in analyzing these requirements. The application domain; critical issues such as safety, security, economic, or environment aspects; and regulations and laws are taken into account. How extensive the coverage of the evaluation should be must also be stated and agreed upon.

Specification of the evaluation

The purpose is to define the scope of the evaluation and the measurements to be performed. The level of detail should be such that the repeatability and reproducibility of the evaluation are ensured. The activity of specifying the evaluation includes three subactivities:

1. Analyzing the product description

2. Specifying the measurements to be performed on the product and its components

3. Verifying the specification produced with regard to the evaluation requirements

This activity may be supported by predefined evaluation specifications. These specifications should be in the form of evaluation module specifications as recommended in ISO/IEC 14598-6.

FIGURE 2 The evaluation process

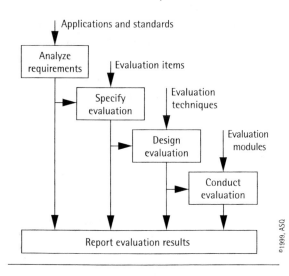

249

Design of the evaluation

The evaluator must produce a plan that describes the resources needed to perform the specified evaluation. This activity is composed of three subactivities:

1. Documenting evaluation methods and producing a draft plan. In most cases this means selecting appropriate evaluation modules.

2. Optimizing the evaluation plan

3. Scheduling evaluation actions with regard to available resources

The goal of this activity is to combine the specified measurements with various product components. The measurements must be selected to ensure an objective and impartial evaluation.

Execution of the evaluation plan

This consists of inspecting, modeling, measuring, and testing elements of the product according to the evaluation plan. The actions performed by the evaluator are recorded, and the results are put in a draft-evaluation report. To execute the evaluation plan the evaluator shall:

1. Manage the product components provided by the client

2. Manage the data produced by the evaluation actions

3. Manage the tools used to perform the evaluation actions

Conclusion of the evaluation

This consists of finalizing and approving the evaluation report and disposing of the product components evaluated.

The MicroScope evaluation procedure complies with the international standard ISO/IEC 14598-5: Process for Evaluators.

Commercial Evaluations

DELTA Software Engineering has obtained considerable experience by offering the MicroScope evaluation service on commercial conditions. MicroScope was launched in 1991, and about 80 software evaluations have already been conducted.

The evaluations cover many application areas, including fire alarms, burglar alarms, offshore systems, gas burners, railway signals, process-control systems, medico systems, automatic weighting

FIGURE 3   Effort used on different application categories

Application category	Effort
Offshore	48%
Fire alarms	23%
Railway	12%
Other	17%

©1999, ASQ

systems, and windmills. The most evaluations have been in safety-critical areas. To identify the main areas of commercial interest in the MicroScope evaluation service, Figure 3 shows the evaluation effort used on different application categories.

The offshore evaluations weigh heavily in this summary because of the size of the evaluations. In numbers, however, they account for less than 10 percent of the evaluations. Software developers learn from their evaluation experiences: The second time a company applies for an evaluation the quality of its software is higher than the first time.

In particular the quality of the development documentation has increased. A few years ago companies seemed to produce limited documentation, whereas now it is common to see extensive and good quality documentation, such as design documents and well-documented source code.

Evaluation Modules

An evaluation module is defined as a package of evaluation technology for a specific software quality characteristic or subcharacteristic. The package includes descriptions of evaluation methods and techniques, inputs to be evaluated, data to be measured and collected, and supporting procedures and tools.

MicroScope includes a set of 12 evaluation modules. They are checklist based and contain more than 1800 questions. A disadvantage of the checklist approach is that answers to the questions often rely on the evaluator's judgment. This loss of objectivity can be minimized by carefully formulating the questions so they can be answered unambiguously and by avoiding very short checklists. Some experiences with checklist-based evaluations are reported in *Software Metrics for Product Assessment* (Andersen and Kyster 1994).

The possible answers to the checklists are such that zero, one, and two points are given, or it is decided that the answer is not applicable (N/A). Two points indicates that the feature is present and the formulation is such that this is positive for the product. Zero points implies an absence of a desired feature.

A score is calculated for each checklist by counting the number of points given and the number of points the product could have received when excluding the N/A questions. The ratio between these two numbers is multiplied by 10 to arrive at a final score for a checklist between zero and 10, independent of the number of questions on the checklist. The evaluation modules cover all quality characteristics identified in ISO/IEC 9126. Figure 4 categorizes the evaluation modules accordingly.

In practice, the application of some evaluation modules may be irrelevant for an evaluation, and in other cases, it may be convenient to restrict the scope of application of some of the chosen evaluation modules to samples from the documentation received for evaluation. In any case, to keep the evaluation within reasonable time and cost limits, an agreement must be reached concerning the choice of evaluation modules and the depth to which they are used.

Before starting an evaluation, the evaluator must ensure that the needed product information is made available by the client. The specific product information requirements are stated in the evaluation modules.

An Evaluation Example

A MicroScope evaluation of the software part of a fire alarm, which is a typical example of a small evaluation, requires one to two weeks' effort. A full evaluation of a fire alarm also requires a thorough hardware and system evaluation, including both design and implementation aspects and practical fire tests of the alarm. It is the combined results of these evaluations that form the basis for the approval decision by the authorities (in this case the Danish Institute of Fire Technology).

Before an evaluation starts the manufacturer must provide the necessary input for the evaluation. This includes product identification information (name, version, date, type, hardware and software platform, programming language, compiler name and version, and so on) design documentation, program description, source code, and user manual. Furthermore, requirements specification, test documentation, executable code, maintenance manual, quality assurance plans, and project plans are also requested.

FIGURE 4 The MicroScope evaluation modules

Quality characteristic	Evaluation module	Description
Functionality	Requirements specification	Checklist for assessing the quality of the requirement-specification document
	Safety	Checklist that takes all product parts and guides the evaluator through a cross examination of the product
	Test documentation	Checklist concerning the test documentation and the test planned and executed
	Fire-alarm regulations	Checklist covering the requirements relating to software of the standard prEN 54-2: Control and Indicating Equipment
	Nonautomatic weighing instrument	Checklist based on the WELMEC guide for examining software of nonautomatic weighing instruments
Reliability	Reliability	Checklist taking as input the design documentation and source code. The asssessment is restricted to qualitative aspects of reliability
Usability	User manual	Checkilst concerning the user manual, not the usability of the system under evaluation
	ISO/IEC 9241	Checklist guiding the assessment of the user interface according to the software-related parts 12 to 17 of ISO 9241
Efficiency	Source code	Checklist guiding the assessment of the source code assessed through the analysis of the software aspects: Time behavior and resource behavior
Maintainability	Design documentation	Checklist concerning the quality of the design documentation for the software product
	Source code	Checklist concerning the quality of the source code as written in any traditional programming language or as logic or ladder diagrams for PLC program
Portability	Source code	Checklist concerning the independence of the source code from any particular hardware and/or operating system platform

This type of MicroScope evaluation usually requires the application of four evaluation modules:

- **Usability: User manual.** A Checklist with 97 questions concerning the user's manual as such for the software (or the system as a whole).

- **Maintainability: Design documentation.** A Checklist with 110 questions concerning the quality of the design documentation for the software product.

- **Functionality: Safety.** A Checklist with 195 questions concerning the safety and security of the software product as a whole.

- **Functionality: Fire-alarm regulations.** The purpose of applying this evaluation module is to demonstrate compliance to European fire-alarm regulations.

The criteria for selecting these four evaluation modules are the requirements from public authorities and the cost of the evaluation. In other words, to answer the questions of evaluation module "Functionality: Fire-alarm regulations" the evaluator must have a thorough understanding of the system. This is obtained by answering the questions of the three other evaluation modules. Since these types of evaluations are cost sensitive (due to competition) the selected evaluation modules constitute a minimal set necessary to carry out the evaluation.

In a real MicroScope evaluation conducted at DELTA Software Engineering the following scores were achieved and observations made:

- **Usability: User Manual: Score 8.6.** The user manual is well structured, with the appropriate level of details for users who have been trained in the operation of the system. On the other hand there lacks an upper-level description of the system including examples of typical systems. There is no identification of the software version for which it is relevant. Of the questions on the checklist, 25 percent were N/A because the system is embedded and the user manual does not need to cover explanations of platform, operating system, software environment, back up, and so on.

- **Maintainability: Design documentation: Score 7.5.** The modularity and breakdown of the system are very good, and it is a convincing reflection of the implementation. The completeness

and consistency of the design documentation is also good. On the other hand, a simple introduction to the system and its design is lacking, together with descriptions of data structures and explanations of variables and constants. The self-descriptiveness of the design documentation is weak, as illustrated through lack of consistent document identification, tables of contents, glossaries, and introductions.

- **Functionality: Safety: Score 7.3.** The self-test facilities and the supervision of the hardware are good from a safety point of view, as well as the user interface. The programming style is well structured. On the other hand, the documentation of fault handling is weak and is mainly restricted to information contained in module headers. Thus, there is no central place to identify what may happen and what the systems' reactions are. Use of interrupts complicates the safety analysis, as does use of the language C. Of the questions on the checklist, 25 percent were N/A because they were related to fail-safe features. No true fail-safe features are present in the software, but because of the application, they are not needed.

- **Functionality: Fire-alarm regulations.** Here "passed" or "failed" is given for each of the requirements from the standard. In this case, 15 out of 16 requirements from fire-alarm regulations were passed.

- **Conclusion of the evaluation.** The software and the corresponding documentation for the fire-alarm unit have been assessed regarding its conformity with the relevant requirements of the fire-alarm regulations. This was done by conducting a MicroScope evaluation to assess the design documentation, the user manual, the safety features of the software system, as well as the conformity with the fire-alarm regulations.

The conclusion is that the software sufficiently conforms with the standard for use in a fire-alarm unit. With regard to the nonconformity found with one of the requirements of the fire-alarm regulations, it should be noted that the judgment is based on the fact that no documentation was found for the requested feature. If the software is in conformance, this may be documented. If the nonconformity is real and the matter is deemed to be sufficiently important, restrictions may be introduced so that the system can only handle 512 fire detectors or manual call points.

Accreditation

At the beginning of 1996 DELTA Software Engineering received an official accreditation of MicroScope according to the European standard EN 45001: General Criteria for the Operation of Testing Laboratories. Accreditation means formal recognition by an authoritative body that an organization is competent. The MicroScope accreditation, which is issued by the Danish Accreditation Service (DANAK), confirms the compliance of MicroScope with ISO/IEC 9126 and ISO/IEC 14598-5. The accreditation gives the right to issue MicroScope evaluation reports using the DANAK logo.

DANAK is a member of the European Cooperation for Accreditation of Laboratories, an organization of the national bodies of all EU/EFTA member countries that accredit testing laboratories. The national accreditation bodies evaluate each other frequently to ensure that each is operating in accordance with international standards. A multilateral agreement exists between national accreditation bodies ensuring that reports issued by accredited testing laboratories have the same degree of credibility in all member countries. The purpose of this European acceptance of reports is to help international business by removing barriers to trade.

To achieve the accreditation, a quality documentation consisting of 39 documents, totaling 2100 pages, was produced. The documentation includes a quality system, relevant standards, operating procedures, and test instructions. The experiences with the accreditation process were positive. The accreditation body handled the process fast and efficiently. It took six months from when the application was forwarded until the accreditation was issued. To keep validity, the MicroScope accreditation must be renewed every year.

It should be noted that European standard EN 45001 is based on the ISO guides listed in Figure 5. In some instances the text from these guides has been modified or clarified for European purposes; however, such changes are the exception rather than the rule.

Licenses

The MicroScope evaluation method and evaluation modules have been licensed to companies in Greece and Hungary, and other companies have expressed interest. Such arrangements provide an efficient start-up of software evaluation services for testing laboratories, which are new in this field.

CONCLUSION

As the number of critical software applications grows, the need and demand for software quality evaluation increases. International standards are being prepared to support evaluation, and practical software product evaluation schemes are available to the market. But the field is not mature yet, and there is still a need to experiment, collect experiences, and improve the evaluation methods and technologies.

FIGURE 5   The ISO guides related to EN 45001

ISO Guide 2:	General terms and their definitions concerning standardization and related activities
ISO Guide 25:	General requirements for the technical competence of testing laboratories
ISO Guide 38:	General requirements for the acceptance of testing laboratories
ISO Guide 43:	Development and operation of laboratory proficiency testing
ISO Guide 45:	Guidelines for the presentation of test results
ISO Guide 49:	Guidelines for development of a quality manual for testing laboratories

© 1999, ASQ

REFERENCES

Anders, U., and R. Flor. 1994. TASQUE-TÜV. In *Software metrics for product assessment,* edited by R. Bache and G. Bazzana. London: McGraw-Hill.

Andersen, O., and H. Kyster. 1994. Reproducibility of checklists. In *Software metrics for product assessment,* edited by R. Bache and G. Bazzana. London: McGraw-Hill.

Battison, R., J. Bengtsson, R. Källgren, L. Piper, M. Ran, H. Samuelsson, and J. Stiernborg. 1996. *Manual för utvärdering av programprodukter enligt ISO 14598-5 och ISO 9126.* Stockholm, Sweden: Föreningen Svensk Programvaruindustri.

Bøegh, J., H. L. Hausen, and D. Welzel. 1992. Guide to software product evaluation: The evaluator's guide. *SCOPE Technical Report* SC.92/099/ECT.jb. GMD.hlh.dw/T2.1.2/DR/04.

Bøegh, J. 1995. Evaluation modules: The link between theory and practice. In *Proceedings of the Second IEEE International Software Engineering Standards Symposium.* Los Alamitos, Calif.: IEEE Computer Society Press.

Bøegh, J., and S. de Panfilis. 1996. SQUID: A method for managing software quality during the development. In *Proceedings of the European Space Agency Product Assurance Symposium and Software Product*

Assurance Workshop. Noordwijk, The Netherlands: ESA Publication Division.

EN 45001: General criteria for the operation of testing laboratories. 1991. CEN/CENELEC.

Geyres, S. 1997. NF Logiciel: Affordable certification for all software products. In *Achieving software product quality*, edited by E. van Veenendaal and J. McMullan (September): 125-135.

ISO Guide 25: *General requirements for the technical competence of testing laboratories*. 1990. Geneva, Switzerland: International Organization for Standardization.

ISO/IEC 9126: Information technology–Software product evaluation–Quality characteristics and guidelines for their use. 1991. Geneva, Switzerland: International Organization for Standardization.

ISO/IEC 9241: Ergonomic requirements for office work with visual display terminals. 1994. Geneva, Switzerland: International Organization for Standardization.

ISO/IEC 12119: Information technology–Software packages–Quality requirements and testing. 1994. Geneva, Switzerland: International Organization for Standardization.

ISO/IEC 12207: Information technology–Software life-cycle processes. 1995. Geneva, Switzerland: International Organization for Standardization.

ISO/IEC 14598: Information technology–Software product evaluation (draft multipart standard). 1998. Geneva, Switzerland: International Organization for Standardization.

ISO/IEC 14598-5: Information technology–Software product evaluation–Process for evaluators. 1997. Geneva, Switzerland: International Organization for Standardization.

Kitchenham, B., A. Pasquini, U. Anders, J. Bøegh, S. de Panfilis, and S. Linkman. 1997. Automating software quality modeling, measurement and assessment. In *Reliability, quality and safety of software-intensive systems*, edited by D. Gritzalis. London: Chapman & Hall.

Kitchenham, B., S. Linkman, A. Pasquini, V. Nanni. 1997. The SQUID approach to defining a quality model. *Software Quality Journal* 6: 211-213.

Knorr, G. 1990. The Gütegemeinschaft software: A major concept in the certification of software quality. In *Approving software products*, edited by W. Ehrenberger (September): 135-138.

Kyster, H. 1995. MicroScope: *The evaluation of software product quality* DQD-5012200. Horsholm, Denmark: DELTA Danish Electronics.

O'Duffy, M. 1997. Certification of software for medical practitioners. In *Achieving software product quality*, edited by E. van Veenendaal and J. McMullan (September): 137-143.

Punter, T. 1998. Developing an evaluation module to assess software maintainability. In *Proceedings of Empirical Assessment in Software Engineering Conference*. Staffordshire, England: University of Keele.

Rae, A., P. Robert, H. L. Hausen. 1995. *Software evaluation for certification*. London: McGraw-Hill.

Robert, P., and A. Roan. 1990. The SCOPE project: An overview. In *Approving software products*, edited by W. Ehrenberger (September): 9-22.

Tectnicher Fachbericht. 1993. Werkzeuge für den standardisierten software-sicherheitsnachweis (SOSAT-3), supported by Bundesministerium für Bildung und Forschung. Hamburg, Germany: Tectnicher Fachbericht. (March).

Tsukumo, A. N., C. R. Capovilla, C. M. Rêgo, M. Jino, and J. C. Maldonado. 1995. ISO/IEC 9126: An experiment of application on Brazilian software products. In *Proceedings of the Second IEEE International Software Engineering Standards Symposium, Montréal*. Los Alamitos, Calif.: IEEE Computer Society Press.

Tsukumo, A. N., A. Oliveira, C. M. Rêgo, G. F. Azevedo, J. C. Maldonado, M. T. Aguayo, M. Jino, and R. Tutumi. 1996. The second experiment of application of ISO/IEC 9126 standards on quality evaluation of Brazilian software products. In *Proceedings of the 6th International Conference on Software Quality, Ottawa, Ontario*.

Tsukumo, A. N., A. Oliveira, C. M. Rêgo, C. S. Salviano, G. F. Azevedo, M. C. Costa, R. M. T. Colombo, and M. Jino. 1997. A framework for incremental evaluation of software product quality based on ISO/IEC 9126. In *Proceedings of the 6th Software Quality Management, Bath, England*.

Welzel, D., H. L. Hausen, and J. Bøegh. 1993. A metric-based software evaluation method. In *Software testing, verification, and reliability*. New York: John Wiley & Sons.

BIOGRAPHY

Jørgen Bøegh has a degree in mathematics and computer science from Aarhus University in Denmark. He is currently a project manager for DELTA Danish Electronics, Light and Acoustics Division.

Bøegh has been involved in research in communication security and personal safety of software-based systems. He was involved in the ESPRIT 1 project REQUEST (Reliability and Quality in European Software Technology) from 1985 to 1987. From 1986 to 1989 he was responsible for DELTA's participation in the MAP projects "Network Security" and "Software Integrity." In 1988 and 1989 he managed an industrial collaborate project on integration of computer-aided engineering tools within the Danish electronics industry.

From 1989 to 1993 he was involved in the ESPRIT II project SCOPE (Software certification program in Europe) and from 1994 to 1996 he was responsible for DELTA's participation in the ESPRIT III project PET (Prevention of errors through test). Since 1995 he has been responsible for DELTA's participation in the ACTS project Prospect, and from 1997 also for the project VALSE (validating SQUID in real environments) and the ESSI project EPIC (exchanging process improvement experiences across SMEs by conferencing on the Internet).

Bøegh is head of the Danish delegation to the international standardization group ISO/IEC JTC1 SC7 and was appointed editor of ISO/IEC 14598 parts 3 and 6. He is the author of several scientific papers and a book on object-oriented software development. His research interests include software quality specification and evaluation, software measurement and testing, and software best practices. Bøegh can be reached by e-mail at jb@delta.dk .

IusWare: a methodology for the evaluation and selection of software products

M. Morisio
A. Tsoukiàs

Indexing terms: Software product evaluation, Methodology, Multicriteria decision aid

Abstract: IusWare (IUStitia SoftWARis) is a methodology designed to evaluate software products in a formal and rigorous way. The methodology is based on the multicriteria decision aid approach and encompasses activities such as comparison, assessment and selection of software artefacts. The methodology defines an evaluation process which consists of two main phases, designing an evaluation model and applying it. The design phase is made up of the following activities: first, identifying the actors relevant to the evaluation, their role, the purpose of the evaluation, the resources available and the object(s) of the evaluation; secondly, identifying the type of evaluation required: either a formal description of products or the ranking of products from the most preferred to the least preferred or a partitioning into two sets of the best and the remaining products; thirdly, defining a nonredundant hierarchy of evaluation attributes, often corresponding with the quality characteristics of quality models; fourthly, associating a measure, a criterion scale and a function to transform the measure scale into the criterion scale to each basic attribute; and finally, choosing an aggregation technique so as to aggregate values on criteria to form a recommendation for the selection. In the application phase attributes of products are measured, measures are transformed into values on criteria and aggregated to form a recommendation.

1 Introduction

The question as to whether product A or product B should be adopted or whether module X developed by a subcontractor should be accepted or whether COTS (component off the shelf) Y or Z should be reused is a question which has to be faced more and more frequently as the use of software becomes more diffuse

© IEE, 1997

IEE Proceedings online no. 19971350

Paper first received 2nd January and in revised form 8th May 1997

M. Morisio is with the Dipartimento di Automatica e Informatica, Politecnico di Torino, Corsa Duca degli Abruzzi, 24, 10129, Torino, Italy

A. Tsoukiàs is with LAMSADE, Université Paris Dauphine, Place du Maréchal de Lattre de Tassigny, F-75775, Paris Cédex 16, France

and it has become increasingly necessary to develop a software quality evaluation technology.

According to Fenton's [1] measurement framework, a product can be evaluated by considering a number of product attributes, which can be either external (functionality, usability, maintainability, etc.) or internal (size, algorithmic complexity, etc.) and they can be either directly or indirectly associated with a measure.

Documents such as [2, 3] define an evaluation process which involves

(a) The identification of the relevant quality attributes of the product

(b) The measurement of the attributes using suitable measures

(c) The aggregation of measures

Other relevant work will be presented and analysed using this evaluation process which will also be discussed. However, the strictly related topic of software production process evaluation will not be dealt with in this paper.

1.1 Software product evaluation

1.1.1 Identification of quality attributes: In fixed quality model approaches [4, 5], quality attributes have been definitely identified and customised for a particular domain and type of evaluation and in such cases the evaluator has only to fill in the scores. This approach is practical but, of course, not general. In a similar way the documents [3, 6] define a set of external quality attributes for CASE tools. In [7], this approach is used to evaluate any software system with a simple model composed of nine factors.

In constructive quality model approaches [2, 8, 9] the evaluator has to customise a general quality model which means that there is maximum flexibility, but there is also need for skilled people and time. To our knowledge only the goal question metric approach [10, 11] has been proposed as an aid in this field.

The need to test the nonredundancy of the quality attributes chosen for the constructed quality model has not been dealt with in any detail in the literature, although this is a very important condition. For instance in cases where some quality attributes are redundant and a weighted sum method is used as an aggregation procedure, the use of this procedure increases the performance of a particular product in an unacceptable way.

1.1.2 Measurement of attributes: The measurement of attributes, especially external ones, is difficult, either because the collection of data is time consuming and impracticable, or because no correlation has been established between the proposed measures and the attribute.

The idea that some form of judgement has to be made in any evaluation can be found in [10, 12, 13].

Measures are numbers or symbols objectively assigned to an attribute [1], *preferences* are subjectively assigned to an attribute in terms of binary relations. For instance the length of an object is a measure (an objective assignment, assuming standard length measurement) while the preference between a long object and a short one is a subjective judgement depending on the purpose and the context of the evaluation. It is important not to confuse the concepts of measures and preferences. Preferences can be defined by starting from measures (they are associated to *measured attributes*) or independently (they are associated to *nonmeasured attributes*). An attribute which is assigned a preference relation is a *criterion*. An *essential judgement* is made using criteria based on measured attributes. A *nonrepeatable judgement* is made using criteria based on nonmeasured attributes [10].

The distinction between measures and preferences has not been defined with sufficient clarity [4, 5, 14–18] and thus there is the risk of confusing preferences, usually presented numerically, with measures, which means that the element of subjectivity is not immediately evident.

An essential judgement is to be preferred as it allows less space to conscious or unconscious bias in evaluations. A nonrepeatable judgement should be used only when the measure does not yet exist or it is impractical or too expensive to use. The choice should always be discussed and justified.

1.1.3 Aggregation techniques: Measures or preferences collected on several attributes and several products constitute a large amount of data. To make a selection decision, these data have to be summarised into the smallest number of aggregated indicators by using an aggregation technique.

The weighted average sum (WAS) aggregation technique is used in [4, 5, 14, 15, 17]. It is also used in most everyday evaluations. However, it should be noted that WAS requires attributes which have at least ratio scales, while the majority of attributes in evaluations can be characterised only by ordinal scales.

Current practice is often to transform an ordinal scale (for instance *very high*, *high*, *fair*, *low*, *very low* associated to attribute *usability*) into a ratio (the scale becomes 5, 4, 3, 2, 1) WAS interprets four as twice two, while it is meaningless to say that *high* is twice *low*. This interpretation is essential to WAS when weights are applied, since weights are in fact trade-offs between attributes, or ratios between the scales. If weight two is assigned to usability, a *low* in usability becomes a *high*. This is meaningless with ordinal scales.

Even when attributes have ratio scales, WAS can have a dangerous effect, called compensation, that hides situations of incomparability with indifference. Given a model with *quality* and *cost*, product A scoring five on quality and one on cost, product B scoring one on quality and five on cost, the aggregated score according to WAS is three for both products, that is to say they are indifferent.

The arbitrary assignment of weights to attributes has another dangerous effect. If quality is assigned weight two, cost weight one, two units of cost compensate one unit of quality. This is not necessarily incorrect. but clients are not usually aware of this relationship, or that its immediate consequence is that a preference of two units in cost can completely compensate for an inverse preference of one unit of quality. Since the assignment of weights is arbitrary, a weight can always be found to make the worst product on attribute quality have the best aggregated score.

The analytic hierarchy process (AHP) (described in [19]) is used in [16, 20]. The hierarchical nature of the data used by the AHP may correspond in some way to hierarchical quality models. However, this is not always the case and the assumption that there should be complete comparability and the imposition of ratio scales at all levels of the hierarchy is very demanding. The AHP technique does not offer an answer in situations where there is incomparability and there is evidence of preferential reversal drawbacks in particular cases [21–23]. A study on a selection of off-the-shelf products [24] reported that the use of WAS and AHP gave different final results and that WAS gave less insight into the evaluation process.

The heuristic approach proposed by [25] is similar to the concordance part in the outranking methods (see [26] and Section 3) but is not sustained methodologically.

The subjective probability and the expected utility theories are used in [27]. This technique has a very strong axiomatisation [28] derived from a normative approach in decision making. Such an approach, however, has been strongly criticised in descriptive and prescriptive situations [29] as being inflexible and unrealistic.

Our fundamental criticism is not that such techniques should not be used, but that the choice of which one is used is arbitrary. The choice of one technique (instead of another) is not always justified and the validation of the technique (different techniques are not suitable for all kinds of problem) is not always discussed. In other words, the aggregation technique is a key variable of the evaluation model, and should be chosen to be consistent with the other components of the model.

1.1.4 Evaluation process: Evaluations involve different people, resources and activities. The need to define a precise evaluation process model in which the roles of people (decision maker, evaluator, user, client and producer) and their responsibilities, the activities, the temporal constraints among activities are described is not recognised in [4, 5, 16, 20].

However, an evaluation process, mainly from a managerial, organisational and legal point of view has been defined in [30, 2, 31] but it considers only the assessment and certification of a product.

There is a need for an evaluation process model which takes into account both the technical issues and a variety of possible evaluations such as the description of products, the ranking of products in a linear scale from the most preferred to the least preferred, the choice of one or more products as acceptable and the others as unacceptable.

1.2 Requirements for an evaluation methodology

In the authors' opinion, the central issue in software product evaluation is to adopt a general approach, so as to provide an evaluator with the conceptual tools

IEE Proc.-Softw. Eng., Vol. 144, No. 3, June 1997

256

which will enable him to build reliable, robust and useful models of his problem. We propose the following requirements for an evaluation methodology.

Decision process: Many actors are involved in an evaluation, each one having different objectives and providing partial information [32]. Many activities are performed and a lot of information is produced. Therefore the evaluation process is not trivial, and should be clearly defined.

Hierarchy of conflicting criteria: An evaluation involves many criteria (also referred to as evaluation attributes, or quality attributes), usually organised in a hierarchy. In most evaluations, some criteria are in conflict with others (for example, quality and cost).

Judgement: An evaluation tries to find which product best fits a need. Since a need depends on people or organisations expressing it, an evaluation also depends on people or organisations. In other words, an evaluation is a subjective, qualitative process that involves judgement. In particular, this requires the use of aggregation techniques capable of handling judgement.

Measures, preferences, uncertainty: In an evaluation different types of information have to be considered: measures (an objective assessment), preferences (a subjective assessment) and uncertainty. These three information sources should not be confused (otherwise meaningless results may appear) and require specific aggregation techniques. For instance uncertainty can be aggregated using a 'max' operator (which is meaningless for the measures and preferences), measures can be aggregated by different kind of means (geometric and arithmetic ones, meaningless for both uncertainty and preferences), preferences can be aggregated using voting procedures (meaningless for measures and uncertainty).

Aggregation technique: The aggregation procedure is not neutral vis-à-vis the information provided (measures, preferences and uncertainty) and the desired result and is therefore part of the evaluation model. Thus it has to be chosen with the same care as the evaluation attributes and should be consistent with the whole evaluation model.

Flexibility and consistency: Each evaluation problem is different, with different criteria, different points of view, different purposes. An evaluation methodology should be flexible enough to address all these points. Conversely, an evaluation methodology should verify the internal consistency of the evaluation. In particular the aggregation technique should not be taken for granted, but chosen to be consistent with the other components of the evaluation.

Most of the above requirements are satisfied by the multicriteria decision aid (MCDA) approach [34–36]. The MCDA approach consists in a conceptual framework, unifying different aggregation techniques (such as multi-attribute value theory, outranking methods, AHP, etc.) under common concepts, while providing some general guidelines for choosing a specific technique which satisfies the following requirements: coherency of all components of an evaluation model to guarantee meaningful results; and suitability of the evaluation model to the decision maker's needs to guarantee useful results. This paper presents IusWare, a methodology that adapts the MCDA approach to evaluations in the software product domain.

2 Method

The IusWare method (IUStitia SoftWARis, to be read as UseWare) will be described in the same terms as the entities which make up the software process, i.e. resources, products and activities.

The software product evaluation process (SPEP), is the set of resources, products and activities consumed, produced and performed between the perception of a software product evaluation problem and the adoption of a formally motivated final solution for the problem. The SPEP is equivalent to the concept of the decision-aid process used in the MCDA approach and involves resources, products and activities which are presented below.

2.1 Resources
Actor refers to the people or organisation involved in the SPEP. An actor can play the role of either buyer, vendor, user, producer of a software product, or its evaluator (the party performing the evaluation). The client is the actor whose point of view is used to build the evaluation model and who will use it. The client and the evaluator are the core actors in the SPEP.

The commitment, knowledge and time which each actor can dedicate to the evaluation are also to be regarded as resources.

2.2 Activities and products
In this Section the activities performed during a SPEP and their respective final products are introduced. Figs. 1–3 contain dataflow diagrams corresponding to the SPEP.

Three top level activities (see Fig. 1) can be identified: the problem formulation, the design of the evaluation model and the application of the evaluation model. The similarity between these activities and the classical decision-making model of Simon [36] should be noted. The top level activities will now be described.

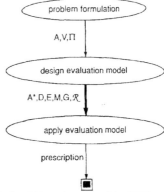

Fig. 1 *Top level activities and products of the SPEP*

2.2.1 Problem formulation:
As soon as it is apparent that a formal decision aid is needed, a number of questions have to be raised and answered to guide the definition of the evaluation model.

The evaluator, on the basis of interviews with the client, defines a problem formulation $\Gamma' = \langle A, V, \Pi \rangle$ where: A is the set of software products on which the SPEP is focused (what will be evaluated?). Great care should be taken in defining A, since the client may consider subsets of a given A, either to test his ideas or as a result of undeclared discrimination. Analogously, unexpressed wishes of the client should be checked for. *V* is the set of points of view (what is the bias of the evaluation?). The points of view depend on the actors (who wants the evaluation?) involved in the SPEP. Typical points of view are those of the user, producer, producer-technician, producer-manager, maintainer and vendor. Normally the point of view of one or more actors is adopted.

Π is a problem statement defining what the final result is expected to be (what is the purpose of the evaluation?). Possible values of Π are

Choice – partition the set products into a set of *best* product(s) and *rest* product(s)

Sorting – partition the set of products following previously defined profiles of *good, bad*, etc.

Classification – rank the products from the *most preferred* to the *least preferred*

Description – provide a formal description of the products, without any ranking

Conceptualisation – identify ideal or quasi-ideal products not available at the moment and possibly conceive new alternatives

different combinations of the above statements

The first three problem statements are called operational.

2.2.2 Design of the evaluation model:
In this activity (see Fig. 2) a detailed evaluation model is defined. The orders of precedence between activities are those shown in Fig. 2. The three main streams of action are the choice of A^*, the definition of D, E, M, G and the choice of $\mathcal{R}$.

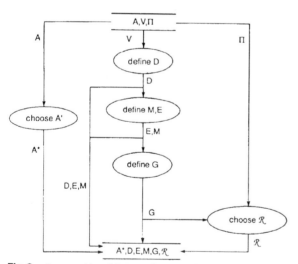

Fig.2 *Decomposition of design evaluation model activity*

Choose A^*: $A^* \subseteq A$ is a subset of the set A defined in the problem formulation. The elements of A^* are assumed to be independent, in the sense that the evaluation of one product should not influence the evaluation of the others. A is purged to A^* to satisfy the independence constraint, to reduce the evaluation effort and eventually to meet any mandatory requirement.

Define D: D is a set of evaluation attributes. Typically they correspond to the quality attributes of quality models and are derived from the points of view

in *V*. Attributes can be decomposed hierarchically. The first level of decomposition introduces *subattributes*, the second level *sub-subattributes*, etc. An attribute which is decomposed is called a *composed attribute*, an attribute which is not decomposed is called a *basic attribute*. The decomposition of an attribute into subattributes means that the attribute depends on the subattributes and that the dependency is qualitative. For instance, the attribute *quality of product* may depend on the subattributes *functionality, operating system, modularity* and *diffusion*.

Define M: M is the set of measures associated to basic attributes. For each basic attribute, the evaluator chooses or defines a measure capable of characterising it. The evaluator can also decide, but should justify any decision, not to measure an attribute. A *measured attribute* is an attribute associated to a measure. An essential judgement is built upon such attributes. A *nonmeasured attribute* is an attribute which is not associated to a measure. Nonrepeatable judgements are built upon such attributes. For instance, *functionality* could be measured in terms of the number of low level functionalities available, *operating system* by classifying the operating system, while *modularity* could be judged and *diffusion* could be measured by the number of licenses sold. *Functionality, operating system* and *diffusion* are measured attributes while *modularity* is not measured.

Define E: E is the set of scales associated to D. The scales can be of any type, including nominal. $e_j(a_i)$ denotes the values obtained by each $a_i \in A^*$ on each measure associated to a basic attribute d_j. For measured attributes the scale usually corresponds to the scale of the measure. For nonmeasured attributes the scale is declared by the client. For instance *functionality* and *diffusion* have scales e_f, e_d sets of positive integers, *operating system* has the scale $e_o = [Unix, Dos, Vms]$, *modularity* has the scale $e_m = [high, medium, low]$.

Define G: The goal of this activity is to define the rules to be used to transform measures into preferences, according to the client's needs [37].

To formalise the concept of preference and the rules to compute it from measures, we introduce the key concepts of preference structure and criterion.

A *preference structure* is a set of preference relations characterised by their properties. In the simplest and most common case such a set collapses to a single binary relation *s*, built in different ways upon the basic relations *p*: strict preference, *i*: indifference and *r*: incomparability. For instance a common definition of *s* is: $\forall x, y \in A^*$ $s(x, y) \equiv p(x, y) \vee i(x, y)$. *s* can have different properties such as completeness, (a)symmetry, transitivity, etc. depending on how it is defined. For instance if incomparability is empty, strict preference is transitive and indifference is not, then *s* is a semi-order [38].

A criterion $g_j^* = \langle d_j, s_j \rangle$ is an attribute equipped with a preference structure. If s_j is a complete binary relation, then a numerical representation exists which is equivalent to it. In that case we introduce for each criterion a function $g_j : \mathcal{E}_j \mapsto R$ (where $\mathcal{E}_j$ is the set of values of the scale e_j) which maps the attribute scale to the reals, satisfying the constraints imposed by the properties of the preference structure and the type of scale. G is the set of all g_j, $g_j(a_i)$ denotes the value of product a_i on criterion g_j.

For instance if s_j is a semi-order, its admissible numerical representation is:

$$\forall x, y \; p(x, y) \Leftrightarrow g(x) - g(y) \geq k$$
$$\forall x, y \; i(x, y) \Leftrightarrow |g(x) - g(y)| < k$$

representing the threshold (constant) at which discrimination is difficult.

Assuming that $\forall j \; s_j$ is a complete binary relation, the goal of this activity is to define G. This activity and the activity *Transform nominal scales* mark the first important transition from measurement to formalised essential judgement, that is to say the first important step in modelling the client's need for the evaluation.

Operationally the evaluator may face the following cases:

(i) Accept the order induced by the scale of the attribute as the preference structure; in this case $\forall x \; g_j(x) = e_j(x)$

(ii) Modify the numerical representation induced by the scale to take into account the specific nature of the client's preferences: any functional transformation (inverting, using logarithms, introducing thresholds, etc.) is possible and actually a scale transformation is carried out; in this case $\forall x \; g_j(x) = g_j(e_j(x))$

(iii) Build s_j directly by performing pairwise comparisons of the elements in A^*, then deduce g_j; this approach is typically used either when the client is not able to declare g_j explicitly or when s_j is not complete (in this case g_j does not exist). Measured attributes with nominal scale (for instance attribute *operatingsystem*) are a particular case. Then, either a direct pairwise comparison of the products may help in defining the associated criterion, or a preference structure is built among the elements of the nominal scale (for instance in the case of *operatingsystem* the user may declare that $[Dos > Unix = Vms]$). In this case the preference structure of the scale applies directly on A^* (if $e_o(a_1) = Dos$, $e_o(a_2) = Unix$, then a_1 is preferred to a_2).

In the two former cases the preference structure is defined implicitly through g_j (and is verified later, see activity *Verify s*), while in the latter case the preference structure is defined and computed explicitly.

In our example the criteria could be defined as

functionality : if the client prefers products with more functionality

$$\forall x, y \in A^* \; s_f(x, y) \Leftrightarrow g_f(x) \geq g_f(y) \text{ with } g_f = e_f$$

if the client prefers products with less functionality

$$\forall x, y \in A^* \; s_f(x, y) \Leftrightarrow g_f(x) \geq g_f(y) \text{ with } g_f = -e_f$$

if the client prefers products with more functionality, besides a threshold

$$\forall x, y \in A^* \; s_f(x, y) \Leftrightarrow g_f(x) \geq g_f(y) + 10 \text{ with } g_f = e_f$$

operating : *system*: $\forall x, y \in A^* \; s_o(x, y) \Leftrightarrow g_o(x) \geq g_o(y)$. with $g_o(Vms) = 0, g_o(Unix) = 0, g_o(Dos) = 1$

modularity : $\forall x, y \in A^* \; s_m(x, y) \Leftrightarrow g_m(x) \geq g_m(y)$. with $g_m(high) = 3, g_m(medium) = 2, g_m(low) = 1$

diffusion : $\forall x, y \in A^* \; s_d(x, y) \Leftrightarrow g_d(x) \geq g_d(y)$ with $g_d = \log(e_d)$ because the client wants to compare orders of magnitude of licences sold.

Choose $\mathcal{R}$: $\mathcal{R}$ is an *aggregation technique*, described by an algorithm, capable of transforming the set of all s_j into a prescription for the client. A *prescription* is an order on A^*. $\mathcal{R}$ can be used only with operational problem statements.

Usually an aggregation of the preferences of the criteria at a certain level of decomposition results in a *global* binary relation which may not be an order. An *exploiting procedure* transforms the global relation into an order.

Four families of techniques are considered: first, multi-attribute value (utility) theory, a marginal value (utility) function is associated to each criterion and a global value (utility) function is computed in an additive or multiplicative form [39]. WAS is a special case of the theory. Utility functions are especially suitable in the stochastic case.

Secondly, interactive techniques, the final prescription is obtained through the interactive exploration of the set of nondominated solutions using the client's preferences (e.g. multi-objective programing, goal programming) [40]. Thirdly, analytic hierarchy processes, the decisional goal is decomposed into a hierarchy of goals and ratio comparisons are performed on a fixed ratio scale. Then overall priorities are computed using an eigenvalue technique on the comparison matrix [19]. Finally, outranking techniques, a global preference relation is computed via direct aggregation of the preference structure and then exploited by the evaluator to compute the prescription. There are many aggregation and exploiting procedures and they enable the evaluator to tune the technique to the problem situation [35]. Unlike the other techniques, outranking techniques distinguish between classification and choice and solve the sorting problem statement.

The choice of $\mathcal{R}$ is constrained by (see [35] for a deeper analysis)

(i) The type of problem statement Π

(ii) A^* being a continuous or discrete set. Actually A^* in software evaluation is always a discrete set. However, several aggregation techniques fit better when A^* is a continuous set (it is the case for several interactive procedures)

(iii) The type of scales of criteria; in the example used above the WAS technique cannot be used because two criteria have ordinal scales, while WAS requires at least ratio scales

(iv) The type of dependency among the criteria (see also [41]). A basic condition to be satisfied is isolability. A criterion g_k is isolable in G iff

$$\forall x, y \in A^* : \forall j \in G \setminus \{g_k\} \; g_j(x) = g_j(y) \text{ and } g_k(x) \geq g_k(y) \text{ then } S(x, y)$$

where S is the global preference relation. $S = P \vee I$ with P global preference and I global indifference. G satisfies the isolability condition if $\forall k \in G \; g_k$ is isolable. When G is nonredundant (see the later activity: verify nonredundancy), then isolability is also satisfied.

A stronger condition is that of additive preferential independence. Let J be a subset of G, J^c its complement. J is preferentially independent in G

if $\forall x, y, z, w$

$$g_j(x) = g_j(y) \wedge \forall j \in J \; g_j(z) = g_j(w)$$
$$g_j(x) = g_j(z) \wedge \forall j \in J^c \; g_j(y) = g_j(w)$$

then

$$P(x, y) \Leftrightarrow P(z, w) \text{ and } I(x, y) \Leftrightarrow I(z, w)$$

where P is global preference and I is global indifference.

if $\forall J \subseteq G \; J$ is preferentially independent in G, then G fulfils the additive preferential independence condition [35]. The WAS technique cannot be used if G does not fulfil the additive preferential independence condition.

(v) The client accepts or rejects compensation among criteria. Multi-attribute value techniques are the best choice if trade-offs among the criteria are to be used.

$\Gamma = \{A, V, \Pi, A^*, D, E, M, G, \mathcal{R}\}$ is the main product of the Design evaluation model activity and is called the evaluation model.

2.2.3 Application of evaluation model:
In this phase (see Fig. 3) the evaluation model is applied and a prescription is obtained.

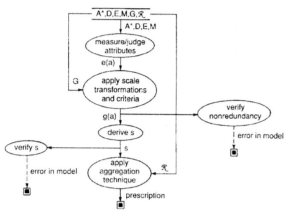

Fig.3 *Decomposition of apply evaluation model activity*

Measure/judge attributes: for each basic measured attribute and for each software product in A^*, a measurement is performed to obtain $e_j(a_i)$. The client judges $e_j(a_i)$ for each basic nonmeasured attribute and for each software product in A^*.

Apply scale transformations and criteria: nominal scales are transformed and $g_j(a_i)$ are computed.

Derive s: for each j s_j is deduced by using the criteria.

Verify s: the evaluator verifies, on relevant attributes, whether the preference structure deduced in this way actually models the client's preferences and needs. In other words, since in real cases often preferences are deduced from existing measures, it is important to verify that the criteria construction respects the user's preferences. A typical example is to verify the necessity to introduce a discrimination threshold. Often the discrimination problem appears only after the preference structure has been built up.

Verify nonredundancy: the nonredundancy of basic and composed criteria is verified by using two tests:

(i) $\forall g_j \in G$ such that $g_j(a) = g_j(b)$ then

$\forall c \ P(c, b) \rightarrow P(c, a)$ and $P(b, c) \rightarrow P(a, c)$

$\forall c \ I(c, b) \rightarrow I(c, a)$ and $I(b, c) \rightarrow I(a, c)$

(ii) $\forall g_j \in G \backslash \{g_k\}$ such that $g_j(d) = g_j(b)$
and $g_k(d) \geq g_k(b)$

and

$\forall g_j \in G \backslash \{g_k\}$ such that $g_j(a) = g_j(c)$
and $g_k(a) \geq g_k(c)$

then

$P(b, a) \rightarrow P(d, c)$

and

$I(b, a) \rightarrow P(d, c)$ or $I(d, c)$

if a reduced set of criteria satisfies the two tests, then G is redundant.

Intuitively the two tests verify what happens if a criterion is eliminated from the set G. The first test says

that two products a, b which are equivalent in all criteria should behave globally in the same way when compared with any third product c (first coherence test). The second test says that if the product d dominates the product b and the product a dominates the product c, then when b is strictly better than a then d should be strictly better than c and when a and b are indifferent then c could not be strictly better than d (second coherence test).

If after eliminating a criterion the two tests are no longer satisfied, then the set G is the minimal set of criteria that guarantees coherency. Conversely, if after eliminating a criterion the tests are still verified, then the set G is no more minimal and hence can be considered redundant.

Apply aggregation technique: $\mathcal{R}$ is applied iteratively to s and a prescription is obtained. A prescription is an order on A^*. In the case of nonoperational problem statements it corresponds to s. In the case of operational problem statements, it is the result of the application of $\mathcal{R}$ to s. In particular

(*a*) If Π is a choice then it corresponds to the *kernel* of the global preference relation, i.e. the elements of A^* which jointly outperform all the others

(*b*) If Π is a sorting then it corresponds to a strict total order of equivalence classes where each class is a cluster of elements of A^*; each cluster is built around an external profile (an imaginary ideal *good* product or *bad* product, etc.)

(*c*) If Π is a classification then it corresponds to a strict total order of equivalence classes where each class is built from products judged to be indifferent

Γ must not change during the application of the model. If this happens (i.e. A and A^* receive or lose elements, G changes) a new iteration of the design phase should be performed.

3 A case study

An account of an evaluation carried out with IusWare is now presented.

3.1 The problem
A CASE tool to support the production of software in a CIM environment has to be selected from the many offered on the market. Basically two functionalities are offered by the products: first, to build a model of a production facility to simulate its behaviour and evaluate its performance; and secondly, to build a model of the software to be used in the production facility so that it can be generated.

CIM software typically has responsibility for production planning, production control and monitoring. The software is event intensive, has (soft) real-time constraints, is embedded and runs in a heterogeneous hardware and software environment.

The simulation model of a facility has to have the model of the software embedded in it, so that the two functionalities can be integrated. First, a model of the whole facility is made, including models of the manufacturing devices, and is used for simulation. Then the model is transformed, by substituting the models of the manufacturing devices with the actual software interfaces which link them, and the software embedded in the facility is generated.

3.2 Application of IusWare

The results of each activity of the SPEP are presented in the same order as in Section 2.

3.2.1 Problem formulation:
The actors of the evaluation are the buyer, the user and the evaluator. The point of view of the evaluation is the one of the buyer and the one of the user, who have jointly decided on a common approach to the evaluation problem.

Three problem formulations, or A, V, Π, were built up

(i) Γ_1' a description of the products. A is the set of CASE products available on the market (more than 20 products). V coincides, for the user, with the software quality attributes listed in the ISO 9126 standard [2]: functionality, portability, efficiency, reliability, usability and maintainability. The buyer's point of view also includes a concern for the life of the purchase. Π is a description, i.e. a description of each product compared with each software quality attribute. Γ_1' is a cautious problem formulation with no aggregation techniques, therefore there is no operational prescription (which product to buy). It is indeed useful to help the client to clarify his ideas so that a more thorough investigation can be carried out if he thinks it is necessary.

(ii) Γ_2', the choice of product. A and V are the same as in Γ_1'. Π is a choice, i.e. the identification of the set of products which jointly outperform all the others. Γ_2' is a more pressing problem formulation which encourages the client to adopt an immediate operational attitude. If the set of outperforming products includes more than one product it is necessary to carry out a more thorough analysis restricted to the products in that set.

(iii) Γ_3', rank the products. A and V are the same as in Γ_1' and Γ_2'. Π is a classification, i.e. a complete ranking of A from the most preferred product to the least preferred one. The related evaluation model Γ_3' is presented later. Γ_3' is an intermediate problem formulation, which can help the client to understand the consequences of his preferences on the whole set of possible purchases and therefore enable him either to decide to carry out a further analysis or to make a purchase.

The difference between choice and classification is that with classification, all the products are ordered, possibly after building many subsets, from best to worst; while with choice, only two subsets are built, best and not best. It should be noted that, given the same initial parameters, the best set computed using classification can be different from the best set computed using choice.

3.2.2 Design of the evaluation model:
The client's choice was Γ_3', because Γ_1' was not operational, and Γ_2' did not provide a complete ranking of the products. Activities and products which correspond to the design of the evaluation model for Γ_3' are now presented.

Choose A^*: A preliminary screening of the set A, based on features considered as absolutely necessary, reduced the set to seven products hereby denoted as $A^* = \{a_1, a_2, a_3, a_4, a_5, a_6, a_7\}$.

Define D: The set of points of view V has been transformed into four evaluation attributes: functionality (d_1), usability (d_2), portability (d_3) and maturity (d_4). These attributes are then decomposed into two hierarchical levels.

The decomposition hierarchy and the definition of attributes are as follows:

d_1 (*functionality*) is decomposed into the subattributes

d_{11} (editing): the possibility of editing the model

d_{12} (executing): the possibility of executing the model

d_{13} (data analysis): the possibility of analysing the data produced by executing the model

d_{14} (debugging): the possibility of debugging the model from inside the product

d_{15} (simulation): the possibility of simulating the model, decomposed into the sub-subattributes

d_{151} (data collection): the collection of statistical data

d_{152} (statistical libraries): the availability of statistical libraries

d_{153} (data structure libraries): the availability of data structure libraries

d_{154} (graphical analysis): the possibility of analysing the data collected graphically

d_{16} (software generation): the possibility of generating software from the model, decomposed into the sub-subattributes

d_{161} (field interfaces): the availability of interfaces to field devices

d_{162} (database interfaces): the availability of interfaces with commercial databases

d_{163} (graphical interfaces): the availability of graphical interfaces

d_{164} (data structure libraries): the availability of data structure libraries

d_2 (*usability*) is decomposed into the subattributes

d_{21} (usability of simulation language): the usability attributes of the language used to build the simulation model, decomposed into

d_{211} (modularity): language modularity

d_{212} (expressiveness): language expressiveness

d_{22} (usability of generation language): the usability attributes of the language used to build the software generation model, decomposed into

d_{221} (modularity): language modularity

d_{222} (expressiveness): language expressiveness

d_{23} (ease of learning): the facility to learn how to use the product

d_{24} (documentation): the quality of written and online documentation about the product

d_{25} (hot-line assistance): the existence of emergency assistance for the product

d_{26} (ergonomics): the ergonomics of the user interface

In building up the attributes d_{15}, d_{16}, d_{21}, d_{22} it was necessary to distinguish between features concerned with the simulation model and those concerned with the software generation model. Actually there were products which performed differently with regard to the same feature (for instance availability of libraries) when it concerned the two different application domains. Therefore d_{153} and d_{164}, d_{211}, d_{221}, d_{212}, d_{222} are not merged.

d_3 (*portability*) is decomposed into two subattributes

d_{31} (portability of the simulation or software generation model): decomposed into two sub-subattributes

Table 1: Scales for basic attributes, or e_j

	Attribute and criterion name	Scale for criterion	Attribute scale type	Criterion scale type
d_{11}	editing	yes > no	nominal	ordinal
d_{12}	executing	yes > no	nominal	ordinal
d_{13}	data analysis	good (g) > normal (n) > no	nominal	ordinal
d_{14}	debugging	integrated (i) > half integrated (hi) > external (e)	nominal	ordinal
d_{151}	data collection	automatic (a) > manual (m) > no	nominal	ordinal
d_{152}	statistical libraries	yes > no	nominal	ordinal
d_{153}	data structure libraries	large (l) > medium (d) > few (f) > no	nominal	ordinal
d_{154}	graphical analysis	yes > no	nominal	ordinal
d_{161}	field interfaces	many (n) > medium (d) > no	nominal	ordinal
d_{162}	db interfaces	many (n) > medium (d) > few (f) > no	nominal	ordinal
d_{163}	graphical interfaces	many (n) > few (f) > no	nominal	ordinal
d_{164}	data structure libraries	many (n) > medium (d) > few (f) > no	nominal	ordinal
d_{211}	modularity	high (h) > medium (d) > no	nominal	ordinal
d_{212}	expressiveness	high (h) > medium (d) > low (l)	nominal	ordinal
d_{221}	modularity	high (h) > medium (d) > no	nominal	ordinal
d_{222}	expressiveness	high (h) > medium (d) > low (l)	nominal	ordinal
d_{23}	ease of learning	good (g) > medium (d) > no	nominal	ordinal
d_{24}	documentation	good (g) > medium (d) > low (l)	nominal	ordinal
d_{25}	hot-line assistance	good (g) > medium (d) > no	nominal	ordinal
d_{26}	ergonomics	good (g) > medium (d) > low (l)	nominal	ordinal
d_{311}	platform	workstation and pc (wpc) > workstation (w) = workstation and other (wo) > pc > other (o)	nominal	ordinal
d_{312}	os	unix and dos and vms (udv) > unix and dos (ud) > unix and vms (uv) > unix (u) = unix and other (uo) > dos (d) > vms (v) > other (o)	nominal	ordinal
d_{321}	platform	workstation and pc (wpc) > workstation (w) = workstation and other (wo) > pc > other (o)	nominal	ordinal
d_{322}	os	unix and dos and vms (udv) > unix and dos (ud) > unix and vms (uv) > unix (u) = unix and other (uo) > dos (d) > vms (v) > other (o)	nominal	ordinal
d_{323}	ui	x and windows (xw) > x = windows (w) > other (o) > no	nominal	ordinal
d_{324}	network protocol	tcp-ip (t) > other (o) > no	nominal	ordinal
d_{41}	diffusion	reals	absolute	ratio
d_{42}	geographical diffusion	USA and Europe (UE) > USA (U) > Europe (E) > Italy (I)	nominal	ordinal

d_{311} (platform): the hardware platform necessary to operate the model

d_{312} (operating system): the operating system necessary to operate the model

d_{32} (portability of the software generated by the software generation model): decomposed into four sub-subattributes

d_{321} (platform): hardware platform

d_{322} (operating system): operating system

d_{323} (user interfaces): supported user interfaces

d_{324} (network protocol): supported network protocols for distributed software

As in attribute d_2 it is necessary to distinguish between simulation and software generation (there are products in which the platform and the operating system are not the same for the two cases, therefore d_{311} and d_{321}, d_{312} and d_{322} are not merged).

d_4 (*maturity*) is decomposed into two subattributes

d_{41} (diffusion): the number of installed licences worldwide

d_{42} (geographical diffusion): the geographical areas of major diffusion of the product

Define M, E: All basic attributes, except d_{13}, d_{153},

d_{21x}, d_{22x}, d_{23}, d_{24}, d_{25} and d_{26} are measured attributes. The scales for the associated measures are of a nominal type, except for d_{41} which has an absolute scale. The values for such measures can be seen in Table 1, they are the values in column *scale*, as long as the symbol > is ignored. The value *no* indicates that a product lacks the feature measured. Nonmeasured attributes all have nominal scales, these values can also be seen in Table 1.

Define G: Table 1 shows the values of the scale for each basic criterion as well as their ordering (with () to indicate an abbreviation for the value, and *and* to indicate a combination of values). For instance when attribute d_{11} was considered the scale is *yes* greater than *no*, showing that the client prefers products capable of editing to the ones which are not capable of supporting this function.

The value *no* is always considered to be the worst value. This is an important assumption and will be discussed in Section 3.3.

The relation s_j is defined as $s_j = p_j \cup i_j$ for every basic and composed attribute, (with p = strict preference and i = indifference).

The mappings g_j are of the form [3, 2, 1] when the scale is of the form [$a > b > c$]. In the case of d_{41} a transformation $g_{41} = \log(e_{41})$ is defined because the client wanted to compare the orders of magnitude of the licenses sold.

The criteria for each attribute d_j, except d_{41}, are of the form $\forall x, y \in A^*$ $s_j(x, y) \Leftrightarrow g_j(x) \geq g_j(y)$. The criterion for d_{41} is $\forall x, y \in A^*$ $s_{41}(x, y) \Leftrightarrow g_{41}(x) \geq g_{41}(y) \wedge g_{41}(x) \geq 10$.

Choose $\mathcal{R}$: The constraints to be considered in choosing $\mathcal{R}$ are

(i) The problem statement is a classification

(ii) A^* is discrete

(iii) The scales of criteria are of an ordinal and absolute type

(iv) The client is not able to indicate trade-offs between the criteria, therefore compensation is not admissible

(v) The criteria are nonredundant (see later *Verify nonredundancy*) and therefore satisfy the isolability condition.

An outranking aggregation technique has been adopted for this step and the one presented in the ELECTRE techniques [26] has been chosen because it satisfies the constraints listed above. The AHP technique has been discarded because the scales are not of a ratio type. Multi-attribute utility theory (and therefore WAS) has not been used because the scales of most criteria are ordinal and because it was not possible to establish trade-offs between criteria.

The basic concept of the chosen $\mathcal{R}$ is the *outranking*

relation or S, which has to be computed between each pair of products of A^* and should be read as *is at least as good as*. The outranking relation holds if the concordance and nondiscordance tests are satisfied.

The *concordance test* is the majority strength to be reached to be able to establish with a certain degree of confidence the outranking relation. Such a majority is generally computed using the relative importance of each criterion.

The *nondiscordance test* is the minority strength below which it is possible to establish the outranking relation. Such a minority is generally computed using the relative importance of each criterion.

In general, S is not complete and transitive and to overcome this problem an *exploiting procedure* is introduced to reduce the global outranking relation to a final complete ranking (this binary relation is denoted by $\geq$; and $>$ represents strict preference and $\approx$ represents indifference).

More formally, and assuming that the criteria are equally important, as in the case study

$$S(x, y) \Leftrightarrow C_o(x, y) \wedge \neg D_o(x, y)$$

or: x is at least as good as y if the ordered pair (x, y) satisfies the concordance test and satisfies the nondiscordance test. Where

$$C_o(x, y) \Leftrightarrow |G^{\pm}| \geq c \wedge |G^+| \geq |G^-|$$

or: (x, y) satisfies the concordance test iff the number of criteria for which x is at least as good as y is not inferior to a certain number of criteria c (majority

Table 2: Measured or judged values of products on basic attributes, or $e_j(a_i)$

		a_1	a_2	a_3	a_4	a_5	a_6	a_7
d_{11}	editing	yes	yes	yes	yes	yes	no	yes
d_{12}	executing	yes	no	no	no	yes	yes	yes
d_{13}	data analysis	no	no	no	n	n	g	g
d_{14}	debugging	hi	hi	hi	i	hi	i	i
d_{151}	data collection	m	m	m	m	m	a	m
d_{152}	statistical libraries	no	no	no	yes	no	yes	yes
d_{153}	data structure libraries	no	no	no	no	l	d	l
d_{154}	graphical analysis	no	no	no	yes	yes	yes	yes
d_{161}	field interfaces	d	n	no	d	no	no	no
d_{162}	db interfaces	f	d	no	f	no	no	no
d_{163}	graphical interfaces	no	n	no	f	f	no	no
d_{164}	data structure libraries	no	no	no	no	n	d	n
d_{211}	modularity	no	d	d	no	h	h	h
d_{212}	expressiveness	d	d	d	l	h	h	h
d_{221}	modularity	no	d	d	no	h	h	h
d_{222}	expressiveness	h	h	h	d	h	h	h
d_{23}	ease of learning	d	g	g	g	no	no	g
d_{24}	documentation	d	g	g	g	l	g	g
d_{25}	hot-line assistance	d	d	d	d	no	no	no
d_{26}	ergonomics	d	d	g	g	g	l	g
d_{311}	platform	wo	pc	w	w	w	pc	wpc
d_{312}	os	uv	u	u	uo	u	udv	ud
d_{321}	platform	w	pc	w	w	w	o	wpc
d_{322}	os	uv	u	u	uv	u	o	d
d_{323}	ui	o	o	o	x	x	no	o
d_{324}	network protocol	t	o	o	no	t	no	no
d_{41}	diffusion	50	500	50	500	5	500	50
d_{42}	geographical diffusion	I	UE	U	UE	I	UE	E

263

Table 3: Preference structure, or s

d_{11}	editing	$a_1 = a_2 = a_3 = a_4 = a_5 = a_7 > a_6$
d_{12}	executing	$a_1 = a_5 = a_6 = a_7 > a_2 = a_3 = a_4$
d_{13}	data analysis	$a_6 = a_7 > a_4 = a_5 > a_1 = a_2 = a_3$
d_{14}	debugging	$a_4 = a_6 = a_7 > a_1 = a_2 = a_3 = a_5$
d_{151}	data collection	$a_6 > a_1 = a_2 = a_3 = a_4 = a_5 = a_7$
d_{152}	statistical libraries	$a_4 = a_6 = a_7 > a_1 = a_2 = a_3 = a_5$
d_{153}	data structure libraries	$a_5 = a_7 > a_6 > a_1 = a_2 = a_3 = a_4$
d_{154}	graphical analysis	$a_4 = a_5 = a_6 = a_7 > a_1 = a_2 = a_3$
d_{161}	field interfaces	$a_2 > a_4 = a_1 > a_3 = a_5 = a_6 = a_7$
d_{162}	db interfaces	$a_2 > a_1 = a_4 > a_3 = a_5 = a_6 = a_7$
d_{163}	graphical interfaces	$a_2 > a_4 = a_5 > a_1 = a_3 = a_6 = a_7$
d_{164}	data structure libraries	$a_5 = a_7 > a_6 > a_1 = a_2 = a_3 = a_4$
d_{211}	modularity	$a_5 = a_6 = a_7 > a_2 = a_3 > a_1 = a_4$
d_{212}	expressiveness	$a_5 = a_6 = a_7 > a_1 = a_2 = a_3 > a_4$
d_{221}	modularity	$a_5 = a_6 = a_7 > a_2 = a_3 > a_1 = a_4$
d_{222}	expressiveness	$a_1 = a_2 = a_3 = a_5 = a_6 = a_7 > a_4$
d_{23}	ease of learning	$a_2 = a_3 = a_4 = a_7 > a_1 > a_5 = a_6$
d_{24}	documentation	$a_2 = a_3 = a_4 = a_6 = a_7 > a_1 > a_5$
d_{25}	hot-line assistance	$a_1 = a_2 = a_3 = a_4 > a_5 = a_6 = a_7$
d_{26}	ergonomics	$a_3 = a_4 = a_5 = a_7 > a_1 = a_2 > a_6$
d_{311}	platform	$a_7 > a_1 = a_3 = a_4 = a_5 > a_2 = a_6$
d_{312}	os	$a_6 > a_7 > a_1 > a_2 = a_3 = a_4 = a_5$
d_{321}	platform	$a_7 > a_1 = a_3 = a_4 = a_5 > a_2 = a_6$
d_{322}	os	$a_1 = a_4 > a_2 = a_3 = a_5 > a_7 > a_6$
d_{323}	ui	$a_4 = a_5 > a_1 = a_2 = a_3 = a_7 > a_6$
d_{324}	network protocol	$a_1 = a_5 > a_2 = a_3 > a_4 = a_6 = a_7$
d_{41}	diffusion	$a_2 = a_4 = a_6 > a_1 = a_3 = a_7 > a_5$
d_{42}	geographical diffusion	$a_2 = a_4 = a_6 > a_3 > a_7 > a_1 = a_5$

strength) and if the number of criteria for which x is strictly preferred to y is not inferior to the number of criteria for which y is strictly preferred to x.

$$\neg D_o(x, y) \Leftrightarrow \forall g_j \in G : \neg v_j(x, y) \wedge |G^-| < d$$

or: (x, y) satisfies the nondiscordance test if there is no criterion on which a veto condition is expressed and if the number of criteria for which y is strictly preferred to x is strictly inferior to a certain number d of criteria (minority strength). A veto represents a negative power which cannot impose a preference, but just make opposition. Where

$$G^+ = \{g_j \in G : p_j(x, y)\}$$
$$G^= = \{g_j \in G : i_j(x, y)\}$$
$$G^- = \{g_j \in G : p_j(v, x)\}$$
$$G^\pm = G^+ \cup G^=$$

$v_j(x, y)$ is the veto expressed on the pair (x, y) on the criterion g_j; c is the concordance threshold; d is the discordance threshold.

The aggregation algorithm follows:

(1) Compute the outranking relation S

(2) If the graph representing the relation S has one or more circuits reduce them to a node. Such a node represents an *equivalence class*, which is a subset of A^* whose elements are considered to be equivalent. Therefore a binary relation S^r is obtained and applied to A^*/C (the set of equivalence classes of A^* defined by S) which is a relation without circuits

(3) Compute its score in S^r for each $x \in A^*/C$, that is

$$f(x, S^r) = |\{z : S^r(x, z)\}| - |\{z : S^r(z, x)\}|$$

in other words the score of x in S^r is the number of products outranked by x minus the number of products outranking x

(4) Rank the elements of A^*/C on the basis of their score. More formally

$$x > y \Leftrightarrow f(x, S^r) > f(y, S^r)$$
$$x \approx y \Leftrightarrow f(x, S^r) = f(y, S^r)$$

3.2.3 Application of the evaluation model:

Measure/judge attributes: Table 2 contains the values for basic attributes, or $e_j(a_i)$.

Apply scale transformations and criteria: Basically Table 2 also shows $g_j(a_i)$, that coincide with $e_j(a_i)$ except for g_{41} whose values are 1.69, 2.69, 1.69, 2.69, 0.69, 2.69, 1.69.

Derive s: The preference structure, deduced by $g_j(a_i)$, is shown in Table 3.

Verify s: The client accepted s as a suitable representation of her preferences.

Verify nonredundancy: The nonredundancy of the criteria has been verified using the tests introduced in Section 2.2.3.

Apply aggregation technique: The prescription is computed by applying $\mathcal{R}$ to s repeatedly. Since the client was not able to define the relative importance of composed criteria, each composed criterion is assumed to have the same importance. No vetos have been expressed by the client. First $\mathcal{R}$ is applied to the preference structures associated to the sub-subattributes. The unanimity rule means $c = |G_j|$, where j identifies a decomposition level. The result is shown in Table 4. $\mathcal{R}$

Table 4

Aggregation of		Ranking	Aggregation parameters
d_{15}	d_{151} to d_{154}	$a_6 = a_7 > a_4 = a_5 > a_1 = a_2 = a_3$	$c = 3, d = 2$
d_{16}	d_{161} to d_{164}	$a_2 > a_4 > a_1 = a_5 > a_7 > a_6 > a_3$	$c = 3, d = 2$
d_{21}	d_{211} to d_{212}	$a_6 = a_7 = a_5 > a_2 = a_3 > a_4 = a_1$	unanimity rule
d_{22}	d_{221} to d_{222}	$a_5 = a_6 = a_7 > a_1 = a_2 = a_3 > a_4$	unanimity rule
d_{31}	d_{311} to d_{312}	$a_7 > a_6 > a_1 > a_2 = a_3 = a_4 = a_5$	unanimity rule
d_{32}	d_{321} to d_{324}	$a_1 > a_4 = a_5 > a_3 > a_2 = a_7 > a_6$	$c = 3, d = 2$

is then applied to the preferences associated to the sub-attributes with the result shown in Table 5.

Table 5

Aggregation of		Ranking	Aggregation parameters
d_1	d_{11} to d_{16}	$a_7 > a_5 > a_1 = a_4 = a_6 > a_2 = a_3$	$c = 5, d = 2$
d_2	d_{21} to d_{26}	$a_7 > a_3 > a_2 > a_5 = a_6 > a_4 > a_1$	$c = 5, d = 2$
d_3	d_{31} to d_{32}	$a_1 > a_4 = a_5 = a_7 > a_3 = a_6 > a_2$	unanimity rule
d_4	d_{41} to d_{42}	$a_2 = a_4 = a_6 > a_3 > a_7 > a_1 > a_5$	unanimity rule

Finally $\mathcal{R}$ is applied to the attributes giving the final ranking, or prescription, as shown in Table 6.

Table 6

Aggregation of	Ranking	Aggregation parameters
d_1 to d_4	$a_7 > a_4 > a_6 > a_5 > a_3 > a_1 > a_2$	$c = 3, d = 2$

3.3 Discussion

The discussion is centred on the most critical points of the SPEP: identification of attributes, decomposition of attributes, selection of metrics, trade-offs between judgement, metrics and decomposition.

3.3.1 Identification of attributes:

The attributes d_1 to d_4 are related exclusively to external attributes. The reasons for this choice are many; first it is difficult to obtain information from the producers about intermediate products (source code, design documents, results of verification and validation activities), then there are constraints on the budget and the time allocated to the evaluation and finally the lack of safety critical issues.

The attributes were chosen from the software quality characteristics (SQC) defined by ISO 9126 [2] and the client considered only functionality, usability and portability as relevant, while maintainability, efficiency and reliability were not considered to be relevant. Maturity, which is not present in ISO 9126, was added to take into account the buyer's point of view.

The maintainability of the CASE tool was not relevant for the user while efficiency and reliability were, but they were discarded for two reasons, there was neither sufficient time nor resources to evaluate them, and these two attributes are much less important than other SQCs.

Maintainability, efficiency and reliability are relevant attributes for software operating in a production facility.

If a CASE tool produces this software, its efficiency and reliability depend both on the CASE tool (especially on the software generator which is contained in it) and on the model of the software defined by the software engineer. The client decided that it was not relevant to evaluate the software generator which might be present in the CASE tools.

Maintainability depends both on the model and on the formalism used to define it, but not on the CASE tool, thus it was not evaluated.

The attribute maturity, defined as the risk of a product disappearing from the market, is not a technical attribute but has been added at the request of the buyer involved in the selection.

3.3.2 Decomposition of attributes:

The decomposition of attributes was a long and hard process, probably the hardest and most intellectualy intensive part of the evaluation process.

One reason for this is that decomposition is another way of drawing up the user's requirements document which either does not exist (as in this case study) or is incomplete, ambiguous, contradictory, redundant and unstable. The decomposition process shares all the difficulties of specifying the user's requirements.

Another reason is the fact that tool evaluation and software process evaluation cannot be easily separated. The CASE tools considered in the evaluation are built upon a number of assumptions regarding the software production process. First the software life cycle (either prototyping, where the production facility is simulated, then the actual control software is rewritten, or incremental refinement, where the production facility is simulated, then the actual control software is automatically generated); secondly, the high level formalism used to define the model of the production facility (either production rules, or Petri nets, or finite state automata) and finally, the low level formalism (C, C++, Smalltalk).

Since the client had not yet made a choice regarding these issues, the selection was a selection of CASE tools and software processes, and this made the evaluation harder. On the other hand, given the constraint that CASE tools be bought on the market and not developed in house, it would be illogical to choose a software process which cannot be supported by available tools.

A further reason is the distance between attributes and basic attributes: given a standard set of attributes (such as ISO 9126), virtually an infinite number of sets of basic attributes can be defined. On the one hand there is no solution to this problem, since an evaluation of quality over external attributes depends, by the definition of external attribute, not only on the product but on the product and its environment (needs, skill, experience and software process of the user, hardware and software platform, etc.). So every evaluation is different and has to be customised to the user's needs. On the other hand, effort should be made to define and standardise the frameworks of those attributes adapted to specific problem domains (in line with [3, 6, 42]) so as to provide a starting point for the customisation process.

3.3.3 Quality measures selection:

The number of nonmeasured attributes used in the evaluation is not negligible.

The use of nonmeasured attributes can be classified under two headings: attributes in which no established measures exist (e.g. d_{212} expressiveness, d_{23} ease of learning, d_{26} ergonomics); and attributes in which measures exist, but where further analysis of the domain and of the client's needs is required (e.g. d_{153} and d_{164} data structure libraries, d_{161} field interfaces, d_{162} db interfaces, d_{163} graphical interfaces, should be improved by identifying which data structure or interface is really needed by the user instead of just counting how many are offered).

The second class was accepted for attributes for which the client decided not to use evaluation resources.

3.3.4 Decomposition, measurement and judgement:

There is dependency between the use of judgement or measurement and decomposition of attributes.

In some cases further decomposition of a nonmeasured attribute facilitates the use of measurements at the lower level. For instance d_{211} has the scale [large, medium, no] and no associated measure; if it were decomposed into, say, d_{2111} *availability of abstract data types*, with scale [yes, no], and d_{2112} *support to encapsulation*, with scale [yes, no], then measurement could be used. However, whatever approach is adopted, judgement, at least partially, determines the decomposition.

Another attribute in which judgement strongly influences the decomposition, even if it is associated only to measures, is d_4: de facto it penalises in the evaluation those products which have just been launched on the market, because very few licenses will have been sold.

d_{24} is a basic attribute, while a full document [42] decomposes it. This demonstrates that judgement is also involved in the decision about where to stop the decomposition.

In other cases a value of a measure could be refined. For instance the value *yes* for d_{152} could be refined with the new values *random number generation* and *statistical data analysis*. Alternatively, the attribute could be refined into two subattributes d_{1521} *random number generation* and d_{1522} *statistical data analysis* both with a scale [*yes, no*].

The relationship between judgement, measurement and decomposition can be summarised in the following statements: first, the depth of decomposition of attributes can vary. It depends on needs, time, budget and information available. Secondly, the level of judgement remains the same, distributed between judgement regarding nonmeasured attributes and decomposition decisions. Finally, as more detail is added through increasing levels of decomposition, the element of judgement intrinsic in an evaluation is more apparent and formalised. In other words it is better to substitute judgement in nonmeasured attributes with further decomposition and measures.

3.3.5 Aggregation technique:
First, it is necessary to emphasise that the choice of the specific aggregation procedure used in the case study does not imply a definite methodological choice. The number of aggregation procedures that are available in MCDA is extremely large. Any technique can be used to aggregate preferences provided that the information about the problem is used correctly and that the client's requirements are satisfied in accordance with the decision process being used. What is claimed is that the arbitrary use of aggregation techniques should be avoided since they may produce meaningless results.

Some specific comments can be made about the case study presented here. In many criteria (e.g. d_{13}, d_{151}) the value *no* on the attribute scale represents the absence of a feature. Whenever this case occurred, the value *no* was considered to be the worst one on the criterion scale. In fact the absence of a feature should be represented with the incomparability of *no* with all the other values, but this violates the complete comparability constraint often imposed by the wish to have a numerical representation. The same situation occurs when preferences on basic criteria are aggregated, since the aggregation produces, as a general rule, a partial order. Aggregation techniques that enable the direct aggregation of partial orders should be used, but at the moment they are at an experimental state [43, 44].

4 Conclusion

A method to evaluate and select software products has been presented. The method satisfies the requirements, stated in Section 1.2, to assure robust and reliable evaluations, and has the following advantages:

The decision process is clearly defined, in terms of activities performed, and information flow. Each item of information corresponds to a choice, and the client and the evaluator are aware of which choices are made in which activity. The client can always understand the detailed motivation of the conclusions of each activity of the process and detect hidden decisions, if any. Essential issues that deeply influence an evaluation (which actors are involved in the evaluation, their points of view, the purpose of the evaluation) are addressed at the very beginning of the process.

An evaluation model is composed of a hierarchy of evaluation attributes. Products are independently evaluated on each basic attribute. The evaluator is asked to define, in a way appropriate to the aggregation technique, the relative importance of attributes. If possible, conflicts are solved by the aggregation technique, otherwise they are signalled to the client and discussed until they are solved.

IusWare assumes that judgement is an essential part of an evaluation. Instead of trying to hide it, IusWare identifies the points where judgement is involved: the decomposition of attributes, the use of nonmeasured attributes, the transformation of nominal scales of measures, the definition of criteria. The client is asked to openly declare, discuss and justify these points. Moreover, IusWare provides tools, such as preferences and aggregation techniques, to handle judgement properly.

IusWare distinguishes between objective assessments of basic attributes (measures) and subjective ratings (preferences). Preferences are needed in an evaluation since they formalise how well a product fits a need, while measures are objective and independent of any need. The method suggests that a start should be made with measures, which should then be transformed into preferences. If measures are not available, it is possible to start directly with preferences. Preferences are aggregated with specific techniques. Preferences involve pairwise comparisons of products: in many cases the client finds it easier to compare products with regard to an attribute rather than to assign absolute ratings.

To provide flexibility, an evaluation model can be created with many degrees of freedom: problem statement (classification, ranking, choice, to be chosen with regard to the purpose of the evaluation); hierarchy of evaluation attributes (to be chosen with regard to the actors in the evaluation and their points of view, starting from the ISO 9126 framework); aggregation technique (to be chosen with regard to the problem statement, hierarchy and scales of attributes).

The whole process is client driven. Attributes, scales, aggregation techniques are not imposed by the method but decided by the client who receives suggestions regarding more technical matters from the evaluator. If the client is not sure that a decision adopted as a prescription will ensure the required result, the process can backtracked and any critical options can be changed.

Building the evaluation model is a creative activity, that uses the degrees of freedom given above. IusWare provides this freedom, but also provides verification and validation activities to check for the internal and external consistency of the evaluation model and its components. Internally, the evaluation model is verified for the independence of evaluated objects, nonredundancy and preferential independence of criteria, constraints within the aggregation technique and the other components of the evaluation model. Externally, the evaluation model is validated to check its suitability for the client's needs.

The aggregation technique is a key variable of the evaluation model and is chosen so that it is coherent with the other components. In other words, no single aggregation technique, such as WAS, is considered as suitable for any evaluation model. A verification activity is defined to check the type of dependency among criteria (such as isolability and preferential independence) and therefore to choose a suitable aggregation technique.

5 Acknowledgments

The authors would like to thank Norman Fenton for his kind help and suggestions, and an anonymous referee for making several useful remarks.

6 References

1 FENTON, N.: 'Software metrics – a rigorous approach' (Chapman and Hall, London, 1991)
2 'International Standard IS 9126 Information technology – software product evaluation – quality characteristics and guidelines for their use'. ISO/IEC JTC1, 1991
3 '1209 A recommended practice for the evaluation and selection of CASE tools'. IEEE, New York, 1992
4 MOSLEY, V.: 'How to assess tools efficiently and quantitatively', IEEE Softw., May 1992, pp. 29–32
5 POSTON, R.M., and SEXTON, M.P.: 'Evaluating and selecting testing tools', IEEE Softw., May 1992, 33–42, pp. 33–42
6 FIRTH, R., MOSLEY, V., PETHIA, R., ROBERTS, L., and Wood, W.: 'A guide to the classification and assessment of software engineering tools'. Software Engineering Institute technical report, CMU/SEI-87-TR-10, 1987
7 BOLOIX, G., and ROBILLARD, P.N.: 'A software system evaluation framework', IEEE Comput., 1995, 28, pp. 17–27
8 KITCHENHAM, B.: 'Towards a constructive quality model. Part 1: software quality modelling, measurement and prediction', Softw. Eng. J., July 1987, pp. 105–113
9 GILB, T.: 'Principles of software engineering management' (Addison Wesley, 1987)
10 BASILI, V.R., and ROMBACH, H.D.: 'The TAME project: Towards improvement-oriented software environments', IEEE Trans., 1988, SE-14, pp. 758–773
11 BASILI, V.R.: 'Applying the GQM paradigm in the experience factory', in FENTON, N., WHITTY, R., and IIZUKA, Y. (Eds.): 'Software quality assurance and measurement' (Thomson Computer Press, London, 1995), pp. 23–37
12 VOLLMAN, T.E.: 'Software quality assessment and standards', IEEE Comput., June 1993, pp. 118–120
13 SCHNEIDEWIND, N.F.: 'New software quality metrics methodology. Standard fills measurement needs', IEEE Comput., April 1993, pp. 105–106
14 MIYOSHI, T., and AZUMA, M.: 'An empirical study of evaluating software development environment quality', IEEE Trans., 1993, SE-19, pp. 425–435
15 'Draft guide for measurement, rating and assessment 2: Buyer's guide', ISO/IEC JTC1/SC7/WG6, 1992
16 ZAHEDI, F.: 'A method for quantitative evaluation of expert systems', Eur. J. Oper. Res., 1990, 48, pp. 136–147
17 MCCALL, J.A.: 'Factors in software quality'. General Electrical technical report, TR-77C1502, 1977
18 BOEHM, B.W., BROWN, J.R., KASPAR, H., LIPOW, M., MACLEOD, G.J., and MERRIT, M.J.: 'Characteristics of software quality' (North Holland, 1978)
19 SAATY, T.: 'The analytic hierarchy process' (McGraw Hill, New York, 1980)
20 ZAHEDI, F., and ASHRAFI, N.: 'Software reliability allocation based on structure, utility, price and cost', IEEE Trans., 1991, SE-17, pp. 345–356
21 BELTON, V.: 'A comparison of the analytic hierarchy process and a simple multiattribute utility function', Eur. J. Oper. Res., 1986, 26, pp. 7–21
22 DYER, J.S.: 'Remarks on the analytic hierarchy process', Manag. Sci., 1990, 36, pp. 249–258
23 MARKER, P.T., and VARGAS, L.G.: 'Reply to remarks on the analytic hierarchy process', Manag. Sci., 1990, 36, pp. 269–273
24 KONTIO, J.: 'A case study in applying a systematic method for COTS selection'. Proceedings of the 18th International Conference on Software engineering, Berlin, Germany, March 1996
25 ANDERSON, E.: 'A heuristic for software evaluation and selection', Softw.-Pract. Exp., 1989, 19
26 ROY, B.: 'The outranking approach and the foundations of the Electre methods', Theory Decis., 1991, 31, pp. 49–73
27 CÁRDENAS-GARCÍA, S., and ZELKOWITZ, V.: 'A management tool for evaluation of software designs', IEEE Trans., 1991, SE-17, pp. 961–971
28 FISHBURN, P.C.: 'Foundations of decision analysis. Along the way', Manag. Sci., 1989, 35, pp. 387–405
29 BELL, D.E., RAIFFA, H., and TVERSKY, A.: 'Descriptive, normative and prescriptive interactions in decision making', in BELL, D.E., RAIFFA, H., and TVERSKY, A. (Eds.): 'Decision making: descriptive, normative and prescriptive interactions' (Cambridge University Press, Cambridge, 1988)
30 'A method for software assessment and certification – the informal model'. SCOPE Consortium technical report, Esprit Project SCOPE, 1992
31 BOEGH, J., HAUSEN, H.L., and WELZEL, D.: 'Guide to software product evaluation – the evaluator's guide'. ISO technical report, ISO/IEC/JTC1/SC7/WG6, 1992
32 ROY, B.: 'Decision aid and decision making', Eur. J. Oper. Res., 1990, 45, pp. 324–331
33 MOSCARÓLA, J.: 'Organizational decision processes and ORASA intervention', in TOMLINSON, R., and KISS, I. (Eds.): 'Rethinking the process of operational research and systems analysis' (Pergamon Press, Oxford, 1984), pp. 169–186
34 ROY, B.: 'Méthodologie multicritère d'aide à la décision' (Economica, Paris, 1985)
35 VINCKE, P.: 'Multicriteria decision aid' (Wiley, New York, 1992)
36 SIMON, H.A.: 'A behavioural model of rational choice'. In 'Models of man' (Wiley, New York, 1957), pp. 241–260
37 EDWARDS, W., and VON WINTERFELDT, D.: 'Decision analysis and behavioural research' (Cambridge University Press, Cambridge, 1986)
38 LUCE, R.D.: 'Semiorders and a theory of utility discrimination', Econometrica, 1956, 24, pp. 178–191
39 KEENEY, R.L., and RAIFFA, H.: 'Decision with multiple objectives' (Wiley, New York, 1976)
40 VANDERPOOTEN, D., and VINCKE, P.: 'Description and analysis of some representative interactive multicriteria procedures', Math. Comput. Model., 1989, 12, pp. 1221–1238
41 ROY, B.: 'Multicriteria methodology for decision aiding' (Kluwer Academic, Dordrecht, 1996)
42 'Draft International Standard DIS 916 software packages – quality requirements and testing, ISO/IEC JTC1, 1991
43 TSOUKIAS, A., and VINCKE, P.: 'A new axiomatic foundation of partial comparability theory', Theory Decis., 1995, 39, pp. 79–114
44 TSOUKIAS, A., and VINCKE, P.: 'Extended preference structures in multiple criteria decision aid'. Proceedings of the XI MCDA International Conference, Heidelberg, 1996, (Springer-Verlag, to appear)

A Model for Software Product Quality

R. Geoff Dromey

Abstract— A model for software product quality is defined. It has been formulated by associating a set of quality-carrying properties with each of the structural forms that are used to define the statements and statement components of a programming language. These quality-carrying properties are in turn linked to the high-level quality attributes of the International Standard for Software Product Evaluation ISO-9126. The model supports building quality into software, definition of language-specific coding standards, systematically classifying quality defects, and the development of automated code auditors for detecting defects in software.

Index Terms—Software quality, product evaluation, ISO-9126, code auditing, quality defect classification, quality model, quality attributes, software characteristics, maintainability, quality-carrying properties.

I. INTRODUCTION

SIGNIFICANT gains in the quality of software will not take place until there is a comprehensive model of software product quality available. Several different models of software product quality have been proposed [1]–[6]. While these models offer interesting insights into various aspects of software quality they have not been strong enough to stimulate significant gains in the quality of software or to gain wide acceptance.

Most recently the international standard ISO-9126 Software Product Evaluation Characteristics (1991) [7] has been put forward as a high-level framework for characterizing software product quality. This standard appears to have drawn considerably on the model originally proposed by Boehm *et al.* [1]. While this standard can provide high-level guidance it does not go nearly far enough to support building quality into software.

What must be recognized in any attempt to build a quality model is that software does not directly manifest quality attributes. Instead, it exhibits product characteristics that *imply* or contribute to quality attributes and other characteristics (product defects) that detract from the quality attributes of a product. Most models of software quality fail to deal with the *product characteristics* side of the problem adequately and they also fail to make the direct links between quality attributes and corresponding product characteristics. We will address these two issues. Our focus will be on the primary software product, the code or implementation. However, the framework we will provide may be equally well applied to other components of software products such as requirements specifications and user-interfaces. To support this claim we

Manuscript received January 1, 1994; revised October 10, 1994. Recommended by R. Jeffery.

R. G. Dromey is with Software Quality Institute, Griffith University, Nathan, Brisbane QLD 4111, Australia.

IEEE Log Number 9407725.

will also sketch part of a quality model for a requirements specification.

There is a wealth of knowledge about software quality available. The greatest challenge in proposing any model for software product quality is to find a framework that can accommodate this knowledge in a way that is constructive, refinable, and intellectually manageable. The prime requirement of any such model is that it makes clear and direct links between high-level *quality attributes* and explicit *product characteristics* at all levels. Beyond this the model must provide:

- systematic guidance for building quality into software,
- a means to systematically identify/classify software characteristics and quality defects, and
- a structure that is understandable at a number of levels, refinable and adaptable

A. Framework for a Model of Software Product Quality

A common approach to formulating a model for software product quality is to first identify a small set of high-level quality attributes and then, in a top-down fashion decompose these attributes into sets of subordinate attributes. The Software Product Evaluation Standard, ISO-9126 is typical of this approach. For example, it decomposes maintainability into the four attributes *analyzability, stability, testability* and *modifiability*. While this provides some indication of what maintainability is about the subordinate terms are still very vague and of little assistance in building quality into software. Seeking even further direct decomposition of such vague attributes is not the best way forward. Instead, it is better to employ a model that places only a *single level* (a set of quality-carrying properties) between the high-level quality attributes and the components of a product. For complex applications like software we will show that such an approach is both simpler and much more powerful. It allows us to approach the task of building a model for software product quality in a systematic and structured way by proceeding from the tangible to the intangible. This is a practical strategy for dealing with concepts as elusive and complex as quality.

Elsewhere we have described a generic model along these lines that supports building quality into products and processes [8]. This quality model consists of three primary entities: *a set of components, a set of quality-carrying properties of components, and a set of high-level quality attributes.* There are at most six binary relations among these entities. The following diagram illustrates the potential relations that must be considered to build quality into designs.

For building quality into a product or process only four of these relations are important (i.e., the ones with solid arrowheads). The model supports the examination of quality

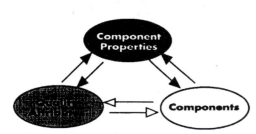

Fig. 1. Generic quality model.

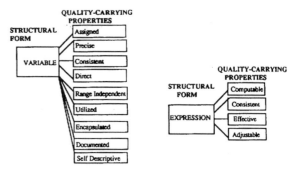

Fig. 2. Quality-carrying properties of variables and expressions.

from two important perspectives. Firstly building in quality from the *bottom-up*. That is, for each component we can identify which quality-carrying properties are important to satisfy and which high-level quality attributes each of these properties impacts. In defining this perspective the quality-carrying properties serve as the intermediaries that link entities to high-level quality attributes. It is also possible to employ this model to look at building in quality from the *top-down*. That is, for each high-level quality attribute we can identify which quality-carrying properties imply that attribute and which product entities possess particular quality-carrying properties. Applying this scheme we can define the scope of the task of building each high-level quality attribute into software products. In adapting this model to software we will replace the term component by *structural form* and we will focus upon the four primary constructive directed relations that may be used to assist building quality into software. The first two of these relations are:

- structural form → quality-carrying property relation
- quality-carrying property → quality attribute relation

Together these two relations allow us to view the task of building high-level quality attributes into software from the bottom-up by ensuring that particular product properties are satisfied. This perspective is most useful to those (that is, the programmers) with the responsibility of implementing quality software. In fact a programming standard can be usefully structured along these lines. The other two relations that are useful are:

- quality attribute → quality-carrying property relation
- quality-carrying property → structural form relation

These two relations allow us to view the task of building high-level quality attributes into software from the top-down by identifying which properties need to be satisfied for each structural form in order to build in a given high-level quality attribute. This perspective is most useful to designers who have the responsibility for specifying and factoring high-level quality attributes into the design of software. Only when we have access to both these perspectives are we in a position to understand what must be done to build quality into software. This bottom-up/top-down model can provide the concrete advice that is so vitally important to implement the process of building quality into software.

In formulating a model for software product quality based upon the generic model we have just sketched we will exploit the property that programs are constructed only using

structural forms (that is, the statement types and the statement components of the implementation language). A basic characteristic of *structural forms* is that they possess, or alternatively, they may each be assigned a set of *quality-carrying properties*. The form-property model can facilitate building quality into software, detecting and classifying quality defects in software and the creation of a framework that is refinable and understandable at a number of levels. A focus on quality defects also makes a positive, if indirect, contribution to building quality into software by telling us what not to do. In considering software the two principal categories of structural forms are:

- computational forms—that describe processes
- representational forms—that describe data

We will first use two simple examples to illustrate the process of applying the form-property model and then proceed to describe the model in more detail.

B. Examples

Consider the fundamental structural forms: *variables* and *expressions*. To be free of quality defects they should possess a number of defined properties. For the moment we will simply list the *quality-carrying* properties of variables and expressions.

To *build-quality-into* variables and expressions when we implement programs we should therefore ensure that all of the above properties are satisfied. In a similar way we can associate a set of quality-carrying properties with each of the other structural forms used in programs for a particular programming language. The syntax of a language identifies all its structural forms.

Violation of any of the quality-carrying properties of a structural form results in a *quality defect* which affects its integrity. Our use of the term *defect* here does not necessarily imply that its presence will cause the functionality or reliability of a software system is to be affected. In some circumstances only nonfunctional properties are impacted by quality defects. In other circumstances defects may point to functionality and reliability problems. Some defects that violate the quality-properties of expressions are:

- uncomputable (e.g., divide by zero)
- inconsistent (e.g., contains side-effects)
- ineffective (e.g., contains computational redundancy)
- unadjustable (e.g., contains numbers)

All of the above types of defects detract from the quality of expressions. Therefore to build quality into expressions when we implement programs they should all be avoided. There are other problems that can arise with expressions. For example, an expression may contain an *unassigned* variable. However, because of the precedence rule used in the classification discipline we impose (see below) this defect will be classified as a *variable integrity* defect rather than as an expression integrity defect even though it impacts the computation of the expression. The classification discipline employed to characterize defects fits our normal intuition. It focuses on the *source of the problem* rather than on the *consequences* of the defect. In the previous example there is no defect directly with the expression. Rather the problem resides elsewhere—the variable should have been assigned before being used in the expression. A crucial requirement in developing such a framework for categorizing quality defects is that the process is *repeatable*. That is, two people confronted with the same defect should arrive at the same classification for that defect. The present proposal sets out to achieve repeatability. In addition, with the proposed model many quality defects can be detected by automatic means. Elsewhere we have described a system for doing this [9].

The conceptual groundwork for constructing a model of software product quality has now been outlined. In the remainder of this paper we will seek to flesh out the model by defining the two important quality perspectives for building in quality by specifying their four supporting relations. To do this we will first examine the various structural forms associated with processes and data for the imperative paradigm. The proposed framework can be extended to handle other programming paradigms, 4GLs, user interfaces and other software product components such as software requirements specifications, etc.

II. STRUCTURAL FORMS FOR PROCESSES AND DATA

To be entirely accurate it is necessary to focus on the structural forms for a particular language. The reason for this is because we find differences like the assignment being an expression in C but a statement in Pascal. Even with this difference it is possible to adopt a style of programming in C where assignments are only used in statements. Putting these sort of difficulties aside, a common set of structural forms for processes within the imperative paradigm, listed in order from the highest level structures to the lowest level structures (increasing numerical order) is given below. The set of structural forms for data (which are ranked below "expressions") within the imperative paradigm, are also ranked from the highest to the lowest structural level, (again in increasing numerical order) are also listed below.

A. Classification Discipline

In classifying quality defects we should always associate them with the lowest level structural form to which they apply.

As an example, if a defect can be associated with either an assignment or an expression we should classify it as an expression defect because of its lower structural level. We will have more to say about this later. To apply this model to a

TABLE I
STRUCTURAL FORMS FOR PROCESSES AND DATA

Level	PROCESS - Structural Forms	Level	DATA - Structural Forms
Highest		Highest	
1	System (set of programs)	12	Records
2	Library (set of reusable ADTs, functions and procedures)	13	Variables
3	Meta-program (e.g. shell script using program I/O)	14	Constants
4	Program	15	Types
5	User-interface	Lowest	
6	Objects (ADT)		
7	Module (encompasses functions and procedures)		
8	Sequence		
9	Statement - > (note precedence in sub-category)		
9.1	Loop		
9.2	Selection		
9.3	Function/procedure call		
9.4	Assignment		
10	Guard		
11	Expression		
Lowest			

particular language it will be necessary to make adjustments to accommodate the differences associated with structural forms. Our intent here is not to completely characterize any particular language but rather to describe the whole process in enough detail so that it can be repeated or adapted as necessary for any particular language, programming environment or other application context.

III. HIGH-LEVEL QUALITY ATTRIBUTES OF SOFTWARE

The quality of software is most often discussed in terms of high-level attributes such as functionality, reliability and maintainability, etc. Ideally, any such choice of high-level quality attributes should be complete, compatible and nonoverlapping. For software this turns out to be a difficult task. Each high-level quality attribute depends on a number of low-level quality-carrying product characteristics that are certainly not mutually exclusive in their high-level quality impact. For example, various forms of redundancy in software affect both its efficiency and its maintainability. Similarly, correctness properties affect both reliability and functionality. There is not much we can do about this overlap problem. Instead we must ensure that the links between low-level quality-carrying product characteristics and high-level quality attributes are clearly established. In addition, we must satisfy ourselves that the high-level quality attributes we choose adequately describe the high-level needs we have for software.

The International Standard ISO-9126 Software Product Evaluation which is built on six quality attributes (*functionality, reliability, usability, efficiency, maintainability, portability*) represents one such attempt that appears to have gained wide acceptance and consensus. Because of the status of this model as an international standard we have chosen to link our model for software product characteristics to it. There is however one serious omission with this standard. It does not emphasize the *reusability* of software. We conjecture that reusability is an important high-level quality attribute of software, which, because of its impact on productivity and quality, deserves a similar status to the other high-level attributes in ISO-9126.

If we accept this minor augmentation of the ISO-9126 model then we must define what we mean by reusability and factor it into the model. A structural form is *reusable* if it uses standard language features, it contains no machine dependencies and it implements a single, well-defined, encapsulated and precisely specified function whose computations are all fully adjustable and use no global variables or side-effects. All ranges associated with computations and data structures in a reusable module should have both their lower and upper bounds parameterized. Also no variable should be assigned to a number or any other fixed constant and all constants used should be declared. Some might argue that reusability is already covered by maintainability and portability. However, it is strongly dependent on a distinctive subset of modularity, structural and descriptive properties. This suggests that reusability is deserving of separate recognition. There is also one other strong reason for giving reuse the status of a high-level quality attribute. It will encourage those responsible for software development to pay more serious attention to constructing software that is reusable.

IV. QUALITY-CARRYING PROPERTIES OF SOFTWARE

In broadest terms the properties associated with structural forms that impact the quality of software involve two fundamental things: *correctness* and *style*. The correctness properties we will use cover characteristics that impinge on the specification-independent minimum requirements for correctness, irrespective of the problem being solved (that is, *weak correctness* criteria rather than strong formally proved correctness criteria). The style properties cover characteristics associated with both high and low-level design, and the extent to which the software's functionality at all levels is specified, described, characterized and documented. It is therefore convenient to divide the *quality-carrying* properties associated with the structural forms of programs into four basic categories. In order of precedence (for classification purposes) these categories are:

- correctness properties (minimal generic requirements for correctness)
- structural properties (low-level, intramodule design issues)
- modularity properties (high-level, intermodule design issues)
- descriptive properties (various forms of specification/documentation)

The next step, which is probably the most difficult and open to question, is to identify a set of properties that adequately cover these four categories. In presenting a set of properties that do what is required we do not pretend that this is the only or the best set of properties for a particular application. What we do however claim is that a model of this form provides a very useful way to tackle the problem of software product quality systematically and constructively. Over time, we may expect with experience of application, that a more refined and accurate set of properties will emerge. Our criteria for selecting and defining these properties has been based on the requirements that they form an *orthogonal* (nonoverlapping), *consistent*, and *complete* set. Quality defects that are discovered that do not result from a violation of any of these properties will provide the constructive force needed to refine the property model and definitions of the properties. It may, for example, be appropriate to have a set of properties that focus much more intermodular issues.

With this model there may be occasions where we must make the choice of classifying a defect as for instance either a correctness problem or perhaps a modularity problem. In this case the precedence (which we have arbitrarily chosen) suggests the problem should be to classified as a correctness problem. The precedence rule is correctness problems before structural, before modularity, before descriptive problems. Our reasoning in choosing this order is based on our perception of their relative impact on the utility of software.

We should not be discouraged by this situation as this sort of framework is used over and over again in science to build any good and useful empirical model. What we propose is a framework for climbing the ladder of software product quality and thrust our foot only on the first rung—the task remains to climb to the top of the ladder. We will list a set of properties that may be associated with structural forms and then provide definitions for each of these properties. Only by examining the definitions of each in detail will it be possible to judge how successful we have been in characterizing the quality-carrying properties of the structural forms of programs. Some quality-carrying properties are much harder to define and characterize than other properties. To assist with the definition process we will use a variety of devices including both positive and negative examples. For example, take the property *structured* which can apply to a number of structural forms. We can at least partially define the property structured in an indirect way by identifying deviations from being structured. When a deviation from being "structured" occurs it results in a quality defect. We claim that a structural form must be *structured* in order not to contribute negatively to the quality of a software product. Exhibiting any of the deviations such as being "unstructured" or ill-structured prevents a given structural form from having the property of being "structured". The "definitions" we will use are always corrigible and open to refinement and improvement. They do however provide a basis for developing a useful constructive model of software product quality.

There are a number of defects associated with structural forms that are language-specific. For example expressions in C may have side-effects whereas expressions in Pascal do not permit side-effects. We identify the impact of each product defect on the high-level quality attributes of the ISO-9126 Software Product Evaluation standard in each case. In the *quality impact* specification, the intent is that the greatest impact is upon the first listed quality attribute and then successively lesser impacts are on the other listed quality attributes. These decisions are empirical.

The order, and hence precedence, of subproperties, within a category has been chosen based on a judgment of the relative impact of a subproperty on its parent property. This is purely an empirical heuristic decision. However it is not hard to justify to most people that a violation of a computability property is likely to have a much more significant impact on correctness than violation of a consistency property (see the following page)—hence the rank of C1 for "computable" compared with C8 for "consistent".

We will now look at a range of properties that are relevant to structural forms. In each case, deviations from particular properties result in quality defects.

A. Correctness Properties

Correctness properties fall broadly into three categories that deal with computability, completeness and consistency. The particular properties we have selected have been chosen in such a way that any violation of one of these properties could potentially mean, that under some circumstances at least, the software may not exhibit its intended functionality. For example, if the structure of a loop indicates that under some circumstances there is a risk that it may not terminate then this risk threatens correctness and hence functionality and is therefore a quality defect. By contrast a loop may be classified as *progressive* if upon examining its structure we find that for all paths through the loop there is evidence of progress towards termination and it is not possible to by-pass the termination point. These characteristics are a weak statement of the formal requirements for a proof of termination. The correctness properties we will use are therefore:

C1.	Computable	Result obeys laws of arithmetic, etc.
C2.	Complete	All elements of structural form satisfied
C3.	Assigned	Variable given value before use
C4.	Precise	Adequate accuracy preserved in computations
C5.	Initialized	Assignments to loop variables establish invariant
C6.	Progressive	Each branch/iteration decreases variant function
C7.	Variant	Loop guard derivable from variant function
C8.	Consistent	No improper use or side-effects

Each of these properties which is ranked from highest to lowest precedence will now be defined and discussed in more detail.

C1. Computable: A structural form is computable if it only involves computations that are defined according to the standard theory of computation and are within the limits defined by the program, the programming language and/or the machine. The property applies to all expressions including subscripts.

Applies to: $\implies$ expressions
Quality Impact: $\implies$ functionality, reliability
Sample Defects: (noncomputable)

— division by zero or other impossible computation
— subscript out-of-range
— writing to an unopened file
— division by a variable of unknown status
— square root of a negative number or number of unknown status.

C2. Complete: A structural form exhibits the property of being *complete* when it has all the necessary elements to define and implement the structural form so that it may fulfil its intended role in a way that will not impact reliability or functionality. As well as using a general completeness property we have chosen to identify three other properties which are specializations of completeness, i.e., *assigned, initialized* and *progressive*. These properties are singled out because of their

key contributions to correctness of loops and other statements.

Applies to: $\implies$ objects, modules, statements
Quality Impact: $\implies$ functionality, reliability, usability, maintainability
Sample Defects: (incomplete)

— if-statements that may abort (language-specific)
— self-assignment (e.g., $x := x$)
— unreachable code in a selection mechanism
— module that generates no output.

C3. Assigned: A variable is *assigned* if it receives a value either by assignment, input, or parameter assignment prior to its use. The property assigned is a specialization of the completeness property that applies specifically to variables and data structures of all types.

Applies to: $\implies$ variables
Quality Impact: $\implies$ functionality, reliability
Sample Defects: (unassigned)

— use of a variable in a term or expression that has not been previously assigned a value.

C4. Precise: A variable or constant is imprecisely typed when its precision is not sufficient to meet the required accuracy of the computation.

Applies to: $\implies$ variables and constants
Quality Impact: $\implies$ functionality, reliability
Sample Defects: (imprecise)

— use of single precision when a computation demands double precision
— use of an integer when problem demands only in the range 0..9.

C5. Initialized: A loop structure is *initialized* if all variables in a loop are initialized prior to loop entry and as late as possible prior to loop entry. The initialized property is a specialization of the assigned property that applies to loops. It is therefore a completeness property. Initialization, is central to the correct and efficient functioning of loop structures. It is also an area of a computation that is vulnerable. The most appropriate initialization is that which establishes the loop invariant for a loop. Defects in initialization can arise largely from doing either too much or too little in the initialization step [10]. Initialization defects identify composition problems between the body of a loop and the initializations chosen for the loop variables. They identify higher level structural problems rather than simply the assignment of variables. The problem of a variable not being initialized for use in a loop is a variable integrity defect, rather than on initialization defect.

Applies to: $\implies$ Loops
Quality Impact: $\implies$ functionality, reliability, maintainability
Sample Defects: (underinitialized, overinitialized, prematurely initialized)

— For a detailed treatment of initialization defects see [10, Ch. 12].

C6. Progressive: A loop or recursive algorithm is *progressive* if there is clear evidence that the structure makes progress towards termination with each iteration or recursive call and the associated variant function is bounded below by zero. Recursive calls must have a reachable base case. The progressive property is a completeness property of iterative and recursive constructs.

Applies to: ⟹ modules (recursive), loops
Quality Impact: ⟹ functionality, reliability, maintainability
Sample Defects: (nonprogressive)

— nested loop where outer loop variables are only changed (make progress) in an inner preguarded loop or called function [10, Ch. 12].

C7. Variant: A loop guard (or inductive guard in recursive structures) is *variant* if it defines a relation (the variant condition) that is congruent with, and derivable from, the variant function used to prove termination of the loop [10] (e.g., for loop that has a variant function $j - i - 1$ which is decreased by $i := i + 1$ and/or $j := j - 1$ an appropriate guard that is variant would be $i \neq j - 1$. A variant guard has a form that makes it easy to assess the termination behavior of a loop.

Applies to: ⟹ guards (for loops and recursive structures)
Quality Impact: ⟹ functionality, reliability, maintainability
Sample Defects: (nonvariant)

— loop that uses a boolean variable flag as a loop guard (e.g., *while* not found *do...*) is nonvariant and not derivable from the variant function for the loop.

C8. Consistent: A structural form is consistent if its usage maintains its properties or functionality and if all its elements contribute to and reinforce its overall intent or effect. Side-effects and any other forms of misuse violate the consistency of a structural form.

Applies to: ⟹ modules, statements, guards, expressions variables and records
Quality Impact: ⟹ functionality, reliability, maintainability, reusability, portability, usability.
Sample Defects: (inconsistent)

— using a variable for more than one purpose in a given scope
— modifying a loop variable on exit from a loop
— using a variable as a constant
— changing a variable in an expression (is a side-effect)
— unused input (read(x);...:read(x))
— output of a variable twice without change
— use of variables/constants of different precision/type in a computation.

B. Structural Properties

The structural properties we have used focus upon the way individual statements and statement components are implemented and the way statements and statement blocks are composed, related to one another and utilized. They enforce the requirements of structured programming and demand that there should be no *logical, computational, representational* and *declarative* redundancy or inefficiency of any form either in individual statements or in sequences or in components of statements. There is a requirement that computations should be expressed directly, efficiently, simply and not in an obscure fashion. Redundant testing is sometimes advocated as a means to increase reliability but this is not defensible at the intramodule level. Another requirement is that every structural form that is declared in a program should be utilized. This applies to such diverse entities as variables and modules. While the main focus of structural properties is intramodular some of these properties also apply at higher levels of organization. These structural properties are:

S1.	Structured	Single-entry/single-exit
S2.	Resolved	Data structure/control structure matching
S3.	Homogeneous	Only conjunctive invariants for loops
S4.	Effective	No computational redundancy
S5.	Nonredundant	No logical redundancy
S6.	Direct	Problem-specific representation
S7.	Adjustable	Parameterized
S8.	Range-independent	Applies to variables (arrays), types, loops
S9.	Utilized	To handle representational redundancy

S1. Structured: A structural form exhibits the property of being *structured* if it follows rules of structured programming [11]. That is, there should be only a single point of entry and exit for every control structure. Too many conditions associated with a guard and poor bracketing of an expression also represent deviations from being structured.

Applies to: ⟹ sequences, guards, and expressions
Quality Impact: ⟹ maintainability, reliability, functionality
Defects: (unstructured, ill-structured)

— exit from the middle of a loop
— multiple returns from a function
— loop guard with too many conditions.

S2. Resolved: A structural form is *resolved* if the control structure of the implementation involved matches the structure of the data [12] or the problem [10] in the sense advocated by Jackson (that is, the control structure matches data structure and thereby satisfies the correspondence principle). At all times the strategy seeks to construct loops that *minimize* the number of variables they change.

Applies to: ⟹ loops
Quality Impact: ⟹ maintainability, efficiency
Defects: (unresolved)

— use of a single loop to process a two-dimensional array [ref. 10, Ch. 12].

S3. Homogeneous: An iterative or recursive form is *homogeneous* if it can be described by an invariant where the major predicates assume a conjunctive form (e.g., the invariant must be of the form "A *and* B *and* ..." but A etc. may involve disjunction). An iterative or recursive form is inhomogeneous if it involves an invariant where major predicates must be combined by disjunction.

Applies to: ⟹ loops, modules (recursive)
Quality Impact: ⟹ maintainability
Defects: (inhomogeneous)

— a loop structure with functionality that is not cohesive (see examples in [ref. 10, Ch. 12].

S4. Effective: A structural form exhibits the property of being *effective* when it has all the necessary elements and only the necessary elements to define and implement the structural form. Elements beyond what are necessary and sufficient to specify the process, computation, data structure or user-interface violate the property of effectiveness for the particular structural form. In other words, unnecessary variables or computations or lack of simplification of structures or computations, violates the property of effectiveness. It applies particularly to expressions and assignment statements and other statements but not to conditions. The redundancy resulting from failing to have a resolved control structure (according to Jackson's methodology) is excluded from an "ineffective" classification. It is treated as unresolved (see above). Note we might at first think an assignment in the body of a loop that does not change its value with each iteration could be classified as a sequence (the loop body) defect. However this structure only shows as a defect in the context of the loop and so it is a defect of the loop structure. Any executable statement that does not change the state of a computation is classified as ineffective. Also if the same result can be achieved more simply then a computation is ineffective (e.g., using $\{N \geq 0\}$ $i := 0$ do $i \neq N \rightarrow i := i + 1$ od instead of $i := N$ makes the sequence consisting of the loop plus the initialization ineffective)

Applies to: $\implies$ expressions, statements
Quality Impact: $\implies$ usability, efficiency, maintainability
Defects: (ineffective)

— assignment that establishes an already-established condition
— expression with unnecessary computation (e.g., $y := x + 1 + 1$).

S5. NonRedundant: A structural form exhibits the property of being *nonredundant* when it has all the necessary logical elements and only the necessary elements to define the structural form. Conditions beyond what are necessary and sufficient to specify the process violate the property of nonredundancy for the particular structural form. In other words, unnecessary conditions or lack of logical simplification of computations, violates the property of nonredundancy. This property is distinguished from "effective" in that it involves some form of logical redundancy rather than computational (arithmetic/algebraic) redundancy. *In other words it applies to conditions not assignment statements.* The redundancy resulting from failing to have a resolved control structure (according to Jackson's methodology) which can be a form of high-level logical redundancy is excluded from a "redundant" classification. It is instead given the more specialized classification of being *unresolved.*

Applies to: $\implies$ guards
Quality Impact: $\implies$ efficiency, maintainability
Defects: (redundant)

— testing a condition that has already been established.

S6. Direct: A computation is expressed *directly* if the abstraction, choice of representation and the structure of the computation are congruent with the original problem being modelled by the computation. An indirect way of framing a computation makes it harder to understand because at least one more level of detail must be considered. When a computation is expressed indirectly there is, from the user's view at least, an inefficiency in the representation. Something additional, that is not present or relevant to the original problem is introduced. The use of boolean flags or numbers to represent other real-world items and clever but obscure computational tricks are all typical of an indirect way of formulating and representing computations. Modern languages through devices like enumerated types make it easy to avoid an indirect style of programming. In early versions of languages like Fortran it was difficult to avoid the use of an indirect style of programming for many applications. Some argue for an indirect way of formulating computations to gain efficiency but this is hard to defend given the power of today's computers.

Applies to: $\implies$ statements, expressions, variables, constants, types
Quality Impact: $\implies$ maintainability, efficiency
Defects: (indirect)

— use of flags (boolean and others)
— use of numbers to represent colours
— use of clever tricks, (e.g., $(I/J)^*(J/I)$ to initialize identity matrix)
— use of boolean variables to represent conditions.

S7. Adjustable (parameterized): A structural form is *adjustable* if it contains no undeclared constants (apart from 1, 0, or -1) and if the minimum number of single-purpose variables needed to support the computation it performs are used.

The word adjustable has been chosen to specifically deal with parameterization internal to the structure of modules and programs.

Applies to: $\implies$ module calls, expressions
Quality Impact: $\implies$ maintainability, reusability, portability
Defects: (unadjustable)

— if a structural form contains numbers instead of defined constants.

S8. Range Independent: A structural form is *range-independent* if both its lower and upper bounds are not fixed numeric or character constants. This property applies particularly to array specifications and iterative structures designed to process a segment of elements in an array. Most often arrays and loops assume a fixed lower bound. For example, an array-sort will be written to sort all the N elements in an array $a[1 \ldots N]$. A more widely useful, range-independent, algorithm is one which sorts a segment of an array $a[L \ldots U]$.

Applies to: $\implies$ declarations (arrays), loops
Quality Impact: $\implies$ reusability, maintainability
Defects: (range-dependent)

— an array type or variable is declared with a fixed lower or upper bound
— an array-processing loop assumes processing starts at 0 or 1.

S9. Utilized: A structural form is *utilized* if it has been defined and then used within its scope. This property applies to all forms of data structures and modules. Its negation identifies any form of redundancy resulting from declaration as opposed to logical, representational or computational redundancy.

Applies to: $\implies$ objects, modules,
all forms of declared data
Quality Impact: $\implies$ maintainability, efficiency
Defects: (unutilized)

— a variable that has been declared but is not used
— a function is declared but is not used.

C. Modularity Properties

The modularity properties employed largely address the high-level design issues associated with modules and how they interface with the rest of a system. These issues include how a module encapsulates its data, how it is coupled to other modules, how loose its functionality is, how flexible it is and what potential does it have for reuse. These modularity properties are:

M1. Parameterized	All inputs accessed via a parameter list
M2. Loosely coupled	Data coupled
M3. Encapsulated	Uses no global variables
M4. Cohesive	The relationships between the elements of an entity are maximized
M5. Generic	Is independent of the type of its inputs and outputs
M6. Abstract	Sufficiently abstract—is no apparent higher level form.

M1. Parameterized: A module is *parameterized* if it contains as parameters all and only the necessary and sufficient inputs and outputs to characterize a particular well-defined function/procedure.

Applies to: $\implies$ modules
Quality Impact: $\implies$ maintainability, reusability, portability
Defects: (unparameterized, over-parameterized, ill-parameterized)

— unparameterized, (e.g., module with no parameters)
— over-parameterized (e.g., swap($i, j, a[i], a[j]$))
— ill-parameterized (e.g., function that modifies input parameters).

M2. Loosely Coupled: A module or a program is *loosely coupled* if all module calls are data-coupled (see Myers [13]) to the calling program/module.

Applies to: $\implies$ module calls
Quality Impact: $\implies$ maintainability, reusability, portability, reliability
Defects: control-coupled, stamp-coupled, content-coupled, common-coupled, externally coupled

— see Myers [13] for a detailed discussion of these defects.

M3. Encapsulated: The way variables are used can have a significant impact on the modularity and hence self-contained quality of modules, programs and systems. A variable (or constant or type) should be used only within the scope in which it is defined. If it satisfies this property it is said to be *encapsulated*. A module that uses global variables or side-effects violates this property. Consistent with the discipline of identifying quality defects with the lowest-level structural form to which they may be associated, encapsulated is treated as a variable-usage property even though it impacts modularity. To build quality software that is easy to maintain and reuse we should ensure that each module is allowed to access and modify only those data items that are absolutely needed by the module. Other data items should be "hidden" in other appropriate modules.

Applies to: $\implies$ variables, constants and types
Quality Impact: $\implies$ maintainability, reusability, portability, reliability
Defects: (unencapsulated)

— use of variable in a module that has not been declared in the module's scope.

M4. Cohesive: A structural form is *cohesive* if all its elements are tightly bound to one another and they all contribute to achieving a single objective or function. Statements within a cohesive component should be organized from the least to the most dependent, that is, the last statement, in a sequence depends on all its predecessors (see [14]). Any interleaving of independent statements destroys cohesion. A variable-dependency graph may be used to assess the cohesion of a given sequence of statements [15]. This concept of cohesion applies at more than one level. That is, for three blocks in sequence, the computations in the third block should depend on the computations in the preceding two blocks, and so on. Identifying statements and blocks that could be executed in parallel is a good way of assessing cohesion and independence.

Applies to: $\implies$ sequences
Quality Impact: $\implies$ maintainability, reusability, portability
Defects: (uncohesive)

— a module with a lot of parameters has low cohesion as it probably implements more than one well-defined function.
— loop with dispersed initialization (see [10]).

M5. Generic: A module is *generic* if its computations are abstracted to a type-parameterized form.
Applies to: $\implies$ modules
Quality Impact: $\implies$ maintainability, reusability, portability
Defects:

— primitive type-dependant (procedure to swap just integers).

M6. Abstract: An object/module is *sufficiently abstract* if there is no obvious, useful higher level concept that encompasses the structural form.
Applies to: $\implies$ Objects
Quality Impact: $\implies$ reusability, maintainability
Defects:

— specialized module/object (e.g., declaring a car object class instead of vehicle object class).

D. Descriptive Properties

There are three primary properties that reflect how well software is described. Explicit *comments* may be added to a program to document how the implementation realizes its desired functionality by manipulating variables with prescribed properties. To precisely characterize the functionality the process can be taken a step further by including *precondition* and *postcondition specifications* for all functions and other significant computations in a program. Also by appropriate choice of identifiers and module names it is possible to make an important contribution to the analyzability and *self-descriptiveness* of programs. The descriptive properties are therefore:

D1. Specified   Preconditions and postconditions provided
D2. Documented   Comments associated with all blocks
D3. Self-descriptive   Identifiers have meaningful names.

D1. Specified: A module or program or other structural form is *specified* if its functionality is described by preconditions and postconditions. A structural form is *fully specified* if all blocks are specified and loops have attached invariants, variants, preconditions and postconditions. The highest level of specification involves the use of a formal specification language. When a structural form is not specified there is always a doubt about its intended functionality. Use of specifications, if done properly, provides the most rigorous form of documentation and description.

Applies to: $\Longrightarrow$ objects, modules, loops, sequences
Quality Impact: $\Longrightarrow$ functionality, maintainability, reliability, usability, portability, reusability

Defects: (under-specified, unspecified, ill-specified)

— functionality is not described by preconditions and postconditons (under-specified)
— contains no preconditions or postconditions (unspecified)
— specification is ambiguous, inaccurate, inconsistent or incomplete (ill-specified)

D2. Documented: A structural form is *documented* if its purpose, strategy, intent and properties are all explicitly and precisely defined within the context of the structural form.

Applies to: $\Longrightarrow$ objects, modules, loops, sequences, module-calls, data structures, variables, constants, types
Quality Impact: $\Longrightarrow$ maintainability, portability, reusability, usability

Defects: (undocumented, under-documented, over-documented, ill-documented).

— structural form contains no comments (undocumented)
— insufficient comments are used to describe purpose (under-documented)
— more comments are used than are needed (over-documented)
— documentation is misleading or wrong (ill-documented)

D3. Self-Descriptive: A structural form is self-descriptive if its purpose, strategy, intent, or properties are clearly evident from the choice of names for modules and various identifiers are meaningful and congruent with the context of the application.

Applies to: $\Longrightarrow$ objects, modules, module-calls, variables, constants, data structures,
Quality Impact: $\Longrightarrow$ maintainability, portability, reusability, usability

Defects: (undescriptive, over-described, ill-described)

— name chosen bears no relation to property (undescriptive)
— name chosen is unnecessarily long (over-described)
— name is ambiguous, misleading or wrong (ill-described)

E. Refining the Definition of Quality-Carrying Properties

The definitions we have provided for the various quality-carrying properties are by no means comprehensive. Our intent, because of the empirical nature of the model, has been to provide base working definitions that can be refined as necessary in a given application context. There are three options for refining these definitions. One way to do this is to aim for completeness by trying to see if the property is applicable to each possible structural form in its *usage* and *representation* and *context*. In our definitions above we have listed the structural forms to which each property applies but we have not detailed how the property is interpreted for each structural form. The second thing we can do is extend the list of examples showing defects and positive instances of the property. For some properties (involving correctness and logical redundancy and incompleteness, etc) it is possible to provide formal definitions. For example, the concept of strongest postconditions $sp(P, S)$ [16] may be used to formally prescribe when a statement S, executed in the presence of a precondition P is redundant. That is, the strongest postcondition *after* executing S under P will be equivalent to P if S is redundant. In other words, S does not change the state of the computation. This may be expressed formally by the following equivalence $sp(P, S) \equiv P$.

V. Model for Software Product Quality

Having defined *a set of structural forms, a set of quality-carrying properties* and *a set of high-level quality attributes* we can proceed to build a constructive model of software product quality by defining the relations among these three sets of entities. The first of these tasks is to identify and associate a set of quality-carrying properties with *each* of the structural forms that may be used in a program (implicitly we have already done this in the previous section). This is the key relation that may be used to support building quality into software. The constructive theorem that supports this task is:

Constructive Theorem: If each of the quality-carrying properties associated with a particular structural form is satisfied when that particular structural form is used in a program, then that structural form will contribute no quality defect to the software.

From this follows the complementary assertion: *if any of the properties associated with a structural form are violated in a program, then each violation will contribute a quality defect to the software.*

Using a model based on these two principles allows us to achieve our two primary goals. It gives us *direct advice* on building quality into software and at the same time it may be used to assist in the systematic classification of quality defects in software. Two important consequences follow if we are willing to accept and adopt this model:

1) *Building Quality into Software:*
   The task of building quality into software reduces to systematically ensuring that all the quality-carrying properties associated with each structural form used in a program are satisfied for all applications of that structural form in the program.

2) *Systematic Detection/Classification of defects:*
   Detecting quality defects in software reduces to systematically checking whether, for each structural form, in all of its occurrences, any of its quality-carrying properties that imply high-level quality attributes are violated}.

In the previous section we have already identified the structural forms to which each of the quality carrying properties apply. To build quality into software it is far more useful to identify all the quality-carrying properties associated with each structural form. As we will see below, for quick reference, this information may also be neatly summarized in tabular form.

We will now systematically work through the product properties that imply quality attributes for each of the main structural forms in imperative programs. For each structural form its properties will be listed according to the precedence rules set out in Section VII below. In this context it is important to define exactly what we mean by a given property when we associate it with each structural form. For example, *inconsistent* translates into something different when applied to an expression compared to what it means for a function/module. In our presentation here we will not fully develop properties in this way. What we will do instead is give instances for various properties and structural forms. For example, we will provide instances of inconsistency as it applies to modules, expressions and so on.

A. The Relation Between Structural Forms and Quality-Carrying Properties

In the previous sections we have identified a set of quality-carrying properties that can be attached to structural forms in programs. We also identified the structural forms to which each of the properties could be attached. For building quality into software it is important to organize this information so we can see at a glance what quality-carrying properties are associated with each structural form. In what follows we will carry out this organization and finally summarize the results in a table. The highest level forms are not dealt with here because we have chosen not to emphasize system-level quality issues. Examples of quality defects associated with each structural form are given.

1) Object Integrity: An object may be realized by declaration of an abstract data type. Its key high-level quality attributes depend on its, specification, completeness and the level of abstraction employed in choosing the data structure and its operations. The internal quality properties of a module are handled by the quality-carrying properties that are assigned to its data structures/variables and its operations or functions.

a) Quality-Carrying Properties: Complete, utilized, abstract, specified, documented, self-descriptive

   Defects:
   — incomplete (does not enable access to all components of data)
   — over-specialized (the abstraction is not at a high enough level)
   — unutilized (declared but not used)
   — unspecified (no precondition/postcondition specifications)
   — undocumented (no comments stating the functions of object)
   — unself-descriptive (poorly chosen name for object).

2) Module Integrity: The term module is used to describe procedures, functions and subroutines, etc. The quality of a module depends on how well its functionality is described, its level of abstraction, its degree of independence and how easy it is to reuse. Its internal quality is covered by a quality-carrying properties that are assigned to the statements from which it is composed.

a) Quality-Carrying Properties: Complete, progressive (recursive modules), consistent, homogeneous, utilized, loosely-coupled, parameterized, generic, abstract, specified, documented, self-descriptive.

   Defects:
   — incomplete (no apparent input and/or output parameters)
   — nonprogressive (not all inductive branches appear to make progress)
   — tightly coupled (control information passed to module)
   — unparameterized (module defines a fixed computation)
   — type-specific (handles data of a predetermined type only)
   — unutilized (module declared but not used)
   — unspecified (no precondition/postcondition specifications)
   — undocumented (no comments stating the purpose of module)
   — unself-descriptive (module name poorly chosen).

3) Sequence Integrity: A sequence is used to describe computations formulated using one or more consecutive executable statements in a given block. The quality of a sequence structure depends on its level of cohesion and whether there is any transfer of control out of the sequence. Other quality problems associated with sequences like, for example, redundant assignments in a sequence are handled at the statement or statement component level. That is, a redundant assignment is *ineffective*. This conforms to the principle of always classifying quality defects at their source. It should be noted that all executable statements in a program (if-statements, assignments, loops, etc.) have the quality-carrying property *effective* associated with them. If they do not change the state of computation or the same overall result can be achieved more simply then an executable statement (or sequence of statements) is ineffective.

a) Quality-Carrying Properties: Structured, effective, cohesive, specified, documented

Defects:

— unstructured (e.g., contains a *goto, break,* etc. in sequence (block))
— ineffective (e.g., $i := 0$; do $i \neq N \rightarrow i := i + 1$ od can be replaced by $i := N$)
— uncohesive (exist interleaved statements in a sequence that are independent).

4) Loop Integrity: The structural form loop is used to characterize the various forms that implement iteration (e.g., the *while, repeat, for,* etc. loop structures used in Pascal and other imperative languages). The quality of a loop depends on its partial and total correctness properties [8], the way it is composed (including its initialization) and on how well its behavior is described. The quality of a loop is also strongly influenced by whether it has a single point of entry and exit. The property is associated with the loop body (rather than the loop itself) which consists of a sequence of statements that possess the property of being *structured.*

a) Quality-Carrying Properties: Complete, initialized, progressive, consistent, resolved, homogeneous, effective, range-independent, specified, documented

Defects:

— incomplete (only decreases variant function)
— nonprogressive (not clear that all branches make progress)
— inconsistent (a loop that does just one iteration)
— underinitialized, overinitialized, uninitialized (see [10])
— ineffective (does not change state of computation)
— unresolved (hidden loop, if-statement and loop-guard are same)
— inhomogeneous (see example [10])
— unspecified (no invariant and variant function specified)
— undocumented (no comment on the purpose of loop)

5) Selection Integrity: The selection structural form is used to characterize if-statements, case statements and switch statements, etc. How selection statements are implemented can have a significant impact on the quality of programs. The key quality property associated with selection is completeness; that is, whether all cases have been covered and also whether all cases are reachable. Another problem with selection statements is the inconsistency associated with switch statements (in C) which allows control to flow from one selection into another. Other problems associated with selection statements are handled as either guard defects or as defects associated with statements that are guarded by the selection structure. For example, when the execution of the statements in the branch of a selection do not change the state of a computation, the defect is classified as its source, that is, as a problem with the guarded statements rather than with the selection statement itself. Of course if no branches change the state of a computation the selection statement is redundant (that is, ineffective).

a) Quality-Carrying Properties: Complete, consistent, effective

Defects:

— incomplete (e.g., not all cases covered, or there is an unreachable statement)
— inconsistent (e.g., fall-through in a C switch statement)

— ineffective (e.g., statement does not change state of computation).

Note: a guard in an if-statement that tests an established condition is classified as a logical defect of the guard rather than a defect of the if-statement.

6) Module-Call Integrity: In the scope where it is employed, a module-call has the purpose of changing the state of a computation by changing the values of one or more variables. The way parameters are used in a module-call can have an impact on quality. There are two main problems: a given variable may be passed more than once and/or fixed constants (e.g., numbers) are passed as parameters. Like other executable statements, a module call is ineffective if it can be demonstrated that it does not change the state of a computation. Other quality problems associated with module calls can be traced back to problems with the use of statements and variables in the body of the module. Module calls that employ either no input and/or output parameters might be thought to violate the property of completeness. However this structural defect should be traced back to a defect in the design of the module in the first place rather than associating it with the module call.

a) Quality-Carrying Properties: Consistent, effective, adjustable, documented

Defects:

— inconsistent (e.g., same parameter passed twice)
— ineffective (e.g., call is computationally redundant)
— unadjustable (e.g., numbers passed as parameters).

7) Assignment Integrity: Most of the quality-carrying properties associated with assignment statements are not associated with the assignment itself but with its components; its variables and the expression being evaluated. The two quality-carrying properties that remain are whether the statement is redundant or not and whether it is complete. It would be possible to consider both these issues in terms of effectiveness because they involve no state change. However the completeness property deals with whether an assignment has been properly formed which may have direct implications for correctness.

a) Quality-Carrying Properties: Complete, effective

Defects

— incomplete (statement lacking an additional term, e.g., $x := x$)
— ineffective (statement does not change state of computation).

8) Guard Integrity: The guard structural form is used to guard state-changing statements in loops and selection statements. Guards are logical constructs and therefore vulnerable to logical redundancies and inefficiencies which may be identified using standard logical equivalence formulas that define simplifications. For loop guards, the ideal form is that they define a relation (the variant condition) that is congruent with the variant function used to prove termination of the loop [10]. Sometimes guards contain numbers or other fixed constants (e.g., *while* $i < 100$ *do*) which make them not adjustable. It may seem appropriate to assign the property adjustable to the guard itself. However following the rule of always associating quality defects with the lowest level structural with which they are associated, this problem is assigned to the component expression that forms part of the relation. That is, the expression should be adjustable ("100" is not) rather than the guard. Guards should be appropriately structured using parentheses.

a) Quality-Carrying Properties: Variant, structured, nonredundant

Defects:

— redundant (e.g., logical redundancy "*while* ch = space & ch ≠ eol *do*")
— nonvariant (e.g., *while* $a[i] \neq x$ *do* ...).

9) Expression Integrity: Expressions are the primary vehicle for implementing computations. The quality-carrying properties associated with expressions relate to computability, side-effects, the presence of any redundancy and the use of fixed constants. Other quality problems associated with expressions relate to their constituent variables and are classified at a lower level accordingly. The appearance of fixed constants in expressions is however definitely an expression defect and not a variable or constant problem.

a) Quality-Carrying Properties: Computable, consistent, structured, effective, direct, adjustable

Defects:

— uncomputable (e.g., divide by zero)
— inconsistent (e.g., contains side-effects)
— inconsistent (e.g., use of variables/constants of different precision)
— ineffective (e.g., contains computational (arithmetic) redundancy)
— unadjustable (e.g., contains numbers or other fixed constants).

10) Record Integrity: A record is just a composite variable. It therefore has associated with it the same quality-carrying properties as variables. These properties are discussed in detail in the next section. An added problem with records is that they may admit the insecurity of only being partially initialized.

11) Variable Integrity: The way variables are used has a significant impact on the quality of programs. A variable possesses correctness, structural, modularity and descriptive properties. In terms of correctness, a variable must always be assigned before it is used, it must be of the appropriate precision and it should only ever be used for a single purpose within a given scope. The only structural obligation for variables is that they be utilized if they are declared. The modularity quality of a variable is that it must only be used (encapsulated) within the scope in which it is declared. Use of a variable at a lower scope, that is, as a global variable, is probably the single most significant thing that detracts from the quality of imperative programs. Assignment to a global variable in such a context results in a side-effect of the lower scope. From an external perspective side-effects are hidden actions which have a severe impact on the analyzability of programs. Another vital quality requirement for variables is that any name chosen should clearly and accurately characterize the property that is ascribed to the variable. It is also wise to strengthen the definition of the intended use of a variable by including a comment that defines its property at the time the variable is declared.

a) Quality-Carrying Properties: Assigned, precise, consistent, encapsulated, direct, range-independent, utilized, documented, self-descriptive

Defects:

— unassigned (e.g., variable not assigned prior to use in expression)
— imprecise (e.g., single precision used when double needed)
— inconsistent (e.g., variable used for more than one purpose in scope)
— unencapsulated (e.g., global variable used in function)
— unutilized (e.g., declared variable not used)
— undocumented (e.g., no comment when variable declared)
— unself-descriptive (e.g., variable 'x' used to store "maximum")
— indirect (e.g., use of a boolean flag).

12) Constant Integrity: A declared constant possesses correctness, structural, modularity, and descriptive properties. In fact it possesses a subset of the quality-carrying properties of variables. It differs from a variable only in that being used for more than one purpose and being assigned are not issues.

a) Quality-Carrying Properties: Precise, encapsulated, direct, utilized, documented, self-descriptive

Defects:

— imprecise (e.g., single precision used when double precision needed)
— unencapsulated (e.g., global constant used in function)
— unutilized (e.g., declared constant not used)
— undocumented (e.g., no comment when constant declared)
— unself-descriptive (e.g., constant 'x' used to store "3.14159265").

13) Type Integrity: The set of quality-carrying properties that apply to types is a contraction of the set of properties that apply to variables and constants. The problems with global use that apply to variables also apply to types. A type should be used if it is declared and it should be both self-descriptive and documented.

a) Quality-Carrying Properties: Encapsulated, direct, utilized, range-independent, documented, self-descriptive

Defects:

— unencapsulated (e.g., global type used in function)
— unutilized (e.g., declared type not used)
— undocumented (e.g., no comment when type declared)
— unself-descriptive (e.g., type 'x' used to represent "job-type").

A table summarizing the quality-carrying properties associated with each structural form is given above.

This table defines two of the sets of relations of our generic quality model: *the quality-carrying properties associated with each structural form* and *the set of structural forms which exhibit a particular quality-carrying property*. The information presented in this way is useful for two purposes: assisting those that implement software to build in quality to the various structural forms that programs are composed of and to assess whether particular quality-carrying properties have been built into software.

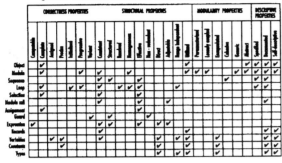

TABLE II
QUALITY-CARRYING PROPERTIES FOR STRUCTURAL FORMS

B. The Relation Between Quality-Carrying Properties and Quality Attributes

Another important way in which we can view product quality-carrying properties is to directly relate them to the high-level quality attributes that are used to characterize the quality of software. For this purpose we will use the high-level attributes advocated in the International Standard ISO-9126 Software Product Evaluation. We will however add to this list the attribute of reusability as we believe (see Section III) this characteristic is important enough in its own right to deserve such high level status. Reusability clearly depends on low-level design.

The intent of this view is to more explicitly identify the requirements for building each of the high-level quality attributes into software. The product properties we have identified and defined provide direct advice, or rather a specification that must be satisfied to build the desired high-level quality attributes into software. This specification is clearly empirical. When we try to construct a systematic process for deciding which product properties contribute to which high-level quality attribute we run into the same difficulty that the naturalist John Muir had: "when *we try to pick out anything by itself, we find it connected to the entire universe*". For example, it is not hard to make an argument that most, if not all quality-carrying product properties make a contribution to the maintainability of software. Given this situation, the issue has to be "which product properties make the most significant contribution to the maintainability of software?" Making this judgement is clearly an empirical step. The criteria we will use to make this judgement are as follows:

- a minimal subset of quality-carrying properties will be selected in each case
- the properties will be ranked in terms of the assessed importance of their contribution to the quality attribute.

We will now examine each of the major quality attributes for software and associate with each a set of quality-carrying properties. Little work has been done on trying to make such direct links. This is a problem which we consider needs to be thoroughly explored.

1) Functionality: The quality attribute functionality depends heavily on two things, correctness properties and the extent to which the functionality of a system is accurately characterized. A program cannot be correct in its own right; it can only be correct with respect to a specification. In a similar way, it makes sense to talk about the functionality of a program with respect to its specification. The product properties that impact functionality are listed in order of their likely impact on functionality (see also the table that follows).

> COMPUTABLE
> COMPLETE
> ASSIGNED
> PRECISE
> INITIALIZED
> PROGRESSIVE
> VARIANT
> CONSISTENT
> STRUCTURED
> ENCAPSULATED
> SPECIFIED

The only problem with this is that it does not say which structural forms possess these properties. To use this information effectively we must link it back to the various structural forms of the product which possess these various characteristics. This information is available in Table II, Section V.A. Properties like *structured* and *encapsulated* are included in this list because of the widely held opinion that there is a much higher risk of their being functional defects in software that is neither structured nor modular in form.

2) Reliability: Functionality implies reliability. The reliability of software is therefore largely dependent on the same properties as functionality, that is, the correctness properties of a program. However where differences arise is in relation to completeness. A program can be correct with respect to its specification, and therefore satisfy its functional requirements and yet fail because the inputs do not satisfy the expected precondition. Unstructured code and side-effects represent high-risk factors for reliability. It is claimed that compliance to the structured and encapsulated properties significantly reduce these risks. For this high-level quality attribute and the remaining attributes the relevant properties are summarized in Table III.

3) Usability: Usability is concerned with the quality of the user interface, its design and performance characteristics. In this specification we have chosen not to describe it in detail as it depends on a completely different set of structural forms (buttons, menus, etc.) which have their own set of quality-carrying properties. At this point we will simply list the quality-carrying properties defined for programs which are also relevant to specifying the quality of a user interface (see Table III).

4) Efficiency: The position taken is that computational and logical redundancy are important factors that effect the efficiency of a program. Ensuring that there is a match between program control structure and data structure also makes a contribution to efficiency. These contributions to efficiency are all independent of the algorithms or strategies used in an implementation. In many instances their contribution to efficiency is not likely to be nearly as great as the contribution of the algorithms. For example, using an $O(N \log_2 N)$ instead of an $O(N^2)$ sorting algorithm will have a dramatic impact

281

on efficiency for large values of N. Unfortunately it will not be practical or even possible to determine the optimal computational complexity for each algorithm in an implementation. We must therefore settle for a much weaker qualitative model for efficiency that is based on excluding various forms of redundancy. The contributing properties are listed in Table III.

5) Maintainability: There is a widely held belief that software which is very easy to maintain is software of high quality [17]. There is a very wide range and a large number of quality-carrying properties that make an important contribution to the maintainability of software. There are two primary concerns for maintaining software: it must be clearly specified and well-documented so the intent of the whole and various fragments of the software is beyond doubt; the software must also be easy to understand. And, for software to be easy to understand, there is a multitude of structural, modularity and descriptiveness factors that need to be satisfied. The most important of these are listed in Table III

6) Portability: A program or system is portable if it requires little or no changes to compile and run it on other systems. The three primary things that affect portability are machine dependencies, compiler dependencies and operating system dependencies. There are two strategies that may be used to minimize portability impact: effective use of parameterization can isolate and minimize machine dependencies, modularization and isolation of compiler/system/language dependencies in a single (or small number of) place can also improve the portability of software. The relevant quality-carrying properties are listed in Table III.

7) Reusability: There are at least two interpretations of reusability. It may used to describe software that is ease to adapt and modify for use in other contexts or, more strictly, it may describe software that has properties that allow it to be used in other application contexts without change. We will apply the latter interpretation here. Using this interpretation, for a module to possess the quality attribute reusability it depends on two things: the functionality of the module must be clearly and precisely described; the module must decoupled and therefore independent of its implementation context. A structural form is *reusable* if it uses standard language features, it contains no machine dependencies, it implements a single well-defined function and all computations are fully adjustable, use no global variables and contain no side-effects. All ranges associated with computations and data structures should have both their lower and upper bounds parameterized. To be completely reusable no variable in a computation should be assigned to a number or any other fixed constant. All constants used should be declared. Type independence also increases reusability. The relevant quality-carrying properties are listed in Table III.

Table III summarizes the relations between high-level quality attributes and the set of quality-carrying properties. The table may be used to answer two questions: *"which quality-carrying properties may be used to satisfy a given high-level quality attribute?"* and *"which high-level quality attributes does a given quality-carrying property impact?"*

The information in this table is useful for assisting the designer to build particular high-level quality attributes into

TABLE III
RELATIONSHIP BETWEEN QUALITY ATTRIBUTES
AND QUALITY-CARRYING PROPERTIES

software and for understanding which product properties impact particular high-level quality attributes.

VI. ASSURING QUALITY HAS BEEN BUILT INTO SOFTWARE

To assure, that the sort of quality properties we have described in our proposed model for software product quality are adhered to, some means of inspection are needed. Code inspection has long been recognized as a powerful method for assuring and improving the quality of software. The only problem is that it is very costly and labour-intensive to perform systematically and rigorously on large amounts of software.

To overcome this problem we have developed a powerful and flexible static analysis system (code auditor) [9] which supports and conforms to the model of software product quality that we have described. This system, which is rule-based, allows users to analyze the quality of software from a number of different perspectives. For example, it is possible to assess the high-level quality attribute *maintainability* of the software by running all the rules that have been classified as impacting this high-level quality attribute. To do this, simply involves selecting maintainability in the quality-attributes menu. In a similar way it is possible to assess high-level product characteristics such as *correctness*. It is also possible to select subordinate correctness properties such as *assigned* which checks whether all variables are assigned before being used. Overall the system for running the various rules is very flexible. Implementation of many of the rules in the system involves a detailed and sophisticated static analysis of the program text.

In analyzing software the PASS (Program Analysis and Style System) tool provides a comprehensive report on the quality of C programs. In the summary part of the report it presents such statistics as number-of-quality-defects-per-thousand-lines-of code, the number of maintainability, reliability, etc defects in the entire file. There is also a summary of how many times each defect was found. The main part of this report uses a format not unlike that used by compilers to report syntax errors. The line number and function where each defect occurs is pin-pointed. This system has been successfully employed to assess the quality of a wide range of industry software. The system allows an industry average to be maintained [9].

VII. DISCIPLINE FOR CLASSIFYING QUALITY DEFECTS

As we have seen programs consist of structural forms that describe data and processes. In order to classify and describe quality defects we need to talk about the properties of structural forms. An alternative approach would have been to use a model where relationships between structural forms were considered but this was rejected because it makes the characterization of defects more difficult. Provided our chosen set of structural forms admits composition (the *sequence* structural form does this) there is no need to speak directly of interrelationships between structural forms. For example suppose, in a sequence of statements, a guard tests a condition that has already been established by prior statements then we say that the guard is "redundant" (it violates the nonredundant usage property of guards). That is, we have assigned a defect to a structural form because of the problem associated with its usage in a particular context.

It was stated earlier that a primary requirement for the proposed model of software product quality was that it should possess a defect classification procedure that was repeatable. That is, two people familiar with the model should arrive at the same classification for any given defect.

The fundamental basis for classification we have employed to achieve repeatable classification involves the use of precedence to establish order. For this to work it is essential to have a fully structured system of precedence rules for classifying defects. Otherwise, we may end up classifying a given defect in an arbitrary number of different ways. One primary and two secondary classification rules are needed to implement system.

A. Primary Classification Rule

Always associate a defect with the lowest level structural form for which it assumes the status of a property.

This rule greatly simplifies the decision process for classification and ensures that defects are characterized in terms of their *origin* rather than in terms of their consequences.

Once the task of deciding which structural form the defect is to be associated with is accomplished the next task it to identify the property of the structural form which is violated. If there is any conflict in making this decision then first intercategory and then, if necessary, intracategory precedence rules may be applied to make the final classification decision.

The high level precedence for the *principal product-property classifications* which dictates the priority order is:

correctness $\rightarrow$ structural $\rightarrow$ modularity $\rightarrow$ descriptive

That is, classification of a defect as violating a correctness property takes precedence over a classification violating a structural property, and so on.

In a similar way, within a given principal property, a precedence order also applies. Take, for example, the correctness properties:

C1.	Computable
C2.	Complete
C3.	Assigned
C4.	Precise
C5.	Initialized
C6.	Progressive
C7.	Variant
C8.	Consistent

Here, if a choice must be made say, between classifying a defect as violating the "complete" property, and the "consistent" property, the former should be given precedence, and so on. Defect classification will now be illustrated by discussion of several examples.

Examples:

1) Unassigned Variable in an Expression of an Assignment Statement:

Defect Classification: We have the choice of associating this defect either with an assignment, with an expression or with a variable:

assignment integrity	$\rightarrow$	incomplete (incorrect)
expression integrity	$\rightarrow$	incomplete (incorrect)
variable integrity	$\rightarrow$	unassigned (correct)

At first glance this defect might seem like an expression integrity problem (e.g., the expression is undefined if one of it's variables is unassigned). However the *source* of the problem is not the expression itself but the variable. The rule that a variable should be assigned before use has been broken.

2) Unreachable Statement in an If-Statement:

Defect Classification: In this case we have the choice between classifying the problem as a defect in the if-statement or as a problem with the statement that is not reachable.

selection integrity	$\rightarrow$	incomplete (correct)

We do not classify a statement as unreachable because this amounts to treating it as a *relation* between structural forms. Instead we classify it as a defect of a structural form at one higher level where it reverts to a *property* of a structural form. We say a statement at a higher level (the if) is incomplete—this is the source of the defect.

3) Modification of a Loop Variable on Exit from a Loop:

Defect Classification: This could be potentially seen as either a defect in the sequence or as a problem with variable usage.

sequence integrity	$\rightarrow$	inconsistent (incorrect)
variable integrity	$\rightarrow$	inconsistent (correct)

Precedence dictates that the source of the problem is variable usage. Changing a loop variable on loop exit means the variable is being used for more than one purpose because the invariant property associated with its use in the loop is destroyed. A formal treatment of this problem is given elsewhere [18].

4) Double Initialization, that is, Initialization of a Variable Prior to Execution of a Loop and then Initialization of the Same Variable Again Prior to Loop Entry: This might potentially be seen as an assignment integrity or a variable integrity problem.

Defect Classification:

assignment integrity	$\rightarrow$	ineffective (incorrect)
variable integrity	$\rightarrow$	inconsistent (correct)

Precedence dictates that the problem be classified as a variable usage problem rather than as a problem with the assignment.

5) Function which Returns no Values but which makes an Assignment to at Least One Variable External to the Function:

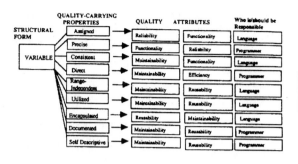

Fig. 3. Quality-carrying properties and programming languages.

QUALITY-CARRYING PROPERTIES

Fig. 4. Quality-carrying properties for a requirements variable.

Defect Classification: This example was chosen because it indicates the presence of a composite defect. There is inconsistent use of a module—it returns no values. And secondly, the module exhibits a side-effect because it makes an assignment to a global variable. Fixing either of these problems would still leave a remaining problem. So we end up with the following two classifications.

module integrity → inconsistent (correct)
variable integrity → unencapsulated (correct).

VIII. Languages and Software Product Quality

The model for software product quality that we have provided raises a number of important issues about programming language design. Most existing languages leave the responsibility for satisfying the various quality-carrying properties in the hands of the designer/programmer. This places a very heavy burden for software quality on the shoulders of the programmer. Design and code inspections and static analysis tools may be used to assist the programmer in ensuring that various quality-carrying properties are satisfied. These approaches however do not offer the best way to deal with the issue.

A far better way to proceed is to shift the major part of this burden from the programmer to the language designer and the compiler writer. By appropriate choices in the design of languages and compilers many of the quality-carrying properties associated with various structural forms can be satisfied or enforced. This means that the programmers have to change their style of implementation and/or submit their programs to much more rigorous compiler checks which insist that quality requirements are satisfied before a compiler will produce executable code. As examples, Fig. 3 illustrates for variables and expressions where the responsibilities for satisfying various quality-carrying properties can/should reside.

Elsewhere we have shown how a simple yet powerful language may be defined to implement the quality requirements that we have defined [19].

IX. Application of the Model to Other Software Products

The model we have described is generic. It can be utilized in many other contexts including for other products of software development. Our intent here is not to develop quality models for such applications but rather to establish the feasibility of the approach by sketching a small part of a quality model for a requirements specification. Such specifications consist of a set of required functions each of which has associated with it a set of input and output variables. In addition, there are usually a set of constraints associated with the variables and functions. Relations are used to define these constraints. As with the model we have developed for software implementations we may associate a comprehensive set of quality-carrying properties with each of the components that are used to define individual requirements (e.g., the input and output variables and any constraints and/or properties associated with the function and its variables). In addition, other quality-carrying properties must be defined which apply to subsets and even the complete set of requirements (e.g., matters relating to consistency and completeness). Proceeding in this way we can develop a comprehensive quality model for software requirements. To illustrate the process let us focus once again on variables. As in programs, the way variables are used in a requirements specification has a key impact on its quality. The quality-carrying properties needed for a variable in a specification are somewhat different from those needed in a program. To specify the quality of a variable in a program it is only necessary to deal with properties that are either only present or absent. In a requirements specification things are different. We need to specify quality-carrying properties that can take on a small set of values. A subset of the quality-carrying properties of variables is given below together with the brief explanation of their role and the identification of defect status.

A. Quality-Carrying Properties of Variables in a Requirements Specification

Fig. 4 shows the quality-carrying properties (category, I/O status, domain, form, name) for variables in a requirements specification. A quality defect occurs when a property has a value marked with "***".

1) Category: For the purposes of specifying requirements the two possible values of category are sufficient. Common is used to characterize variables whose properties are commonly known (e.g., phone-book) and technical describes variables whose properties are context-dependent. There is a tendency in requirements to refer to common variables and not to bother to define them for the purposes of shorthand. While this is a defect in a requirements specification it is not a problem that is hard to overcome. However when a technical variable (e.g., reentry-velocity) is not defined this is a much more serious quality defect that needs rectification.

phone-book → common → undefined → not serious defect
reentry-velocity → technical → undefined → serious defect

. Note to *define* common variables we can use an example or cite a reference (e.g., Brisbane telephone book). We may also refer to a certain page in an organization's data model.

2) I/O-Status (source/sink properties): The quality of a requirement's specification depends very much on the source/sink properties of variables. If this is defined/explicit this is important, if it is unknown then it detracts from the quality of a requirement. Each variable should have a *source* and at least one *sink*. If there is more than one source there could be a problem. If this information is not known then it detracts from the quality of the requirement. The source could be EXTERNAL (e.g., user input, an existing database etc.) or the source may be the output of a function/process. A sink might be the input to a function. Variables can also be input to and output from a function—in this case a variable must also have some other source.

3) Domain: The domain of a variable must be defined.

4) Form: From a requirement it should be possible to determine a variable's form. If this is not be possible—it represents a quality defect.

5) Alias: Defect when more than one name is used to refer to a particular variable

Using the approach we have begun to outline here for variables it is possible to build a comprehensive quality model for a requirements specification. A similar approach can also be taken to construct quality models for user interfaces and other software products.

X. CONCLUSION

The model we have defined and illustrated here provides an explicit process for building quality-carrying properties into software. These properties in turn imply particular quality attributes. In other words we have proposed a model that establishes the link between tangible product characteristics and less tangible quality attributes.

An important advantage of this model is that it can assist in conducting a systematic search for quality defects. The model guides us where to look for defects and also indicates the properties that will need to be violated to create defects. This information provides constructive guidance for building a comprehensive set of defects for any particular language environment.

No claim is made that the model we have proposed is "correct" or that it is the only one that might be employed.

The model is empirical and therefore corrigible and open to refinement. Irrespective of disputes or disagreement over the details of the model the framework provided offers a means for, in the longer term, providing direct guidance for building quality into software both from the top-down (during design) and from the bottom-up (during implementation). In addition the model supports assuring the quality of software and systematic classification of quality defects. While the details of the model might need to be changed and refined the framework should provide a sound constructive foundation for achieving a better understanding of software product quality.

REFERENCES

[1] B. W. Boehm, J. R. Brown, M. Lipow, G. J. MacLeod, and M. J. Merritt, *Characteristics of Software Quality.* New York: Elsevier North-Holland, 1978.
[2] B. Kitchenham, "Towards a constructive quality model," *Software Eng. J.,* pp. 105–112, July 1987.
[3] B. W. Kernighan and P. J. Plaugher, *The Elements of Programming Style.* New York: McGraw-Hill, 1974.
[4] M. Deutsch and R. Willis, *Software Quality Engineering.* Englewood Cliffs, NJ: Prentice-Hall, 1988.
[5] T. P. Bowen, "Specification of software quality attributes," Rome Laboratory, New York, Tech. Rep. RADC-TR-85-37, vols. 1–3, 1976.
[6] R. Nance, "Software quality indicators: An holistic approach to measurement," in *Proc. 4th Ann. Software Quality Workshop,* Alexandria Bay, New York, Aug. 1992.
[7] Software Product Evaluation—Quality Characteristics and Guidelines for Their Use, ISO/IEC Standard ISO-9126 (1991).
[8] R. G. Dromey, "A generic model for building quality into products and processes," in preparation.
[9] R. G. Dromey and K. Ryan, *PASS-C: Program Analysis and Style System User Manual,* Software Quality Inst., Griffith Univ., 1993.
[10] R. G. Dromey, "Program Derivation," in *International Series in Computer Sciences.* London, England: Addison-Wesley, 1989.
[11] N. Wirth, "Program development by stepwise refinement," *CACM,* vol. 14, pp. 221–227, 1971.
[12] M. Jackson, *Principles of Program Design.* London, England: Academic, 1975.
[13] G. Myers, *Software Reliability; Principles and Practices.* New York: Wiley, 1976.
[14] R. G. Dromey and A. D. McGettrick, "On specifying software quality," *Software Quality J.,* vol. 1, no. 1, pp. 45–74, 1992.
[15] R. G. Dromey, "A framework for engineering quality software," keynote address, *7th Australian Software Eng. Conf.,* Sydney, Australia, Sept. 1993.
[16] E. W. Dijkstra and C. S. Scholten, *Predicate Calculus and Program Semantics.* New York: Springer-Verlag, 1989.
[17] T. Manns and Coleman, *Software Quality Assurance.* London, England: MacMillan, 1988.
[18] Si Pan and R. G. Dromey, "A formal basis for measuring software product quality," *17th Australian Comput. Sci. Conf.,* Christchurch, NZ, Jan. 1994.
[19] B. Oliver and R. G. Dromey, "SAFE: A programming language for software quality," *1st Int. (Asia-Pacific) Conf. Software Quality and Productivity,* Hong Kong, China, Dec. 1994.

R. Geoff Dromey is the Foundation Professor of the School of Computing and Information Technology at Griffith University. He founded the SQI in 1989.

Through the SQI, he has worked closely for a number of years with industry, national and international standards bodies and government. He has worked at Stanford University, the Australian National University, and Wollongong University before taking up the Chair at Griffith University in Brisbane Australia. His current research interests are in applying formal and empirical methods to improve the quality of software and the productivity of software development.

Dr. Dromey has authored/co-authored two books and over fifty refereed research papers. He is on the Editorial Board of four international journals.

Chapter 7

ISO 9000 Series and TickIT

1. Introduction to Chapter

This chapter discusses what was originally a UK initiative, the application of the generic quality management series of standards ISO 9000 to software. The UK scheme, which was launched in 1989, is known as TickIT. One of the issues involved in the use of TickIT was the extent to which software products and the processes used to develop and maintain them are similar to other manufactured products and processes. Earlier studies commissioned by the UK government found that

- it was appropriate to apply the ISO 9000 series to software (the Logica report[4]);

- the anticipated costs and benefits of applying the ISO 9000 series of standards to software suggested that it was cost effective to do so (the Price Waterhouse report[5]).

The part of the ISO 9000 series considered most appropriate for application to software was ISO 9001 [2] (equivalent to BS 5750 part 1, which preceded it, and EN 29001, the European version of the standard) and a guide to the application of ISO 9001 to software entitled "Guidelines for the Application of ISO 9001 to the Development, Supply and Maintenance of Software" was produced. This guide was known as ISO 9000-3[1].

The requirements of ISO 9001 (according to the 1994 version of the standard) are arranged under the 20 clauses of section 4 of the standard, namely

4.1   Management responsibility

4.2   Quality system

4.3   Contract review

4.4   Design control

4.5   Document and data control

4.6   Purchasing

4.7   Control of customer-supplied product

4.8   Product identification and traceability

4.9   Process control

4.10   Inspection and testing

4.11   Control of inspection, measuring, and test equipment

4.12   Inspection and test status

4.13   Control of nonconforming product

4.14   Corrective and preventive action

4.15   Handling, storage, packing, preservation, and delivery

4.16   Control of quality records

4.17   Internal quality audits

4.18   Training

4.19   Servicing

4.20   Statistical techniques

TickIT is supported by a Guide, subtitled "making a better job of software", at the time of writing (2001) in its fourth edition and updated to bring it into line with the 1997 revision of ISO 9000-3 and the 1995 edition of the standard ISO/IEC 12207 [3] on software lifecycle processes. The Guide defines the scope of TickIT and describes the organization behind it. It provides guidance for software customers and software suppliers as well as for auditors. It also contains listings of other relevant standards and associated reading, as well as guidance to relevant standards information on the internet. Information concerning the Guide is available at the TickIT web site [6]. Information concerning other support material for TickIT including a video, details of case studies, and a quarterly international journal entitled TickIT International, are also available at the web site.

The bulk of TickIT certifications have taken place in the United Kingdom. In August 1999, 70% of the 1437 active certificates were held in the UK. However, in the previous six months only 62% of the certificates granted were in the UK, suggesting a gradual spread of TickIT to other countries. Approximately 9% of certificates are held in North America (US and Canada), and the European countries (apart from the UK) where TickIT has made the most impact are Ireland and Sweden. Elsewhere in the world TickIT has made the largest impact in India and Japan. Overall, there has been a steady growth over the last few years in the number of TickIT certificates held from just over 600 in 1994 to over 1400 in 1999.

A list is maintained (accessible over the internet) of bodies currently able to award TickIT certificates, all of which have been approved for the purpose by UKAS (United Kingdom Accreditation Service), formerly NACCB (National Accreditation Council for Certification

Bodies). UKAS lays down detailed criteria which certification bodies should conform to in the areas of:

- Impartiality
- Confidentiality
- Competence
- Maintenance of records
- Appeal procedures

While TickIT has clearly made its greatest impact in the United Kingdom, there is also no doubt that it has considerable influence world-wide.

At the time of writing, the ISO 9000 series of standards is undergoing a major revision. The first article in this chapter is based on the new series of standards.

2. Description of Articles

The first paper in this chapter is entitled "ISO 9001: A Tool for Systematic Software Process Improvement" and is by Victoria Hailey. It is written in the context of the emerging standard ISO 9001:2000, and describes the evolution of software quality from quality control to quality management. The contribution of the ISO 9000 series of standards (first published in 1987) is emphasized.

ISO 9001 views software production and maintenance as a system of processes which must be linked in a logical and cost effective manner in order to allow a systematic approach to (software) quality to be adopted. Systems theory suggests that the production and maintenance of a quality management system has much in common with the production and maintenance of a software system. In the case of a quality management system (QMS), the internal interfaces and interdependencies are critical unless there is maximum commitment, especially from top management.

Hailey maintains that cost benefit justifications are critical in retaining the support of top management and quotes the four principles of the Taguchi method:

- Quality can be improved without increasing cost;
- Costs cannot be reduced without affecting quality;
- Costs can be reduced by improving quality;
- Costs can also be reduced by reducing variation.

The paper concludes by discussing improvement paradigms.

The second paper in this chapter, entitled "Benefits and Prerequisites of ISO 9000 Based Software Quality Management," by Dirk Stelzer, Mark Reibnitz, and Werner Mellis, presents a study of the experiences of twelve European software organizations which have sought ISO 9000 certification. In particular it summarizes the benefits of and prerequisites for seeking such certification, as seen by the twelve organizations.

The benefits are much as would be expected in the circumstances: improved project management, improved productivity, improved customer satisfaction, improved product quality, and so on. In 26 per cent of cases, a positive return on investment also resulted.

The two most important prerequisites—management commitment and support and staff involvement—were also fairly predictable. However, the next two prerequisites—providing enhanced understanding (acquiring and transferring knowledge of current practices) and tailoring improvement initiatives (adapting quality management practices to the   specific strengths and weaknesses of different teams and departments) —are perhaps less obvious.

The third paper in this chapter, entitled "How ISO 9001 Compares with the CMM" is by Mark Paulk and is concerned with comparing ISO 9001 and the SW-CMM. The paper answers the questions,

- At what level in the SW-CMM would an ISO 9001-compliant organization be?

- Can a SW-CMM level 2 (or 3) organization be considered compliant with ISO 9001?

The comparison between ISO 9001 and the SW-CMM is not simple, as the two have different scopes. For example, certain aspects of ISO 9001 are not addressed at all by the SW-CMM. However, a mapping can be made from the ISO 9001 requirements on to the key process areas at each level of the SW-CMM, and from this a reasonable level of equivalence may be established.

References

[1] ISO 9000-3, *Quality Management and Quality Assurance Standards: Guidelines for the Application of ISO 9001:1994 to the Development, Supply Acquisition and Maintenance of Computer Software,* ISO, 1997.

[2] ISO 9001, *Quality Systems - Model for Quality Assurance in Design, Development, Production, Installation and Servicing,* ISO, 1994.

[3] ISO/IEC 12207, *Information Technology - Software Life Cycle Processes,* ISO/IEC, 1995.

[4] Logica Report, *Quality Management Standards for Software,* Logica Consultancy Ltd, London, 1988.

[5] Price Waterhouse Report, *Software Quality Standards: The costs and Benefits,* Price Waterhouse, London, 1988.

[6] TickIT web site http://www.tickit.org

ISO 9001[1]: A Tool for Systematic Software Process Improvement

Victoria A. Hailey, CMC

The Victoria Hailey Group Corporation
P.O. Box 334, Thornhill, Ontario Canada L3T 4A2
Tel: +1 416 410-3400 vah@vhg.com

Abstract

During the past several decades, the quality gurus have helped us to understand that the quality of software can only be improved by the focusing on the processes used to build it.[2] This tutorial presents ISO 9001:2000 as a software process improvement tool for the software organization that is systematically striving to improve both process effectiveness and product quality. Borrowing from the basic concepts of systems theory, the software organization can use ISO 9001 as a "system" for managing the quality of its products through the adoption of a disciplined approach to the management of its people, processes, and technology. In doing so, it becomes possible to see more clearly into the process interactions and structures that contribute to the development of software. ISO 9001's quality management system requirements embrace the process approach as fundamental to controlling, through measurement, the design and development of the product. Consequently, once the organization has implemented this system and collected performance data regarding the execution of its processes, it can manipulate, via measured change under controlled conditions, whatever aspect of the system is appropriate, to directly affect the quality of its products.

Introduction

For more than two decades, software engineering experts have been writing about the software crisis and the risks associated with it. Some say the crisis is over because we can now see clearly into the processes where the root cause of the problems originate. We have proven that effective methods can produce reliable, high-quality software on time and on budget.[3] Others warn that our problems have only just begun, with cybercrime being the biggest threat since the invention of the atomic bomb. Regardless of who you believe, the one issue that always gains consensus is that software systems now pervade every aspect of our lives, from the digital alarm clock that wakes us up in the morning to the way we get ourselves to work and to the aircraft with which we trust our lives.

While our societal dependence on software has increased exponentially, our ability to manage its quality has not kept pace. Still, software engineering as a discipline has made significant progress with the development of tools to measure process capability. The only problem is that their take-up is also falling behind the need to embrace these tools. The *vast majority* of software organizations (roughly 80 percent) are at the *lowest ratings of maturity*.

The software industry's self-propelled momentum for change will never slow even as demands for reliability increase. The effects of this breakneck speed are manifested in a number of ways:

- Software engineers are expected to stay current with technology that changes at unprecedented rates, placing enormous learning challenges on scarce, skilled resources.

- The interconnectivity of the Internet means interfacing new, sometimes unproven, technologies with legacy systems to take advantage of e-business market forces.

- Required reliability and integrity levels are unmet because new technologies and methods preclude accurate verification and validation.

- Processes are bypassed because formality is perceived to be unnecessary when doing extreme or fast-to-market programming and small Java/C++ projects.

- Management's perception is that tangible and quantifiable (including cost) gains are not obviously a direct result of process improvement efforts. To invest in gains requires a base of current costs that is not always available.

Yet never before has there been such a need for a systematic approach to improving software. ISO 9001:2000 (ISO 9001 hereafter) offers a closed-loop, continuous process improvement system as a toolkit for defining and establishing a consistent and improving process that produces quality software *and* meets the software organization's business objectives. Using this toolkit, the software organization can gradually shift from a reactionary stance, with putting out fires as its principal means of control, to one that is proactive, where planning incremental improvements with measured and predicable control becomes the norm.

ISO 9001 offers an alternative to the common perception that if the software engineer cannot deal with and understand the technology issues, an improved process will not help. It provides a "system" infrastructure that encourages and even rewards—through the product improvements that result—an institutionalized process discipline where even time-to-market priorities would not cause processes to be bypassed.[4] The belief that software process improvement is only for organizations that are large enough or rich enough to be able to afford an independent process group is countered by the fact that regardless of the size of a company or its priorities, a process of some sort is being followed, so the intent should be to ensure that it is an effective one.

Not every organization must be big or rich to benefit from software process improvement, however, it does have to be disciplined. A software organization can use ISO 9001 to implement a systems approach to designing and developing quality software. By applying the ISO 9001 quality management system framework to the building of software, the organization can almost, as if by default, implement a systematic approach to improve the software being developed.

The Evolution of Software Quality

Quality has to be *caused*, not controlled.[5]

Quality and its cohort, continuous improvement, have been evolving since humans first made tools. The concept is not new. As a species, we have learned that trial and error is not the most efficient or profitable methodology with which to reach our goals (even though sometimes it is the only way). Instead, we have reached toward mathematical models and statistical process control, introduced largely as a result of war efforts.[6] In a few decades, we have moved from quality control to quality assurance to quality management to today's goal of quantitative improvement based on measured and controlled change. We have probably witnessed more formalization of the quality discipline in the last half-century than in all of history combined.

More than a century ago, thinkers and philosophers understood measurement to be the basic principle behind quantitative or statistical control: "When you can measure what you are speaking about, and express it in numbers, you know something about it."[7] Following along this evolutionary path, we have learned that measuring our processes will help us to determine whether or not their performance is inherently stable and consistent. The levels of stability and consistency will tell us whether or not the processes are predictable and, hence, whether or not the product and its future performance will be predictable. These factors are measured by establishing process performance parameters and then determining the variations according to the established statistical process control limits set out for the process.[8] "Quantification is mandatory for control, therefore evaluation must be scientific. Scientific means that the results must be predicted before the measurements are made, and the difference used to guide adjustments. Projects should choose their tools and methodologies based on quantitative criteria, measuring their effects on reliability, schedule, and cost with respect to the cost of implementation."[9] What this means is that quantitative process control[10] provides a measure of predictive ability to help determine the process's performance. Once the process adjustments have been calculated, they can be proven empirically prior to making the changes. Once proven, they can be implemented with minimal disruption to the existing processes in production.

The software quality equation has advanced with a definition of the practices required to develop the right product with the right characteristics so that measurement can be applied, adjustment can be made to the variables, and improvement opportunities can be identified according to the software process model definition.

The ISO (International Organization for Standardization) standards development community represents the minimum best practice as reached by worldwide consensus. Only within the last 20 or so years has a definition of the software development process reached *any* degree of consensus, as culminated by the publication in 1995 of ISO/IEC 12207.[11,12] Although it has been evolving since the earliest days, no clear and concise definition of the software process and its various components (such as purpose, objectives, outcomes, inputs, outputs, and activities) has been available. Reliable measurements have previously not been possible because there was no basis with which to determine what needed to be measured and how. To be able to define a software process succinctly, all of the processes involved with the development of a software system must first be identified and then defined at a basic *performed*[13] capability level, with additional process management attributes normalized so they can be measured. Equipped with a baseline definition of what needs to be done to design, develop, and deliver software, a software organization can then consider measuring its software process performance. "Unless you know how you're doing as you go along, you'll never know when you're done, or if you've succeeded."[14]

Practitioners in the software engineering field have recognized the importance of statistical methods and have produced a number of measurement models for software process assessment. ISO/IEC (International Electrotechnical Commission) published a Technical Report (TR) on software process assessment, ISO/IEC TR 15504.[15] The Software Engineering Institute (SEI) at Carnegie Mellon University (CMU) published several Capability Maturity Models®.[16] These models, as well as others, are gaining steady acceptance among software organizations largely because they provide the parameters within which variation can be identified. The performance of the software process and, hence, the risk of impacts on product quality can be detected through measurement, with the resulting analysis providing the specifics on which to focus process improvement efforts.

To date, the biggest impact on quality since Deming and Juran shared their experiences and philosophies has been the introduction of the ISO 9000 family of standards. Since the first edition of ISO 9000 was published in 1987, innumerable volumes of information have been written about it and the benefits, pain, and costs of its implementation and practice. It has been criticized vigorously since its introduction, yet the number of certifications continues to grow. Hundreds of thousands of organizations from virtually every industry sector have become registered to one of its versions, and the momentum has not yet slowed. "Up to the end of December 1999, at least 343,643 ISO 9000 certificates had been awarded in 150 countries worldwide."[17] This trend is either a testimonial to the value of the model or to the competitive market pressures of conformance.

Since it was first introduced, however, this promoter of product consistency has not fared well in the software industry because of its heavy manufacturing bias. The requirements for procedures in the early editions did not seem to resemble software development life cycle activities. Software organizations were already struggling to ensure that they were just performing the basic processes without having to tackle another challenge that resembled translation into software development terminology.

The number of certifications for those organizations whose primary focus is on software systems still remains relatively low compared to other industry sectors. With each new version of the standard, the benchmark is set higher and becomes more difficult to reach. Criticisms that ISO 9001 is too generic and does not meet the demands of the software process will continue to flourish. Nevertheless, software engineering practitioners with a modest amount of perseverance with which to interpret the standard's meaning and with enough creativity to challenge it to a degree sufficient to extract its value, will find that this internationally accepted quality management system model can and will provide a disciplined structure within which to plan, implement, monitor, and measure software process improvement.

The work done to date in the sometimes disparate worlds of software engineering and quality management can be integrated systematically using the ISO 9001 model. To be effective, the software organization's quality management system must be designed and built to encourage change (à la improvement). To accommodate this design, the system must be flexible enough to allow the organization's objectives, once defined, to evolve according to both the organization's and the customer's requirements. Continuous process improvement as rendered in this standard can be likened to a self-repairing model that endlessly loops back to monitor its own performance as it strives toward achieving its objectives and sustaining a balance of need, opportunity, and resource.

ISO 9001 Is a System of Processes

The system of quality is prevention.[18]

The Process Approach

In ISO 9001, everything is a process. Every activity that is performed, whether directly or indirectly, with the intent of producing a work product is part of a product-producing process. Similarly, every activity that either supports the production of the final product or integrates with it is part of a product-producing process. If the activity has no value in supporting these objectives, then it probably has little or no value and will not survive in an effective quality management system (although it may serve elsewhere, such as finance). The standard adopts a "process approach" to quality so that the individual activities that work together to produce the product can be formally identified, defined, designed, and planned for together as processes. Once these processes are organized, managed, and linked, they form a system that can be tracked and measured to ensure each process achieves its objective.

These processes must be linked in a logical and cost-effective manner to permit the organization to identify and control the inputs on which to perform the appropriate activities. The inputs then can be transformed into a set of outputs that meet the customer's (and other applicable) requirements. As shown in the simple customer model below in Figure 1, each of the four boxes represents a process that is linked, according to its sequence, to the others through the controls of the quality management system. This chain effect of linked processes begins with the identification of customer requirements and ends with delivery of the product to the customer. The ongoing management of these processes and the application of quality management system controls that ensure links are not broken both comprise the quality management system or the "systematic" approach to managing quality. Each process is cycled through as often as necessary to ensure that defects are eliminated and quality process objectives are being met.

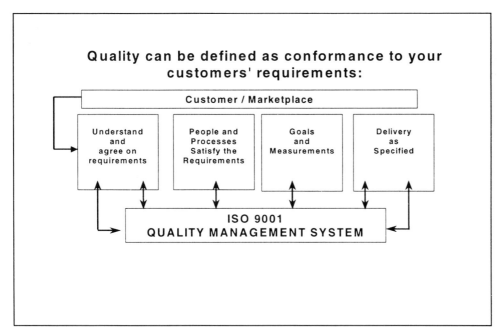

Figure 1. Simple customer model.

When the process approach has been used within a software organization to represent its software development process, a systematic approach to quality can be adopted. That this model is generic is irrelevant, since the quality management system requires the organization to determine for itself the processes it should use to develop its products. Consequently, this model makes as much sense for designing and developing software as it does for building cars. That the software development and measurement processes have been standardized (through ISO/IEC 12207, ISO/IEC TR 15504, ISO/IEC 9126, and IEEE software engineering standards, among others) means that the software industry has a mechanism for take-up of the best practices by looking at industry-defined models.

Satisfying Requirements—The Customer's and the Organization's

The ISO 9001 model is a simple (though not easy) system that works if the design of the quality management system is based on the *organization's own requirements to satisfy its customer's requirements*. Each software organization is different, from its customer profile, application domain, and set of products to its definition of quality. Other than senior management's commitment to its implementation, the criterion of critical importance as a success factor for an effective quality management system is the organization's ability to define a system that works for itself[19] and its customers.

Priorities, strategies, and schedules for change must be unique to the organization. By adopting a process approach to quality, the organization must consider how well each process within the system contributes value. Whether the need is for radical reengineering methods to provide accelerated and dramatic change or incremental continuous process improvement for slow, controlled change or a hybrid, issues-based approach that ensures attention is paid to visible problems, the process approach that the organization adopts must fit the environment. By setting measurable objectives for each process, and by ensuring that these objectives relate to the overall quality of the product being produced, fulfillment of these objectives can be tracked throughout the design and development of the process.

Every quality management system, whether it is for software or widgets, is similar and yet distinctly unique, reflecting its own unique culture and purpose. The uniqueness of the quality management system can be seen in the blend of characteristics that form the software organization's identity. These characteristics help to determine the software organization's requirements for the quality management system, its measurement goals, and thus the measurable attributes that determine the improvement equation. This blend also contributes to the unique or custom aspects of the software process. The "personality traits" of the organization, such as size, organizational structure, application domain, and type of and relationship with customers, also contribute to the specification of the quality management system requirements. The specific organizational objectives and strategies must contribute to the definition of the quality management system so that once its unique aspects have been considered, the software organization can overlay a suitable software process model onto its quality requirements definition to design and develop a customized system that specifies how the organization should approach its software quality objectives.

ISO 9001 As a Closed-Loop System

The following description of ISO 9001's five sections (numbered 4 to 8 in Table 1) specifies how the requirements to define this closed-loop, quality management system can be applied:

4 *Quality Management System*	Specifies how the system is to be designed and developed: • Structure the quality management system by ensuring requirements for demonstrating effectiveness and continuous improvement. • Use a process approach to define the system of processes that ensures the delivery of quality to the customer. • Document this approach in a controlled manner including the policies, processes, and procedures used to develop the product and keep the system working together as a whole. • Keep records as evidence of conformance and to assist in both the collection of data regarding process and product performance as well as the reconstruction of an audit trail of activities.
5 *Management Responsibility*	Defines the level of commitment management should devote to the system: • Focus on the customers. • Have management play an active role in the system, not only in defining it and the policies surrounding quality, but in ensuring its effectiveness, continual improvement, and longevity. • Set targets and *measurable* objectives. • Ensure effective communication throughout the organization as well as with customers. • Make staff resources available and educate them on their role. • Plan, define, design, monitor, measure, and track the quality management system.
6 *Resource Management*	Ensures that people (through competence, skills, training, and experience), the infrastructure, and the environment can do the job

	of supporting quality as the output of every process.
7 ***Product Realization***	Defines the set of processes used to design and develop the product for the customer: • Plan how to design and develop the product (and the processes that create them). • Define requirements, their review, and change management. • Design and develop the product (planning, requirements, build, verification, validation, and change management). • Control the acquisitions and purchasing processes, including outsourcing. • Control the processes to ensure management of the process variables. • Manage the configuration of all work products (including interim and customer-owned products). • Verify test tools to ensure the integrity of measurement data.
8 ***Measurement, Analysis, and Improvement***	Supports the closed-loop improvement cycle of the system to ensure both the products and processes: • Monitor to detect/prevent problems. • Measure to ensure conformance to requirements. • Analyze to identify the current status of the product, processes, customer perception, and relationship with suppliers. • Correct the root cause when defects are found. • Improve so as to prevent potential defects.

Table 1. ISO 9001:2000's Five Sections

The intelligence and common sense underlying ISO 9001's process-oriented requirements place the onus on the organization to identify the processes it needs to satisfy customer requirements and to then build a system *that works and is effective*. The model can be considered to be recursive, because it applies its own requirements to its product—the quality management system—to ensure that the correct output is obtained. As stated in 4.1, General Requirements:

"The organization shall

a) identify the processes needed for the quality management system and their application throughout the organization (see 1.2),

b) determine the sequence and interaction of these processes,

c) determine criteria and methods needed to ensure that both the operation and control of these processes are effective,

d) ensure the availability of resources and information necessary to support the operation and monitoring of these processes,

e) monitor, measure and analyse these processes, and

f) implement actions necessary to achieve planned results and continual improvement of these processes."[20]

Systems Theory

According to *Merriam Webster,*[21] a *system* is "an organized integrated whole made up of diverse but interrelated and interdependent parts." This simple definition can be applied to both a software system and a quality management system. It is by extracting the simplicity of this approach that software engineers can apply the principles and requirements of ISO 9001 to the manner in which they build software systems and achieve results in improved product quality.

Systems theory promotes the idea that it is the similarities in the way in which systems function that allow them first to be compared and then to be likened to each other to extract the truths behind the principles and the patterns that allow them to be universal. "Systems theory...argues that however complex or diverse the world that we experience, we will always find different types of organization[s] in it, and such organization[s] can be described by concepts and principles which are independent from the specific domain at which we are looking. Hence, [by] uncover[ing] those general laws, we [can] analyse and solve problems in any domain, pertaining to any type of system. The systems approach distinguishes itself from the more traditional analytic approach by emphasizing the interactions and connectedness of the different components of a system. Although the systems approach in principle considers all types of systems, it in practice focuses on the more complex, adaptive, self-regulating systems...."[22]

In the software domain, both the software system and the quality management system must be engineered first to work and then to be effective. The process of designing and developing a quality management system resembles the process of designing and developing software:

1. Both systems are based on requirements from customers.

2. Both systems are designed and developed using people, processes, and technology (even if that technology is the process itself).

3. In both cases, the organization is designing and building a system of abstract relationships, concepts, and information flows.

4. No one knows precisely what the system will look like until it is finished, although experience and a detailed project plan will provide a fair representation.

5. As in software systems, change/configuration management within the quality management system is critical to ensure control over work products and deliverables.

6. Like software, the only guidance for the project is a policy or requirements definition and various levels of interpretations of those requirements.

The similarities between the two types of systems become visible when both are viewed as an infrastructure of interdependent processes and relationships that combine to comprise a whole that is designed to meet the objective of satisfying customer requirements.

Systems Building Blocks

The definition of any complex system requires the definition of its components. The first step in defining a software quality management system is to ensure that the architectural building blocks listed below are defined to ensure the structural integrity of the system. By planning the activities that integrate the various parts of the system into a whole, integrity can be ensured between the various aspects of the process. This formalization includes ensuring that the outputs of a process match the input requirements of the connecting process, without dangling or broken links occurring that could disconnect them. These building blocks include:

- Policies;

- Measurable objectives;

- Identified purpose and outcomes of the process;

- Process activities (which may be comprised of the software life cycle processes of, for example, ISO/IEC 12207);

- Links between processes;

- Inputs/outputs;

- Entrance/exit criteria;

- Process controls;

- Roles, responsibilities, accountabilities;

- Customer–organization–supplier relationships;

- Documents;

- Records; and

- Metrics.

To provide a foundation for growth and improvement, the software organization must manage the complexities and interactions of the software development processes and build an open system that provides a closed feedback improvement loop as illustrated in the process map shown in Figure 2. "Systems theory emphasize[s] that real systems are open to, and interact with, their environments, and that they can acquire qualitatively new properties through emergence, resulting in continual evolution. Rather than reducing an entity...to the properties of its parts or elements...systems theory focuses on the arrangement of and relations between the parts which connect them into a whole...[which] determines a system, which is independent of the...elements.... Thus, the same concepts and principles of organization underlie the different disciplines...providing a basis for their unification."[23]

As a complex system, once the components have been defined, unless they are integrated into the whole, they have limited value. It has been said that it is the interfaces that cause the problems, not the components themselves, because "the value of a system lies in its interfaces."[24] The interfaces allow movement of information and activities to occur. Support for this system of interconnectivity without the infrastructure collapsing from the sheer complexity of their interactions requires that each component within this system be developed correctly, one step at a time. ISO 9001 presents a model against which to define a working system, but unless the various aspects or components have been designed to work together effectively, the system will have no more value that any other poorly designed entity. If any of the system's process linkages are disconnected, the system will "crash."

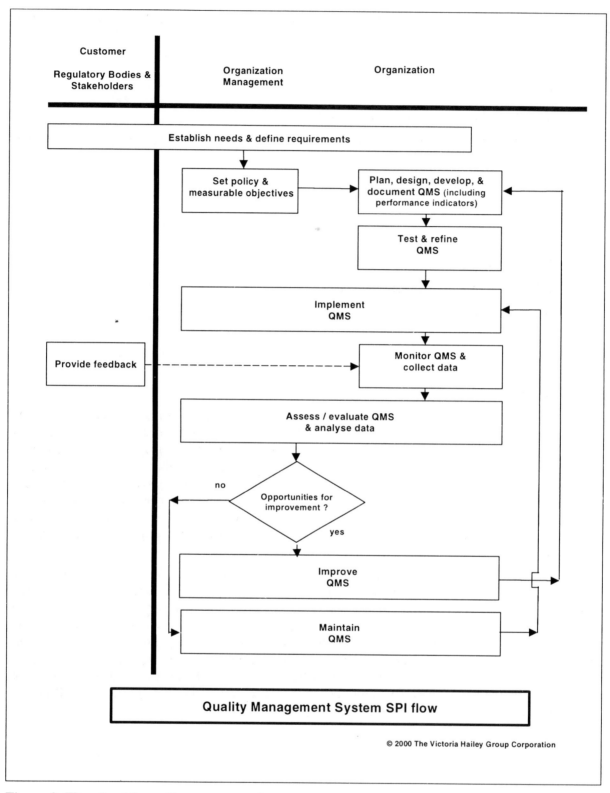

Figure 2. Flowchart for software process improvement.

System Interfaces

The interfaces and interdependencies within the quality management system are vulnerable. It is up to each individual participant to commit, support, and comply, since each role plays an integral part in the quality puzzle. While top management must initiate, lead, and support the system, each software manager or engineer must become an integral part of the system. Discipline must be maintained by everyone working within the process and all must agree to ensure that the agreed requirements are met. It becomes everyone's responsibility to be aware and cognizant of the effects of noncompliance and of the problems that can affect the entire system. It is also critical to exercise as much discipline as is required and appropriate to ensure that change only occurs within the acceptable parameters as defined by the system. Full and effective participation and practice by everyone within the quality management system is their job. It is not separate or distinct from it.

At some point, agreement must be reached that the requirements of any system must be frozen so the product can be built and delivered. However, the similarities between quality management and software systems continue past the final product build stages because maintenance and improvement are continuous for both. The similarities finally end between them at the end of the software system's finite life cycle when it faces retirement, whereas ISO 9001 can continue as long as the organization continues. Once conformance with ISO 9001's requirements is achieved, the system requires that it continually regenerate itself through process maintenance, self-repair, and self-propulsion toward improvement.

Management Commitment

It is management's responsibility to ensure that the requirements and processes of the organization are addressed by the ISO 9001 system. One of the most common pitfalls executive sponsors encounter is the lack of cohesion between the quality management system and the practices of the organization. It becomes difficult to justify an investment that shows little return. In every aspect of the system, the organization's and customer's objectives must be aligned *through* ISO 9001 if it is to work effectively.

One of the main reasons that quality management systems fail is because the organization has neglected to gather *its own requirements for its own system from its own users.* This situation often occurs whenever the organization just "puts in" the system. Without constant interaction and involvement in defining the requirements of any system, the developers cannot just guess at how to build an acceptable product. Experienced developers know they must extract their customers' requirements in order to provide a blueprint from which to help the customer translate its requirements into a working, compliant system and so guide them through to successful implementation.

The importance of software engineers and software managers defining their own quality management system requirements is a critical step. Consider that the quality management system is built for and by people trying to envisage an entire complex system of interactions and exchanges. Consider that the ISO 9001 requirements are introduced as the benchmark against which a quality audit will determine conformance. Consider that there are probably a myriad of external or regulatory requirements, depending on the application domain. Consider the impact on existing organizational activities. While not conflicting, neither are these factors mutually supportive. Top management has the responsibility and authority to specify the business requirements for survival, growth, success, compliance, achievement, recognition (or whatever the motivation). When top management does not participate—and instead just provides approval to just "go do it"—the opportunities for failure of the system to achieve objectives and payback increase exponentially. ISO 9001 does not dictate the level of participation that top management must take, but the more participation and direct involvement of top management, the clearer their visibility will be into the overall improvement of it.

The *quality manual*, often considered to be superficial "fluff," is the main vehicle for specifying the quality management system requirements from the senior management perspective by articulating the quality policy, measurable objectives, organizational structure, and processes required to inform and empower staff about strategies, direction, processes, how the work is being done, what decisions have been agreed to, by whom, and who is responsible and accountable. Together with the documentation that defines them, supporting or infrastructure processes that have been defined and documented provide a form of "organizational user's manual" that describes the entire development and support (maintenance) life cycles for a software product, including all activities associated with ensuring quality (quality planning).

The organizational policies must reflect the strategic decisions of the organization and, hence, require top management's involvement, direction, commitment, and support. These latter factors are critical regardless of whether the process or management style reflects a team-based, autocratic, self-guiding, or customer relations management (CRM)-empowered strategy. The policies (like software requirements) must meet the following criteria. They must:

- Synchronize such that process interrelationships do not cause or create conflict (management's policies should define an escalation path to resolution);

- Not be contradictory or mutually exclusive to enable them to guide the operational performance and quality objectives;

- Be measured so as to enable monitoring of process and product performance and to facilitate improvement.

When policies are defined that address the organization's own requirements, the system can operate as a cohesive unit. If the job is done right and if the software organization has taken advantage of this opportunity to design and develop an effective quality management system—according to not only the ISO 9001 requirements but also its own and the customer's requirements—then it has internalized its responsibility. By taking this first step, the software organization has adopted a path toward self-determination on the road to process improvement and maturity.

Open Systems and the Supplier→Organization→Customer Relationship

By definition, a quality management system is an open system since it involves customer, suppliers, regulatory bodies, and a myriad of relationships among these entities. "The peculiarity of open systems is that they interact with other systems outside of themselves. This interaction has two components: input, that [which] enters the system from the outside, and output, that [which] leaves the system for the environment. In order to speak about the inside and the outside of a system, we need to be able to distinguish between the system itself and its environment. System and environment are in general separated by a boundary.... The output of a system is in general a direct or indirect result from the input."[25] When implementing an ISO 9001 system, the software organization must carve out its own universe by defining its boundaries, relationships, and interactions with other organizations. It must then put controls in place to ensure that these definitions and boundary rules are respected.

The model fits all roles and structures, regardless of what activity is being performed and how the relationship is defined. The "supply chain," as represented by the "supplier→organization→customer" relationship, works well in any organization, for instance, in a business (as the customer) with an internal department (the organization) supporting the organization's information technology requirements using any of the following as external suppliers: customized purchased software, hardware, networks, and supporting infrastructure services such as backup, off-site disaster recovery support, and contract agencies that supply technical staff. Internal suppliers could include corporate purchasing, parts of human resources, finance, or facilities. The model works equally well for government IT departments (organization) that provide products and services to the government agencies (customer) they support. The commercial software organization has the easiest time deciphering its relationships: they most closely reflect reality without having to perform abstract relationship gymnastics to determine who is supplying what to whom.

The complexity of the quality management system grows for those software organizations that are encapsulated within another organization as a system within a system or subsystem. In such a scenario, whether or not the parent organization has a quality management system in place, the parent often become the client of the software organization. This definition of their relationship is dictated by the software organization having defined its scope to be its own operations—that is, the limits of its direct control as determined through customer–supplier agreements.

Regardless of whether the organization's quality management system structure reflects actual or constructed boundaries or whether it is an independent or component part of another organization (i.e., an independent organization or a department or division serving the parent organization), one of the keys to successfully implementing ISO 9001 is in clearly defining how these relationships interact.

One Strategy for Implementation and Improvement

For the quality management system to work, top management must commit to a systematic approach to improving the software organization's processes. If the commitment is there, and if it is strong, disciplined, and participatory, then external certification may or may not be required, depending on the needs of the organization's customers. If the adoption of the quality management system is designed with the principles of total quality management in mind, then the consequences of nonconformance are very real in the recognition that failure affects the organization and its ability to function effectively. If this system is not performing to stipulated, self-imposed requirements, the consequences are the loss of real value. Top management commitment is always much higher when consequences are reality based and do not merely represent the loss of an ISO 9001 registration certificate. Resources tend to be devoted to determining why problems occurred to begin with, what should change, the effective implementation of the change, and most importantly that the change was effective because the true root cause of the problem was addressed appropriately.

The systematic process approach to achieving true software quality requires definition, development, documentation, implementation, monitoring, and improvement of the software development life cycle processes of the organization, not simply the specification of procedures as required by previous versions of the ISO 9001 standard. Rather than attempting to approach the challenges of software quality through compliance to ISO 9001, consideration should be given as to how to design a software quality management system that meets the requirements of the organization, the software engineers working within it, the customers it is trying to serve, and the stakeholder or regulatory requirements placed on it. By defining a system that works and focuses on what is really needed to meet true preexisting quality requirements, ISO 9001 requirements just happen to be met.

Cost–Benefit Justifications

One of the keys to sustaining a software quality program that continues to enlist the support of top management is being able to demonstrate how costs justify the improvement efforts. The tools are already in place within the ISO 9001 system as a result of senior management setting the organization's measurable objectives (5.4.1, Quality Objectives). Within the ISO 9001 framework, management already must determine the infrastructure within which to develop its software products. Since it can set its own formula for determining how to place a value on the improvements to the system by measuring the system's performance against software process improvement targets and tracking them against actual achievements, by investing the extra effort required to correlate this information, tracking planned versus actual achievements becomes possible at this level of management. By establishing and setting measurable business goals (such as reducing the number of support calls by 20 percent) that are specific and meaningful, true improvement and increased value can be demonstrated.

Consider the rework necessary to account for the loss of quality that is incurred by attempting to increase productivity by bypassing the process. Table 2 shows the relative costs of fixing problems after the fact.

Stage[26]	Relative Repair Cost
Requirements	1–2
Design	5
Coding	10
Unit test	20
System test	50
Maintenance	200

Table 2. Relative Cost to Repair a Software Error in Different Stages of Development

Often the only additional cost incurred in the ongoing improvement of the quality management system—other than maintenance—is the up-front overhead of implementing it (the cost of setting up an infrastructure that is necessary anyway before any work can be performed). Consider what is spent in capital expenditures on software tools and hardware, with accelerated depreciation typically turning over equipment every 2 to 3 years. Compare these numbers to an investment in people and processes that continues to provide a return, and perhaps even appreciation over time through a satisfied and growing customer base and knowledge and system assets. If the latter is added to any sustained improvements in effectiveness and efficiency, a quality management system appears to be a good investment. The quality management system, properly implemented, ensures that quality is built into the product because the appropriate controls, checks, and balances within the process have been satisfied and have been justified through costs demonstrating the worth of achieving targets.

"Quality costs are a measure of the costs specifically associated with the achievement or nonachievement of product or service quality—including all product or service requirements established by the company and its contracts with customers and society. Requirements include marketing specifications, end-product and process specifications, purchase orders, engineering drawings, company procedures, operating instructions, professional or industry standards, government regulations, and any other document or customer needs that can affect the definition of product or service. More specifically, quality costs are the total of the cost incurred by (a) investing in the *prevention* of nonconformances to requirements; (b) *appraising* a product or service for conformance to requirements; and (c) *failure* to meet requirements."[27]

The Taguchi method, which combines engineering and statistical methods to improve product quality, states four principles[28]:

1. *Quality can be improved without increasing cost.*

If top management participates in the design and implementation of the quality management system, it can ensure that the organization's requirements—including financial—are addressed, with the appropriate cost-of-quality system indicators built in. This commitment can help to ensure that a suitable infrastructure is built in line with organizational goals and budgets. Then project costs can be estimated intelligently, knowing the overhead that must be factored into the estimates.

2. *Costs cannot be reduced without affecting quality.*

To arbitrarily reduce established budgets within an existing infrastructure is forcing shortcuts to happen. As with anything else, to make changes effective and allow them to integrate smoothly into the existing environment, regression analysis, planning, goal-setting, requirements, and design are all prerequisites to making such changes without disastrous results. Change management works with this type of system change as well.

3. *Costs can be reduced by improving quality.*

Process efficiencies can often be gained through a simple review of the current operation. The organization can perform radical reengineering or it can set incremental, measurable cost-reduction goals as the criteria for acceptance of quality improvement activities.

4. *Costs can also be reduced by reducing variation.*

With quantitative measures of process performance in place, the software organization can plot its data to see where variations are occurring. By predicting a model based on current performance, and then experimenting with small changes to validate the model, future performance can be predicted. As a result, more accurate planning is possible.

"Reducing waste and increasing productivity are natural by-products of a systematic process of quality improvement. Less waste and greater productivity lower costs, which improves both margins and the use of assets. With respect to perceived quality, products and services that exceed customer requirements are of greater value to the customer than competitors' products and services. Increasing numbers of customers are likely to purchase such quality, and that improves margins and grows revenues. Revenue growth and improvements in asset utilization and margins mean improved profitability—and higher projected cash flows...."[29]

Improvement Paradigms

"Two general paradigms to SPI have emerged, as described by Card.[30] The first is the analytic paradigm. This is characterized as relying on *'quantitative evidence to determine where improvements are needed and whether an improvement initiative has been successful.'* The second, what Card calls the benchmarking...paradigm, *'depends on identifying an "excellent" organization in a field and documenting its practices and tools.'* The analytic paradigm 'is exemplified by the work [a software organization would perform if it were to carry out statistical process control over its quality management system processes]. The benchmarking paradigm is exemplified by...the emerging ISO/IEC 15504 international standard.'[31] Benchmarking assumes that if a less-proficient organization adopts the practices of the excellent organization, it will also become excellent."[32]

The former paradigm involves the organization defining and mapping all of the components and relationships within the quality management system and, through a disciplined process of measurement and trial and error, plotting out its improvement path. While this approach has worked for countless generations, the benchmarking paradigm takes advantage of work performed by experts in the field. While it assumes a leap of faith in what are considered to be the generally accepted software engineering principles and processes, the advantages to the organization are the ease of process definition, measurement, analysis, and improvement.

Consideration of how to improve is relevant to ISO 9001's measurement requirements:

"The organization shall plan and implement the monitoring, measurement, analysis and improvement processes needed

a) to demonstrate conformity of the product,

b) to ensure conformity of the quality management system, and

c) to continually improve the effectiveness of the quality management system.

This shall include determination of applicable methods, including statistical techniques, and the extent of their use."[33]

Adoption of the benchmarking paradigm provides a number of distinct advantages. The software organization can adopt, as components of its closed-loop quality management system, an implementation of the following standards:

1. ISO/IEC 12207 as a software life cycle model for identification and customization of its processes;

2. ISO/IEC TR 15504 as a software process assessment standard to measure project and process performance and improvement;

3. ISO/IEC 9126[34] as a product measurement standard to assist in establishing not only requirements but also acceptance criteria; and

4. ISO/IEC 15939[35] (soon to be published) as a software process measurement framework to lend integrity to the entire measurement and improvement cycle.

The objective is a working quality management system that is self-propelled toward improvement opportunities by active participants. Communication throughout the organization about the importance of demonstrating conformance through measurement will help to keep everyone directed toward achieving the same goals. A system working according to these principles can only get better at what it does.

Conclusions

Adopting a systems approach to the design and development of an ISO 9001 quality management system can offer staff a familiar framework within which to identify, plan, and manage continuous improvement of the activities being performed on a daily basis. By modeling the quality management system after the concepts of the software system, software engineers may gain a more insightful perspective of what is involved to make the system work. Performing good process work always requires discipline, and if standards are available to assist in the identification and definition of the system, then reusability of best practices may even play a role here. Of course, as Deming said, none of the above is necessary, if survival is not deemed to be essential.

The quality management system will work, given structure, discipline, and a model to follow—but the initiative must be started. The irony that the industry faces is that those software organizations, or the troubled projects within them, that are most resistant to change are also the ones most in need of it.

Acknowledgments

Grateful appreciation is extended to the reviewers of this tutorial: Andy Coster, UK, ISO/IEC JTC1/SC7/WG18, and ISO 9000-3 Revision Project Editor, Bob Marshall, Canada TC176 Liaison to

ISO/IEC JTC1/SC7/WG18, Peter Voldner, Former Canadian Chair, ISO/IEC JTC1/SC7, and Antonio Coletta, Italy, SC7/WG10 ISO/IEC 15504-3 Editor.

About the Author

Victoria A. Hailey is president of The Victoria Hailey Group Corporation, a certified management consultancy specializing in helping the software, systems, and service industries improve their processes and best practices via standards such as ISO 9001, ISO/IEC TR 15504, TL 9000, and CMM. Victoria is a certified management consultant, an ISO 9000 quality management system lead auditor (IRCA), a TickIT auditor, a SPICE lead assessor, an SEI-CMM software capability evaluator, and a TL 9000 lead auditor.

She is convener of ISO/IEC JTC1/SC7/WG18 on Quality Management, the working group responsible for updating ISO 9000-3 as well as a working group member of ISO/IEC JTC1/SC7/WG10 on Process Assessment (ISO/IEC TR 15504). Victoria has 20 years of experience in the software industry, having started her career with the IBM Toronto Laboratory in Product Assurance, which she left in 1985 to start her own consultancy. Her clients include Bell Canada, Hydro One Networks, Microsoft, Metafore, and Sony.

[1] ISO 9001:2000(E), *Quality Management Systems—Requirements*, International Organization for Standardization, Geneva, 2000.

[2] Software Engineering Institute, *The Capability Maturity Model: Guidelines for Improving the Software Process,* Addison Wesley, Reading, MA, 1995.

[3] Paulk, M.C., "Foreword," *Software Process Improvement: Practical Guidelines for Business Success,* S. Zahran, ed., Addison-Wesley, Reading, MA, 1998.

[4] The common perception is that process conformance causes excesses in schedule, cost, and resources, when, in fact, a good process will accommodate new technologies and increase the speed to market by, for example, enabling an organization to manage new technologies better using such techniques as risk assessment. In fact, the more critical the pressures, the more imperative it is to ensure the process will withstand them and deliver as expected.

[5] Crosby, P., *Philip Crosby's Reflections on Quality*, McGraw-Hill, New York, 1996.

[6] See Deming, W.E., *Out of the Crisis,* Massachusetts Institute of Technology, Center for Advanced Engineering Study, Cambridge, 1982, for an informative discussion of early quality efforts.

[7] Dunham, J.R., and E. Kruesi, "The Measurement Task Area," *IEEE Computer,* vol. 16, no. 11, 1983.

[8] Deming, W.E., *Out of the Crisis,* Massachusetts Institute of Technology, Center for Advanced Engineering Study, 1982.

[9] E-mail containing the final results of the first Delphi study" on *Fundamental Principles of Software Engineering*, from Pierre Bourque, University de Québec à Montréal, 1997, http://www.lrgl.uqam.ca/fpse/index.html.

[10] See ISO/IEC TR 15504-2's discussion of the capability levels.

[11] ISO/IEC 12207, *Information Technology—Software Life Cycle Processes*, International Organization for Standardization, Geneva, 1995.

[12] A software process model that can be measured by the emerging process assessment standard ISO/IEC 15504 is currently the focus of work by the ISO/IEC JTC1/SC7 WG7. WG7 is working with WG10 (SPA WG) to revise ISO/IEC 12207 to produce a software process model for the process

dimension that would adequately define each process in terms of purpose and outcomes that achieve level 1 capability. Prior to i5504, the software process was defined by process models such as the SEI's Capability Maturity Model.

[13] "Performed" is the level 1 capability represented in the ISO/IEC TR 15504-2 software process assessment capability model. It means that "the purpose of the process is generally achieved. The achievement may not be rigorously planned and tracked. Individuals within the organization recognize that an action should be performed, and there is general agreement that this action is performed as and when required. There are identifiable work products for the process, and these testify to the achievement of the purpose" (ISO/IEC TR 15504-2: *Information Technology—Software Process Assessment—Part 2: A Reference Model for Processes and Process Capability*, 1998, http://wwwsel.iit.nrc.ca/spice/).

[14] Crosby, P., *Philip Crosby's Reflections on Quality*, McGraw-Hill, New York, 1996.

[15] ISO/IEC TR 15504, *Information Technology—Software Process Assessment*, 1998, is expected to be revised and published as an international standard on process assessment by around 2003.

[16] ® CMM and Capability Maturity Model are registered in the U.S. Patent and Trademark Office. SM CMM and CMMI are service marks of Carnegie Mellon University. The Software Engineering Institute (SEI) is a federally funded research and development center sponsored by the U.S. Department of Defense and operated by Carnegie Mellon University.

[17] *The ISO Survey of ISO 9000 and ISO 14000 Certificates –Ninth Cycle–1999*, International Organization for Standardization, Geneva, http://www.iso.ch/presse/survey9.pdf.

[18] Crosby, P., *Philip Crosby's Reflections on Quality*, McGraw-Hill, New York, 1996.

[19] Throughout this discussion of the organization's requirements, all applicable regulatory requirements should be understood as forming part of these requirements.

[20] ISO 9001:2000(E), *Quality Management Systems—Requirements,* International Organization for Standardization, Geneva, 2000.

[21] *Merriam-Webster's Collegiate Dictionary*, Merriam-Webster, New York, 2000, http://www.m-w.com. Go to the thesaurus "Look It Up" reference for "system."

[22] Heylighen, F., C. Joslyn, and V. Turchin, eds., "What Are Cybernetics and Systems Science?," *Principia Cybernetica Web,* Principia Cybernetica, Brussels, 1999, http://pespmc1.vub.ac.be/CYBSWHAT.html.

[23] Heylighen, F., and C. Joslyn, , eds., "What Is Systems Theory?," *Principia Cybernetica Web,* Principia Cybernetica, Brussels, 1992, http://pespmc1.vub.ac.be/SYSTHEOR.html.

[24] Reinertsen, D.G., *Managing the Design Factory: The Product Developer's Toolkit*, The Free Press, New York, 1997.

[25] Heylighen, F., "Basic Concepts of the Systems Approach," Principia Cybernetica Web, F. Heylighen, ed., Principia Cybernetica, Brussels, 1998, http://pespmc1.vub.ac.be/SYSAPPR.html.

[26] Faulk, Stuart, R. "Software Requirements: A Tutorial," *Software Engineering: Project Management,* R.H. Thayer, ed., IEEE Computer Society Press, Los Alamitos, CA, 1997.

[27] Campanell, J., ed., *Principles of Quality Costs: Principles, Implementation, and Use*, ASQC Quality Press, Milwaukee, WI, 1990.

[28] Campanell, J., ed., *Principles of Quality Costs: Principles, Implementation, and Use*, ASQC Quality

Press, Milwaukee, WI, 1990.

[29] George, S., and A. Weimerskirch, *Total Quality Management,* John Wiley & Sons, New York, 1994.

[30] Card, D., "Understanding Process Improvement," *IEEE Software*, 1991.

[31] El Emam, K., J.N. Drouin, and W. Melo, *The Theory and Practice of Software Process Improvement and Capability Determination,* IEEE Computer Society Press, Los Alamitos, CA, 1998.

[32] El Emam, Khaled and Dennis R. Goldenson, *"An Empirical Review of Software Process Assessments"*, ERB-1065 National Research Council, Canada, 1999

[33] ISO 9001:2000(E), *Quality Management Systems—Requirements,* International Organization for Standards, Geneva, 2000.

[34] ISO/IEC 9126, *Information Technology—Software Quality Characteristics and Metrics*, International Organization for Standards, Geneva, 1991.

[35] ISO/IEC CD 15939, *Software and Systems Engineering—Software Measurement Process Framework* International Organization for Standards, Geneva (in press).

Benefits and Prerequisites of ISO 9000 Based Software Quality Management

Dirk Stelzer, Mark Reibnitz, Werner Mellis

University of Koeln

The ISO 9000 quality standards were released a decade ago. Since then thousands of software companies have implemented ISO 9000 based quality systems. In Europe, the ISO 9000 standards are the prevalent model for implementing software quality management. However, only few empirical studies on ISO 9000 based quality management in software companies have been published [1][8][16][23][29][33]. Little is known about benefits software companies have achieved with the help of ISO 9000 based quality systems. Furthermore, a profound knowledge of the enabling and inhibiting factors, i. e. the prerequisites of successful software quality management, is still lacking.

The objective of this paper is (1) to describe benefits that software companies have achieved by implementing ISO 9000 based quality systems, and (2) to identify prerequisites of conducting successful software quality management initiatives.

Research Method

Between October 1996 and December 1997 we analyzed published experience reports of 25 software organizations that had implemented an ISO 9000 quality system and sought certification. By examining the experience reports we identified benefits and prerequisites of implementing ISO 9000 based quality management initiatives in software companies.

The study covers experience reports of 12 organizations located in the UK, eight German organizations, two French organizations, and one organization each in Austria, Greece, and the US. The study includes published reports of software organizations at ACT Financial Systems Ltd. [3], Alcatel Telecom [5], ALLDATA [20], Answers Software Service [37], AVX Ltd. [34], BR Business Systems [13], Bull AG [25, 26], Cap Gemini Sogeti [31], CMS (British Steel) [14], Danet-IS GmbH [2, 21], Dr. Materna GmbH [32], IBM Deutschland [6], IDC-UK [28], INTRASOFT [11], Logica [9, 10], Oracle [35], Praxis [15], PSI AG [38], SAP AG [7, 36], Siemens AG [39, 40], Sybase [24], Tembit Software GmbH [30], Triad Special Systems Ltd. [12], Unisys Systems and Technology Operations [4], and an anonymous British software company [27].

The authors of the experience reports are quality managers or senior managers of the software companies. At the time the experience reports were written, the size of the companies ranged from 10 to 2700 employees (mean: 674 employees). The time needed to implement the quality systems ranged from 10 to 96 months (mean: 21 months). The time between certification of the quality system and the publication of the experience reports ranged from 0 to 60 months (mean: 36 months); 72 % of the companies had gathered experience with the quality system for more than two years.

Benefits

In the following section we will describe benefits that the authors of the experience reports have attributed to the implementation of ISO 9000 based quality systems.

Twenty-three (of 25) reports explicitly describe benefits that were achieved by implementing the quality system. We have summarized these benefits in seven categories: improved project management, improved productivity and efficiency, improved customer satisfaction, improved product quality, more on-time deliveries, positive return on the investment in software quality management, and improved corporate profitability.

Figure 1 shows the percentage of reports that mention benefits relating to each of the categories.

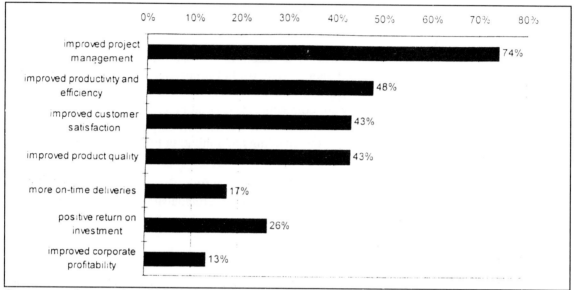

Percentage of companies addressing benefit categories (n=23)

Figure 1: Benefits of ISE 9000 based Software Quality Management

Improved project management is reported by 74 % of the companies. This usually results from better documentation of the software process and from improved communication among staff members and managers in different organizational units of the company. ISO 9000 based quality systems lead to better visibility of the software process, improved documents and checklists, clearer definition of responsibilities, and making use of experience and best practices of other projects. Improved project management leads to a variety of other benefits:

- 48 % of the companies report improved productivity and efficiency of software development.

- 43 % of the companies report improved customer satisfaction.

- 43 % of the companies report improved product quality (usually described in a reduction of defects delivered to customers).

- 17 % of the companies report more on-time deliveries.

26 % of the companies explicitly mention a positive return on the investment in software quality management. 13 % of the companies report improved corporate profitability that they attribute to the implementation of ISO 9000 based software quality management.

However, only 6 out of 23 companies (26 %) support their statements on benefits with quantitative data. Examples are a reduction of budget overruns by 50 % in 4 years [31], a reduction of defects found in user acceptance tests by a factor of 9 [13], a reduction of 13 % in post-installation support costs [13], a reduction of programmers' time spent for hotline support by a factor of 3 [27], and a reduction of overall software development cost by 20 % [38]. The other 17 companies that address benefits of ISO 9000 based quality management do not give any quantitative data. Presumably, the statements on benefits in these reports primarily reflect perceived advantages of implementing quality systems.

Prerequisites

The term "prerequisites" summarizes factors that authors of the experience reports covered in our study regard as essential when implementing an ISO 9000 based quality system. Implementation of the factors has facilitated the success of software quality management; a lack of compliance with the factors has delayed progress in quality management or made it difficult to achieve.

Prerequisites of successful software quality management	Percentage of experience reports addressing the factors
Management commitment and support	84%
Staff involvement	84%
Providing enhanced understanding	72%
Tailoring improvement initiatives	68%
Encouraging communication and collaboration	64%
Managing the improvement project	56%
Change agents and opinion leaders	52%
Stabilizing changed processes	52%
Setting relevant and realistic objectives	44%
Unfreezing the organization	24%

Figure 2: Prerequisites of successful software quality management (n=24)

We identified 10 prerequisites of successful software quality management efforts. Figure 2 shows the factors and the percentage of experience reports addressing these factors.

Management commitment and support is the degree to which management at all organizational levels sponsor the implementation of the quality system. The necessary investment of time, money, and effort and the need to overcome staff resistance are potential impediments to successful ISO 9000 based improvement initiatives. These obstacles cannot be overcome without management commitment. Active participation and visible support of senior management may give the necessary momentum to the initiative. This positively influences the success of the quality system. 84 % of the experience reports emphasize the importance of management commitment and support.

Staff involvement is the degree to which staff members participate in quality management activities. Staff involvement is essential to avoid a schism between software engineers in development projects and quality managers responsible for implementing the quality system. Staff members have detailed knowledge and first hand experience of strengths and weaknesses of the current processes. Using the skills and experience of employees guarantees that the resulting quality system is a consensus that reflects the practical considerations of diverse projects. 84 % of the authors address this point.

Providing enhanced understanding to managers and staff members comprises acquiring and transferring knowledge of current practices. Managers usually have a general idea of the software process, but they do not have complete understanding of essential details. Employees often do not understand how their work contributes to the corporate mission and vision. Successful quality management initiatives give managers a clearer picture of current practices and they give staff members the opportunity to better understand the business of their organization. 72 % of the authors emphasize the significance of this topic.

Tailoring improvement initiatives means adapting quality management efforts to the specific strengths and weaknesses of different teams and departments in the company. Standardized and centralized quality systems are usually not well accepted. Quality management must clearly and continually demonstrate benefits to projects. Tailoring increases the compatibility of improvement plans with existing values, past experience, and needs of various projects within an organization. Tailoring helps to implement a quality system that responds to the true needs of the organization. 68 % of all reports stress this point.

Successful quality management initiatives have encouraged communication among staff members. This has helped to rectify rumors, to preclude misunderstandings, and to overcome resistance of staff members. Successful quality management efforts have also emphasized collaboration of different teams and divisions. Close cooperation of organizational units provides natural feedback loops, enhances staff members' understanding and knowledge, encourages people to exploit synergy, and consequently improves productivity and quality. Intensive communication and collaboration help to create a coherent organizational culture that is necessary for achieving substantial improvements. 64 % of the authors mention the importance of communication and collaboration.

Managing the improvement project means that the implementation of the ISO 9000 based quality system is treated like a professional project. At the beginning, in some organizations the quality management projects had neither specified requirements nor had they elaborated a formal project plan, defined milestones, or outlined a schedule. Areas of responsibility were not accurately determined and the initiative was lacking effective interfaces between quality management and software development teams. Successful initiatives set up and ran the quality management project like a software development project. They used existing project management standards, analyzed requirements, defined explicit objectives, established milestones, and monitored progress. 56 % of the reports address this factor.

Change agents are individuals or teams external to the system that is to be improved. Quality managers or consultants usually play the role of change agents. Often, they initiate the quality projects, request resources, and encourage local improvement efforts. They also provide technical support and feedback, publish successes, and keep staff members aware of the quality management efforts. Opinion leaders are members of a social system in which they exert their influence. Experienced project managers or proficient software engineers usually act as opinion leaders. They are indispensable for overcoming the potential schism between software development and quality management. They help to tailor the improvement suggestions to the needs of different teams and organizational units. 52 % of the authors mention this issue.

Stabilizing changed processes means continually supporting maintenance and improvement of the quality system at a local level. Staff members adopting new activities need continuous feedback, motivation, recognition, and reinforcement to stay involved in the improvement effort. They also need guidance and support to overcome initial problems and difficulties. Stabilizing changed processes prevents that improved performance slides back to the old level. 52 % of the reports emphasize the need to stabilize changed processes.

Setting relevant objectives means that the quality management efforts attempt to contribute to the success of the organization. Mere conformance to the standards or attaining certification usually is not a relevant goal for staff members. It is essential that staff members understand the relationship between quality management and business objectives of the organization. Setting realistic objectives means that the goals may be achieved in the foreseeable future and with a reasonable amount of resources. 44 % of the authors address this point.

Lewin [22] has introduced the importance of "unfreezing" organizations before substantial improvements can be achieved. He emphasizes that social processes usually have an "inner resistance" to change. To overcome this resistance an additional force is required, a force sufficient to break the habit and to unfreeze the custom. In software companies that have successfully implemented ISO 9000 based software quality systems perceived deficiencies in software development, management commitment, and competitive pressure have contributed to unfreezing the organization. 24 % of the reports mention this topic.

Discussion

The findings of our study are based on experience reports written by managers of software organizations. Of course these sources primarily reflect the personal views of the authors of the reports. Nevertheless, the findings give interesting insights into benefits software companies might achieve and factors they should consider when implementing ISO 9000 based software quality management.

Benefits

One would expect that quality managers will tend to publish their experiences with software quality management if the improvement efforts have been successful. Experiences with less successful quality systems are less likely to be published. Therefore, our findings may be biased because we analyzed published experience reports only. Presumably, representative studies covering successful and unsuccessful quality systems would reveal lower percentages of companies addressing benefits.

We have summarized the benefits described in the experience reports in seven categories. Improved project management is the prevailing benefit category. In most companies it leads to higher productivity and efficiency, improved customer satisfaction, or to improved product quality. However, more on-time deliveries are reported only by 4 of 23 companies. In the majority of the companies the implementation of ISO 9000 based quality systems does obviously not help to meet schedule commitments more often. This is astonishing since the ability to meet schedules more often is usually one of the benefits expected from the implementation of quality systems.

Twenty three of 25 experience reports explicitly mention at least one benefit of the quality system. Surprisingly, only 6 of 23 companies report a positive return on the investment in software quality management, and only 3 of 23 companies mention improved corporate profitability. This might lead to the conclusion that the majority of the companies have not achieved a positive return on investment in software quality management. One might also conclude that ISO 9000 based quality systems will usually not improve corporate profitability. However, not a single experience report explicitly mentions that the quality efforts have not produced a positive return on investment or have not lead to a higher profitability.

It is more likely that the small number of companies reporting positive returns on investment and improved profitability can be put down to the fact that most companies do not conduct comprehensive measurements of costs and benefits of software quality management.

Only 26% of the companies support their statements on benefits of ISO 9000 based quality management with quantitative data. This is remarkable because ISO 9001 [18] and ISO 9000-3 [17] suggest to use measurement and statistical techniques to establish, control and verify process capability. Furthermore, ISO 9004-1 [19] states: "It is important that the effectiveness of a quality system be measured in financial terms". However, a previous empirical study [33] has already shown that many software companies ignore the suggestions of the ISO 9000 standards to conduct measurements.

Prerequisites

Surprisingly, only 3 of the 10 prerequisites identified in our study are explicitly mentioned in ISO 9001: management commitment and support in clause 4.1 (management responsibility), managing the improvement project in clause 4.2 (quality system), and setting relevant and realistic objectives in clause 4.1.1 (quality policy) of ISO 9001. This means that companies that strictly stick to the elements of ISO 9001 will probably ignore other essential prerequisites of successful software quality management. Therefore, it is necessary to implement a more comprehensive approach to achieve substantial improvements.

Most of the prerequisites identified in our study address the management of change, that is transforming assumptions, habits, and working routines of managers and staff members so that the quality system may become effective. Implementing ISO 9000 based software quality management requires various changes to an organization. Our study has shown that many software companies have obviously underestimated the effort needed to accomplish the change process. This indicates that change management is not sufficiently accounted for in the ISO 9000 standards.

At first glance, the prerequisites discussed in this paper may be taken for granted. At least, they seem to be basics of software management. However, when one looks at the experience reports a second time it becomes clear that the factors are regularly described as lessons learned. Some organizations have obviously not paid enough attention to the implementation of the factors at the beginning of the initiative. Other organizations may not have fully understood the significance of the prerequisites until the improvement objectives had been accomplished. Obviously, most quality managers do not pay sufficient attention to the management of change when implementing ISO 9000 based software quality systems.

Concluding Remarks

Most software companies achieve benefits with the implementation of ISO 9000 based quality systems. Only few companies, however, report a positive return on the investment in software quality management and improved corporate profitability. This might lead to the conclusion that the majority of the companies have not achieved a positive return on investment and improved corporate profitability. However, one might also conclude that the small number of companies reporting economic success can be put down to the fact that most companies do not conduct comprehensive measurements of costs and benefits of software quality management.

Most of the prerequisites of successful software quality management identified in our study address the management of change. The fact that the authors of experience reports emphasize these prerequisites as lessons learned shows that the factors are obviously not sufficiently accounted for in the ISO 9000 standards. Change management should therefore be a central element of future versions of the ISO 9000 family.

References

[1] M. Beirne, A. Panteli, and H. Ramsay, "Going soft on quality?: Process management in the Scottish software industry". In Software Quality Journal, no. 3, pp. 195-209, 1997.

[2] G. Bulski and H. Martin-Engeln, "Erfahrungen und Erfolge in der SW-Projektabwicklung nach 4 Jahren DIN ISO 9001 Zertifizierung". In H. J. Scheibl, editor, Technische Akademie Esslingen - Software-Entwicklung - Methoden, Werkzeuge, Erfahrungen '97. 23.-25. September 1997, pp. 403-406, Ostfildern, 1997.

[3] H. Chambers, "The implementation and maintenance of a quality management system". In M. Ross et al., editors, Software Quality Management II, vol. 1: Managing Quality Systems, pp. 19-33, Southampton - Boston, 1994.

[4] A. Clarke, "Persuading the Staff or ISO 9001 without Tantrums". In SQM, no. 9, pp. 1-5.

[5] D. Courtel, "Continuous Quality Improvement in Telecommunications Software Development". In The first annual European Software Engineering Process Group Conference 1996. Amsterdam 24-27th June 1996, pp. (C309) 1 - 9, Amsterdam, 1996.

[6] W. Dette, "Einfuehrung eines QM-Systems nach DIN ISO 9001 in der Entwicklung". In SQS, editor, Software-Qualitaetsmanagement 'Made in Germany' - Realitaet oder Wunschdenken?. SQM Kongress 1996. Koeln, 28th-29th March 1996, Cologne, 1996.

[7] A. Dillinger, "Erfahrungen eines Softwareherstellers mit der Zertifizierung eines Teilbereiches nach DIN ISO 9001". In BIFOA, editor, Fachseminar: Aufbau eines Qualitaetsmanagements nach DIN ISO 9000. Koeln, 26./27. April 1994, pp. 1-24, Cologne, 1994.

[8] K. El Emam and L. Briand, "Costs and Benefits of Software Process Improvement". In International Software Engineering Research Network technical report ISERN-97-12, 1997.

[9] M. Forrester, "A TickIT for Logica". In SQM, no. 16, 1996. [10] M. Forrester and A. Dransfield, "Logica's TickIT to ride extended for 3 years!". In TickIT International, no. 4, 1994.

[11] S. A. Frangos, "Implementing a quality management system using an incremental approach". In M. Ross et al., editors, Software Quality Management III, vol. 1: Quality Management, pp. 27-41, Southampton - Boston, 1995.

[12] A. M. Fulton and B. M. Myers, "TickIT awards - a winner's perspective". In Software Quality Journal, no. 2, 1996.

[13] R. Havenhand, "TickIT Case Study: British Rail Business Systems". In SQM, no. 18, pp. 1-6, 1996.

[14] B. Hepworth, "Making the best the standard. Users experiences of operating an ISO 9001 compliant quality management system and total quality management culture". In SAQ and EOQ-SC, editors, Software Quality Concern for People. Proceedings of the Fourth European Conference on Software Quality. October 17-20, Basel, Switzerland, pp. 208-223, Zuerich, 1994.

[15] M. Hewson, "TickIT Case Study: Praxis". In SQM, no. 22, 1996.

[16] A. Ingleby, J. F. Polhill, and A. Slater, "A survey of Quality Management in IT. Progress since the introduction of TickIT. Report form a survey of both certificated and non certificated companies". London, 1994.

[17] International Organization for Standardisation, "ISO 9000-3:1991. Quality management and quality assurance standards. Part 3: Guidelines for the application of ISO 9001 to the development, supply and maintenance of software". Geneva, 1991.

[18] International Organization for Standardisation, "ISO 9001:1994. Quality systems. Model for quality assurance in design, development, production, installation and servicing". Geneva, 1994.

[19] International Organization for Standardisation, "ISO 9004-1:1994. Quality management and quality system elements. Part 1: Guidelines". Geneva, 1994.

[20] K. Kilberth, "Einfuehrung eines prozess-orientierten QM-Systems bei der ALLDATA". In H. J. Scheibl, editor, Technische Akademie Esslingen - Software-Entwicklung - Methoden, Werkzeuge, Erfahrungen '97. 7. Kolloquium - 23.-25. September 1997, pp. 377- 392, Ostfildern, 1997.

[21] H.-G. Klaus, "Zertifizierung eines Softwareherstellers nach DIN ISO 9001 -Voraussetzungen, Ablauf, Vorgehensweise-". In BIFOA, editor, Fachseminar: Aufbau eines Qualitaetsmanagements nach DIN ISO 9000. Koeln, 26./27. April 1994, Cologne, 1994.

[22] K. Lewin, "Group decision and social change". In Holt, Rinehart, and Winston, editors, Readings in social psychology, 3rd ed., pp. 197-211, New York, 1958.

[23] C. B. Loken and T. Skramstad, "ISO 9000 Certification - Experiences from Europe". In: American Society for Quality Control

(ASQC) et al., editors, Proceedings of the First World Congress for Software Quality, June 20-22, 1995, Fairmont Hotel, San Francisco, CA, Session Y, pp. 1-11, San Francisco, 1995.

[24] M. L. Macfarlane, "Eating the elephant one bite at a time". In Quality Progress, no. 6, pp. 89-92, 1996.

[25] H. Mosel, "Erfahrungen mit einem zertifizierten QMS im Bull- Softwarehaus". In BIFOA, editor, Fachseminar: Von der ISO 9000 zum Total Quality Management? Koeln, 16./17. April 1996, pp. 1- 25.

[26] H. Mosel, "Vier Jahre Zertifikat und was sonst noch notwendig ist". In SQS, editor, Software- Qualitaetsmanagement 'Made in Germany' - Realitaet oder Wunschdenken?. SQM Kongress 1996. Koeln, 28.-29. March 1996, Cologne, 1996.

[27] B. Quinn, "Lessons Learned from the Implementation of a Quality Management System to meet the Requirements of ISO9000/TickIT in two small Software Houses". In Fifth European Conference on Software Quality - Conference Proceedings, Dublin, Ireland, September 16-20, 1996, pp. 305-314, Dublin, 1996.

[28] C. Robb, "From quality system to organizational development". In M. Ross et al., editors, Software Quality Management II, vol. 1: Managing Quality Systems, pp. 99-113, Southampton - Boston, 1994.

[29] K. Robinson and P. Simmons, "The value of a certified quality management system: the perception of internal developers". In Software Quality Journal, no. 2, pp. 61-73, 1996.

[30] M. Schroeder and R. Wilhelm, "Flexibilitaet staerken. Erfahrungen beim Aufbau eines QM-Systems nach ISO 9000 in einem kleinen Softwareunternehmen". In QZ - Qualitaet und Zuverlaessigkeit, no. 5, pp. 530-536, 1996.

[31] J. Sidi and D. White, "Implementing Quality in an International Software House". In American Society for Quality Control (ASQC) et al., editors, Proceedings of the First World Congress for Software Quality, June 20-22, 1995, Fairmont Hotel, San Francisco, CA, Session W, pp. 1-13, San Francisco, 1995.

[32] S. Steinke, "Erfahrungen bei der Einfuehrung und Verbesserung eines QMS". In SQS, editor, Software- Qualitaetsmanagement 'Made in Germany' - Modeerscheinung oder Daueraufgabe. SQM Kongress 1997. Koeln, 17.-18. April 1997, Cologne, 1997.

[33] D. Stelzer, W. Mellis, and G. Herzwurm, "Software Process Improvement via ISO 9000? Results of Two Surveys Among European Software Houses". In Software Process – Improvement and Practice, no. 3, pp. 197-210, 1996.

[34] A. Sweeney and D. W. Bustard, "Software process improvement: making it happen in practice". In Software Quality Journal, no. 4, pp. 265-273, 1997.

[35] S. Verbe and P.W. Robinson, "Growing a quality culture: a case study - Oracle UK". In M. Ross et al., editors, Software Quality Management III, vol. 1: Quality Management, pp. 3-14, Southampton - Boston, 1995.

[36] M. Vering and V. Haentjes, "Ist ISO 9000 ein geeignetes Werkzeug fuer Process Engineering? Ein Erfahrungsbericht aus der SAP- Entwicklung". In m & c - Management & Computer, no. 2, pp. 85- 90, 1995.

[37] S.D. Walker, "Maintaining your quality management system – what are the benefits?". In M. Ross et al., editors, Software Quality Management II, vol. 1: Managing Quality Systems, pp. 47-61, Southampton - Boston, 1994.

[38] A. Warner, "Der Weg von der Qualitaetssicherung nach ISO 9001 zum Qualitaetsmanagement in einem Systemhaus". In H. J. Scheibl, editor, Technische Akademie Esslingen - Software- Entwicklung - Methoden, Werkzeuge, Erfahrungen '97. 7. 23.-25. September 1997, pp. 407-423, Ostfildern, 1997.

[39] S. Zopf, "Ein Erfahrungsbericht zur ISO 9001 Zertifizierung". In Softwaretechnik-Trends, pp. 15-16, August 1994.

[40] S. Zopf, "Improvement of software development through ISO 9001 certification and SEI assessment". In SAQ and EOQ-SC, editors, Software Quality Concern for People. Proceedings of the Fourth European Conference on Software Quality. October 17-20, 1994, Basel, Switzerland, pp. 224-231, Zuerich, 1994

HOW ISO 9001 COMPARES WITH THE CMM

Organizations concerned with ISO 9001 certification often question its overlap with the Software Engineering Institute's Capability Maturity Model. The author looks at 20 clauses in ISO 9001 and maps them to practices in the CMM. The analysis provides answers to some common questions about the two documents.

MARK C. PAULK
Software Engineering Institute

The Capability Maturity Model Model for Software, developed by the Software Engineering Institute, and the ISO 9000 series of standards, developed by the International Organization for Standardization, have the common concern of quality and process management. The two are driven by similar issues and are intuitively correlated, but they differ in their underlying philosophies: ISO 9001, the standard in the 9000 series that pertains to software development and maintenance, identifies the minimal requirements for a quality system, while the CMM underlines the need for continuous process improvement. This statement is somewhat subjective, of course; some members of the international standards community main-tain that if you read ISO 9001 with insight, it *does* address continuous process improvement. Corrective action, for example, can be construed as continuous improvement. Nonetheless, the CMM tends to address the issue of continuous process improvement more explicitly than ISO 9001.

This article examines how the two documents relate. I have essentially mapped clauses of ISO 9001 to CMM key practices. The mapping is based on an analysis of ISO 9001, ISO 9000-3, TickIt (a British guide to using ISO 9000-3 and 9001), and the TickIt training materials.[1] ISO 9000-3 elaborates significantly on ISO 9001, while the TickIt training materials help in interpreting both ISO 9000-3 and ISO 9001.

As part of the analysis, I attempt to answer some frequently asked questions, including

• At what level in the CMM would an ISO 9001-compliant organization be?

• Can a level 2 (or 3) organization be considered compliant with ISO 9001?

• Should my software-quality-management and process-improvement efforts be based on ISO 9001 or on the CMM?

I assume the reader is familiar with or has ready access to both ISO 9001 and the CMM. For those who need a refresher, the box on pp.76-77 gives an overview.

MAPPING SPECIFICS

My analysis involved mapping ISO 9001's 20 clauses to CMM key practices at the sentence to subpractice level.[2,3] The analysis is admittedly subjective — others may interpret both ISO 9001 and the CMM differently (indeed, reliable and consistent interpretation and assessment are common challenges for CMM-based appraisals and ISO 9001 certification) — but hopefully there is enough objectivity to make the analysis worthwhile to those who wonder where ISO 9001 certification fits into a continuous quality-improvement strategy.

Table 1 is an overview of the mapping from ISO 9001 clause to CMM key process areas and key practices. The column labeled "Strong relationship" contains key process areas and common features for which the relationship is relatively straightforward. The column labeled "Judgmental relationship" contains key process areas and common features that may require a significant degree of subjectivity in determining a reasonable relationship. Table A in the box on pp. 76-77 describes the focus of the key process areas and common features. In the Activities Performed common feature, key practices focus on systematically implementing a process, while the key practices in other common features focus on institutionalizing it.

Clause 4.1: Management responsibility. ISO 9001 requires an organization to

• define, document, understand, implement, and maintain a quality policy;

• define responsibility and authority for personnel who manage, perform, and verify work affecting quality; and

• identify and provide verification resources.

A designated manager ensures that the quality program is implemented and maintained.

The CMM addresses responsibility for quality policy and verification at level 2. This includes identifying responsibility for performing all project roles, establishing a trained software quality assurance group, and assigning senior management oversight of SQA activities.

As practices within common features, the CMM identifies management's responsibility at both the senior- and project-management levels to oversee the software project, support SQA audits, provide leadership, establish organizational structures to support software engineering, and allocate resources.

You could argue that this clause also addresses the quality policy described at level 4, but the level 4 quality policy is quantitative. ISO 9001 is somewhat ambiguous about the role of measurement in the quality-management system (see discussion under "Clause 4.20: Statistical techniques"); an organization is required to define and document quality objectives, but it does not have to quantify them.

Clause 4.2: Quality system. ISO 9001 requires an organization to establish a documented quality system, including a quality manual and plans, procedures, and instructions. ISO 9000-3 characterizes this quality system as an

> THIS ANALYSIS IS SUBJECTIVE, BUT I HOPE IT IS OBJECTIVE ENOUGH TO BE WORTHWHILE.

integrated process throughout the life cycle.

The CMM addresses quality-system activities for verifying compliance and for management processes at level 2. The specific procedures and standards a software project would use are specified in the software-development plan. At level 3, the organization must have defined software-engineering tasks that are integrated with management processes, and it must be performing them consistently. These requirements correspond directly with the ISO 9000-3 guidance for interpreting this clause.

As a practice in the Verifying Implementation common feature, the CMM identifies auditing to assure compliance with the specified standards and procedures.

One arguable correspondence is to the software process assets, including standards, procedures, and process descriptions, defined across the organization at level 3. Establishing such organizational assets would certainly contribute to implementing the quality system, but the standards and procedures in this clause could be addressed at the project level. ISO 9001 discusses the supplier's quality system, but it does not specifically address the relationship between organizational support and project implementation, as the CMM does. ISO 9000-3, on the other hand, has two sections on quality planning: clause 4.2.3 discusses quality planning across projects; clause 5.5 discusses quality planning within a particular development.

Clause 4.3: Contract review. ISO 9001 requires organizations to review contracts to determine if requirements are adequately defined, agree with the bid, and can be implemented.

The CMM addresses establishing a contract at level 2. The organization must document and review customer requirements, as allocated to software, and clarify any missing or ambiguous requirements. However, because the CMM is constrained to the software perspective, customer requirements in general are beyond the scope of the Requirements Management key process area.

Also at level 2, the CMM describes the proposal, statement of work, and software-development plan that establish external (contractual) commitments, which the software-engineering group and senior management review.

Finally, the CMM explicitly addresses how the organization can acquire software through subcontracting with an external customer or other type of subcontractor (the supplier may also be a customer). ISO 9001's contract-review clause does not explicitly describe the supplier's role when it is acting as a customer to a subcontractor.

CMM AND ISO 9000 DOCUMENT OVERVIEW

Below are highlights of the Capability Maturity Model Version 1.1 and ISO 9001 and 9000-3, the ISO 9000 standards that apply to software development and maintenance. For more detail on the CMM, see the CMM document.[1,2] For more details on using ISO 9000-3 and 9001, see those documents[3,4] and TickIt, the British guide for applying ISO 9001 to software.[5]

CMM. The Capability Maturity Model describes the principles and practices underlying software-process maturity and is intended to help organizations improve the maturity of their software processes through an evolutionary path from ad hoc, chaotic to mature, disciplined. It may also be used by an organization's customers to identify the strengths, weaknesses, and risks associated with their software suppliers. Authorized appraisers must go through both CMM and appraisal training. (For more information on CMM-based appraisal programs, contact SEI customer relations at (412) 268-5800.)

As Table A shows, the CMM is organized into five levels. Except for level 1, each level has a set of key process areas that an organization should focus on to improve its software process. Each key process area comprises a set of key practices that indicate if the implementation and institutionalization of that area is effective, repeatable, and lasting.

For convenience, the key practices in each key process area are organized by common features:

♦ *Commitment to Perform.* What actions must the organization take to ensure that the process is established and will endure? Includes practices concerning policy and leadership.

♦ *Ability to Perform.* What preconditions must exist in the project or organization to implement the software process competently? Includes practices that concern resources, training, orientation, organizational structure, and tools.

♦ *Activities Performed.* What roles and procedures are necessary to implement a key process area? Includes practices on plans, procedures, work performed, tracking, and corrective action.

♦ *Measurement and Analysis.* What procedures are needed to measure the process and analyze the measurements? Includes practices on process measurement and analysis.

♦ *Verifying Implementation.* What steps are needed to ensure that activities are performed in compliance with the established process? Includes practices on management reviews and audits.

Satisfying a key process area depends on both implementing and institutionalizing the process. Implementation is described in the Activities Performed common feature; institutionalization is described by the other common features.

ISO 9001, 9000-3. The ISO 9000 standards specify quality-system requirements for use when a contract between two parties requires the demonstration of a supplier's capability to design and supply a product. The two parties could be an external client and a supplier, or both could be internal, such as the marketing and engineering groups within the same company.

Of the ISO 9000 series, ISO 9001 is the standard most pertinent to software development and maintenance. Organizations use it when they must ensure that the supplier conforms to specified requirements during several stages of development, including design, development, production, installation, and servicing. ISO 9000-3 provides guidelines for applying ISO 9001 to the development, supply, and maintenance of software.

Organizations typically use ISO 9000 standards to regulate their internal quality system and assure the quality system of their suppliers. In fact, the standards are frequently used to register a third-party's quality system. Certificates of registration have a defined scope within an organization and are issued by quality-system registrars. Auditors are trained in the ISO 9000 standards, but they may not be trained in or knowledgeable about software-specific issues. If the scope of an audit specifies software, software-knowledgeable auditors should be included on the auditing team.

Status. Version 1.1 of the CMM was published in February 1993. The SEI is now collecting change requests and investigating

Clause 4.4: Design control. ISO 9001 requires an organization to establish procedures to control and verify design. These include

♦ planning, design, and development activities;

♦ defining organizational and technical interfaces;

♦ identifying inputs and outputs;

♦ reviewing, verifying, and validating the design; and

♦ controlling design changes.

ISO 9000-3 elaborates this clause with clauses on the purchaser's requirements specification (5.3), development planning (5.4), quality planning (5.5), design and implementation (5.6), testing and validation (5.7), and configuration management (6.1).

The CMM describes the life-cycle activities of requirements analysis, design, code, and test at level 3. Level 2 addresses planning and tracking of all project activities, including these, as

TABLE A KEY PROCESS AREAS IN THE CMM	
Level	Key Process Areas
5 Optimizing Continuous process improvement is enabled by quantitative feedback from the process and from piloting innovative ideas and technologies.	Defect prevention Technology change management Process change management
4 Managed Detailed measures of the software process and product quality are collected. Both the software process and products are quantitatively understood and controlled.	Quantitative process management Software quality management
3 Defined The software process for both management and engineering activities is documented, standardized, and integrated into a standard software process for the organization. All projects use an approved, tailored version of the organization's standard software process for developing and maintaining software.	Organization process focus Organization process definition Training program Integrated software management Software product engineering Intergroup coordination Peer reviews
2 Repeatable Basic project-management processes are established to track cost, schedule, and functionality. The necessary process discipline is in place to repeat earlier successes on projects with similar applications.	Requirements management Software project planning Software project tracking and oversight Software subcontract management Software quality assurance Software configuration management
1 Initial The software process is characterized as ad hoc, occasionally even chaotic. Few processes are defined, and success depends on individual effort and heroics.	———

potential additions. The next release, planned for late 1996, may add key process areas and will harmonize the CMM with ISO 9001 and other standards. The ISO 9000 series was published in 1987. A minor revision to ISO 9001 was published in July 1994, and a major revision of the entire series is planned for 1996.

REFERENCES

1. M. Paulk et al., *Capability Maturity Model for Software, Version 1.1*, Tech. Report CMU/SEI-93-TR-24, Software Eng. Inst., Pittsburgh, 1993.

2. M. Paulk et al., *Key Practices of the Capability Maturity Model, Version 1.1*, Tech. Report CMU/SEI-93-TR-25, Software Eng. Inst., Pittsburgh, 1993.

3. *ISO 9000-3: Guidelines for the Application of ISO 9001 to the Development, Supply, and Maintenance of Software*, Int'l Org. for Standardization, Geneva, 1991.

4. ISO 9001: Quality Systems — Model for Quality Assurance in Design/Development, Production, Installation, and Servicing, Int'l Org. for Standardization, Geneva, 1994.

5. *TickIT: A Guide to Software Quality Management System Construction and Certification Using EN29001, Issue 2.0*, UK Dept. of Trade and Industry and the British Computer Society, London, 1992.

ISO 9001 Clause	Strong Relationship	Judgmental Relationship

TABLE 1
SUMMARY MAPPING BETWEEN ISO 9001 AND THE CMM

ISO 9001 Clause	Strong Relationship	Judgmental Relationship
4.1: Management responsibility	Commitment to perform Software project planning Software project tracking and oversight Software quality assurance	Ability to perform Verifying implementation Software quality management
4.2: Quality system	Verifying implementation Software project planning Software quality assurance Software product engineering	Organization process definition
4.3: Contract review	Requirements management Software project planning	Software subcontract management
4.4: Design control	Software project planning Software project tracking and oversight Software configuration management Software product engineering	Software quality management
4.5: Document and data control	Software configuration management Software product engineering	
4.6: Purchasing	Software subcontract management	
4.7: Control of customer-supplied product	——	Software subcontract management
4.8: Product identification and traceability	Software configuration management Software product engineering	
4.9: Process control	Software project planning Software quality assurance Software product engineering	Quantitative process management Technology change management
4.10: Inspection and testing	Software product engineering Peer reviews	
4.11: Control of inspection, measuring, and test equipment	Software product engineering	
4.12: Inspection and test status	Software configuration management Software product engineering	
4.13: Control of nonconforming product	Software configuration management Software product engineering	
4.14: Corrective and preventive action	Software quality assurance Software configuration management	Defect prevention
4.15: Handling, storage, packaging, preservation, and delivery	——	Software configuration management Software product engineering
4.16: Control of quality records	Software configuration management Software product engineering Peer reviews	
4.17: Internal quality audits	Verifying implementation Software quality assurance	
4.18: Training	Ability to perform Training program	
4.19: Servicing	——	
4.20: Statistical techniques	Measurement and analysis	Organization process definition Quantitative process management Software quality management

well as configuration management of software work products.

ISO 9001, as revised in 1994, requires design reviews. ISO 9000-3 states that the supplier should carry out reviews to ensure that requirements are met and design methods are correctly carried out. However, although design reviews are required, organizations have a range of options for satisfying this clause, from technical reviews to inspections. In contrast, the CMM specifically calls out peer reviews at level 3 and identifies a number of work products that should undergo such a review.

TickIt training clarifies the ISO 9001 perspective by listing three examples of design reviews: Fagan inspections, structured walkthroughs, and peer reviews (in the sense of a desk check). The training also states (on page 17.10) that "an auditor will need to be satisfied from the procedures and records available that the reviews within an organization are satisfactory considering the type and criticality of the project under review."[1]

The CMM describes more formal, quantitative aspects of the design process at level 4, but ISO 9001 does not require this degree of formality.

Clause 4.5: Document and data control. ISO 9001 requires an organization to control the distribution and modification of documents and data. The CMM describes the configuration-management practices characterizing document and data control at level 2. The documentation required to operate and maintain the system is specifically called out at level 3. The specific procedures, standards, and other documents that may be placed under configuration management are identified in the different key process areas in the Activities Performed common feature.

Clause 4.6: Purchasing. ISO 9001 requires organizations to ensure that purchased products conform with specified requirements. This includes

evaluating potential subcontractors and verifying purchased products.

The CMM addresses custom software development at level 2, including the evaluation of subcontractors and acceptance testing of subcontracted software.

Clause 4.7: Control of customer-supplied product. ISO 9001 requires an organization to verify, control, and maintain any customer-supplied material. ISO 9000-3 discusses this clause in the context of included software product (6.8), also addressing commercial-off-the-shelf software.

The only CMM practice describing the use of purchased software is a subpractice at level 3, and the context is identifying off-the-shelf or reusable software as part of planning. The integration of off-the-shelf and reusable software is one of the CMM's weaker areas. In fact, this clause, especially as expanded in ISO 9000-3, cannot be considered adequately covered by the CMM. It would be reasonable, though not sufficient, to apply the acceptance testing practice for subcontracted software at level 2 to any included software product.

I have written a change request to CMM version 1.1 to incorporate practices that address product evaluation and the inclusion of off-the-shelf software and other types of software that have not been developed internally.

Clause 4.8: Product identification and traceability. ISO 9001 requires an organization to be able to identify and trace a product through all stages of production, delivery, and installation. The CMM covers this clause primarily at level 2 in the context of configuration management, but states the need for consistency and traceability between software work products at level 3.

Clause 4.9: Process control. ISO 9001 requires an organization to define and plan its production processes. This includes carrying out production under controlled conditions, according

to documented instructions. When an organization cannot fully verify the results of a process after the fact, it must continuously monitor and control the process. ISO 9000-3 clauses include design and implementation (5.6); rules, practices, and conventions (6.5); and tools and techniques (6.6).

In the CMM, the specific procedures and standards that would be used in the software-production process are specified in the software-development plan at level 2. The definition and integration of software-production processes, and the tools to support these processes, are described at level 3. Level 4 addresses the quantitative aspect of control, exemplified by statistical process control, but an organization typically would not have to demonstrate this level of control to satisfy this clause. Also, clause 6.6 in ISO 9000-3 states that "the supplier should improve these tools and techniques as required." This corresponds to transitioning new technology into the organization, a level 5 focus.

Clause 4.10: Inspection and testing. ISO 9001 requires an organization to inspect or verify incoming materials before use and to perform in-process inspection and testing. The organization must also perform final inspection and testing before the finished product is released and keep inspection and test records.

I have already described how the CMM deals with issues surrounding the inspection of incoming material ("Clause 4.7: Control of customer-supplied product"). The CMM describes testing and in-process inspections (strictly for software) at level 3.

Clause 4.11: Control of inspection, measuring, and test equipment. ISO 9001 requires an organization to control, calibrate, and maintain any equipment used to demonstrate conformance. When test hardware or software is used, it must be checked before use and rechecked at prescribed intervals. ISO 9000-3 clarifies this clause with clauses on testing and validation (5.7); rules, practices, and conventions (6.5); and tools and techniques (6.6).

The CMM generically addresses this clause under the testing practices in Software Product Engineering. Test software is specifically called out in the Ability to Perform common feature in the practice that describes tools that support testing (Ability 1.2).

Clause 4.12: Inspection and test status. ISO 9001 requires an organization to maintain the status of inspections and tests for items as they move through various processing steps. The CMM addresses this clause with practices on problem reporting and configuration status at level 2 and by testing practices at level 3.

Clause 4.13: Control of nonconforming product. ISO 9001 requires an organization to control a nonconforming product — one that does not satisfy specified requirements — to prevent inadvertent use or installation. ISO 9000-3 maps this concept to clauses on design and implementation (5.6); testing and validation (5.7); replication, delivery, and installation (5.9); and configuration management (6.1).

The CMM does not specifically address nonconforming products. In ISO 9000-3, the control issue essentially disappears among a number of related processes spanning the software life-cycle. In the CMM, the status of configuration items, which would include the status of items that contain known defects not yet fixed, is maintained at level 2. Design, implementation, testing, and validation are addressed at level 3.

Clause 4.14: Corrective and preventive action. ISO 9001 requires an organization to identify the causes of a nonconforming product. Corrective action is directed toward eliminating the causes of actual nonconformities. Preventive action is directed toward eliminating the causes of potential nonconformities. ISO 9000-3 quotes this clause

verbatim, with no elaboration, from the 1987 release of ISO 9001.

A literal reading of this clause would imply many of the CMM's practices in the level 5 key process area, Defect Prevention. According to the TickIt auditors' guide[4] (pages 139-140) and discussions with ISO 9000 auditors, corrective action is driven primarily by customer complaints. The software-engineering group should look at field defects, analyze why they occurred, and take corrective action. This would typically occur through software updates and patches distributed to the fielded software.

Under this interpretation of the clause, an appropriate mapping would be to level 2's problem reporting, followed by controlled maintenance of baselined work products.

Another interpretation described in section 23 of the TickIt training literature[1] is that corrective action is to address noncompliance identified in an audit, whether external or internal. This interpretation maps to the CMM's level 2 key process area, Software Quality Assurance.

How you interpret "preventive action" is a controversial issue in applying ISO 9001 to software. Some auditors seem to expect a defect-prevention process similar to that found in a manufacturing environment. Others require only that an organization address user-problem reports. It is debatable how much of the CMM's level 5 in-process causal analysis and defect prevention is necessary to satisfy this clause.

Clause 4.15: Handling, storage, packaging, preservation, and delivery. ISO 9001 requires organizations to establish and maintain procedures for handling, storage, packaging, and delivery. ISO 9000-3 maps this to clauses on acceptance (5.8) and replication, delivery, and installation (5.9).

The CMM does not cover replication, delivery, and installation. It addresses the creation and release of software products at level 2, and

acceptance testing at level 3. The CMM does not, however, describe practices for delivering and installing the product. I have written a change request to CMM version 1.1 to incorporate a practice for these areas.

Clause 4.16: Control of quality records. ISO 9001 requires an organization to collect and maintain quality records. In the CMM, the practices defining the maintenance of quality records are distributed throughout the key process areas as part of the Activities Performed common feature. Specific to this clause are the problem reporting described at level 2 and the testing and peer review practices, especially the collection and analysis of defect data, at level 3.

Clause 4.17: Internal quality audits. ISO 9001 requires an organization to plan and perform audits. The results of audits are communicated to management, and any deficiencies found are corrected.

The CMM describes the auditing process at level 2. Auditing practices to ensure compliance with the specified standards and procedures are identified in the Verifying Implementation common feature.

Clause 4.18: Training. ISO 9001 requires an organization to identify training needs, provide training (since selected tasks may require qualified personnel), and maintain training records.

The CMM identifies specific training needs in the training and orientation practices in the Ability to Perform common feature. It describes the general training infrastructure, including maintaining training records, at level 3.

Clause 4.19: Servicing. ISO 9001 requires an organization to perform servicing activities when such activities are part of a specified requirement. ISO 9000-3 addresses this clause as maintenance (5.10).

Although the CMM is intended to

be applied in both the software development and maintenance environments, the practices in the CMM do not directly address the unique aspects that characterize the maintenance environment. Maintenance is embedded throughout the CMM, but organizations must correctly interpret these practices in the development or maintenance context. Maintenance is not, therefore, a separate process in the CMM. Change requests for CMM version 1.0 expressed a concern about using the CMM for maintenance projects, and the SEI changed some wording for CMM version 1.1 to better address the maintenance environment. The SEI anticipates that this will remain a topic of discussion as it provides guidance for tailoring the CMM to different environments, such as maintenance, and begins the next revision cycle for the CMM.

Clause 4.20: Statistical techniques. ISO 9001 states that organizations must identify adequate statistical techniques and use them to verify the acceptability of process capability and product characteristics. ISO 9000-3 simply characterizes this clause as measurement (6.4).

In the CMM, product measurement is typically incorporated into the various practices within the Activities Performed common feature. Process measurement is described as part of the Measurement and Analysis common feature.

Level 3 describes the establishment of an organization-wide process database for collecting process and product data. It seems likely that most auditors would accept project-level data (as described at level 2) to satisfy this clause. However, at least a few auditors require an organization-level historical database and the use of simple statistical control charts.

If you infer statistical process control from this clause, an organization would satisfy it at level 4. To quote ISO 9000-3, however, "there are currently no universally accepted measures of software quality." Some auditors

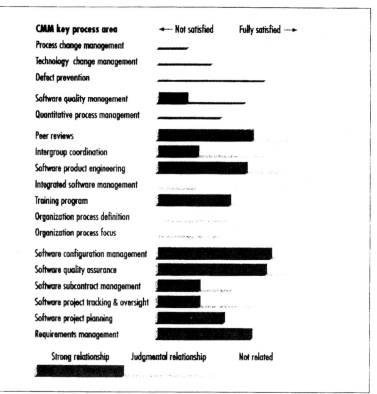

Figure 1. Key process area profile for an ISO 9001-compliant organization. Dark shading represents practices that ISO 9001 or ISO 9000-3 directly address; light shading indicates practices that may be addressed, depending on how you interpret ISO 9001; and unshaded areas indicate practices not specifically addressed.

look for the use of statistical tools, such as Pareto analysis. Others are satisfied by any consistently collected and used measurement data. In general, the only absolute is that auditors vary significantly in how they interpret this clause.

Summary. Clearly there is a strong correlation between ISO 9001 and the CMM, although some issues in ISO 9001 are not covered in the CMM, and vice versa. The level of detail differs significantly: section 4 in ISO 9001 is about five pages long; sections 5, 6, and 7 in ISO 9000-3 comprise about 11 pages; and the CMM is more than 500 pages. Judgment is needed to determine the exact correspondence, given the different levels of abstraction.

As Table 1 shows, the clauses in ISO 9001 with no strong relationships to the CMM key process areas, and that are not well addressed in the CMM, are control of customer-supplied product (4.7) and handling, storage, packaging, preservation, and delivery (4.15). The clause in ISO 9001 that is addressed in the CMM in

a completely distributed fashion is servicing (4.19). The clauses in ISO 9001 for which the exact relationship to the CMM is subject to significant debate are corrective and preventive action (4.14) and statistical techniques (4.20).

As I stated earlier, the biggest difference between the two documents is the explicit emphasis of the CMM on continuous process improvement. ISO 9001 addresses only the minimum criteria for an acceptable quality system. Another difference is that the CMM focuses strictly on software, while ISO 9001 has a much broader scope that encompasses hardware, software, processed materials, and services.

The biggest similarity between the two documents is their bottom line: "Say what you do; do what you say." The fundamental premise of ISO 9001 is that organizations should document every important process and check the quality of every deliverable through a quality-control activity. ISO 9001 requires documentation that contains instructions or guidance on what should be done or how it should be done. The CMM shares this emphasis on processes that are documented and practiced as documented. Phrases such as conducted "according to a documented procedure" and following "a written organizational policy" characterize the key process areas in the CMM.

On a more detailed level, some clauses in ISO 9001 are easily mapped to their equivalent CMM practices. Other relationships map in a many-to-many fashion, since the two documents are structured differently. For example, the training clause (4.18) in ISO 9001 maps to both the Training Program key process area and the training and orientation practices in all the key process areas.

COMPLIANCE ISSUES

At first glance, an organization with an ISO 9001 certificate would have to be at level 3 or 4 in the CMM. In reality, some level 1 organizations have been certified. One reason for this discrepancy is ISO 9001's high level of abstraction, which causes auditors to interpret it in different ways. If the auditor certifying the organization has had TickIt training, for example, the design reviews in ISO 9001 will correspond directly to the CMM's peer reviews, which are at level 3. But not all auditors are well-versed in software development. The virtue of a program like TickIt is that it produces auditors who understand how to apply ISO 9001 to software.

Another reason for the discrepancy is that an auditor may not require mastery to satisfy the corresponding ISO 9001 clause.

Figure 1 shows how an ISO-9001-compliant organization that has implemented no other management or engineering practices except those called out by ISO 9001 rates on the CMM. The size of the bar indicates the per-

centage of practices within the key process area that are addressed in either ISO 9001 or ISO 9000-3. The figure shows areas that have a direct relationship to clauses in these documents (dark shading), areas for which the relationship is subject to interpretation (light shading), and areas that the clauses do not directly address (white).

Note the following about Figure 1:
♦ Every key process area at level 2 is strongly related to ISO 9001.
♦ Every key process area is at least weakly related to ISO 9001 under some interpretation.

On the basis of this profile, an organization assessed at level 1 could be certified as compliant with ISO 9001. That organization would, however, have to have significant process strengths at level 2 and noticeable strengths at level 3. Private discussions indicate that many level 1 organizations have received ISO 9001 certificates. If an organization is following the spirit of ISO 9001, it is likely to be near or above level 2. However, organizations have identified significant problems during a CMM-based assessment that had not surfaced during a previous ISO 9001 audit.[5] This seems to be related to the greater depth of a CMM-based investigation.

Although the CMM does not adequately address some specific issues, in general it encompasses the concerns of ISO 9001. The converse is less true. ISO 9001 describes only the minimum criteria for an adequate quality-management system, rather than addressing the entire continuum of process improvement, although future revisions of ISO 9001 may address this concern. The differences are sufficient to make a rigid mapping impractical, but the similarities provide a high degree of overlap.

To answer the three questions I listed in the beginning of this article:
♦ An ISO 9001-compliant organization would not necessarily satisfy all the key process areas in level 2 of the CMM, but it would satisfy most of the level 2 and many of the level 3 goals. Further, because ISO 9001 doesn't address all the CMM practices, a level 1 organization could receive ISO 9001 registration.
♦ A level 2 (or 3) organization would probably be considered compliant with ISO 9001 but even a level 3 organization would need to ensure that it adequately addressed the delivery and installation process described in clause 4.15 of ISO 9001, and it should consider the use of included software products, as described in clause 6.8 of ISO 9000-3. With this caveat, obtaining certification should be relatively straightforward for a level 2 or higher organization.
♦ As to whether software process improvement should be based on the CMM or ISO 9001, the short answer is that an organization may want to consider both, given the significant degree of overlap. A market may require ISO 9001 certification; addressing the concerns of the CMM would help organizations prepare for an ISO 9001 audit. Conversely, level 1 organizations would certainly profit from addressing the concerns of ISO 9001. Although either document can be used alone to structure a process-improvement program, the more detailed guidance and software specificity provided by the CMM suggests that it is the better choice, although admittedly this answer may be biased.

In any case, organizations should focus on improvement to build a competitive advantage, not on achieving a score — whether that is a maturity level or a certificate. The SEI advocates addressing continuous process improvement as encompassed by the CMM, but even then there is a need to address the larger business context in the spirit of Total Quality Management. ♦

> **EVERY CMM KEY PROCESS AREA IS AT LEAST WEAKLY RELATED TO ISO 9001 IN SOME WAY.**

ACKNOWLEDGMENTS

I thank the many people who commented on the early drafts of this article and who discussed the relationships between ISO 9001 and the CMM. In some cases, we have agreed to disagree, but the discussions were always interesting. Specifically, I thank Peter Anderson, Robert Bamford, Kelley Butler, Gary Coleman, Taz Daughtrey, Darryl Davis, Bill Deibler, Alec Dorling, George Kambic, Dwight Lewis, Stan Magee, Helen Mooty, Don O'Neill, Neil Potter, Jim Roberts, John Slater, and Charlie Weber.

This work is sponsored by the US Department of Defense under contract F19628-90-C-003.

REFERENCES

1. *Lloyd's Register TickIT Auditors' Course, Issue 1.4*, Lloyd's Register, Mar. 1994.

2. Mark C. Paulk, "A Comparison of ISO 9001 and the Capability Maturity Model for Software," Tech. Report CMU/SEI-94-TR-2, Software Eng. Inst., Pittsburgh, July 1994.

3. M. Paulk, "Comparing ISO 9001 and the Capability Maturity Model for Software," *Software Quality J.*, Dec. 1993, pp. 245-256.

4. *TickIT: A Guide to Software Quality Management System Construction and Certification Using EN29001, Issue 2.0*, UK Dept. of Trade and Industry and the British Computer Society, London, 1992.

5. F. Coallier, "How ISO 9001 Fits Into the Software World," *IEEE Software*, Jan. 1994, pp. 98-100.

Mark C. Paulk is a senior member of the technical staff at the Software Engineering Institute, where he is product manager for version 2 of the Capability Maturity Model. At the SEI, he was also project leader for the CMM version 1.1 development. Before joining the SEI, Paulk worked on distributed real-time systems for System Development Corp. (later Unisys Defense Systems) at the Ballistic Missile Defense Advanced Research Center.

Paulk received a BS in mathematics from the University of Alabama, Huntsville, and an MS in computer science from Vanderbilt University. He is a senior member of the IEEE and a member of the American Society for Quality Control.

Address questions about this article to Paulk at Software Engineering Institute, Carnegie Mellon University, Pittsburgh, PA 15213-3890; mcp@sei.cmu.edu.

Chapter 8

The SPICE Project

1. Introduction to Chapter

The SPICE (Software Process Improvement and Capability dEtermination) project is supporting the production of an international standard suite for software process assessment, software process improvement, and capability determination. The project has its roots in a UK study entitled ImproveIT [1]. ImproveIT was sponsored by the UK government and the Defence Industry Trade Association to investigate how to select competent suppliers of software intensive systems.

The report of the ImproveIT study found that there was, at the time, a range of methods in use for software process assessment, and a desire and need for a common approach. The report also recommended that there should be an emphasis on self-assessment.

An edited version of the ImproveIT report was presented at the 4th plenary meeting of ISO/IEC JTC1/SC7, held in Stockholm in 1991, with the aim of obtaining approval for a study period to investigate the need for and requirements of an international Software Process Assessment standard.

The study period was approved, and the report from this study was submitted to the 5th plenary meeting of ISO/IEC JTC1/SC7, held in London in 1992. The result of this report was that a new work

item was approved to create the new international standard, and a new working group (WG 10) was created to manage its development.

The strength of the SPICE project is that it contains the key personnel who have been, and continue to be, involved in developing the principal software process assessment methods in use throughout the world and throughout a wide range of industries. These include representatives from the SEI (responsible for the SW-CMM), the Bootstrap Institute, Bell Canada (for TRILLIUM), BT (for Healthcheck), Compita (for the Software Technology Diagnostic), and so on. In addition, the project includes researchers in the area and involves international research centers such as the SEI, European Software Institute (ESI), Australian Software Quality Institute (SQI) in Brisbane, Centre de Recherche Informatique de Montréal (CRIM), and the Fraunhofer Institute for Experimental Software Engineering in Kaiserslautern in Germany. The fact that the project was able to bring together so many influential workers in the area is almost entirely due to the hard work and diplomatic skills of the project leader, Alec Dorling.

As an international standardization project, SPICE is unique in two ways:

- During its development the standard is being extensively trialed throughout the world;
- It is using a "fast track" route to standardization via a series of technical reports.

We will say more about the trials in Chapter 9.

The normal route to standardization goes through the following stages:

- New work item;
- Working draft;
- Committee draft;
- Draft international standard;
- International standard.

The technical report route, however, has different stages after the working draft stage, namely:

- Proposed draft technical report;
- Draft technical report;
- Technical report.

The technical report route is sometimes used by a standards working group when it is not sure that the degree of consensus required for an international standard is present. The technical report produced is known as Technical Report (type-2) or a TR-2, and is expected to be replaced by a full international standard within two years of its publication. The SPICE standard is currently at the TR-2 stage and is known as ISO/IEC TR 15504:1998.

Considerable thought went into the management of the SPICE project. A regional structure was adopted with technical centers for four (later five) regions of the world, initially the USA, Canada and Latin America, Europe and Africa, and the Asia Pacific region. Later the Asia Pacific region was split into two: Northern Asia Pacific (mainly Japan and South Korea) and Southern Asia Pacific (centered on Australia). The project makes extensive use of modern means of communication, including email, websites, document circulation via servers, etc. Since the project started, this type of technology has developed rapidly and the SPICE methods of communication, which seemed innovative in the early stages of the project, now seem commonplace.

Those interested in more details of the SPICE project should consult El Emam, et al., *The Theory and Practice of Software Process Improvement and Capability Determination* [2].

2. Description of Articles

The first paper in this chapter, entitled "The SPICE Approach to Software Process Improvement," is by Terence P. Rout, a Senior Lecturer in the Australian Software Quality Institute in Griffith University in Brisbane. He has been heavily involved in the SPICE project from the start, as manager of the Asia Pacific (later the Southern Asia Pacific) technical center. He is now also the editor of the ISO/IEC 15504 document set.

Rout's paper introduces the SPICE project and explains its role in supporting the work of producing the international standard ISO/IEC 15504. The paper describes the two-dimensional structure of the 15504 reference model in terms of *process categories, process attributes,* and *capability levels.* The process assessment framework described in the standard and the approach to software process improvement are both described. The paper concludes by introducing the SPICE trials and indicating the future directions in the development of the ISO/IEC 15504 standard.

The second paper in this chapter is from the book *SPICE: The Theory and the Practice of Software Process Improvement and Capability Determination,* edited by El Emam, Drouin and Melo [2], and published by the IEEE Computer Society Press. It is entitled "Assessment Using SPICE: A Case Study," and was written by Jean-Martin Simon. The case study concerns a software company with ISO 9001 registration, which sought to maintain its quality management systems in a changing environment. The company used the SPICE documents as the basis of an assessment, determined the assessment scope from the assessment purpose, and selected the process instances based on the assessment scope. Simon graphically describes the results of the assessment and comments on the differences between successive versions of the SPICE model.

The third paper in this chapter is by T. P. Rout, A. Tuffley, B. Cahill, and B. Hodgen, and is entitled "The Rapid Assessment of Software Process Capability." Software Process Assessment tends to be a rather expensive process, whether it is measured in terms of effort required or money expended. There are therefore very compelling financial reasons for endeavoring to minimize the effort required.

In this paper, Rout, et al., describe a method of performing a rapid assessment of software processes for the purposes of process improvement with the following characteristics (among others):

- a duration of one day;

- assessment of a specific set of eight SPICE processes;

- use of only experienced and competent assessors.

The method described brings software assessment within the reach of small organizations, and the authors claim that it benefits large organizations as well. There are plans to validate the method by comparing its results with the results of more conventional assessments made of some of the same organizations.

The fourth paper in this chapter is by Ann Cass, Christian Völcker, Paolo Panaroni, Alec Dorling, and Lothar Winzer, entitled "SPICE for Space: A Method of Process Assessment for Space Software Projects."

The paper describes an ISO/IEC 15504-conformant method for software process assessment developed for use within the European Space Agency. It is based on the 15504 exemplar assessment model, which is significantly extended to include:

- new processes such *as contract maintenance, safety and dependability,* and *information management;*

- new component processes such as *supply preparation* and *delivery;*

- new base practices for processes such as *supplier selection, documentation* and *configuration management;*

- new notes to implement ESA standard requirements for the production of space software.

A software tool has been developed to support SPICE for Space (or S4S) assessments, and a number of pilot assessments have been performed.

The fifth paper, entitled "Relating the SPICE Framework and SEI Approach to Software Process Assessment," is by Dave Kitson of the SEI, who has also been involved in the SPICE project from the early days. The paper includes a good history of the development of the SW-CMM to complement the papers published in Chapter 2 of this tutorial, as well as a brief history of the SPICE project. Kitson compares and contrasts the two efforts, noting that at the highest level the two approaches have no significant differences, both being concerned with continuous process improvement, based on a clear reference model for assessment, and recognizing repeatability and reproducibility of assessment results as important issues.

Key differences between the two approaches identified include

- the fact that SPICE provides a framework for assessment methods, but no specific method, whereas the SW-CMM provides a specific method;

- SPICE ratings are based on a four-point ordinal scale, whereas the SW-CMM ratings are based on a three-point scale;

- the scope of a SPICE assessment is broader than that of a SW-CMM assessment, since SPICE assessments are concerned with acquisition, supply, and operation of software products. In fact, aspects of SPICE conformant assessments are within the scope of other CMMs, such as the Software Acquisition CMM

The paper concludes that since there are no major conflicts between the SPICE framework and the SW-CMM method, then the SW-CMM, possibly augmented by aspects of other CMMs, could to a large extent be considered a SPICE conformant software process assessment method. However, it is worth noting the this is a matter that has also been considered in depth elsewhere [3].

References

[1] A. Dorling, P. Simms, *ImproveIT Study Report*, UK Ministry of Defence, 1991.

[2] K. El Emam, J.-N. Drouin, W. Melo, *SPICE: The Theory and Practice of Software Process Improvement and Capability Determination*, IEEE Computer Society, 1998.

[3] T. P. Rout; "SPICE and the CMM: Is the CMM Compatible with ISO/IEC 15504?,"*4th International Conference on Achieving Quality in Software (AQUIS '98)*, pp. 97- 104, Venice, 1998.

The SPICE Approach to Software Process Improvement

Terence P. Rout

Software Quality Institute
Griffith University
Queensland, Australia 4111

1. Introduction

The techniques generically described as *software process assessment* have their origin in the total quality management (TQM) movement, and derive from the basic premise that the quality of manufactured products is largely determined by the quality of the processes that produce them [1]. As Humphrey [2] points out, the first step in any program to improve software capability is to understand the current status of the development process. Process assessment is the means of achieving this; the technique is defined as:

> *The disciplined examination of the processes used by an organisation against a set of criteria to determine the capability of those processes to perform within quality, cost and schedule goals. The aim is to characterise current practice, identifying strengths and weaknesses and the ability of the process to control or avoid significant causes of poor quality, cost and schedule performance.* [3]

The increasing number of assessment methods and models available and the increasing use of the technique in commercially sensitive areas were the key motivating factors behind the development and acceptance of a proposal to develop an international standard for software process assessment. The SPICE (Software Process Improvement and Capability dEtermination) project is an international collaborative effort to support the development of the international standard. The project was established by the international committee on software engineering standards, ISO/IEC JTC1/SC7, through its Working Group 10 on software process assessment, in January 1993. This followed the recommendations of the committee's Study Group on Needs and Requirements for a standard for software process assessment, which in 1992 recommended:

"(These) considerations lead to the following approach:

a) that development should be carried out by a dedicated project team;

b) that development should be closely linked with a period of field trials and experimentation;

c) that the standard should be published initially as a Technical Report (Type 2)[1] to enable the method to stabilise and user feedback to be obtained prior to committing to a full standard.

Development by a dedicated team, with a core team staffed by full-time resource, will provide greater scope for more intensive technical design and development and should result in a reduction in timescales." [3]

At the time of the study group report, a number of process assessment methods were in use. Many of these had proven themselves effective within a variety of software and business domains. However, significant concerns were raised that the presence of multiple incompatible assessment approaches would result in additional costs for both acquirers and developers. The development of an international standard provided the opportunity to build on the best attributes of each method and

---

[1] The ISO/IEC JTC1 directives [4] provide that "When the subject in question is still under technical development or where for any other reason there is the possibility of an agreement at some time in the future, JTC1 may decide that the publication of a TR2 would be more appropriate."

harmonize the efforts of their developers. This was seen as advancing the "state of the art" while producing a public and shared model for assessment.

The major benefits of a standard for process assessment were considered to be as follows: It would

1. Provide a public and shared model for process assessment.

2. Lead to a common understanding of the use of process assessment for process improvement and capability evaluation.

3. Provide a baseline for measurement.

4. Provide the means to reflect differences between industry sectors.

5. Give industry the motivation to improve.

6. Provide a route to external recognition of best practice.

7. Facilitate capability evaluation in open procurement.

8. Assist in removing barriers to trade through increased visibility of capability.

9. Improve people's understanding of their duties.

10. Be controlled and regularly reviewed in the light of experience with its use.

11. Be changed only by international consensus.

12. Encourage harmonization of existing schemes [3].

Looking back on the history of the project, we can see that many of these benefits have been delivered. The most interesting issue is that they have largely been provided by the operation of the SPICE [project, and its success in raising awareness of assessment as a technique of value. The SPICE project, when established, had three defined goals:

1. To assist the standardization project in its preparatory stage to develop initial working drafts;

2. To undertake user trials in order to gain early experience data, which will form a basis for revision of the published technical reports prior to review as full international standards; and

3. To create market awareness and take-up of the evolving standards.

The first of these goals was achieved with the release of the working drafts for ISO /IEC 15504 in 1995. The second now forms the principal focus for project activities; the first and second phases of SPICE trials have been concluded, and the third phase was under way at the time of this writing. The third goal has been addressed through a series of publications and symposia, and through the overall efforts of project members, which has resulted in a generally high profile for the project and for the use of process assessment. This role has in recent years been adopted by the SPICE Users Group.

Following on the acceptance of the study group report, the task of defining a standard was assigned to a new working group, WG10, which established the SPICE project in 1993. The origins of the project are described in more detail by Dorling [5], together with the management structure adopted to direct the project.

Four international technical centers (covering Europe, the United States, Canada, and Latin America) were established to coordinate the international effort on the project. Its conduct has brought together a unique combination of standards developers, software developers, and academics from more than 20 countries to generate a consistent and validated framework for assessment in a remarkably short period of time. The success of the approach can be gauged from the results: Although the project fell behind its initial schedule, it produced a full suite of documents suitable for extensive industry trials in a period of 2 years. Following the production of the working draft document set, the SPICE project handed this material over to WG10 to do the work needed to create an international standard, and turned its attention to the conduct of extensive industry trials of the emerging standard.

The development process has at present resulted in the publication of ISO/IEC TR 15504:1998 *Information Technology—Software Process Assessment* [6], as a series of technical reports (type 2), as envisaged in the initial proposal . Work is now in progress that will result in the release of a full international standard for process assessment.

For the purposes of this paper, I have regarded the "SPICE approach to process improvement" as referring to a program for software process improvement that is:

1. Based on the use of process assessment techniques;

2. Where such process assessment is conducted according to the requirements of ISO/IEC TR 15504-3;

3. Where the model used as the basis for assessment is ISO/IEC TR 15504; and

4. Where the general guidance for process improvement is drawn from ISO/IEC TR 15504-7 (Guide for Use in Process Improvement).

2. A Framework for Software Process Assessment

ISO/IEC 15504 describes an overall framework for software process assessment that is designed to result in reliable and consistent assessments that yield results that allow comparison between different assessment methods. The basic elements of the framework are shown in Figure 1.

The framework effectively provides the basic elements of a defined process for performing assessments, through prescribing minimum required inputs and outputs, and a

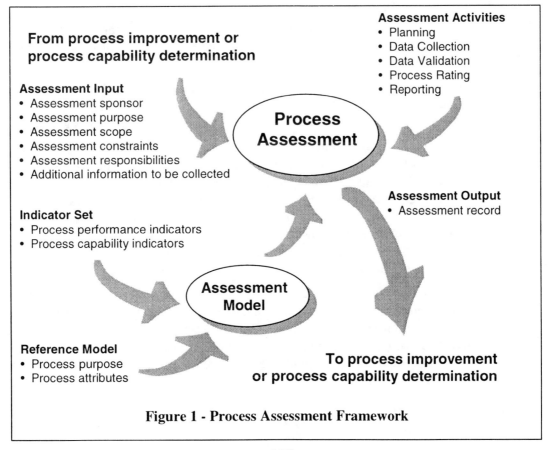

Figure 1 - Process Assessment Framework

required set of activities. The definitions of inputs, outputs, and activities are designed to ensure repeatability and consistency in the assessment process, in order to provide confidence that assessment results can be seen as reliable and objective.

The other significant component of the assessment framework is the use in the assessment of a process model as the basis for the comparisons and ratings of process capability. The use of such process models is a common feature of all approaches to process assessment; the value of ISO/IEC 15504 is that it requires that the model be "compatible" with a defined reference model for processes and process capability.

The reference model defined in ISO/IEC 15504-2 is described as a "two-dimensional model of processes and process capability." It provides a common scale for the expression of the results of process assessment. The *process dimension* effectively defines the entities that are evaluated in a process assessment; the *capability dimension* defines a measurement scale for expressing the rating of capability.

1.1.   The Process Dimension

In the process dimension, the model defines 40 processes that comprise and characterize the software life cycle. These processes are classified into five process categories:

1. The *customer-supplier* process category consists of processes that directly impact the customer, support development and transition of the software to the customer, and provide for its correct operation and use.

2. The *engineering* process category consists of processes that directly specify, implement, or maintain a system and software product and its user documentation.

3. The *support* process category consists of processes that may be employed by any of the other processes (including other supporting processes) at various points in the software life cycle.

4. The *management* process category consists of processes that contain practices of a generic nature, which may be used by anyone who manages any sort of project within a software life cycle.

5. The *organization* process category consists of processes that establish the business goals of the organization and develop process, product, and resource assets that, when used by the projects in the organization, will help the organization achieve its business goals.

Each process is defined through a detailed statement of the purpose of the process, together with a list of the expected outcomes of executing the process. The process purpose statement is a paragraph stating at a high level the overall objectives of performing the process, with an optional additional paragraph to further define the purpose statement. The process outcomes are observable results of the successful implementation of a process. Outcomes are measurable statements describing the achievement of the purpose of the process, in terms of the production of an artifact; a significant change of state; or the meeting of specified constraints, for example, requirements or goals.

The processes are shown in Figure 2, which also demonstrates the higher level architecture of the reference model: Some of the processes are seen as "components" of others. (Thus, the acquisition process contains within its scope the processes of acquisition preparation, supplier selection, supplier management, and customer acceptance.) This feature primarily allows for exact equivalence of processes in the reference model to those defined in

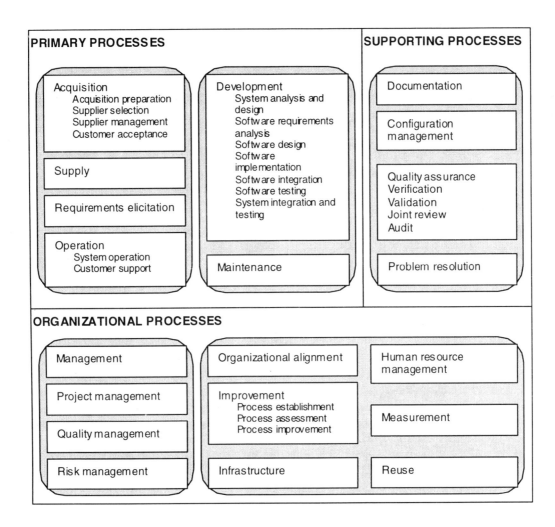

Figure 2 - Processes defined in the Reference Model in ISO/IEC 15504

ISO/IEC 12207 [7], which has a lower level of granularity. Each of the processes defined in the reference model, however, is separately assessable.

3.1.   *The Capability Dimension*

The capability dimension of the reference model defines an ordinal scale for expressing the rated capability of a process. Six points are defined on the scale, and described as capability levels:

Level 0 – *Incomplete:* There is general failure to attain the purpose of the process. There are no easily identifiable work products or outputs of the process.

Level 1 – *Performed:* The purpose of the process is generally achieved. The achievement may not be rigorously planned and tracked. There are identifiable work products for the process, and these testify to the achievement of the purpose.

Level 2 – *Managed:* The process delivers work products according to specified procedures and is planned and tracked. Work products conform to specified standards and requirements. The primary distinction from the performed level is that the performance of the process now

337

delivers work products that fulfill expressed quality requirements within defined timescales and resource needs.

Level 3 – *Established:* The process is performed and managed using a defined process based on good software engineering principles. Individual implementations of the process use approved, tailored versions of standard, documented processes to achieve the process outcomes. The resources necessary to establish the process definition are also in place. The primary distinction from the managed level is that the process of the established level is using a defined process that is capable of achieving its process outcomes.

Level 4 – *Predictable:* The defined process is performed consistently in practice within defined control limits to achieve its defined process goals. Detailed measures of performance are collected and analyzed. This leads to a quantitative understanding of process capability and an improved ability to predict and manage performance. Performance is quantitatively managed. The quality of work products is quantitatively known. The primary distinction from the established level is that the defined process is now performed consistently within defined limits to achieve its process outcomes.

Level 5 – *Optimizing:* Performance of the process is optimized to meet current and future business needs, and the process achieves repeatability in meeting its defined business goals. Quantitative process effectiveness and efficiency goals (targets) for performance are established, based on the business goals of the organization. Continuous process monitoring against these goals is enabled by obtaining quantitative feedback, and improvement is achieved by analysis of the results. Optimizing a process involves piloting innovative ideas and technologies and changing ineffective processes to meet defined goals or objectives. The primary distinction from the predictable level is that the defined and standard processes now dynamically change and adapt to effectively meet current and future business goals.

3.2. *Rating Process Capability*

The achievement of a capability level is evaluated by rating the extent of achievement of a set of defined process attributes, as listed in Table 1. The rating of process capability is performed by evaluating the extent of achievement of the nine defined process attributes for each process within the scope of the assessment. The rating scale is a percentage scale from 0 to 100 percent that represents the extent of achievement of the attribute. A four-point ordinal rating scale is used to calibrate the levels of achievement of the defined capability of the process attributes: **N**ot achieved, **P**artially achieved, **L**argely achieved, and **F**ully achieved. The minimal output from an assessment of capability is thus a series of profiles of ratings of process attributes, for each process within the scope of the assessment.

Table 1. Capability Levels and Process Attributes

ID	Title
Level 1	**Performed Process**
1.1	Process performance attribute
Level 2	**Managed Process**
2.1	Performance management attribute
2.2	Work product management attribute
Level 3	**Established Process**

ID	Title
3.1	Process definition attribute
3.2	Process resource attribute
Level 4	**Predictable Process**
4.1	Process measurement attribute
4.2	Process control attribute
Level 5	**Optimizing Process**
5.1	Process change attribute
5.2	Continuous improvement attribute

The process profile can be used as the basis for expressing a rating of the capability level achieved in the implementation of a process, according to the decision table shown in Table 2. This allows the expression of capability in either of two equivalent ways: as a profile of attribute achievement, or as a capability level rating.

Table 2. Capability Level Ratings

Scale	Process Attributes	Rating
Level 1	Process performance	Largely or fully
Level 2	Process performance	Fully
	Performance management	Largely or fully
	Work product management	Largely or fully
Level 3	Process performance	Fully
	Performance management	Fully
	Work product management	Fully
	Process definition and tailoring	Largely or fully
	Process resource	Largely or fully
Level 4	Process performance	Fully
	Performance management	Fully
	Work product management	Fully
	Process definition and tailoring	Fully
	Process resource	Fully
	Process measurement	Largely or fully
	Process control	Largely or fully

3. Process Improvement Based on Assessment

Process assessment has been strongly linked with attempts to improve quality and productivity in software development. The technique had its origins in traditional approaches to TQM, and the formalized approaches now consolidated in ISO/IEC 15504 derived in part from traditional approaches to TQM [2]. While the initial impetus behind the development was the evaluation of developer capability, the application of the approach to process improvement was always seen as a strong motivator and the first reports on application of the technique [8] focused on improvement and the returns from such activity.

The SC7 Study Group Report [3] saw process improvement as one of the key areas of application of any standard for process assessment, and a key requirement for the standard was its applicability for both process improvement and capability determination. As a response to this requirement, ISO/IEC TR 15504-7 (Guide for Use in Process Improvement) [6] provides explicit guidance for the use of process assessment in process improvement. The guidance includes an eight-step model for improving software processes (Figure 3); these eight steps form a continuous cycle of improvement.

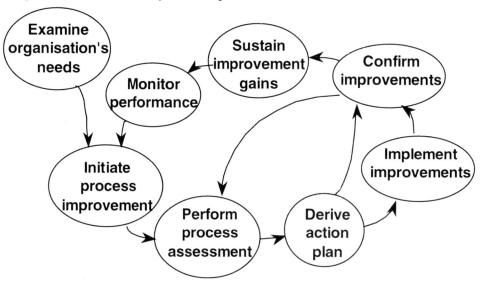

Figure 3 - Process Improvement Steps in ISO/IEC 15504-Part 7

3.3.   *Examine the Organization's Needs*

Any improvement project should be undertaken because it is intended to place the organization in a better position in its environment; that is, improvement should be designed to positively influence the competitive position of the organization, its ability to retain existing markets and to capture new ones. It is surprising how often this basic truism is overlooked or ignored; it should really provide the basic driver for improvement.

The first step in improvement, then, should be to examine the overall business goals of the organization, and from these establish the current needs and priorities. These can then be used to establish the goals of the process improvement initiative. Two types of objectives can typically be addressed by software process improvement: product-related goals and risk-related goals. Product-related goals are, for example, quality, time to market, and production cost. Risk-related goals include ability to predict development time and ability to control development time.

Once the goals have been set, the priorities of the improvement goals can be established. The improvement goals direct the choice of the processes to be assessed, the definition of improvement targets, and ultimately the identification of the most effective improvement actions. In this part of the improvement process, it is important to build the necessary management commitment.

3.4. Initiate Process Improvement

The improvement program should be treated as a project in its own right, with a plan against which progress is monitored. The improvement project should have its own resources and its plan should address all the issues required for a project, with defined milestones, review points, and so forth. The establishment of such a project should occur either following the examination of organization's needs or following the monitor performance step to initiate a second or subsequent cycle of improvement. This means that the commitment of management— at least in terms of recognizing the resource commitment required — is established from the beginning of the initiative.

The improvement plan should include [9]:

- A description of the current status of software engineering practices in the organization,

- Business needs,

- Preliminary improvement goals,

- Processes targeted for improvement,

- Expected benefits,

- Time frame, and

- Budget constraints.

A process improvement initiative should be planned at three levels. At the organizational level, process improvement initiatives should be included in the business plan, at which level it is integrated with the overall plans for the organization. The initiative also needs a program plan that addresses the whole of the process improvement initiative. This plan can cover more than one improvement cycle. Each process improvement project also needs its own detailed project plan.

In addition to defining an initial plan, this stage in the improvement initiative should commence the establishment of an effective infrastructure for process improvement. The primary purpose for establishing an infrastructure for an improvement program is to build the mechanisms necessary to help the organization institutionalize continuous process improvement [10]. The infrastructure established for any improvement program is critical to the success of that program. A solid and effective infrastructure can sustain a developing program until it begins to produce visible results. A good infrastructure can mean the difference between success and failure for the improvement program. The infrastructure includes the organizational structures set up with specific roles and responsibilities for improvement. This should include a steering group of senior management, as well as an implementation team centered around the "champion" of the program within the organization.

3.5. Perform Process Assessment

A detailed evaluation of the current status of the processes in the organization is needed at an early stage in the improvement program; this should be achieved by performing an assessment of process capability. The assessment provides an understanding of the current status of the relevant processes within the organization. Before this assessment can be undertaken, a number of assessment inputs need to be identified. The senior managers who will sponsor and own the assessment have to be identified. A competent assessor to take the responsibility for conformance of the assessment will be needed. Responsibilities for the assessment must be assigned and accepted. The purpose and scope of the assessment have to be documented, and any constraints on the freedom of the assessment team must also be documented.

During an assessment, an organization need cover only the subset of processes that are relevant for its business objectives. In most cases, it is not necessary to assess all of the processes in the process dimension. In the absence of other information (for example, evidence from an ISO 9001 audit), or where there is general recognition within the organization of a pressing problem to be addressed (e.g., the absence of effective configuration and change control), when an improvement project is being initiated in an organization, the scope of the initial assessment should incorporate those "primary" [2] processes that are seen as most important to the organization's business, without (in the first instance) examining other management or supporting processes.

Thus, for an organization that is normally involved in the development of software in contractual relationships, the initial assessment might focus on the component processes of software development, and possibly the requirements elicitation process. The results of such an assessment will focus concentration on issues related to the organization's business needs, and will also highlight those supporting and management processes that have the most impact on the ability to address these needs.

Once the inputs are defined, the assessment should be conducted. The assessment will result in a profile for all of the processes in the scope, a record of the context of the assessment, and additional information. In the context of process improvement, this additional information could be about existing localized good practices that could be extended to the whole organization; experiences from the introduction of previous new methods or tools; cultural issues that need to be taken into account when introducing improvements; organizational issues that need to be taken into account when introducing improvements; and training that will be required before improvements can be introduced.

Assessments take place either at the start of a new improvement cycle or may be requested at a later stage, in order to confirm improvements after they are implemented. The fine granularity inherent in the SPICE approach — deriving from the process-based approach to assessment — allows for multiple small assessments to be performed within a limited timescale, enabling additional diagnostic information to be collected quickly following an initial assessment. The assessments should, as far as possible, be conducted according to the requirements of ISO/IEC 15504-3 (Performing an Assessment); note, however, that nonconforming assessments of small scope may be of considerable value in an improvement project. This paper does not address how assessments are performed or what tools can be used to support assessment; these issues are addressed in other sources [9, 11].

---

[2]   This term refers to the process model from ISO 12207, which classifies processes as primary, supporting, or organizational. It incorporates the customer-supplier and engineering categories from ISO/IEC TR 15504-2.

3.6. Analyze Results and Derive Action Plan

Using the output from the assessment, the areas requiring improvement should be identified. Then, using the goals identified for the improvement initiative, these areas should be put in order of priority. As a result of this analysis, a set of specific targets for improvement should be established for the priority areas. First, qualitative goals should be set. Then ways of measuring the achievement of each goal should be found. Finally quantified targets for improvement should be defined. Targets may be values for process effectiveness, or they may be target capability profiles.

Once the measurable improvement targets are established, a plan of action aimed at achieving these targets should be established. Each action in the plan should be linked to one of the targets, and the way in which the success of the action will be checked should be identified. The plan should include the responsibilities, estimated costs, timescales, and so on, for the improvement actions. The action plan (or plans) will amplify and extend the original improvement plan, and these plans should be maintained to be consistent with each other.

3.7. Implement Improvements

Once the action plan is established, projects to implement the specific improvement actions should be initiated. These can address one or more of the actions. These projects may also include the confirmation of the improvements and sustaining of the improvement gains that are the subject of the next two steps.

It is common to use pilot projects to validate an intended improvement, and this approach can be particularly useful in larger organizations. This has the advantage of allowing risks associated with the proposed changes to the processes to be exposed in advance of full organizational implementation. It is important to ensure that measures of success for the improvements are identified and monitored throughout the pilot, so that the success or otherwise of the selected strategy is apparent.

3.8. Confirm Improvements

Once an improvement action has been completed, it is important to evaluate whether it has achieved the required target. This is principally done by examination of the measurements defined during analysis of the assessment results. This may also involve a reassessment where the target is defined as a process profile. This could be a limited scope assessment where the processes affected by an action are few. Side effects of the change should also be considered in this step, such as possible effects on organizational culture. The costs and benefits of the improvement exercise should be calculated to assist with future planning.

3.9. Sustain the Improvement Gains

A defined approach to monitoring the continued effectiveness of the improvement should be established. Use of measurements is the preferred approach, but consideration must be given to nonmeasurable factors as well. A point to remember is that a process change in one area may have a side effect of reducing the effectiveness of another process by, for example, redistributing limited resources. For instance, introducing an extensive peer review of design documentation may reduce the time available for analysis of the design by the designer and lead to a reduction in time available for monitoring progress by the project leader. Care should be taken that the overall effect of a change is beneficial.

This step also includes the deployment of improvements piloted in a restricted area across the organization. Again, this should be done in a planned and controlled way.

3.10. Monitor Performance

The software improvement process of the organization should be continuously monitored, to select areas for new improvement initiatives. Measurements of key quality and process indicators and periodic assessments can be a useful basis for this monitoring activity. New improvement cycles will be initiated based on the results of this step.

Measurement has a central role in the approach to process improvement presented here. Two types of measures are involved: measures of process capability (the assessment results) and measures of process effectiveness, specific to the specific processes in an organization. The process capability measures (the assessment profiles) are based on the generic goals of the process model. An improvement goal might be expressed in terms of achieving a particular profile of capability.

The effectiveness measures are specific to the organization and can be used to measure specific values of interest; for example, faults introduced into software at different stages of the design process may be counted and an improvement goal expressed as a ratio of number of faults against a measure of program size. In this example it is easy to relate the measured value to the quality of the product, which could be a process improvement goal. For some processes it will be less easy to define specific metrics that relate to the improvement goals. In these cases, using SPICE assessment profiles to measure improvement will be useful.

4. Using Assessment Results

An assessment can provide a detailed analysis of the strengths and weaknesses of an organization, expressed in terms of its ability to establish and maintain capable processes to achieve its key business goals. These results generally come in two forms: the detailed *findings* in terms of observed items and conclusions drawn from the available evidence; and the *process profiles,* which record the capability as a series of measurements across the processes within the scope of the assessment. The challenge facing the organization now is to use these results as the basis for a plan of prioritized improvement actions that will reinforce the strengths and address the weaknesses identified.

3.11. Prioritizing Improvement Opportunities

In many improvement approaches, the mechanism for determining the relevant priorities for action is built into the assessment model employed. This is generally the case for a model of the "staged" type, such as the Capability Maturity Model (CMM®). Where the model is continuous in nature, expressing capabilities for individual processes on a continuous scale (as is the case for ISO/IEC 15504-5), the organization must determine its own priorities for improvement based on its perceived business needs and goals.

The structure of the process model can however help in the determination of priorities. The basic architecture of the model is as defined in ISO/IEC 12207 (*Information Technology — Life Cycle Processes*) [7]. In this model, the key processes — those associated with the core business activities of the organization — are the primary processes. The primary interest of the organization, therefore, should be in building an adequate level of capability in the relevant primary processes — acquisition, supply, development, maintenance, and operation. The first step in developing the improvement plan, therefore, is to identify — from a consideration of the organization's strategic and competitive position —the core primary processes for the organization.

With the structure of the reference model providing for component processes within certain of these primary processes, a more refined view of the key processes is available that is tailored to the specific life cycle models in use within the organization. With a profile of key primary processes defined, the organization is now in a position to employ the structure of the process model to establish priorities for improvement.

With basic (level 1) capability achieved in all key primary processes, efforts should next be directed to achieving repeatable, managed performance. This will be demonstrated by the achievement of process attributes 2.1 (performance management attribute) and 2.2 (work product management attribute) in the primary processes. When we examine the nature of these processes, we see that their achievement depends on the implementation of related management and support processes.

Specifically, in seeking to achieve the performance management attribute of a primary process, we will need to have established at least basic project management performance. Equally, achievement of the work product management attribute requires performance of a range of supporting processes — at minimum, configuration management and the processes associated with quality assurance.

Thus, achievement of managed capability in the primary processes comes not from focusing on individual instances of these processes (i.e., working on a "project-by-project" basis), but rather by implementing management and supporting processes that operate across the organizational unit as a whole. The conclusion is similar to the outcome from using a staged model; however, the emphasis on the key primary processes ensures that the overall outcomes of the organization are effective in themselves. To this extent, the model itself provides good guidance on the appropriate priorities and actions to take in the initial stages of an improvement program.

Beyond this level, the picture becomes less clear-cut and more dependent on the business environment within which the organization operates. In achieving established capability (level 3) in the key primary processes, it is reasonably obvious that basic performance of the process establishment process is the key to success. However, at this level, we begin to raise questions as to priority that are complex and not readily resolved. For example, is it more important to have a defined process for design or a defined process for project management? There is no simple answer to these questions; basically, the priority depends on the business environment of the organization. If the key goal is reliability in design and implementation, then the design process may be more important; if the critical issues are schedule and project control, then the project management process will demand priority. The assumption is made — as with most model-based improvement programs — that establishing a defined process is a key milestone on the road to maturity.

3.12. Target Profiles for Improvement

The business goals of the organization become critical to the determination of the overall priorities for improvement. A useful starting point for the development of a profile of desired capability is to consider the required quality characteristics for the product(s) being provided by the organization. Techniques such as quality function deployment [12] can be applied to define the required qualities for the products; and it should be possible to relate these to a target capability profile.

No defined rules are available for the generation of such target capability profiles, and as with the current experience of use of the SPICE framework, a reliable heuristic does not exist to support the task. A strategy has been proposed for defining "target capability profiles" [13] based principally on the desired product characteristics. The strategy makes use of the key role of work products in the SPICE framework, as indicators of process and practice adequacy. A four-stage process is proposed:

1.   Identify the attributes and issues that are of importance to meeting the requirements.

2.   Map these issues to the relevant process indicators and process management indicators in the SPICE framework (from ISO/IEC TR 15504-5).

3.   From these indicators, identify the processes and capability attributes that are important in meeting the requirements.

4.   Complete the profile by identifying processes and attributes that support, or are supported by, those already identified.

Once determined, the target profile can be used flexibly to determine priorities for process improvement. The key issue should be the identification of potential business risks arising from weaknesses in the current processes, and the implementation of improvements to mitigate these risks.

As the overall levels of capability increase, the role of the assessment model in helping to define priorities for improvement actions is reduced. The use of a multiprocess continuous model of capability makes visible the many interactions and options within the organization, ensuring that the real business goals of the enterprise become the key driver for improvement.

5. The SPICE Trials

The SC7 study group report [3] recognized the possible impact of commercial and political influences within the standardization system and the potential that these might have on influencing the development schedule for the new standard. The report concluded:

> *The new standard must be soundly based on meeting user needs. It is therefore essential that the primary users of the standard are closely associated with its development. In particular, there will be a need to conduct a series of field trials to gain early feedback prior to full standardisation.*

As a result of this, a comprehensive series of user trials was incorporated into the SPICE plans [14]. Today, following the completion of the initial working draft development, the conduct of the trials is the principal function of the project. The trials have led to significant use of the draft versions of ISO/IEC 15504; it is estimated [15] that more than 1,200 assessments were performed internationally using the draft versions of the technical report.

To fit in with the differing delivery schedules of the various SPICE products and with the ISO review stages, a phased approach was adopted for the trials. The three phases were identified as having different goals:

Phase 1: Design decision and usability testing of the core products — Parts 2, 3, 4 and 5.

Phase 2: Product integration and repeatability testing — covering the full product set.

Phase 3: Validation of overall SPICE goals and standards requirements.

3.13. Findings from the Trials

The Phase 1 trials provided a unique opportunity for testing the key components of the SPICE document set [16]. Thirty-five trials were conducted throughout the world. These achieved reasonable coverage of the SPICE model for process management in a good cross-section of application domains. The results of these trials were generally positive about SPICE, although a number of issues were highlighted that needed to be addressed in the revision of the framework. [16–18] These issues, and the analysis of their impact, formed the key input for reworking of the draft documents.

Phase 2 of the trials commenced in September 1996 and extended until June 1998 [19]. Trials in this phase used primarily the preliminary draft technical report versions of ISO/IEC 15504. The internal consistency of the measurement framework for process capability (the *capability dimension*) was shown to be high [19–21]. In addition, inter-rater agreement (an important component of assessment reliability) was also shown to be high [22]. Thus, the goal of achieving a reliable approach to assessment was established.

With the formal publication of ISO/IEC 15504 as a technical report, Phase 3 of the SPICE trials has commenced. A key goal here is the ongoing collection of data to confirm the value of applying the technique of process assessment in the two key areas: process improvement and capability determination. The availability of a standard definition of the processes of the software life cycle and of a defined measurement scale for reporting evaluations of process capability also provide the opportunity to add detailed benchmarking to the tools of software process improvement [19]. The availability of such a service through Phase 3 of the SPICE trials [23] should add to the awareness of this.

6. Future Directions and Conclusions

Software process assessment is a technique that has proven value as a driver of process improvement. Evidence from the application of approaches based on the CMM [24, 25] has demonstrated that effective process improvement based on assessment can yield strong positive returns on investment Case studies of projects based on the SPICE approach [26–30], while not yet as numerous, are still indicative of similar levels of return [11].

The high level of detail and fine granularity in the SPICE assessment model offers the opportunity to obtain additional diagnostic information from an assessment, and also to scope the assessment to closely reflect the business needs and priorities of the organization, with the use of fewer resources overall. Small-scale SPICE assessments can also be used in conjunction with other approaches to validate the results of pilot-scale improvement experiments or to monitor the ongoing progress of an overall initiative.

The ongoing evolution of ISO/IEC 15504 should see its refinement into a more generic standard, applicable to the assessment of processes from a wide range of domains, and not limited to the processes of the software life cycle. The experiences with the use of the initial document set, monitored through the SPICE trials, together with the ongoing maturity of understanding of process management in systems and software engineering, have led to a significant redesign of the assessment framework [31].

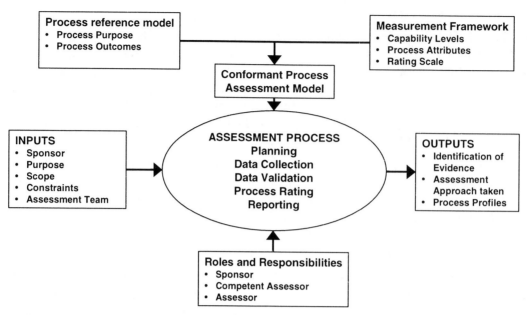

Figure 4. Revised view of the assessment process.

The most significant proposed change is to remove the process reference model (the current Part 2 of the document set) from the scope of the standard. The intent is to incorporate requirements for process reference models that will be met by current and emerging standards within the domain of JTC1/SC7 — in particular, the forthcoming amendment to ISO/IEC 12207, *Software Life Cycle Processes,* and the emerging standard for *System Life Cycle Processes,* ISO/IEC 15288. The new framework is shown in Figure 4.

The major benefit of this change is that it expands the available scope of the standard substantially. Instead of being constrained to the processes of the software life cycle, it now will define a common assessment process that can be applied to any processes defined in the required manner. The benefits of a formal assessment-based approach to process improvement will thereby be extended to any domain for which a set of suitable and generally accepted process definitions is available; in the short term, this will encompass both the software and systems life cycles and also processes associated with achieving effective usability in products.

Assessment is but one of the tools available to management in the search for improvement. Others are available — notably the quality improvement paradigm developed by Basili and others [32]. Key to the success of any improvement project, however, whatever the tools or techniques selected, is the commitment of the management of the organization.

7. References

1. Deming, W.E., *Out of the Crisis,* Cambridge, MA: MIT Center for Advanced Engineering Study, 1982.

2. Humphrey, W.S., *Managing the Software Process,* Reading, MA: Addison-Wesley, 1989.

3. ISO/IEC, *The Need and Requirements for a Software Process Assessment Standard,* Study Report, Issue 2.0, JTC1/SC7 N944R, International Organization for Standardization, Geneva, June 11, 1992.

4. ISO/IEC JTC1, *Procedures for the Technical Work of ISO/IEC JTC1*, International Organization for Standardization, Geneva, February 2000.

5. Dorling, A., "SPICE: Software Process Improvement and Capability dEtermination," *Software Quality Journal*, vol. 2, 1993, pp. 209–224.

6. ISO/IEC TR 15504:1998, *Information Technology — Software Process Assessment*, Parts 1–9, International Organization for Standardization, Geneva, 1998.

7. ISO/IEC 12207:1995, *Information Technology — Life Cycle Processes,* International Organization for Standardization, Geneva, 1995.

8. Humphrey, W.S., T.R. Snyder, and R.R. Willis, "Software Process Improvement at Hughes Aircraft," *IEEE Software,* vol. 8, no. 4, July 1991, pp. 11–23.

9. Sanders, M., ed., *The SPIRE Handbook — Better, Faster, Cheaper: Software Development in Small Organisations.* Dublin: Centre for Software Engineering, 1998.

10. McFeeley, B., "IDEAL^{SM}: A User's Guide for Software Process Improvement," CMU/SEI-96-HB-001, Software Engineering Institute, Pittsburgh, PA, 1996.

11. El Emam, K., J.-N. Drouin, and W. Melo, eds., *SPICE: The Theory and Practice of Software Process Improvement and Capability Determination,* Los Alamitos, CA: IEEE Computer Society Press, 1997.

12. Reed, B.R., and D.A. Jacobs, *Quality Function Deployment for Large Space Systems: Guidelines for Implementation of Quality Function Deployment (QFD) in Large Space Systems,* prepared for NASA by Old Dominion University, Contract NAS1-19859, Task 28.

13. Rout, T.P., "Defining Target Profiles for Determining Software Process Capability," *Proc. European Software Quality Conf.,* Dublin, September 1996.

14. Maclennan, F., and G. Ostrolenk, "The SPICE Trials: Validating the Framework," *Proc. 2nd Int'l. SPICE Symp.,* Brisbane, June 1995.

15. El Emam, K., and I. Garro, "Estimating the Extent of Standards Use: The Case of ISO/IEC 15504," *Journal of Systems and Software,* vol. 53, 2000, pp. 137–143.

16. SPICE Project, *Phase 1 Trials Report*, Version 1.00, October 12, 1995.

17. Maclennan, F., G. Ostrolenk, and M. Tobin, "Introduction to the SPICE Trials," *SPICE: The Theory and Practice of Software Process Improvement and Capability Determination,* K. El Emam, J.-N. Drouin, and W. Melo, eds., Los Alamitos, CA: IEEE Computer Society Press, 1997, pp. 269–286.

18. Marshall, P., F. Maclennan, and M. Tobin, "Analysis of Observation and Problem Reports," *SPICE: The Theory and Practice of Software Process Improvement and Capability Determination,* K. El Emam, J.-N. Drouin, and W. Melo, eds., Los Alamitos, CA: IEEE Computer Society Press, 1997, pp. 343–356.

19. SPICE Project, *Phase 2 Trials Interim Report,* June 10, 1998.

20. El Emam, K., and A. Birk, "Validating the ISO/IEC 15504 Measures of Software Development Process Capability," *Journal of Systems and Software,* vol. 51, pp. 119–149.

21. El Emam, K., and A. Birk, "Validating the ISO/IEC 15504 Measure of Software Requirements Analysis Process Capability," *IEEE Trans. Software Engineering,* vol. 26, no. 26, pp. 541–566.

22. El Emam, K., and P. Marshall, "Interrater Agreement in Assessment Ratings," *SPICE: The Theory and Practice of Software Process Improvement and Capability Determination,* K. El Emam, J.-N. Drouin, and W. Melo, eds., Los Alamitos, CA: IEEE Computer Society Press, 1997, pp. 357–362.

23. SPICE Project, *Phase 3 Trials — Call for Participation,* October 1998.

24. Herbsleb, J., A. Carleton, J. Rozum, J. Siegel, and D. Zubrow, *Benefits of CMM Based Software Process Improvement: Initial Results,* CMU/SEI-94-TR-13, Software Engineering Institute, Pittsburgh, PA, August 1994.

25. Brodman, J.G., and D.L. Johnson, "Return on Investment (ROI) from Software Process Improvement as Measured by U.S. Industry," *Software Process Improvement and Practice,* pilot issue, 1995.

26. Michielsen, C., and G. Fischer, "OSIRIS, A SPICE Based Improvement Approach towards IT Maintenance and Support Organizations," *Proc. SPICE 2000,* Limerick, Ireland, June 2000, p. 57.

27. O'Brien, S., "Using ISO/IEC TR 15504 for Software Process Improvement," *Proc. SPICE 2000,* Limerick, Ireland, June 2000, p. 107.

28. Hamann, D., P. Derks, and P. Kuvaja, "Using ISO 15504 Compliant Assessment Combined with Goal-Oriented Measurement for Process Improvement at Dräger Medical Technology," *Proc. SPICE 2000,* Limerick, Ireland, June 2000, p. 117.

29. van Loon, H., "Applying SPICE," *Proc. SPICE 2000,* Limerick, Ireland, June 2000, p. 131.

30. van Zyl, J., and A. Walker, "Process Innovation — Using the ISO/IEC TR 15504 and Additions for Building a Capable Software Development Organization," *Proc. SPICE 2000,* Limerick, Ireland, June 2000, p. 151.

31. Rout, T.P., "Evolving SPICE — The Future for ISO/IEC 15504," *Proc. SPICE 2000,* Limerick, Ireland, June 2000.

32. McGarry, F., R. Pajerski, G. Page, S. Waligora, V. Basili, and M. Zelkowitz, "Software Process Improvement in the NASA Software Engineering Laboratory," CMU/SEI-94-TR-22, Software Engineering Institute, Pittsburgh, PA, 1994.

Assessment Using SPICE: A Case Study

Jean-Martin Simon
CISI, France

A software organization with a strong quality background and an ISO 9001 registration needs to maintain the efficiency of its Quality Management System (QMS) over time. The registration program will have consumed much effort, cost, and individual investment. Once this goal has been reached, a major quality challenge will have been met and completed. However, the QMS must be maintained to support the (often new) business goals of the organization.

A common practice to check the applicability and use of the QMS' procedures is to perform internal quality audits. This basic action for quality assurance is required by the ISO 9001 standard and provides good results. Nevertheless, it is usually considered by the software practitioners of the organization to be a *control* action, rather than an opportunity to participate in the improvement of the practices and procedures.

It was for this reason that we decided to consider the Software Process Assessment (SPA) emerging standard as a new way to involve software personnel in the evolution of internal software best practices. We felt that the performance of assessments dedicated to process improvement should contribute to the overall quality of the software development activities and should provide inputs to the evolution of the QMS' procedures.

This chapter presents the results of a standalone-assessment case study using the SPICE framework. The study had been conducted during the PEACE project (ProcEss Assessment for Certification) in the context of the European Systems and Software Initiative (ESSI) June 95 call. The goals of the project were to experiment with the latest deliverables of the SPICE document set and to consider the software assessment method as a tool for quality management. This chapter also provides some practical recommendations and advice to the reader wanting to use the SPICE documents. The preparation and performance of the assessment as required by the SPICE documents in Part 3[5] and guided by Part 4[6] is explained.

Version 2.00 of the SPICE assessment model was used during the project. The results show that in the new SPICE model the *capability dimension* is more usable and the *process dimension* is more coherent. We now have an efficient model for SPA that can be used to complement internal quality audits to maintain and improve the QMS of an organization.

The PEACE project's goals

This section presents the global context of the PEACE project and discusses specific issues, mainly related to the purpose—the *assessment goals*—of the case study.

The 1995 ESSI call that was dedicated to Standalone Assessment Tasks was the perfect opportunity to evaluate the usability of a new assessment framework. At the same time, the SPICE Project had just completed the Phase 1 Trials based on Version 1.00, the results of which had been used as input to the development of Version 2.00. With a new version available, the PEACE project decided to experiment with the new version to evaluate how the assessment technique could be used to maintain a registered QMS. The assessment clearly had two goals:

1. to experiment with the new version of the SPICE software process model and assessment framework
    Since we had participated in the Phase 1 Trials,[1, 9, 12, 13, 14] we easily could compare the added value of Version 2.00 to Version 1.00.
2. to add the assessment technique to the tool set available to quality managers and quality engineers to assist them in maintaining and improving the QMS procedures.

The next section shows how these two goals influence the assessment preparation.

Performing the assessment

The following description illustrates one possible way to perform a SPICE assessment. Some of the requirements expressed in Part 3, as well as the tasks achieved in each step of the assessment, are illustrated below.

Even though the case study was not dedicated to an actual process improvement or capability determination initiative, we decided to follow the rules of assessment to perform a SPICE-conformant assessment. These rules are:

- use a model compatible with the reference model—Part 5[7] was selected

- review the defined inputs and record and document the justification of the assessment results

- satisfy the requirements of the Part 2 document[4]

- plan the expected outputs (process profiles, improvement orientations, and so on)

- include in the assessment team a qualified assessor: the author had acted as qualified assessor during the Phase 1 Trials and for other SPICE assessments.[12]

How to use the SPICE documents

Figure 18.1 shows how the different documents are combined together for use in assessing process capability and to either improve capability or consider how to determine capability using the results of the assessment.

When preparing for an assessment, the requirements of Parts 2[4] and 3[5] must be considered if the assessment is to be SPICE-conformant. Part 2 describes the two dimensions of the reference model: the process dimension and the capability dimension with its six levels. It gives a reference framework for the existing assessment methods so that the assessment results can be input into the SPICE framework and be compared. The SPICE document set also provides an assessment model in Part 5[6] that can be used for the assessment, independent of other models. The PEACE project used Part 5 as the assessment model. Chapter 7 of this book describes how the reference model in Part 2 is embedded within the Part 5 assessment model. Finally, helpful guidance is given to the qualified assessor in Part 4[6] to organize the assessment and develop the assessment plan.

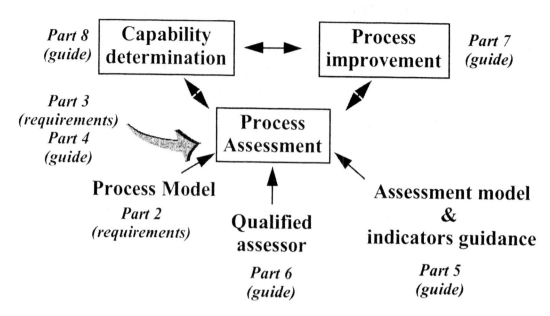

Figure 18.1: Using the SPICE document set.

The document set might be read in the following sequence:

1. the introduction in Part 1, with the help of the *Vocabulary* in Part 9 (these documents are not shown in Figure 18.1)
2. an overview of the SPICE reference model in Part 2
3. Parts 7 or 8 according to the organizational unit's (OU) assessment goals
4. Part 3 requirements and Part 4 guidance to prepare the assessment and develop the assessment strategy, with the help of Part 5 if the experiment is planned in a full SPICE context.

Assessment organization and planning

The PEACE project lasted over two and one-half months and included:

- a phase for project initialization to establish a detailed plan, to determine the requirements for the output documents, and to write the assessment plan

  During this phase, the first goal required the development of documents and forms to support the assessment process itself. To contribute to the achievement of the second goal, a preliminary analysis of the SPICE framework with the QMS of the organization was undertaken.

- an assessment phase to assess the process instances of the process within the assessment scope (see below)
- a phase to analyze the assessment output data and write the assessment and PEACE project experiment reports

At this phase of the project, a strategy was suggested for using the results of the SPICE assessments.

For the case study, the assessment tasks had been planned over a period of four weeks according to the plan presented in Figure 18.2. The assessment scope included nine processes at the project level and five processes addressing the OU. Two process instances were selected (as described in "Selecting the processes" below).

This type of planning usually provides only a high-level view and should be completed as part of the assessment plan in more detail, indicating precisely when (date and time) the meetings and interviews will be performed. The detailed schedule should be established in collaboration with the OU facilitator to guarantee the availability of each individual involved in the assessment. To define the detailed schedule, the following points must be identified clearly:

- assessment tasks to be performed—inspections of documents, meetings, interviews, feedback sessions, and so on
- assessment scope, according to the assessment purpose
- process instances, according to the assessment scope
- time allocated for each interview or meeting, according to the resources and infrastructure availability and considering the assessment budget
- project team and individuals involved
- availability of documents—*assessment inputs*
- expectations of the assessment sponsor.

A draft version of the detailed schedule should be given to the OU as soon as possible to establish the final schedule, encouraging a collaborative approach between the assessment team and the OU.

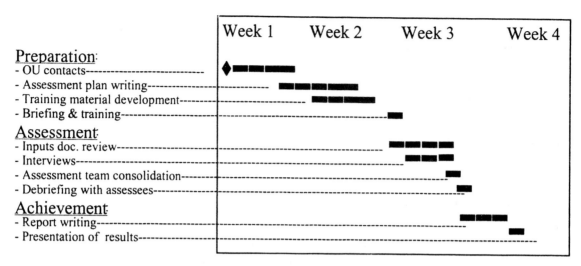

Figure 18.2: Assessment planning.

Assessment inputs

The assessment team must identify and describe in the assessment plan all the inputs to be used during the assessment, including:

- **assessment goals/purpose:** a very clear understanding of the assessment goals as defined by the sponsor is a key prerequisite for the success of the assessment

  For example, the assessment may be to assess process improvement, however, the improvement strategy will impact the assessment scope. If the experiment is based on using an assessment technique and/or participation in the SPICE Trials, the approach would be different.

- **process context:** guidance for the SPICE assessment method requires the assessment team to consider the process environment when making its judgments and determining the process attribute ratings and process capability level(s)

  As an example of specific processes, consider that ENG.3 *Develop software design* or MAN.3 *Manage risks* might have different requirements if the process is instantiated for a real-time embedded system or a client-server application lasting only three person-months.

- **level to be assessed:** indicates the investigation coverage of either the six capability levels or only a subset

- **selected processes:** the processes to be assessed are identified according to the inputs described above (see also Reference 11)

  A mapping between the SPICE standard processes and the processes of the OU might be necessary. This mapping might be the occasion to develop *extended processes* that do not exist in the standard model.[4]

- **process instances/projects:** the selected processes are assessed with *process instances* at the level of the project and/or the organization (units, department, teams, and so on)

- constraints: any constraint to be considered during the assessment must be identified, such as resource availability, confidentiality issues, sponsor requirements, assessment output data collection, and so on

- principles: a brief explanation of what the SPICE assessment philosophy is to those (such as executives) who receive the assessment plan and may not attend the training sessions, interviews, or debriefings

- **additional information to be collected:** by means of interviews (if this basic assessment technique is used), the assessment gives the opportunity to collect additional data such as improvement actions to be conducted and difficulties identified in performing project tasks or implementing internal standards and procedures.

Assessment plan

The assessment process is described in an assessment plan written by the qualified assessor, checked by the coassessor, and approved by the sponsor. For the PEACE project, the assessment plan contained the items in Figure 18.3. Some of these items are described later in this chapter.

The plan is used as a roadmap throughout the assessment. Part 4[6] gives other guidance to organize an assessment and write an assessment plan.

1. Introduction—Context
2. Terminology
3. Reference documents
4. Confidentiality agreement
5. Assessment inputs

   Assessment goals
   Assessment scope
   > *Process context*
   > *Selected processes*
   > *Levels to be assessed*
   > *OU's units concerned*
   > *Process instances/projects*

   Constraints
   Principles
6. Assessment outputs

   Process capability profiles
   Process capability levels
   Assessment report
   Experiment report
7. Role and responsibilities

   Assessment sponsor
   Qualified assessor
   Coassessors
   OU facilitator
   Participants
8. Progress tracking and quality control
9. Assessment performance

   Planning
   Briefing and training
   Assessment technique and tools
   Resources—Infrastructure—Logistics
   Document inputs
   Data collection
   Data validation
   Debriefing
   Results presentation
   Next action
10. Detailed planning

Figure 18.3: Contents of an assessment plan.

Responsibilities

The roles and responsibilities of the participants involved in the assessment process are described in the assessment plan (see Part 4). Some specific issues described are:

- **assessment sponsor:** has a strong influence on the attitude of the assessment participants—the assessees—to have (or not have) a positive and collaborative approach during the interviews
- **qualified assessor:** the assessment success depends on knowledge of the SPICE framework and assessment techniques
- **coassessors:** provides assistance and support of the qualified assessor by sharing their expertise of the processes and establishing their own judgment and ratings to compare and validate against the qualified assessor's
- **OU facilitator:** very useful when the assessment team does not know the business sector of the assessed OU, acting, in some cases, as a moderator in the event of a conflicting situation during an interview with a participant
- **participants:** require a briefing about the assessment before the interviews.

Selecting the processes

The two goals of the project, as well as the availability of internal resources for the assessment phase, determined the project's assessment scope. Nine processes addressing the software projects and five processes concerning the organization were selected:

Goal #1 suggested considering some uncommon processes from the process dimension of the model to try them out during this assessment—for example, ORG.1 *Engineer the business*. We also included in the scope processes that were not assessed during our Phase 1 Trials participation.

Goal #2 suggested considering processes that would fit closely with some of the QMS procedures—for example, the ENG process category.

Table 18.1 and Table 18.2 contain, for each assessed process, the reference to its process category and a comment to explain why it was selected. A process is supposed to contribute to the achievement of one or both of the assessment goals (see Goals #1 or #2 indicated in the tables).

One instance of each process was assessed for the organization and two instances at the project level.

Table 18.1: Processes addressing the OU.

CUS	CUSTOMER SUPPLIER PROCESS CATEGORY
CUS.5	**Provide customer service—Goal #2** The QMS and ISO 9001 are strongly oriented to the customers' satisfaction. One of the OU's business goals is to guarantee the customers' satisfaction. This satisfaction is a key issue of the QMS and should be correlated to the capability of this process.
SUP	**SUPPORT PROCESS CATEGORY**
SUP.5	**Perform work product validation—Goal #2** The validation activities are performed throughout the software life cycle. A global assessment of this process should give information on the mean capability of the validation practices inside the OU.
MAN	**MANAGEMENT PROCESS CATEGORY**
MAN.3	**Manage risks—Goal #1** This process is considered important because it might have an influence on project achievement and the satisfaction of quality requirements. The process corresponds to a recent evolution of the QMS by means of an additional procedure. This process had not been assessed before.
ORG	**ORGANIZATION PROCESS CATEGORY**
ORG.1	**Engineer the business—Goal #1** This process addresses any kind of business and is not specific to software engineering activities. It is close to the TQM approach and contributes to the global efficiency of the OU which impacts customer satisfaction. It also allows an assessment of how the internal culture is spread inside the company. This process was not assessed before.
ORG.4	**Provide skilled human resources—Goal #2** This process is also dependent on the kind of business the OU is in. Its capability reflects how management considers individuals with respect to the strategic goals of the company.

Table 18.2: Processes at the software project level.

CUS	CUSTOMER-SUPPLIER PROCESS CATEGORY
CUS.2	**Manage customer needs—Goal #1** This process was selected to determine the scope of the *needs* that are not exclusively functional and because of the impact of its capability on the relationship with the customer.
CUS.5	**Provide customer service—Goal #2** This process was selected to determine the instantiation of the process at the project level.
ENG	**ENGINEERING PROCESS CATEGORY**
ENG.3 ENG.5	**Develop software design—Goal #2** **Integrate and test software** These two processes are supported by internal procedures that should be covered by the SPICE processes.
SUP	**SUPPORT PROCESS CATEGORY**
SUP.3	**Perform quality assurance—Goal #2** This process was selected to estimate how the model covers the quality assurance and quality control activities as they are implemented in the organization according to its internal culture. The process, with MAN.2 *Manage quality* (see below), gives complementary data about quality management.
SUP.4	**Perform work product verification—Goal #2** This process was selected because the verification activities are widely addressed by the QMS procedures.
MAN	**MANAGEMENT PROCESS CATEGORY**
MAN.1	**Manage the project** This process was selected to have a global overview of the project management of the instantiated processes.
MAN.2	**Manage quality—Goal #2** See SUP.3 *Perform quality assurance*.
MAN.3	**Manage risks—Goal #1** This process was included in the assessment scope, first to evaluate how the standard procedure for risk management is implemented, and second to experiment with its assessment at the project level.

Assessment techniques

The assessment can be based on one of the following techniques:

- interviews
- individual discussions

- group discussions
- closed-team sessions where the assessment team discusses findings among themselves
- documentation inspections
- feedback sessions where the assessment team discusses findings with OU representatives
- questionnaires

Interviews are considered the most efficient means with which to collect the output data because of the interactiveness of this approach. This technique also minimizes the validation activities: the assessment plan includes a step to validate the data collected during the interviews. Feedback from a previous assessment[12] influenced the choice of interviews as the main assessment technique. The assessment team interviewed the process owners, referring (if needed) to paper-based SPICE documents and collected the assessment data online with a PC laptop. Because validated assessment tools, specific files, forms, and documents were unavailable, they were developed during the initialization phase to support the assessment.

Performance and capability rating

The process rating is made by the assessment team, using *indicators* described in Part 5[7]). Two kinds of *process performance indicators* exist:

- *base practices* corresponding to software engineering or management activities that address the purpose of a particular process: a process has between 3–12 base practices
- *work products*: process inputs and outputs—data and documents.

The *process capability indicators* are:

- *management practice*: a management activity or task that addresses the implementation or institutionalization of a specified process attribute
- *management practice characteristics*: objective attributes or characteristics dedicated to the management practice's performance, resources, and infrastructure that validate the judgment of the assessment team as to the extent of achievement of a specified process attribute.

The process performance estimations, as well as the process capability evaluations, are made using a specific *rating* scale. For each assessed process instance, the ***first step*** is to estimate the base practice's *existence* by using the following rating scale:

- *Nonexistent*: the base practice is either not implemented or does not produce any identifiable work products
- *Existent*: The implemented base practice produces identifiable work products.

The base practice adequacy is evaluated by the assessment team using a four-point adequacy rating scale (see Figure 18.4 and Figure 18.5 for the Level 1 rating).

The ***second step*** when assessing a process instance is to estimate and rate the adequacy of the management practices, using the management practice adequacy rating scale:

- ***Not adequate***: the management practice is either not implemented or does not to any degree satisfy its purpose
- ***Partially adequate***: the implemented management practice does little to satisfy its purpose
- ***Largely adequate***: the implemented management practice largely satisfies its purpose
- ***Fully adequate***: the implemented management practice fully satisfies its purpose.

This scale is very practical to assist qualified assessors in making their judgments. Instead of answering only Yes/No questions, the assessment team must consider the assessment context to estimate the adequacies with respect to the requirements of the SPICE model. All the members of the team are involved, must have a good knowledge of the SPICE process model, and also must have a fair understanding of the rating principles.

Assessment team preparation

The assessment team usually includes a qualified assessor and a coassessor. The qualified assessor has a deep understanding of the SPICE framework: the main items of concern are the process dimension of the model, the capability dimension, the assessment requirements, and the rating principles. The coassessor is experienced in software quality, software engineering, and has a good knowledge of SPICE. This assessment team in the PEACE project had already performed SPICE assessments before.

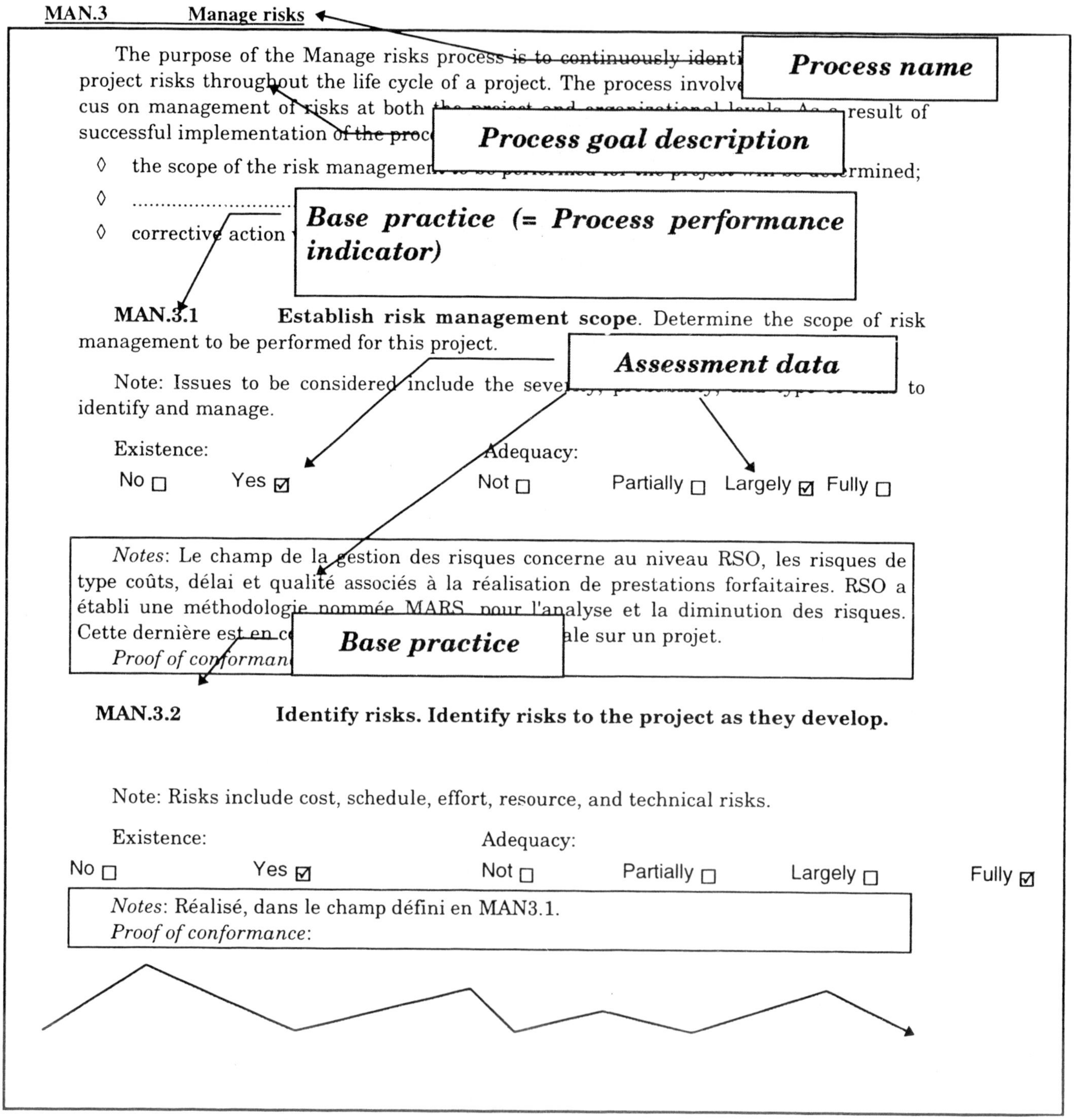

MAN.3   **Manage risks**

The purpose of the Manage risks process is to continuously identi~~fy~~ project risks throughout the life cycle of a project. The process involve~~s~~ ~~fo~~cus on management of risks at both ~~the project and organizational levels. As a~~ result of successful implementation of the proc~~ess~~

◊   the scope of the risk managemen~~t to be performed for the project will be deter~~mined;

◊   ....

◊   corrective action

> **Process name**

> **Process goal description**

> **Base practice (= Process performance indicator)**

MAN.3.1   **Establish risk management scope**. Determine the scope of risk management to be performed for this project.

Note: Issues to be considered include the seve~~rity, probability, and type of risk~~ to identify and manage.

> **Assessment data**

Existence: Adequacy:

No ☐   Yes ☑   Not ☐   Partially ☐   Largely ☑ Fully ☐

Notes: Le champ de la gestion des risques concerne au niveau RSO, les risques de type coûts, délai et qualité associés à la réalisation de prestations forfaitaires. RSO a établi une méthodologie nommée MARS pour l'analyse et la diminution des risques. Cette dernière est en c~~ours de mise en app~~le sur un projet.

Proof of conforman~~ce:~~

> **Base practice**

MAN.3.2   **Identify risks. Identify risks to the project as they develop.**

Note: Risks include cost, schedule, effort, resource, and technical risks.

Existence: Adequacy:

No ☐   Yes ☑   Not ☐   Partially ☐   Largely ☐   Fully ☑

Notes: Réalisé, dans le champ défini en MAN3.1.
Proof of conformance:

Figure 18.4: Form to collect assessment outputs (extract).

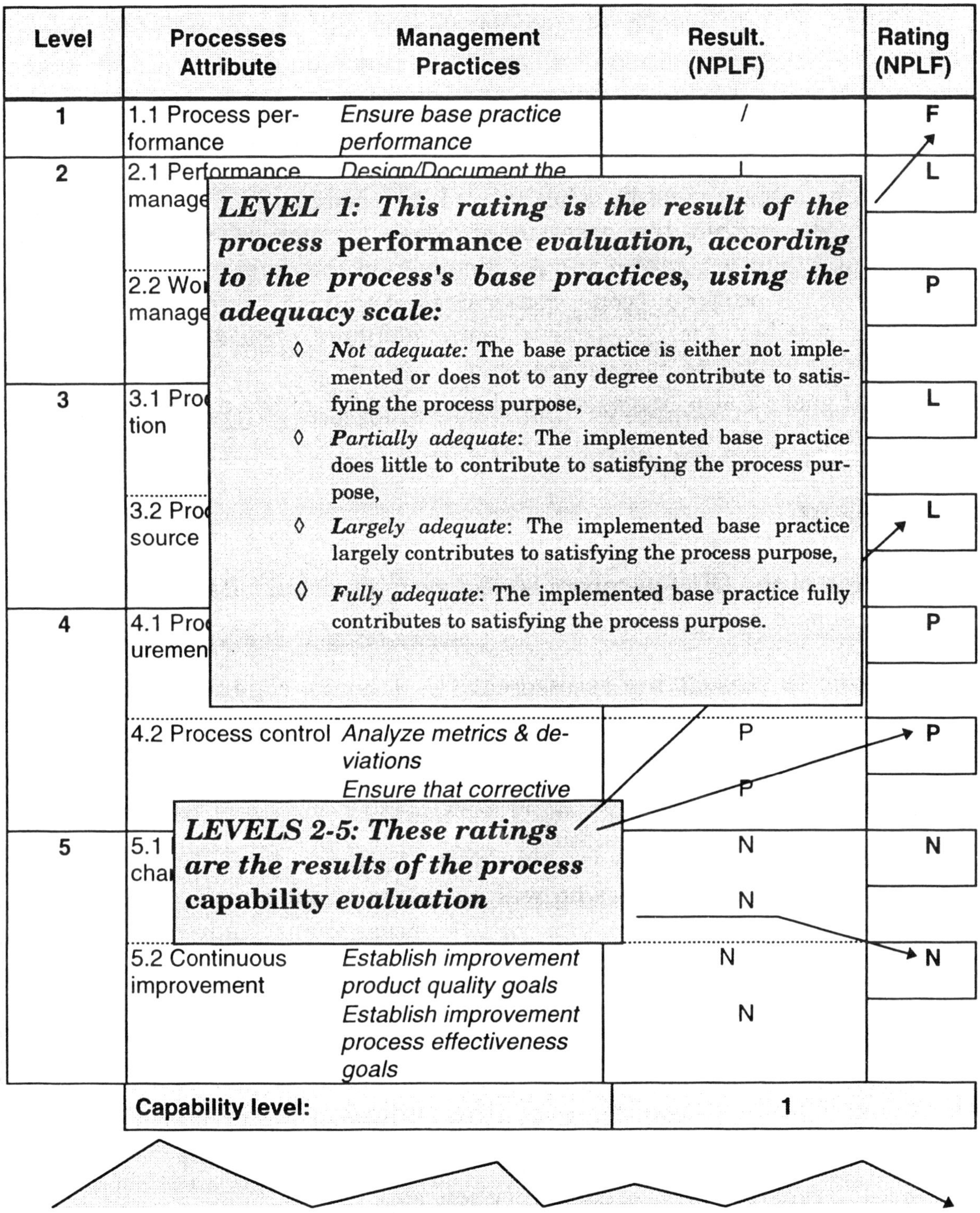

Level	Processes Attribute	Management Practices	Result. (NPLF)	Rating (NPLF)
1	1.1 Process performance	Ensure base practice performance	/	F
2	2.1 Performance manage...	Design/Document the...		L
	2.2 Wo... manage...			P
3	3.1 Pro... tion			L
	3.2 Pro... source			L
4	4.1 Pro... uremen...			P
	4.2 Process control	Analyze metrics & deviations	P	P
		Ensure that corrective	P	
5	5.1 ... cha...		N	N
			N	
	5.2 Continuous improvement	Establish improvement product quality goals	N	N
		Establish improvement process effectiveness goals	N	
	Capability level:		1	

> **LEVEL 1: This rating is the result of the process performance evaluation, according to the process's base practices, using the adequacy scale:**
>
> ◊ *Not adequate*: The base practice is either not implemented or does not to any degree contribute to satisfying the process purpose,
>
> ◊ *Partially adequate*: The implemented base practice does little to contribute to satisfying the process purpose,
>
> ◊ *Largely adequate*: The implemented base practice largely contributes to satisfying the process purpose,
>
> ◊ *Fully adequate*: The implemented base practice fully contributes to satisfying the process purpose.

> **LEVELS 2-5: These ratings are the results of the process capability evaluation**

Figure 18.5: Form for recording ratings.

A minimum of two people is usually needed for the assessment team. Depending on their experience and approach, a single qualified assessor might feel uncomfortable in having to manage the interview, listen to and record the answers and proofs of conformance, prepare the next question, and refer to SPICE documents.

The assessment team must be cohesive and knowledgeable about the parts of the SPICE model within the assessment scope (rating scheme, concept of achievement of attributes, and so on). All members of the team must be aware of the assessment: its purpose, scope, constraints, approach, planning, schedule, and so on. If possible, the assessment team members should be involved in writing and/or verifying the assessment plan.

Assessment goal #2 also suggests establishing a draft of the mapping between the scope of the QMS procedures and the processes of the SPICE model.

Preparing the OU

The preparation of the OU's members is also very important. Basically, at least two meetings should be organized:

1. a meeting to present the assessment (+/- 1 hour), conducted by the sponsor and the qualified assessor: both present to the OU staff the assessment purpose, scope, constraints, how the assessment will be conducted, the benefits of assessment results, and the principles for confidentiality and ownership

2. a training session (a ½ day is a minimum) for the assessment participants, in particular those who will be interviewed: members of the assessment team explain the SPICE assessment approach and method they will use.

   During the half-day course for the PEACE project, the following items were presented:

   1.   process improvement for software quality improvement
   2.   software process concepts: the ISO 12207[2] standard
   3.   software process capability concepts
   4.   other models for assessing software process capability
   5.   the ISO/SPICE Project
   6.   the ISO/SPICE Part 2 reference model—rating rules
   7.   the assessment technique and method

8.   the SPICE Part 5 assessment model

9.   assessment performance and output examples.

To provide a short overview of the SPICE framework, Part 1[3,] the introduction document, might also be distributed to the participants.

Risk analysis

When preparing the assessment, a risk analysis should be done to guarantee the achievement of the assessment goals. Potential risks include unavailability of documentation, OU individuals' availability, resistance from the OU to provide information, changes to the purpose or scope of the assessment, and lack of confidentiality.

Assessment results

Assessment report

The assessment outputs, shown below as graphical representations, are useful to provide a global overview of process capability. Nevertheless, it is essential to write a full assessment report and to record all the collected data. Depending on the assessment goals, other documents might be necessary, such as an improvement plan and an assessment experiment report. Table 18.3 is an example of an assessment report that includes comments for each process instance—typically improvement opportunities—as well as feedback about the assessment process itself.

The assessment report is dedicated mainly to the assessment sponsor, but it also should be distributed to those who have collaborated in the assessment: we observed that the people interviewed had a strong expectation of feedback as a result of their collaboration.

The capability of each process instance was included in the assessment report to represent graphically (Figure 18.6) the detailed achievement of the different attributes.

This representation gives a detailed view of process capability, compared to Figure 18.8 which shows only the global process capability level.

Table 18.3: Elements of an assessment report.

1. Introduction—Context
2. Terminology
3. Reference documents
4. Confidentiality agreement
5. Assessment inputs overview
     Assessment goals
     Assessment scope
     Process context
     Selected processes
6. Assessment results
     Process capability profiles
     Process capability levels
7. Comments per process instances
     Process instances from project 1
     Process instances from project n
     Process instances from Organization 1
     Process instances from Organization n
8. Assessment feedback
     Resources—Infrastructure—Logistics
     Assessment technique and performance
     Meeting—Training—Presentation
     Planning—Schedule
9. Further actions
10. Quality control records
11. Annexes:
     A1: Assessment records
     A2: SPICE process dimension
     A3: SPICE capability dimension

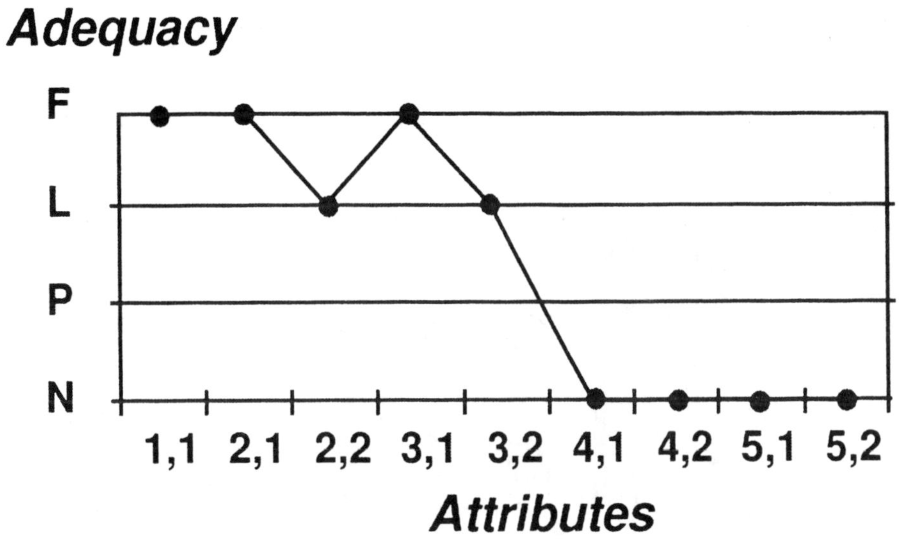

Adequacy

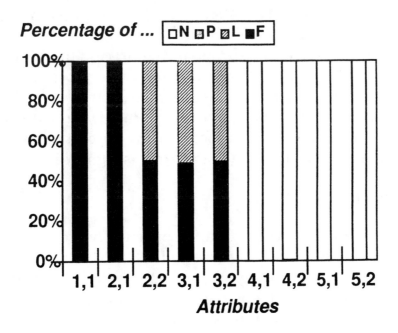

Figure 18.6: Example of process capability profile (Level = 2).

The attributes achievement represented in Figure 18.6 is useful for revealing the strength and weakness in the process capability and also to compare two processes capabilities (see Figure 18.10).

By combining the attribute ratings of different instances of the *same process*, we obtained derived ratings showing the attribute rating distribution (Figure 18.7). This representation highlights the global process capability.

Figure 18.7: Attribute rating distribution.

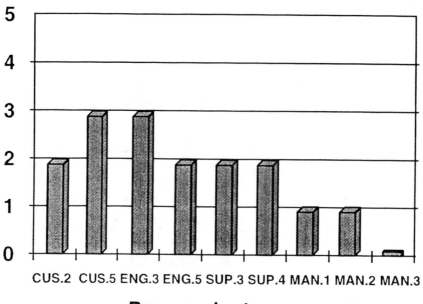

Capability Level

Process Instance

Figure 18.8: Process capability level.

Process capability level

The reference model for process assessment[4] indicates how to determine the capability level for a process instance by using the attribute ratings (also see chapter 6). Complementing the capability profile represented in Figure 18.6, the capability level gives a global value of the process capability.

By combining the capability levels from all the process instances, we obtained another derived rating. Figure 18.9 represents the process capability level distribution for all processes within the assessment scope:

Other representations can be used, but these graphical results are based only on assessment records and do not correspond to any absolute measurements: any variation of +/- 10 percent must not be considered as significant.

Improvement opportunities

An assessment is (almost) always an opportunity to identify potential suggestions for improvements. In the case of PEACE, the assessment report contained a mean value of two significant improvement actions per process instance. This assessment output was not expected initially to satisfy any of the goals, but provided added value to the experiment.

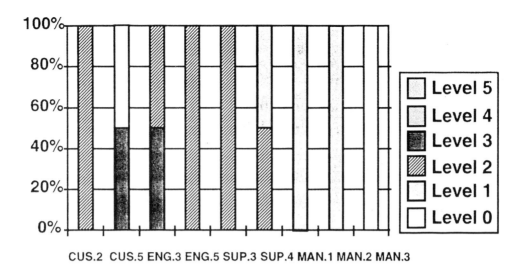

Figure 18.9: Process capability distribution.

Participants' feedback

Whenever an assessment has been performed within an organization or project that initially had no awareness of the SPA philosophy, we have observed a high degree of interest from participants, even if they already had a quality-oriented culture. The assessment is a good opportunity to introduce new concepts for managing the processes. During the PEACE project, everyone collaborated very positively and we did not have any problem collecting the data. Other experiences show an average of 4 percent of participants have a negative attitude against the assessment approach and the SPICE framework.

From the assessment sponsor's point of view, we have always been able to provide a satisfying appreciation of the assessment performance and results.

Case study results

This section describes some of the problems and remarks made during the assessment about the process and capability dimensions of the model described in Part 5, Version 1.00. At the end of 1996, the SPICE Project had integrated changes into the model for assessment to establish Version 2.00. Nevertheless, some problems are still significant, even for the reference model in Part 2 and should be tracked during the Phase 2 SPICE Trials.

Process dimension

The major changes in Version 2.00 were:

- changes or clarification of some areas
- a new distribution of activities and a global reduction of the number of processes from 35 to 29.

Below are examples of comments concerning the assessed processes:

- CUS.2 *Manage customer needs*: this process requires the OU to manage all types of requirements, functional and nonfunctional. Its assessment interferes with process ENG.2 concerning software requirements.

- CUS.5 *Provide customer service*: the constitutive base practices make it difficult to assess an instance at the level of the organization

- ENG.5 *Integrate and test software*: the distribution of the base practices are not clear enough: the tasks for integration testing, validation testing, and qualification should be more explicit

- SUP.3 *Perform quality assurance*: the base practices are not coherent enough: the process should be more specific, such as "Define the project quality framework"

- SUP.5 *Perform work product validation*: the process description addresses any kind of validation, but the base practices only address code validation and overlap with the ENG.5 process for *Integration and test*.

- MAN.1 *Manage the project*: the process description should include *effective project tracking* (see the base practice MAN.1.11). The base practice MAN.1.10 could be removed

- MAN.2 *Manage Quality*: the process has a strong quality goals orientation that is barely implemented in actual situations and anticipates the state-of-the art

- MAN.3 *Manage risks*: the process description should contain actions at the organizational level since the process is not implemented at only the project level. The base practice MAN.3.5 *Define risk metrics* belongs in Level 4. An adaptation could be made with the notion of risk tracking indicators.

Capability dimension

The evolution of this dimension corresponds to a major change in the SPICE software process model architecture. The Part 2 reference model used during the case study has a six-level capability dimension, each of which has two attributes (except for Levels 0 and 1).

For level determination, the rule to apply to determine the capability of a process makes it possible to give the same capability to two processes with strong differences in the achievements of the attributes. For example, see Figure 18.10.

The process instance A presents a higher capability than the instance B because the attributes 2.2, 3.1, 4.1, and 4.2 have attained a higher achievement. This aspect of the level's determination is not a real problem if the mechanism is clearly known and understood by those using the assessment results. On the other hand, the new concept of process capability level is useful for global comparison or improvement tracking.

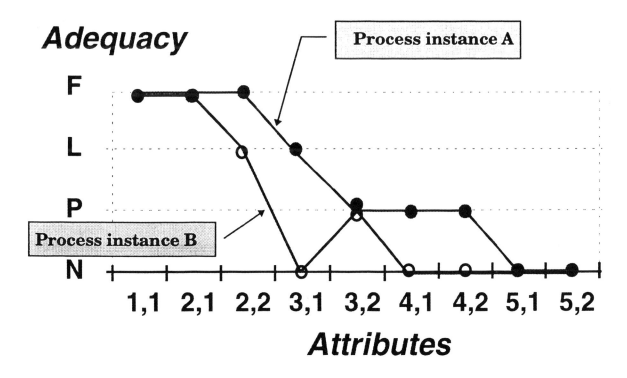

Figure 18.10: Two processes A and B at Level 2.

- *attribute 1.1 rating*: The attribute 1.1 indicates process performance and by using Part 5, Version 1.00, indicators are available: base practices and work products' input/output. There is no formal rule to determine the attribute rating after having estimated the existence and adequacy of the base practices.

- *ratings of the attributes 2.1 to 5.2*: Similarly, the principle to determine the rating of these attributes from their two management practices is not defined

- *attribute 3.1 process definition*: This attribute stipulates that the business goals are defined: they should be adapted. Also, 3.1 interacts with ORG.1

Using SPICE for managing quality

The second goal of the assessment was to consider the SPICE assessment to support the implementation and evolution of standard procedures. The assessment allowed us to estimate the implementation of a specific procedure's scope as covered by some processes of the model—*project management* in the case of the experiment. Using this approach, we mapped the whole set of procedures included in the QMS to the SPICE process model so that assessments could be performed during the quality assurance actions that had been planned to maintain the QMS. The mapping also has the benefit of being a complementary analysis of the ISO 9001 requirements.[10]

Project statistics

The two months of the project were divided roughly into

- Phase 1—initialization: one month
- Phase 2—assessments: two weeks
- Phase 3—assessment results and experiment analysis: one additional month.

The initial estimations for costs and effort were followed closely and were adequate. The overall method for the assessment preparation, planning, data collection, and validation was satisfactory because it was based on experience gained in previous assessments.

Nevertheless, this kind of experience might be improved upon with a less-conflicting selection of the assessment goals: Goal #1 suggested selecting some processes with which to experiment with the SPICE model, some specific or new processes of SPICE available only in Version 2.00. However, Goal #2 involved selecting some processes covering clearly some of the QMS procedures.

Conclusion

The PEACE project allowed us to experiment with the new version of the SPICE framework for process assessment. The case study confirmed that the SPICE documents are an operational tool for managing software quality. Both the process model that gives a reference framework for SPA and the assessment model are operational.

One of the most efficient approaches to using the assessment technique for internal quality improvement is to tailor the process assessment model to the specifics of the QMS, with the result being a customized model. This activity would involve changing and adapting base practices, work products, or even adding specific processes, called *extended processes*. All these actions can be performed by keeping compliance with the assessment reference model. Further action should also include adding new processes to the QMS and planning assessments to occur at the same time as the internal quality audits.

References

1. El Emam, K. and D.R. Goldenson, "Some Initial Results from the International SPICE Trials," *IEEE TCSE Software Process Newsletter*, No. 6, Spring 1996.

2. ISO/IEC 12207, *Information technology—Software Life Cycle Processes*, 1st Ed., Aug. 1995.

3. ISO/IEC/JTC1/SC7/WG10/N101, *Software Process Assessment—Part 1: Concepts and Introductory Guide*, July 1996

4. ISO/IEC/JTC1/SC7/WG10 WD N102, *Software Process Assessment—Part 2: A Reference for Process and Process Capability*, July 1996.

5. ISO/IEC/JTC1/SC7/WG10 WD N103, *Software Process Assessment—Part 3: Performing an Assessment*, July 1996.

6. ISO/IEC/JTC1/SC7/WG10 WD N104, *Software Process Assessment—Part 4: Guide to Performing an Assessment*, July 1996.

7. ISO/IEC/JTC1/SC7/WG10/OWG WD N103, *Software Process Assessment—Part 5: An Assessment Model and Indicator Guidance*, Version 1.006, 18 Aug. 1996.

8. ISO/IEC/JTC!/SC7/WG10, *Software Process Assessment—Part 5: An Assessment Model and Indicator Guidance*, Version 2.00, 1996.

9. Marshall, P., F. Maclennan, and M. Tobin, "Analysis of Observation and Problem Reports from Phase 1 of the SPICE Trials," *IEEE TCSE Software Process Newsletter*, No. 6, Spring 1996.

10. Radice, R.D., *ISO 9001 Interpreted for Software Organizations*, Paradoxicon Publishing, 1995.

11. Simon, J.M., "Choosing the Process for the Assessment Scope: A Key Factor for SPICE Assessment Success," *Proc. European Conf. Software Process Improvement — SPI95*, 1995.

12. Simon, J.M., "Experiences in the Phase 1 SPICE Trials," *IEEE TCSE Software Process Newsletter*, No. 8, Winter 1996.

13. SPICE Project. *Phase 1 Trials Report*, Version 1.00, Oct. 1995.

14. Woodman, I. and R. Hunter, "Analysis of Assessment Data from Phase 1 of the SPICE Trials," *IEEE TCSE Software Process Newsletter*, No°6, Spring 1996.

The Rapid Assessment of Software Process Capability

T.P. Rout, A. Tuffley, B. Cahill and B. Hodgen

Software Quality Institute, Griffith University, Queensland, Australia

Abstract

There is a strategic need for a cost-effective method of conducting ISO/IEC 15504 conformant assessments of the capability of software development projects. This applies particularly in the case of SMEs for whom the cost of a full three to four day assessment may be prohibitive. The **R**apid **A**ssessment for **P**rocess **I**mprovement for software **D**evelopment (RAPID), has been developed to address this need. The RAPID method, which is intended for use by experienced ISO 15504 assessors is specifically for process improvement and is not suitable for supplier management. By limiting the scope of the assessment to eight key processes and limiting the collection of evidence to facilitated discussion between key organizational personnel and the assessors, a RAPID assessment can be conducted in one day.

1.   Introduction

The techniques generically described as Software Process Assessment have their origin in the TQM movement, and derive from the basic premise that the quality of manufactured products is largely determined by the quality of the processes which produce them[1]. As Humphrey[2] points out, the first step in any program to improve software capability is to understand the current status of the development process. Process Assessment is the means of achieving this; the technique is defined as:

> "The disciplined examination of the processes used by an organisation against a set of criteria to determine the capability of those processes to perform within quality, cost and schedule goals. The aim is to characterise current practice, identifying strengths and weaknesses and the ability of the process to control or avoid significant causes of poor quality, cost and schedule performance."[3]

The increasing number of assessment approaches available, and the increasing use of the technique in commercially-sensitive areas, were the key motivating factors behind the development and acceptance of a proposal to develop an International Standard for software process assessment. ISO/IEC TR 15504:1998 [4] sets out requirements for the assessment of process capability for processes in the software life cycle. ISO 15504 describes an overall framework for software process assessment that is designed to result in reliable and consistent assessments that yield results that allow comparison between different assessment methods. The framework effectively provides the basic elements of a defined process for performing assessments, through prescribing minimum required inputs and outputs, and a required set of activities. The definitions of inputs, outputs and activities are designed to assure repeatability and consistency in the assessment process, in order to provide confidence that assessment results can be seen as reliable and objective.

Process assessment is typically seen as requiring intensive use of resources. Wiegers and Sturzenberger [5] point out that many organizations have developed small-scale assessment approaches to support improvement projects in between full scale assessments, and a similar strategy is described by Natwick et al [6]. The SPIRE Project [7] points out the importance of assessment in improvement projects for small and medium size enterprises, and correctly identifies the need for a specific approach to such assessment. The approach they select, however, while adequately diagnostic, does not claim to be conformant with the international standard, and the results are seen as applicable within the organization, with only limited applicability of comparisons such as benchmarking.

A key issue for many small and medium size companies - in particular - is the ability to obtain meaningful and reliable evaluations of capability with limited investment of time and resource. The **R**apid **A**ssessment for **P**rocess **I**mprovement for software **D**evelopment (RAPID), has been developed to address this need. The RAPID method is purely designed for process improvement and is not intended to be adopted for supplier management.

2.   Design Concerns

RAPID defines an approach to assessment that delivers consistent evaluations of process capability based upon an intensive investigation of the operations of the organization. The approach is based upon the following principles:

1. The assessment is conducted within a one-day timeframe to minimise the cost and investment of time and resource required by small to medium sized companies.

2. The assessment is based upon an assessment model of limited scope, with a standard set of eight processes; the high level Software Development process (ENG.1) is assessed as a whole, without disaggregation into its component processes.

3. The competence and experience of the assessors is seen as of primary importance. A team of two assessors with experience in performing full-bodied assessments based upon ISO 15504 is used for a RAPID assessment. Competency is focussed on assessors who have completed training as ISO/IEC 15504 assessors, with formal education relevant to the field of software engineering, and experience in the performance and management of software development.

4. Data collection is limited to the single technique of moderated discussion by performers of the processes - the management team and other members of the organization.

5. Generation of ratings of capability is performed by a process of consensus-gathering involving all of the participants in the discussion, rather than by judgement of the assessors.

Restricting the assessment to one day rather than a more intense three to four day assessment, enables small organizations to participate in a process capability assessment. Most organizations are willing to invest a day of their time and resource without feeling the impact of the assessment on their commitments. It also allows the cost of the assessment to be more attractive.

The RAPID method employs a defined assessment model of restricted scope, based upon and compatible with the Process Reference Model of ISO 15504-2. The model includes only the eight processes listed in Table 1.

Table 1. - Process Scope of the RAPID Assessment Model

Requirements Gathering	CUS.3
Software Development	ENG.1
Project Management	MAN.2
Configuration Management	SUP.2
Quality Assurance	SUP.3
Problem Resolution	SUP.8
Risk Management	MAN.4
Process Establishment	ORG.2.1

The core of the model is the primary processes of Requirements Gathering (identical to the Requirements Elicitation process of ISO 15504-2) and Software Development. As discussed above, the development process is not disaggregated into its component processes. The remaining processes have been selected on the basis of their support for the capabilities associated with Levels 2 and 3 on the capability scale; they include Project Management, Configuration Management, Quality Assurance and Problem Resolution, which are critical to achievement of the attributes of Process Performance and Work Product Management. Finally, the "strategic" processes of Risk Management and Process Establishment have been included as providing a platform for improvement beyond the Managed level. The Capability Dimension of the assessment model is identical in structure to that in ISO 15504-2; for most assessments, the scope of the model is limited to Levels 1, 2 and 3. Ratings of capability at Levels 4 and 5 are possible if required.

The indicators employed in the assessment model are based upon the design decision to limit data collection to interviews only. The principal indicators are a series of questions designed to facilitate the structured discussion that is at the heart of the assessment. Table 2 lists the questions applicable to the Requirements Gathering process at Level 1.

There is a complete set of questions / indicators for each process across all capability levels; this provides in the end a set of 210 questions in the model. The questions / indicators are based on an analysis of the outcomes of the processes, and the results of achievement of the various process attributes for each capability level. The assessment model is incorporated into a paper-based assessment instrument which is employed as the basis for the discussions in the assessment; all participants are provided with a copy of the instrument.

Table 2 - Capability Indicators for Requirements Gathering - Level 1

Does the process for gathering requirements as implemented in this organization achieve its expected outcomes?
Do the company personnel understand the scope of the requirements gathering process ?
Are there identifiable input work products for requirements gathering? Identify
Are there identifiable output work products from requirements gathering? Identify
Has your company established continuing communications with your key customers?
Do you have a clear understanding of the customer's requirements for each project?
Is there a means for identifying new customer needs and reflecting this in the requirements?
Do you monitor the needs of your customers on a continuous basis?
Can your customers readily establish the status of their requests?
Do you have a program for ongoing enhancement of your products?

Results from the SPICE Trials [8] indicate that the experience and competence of the assessment team are significant factors in determining the reliability of the assessment results. Accordingly, RAPID places substantial emphasis on assessor competence for the method. The two assessors conducting the assessment adopt two roles: team leader and support assessor. The team leader prepares the plan of the assessment with the sponsor of the organization and during the assessment facilitates the discussion of the capabilities of the processes by encouraging frank and open discussion about the activities of the organization. The support assessor's primary duty is to record the evidence discussed against the relevant sections of the assessment instrument.

Restricting the data collection to moderated discussions places the onus on the organization to present a fair and accurate report of their activities within the processes assessed. It is stressed that by not doing this, the assessors will be unable to identify areas of improvement for the organization and hence would not gain the benefit of having a RAPID assessment conducted.

The consensus on ratings is discussed at the end of the assessment allowing the participants to understand where their strengths and weaknesses lie and areas that present opportunities for improvement. This reduces any surprises occurring when the assessment is report is presented after the assessment.

2.1   Issues in Conducting Assessments

Before conducting a RAPID assessment, the team leader contacts the sponsor of the organization to be assessed, to determine the organizational demographics. These demographics are recorded utilising a standard questionnaire, which is then used as an input to the RAPID assessment plan again using a standard template. From the demographics and discussions with the sponsor, it can be determined which instances of the organization will be assessed using RAPID. Generally, due to the small size of the organizations for which this method is targeted, the entire organization is assessed, however for larger organizations, specific instances of projects or product streams will be the focus of the RAPID assessment.

The team leader is responsible for facilitating the discussions of the process attributes by asking the participants about "How" they perform the processes assessed. As far as possible, the team leader does not "tell" the organization about the processes except when clarification is required. This reduces the possibility of the participants trying to give the "right" answer rather than the actual "correct" answer. The team leader has to elicit the answers from the discussions with the organization. The primary role of the support assessor is to record the evidence against the relevant sections in the assessment instrument. This ensures that all aspects of the process are investigated and the support assessor can point out any areas that require further evidence.

When conducting the RAPID assessment most of the morning of the site visit to assessing the first two processes, Requirement Gathering and Software Development with the possibility of touching on Project Management. After a lunch break the remaining five to six supporting processes are assessed much more quickly, as much of the evidence has been noted while discussing the first two processes. On one occasion the management processes needed to discussed first due to the availability of relevant personnel; interestingly, the assessment was performed within the same constraints without difficulty, with only two touching on three processes assessed in the initial discussions and the remaining assessed later. Again, much of the evidence was noted while assessing the first two processes.

At the completion of the RAPID assessment, the team leader presents key findings from the day. The findings firstly focus on the strengths of the organization highlighting what they actually are performing well. Then the weaknesses which present opportunities for improvement are discussed and agreed with the customer. Any differences of opinion can be addressed immediately and a resolution agreed before the assessment is concluded. To date, there have been very few instances of disagreement between the assessors and the customers, rather the customers have already realised from the discussions during the day, what their strengths and weaknesses are.

The method makes extensive use of templates for the assessment plan, organizational context, and reports thereby reducing the cost and the time required by the assessors to manage the assessment and produce the required documentation.

3.   Application and Results

RAPID assessments have been conducted in South East Queensland, Australia during the last six months of 1999, involving to date 25 organizations with a further five assessment planned for the early part of 2000. It is also planned in 2000, to transition this method nationally to all states of Australia.

The size of the organizations assessed so far ranges from 3 to 120 employees with an average size of 10 - 12 employees. All organizations are based in South East Queensland, primarily in the Brisbane region. All of the organizations are in the software development industry most of which are using leading edge technologies.

These technologies include object orientated development (OOD), fourth generation languages (4GL) and Internet technologies.

Organizations participating in the process improvement program tend to have intimate knowledge of their selected market. The organizations have fostered a very close relationship with their clientele and have a good understanding of their clientele's requirements. The assessors conducting the RAPID assessment were drawn from a pool of nine people. These assessors ranged from highly experienced ISO/IEC 15504 assessors, who have conducted numerous SPICE assessments over the past six years to assessors who have completed ISO/IEC 15504 SPICE Assessor Training and have limited additional experience. In all cases, the less experienced assessors filled positions of support assessor. All assessors are registered with the Software Quality Institute, Australia.

The effort required to conduct RAPID assessments is minimised by limiting the scope of the assessment and utilising standard templates for the organizational demographics, the assessment plan, and the assessment report. Table 3 gives a breakdown of the typical effort required by participants to conduct a completed RAPID assessment.

Table 3 – Breakdown of Typical Effort for a RAPID Assessment

Task	Person(s) involved	Typical Effort
Prepare and send demographic questionnaire	Team leader	15 minutes
Complete demographic questionnaire	Sponsor	15 minutes
Prepare Assessment Plan	Team leader	30 minutes
Prepare Assessment Instrument	Team leader	30 minutes
Conduct RAPID Assessment	Team leader Support Assessor Organization Participants	8 hours 8 hours 8 hours
Prepare Assessment Report	Team leader Support Assessor	6 hours 4 hours

Feedback from the RAPID assessments has been favourable, with organizations expressing further interest in adopting process improvement programs. Figure 1 shows the results expressed as Capability Level ratings from 15 of the assessments conducted so far, across the eight processes in the RAPID model. The profile of results is consistent with results from the SPICE Trials in Australia, and indicate generic areas of strength and weakness that are not unusual for the small - medium size enterprise. It is noteworthy that there are significant weaknesses in Process Establishment (not surprising, since most of the participants have not attempted to establish formal quality management systems at this stage) and notably in Problem Resolution (which would imply a significant opportunity for improvement).

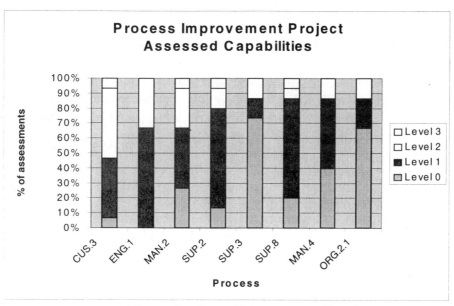

Figure 1 - Overall Assessment Results

It was noted – though the process was not formally assessed – that measurement practices were either non-existent or poorly performed across all of the organizations in the process improvement program. The lack of measurement included critical areas such as estimation and resourcing of projects, where proper measurement would mean better estimation of time and resources for future projects. Also due to the lack of measurement there is often no warning of slippage in projects. The problems with measurement are related to the lack of documentation within most of these organizations in that many of the processes are not defined nor documented, in order to have a baseline to measure from.

4. Validation Strategy

In order to validate the RAPID assessment profiles, five of the organizations that have had a RAPID assessment conducted are participating in a more detailed three to four day assessment of their process capabilities incorporating the scope of the RAPID method. These assessments are currently in progress and will be conducted within the next one to two months.

The purpose of these assessment is to develop a detailed process improvement plan to be implemented over 10 to 12 months. During this period, the organization will be mentored by a quality consultant to ensure that the process improvement activities are being performed. At the end of the period, another detailed assessment will be conducted to gauge the effectiveness of the process improvement activity.

It is expected that during this validation of RAPID, any weaknesses with the model will be uncovered. Possible weaknesses could be the accuracy of ratings, and design constraints such as employing only interviews as the evidence collection rather than work product inspections and assessing the development process as a whole rather than at the component level.

5.   Summary and Conclusions

One of the strengths of RAPID lies in the customer's involvement with the assessment. By participating throughout the whole assessment, they buy-in to the results of the assessment. The customer is able to identify the strengths and weaknesses in their own processes, via the facilitated discussions of their practices led by the team leader. This is evidenced at the conclusion of the assessment when the findings of the assessors are being discussed and agreed with the customers. It is at this point that the customer agrees on the findings and any discrepancies can be fully discussed, although to date

The restricted scope of RAPID and the timeframe of one-day, makes RAPID a feasible assessment for small organizations, since the cost of having the assessment is not exorbitant.. It only requires one day of their key personnel time as opposed to three or four days and most organizations can afford to dedicate one day to the assessment without significantly impacting any work in progress. In addition, if an unforeseen event occurs, it is much easier to re-schedule another day that suits all the participants.

RAPID was developed specifically for small organizations, however, it has been successfully performed in larger organizations, and it seems that it has strong potential for performance of snapshot assessments on projects within the larger organization. The RAPID method could be improved by the development of an appropriate automated assessment instrument to record the evidence rather than using the current paper based version; members of the RAPID team are investigating this possibility during the coming year.

By restricting and fixing the scope of the assessment to the eight processes, it is possible to quickly provide benchmarking information for organizations assessed using RAPID. Also, since RAPID is conformant with ISO 15504 assessments, the results of the RAPID assessment can be benchmarked against other assessment models. The results of RAPID assessments will be submitted to Phase 3 SPICE Trials database. This will provide participants with benchmarking against organizations internationally.

The most significant finding from the improvement exercise has been the positive feedback from the participating companies. Without exception there has been agreement that the findings were consistent with the experiences of the companies, and it appears that the program has provided significant impetus for the implementation of appropriate improvement initiatives.

6.   References

1. Deming, W.E., *Out of the Crisis*. Cambridge, MA: MIT Center for Advanced Engineering Study, 1982.

2. Humphrey, W.S., *Managing the Software Process*. Reading, MA: Addison-Wesley, 1989.

3. ISO/IEC JTC1/SC7, *The Need and Requirements for a Software Process Assessment Standard*, Study Report, Issue 2.0, JTC1/SC7 N944R, 11 June 1992.

4. ISO/IEC TR 15504: 1998, *Information technology - Software process assessment*, Parts 1 - 9.

5. Wiegers, K.E. and D.C Sturzenberger, "A Modular Software Process Mini-Assessment Method", *IEEE Software,* January 2000, pp 62 - 69.

6. Natwick, G., G. Draper, and L. Bearden, "Software Mini-Assessments: Process and Practice", *CROSSTALK: The Journal of Defense Software Engineering*, October 1999, pp 10 - 14.

7. SPIRE Project Team, *The SPIRE Handbook: Better, Faster, Cheaper Software Development in Small Organizations*, Centre for Software Engineering, Dublin, 1998.

8. SPICE Project, *Phase 2 Trials Interim Report*, June 1998.

9. Software Quality Institute, *Method for the RAPID Assessment of Process Capability,* Griffith University, Brisbane, Queensland, Australia, 30 August 1999

10. Software Quality Institute, *Process Model for the RAPID Assessment of Process Capability,* Griffith University, Brisbane, Queensland, Australia, 30 June 1999.

SPiCE for Space: A Method of Process Assessment for Space Software Projects

Ann Cass, Christian Völcker, Paolo Panaroni[1], Alec Dorling[2] and Lothar Winzer[3]

SYNSPACE AG

Binningen, Switzerland

Abstract

As part of a programme[4] for software process improvement sponsored by the European Space Agency (ESA), an ISO 15504 conformant method for software process assessment has been developed. Called SPiCE for Space™, or S4S, the method aims to encourage the production of the best possible software products and services within the European space industry.

The S4S method includes an assessment model based on the ISO 15504 exemplar model, with the process dimension considerably refined to incorporate space software practices. Four new processes, approximately 50 new base practices, and an even larger number of new notes have been added following ESA standard requirements for the production of space software. A documented method leads space assessors step by step from Initiation to Reporting. Finally, a software tool based on the product SPICE 1-2-1 and templates of key outputs support the performance of S4S assessments.

Four pilot assessments of space software projects were performed in October 1999 and a further series of trial assessments began in February 2000. By promoting the best practice concepts of SPICE and addressing the specific needs of space software, ESA expects S4S to emerge as the prevailing tool of process improvement within the European space software industry.

1 Background

The Product Assurance and Safety Department of the European Space Agency is developing a method of process assessment as part of a programme of software process improvement within the European space industry. As increasingly more critical functions in space systems are implemented in software, the need grows for high quality software products. Experience in the software industry has shown that an effective

---

[1] Intecs Sistemi S.p.a., Rome, Italy
[2] InterSPICE Ltd, London, England
[3] European Space Agency, Noodwijk, Netherlands
[4] Supported under ESTEC Contract Number 10662/93/NL/NB CCN4

means of improving a company's software products is by improving its process of producing software [1]. Thus, it is desirable to provide space software suppliers with a method to evaluate their processes in order to identify potential improvements within their organisations. The same assessment method may be used by space software customers to evaluate the capability of current and potential suppliers. Furthermore, the method may be used by suppliers to verify their compliance with ESA process requirements.

As a first step, three approaches for assessing software processes, CMM [2], BOOTSTRAP [3,4] and ISO/IEC TR 15504 [5], were examined for their compatibility and adaptability to space specific requirements. None of the evaluated assessment schemes could be used as-is for ESA purposes, as space specific aspects like safety, dependability and in-flight software maintenance are not addressed explicitly in any of the approaches. As the emerging international standard based on software best practices, ISO/IEC TR 15504 (hereafter referred to as ISO 15504) was considered the most suitable baseline of an ESA method of process assessment [6]. SYNSPACE AG was selected to lead the development of the new method with technical support from Intecs Sistemi, Objectif Technologie and InterSPICE. DNV provided managerial support for the project.

2 Introduction to SPiCE for Space

SPiCE for Space, or S4S, is the method of space software assessment for ESA developed by SYNSPACE. S4S consists of an assessment model based on the exemplar model of Part 5 of ISO 15504; a documented process, including expert guidance for performing the assessment; and a software tool to assist in rating, record keeping, and reporting. Templates for assessment outputs, such as assessment plans and reports, are also included in S4S.

The S4S assessment method is published by ESA in the form of a two-part internal Technical Note [7]. Part A contains the S4S assessment model. Part B presents the assessment method. The S4S method and model have been independently verified as meeting the requirements for conformant assessments and compatible models as laid down in ISO 15504 [8].

2.1 The S4S Assessment Model

In designing the S4S assessment model, the exemplar assessment model from Part 5 of ISO 15504 was taken as a basis. Internal ESA requirements on the production of space software and software process models developed by ESA in previous study projects were used to tailor the process dimension of the model. The capability dimension from the Part 5 exemplar assessment model was adopted as-is with no modifications or additions.

ESA space systems must be developed according to the requirements published by the European Cooperation for Space Standardization (ECSS). These standards are to be applied in the management, engineering, and product assurance of space projects and applications. The standards are written in the form of requirements and expected outputs. All of the ECSS Level One standards and several Level Two standards were used as primary input in developing the S4S assessment model. A complete list of the ECSS standards applicable to S4S is found in Section 6 [9-24]. Of particular importance were the two standards that focus on software, ECSS-E-40, "Space Engineering–Software" and ECSS-Q-80, "Space Product Assurance–Software Product Assurance" [10, 24]. In addition, several internal space software process models derived from these standards were used to refine the S4S assessment model [25, 26].

In forming the S4S process dimension, all processes and base practices were adopted as-is from the ISO 15504 exemplar assessment model in Part 5 of ISO 15504 (ISO 15504-5). Requirements from ECSS documents or activities from space software process models were matched with assessment model processes and base practices. In addition, the process dimension was augmented with processes, base practices and notes created to reflect activities not present in ISO 15504-5. All of the exemplar model work products were either matched with the expected outputs of ECSS requirements or, where no match was found, were kept in S4S as-is. New work products and work product characteristics were formed to represent ECSS outputs not covered by the exemplar model. These new processes and process indicators incorporate space software needs into S4S. The common origin of ECSS-E-40 and ECSS-Q-80 (e.g. ISO 12207 [27]) made this tailoring approach feasible.

As a result of these efforts, the process dimension of S4S has been considerably expanded from the exemplar model. Four new processes, about 50 base practices, and about 60 new notes have been added to reflect ECSS activities. The process dimension

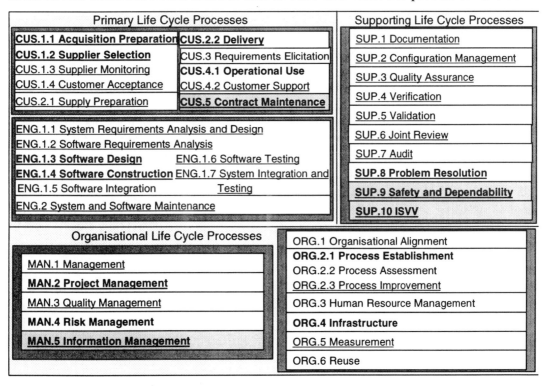

Figure 1: S4S Processes and process categories. Processes new to the ISO 15504 exemplar assessment model are shaded in light grey. Processes with base practices added are represented in bold. Processes with notes added are underlined. Note that CUS.2 from ISO 15504 has been split into two component processes, CUS.2.1 and CUS.2.2.

of the S4S model is shown in Figure 1. Processes new to the ISO 15504 exemplar assessment model are shaded in light grey. Processes with base practices added are represented in bold. Processes with notes added are underlined. Figure 1 shows clearly that enhancements have been made throughout the entire process dimension.

Of the four new processes, two extend the exemplar model to cover issues particular to the highly complex and often safety-critical software produced by the space industry. The new process *Independent Software Verification and Validation (ISVV)* describes the activities that occur when, for highly critical software, a subset of the standard life cycle processes is repeated by a third party completely independent from the supplier. The *Safety and Dependability Assurance* process ensures that the requirements on safety and dependability are defined, that the criticality of each software module is analysed and that the analyses are updated in accordance with modifications to the software design. Both the *ISVV* and the *Safety and Dependability Assurance* processes have been added to the Support category, as SUP.9 and SUP.10 respectively.

Two new processes address general customer and management activities not found in the exemplar model. In the customer category, CUS.5, *Contract Maintenance*, describes the process of maintaining and modifying the contract. MAN.5, *Information Management*, is added to the Management category. This process concerns the installation, maintenance and use of a project information system. Such systems are often used in space projects to facilitate exchange of project information when actors work in different locations at different organisations.

Finally, two new component processes stem from splitting the exemplar model process CUS.2, *Supply* process, into two processes, CUS.2.1, *Supply Preparation*, and CUS 2.2, *Delivery*. This change occurred based on the feedback from S4S pilot assessments and is described in Section 3.

In addition to the processes and process indicators created for S4S, the work products of ISO 15504-5 have been restructured to reflect ESA defined deliverables and its milestone-based life cycle. Two categories of work product types have been added. Also, the model is readily tailored to software classes of risk and safety criticality, as certain process indicators are listed as a function of criticality class [28].

In the following section, the reasoning behind the strategy used to tailor the exemplar model to space software needs is described in more detail, illustrated by a few examples.

2.2 Developing the S4S Model

Each ECSS standard is organised into groups of requirements, or sections, that describe processes which occur during different phases of project development. Indeed, ISO 12207 was used as a primary input for the development of the ECSS software standards. As such, the requirements in these standards are readily analogous to the base practices of ISO 15504 exemplar model processes. The relationship between ISO 12207, ECSS-E-40, ECSS-Q-80, Part 5 of ISO 15504, and the S4S assessment model is depicted in Figure 2.

One example of an "easy" match between ECSS and the exemplar model was the requirement ECSS-E-40 5.4.2.3 that describes the evaluation of software requirements. According to the standard, space software suppliers "shall evaluate the software requirements" considering, among other criteria, "traceability to system partitioning" and "inconsistency". This requirement clearly addresses activities within the *Software*

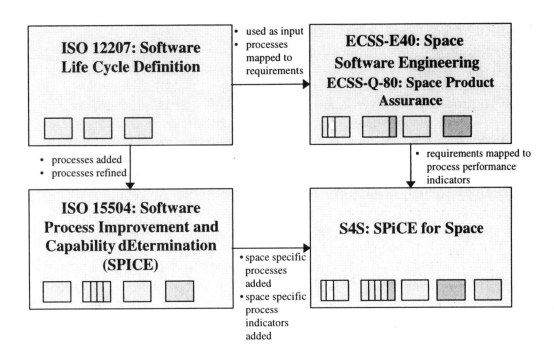

Figure 2: The relationship between S4S, ECSS-E-40, ECSS-Q-80, ISO 12207, and ISO 15504.

Requirements Analysis process (ENG.1.2). In particular, it is readily associated with base practice ENG 1.2 BP8, "Evaluate the software requirements". The purpose of this base practice includes evaluating "consistency" and establishing "traceability between software requirements and system requirements". Thus, in this case, the ECSS requirement is a good match to the exemplar model base practice.

In other cases, appropriate ISO 15504 indicators did not exist in the exemplar model and had to be derived from the ECSS requirement. For example, ECSS-E-40 contains requirements on the reuse of software from other space projects and from third party "commercial off-the-shelf"(COTS) software. ECSS-E-40 6.4.2.1 states that, if required by the customer, the supplier shall "consider the 'reuse' of already developed, commercial off-the-shelf and modifiable off-the-shelf software". For the project at hand, the supplier is required to identify the "reuse components with respect to the functional requirements baseline" and perform "a quality evaluation of these components". These requirements clearly describe engineering and product assurance activities that would be performed in the project when formulating the architectural or detailed design.

In the exemplar model of ISO 15504, ORG.5 treats the reuse of software, describing the establishment of a reuse strategy and a reuse library for the organisation. The topic is also broached through the characteristics of the work product Acquisition Strategy (45), which includes the potential acquisition of off-the-shelf products. However, neither of these addresses the ECSS engineering analysis necessary to incorporate a reused or COTS product into a new design. To integrate reuse activities into the engineering chain, as required by the ECSS standards, two base practices were added to the *Design* process, ENG.1.3. These new base practices are ENG.1.3 BP6, "Identify and analyse reusable components" and ENG.1.3 BP7, "Identify and analyse commercially available software components". As with all new S4S base practices, they were written using the style guidelines found in Annex C of ISO 15504-5 and were assigned base practice numbers greater than the practice numbers of the exemplar model indicators.

As artefacts produced by the performance of required activities, the expected outputs of ECSS requirements are clearly analogous to work products in the exemplar model. In order to incorporate them easily into the model, a new work product structure was devised. In the first example about evaluating the software requirements, the expected outputs of the ECSS-E-40 requirement include a Requirements Traceability Matrix and a Requirements Verification Report. Neither of these work products is found in ISO 15504-5, although a generic Traceability Matrix (58) exists in the exemplar model. The Requirements Traceability Matrix from ECSS-E-40 is an instantiation of this work product type, as are other traceability matrices required by the same standard, such as the Software Code Traceability Matrix and the Design Traceability Matrix. In fact, many other such instantiations of generic exemplar model work products are listed as outputs of the ECSS-E-40 requirements. Rather than adding all of these as new indicators, a new class of work product, the "ECSS instance" was created. ECSS instances share the characteristics of the generic work product type (in this example, the Traceability Matrix) but each instance includes additional characteristics that differentiate it from the rest.

Some areas of software development described by the ECSS standards as mandatory for space software are not covered at all in the ISO 15504 exemplar model. For example, two separate standards address the topics of Safety [23] and Dependability [22] in space software. In these standards, safety and dependability efforts are described within the context of an overall programme. The management of safety and dependability efforts is addressed as well as the performance of technical analyses, verification, and other engineering activities. The philosophy of both standards is expressed in the introduction to ECSS-Q-30, which states that "Dependability assurance shall be a continuous and iterative process throughout the project life cycle". Likewise, ECSS-Q-40 describes the implementation of a "safety programme" that "shall be integrated in all project activities".

This approach is shared by the Support category processes of the ISO 15504 reference model. According to Part 2 of the standard, support processes "may be employed by any of the other processes (including other supporting processes) at various points in the software life cycle" [5]. Support processes such as SUP.1, *Documentation*, or SUP.2, *Configuration Management*, describe areas of focus that support all other development activities. For the requirements from ECSS-Q-30 and ECSS-Q-40, it was decided to follow the reference model approach by incorporating Safety and Dependability as a new process within the Support category, SUP.9. The topics of safety and dependability were combined in a single process because, at least for software, the same activities are performed for both. As with the case of the *Safety and Dependability* process, the new processes SUP.10, CUS.5, and MAN.5 arose from missing areas of activity in ISO 15504-5.

2.3   The S4S Assessment Process

S4S contains a documented assessment process, which includes a step-by-step breakdown of assessment activities, definition of key assessment roles and description of assessment input and output work products. Following the process outlined in ISO 15504, a S4S assessment is divided into the following seven activities: Initiation,

Planning, Briefing, Data Acquisition, Data Validation, Process Rating, and Reporting. In addition to describing the assessment activities, the method offers detailed guidance to assist S4S assessors at each phase in the assessment. For example, experiences from the pilot assessments revealed that during the planning phase, assessors need to clearly understand the customer-supplier contractual relationship and the applicability of standards used in the project to be assessed. Space projects tend to be based on multi-tiered contracts with many levels managed by a prime contractor. Thus when evaluating space projects, S4S pilot assessors found they had to carefully separate the responsibilities of the project from those of the next level customer. Expert guidance of this type added to the assessment process incorporates lessons from the space software perspective into each phase of an S4S assessment.

The method was also subjected to an independent check of its conformance to ISO 15504. Alec Dorling of InterSPICE performed an independent verification that the S4S method meets the requirements for conformant assessments and compatible models as described in ISO 15504 [8].

2.4 S4S Tools

A software tool has been developed to support the performance of S4S assessments. The tool may be used to view the process model during the assessment, to record process ratings and to produce the assessment report. Experiences with BOOTSTRAP have shown that without tool support the efficient performance of an assessment is virtually impossible [29].

The tool couples the popular and proven SPICE 1-2-1 user interface with a database containing the entire S4S process model. For a given process, assessors may view the process purpose, outcomes, base practices and input and output work products. Pop-up windows provide work product characteristics or attribute definitions.

A dedicated window allows the user to record the ratings of all nine process attributes. Under tabs, the assessor may record notes describing the objective evidence found to support his or her judgement. Ratings are displayed in easy-to-read charts. Target profiles may be loaded into the tool and compared with actual results. The S4S data file created by the tool may serve as the assessment record and can be easily re-examined for future analysis.

Charts, assessor notes, and raw scores recorded in the tool may be exported in standard formats to assist in the production of the assessment report. A standard S4S assessment report template is provided with macros that automatically import assessment data.

In subsequent versions of the tool, an additional tab will display expert guidance for each process and each process attribute, placing the knowledge accumulated from S4S assessments at the space assessor's fingertips.

Templates of all S4S assessment work products are provided with the method, including Pre-Assessment Questionnaires, Assessment Plans, a Statement of Confidentiality, and Assessor Logs. A sample presentation briefing the assessed organisational unit on the S4S method and model is also included.

3 The Pilot Assessments

To validate the new method, four S4S pilot assessments were performed in October 1999 at two software suppliers within the space industry. The primary purpose of the pilot assessments was to validate S4S and to provide feedback to further refine the method. A second goal was for the assessors to gain experience in performing assessments in the context of space projects. A third and final goal was to provide potential improvement suggestions to the assessed organisations.

Assessments were performed at Intecs Sistemi in Pisa and Rome and at Aerospatiale (now Alcatel) in Cannes. In total, thirty of the (then) forty S4S processes were assessed, including all of the new processes. Nine different assessors from ESA, SYNSPACE, and InterSPICE participated in the pilots.

During the pilot assessments, the assessment team leaders guided the assessment team through a step-by-step "walk through" of the method. Feedback was collected from assessors and participants in the form of problem reports. A total of 210 problem reports were generated during the pilot programme. SYNSPACE collected the problem reports and classified them according to category and difficulty to implement. In November 1999, all pilot assessors met for a one-day workshop where actions were determined on the basis of the problem reports. With this feedback, the method was revised to its current version.

An analysis of the types of problems recorded revealed that the method contained no serious flaws. Seventy percent identified minor modifications to the assessment model. An additional ten percent represented requests for clarification of the text describing the assessment process. Only ten percent of the problem reports recorded addressed structural changes to the model or method. In addition to statistics on the data collected, reaction from the host organisations was overwhelmingly positive. It was clear that the assessments proved highly effective at targeting areas of potential improvement.

Several important changes resulted from the pilot assessments. Assessment teams found the *Supply* process, CUS.2, too broad in scope to assess effectively. As the process is defined in Part 2 of ISO 15504, the CUS.2 activities span the life of the entire project from proposal preparation to the delivery of the final product. When assessing projects in the middle of software development, the assessment teams found that parts of CUS.2 were not applicable. To allow assessments to focus on crucial activities either at the beginning or at the end of the project life cycle, it was decided to split CUS.2 into two components. CUS.2.1, *Supply preparation* process, addresses the activities involved in establishing a contractual framework that defines the requirements at the beginning of the project, while CUS.2.2, *Delivery* process, focuses on providing software to the customer that meets the agreed requirements.

Another important enhancement to S4S that resulted from the pilot assessments was the addition of product and process metrics. When assessing the *Measurement* process, ORG.5, and processes up to Capability Level Four, S4S assessment teams reported that having examples of the types of metrics to collect for each process would be helpful in supporting the judgement of the assessor. Fortunately, another ESA study project, SPEC, was in the process of collecting industry best practice metrics and evaluating their use for space software [30]. The SPEC project identified specific metrics relevant for each S4S process as well as a list of generic metrics that apply to every S4S process and a list of product metrics. These metrics are included in an annex of the S4S method.

4 Future Plans

To promote the new method, the European Space Agency is sponsoring several S4S trial assessments. Five space software suppliers will receive a S4S assessment, funded by ESA. As opposed to the pilot assessment programme, the primary purpose of the trial assessments is to provide benefit to the host organisation.

The first trial assessment took place in February 2000, at Austrian Aerospace GmbH (AAE) in Vienna. Funding was provided for two external assessors, Alec Dorling and Ann Cass, to perform a week long assessment and support AAE in the development of a process improvement plan, using the assessment results as main input. A case study report describing Austrian Aerospace's experiences with S4S is available on request.

In the meanwhile, the method expands into a new dimension: Risk. A future study project will add process risk as a third dimension to the S4S model, with four categories reflecting the risk of poorly performed or implemented processes. With this additional information, assessors can assist organisations in prioritising improvement actions, helping organisations to make the most of improvement budgets. Future goals of the S4S project also include the definition of target profiles for the different safety criticality classes of space software.

5 Summary

SPiCE for Space (S4S), an ISO 15504 conformant method for software process assessment, has been developed by SYNSPACE AG for the European Space Agency. S4S consists of an assessment model tailored to the production of space software; a documented process; and a software tool to assist in rating, record keeping, and reporting.

The method has been validated through pilot assessments and is currently being used in a series of trial assessments of space software suppliers. Based on a synergetic combination of ISO 15504 and space software standards, the S4S assessment method is the cornerstone of an emerging initiative of process improvement across the European space industry.

6 References

[1]   Stevens, R.:Creating Software the Right Way. Byte, Aug. 1991, pp. 31–38.

[2]   Capability Maturity Model for Software, Version 1.1. Mark Paulk, Bill Curtis, Mary Beth Chrissis, Charles Weber, CMU/SEI-93-TR-24, Software Engineering Institute, February 1993.

[3]   Kuvaja, P., et.al.: BOOTSTRAP: Europe's assessment method. IEEE Software, Vol. 10, No. 3, 1993, pp. 93–95.

[4]   Kuvaja, P., et.al.: Software Process Assessment & Improvement–The BOOTSTRAP Approach. Blackwell, 1994, ISBN 0-631-19663-3.

[5]   ISO/IEC TR 15504:1998/99(E), Information Technology - Software Process Assessment, Parts 1-9: Type 2 Technical Report.

[6] PASCON/WO6 CCN2/TN6: Analysis of Software Process Assessment Schemes and Recommended Scheme for Space Systems. H. Gierszal, C. Völcker, Technical Note No. 6, Issue 2.0, 19.5.1999.

[7] PASCON/WO6 CCN4/TN7: ISO/IEC TR 15504 Conformant Method for the Assessment of Space Software Processes. C. Völcker, A. Cass, Technical Note No. 7, Issue 1.0, Draft C, 19.02.00.

[8] PASCON/WO6 CCN4/TN15: Verification Report and ISO/IEC Compliance Statement for the ISO/IEC TR 15504 Conformant Method for the Assessment of Space Software Processes. A. Dorling, Technical Note No. 15, Issue 1.0, Draft A, 19.02.00.

[9] ECSS–E–10: Space Engineering - System Engineering. ESA-ESTEC Requirements & Standards Division, Noordwijk, 19.4.1996.

[10] ECSS–E–40: Space Engineering – Software. ESA-ESTEC Requirements & Standards Division, Noordwijk, 13.4.1999.

[11] ECSS-M-00: Space Product Management - Policies and Principles. ESA-ESTEC Requirements & Standards Division, Noordwijk, 19.4.1996.

[12] ECSS-M-00-03 Draft 7: Space Product Management – Risk Management. ESA-ESTEC Requirements & Standards Division, Noordwijk, 9.9.1998.

[13] ECSS-M-10: Space Product Management - Project Breakdown Structures. ESA-ESTEC Requirements & Standards Division, Noordwijk, 19.4.1996.

[14] ECSS-M-20: Space Product Management - Project Organisation. ESA-ESTEC Requirements & Standards Division, Noordwijk, 19.4.1996.

[15] ECSS-M-30: Space Product Management - Project Phasing and Planning. ESA-ESTEC Requirements & Standards Division, Noordwijk, 19.4.1996.

[16] ECSS-M-40: Space Product Management - Configuration Management. ESA-ESTEC Requirements & Standards Division, Noordwijk, 19.4.1996.

[17] ECSS-M-50: Space Product Management - Information/Documentation Management. ESA-ESTEC Requirements & Standards Division, Noordwijk, 19.4.1996.

[18] ECSS Glossary of Terms, Rev. 1.

[19] ECSS-Q-00: Space Product Assurance - Policies and Principles. ESA-ESTEC Requirements & Standards Division, Noordwijk, 19.4.1996.

[20] ECSS-Q-20: Space Product Assurance - Quality Assurance. ESA-ESTEC Requirements & Standards Division, Noordwijk, 19.4.1996.

[21] ECSS-Q-20-09: Space Product Assurance - Nonconformance control system. ESA-ESTEC Requirements & Standards Division, Noordwijk, 19.4.1996.

[22] ECSS-Q-30: Space Product Assurance - Dependability. ESA-ESTEC Requirements & Standards Division, Noordwijk, 19.4.1996.

[23] ECSS-Q-40: Space Product Assurance - Safety. ESA-ESTEC Requirements & Standards Division, Noordwijk, 19.4.1996.

[24] ECSS-Q-80: Space Product Assurance - Software product Assurance. ESA-ESTEC Requirements & Standards Division, Noordwijk, 19.4.1996.

[25] ESTEC Contract 12798/98/NL/PA, ECSS-PMod Study Deliverables

[26] PASCON/WO6 CCN2/TN5: Tailoring of the Space SW PA Model with Instantiation. P. Panaroni, G. Marcucci, Technical Note No. 5, Issue 1.0, 15.9.1998.

[27] ISO/IEC 12207: Information technology - Software life cycle processes. International Standardisation Organization, 1995.

[28] PASCON/WO6 CCN2/TN1: Definition of Space Software Classes. P. Panaroni, G. Marcucci, Technical Note No. 1, Issue 1, 23.9.1997.

[29] Stienen, H., et.al.: BOOTSTRAP: Five Years of Assessment Experience. Proc. ICSE '97, Boston, IEEE.

[30] SPEC/TN3: Space Domain Specific Software Product Quality Models, Requirements and Related Evaluation Methods. Technical Note No. 3, Issue 3.0, Draft A, November 5, 1999.

Relating the SPICE Framework and SEI
Approach to Software Process Assessment

D. H. Kitson

Carnegie Mellon University. USA

In June 1993, an international effort (SPICE) was launched to develop a standard for software process assessment. An important goal of this effort is to harmonize existing process assessment approaches. This paper describes and characterizes SEI and SPICE software process assessment work and then highlights the similarities and differences. The following aspects are considered -underlying philosophy, goals, scope/domain, rating processes, underlying reference model, tailorability and impact on the international software community.

1. Introduction

More and more software managers and engineers are becoming aware of initiatives that focus on improving software production processes. Name recognition of terms such as process improvement, process assessment, CMM (CMM is a service mark of Carnegie Mellon University), Bootstrap, and Trillium is high. Less well known to most software practitioners is the fact that there is a significant international effort, known as SPICE, underway to develop a software process assessment standard.

Interest in software process assessment methods has grown steadily during the past 10 years. IBM was one of the first to develop and conduct appraisals of software process in an orderly and defined manner [1]. Following the spirit of the approach developed at IBM [2] the SEI fielded an assessment method [3] in 1987 which has evolved into a de facto, standard within the United States.

This activity in the United States, coupled with similar activity and interest in Europe and the Asia-Pacific region, has provided the impetus for an international collaborative effort to develop an international standard in the area of software process assessment.

Because significant investments have been made by a number of method providers and their installed base of users—including, but not limited to, the Software Engineering Institute (SEI)—one of the most challenging aspects of the SPICE effort will be to incorporate the best aspects of existing successful approaches and pave the way for future improvements in software process assessment without precluding the continued use of successful approaches to software process improvement. Many software supplies already feel compelled to pay attention to a number of quality thrusts.

For example, a typical US-based international corporation might be engaged in many of the following quality improvement activities:

- internal company proprietary audits or quality reviews

- ISO 9000-related audits

- CMM-based appraisal methods—software capability evaluations (externally imposed) and/or software process assessments (internally imposed)

- Malcolm Baldrige National Quality Award competition

- Bellcore Process Maturity Level audit

- Trillium appraisal

The arrival of yet another approach which must be considered could demotivate continued investment in process improvement by the software acquisition and software supplier communities. If the SPICE effort can provide an *integrating framework while still advancing the state of practice in software process assessment, it will be a very significant and positive accomplishment.*

This paper presents a high-level comparative analysis and review of the relevant SEI products and the current and anticipated SPICE products. The analysis and discussion assumes the successful implementation of a number of key changes formulated at the WG10 meeting in Kwa Maritane, South Africa in November, 1995 [4].

2. SEI Software Process Assessment Overview

The SEI, located in Pittsburgh, Pennsylvania, is a Federally Funded Research and Development Center (FFRDC) created in 1984 with a mission to provide leadership in advancing the state of the practice of software engineering to improve the quality of systems that depend on software. The contract for the SEI was awarded to Carnegie Mellon University based on a competitive procurement process and has been re-awarded twice at 5-year contract review cycles. It is managed by the Department of Defense Advanced Research Projects Agency and administered by the US Air Force (USAF) Electronic Systems Center. FFRDCs are operated on a not-for-profit basis.

The SEI has a number of technical focus areas in addition to software process; among these are software risk management and trustworthy systems. The software process focus area began in earnest in February 1987 with the first SEI-assisted software process assessment which used as its reference framework a five-level maturity model and a set of approximately 100 practice-oriented questions. Table 1 summarizes key events and milestones as well as identifying additional products and services relating to the SEI's work in the area of software process assessment.

In addition to the CMM for Software (SW-CMM) and its associated appraisal methods there are Capability Maturity Models[sm] (Capability Maturity Model is a service mark of Carnegie Mellon University) which cover other domains; Table 2 provides a summary of these models and their domains.

3. SPICE Overview

The SPICE (Software Process Improvement Capability dEtermination) project is an international effort to develop a standard for software process assessment. Approximately 40 countries are actively contributing resources to this effort. The effort is being managed by Working Group 10 (ISO/IEC JTC1/SC7/WG10). IEC is the International Electrotechnical Commission; JTC1 is a joint ISO and IEC technical committee which deals with information technology. SC7 is the subcommittee responsible for software engineering standards.

Interest in developing an international standard on software process assessment was sparked by an investigative study sponsored by the UK Ministry of Defence (MOD) into methods for assessing the development capability of software supplies. The study [14] identified and reviewed two dozen existing methods already in use and put forth these findings:

- 'there is a general need to supplement reliance of software procurers on ISO 9001;

- there is a wide support for a software assessment scheme which is in the public domain, widely recognized, and preferably backed by an international standard;

- some organizations using or developing their own assessment schemes have registered interest in supporting a public domain, standardized scheme, in preference to their own schemes;

- an initiative to develop such a scheme would be directed toward continuous process and quality improvement matched to business needs. The initiative would be focused around an international standard on process management which would itself provide a framework for a capability assessment scheme supporting both self-improvement for software suppliers and capability determination as a means of evaluating contract risk'.

Based on the conclusions reached by the MOD study, the British Standards Institution (BSI) proposed to ISO/IEC JTC1/SC7 that software process assessment be considered as an area for standardization and that a three part approach be used. A study period would be undertaken to be followed by the development of a draft international standard (Technical Report Type 2), resulting in registration as a full international standard.

The case for an international standard on software process assessment was further developed during the ensuing study period (June 1991-June 1992) by a Study Co-ordination Team (sponsored by the UK Ministry of Defense) within JTC1/SC7/WG7 which drew upon the resources of a UK Technical Experts Group. The study resulted in the following conclusions [16]:

- 'there is international consensus on the need for a standard for process assessment,

- the standard should be concerned with the processes used in the procurement, development, delivery, operation, evolution and related service support of software and software-dependent systems,

- the standard should be applicable by procurers for the evaluation of supplier capability and by suppliers for the purpose of self-improvement,

- the development of the standard should aim to utilise the proven and best features of existing assessment methods, and to draw on existing material wherever relevant,

- the developers of several existing schemes are supportive of the concepts of the new standard and are willing to contribute to its development.

- there is consensus on the need for a rapid route to development and trialling to provide usable output in an acceptable timescale and to ensure that the standard fully meets the needs of its users.'

In addition, the report contained a set of requirements, success criteria and a proposed architecture for the standard.

In 1993, ISO/IEC JTC1 approved a new work item proposal [17, 18], thus effectively establishing the SPICE project organization WG10. A more detailed account of the history of the SPICE project can be found in [19]. Table 3 provides a summary of key events and milestones.

The SPICE project is composed of six phases: (a) project initiation; (b) product development; (c) trials; (d) product revision; (e) awareness/technology transfer; and (1) closure; it is currently in the trials phase.

The scope of the standard is process assessment, process improvement, and capability determination [20]. Software process domains to be assessed are acquisition, supply, development, operation, maintenance, supporting processes and service support.

Table 1. Selected events – SEI software process technical focus area

Year	Event
1986	– SEI tasked by USAF to provide a method for determining software competency of bidders – Process Program initiated
1987	– First SEI-assisted assessment conducted – Software Process Feasibility project initiated – Publication of 'maturity questionnaire' [5] – Software Process Assessment project initiated – Contractor Software Engineering Capability Assessment project initiated (predecessor to SCE project)
1988	– Self-assessment training offered – 1st Software Engineering Process Group workshop
1989	– Publication of initial report on assessment results [6] and Managing the Software Process [7]
1990	– Commercialisation program (for software process assessment) initiated – Field studies of Japanese software process maturity [8] – Initial delivery of assessment training to vendors
1991	– Publication of Capability Maturity Model for Software V1.0 – 1st International Conference on the Software Process
1992	– Publication of second SEI report on analysis of assessment results [9]
1993	– Capability Maturity Model for Software V1.1 [10] – SPA Alpha 2 field exercises conducted
1994	– CBA-IPI field exercises conducted – Lead Assessor program launched – Publication of initial report on benefits of CMM-based software process improvement [11] – Publication of upgraded 'maturity questionnaire' [11a] – Disciplined Software Engineering (PSP) training offered
1995	– Publication of A Discipline for Software Engineering [12], CMM Appraisal Framework [13], report on impact of CMM-based software process improvement [13a]

Table 2. Selected capability maturity models

CMM Name	Domain Covered	Remarks
CMM for Software (SW-CMM)	Software management and technical processes	Baselined February 1993 – V1.1
People CMM (P-CMM)	Management of human resources in software organizations	Baselined September 1995 – V1.0
Software Acquisition CMM (SA-CMM)	Software acquisition management and technical processes	This CMM is under development.
Systems Engineering CMM (SE-CMM)	Systems Engineering management and technical processes	Baselined January 1996 – V1.2. SEI facilitated the development of this CMM.
Trusted Software CMM (T-CMM)	Software management and technical process for trusted software	This CMM is under development.

402

Table 4. SPICE product set summary

Part ID/Name	Topics	Size (pages)	Norm/Inf
1. Concepts and Introductory Guide	• Overview • Conformance requirements	24	Inf
2. A Model for Process Assessment	• Conformance requirements • Process Definitions • (mapping to 12207)	114	Norm
3. Rating Processes	• Conformance requirements • Rating processes	12	Norm
4. Guide to Conducting Assessments	• Assessment process overview • Assessment process guidance	30	Inf
5. Construction, Selection and Use of Assessment Instruments and Tools	• Assessment instrument conformance requirements	138	Norm
6. Qualification and Training of Assessors	• Defines initial and ongoing qualification of assessors • Assessment method	33	Inf
7. Guide for Use in Process Improvement	Discusses management of organizational process improvement efforts	49	Inf
8. Guide for Use in Determining Supplier Process Capability	Discusses application of the standard in the context of supplier selection	28	Inf
9. Vocabulary	• SPICE product set term definitions • Identifies normative references to terms defined elsewhere	17	Inf

Table 5. Product levels of abstraction

Level Attribute	Method/Model	Meta-method/Model
Usage	Directly usable with little or no customization for software process improvement activities	Provides framework and requirements for building conformant models and methods
Primary Customers	Assessment teams, process improvement teams	Method/model builders and providers
Example Artefacts	• SEI – SW – CMM, CBA/IPI Lead Assessor Guide, Team Training Participant's Guide • SPICE – Embedded conformant model in informative portion of standard (base practices, generic practices)	• SEI – CMM Appraisal Framework (method) • SPICE – parts 2 (model), 3 and 5 (method)

Table 3. Selected events – international standardization effort for software process assessment

1991	– UK MOD investigative study report issued [14] – ISO/IEC JTC1/SC7 approves study period [15]
1992	– ISO/IEC JTC1/SC7 study period report published [16] – SPICE project organization procedures drafted
1993	– JTC1 approves new work item proposal [17, 18] – First meeting of SPICE 'group' (Dublin) – SPICE project organization formally established – Product and requirements specifications baselined [20, 21]
1994	– Development stage of SPICE project ends – Trials stage of SPICE project begins
1995	– Phase 1 trials conducted; analysis report completed – Draft technical reports type 2 released to ISO/IEC JTC1/SC7 for review and balloting – Adoption in principle of key changes to SPICE at Kwa Maritane, South Africa meeting [4]
1996	– New baseline developed to incorporate Kwa Maritane changes – Phase 2 trials begin (planned for March)

The overall goals of the standard [20] are to encourage predictable quality products, encourage maximum productivity, promote a repeatable software process, not be used for trade restraint, and be subject to continuous improvement through periodic reviews to maintain consistency with current good practice.

Additional insight into the SPICE project can be found in [22-24].

Frequently the assumption is made that SPICE is a software variant of ISP 9001. This is not the case, although one of the SPICE requirements is to be supportive of, and consistent with, the ISO 9000 series of standards. The SPICE project is under JTC1/SC7. The ISO 9000 series of standards is under TC176, which is responsible for quality management.

The current SPICE product set consists of a nine-part document set; key aspects of these documents are summarized in Table 4 (the contents reflect the pre-Kwa Maritane SPICE product set). The column labelled 'Norm/Inf'' refers to the distinction between normative and informative provisions of an international standard. A requirement is classified as normative if satisfaction of the requirement is considered mandatory for conformance to be claimed. Anything else is classified as informative and typically consists of guidance for country or domain specific implementation. At the time this paper was written the SPICE Management Board had decided to release the SPICE product set into the public domain. This action is intended to further raise awareness of the SPICE activity within the software community and stimulate interest in trialling (see [26, 27] for a discussion of the trialling phase of the SPICE project). These materials will be accessible via FTP and world-wide web as well as in paper form for a nominal cost recovery fee.

4. Comparing and Contrasting the Two Efforts

There are two significantly different levels of abstraction (with correspondingly distinct customer and supplier communities) represented in the SPICE and SEI product sets:

- the method/model level—this level has as its focus specific assessment methods and reference models;

- the meta-method/model level -this is one level of abstraction removed from the method/model level. Its focus of discussion is families of assessment methods and reference models. For example, one family might be that which is SPICE-conformant.

Table 5 summarizes the levels, customer and supplier communities and provides product examples.

4.1 Underlying Philosophy and Goals

At the highest level, the two approaches have no significant differences in terms of underlying philosophy and goals. The following list identifies key elements of the underlying philosophy shared by both approaches:

- a focus on continuous process improvement;

- a public and defined assessment approach;

- an underlying reference model for assessment;

- recognition that results from different modes of method use must be comparable and consistent.

Goals shared by the approaches include the following:

- elevate the importance of continuous process improvement in both the software supplier community and the software acquisition community;

- provide means by which objective measures of process quality can be determined in a repeatable and valid manner .

An unstated implicit difference is that the resulting international standard will provide a unifying basis for existing and future models and methods.

4.2 Scope and Domain

At one level the two approaches have similar scopes in that both are intended to be used for self-improvement by software producers and supplier selection by acquisition agents. However, in terms of technical scope, there is a difference -this is discussed in more detail in Section 4.5.

4.3 Appraisal Method(s) and Rating Processes

As indicated earlier, the SPICE product set sets out a framework for conformant assessments but does not provide a method per se. The SEI product set does include an assessment method (CBA-IPI) and a contractor evaluation method (SCE). Note that this is not only a significant point of differentiation but also an intentional one.

Because there are a number of existing and successful assessment approaches, a key implicit assumption/requirement underlying the SPICE effort was that the investments made by method providers and their community of users would not be undermined by the emerging international standard.

The CMM Appraisal Framework, or CAF [13], is the SEI analogue to the parts of the SPICE product set dealing with the assessment process.

The approach to rating used in the SPICE product set is to use a four-point ordinal rating scale of adequacy (Fully, Largely, Partially, Not) for each process included within the scope of the assessment.

The approach to rating used by CMM-based appraisal methods is to rate at two levels—goal and key process area (KPA). There are two to four goals associated with each KPA. Both goals and KPAs use the same four-point rating scale (satisfied, unsatisfied, not applicable, not rated). Note that goal-level rating is based on the collection of objective data and is subject to coverage requirements; ultimately it is a team judgement based on the available data and collective team experience and wisdom. KPA-level rating is essentially a mechanical roll-up of the ratings for the KPA's goals.

A key outcome of each approach is a rating profile -that is, identification of each rated process and the rating assigned. Beyond this, it is especially significant that the intent of the SPICE approach is that conformant assessments would result in rating outcomes which could be mapped into a SPICE process profile (see Fig. 1).

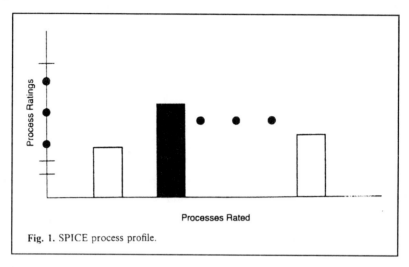

Fig. 1. SPICE process profile.

4.4 Reference Model

The scope of the CMM for Software is software management and technical processes; these areas are covered by eighteen key process areas (KPAs). Each KPA is defined in terms of goals and specific practices.

The SPICE product set also explicitly identifies and characterizes (in terms of goals and purpose statements) a set of processes which are the domain for SPICE-conformant assessments. These processes have been aligned to relevant processes defined in the recent international standard on software life-cycle processes ISO/IEC 12207 [28]. Specification at the practice level is intentionally omitted from the normative portion of the SPICE product set. A conform ant reference model has been constructed and will be included as an exemplar in an informative section of the SPICE product set; this model does provide specificity at the practice level of detail.

The scope of a SPICE-conformant model can extend beyond that of the SW-CMM to include processes involved in the acquisition, supply, operation and support of software; Table 6 provides further information on these areas. Note that none of the areas mentioned are incompatible with the SW-CMM and that many of the areas are within scope of one or more of the CMMs noted in Table 2.

A significant difference between the two models is the underlying architecture used to express the model. SPICE uses what is called a continuous model; in this approach, process management considerations are explicitly applied to individual domain-specific processes (e.g. requirements management, configuration management) and rated accordingly. This approach provides a natural fit with the rating profile scheme depicted in Fig. I. Stated another way, process capability is measured on a process-by-process basis.

The SW -CMM uses a staged model in which individual key process areas are assigned to a specific level of organizational process capability. The focus is on the extent to which goal satisfaction has been

Table 6. Selected domains from SPICE process model

Domain	Description	Sample processes
Customer-Supplier	Consists of activities that directly impact the customer, support development and transition of the software to the customer, and provide for its correct operation and use	Acquire software, operate software, provide customer service (SA-CMM, SE-CMM)
Engineering	Processes that directly specify, implement, or maintain a system and software product and its user documentation	Develop system requirements and design (SE-CMM)
Organization	Establish the business goals of the organization and develop process, product, and resource assets which, when used by the projects in the organization, will help the organization achieve its business goals	Engineer the business (PD-CMM)

achieved. Overall process capability of the organizational unit assessed is then a roll-up of individual KPA ratings.

Among the implications of the choice of architecture is that a staged approach necessarily has a built-in implicit improvement roadmap which provides guidance on the order in which processes should be improved.

Additional insight into the topic of staged versus continuous models is provided in (29].

4.5 Tailorability

Both approaches acknowledge the need for tailoring. CMM-based appraisal methods have built-in tailorability which allow them to be adapted to a range of commonly encountered situations (e.g. small organizations, distributed organizations).

The SPICE product set also allows for tailoring in the sense that conformant models have the following degrees of freedom:

- guidance can be provided to aid in appropriate interpretation of the processes;
- existing model processes can be extended by supplementing them;
- entirely new processes can be added.

4.6 Impact on Software Community

CMM-based products have had an impact on the US DOD contractor community as well as the US commercial software community; the former primarily due to use by the government acquisition community, the latter primarily due to the belief that there is business value in focusing on process improvement. In addition, many other countries are using CMM-based products. In a recent SEI maturity profile update, 16% of the 515 reporting sites were outside of the US. Coupled with the assumption that only 10-20% of assessments conducted are actually reported formally to the SEI, this means that there is a significant amount of international SEI assessment activity. Cooperative partnerships with the SEI for the distribution of SEI products and services have been formed with the Applied Software Engineering Center in Montreal, Canada and the European Software Institute in Bilbao, Spain. The first international Software Engineering Process Group Conference will be held in Amsterdam in June 1996. This conference is modelled after the Software Engineering Process Group Conferences conducted in the US every year since 1988.

The impact on the international software community of the SPICE effort is likely to be several fold—it encompasses the opportunity to:

- provide an international forum for advancing the state of practice in the area of software process assessment as well as related areas;

- provide the software community a common framework for the expression of software process capability (e.g. SPICE process profiles). This should make it easier to compare and contrast results obtained from differing methods;

- allow greater freedom of choice for method/model users since SPICE does not impose a specific method or model but only requires that certain conformance criteria are met.

5. Conclusions

The existence of a significant and sustained international effort to develop a standard on software process improvement is a clear and compelling indication of the extent to which the premise that quality software processes are critical to business success and an organic source of competitive advantage has been embraced by the international software community.

While nominally labelled a standard for software process assessment, the SPICE product set has a far wider scope, including the domains of acquisition, support and process improvement.

In terms of similarities, the CMM and SPICE approaches are both based upon the notions of process focus based on business need and continuous process improvement as the end goal. Both use the paradigm of appraisal based on review of software practices (in the context of 'live' projects) relative to a reference model.

In terms of significant differences between the CMM approach and the SPICE approach, at the normative level, the primary distinction is that SPICE provides a framework for a model and a method while the SEI provides a conformant model (e.g. the CMM) and conformant methods (e.g. IPI, SCE). The domain space of the SPICE product set is broader than that of the CMM for Software, with the CMM focusing on software management and technical processes, while SPICE includes additional such areas as acquisition and operational support. However, when additional existing or developing CMMs are considered, the domain gap is somewhat smaller .

There are no key incompatibilities between the two approaches at the time this review was conducted (see caveat mentioned earlier in this paper regarding recent changes in SPICE direction).

The arrival of yet another approach which must be considered could demotivate continued investment in process improvement by the software acquisition and software supplier communities. If the SPICE effort can provide an *integrating framework while still advancing the state of practice in software process assessment, it will be a very significant and positive accomplishment.*

Acknowledgements

Undertaking the development of an international standard, especially in the software arena, is somewhat like marriage—not to be entered into lightly. Beyond this, the specific area of software process assessment is somewhat of a linchpin in the sense that it is becoming an increasingly significant driver for contract award decisions both in the government sector and in the private sector. Accordingly, there is a lot at stake for members of the software community and, in a larger sense, for society at large which has become dependent on systems that are software-based.

It is with great pleasure and the highest regard that I recognize the efforts (both past and future) of the many colleagues around the world who have participated in this effort. Unfortunately there are too many to mention by name and I would hesitate to risk missing even one of them.

Finally, I would like to thank the reviewers of this paper for their helpful comments. My friends and colleagues Suzie Gardia, Dr Mike Konrad and Steve Masters provided many helpful comments and insights. My friend, colleague and wife Jeanie also provided very useful comments despite the fact that she was recovering from surgery at the time; for this I am deeply grateful.

This work is sponsored by the US Department of Defense.

References

I. Houston Begins Site Programming Study, *Houston Today* (FSD Communications Department, Houston, Texas, August 20, 1984).

2. R. Radice, J.T. Harding, P.E. Munnis and R.W. Phillips, A Programming Process Study, *IBM Systems Journal*, 1985, volume 24, pages 91-101.

3. W.S. Humphrey and D.H. Kitson, *Preliminary Report on Conducting SEI-Assisted Assessments of Software Engineering Capability* (Software Engineering Institute, Carnegie Mellon University, 1987).

4. WG10 Meeting Kwa Maritane: Proposal for Changes to the Architecture, 1995, ISO/IEC JTCl/SC7/ WG10 N080.

5. W.S. Humphrey and W.L. Sweet, *A Method for Assessing the Software Engineering Capability of Contractors* (Software Engineering Institute, Carnegie Mellon University, 1987).

6. W.S. Humphrey, D.H. Kitson and T. Kasse, *The State of Software Engineering Practice: A Preliminary Report* (Software Engineering Institute, Carnegie Mellon University, 1989).

7. W.S. Humphrey, *Managing the Software Process* (Addison-Wesley, 1989).

8. W.S. Humphrey, D.H. Kitson and J. Gale, *A Comparison of U.S. and Japanese Software Process Maturity* (Software Engineering Institute, Carnegie Mellon University, 1991).

9. D.H. Kitson and S.M. Masters, *An Analysis of SEI Software Process Assessment Results: 1987-1991* (Software Engineering Institute, Carnegie Mellon University, 1992).

10. M.C. Paulk, B. Curtis, M.B. Chrissis and C. v. Weber, *The Capability Maturity Model: Guidelines for Improving the Software Process* (Addison-Wesley, 1995).

11. J. Herbsleb, A. Carleton, J. Rozum, J. Siegel and D. Zubrow, *Benefits of CMM-based Software Process Improvement: Initial Results* (Software Engineering Institute, Carnegie Mellon University, 1994).

11a. D. Zubrow, W. Hayes, J. Siegel and D. Goldenson, *Maturity Questionnaire* (Software Engineering Institute, Carnegie Mellon University, 1944).

12. W.S. Humphrey, *A Discipline for Software Engineering* (Addison-Wesley, 1995).

13. S. Masters and C. Bothwell, *CMM Appraisal Framework, Version 1.0* (Software Engineering Institute, Carnegie Mellon University, 1995).

13a. D. Goldenson and J. Herbsleb, *A Systematic Survey of Process Improvement, Its Benefits. and Factors that Influence Success* (Software Engineering Institute, Carnegie Mellon University, 1995).

14. ImprovelT, 1991, ISO/IEC JTCl/SC7 N865.

15. Proposal for a Study Period on Process Management, 1991, ISO/IEC JTCl/SC7 N872.

16. Study Report: The Need and Requirements for a Software Process Assessment Standard, 1992, ISO/IEC JTCl/SC7 N944R.

17. New Work Item Proposal to Develop A Standard for Software Process Assessment, 1993, ISO/IEC JTCl N2104.

18. Summary of Voting on JTC1/N2104 Proposal for NWI: Software Process Assessment, 1993, ISO/IEC JTCl N2312.

19. A. Dorling, History of the SPICE Project, *2nd International SPICE Symposium*, Brisbane, Australia, 1995, pp. 1- 7 (Australian Software Quality Research Institute, Griffith University).

20. Product Specification for a Software Process Assessment Standard, 1993, ISO/IEC JTC1/SC7/WG10 No16.

21. Requirements Specification for a Software Process Assessment Standard, 1993, ISO/IEC JTC1/SC7/WG10 NO17.

22. M. Paulk and M. Konrad, An overview of ISO's SPICE project, *American Programmer*, 7, (1994) 16-20.

23. M. Paulk, A perspective on the issues facing SPICE, *Proceedings of the Fifth International Conference on Software Quality*, Austin, Texas, USA, 1995, pp. 415-424.

24. M. Konrad, M. Paulk and A. Graydon, An overview of SPICE's model for process management, *Proceedings of the Fifth International Conference on Software Quality*, Austin, Texas, USA, 23-26 October 199~, pp. 291-301.

25. T. Rout, (ed.) *Proceedings of the 2nd International SPICE Symposium*, 1995 (Australian Software Quality Research Institute, Griffith University).

26. F. Maclennan and G. Ostrolenk. The SPICE trials: validating the framework, *2nd International SPICE Symposium*, Brisbane, Australia, 1995, pp. 109-117 (Australian Software Quality Research Institute. Griffith University).

27. K. El Emam and D. Goldenson, SPICE: an empiricist's perspective, *2nd International Software Engineering Standards Symposium*, Montreal, Quebec, Canada, 1995, pp. 84~97 (IEEE Computer Society Technical Council on Software Engineering).

28. International Standard ISO/IEC 12207, Information Technology -Software Life Cycle Processes, International Organisation for Standardisation, International Electrotechnical Commission, 1995.

29. M. Paulk, M, Konrad and S. Garcia, CMM versus SPICE architectures, *Software Process Newsletter.* IEEE Computer Society Technical Council on Software Engineering, No.3, Spring 1995, pp. 7-11.

Chapter 9

Experiences of Software Process Assessment

1. Introduction to Chapter

In this chapter we describe some of the experiences of software process assessment gained in the last decade or so. These experiences are based on data collected routinely from process assessments, and on special studies performed in connection with specific process assessments.

For some time now, the SEI has been publishing summaries of the process assessments that it has performed, via its web site [5]. While these summaries are not sufficiently representative to give a clear indication of the state of the practice, even in the U.S., to which most of them relate, they make interesting reading nonetheless. It is probably safe to assume that they present an optimistic picture of the state of the industry as a whole, since it is the organizations that are closest to the state of the art who are most likely to have their software processes assessed.

While a great deal of such experience data must have been collected over the last fourteen or so years, much of it has been based on the use of propriety systems and is not in the public domain, though high-level summaries of the data often are. The following is a selection of the organizations that make at least some software process improvement or improvement-related data available in the

411

public domain.

- Software Engineering Institute (SEI)
- European Software Institute (ESI - Vasie project[8])
- Software Productivity Consortium
- SPICE

Within Europe, the ESSI (European Systems and Software Initiative) has funded process improvement activities. The two principal types of activities supported have been:

- Process Improvement Experiments (PIEs);
- Dissemination activities.

The largest part of the funding has gone to the PIEs. These have been widely reported via dissemination activities such as VASIE, which has used the ESI's website to make reports available to the public. Reports of PIEs have also featured at a number of European conferences.

As already mentioned, the SEI reports its experiences via its website. A typical six-month report characterizes the data accumulated to date with respect to organization type and organization size. It also reports on the overall maturity profiles observed since 1992 and how these profiles relate to organization type and organization size. In addition, it reports on trends observed in the data over a period of time, such as the number of organizations assessed in a given period, the maturity profiles observed, and the process improvements achieved. As an example, the March 2000 summary of SEI results showed that 40% of organizations assessed were at the *initial* level, 36% at the *repeatable* level, 18% at the *defined* level, 5% at the *managed* level and 2% at the *optimizing* level of the SW-CMM.

As already mentioned in the previous chapter, the SPICE standardization project is unique in that a large number of trial assessments have been performed and are being performed, in order to:

- identify shortcomings in the ISO/IEC 15504 document sets;
- seek evidence that the results of 15504-conformant assessments are valid, repeatable and comparable across organizational units;
- initiate the collection of data concerning the benefits resulting from the use of the 15504 document set;
- confirm that the 15504 document sets satisfy the requirements document for the standard.

These requirements are further elaborated in Maclennan, et al., [4]. The SPICE trials activity is structured into three non-overlapping phases, each with its own objectives and time scale. At the end of the year 2000, phases 1 and 2 were complete and phase 3 was well under way. The reports produced by the project for phases 1 and 2 [6,7] have been written and are available in the public domain.

These are just some of the sources of software improvement data. Comparisons across the various data sources are difficult because of the different assumptions that may have been made in defining the data collected, and the lack of commonly accepted definitions of the metrics and classifications used. Were these issues to be overcome, then the totality of the data would certainly be worth more than the sum of its parts.

2. Description of Articles

The first paper in this chapter, entitled "Software Quality and the Capability Maturity Model," is by James Herbsleb of Bell Laboratories, and David Zubrow, Dennis Goldenson, Will Hayes and Marc Paulk, all of the SEI. The authors investigated the following questions concerning software process improvement (SPI):

- How long does it take, and how much does it cost?

- **What are the factors that affect the success or failure of SPI?**

- **Is the SW-CMM an appropriate framework for guiding improvements?**

The authors investigated the outcomes of process assessments performed between one and three years previously in the US and Canada, by means of follow-up questionnaires addressed to senior technical staff involved in the assessments, project managers, and members of Software Engineering Process Groups (SEPGs). The questions were concerned with the value and accuracy of the assessment, the current performance of the organization, and the degree of success in implementing the recommendations that arose from the assessment, etc.

The paper concludes with some observations on what is now known about the relationship between the SW-CMM and software quality.

The second paper in this chapter is by Bob Smith and is entitled "SPICE Trials Phase 2." It describes the aims of phases 1 and 2 of the SPICE trials and summarizes the results of the phase 1 trials.

Smith also enumerates the requirements for participation in the phase 2 trials, as well as the main studies planned using the phase 2 data. These include:

- repeatability studies;

- harmonization studies;

- process capability determination studies;

- process improvement studies;

- applicability studies.

The paper ends with a call for participation in the phase 2 trials.

The third paper in the chapter, "SPICE Trials Assessment Profile," by Robin Hunter, describes the results of the phase 2 trials of the SPICE project. It is based on the contents of the interim phase 2 trials database of 30 trials in 23 organizational units, and contains the ratings collected from 341 process instances.

Hunter summarizes the trials data with respect to the:

- characteristics of the organizational unit involved;

- characteristics of the software product produced;

- process coverage achieved;

- attribute ratings observed;

- process capability levels achieved.

This paper also contains a limited study of the relationship between criticality of the product and process capability.

Hunter's paper is only one of a number of papers published describing the results of the SPICE trials. The results of the phase-1 trials were described in a special issue of the *IEEE Software Process Newsletter* [3] as well as in a textbook [1]. Another paper describing the phase-2 trials is [2]. Each phase of the SPICE trials has benefited from the experiences gained from the previous phases in terms of data storage methods, types of analysis performed, presentation of results, etc.

The fourth paper in the chapter, entitled "The Reliability of ISO/IEC PDTR 15504 Assessments," is by Jean-Martin Simon, Khaled El Emam, Sonia Rousseau, Eric Jacquet and Frederic Babey. The paper is concerned with the reliability of SPICE assessments and the issue of interrater agreement. It also provides a good introduction to the PDTR (Preliminary Draft Technical Report) version of ISO/IEC 15504.

Generally, interrater agreement seems to be high, though in the studies undertaken this depended somewhat on the process attribute that was assessed. Of the attributes at levels 1 through 3, the agreement was highest for the *process performance attribute* and the *process resource attribute*, and lowest for the *work product management* attribute.

The authors also consider whether interrater agreement would be higher if the four-point scale (*fully, largely, partially, not*) were replaced by a three-point scale formed by merging adjacent values in the scale. However, they found no evidence to suggest this.

The fifth paper in this chapter is by Fran O'Hara and is entitled "European Experiences with Software Process Improvement." The paper is written in the context of the European ESSI (European Systems and Software Initiative) program, which, among other things, provided financial support to organizations that embarked on software process improvement (SPI) programs.

O'Hara describes the experiences of four organizations that embarked on SPI programs. Between them, they used all of the "big three" assessment models: SW-CMM, ISO 9001 and SPICE/15504. For each case study the paper describes the business drivers, the sponsors' roles, the assessment approaches and the improvement strategies.

The paper concludes by describing the training approaches used in each of the case studies, the effect of cultural issues, and the lessons learned, concluding that focusing on improvement rather than compliance (with, for example, a SW-CMM level) was crucial.

References

[1] K. El Emam, J.-N. Drouin, W. Melo, *SPICE: The Theory and Practice of Software Process Improvement and Capability Determination*, IEEE Computer Society, 1998.

[2] R. B. Hunter; "Software Process Assessment: Difficulties and Benefits"; 6*th*. *European Conference on Software Quality*, Vienna, 1999.

[3] *IEEE Software Process Newsletter*, number 6, Spring 1996.

[4] F. Maclennan, G. Ostrolenk; "Introduction to the SPICE Trials", Chapter 12 of *SPICE: The Theory and Practice of Software Process Improvement and Capability Determination*, edited by El Emam, Drouin, Mel; IEEE Computer Society Press, 1998.

[5] *SEI website:* http://www.sei.cmu.edu

[6] *SPICE Trials Phase-1 Report*, SPICE project 1996.

[7] *SPICE Trials Phase-2 Interim Report*, volume 1, SPICE project, 1998.

[8] *Vasie, ESI website:* http://www.esi.es/

Software Quality and the Capability Maturity Model

James Herbsleb, David Zubrow, Dennis Goldenson, Will Hayes, and Mark Paulk

About the time Fred Brooks was warning us there was not likely to be a single, "silver bullet" solution to the essential difficulties of developing software [3], Watts Humphrey and others at the Software Engineering Institute (SEI) were busy putting together the set of ideas that was to become the Capability Maturity Model (CMM) for Software.[1] The CMM adopted the opposite of the quick-fix silver bullet philosophy. It was intended to be a coherent, ordered set of incremental improvements, all having experienced success in the field, packaged into a roadmap that showed how effective practices could be built on one another in a logical progression (see "The Capability Maturity Model for Software" sidebar). Far from a Quick fix, it was expected that the

improvements would take considerable time and effort to put into place and would usually require a major shift in culture and attitudes.

Judging by its acceptance in the software industry, the CMM bas already been a major success. It has spread far beyond its origins in military avionics applications, and is not used by major organizations in every sector of the economy around the globe (see box "Adoption of the CMM: A Growing Phenomenon" sidebar). While we haven o accurate estimates of its penetration in the global industry, based on what we do know it surely includes thousands of organizations, and the resources expended on CMM-based software process improvement (SPI) are certainly in the billions of dollars. However, the CMM is not without it critics [1]. It is sometimes claimed that adopting the CMM encourages too much bureaucracy

---

[1] CMM and the Capability Maturity Model are service marks of Carnegie Mellon University.

"Software Quality and the Capability Maturity Model" by James Herbsleb from *Communications of the ACM*, Volume 40, number 6, pp. 30-40, Association for Computing Machinery, Inc., June 1997. Reprinted by permission.

The Capability Maturity Model for Software

The Capability Maturity Model for Software (CMM or SW-CMM) is a reference model for appraising software process maturity and a normative model for helping software organizations progress along an evolutionary path from ad hoc, chaotic processes to mature, disciplined software processes. The CMM is organized into five maturity levels as shown in Box 1.

Except for Level 1, each maturity level is decomposed into several key process areas that indicate the areas an organization should focus on to improve its software process. These "vital few" areas are listed as shown in Box 2.

The rating components of the CMM, for the purpose of assessing an organization's process maturity, are its maturity levels, key process areas, and their goals. Each key process area is further described by informative components: key practices, subpractices, and examples. The key practices describe the infrastructure and activities that contribute most to the effective implementation and institutionalization of the key process area.

CMM Level	Major Characteristics
1) **Initial**	The software process is characterized as ad hoc, and occasionally even chaotic. Few processes are defined, and success depends on individual effort and heroics.
2) **Repeatable**	Basic project management processes are established to track cost, schedule, and functionality. The necessary process discipline is in place to repeat earlier successes on projects with similar applications.
3) **Defined**	The software process for both management and engineering activities is documented, standardized, and integrated into a standard software process for the organization. Projects use an approved, tailored version of the organization's standard software process(es) for developing and maintaining software.
4) **Managed**	Detailed measures of the software process and product quality are collected. Both the software process and products are quantitatively understood and controlled.
5) **Optimizing**	Continuous process improvement is facilitated by quantitative feedback from the process and from piloting inovative ideas and technologies.

Box 1.

CMM Level	Focus	Key Process Areas
1 **Initial**	Competent people and heroics	
2 **Repeatable**	Project management processes	Requirements management Software project planning Software project tracking and oversight Software subcontract management Software quality assurance Software configuration management
3 **Defined**	Engineering processes and organizational support	Organization process focus Organization process definition Training program Integrated software management Software product engineering Intergroup coordination Peer reviews
4 **Managed**	Product and process quality	Quantitative process management Software quality management
5 **Optimizing**	Continuous process improvement	Defect prevention Technology change management Process change management

Box 2.

or that the CMM is incomplete or flawed. This debate is partly concerned with scope, policy issues, and conceptual questions (such as whether the model harmonizes appropriately with international standards such as ISO-9000). But the debate also focuses on the supposed consequences of adopting the CMM as the basis for SPI efforts. Will the organization get bogged down in red tape or suffer other damage, or will it benefit and show improved performance?

Within the last several years, a significant evolution has taken place as the debate has evolved into a more scientific investigation. Many of the most important questions about the CMM can be

416

addressed by careful collection and analysis of data, rather than the exchange of rhetoric and undocumented anecdotes that has often characterized this sort of discussion in the past. In this article, we will present the results to date of the SEI's efforts to test critical claims and assertions about the CMM. The effort is still under way, but we believe the current findings are significant. While we will focus on our own efforts, we will also briefly discuss other relevant work.

Claims about the CMM

In order to organize our CMM studies, we worked extensively with users and potential users of the CMM to identify the questions of greatest practical concern. At a high level, the most pressing issues are:

* Process maturity: How long does it take, how much does it cost, and how will it benefit the business?
* What are the factors that influence the success and failure of CMM-based SPI?
* Is the CMM an appropriate framework for guiding improvements in a way that can be understood and applied to the full variety of software organizations?

We have completed three studies to date. Each employed a different approach and different data sources. Through the use of multiple studies and methods, we reduced our vulnerability to the inevitable weaknesses of any single effort.

Multiple-case study. When we began this effort, several case studies had already been published [such as 4, 5, 9, 12]. These studies showed dramatic improvements in such important organizational performance parameters as productivity, reduction of rework, and improvements in cycle time. In our initial effort [7], we tried to locate any additional existing data of this sort that organizations undergoing SPI might already have available. We eventually received usable data from 13 organizations. In order for us to consider the data usable, we had to understand the data collection and analysis process well enough to have a reasonable degree of confidence the data point was meaningful, and ensure the organization was engaged in a CMM-based SPI effort, which appeared to be causing these results.

We presented these results as changes over time¹ within the organization, in order to avoid comparing results from different organizations, which typically defined data in very different ways.

After-the-appraisal survey. The case study evidence (from both the previously published case studies and our own multiple-case study) has several inherent limitations:

* Are these cases typical, or are we only studying a select group of success stories?
* In most cases, only a few types of data are reported from each organization, leaving open the possibility that the organization traded off other performance dimensions (like quality for cycle time) to get these results.
* Did CMM-based SPI cause the improvements in performance, or merely coincide with them?

We undertook the survey described in this section specifically to address these shortcomings. In order to address the first two concerns, we needed to look more broadly across organizations using the CMM, and try to get some small but comprehensive set of performance indicators from them. A survey is an effective tool for this purpose. The third concern—establishing the causal connection between process improvement and performance—must be addressed by accumulating evidence from a number of different studies, using different methods and relying on different assumptions. The survey provides a cross-sectional view of organizations with a wide range of characteristics, and hence provides a good complement to the longitudinal case studies of a few successful organizations.

The goals of this survey [8] were to find out what typically happens to SPI efforts after assessments, to learn as much as possible about the reasons for success or failure, and to see if the performance reported by more mature organizations is, in fact, superior to the performance reported by less mature organizations.

We used our database, which contained over 450 assessments at that time, to select appraisals conducted no less that one year ago (so there was time for change to take place) and no more than three years ago (so we could find people able to give good

---

¹Our basic analysis was percentage change per year, which is much like a compound interest rate. A threefold increase over three years, for example, works out to about a 44% increase per year for three years.

accounts of what happened after the appraisals). In order to get a broad and balanced perspective, we decided to try to contact a senior technical person and a project manager as well as a member of the software engineering process group (SEPG) for each appraisal.

All told, we were able to obtain contact information for about 167 individuals representing 61 assessments. Of the 167 questionnaires we sent out, we received completed and usable data from 138 of them, for a return rate of 83%. We also succeeded in obtaining responses from individuals in several roles. Of the 138 questionnaires returned, 47 were from senior members of the technical staff, 47 were from project managers, and 44 were from members of an SEPG. Interestingly, and perhaps surprisingly, we found no systematic differences among the responses of these three groups.

Appraisals from reassessed organizations. Since the SEI developed the Software Process Assessment (SPA) method, it has been collecting SPA results from organizations using the method. The results include the maturity level of the organization, the identified process strengths and weaknesses, the organizational scope of the assessment, and the date the SPA was conducted. In this study [6], we used the information in our SPA database to address these two questions:

• How long does it take for an organization to move up a maturity level?
• What are the process challenges that distinguish those who move from the initial level (Level 1) to the repeatable level (Level 2) and those who remain at the initial level?

To address these questions, we focused on organizations that have undergone multiple SPAs. This allowed us to investigate the experiences and changes in individual organizations. From the database housing the SPA results, we extracted the data for 48 organizations that had conducted two or more SPAs. As a group, these organizations have conducted 104 assessments. To address the first question, we looked at the elapsed time between assessments in those cases where organizations moved up in level on a subsequent assessment. To address the second question, we categorized the "weakness" findings according to which key process area (KPA) they served,[3] and compared the weaknesses in organizations that improved their maturity levels with those that did not (see CMM sidebar).

Process maturity: How long does it take, how much does it cost, and how will it benefit the business?

The CMM is best regarded as a tool to be used to pursue an organization's business goals. So it is extremely important to determine the time and effort that must be invested as well as the effects of SPI on organizational performance.

An examination of reassessments shows the median time between assessments (where organizations have moved up on a subsequent assessment) is about two years (see Figure 1). No doubt this interval is, in part, a reflection of the "common wisdom" about timing of assessments, a frequent recommendation being 1.5 to 2.5 years. Only about 25% move from Level 1 to Level 2 in 21 months or less, and about 25% take 37 months or more. Moving from Level 2 to Level 3 appears to be a little quicker, with 25% moving up in 17 months or less and 25% taking 31 months or more.

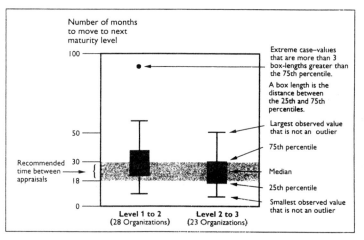

Figure 1. Time to move from Level 1 to Level 2, and from Level 2 to Level 3. The medians are 26.5 months for Level 1 to Level 2, and 24 months for Level 2 to Level 3. (This data is updated regularly; at press time, this summary is accurate.)

We have only a few data points about the actual cost of a SPI program, all of which came from our multiple-case study. We normalized the cost by the number of software engineers in the organization. The range was $490 to $2,004 per software engineer per year, with a median figure of $1,375. What was included in these costs varied somewhat depending on the accounting practices of each organization, but

---

[3] We established the reliability and validity of this categorization scheme which is described in [6].

in general it included the cost of any assessments, any CMM-related training, and the cost of staffing the SEPG.

The cost and time required for a SPI program apparently exceeded the expectations of many people. In our survey we found that slightly over three-fourths (77%) agreed or strongly agreed that SPI "took longer than expected," and slightly over two-thirds (68%) said it "cost more than expected."

Table 1. Summary of case study performance results [7].

Category	Range	Median	Data pts.
Productivity gain/year	9%–67%	35%	4
Time to market (reduction/year)	15%–23%	—	2
Post-release defects (reduction/year)	10%–94%	39%	5
Business value ratio	4.0–8.8:1	5.0:1	5

Almost half (49%) said there was "lots of disillusionment over lack of progress." CMM-based SPI is not a cheap nor a quick fix.

It is difficult to tell from these results alone whether the time and cost is exceeding expectations because the actual numbers are high relative to the benefit or because the organization had little information or experience with which to set realistic expectations.

The results from our multiple case study are consistent with those from previous case studies in organizations such as Hughes Aircraft [9], Raytheon [5], Schlumberger [12], and Tinker AFB [4]. For all the data points that satisfied our criteria, organizations engaged in CMM-based SPI tended to improve substantially in quality, cycle time, and productivity. The business value ratios (benefits divided by cost) were also substantially above 1. Table 1 shows a summary of the data we reported.

Our survey, which allowed us to look at a much broader sample of software organizations, gave us similarly encouraging results. We asked our respondents to rate their organization's performance on a number of dimensions, such as ability to meet schedules, ability to stay within budgets, product quality, and so on. For each of these dimensions, they rated their organization's performance as "excellent," "good," "fair," or "poor."' We combined the percentages of excellent and good responses then cross tabulated these responses with the organization's maturity level to produce the results shown in Figure 2.

With the exception of customer satisfaction, all these comparisons show improved performance with increased maturity level. These differences are statistically significant for all but "ability to meet budget." Ratings of customer satisfaction show a dip from Level 1 to Level 2, before reaching 100% good or excellent at Level 3. While this pattern is statistically significant, that is, different from a horizontal line, the difference between levels 1 and 2 is not sig-

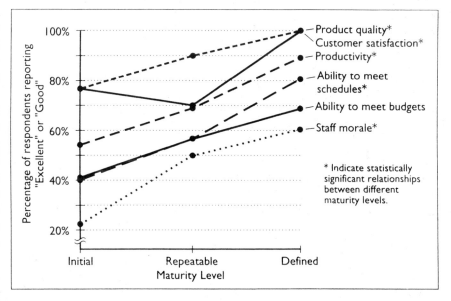

Figure 2. The percentage of respondents who reported that their organization had "excellent" or "good" performance in each area. The asterisks indicate statistically significant relationships between different maturity levels.

nificant. This means we are not able to tell whether this is a genuine difference or if it is just noise in the data. We hope future studies will sort this out. There have been several plausible suggestions about why this dip might occur, including the possibilities that

---

'We'd like to be as clear as we can about what these numbers do and do not mean. We do not know the actual bases for the respondents' answers. All we need to assume, however, is that if 138 people are asked "How good is your ability to meet schedule?" those answering it is "good" or "excellent" are, on average, better able to meet schedules than are those who answer their ability is "fair" or "poor."

some customers do not initially like the discipline that requirements management brings to customer interactions, and that customers suffer as attention is focused internally as SPI gets under way.

In addition to these studies by the SEI, an elegant study of software produced under contract for the U.S. Air Force was recently published [11]. Their results also indicate the ability to meet schedules and stay within budget was substantially better in higher maturity organizations. In another study, Krishnan [10] examined the relationship of CMM process maturity and software quality and cost. His sophisticated statistical analysis of data from a large software development laboratory in a Fortune 100 company showed that process maturity significantly increased quality, but did not show evidence of a direct effect on cost. Higher product quality, however, significantly reduced both development and support cost, so to the extent that process maturity increased quality, it may also have indirectly decreased cost.

Note that virtually all the reports on the benefits of process maturity come from comparisons among organizations at the *initial. repeatable.* and *defined* levels, or from observations of organizations over time as they move through these three stages. Very little is known at this point about the benefits of the higher maturity levels, since there has been relatively little experience to draw on.

Criticisms of the CMM

As we mentioned, several criticisms have been made of CMM-based improvement. The ones that seem to have received the most attention are that CMM-based SPI will be counterproductive, will cause the organization to neglect important non-CMM issues, to its detriment, and will cause the organization to become rigid and bureaucratic, making it more difficult to find creative solutions to technical problems.

Adoption of the CMM: A Growing Phenomenon

The CMM was originally developed to assist the U.S. Department of Defense (DoD) in software acquisition. The rationale was to include likely contractor performance as a factor in contract awards. The model for determining likely contract performance also became a guide or framework for software process improvement. DoD contractors quickly learned they needed to mold and guide their organizations to become more aligned with the CMM if they were to be successful in winning DoD contracts.

This focus is clearly seen in the data on the number and proportion of assessments conducted by DoD contractors in the period from 1987 through 1992. Most, if not all, of the major DoD contractors began CMM-based software process improvement initiatives as they vied for DoD contracts.

But the CMM has not remained a "stick" in the DoD contracting community. Through the efforts of the SEI to obtain broad participation in the development and improvement of the CMM, the model gained visibility in the wider software engineering community. Gradually, commercial organizations began to adopt the CMM as a framework for their own internal improvement initiatives. In 1989, only a handful of commercial organizations conducted software process assessments, but each year since 1993, commercial organizations have performed more assessments than all DoD and other Federal contractors combined. Furthermore, since 1994, several case studies of the impact of using the CMM in commercial organizations have appeared, including Motorola, Schlumberger, Bull HN, and Siemens.

Many of these companies are multinational in scope. As they acknowledged the benefits of software process improvement in their U.S. sites, they sought to apply this improvement strategy to their sites around the world. Furthermore, many organizations outside of the U.S. compete in markets with U.S. organizations and were stimulated to adopt a CMM approach to improvement through competitive pressure.

Today we see growing indications of the global adoption of the CMM. One indicator of the adoption is the number of CMM-based software process assessments conducted outside of the U.S. There has been a steady increase in this number over the past few years. According to the most recent software process maturity profile, 17% of the assessments on file at the SEI were conducted at sites located outside of the U.S.

Additionally, the number of Software Process Improvement Network (SPIN) groups outside of the U.S. is on the rise. SPINs are local organizations whose members have an interest in software process improvement. Twenty-six such groups have been established outside of the U.S. and can be found in Australia, Europe, Asia, and South and North America. They were established to facilitate communication of field experiences and lessons learned among champions and practitioners of software process improvement.

In our survey, we asked about whether any of these performance problems had actually occurred. In each case, the overwhelming majority of respondents (84% to 96%) disagreed or strongly disagreed that they had experienced the problem (see Table 2). These concerns appear to be misplaced for all but a relatively few organizations.

Another criticism occasionally made is that CMM-based SPI causes organizations to become

Table 2. Percentage of respondents that disagreed or strongly disagreed that CMM-based SPI caused these problems with organizational performance.

Question	Disagree or strongly disagree
SPI was counterproductive	96%
Neglect non-CMM issues	90%
Became more rigid and bureaucratic	84%

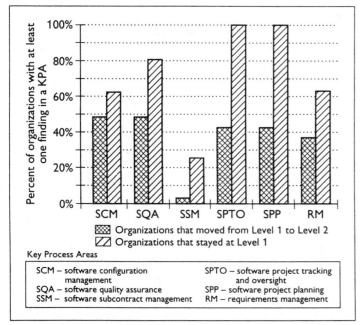

Key Process Areas

SCM – software configuration management	SPTO – software project tracking and oversight
SQA – software quality assurance	SPP – software project planning
SSM – software subcontract management	RM – requirements management

Figure 3. Percentage of organizations that had at least one finding in each of the Level 2 key process areas. (These are results from a second assessment.) All of the organizations were originally assessed at Level 1.

risk-averse. The argument apparently is that mature organizations will not pursue risky (but potentially high-payoff) projects for fear of "losing their maturity rating." On the other hand, one might argue that if process maturity lowers the level of risk on typical projects, the organization can more easily add high-risk projects to its portfolio. We have data from our survey that bear on this

issue. One question asked "How much risk is management generally willing to take?" In Level 1 organizations, only 42% responded "substantial" or "moderate" (the other choices were "some" and "little if any"). The figure for Level 2 organizations was 74%, and it rose to 79% in Level 3 organizations. This difference is statistically significant. This data indicates that people from higher maturity organizations report their managers are more willing, not less willing, to take risk.

The time and cost of a CMM-based SPI program often exceeds the expectations of those involved. However, substantial evidence has now accumulated that software process maturity, as defined by the CMM, has significant business benefits. A number of case studies, two correlational studies, and the survey we reported here all point toward this conclusion. There is also little evidence to suggest that using the CMM leads to the adverse effects predicted by its critics.

What are the factors that influence the success and failure of CMM-based SPI?

Clearly, not every organization that has attempted process improvement has succeeded. It is very important to learn more about what it takes to succeed so that more organizations can reap the benefits earlier.

In our analysis of reassessments, we examined the weaknesses that were most typical of organizations that were initially assessed at Level 1, then assessed again at Level 1 on a subsequent assessment. If we contrast these weaknesses with those found in organizations that succeeded in achieving Level 2, we can see the areas in which these organizations seemed to have the most difficulty.

As Figure 3 shows, the organizations not moving up were more likely to have a finding in each of the Level 2 KPAs. But the largest differences are in the areas of planning and tracking software projects. Every organization that failed to move up to Level 2 had a finding in both of these areas. This strongly suggests that these areas are either the most neglected or are the most difficult types of practices to put in place, or both.

Our survey revealed several problems which are encountered frequently in SPI efforts. Two of them are probably very general problems with organizational change efforts. Of the respondents, 42%

agreed or strongly agreed with statements that SPI had "been overcome by events and crises;" 72% agreed or strongly agreed that it has "often suffered due to time and resource limitations."

Another frequent problem stems from the characteristics of the CMM itself. Two thirds of the respondents agreed with the statement, "We understood what needed to be improved, but we needed more guidance about how to improve it." Similarly, over half agreed that they needed more mentoring and assistance. We had heard anecdotal evidence of these types of problems before, but the survey gave us a better sense of how widespread they really are. What is needed is clear, practical guidance on how to introduce the CMM into a software organization. This is currently being addressed in several ways at the SEI.[5]

In order to investigate the overall success rate of CMM-based SPI, we included a question on our survey which simply asked: "How successfully have the findings and recommendations of the assessment been addressed?" The distribution of responses is shown in Figure 4.

These results clearly indicate that success is not guaranteed, and that it is very important to learn about factors that distinguish the successes from the failures.

Lessons Learned

In our multiple case study, we identified a number of lessons learned by successful organizations. Many of these lessons are factors identified by those involved in the SPI effort as critical to the effort's success. The factors most often identified as important were the following:

- The SPI effort requires visible support and commitment from senior management.
- Middle management support is important and often hard to get because they have major project responsibility and often no additional resources for process improvement.
- Grassroots support and involvement is also extremely important.

- Obtaining observable results, backed up with data if possible, is important early on to keep the effort visible, and to motivate and sustain interest.
- The process improvement effort must be planned, managed, and given sufficient dedicated resources.
- The SPI effort must serve business interests and

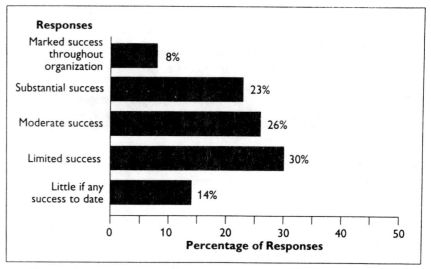

Figure 4. Distribution of responses to question about the degree of success in addressing the assessment findings and recommendations. (The numbers do not add up to 100 because of rounding error.)

must be coordinated with other parts of the business in order to have the necessary foundation for the cultural change required by successful SPI.

In our survey, we were able to examine success factors in a more systematic way. We asked a number of questions about characteristics of the organization and of the SPI effort, and identified a number of characteristics associated with successful and with unsuccessful efforts. There is considerable agreement with the more informally developed lessons learned. Highly successful efforts tended to have the following characteristics:[6]

- Senior management actively monitors SPI progress
- Clearly stated, well understood SPI goals
- Staff time/resources dedicated to process improvement
- Clear, compensated assignment of responsibility
- SEPG staffed by highly respected people
- Technical staff is involved in improvement

On the other hand, agreement with the following was associated with less successful SPI efforts:

[5]See the SEI web site for more information. http://www.sei.cmu.edu.
[6]Agreement with these statements was statistically associated (at the .05 level) with the higher categories of "success" as shown in Figure 4.

- High levels of "organizational politics"
- Turf guarding
- Cynicism from previous unsuccessful improvement experiences
- Belief that SPI "gets in the way of real work"
- Need more guidance on how to improve, not just what to improve

As these studies suggest, a number of factors appear to be associated with success or failure of a process improvement effort. In order to get off the ground, particular attention should be given to planning and tracking projects, an area that seems to be holding many Level 1 organizations back from achieving Level 2. There are several factors under management control that also appear to be critical to success, including active monitoring, giving the effort adequate resources, and staffing it with highly respected people. Participation and buy-in at all levels, including middle management and technical staff, is also very important. Showing concrete results quickly may help with this. Organizations that have dysfunctional attitudes such as turf guarding, internal political contention, and cynicism about the effort are going to have a more difficult time. There is also a tendency for SPI programs to be starved for resources and to be overcome by events. A common problem, which has not yet been adequately addressed, is the need for more guidance on how to go about making the improvements.

Is the CMM an appropriate framework for guiding improvements in a way that can be understood and applied to the full variety of software organizations?

It is sometimes suggested that some features of the CMM are inappropriate for organizations that differ substantially from the large-project defense avionics environment for which the CMM was originally developed. In particular, it is often suggested that small organizations [2] and commercial companies may find the CMM less useful or more difficult to apply.

In our survey, we were able to compare success rates of organizations of various sizes operating in different sectors in order to see if these factors played a major role in determining success. Most organizations in the survey were in the commercial (23), government contractor (19), or government (12) sectors, and our results show no systematic differences in the success rates among these sectors.

We also had a number of sizes of organizations represented. The smallest 25% had fewer than 54 software engineers, while the largest 25% had 300 or more. Again, there was no systematic difference in success rate due to organizational size. Interestingly, we found that small organizations had fewer of the problems such as organizational politics and turf guarding that appeared to inhibit success.

Despite these findings, there is some limited evidence which suggests it may be more difficult to apply the CMM, or at least parts of the CMM, in small organizations and in commercial organizations. The evidence is from an unpublished survey that we conducted of 84 people who took the SEI's "Introduction to the CMM" course during the period from late 1993 until early 1995. The survey was conducted by mail from late 1995 to early 1996 with a return rate of over 60%. Approximately one to two years passed between the survey and the time the students had completed the course—enough time for them to make informed judgments about its value added in practice.

Figure 5 shows the distribution of responses to the question: "How much of the subject matter that was covered in the course is applicable/relevant to your work?" In all of the organizational size categories, well over 60% answered that much or most of the material was applicable. However, all of the "little, if any" responses came from the two smallest categories of organizations. There is a similar pattern of results, although it did not achieve statistical significance, for how well they have been able to use the material in their organization.

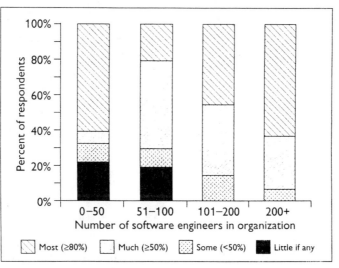

Figure 5. Distribution of responses to question about relevance of CMM course material. The overall pattern of results is statistically significant.

There are similar hints in the data broken down by type of company. The rates for relevance and ability to actually use the material were quite high for each type of organization, again with well over 60% saying "much" or "most" was applicable. As before, these rates are slightly lower (although the differences did not quite achieve statistical significance) for commercial companies than for defense contractors.

In summary, the data to date does not point to any actual differences in success in using the CMM for companies of various sizes and types. There are some hints, however, that small companies and commercial companies may find some of the CMM irrelevant or hard to apply. These differences do not appear to be large.

What do We Know Now About The CMM and Software Quality?

In the past several years the empirical studies of organizations using the CMM— both studies performed by the SEI and by others—have produced significant advances in our understanding of the costs, benefits, problems, and risks of CMM-based SPI. The most broadly supported claim is that CMM-based SPI has substantial business benefits for those moving from the initial through the defined levels. A number of individual case studies, a multiple-case study, a survey, and two correlational studies are quite consistent in showing important organizational performance improvements associated with process maturity. Future work should aim to identify the precise mechanisms that relate process and performance so the existence and nature of the causal relationship can be determined.

Many factors associated with success and failure are fairly well established, since they crop up in many case studies and were also good predictors of successful efforts in the surveyed organizations. The results about how widely the CMM applies to organizations of various sizes and types should still be regarded as tentative.

There are several important areas where there has been very little work to date. There have been no published studies we are aware of on the results of moving to the highest maturity levels, although there have been studies of some of the individual practices included in those levels. There is also a whole set of issues about change, resistance, and institutionalizing new ways of working in software organizations that we need to better understand in order to become more effective at putting innovations into practice. ◼

ACKNOWLEDGMENTS
The authors would like to thank all of those who shared data or took the time to fill out questionnaires. This work would not be possible without their gracious cooperation.

REFERENCES

1. Bach, J. Enough about process: what we need are heroes. *IEEE Soft.* 12, 2 (1994), 96–98.
2. Brodman, J. G. and Johnson, D. L. What small businesses and small organizations say about the CMM. In *Proceedings of ICSE '94* (Sorrento, Italy, May 16–21).
3. Brooks, F.P. No silver bullet: Essence and accidents of software engineering. *IEEE Comput.* 20, 4 (1987), 10–19.
4. Butler, K.L. The economic benefits of software process improvement. *CrossTalk* (July 1995), 14–17.
5. Dion, R. Process improvement and the corporate balance sheet. IEEE Soft. 10, 4 (July 1993), 28–35.
6. Hayes, W. and Zubrow, D. Moving on up: Data and experience doing CMM-based software process improvement. Software Engineering Institute, Carnegie Mellon University, Pittsburgh, PA CMU/SEI-95-TR-08, Sept. 1995.
7. Herbsleb, J., Carleton, A., Rozum, J. Siegel, J, and Zubrow, D. Benefits of CMM-based software process improvement: Initial results. Software Engineering Institute, Carnegie Mellon University, Pittsburgh, PA CMU/SEI-94-TR-13, Aug. 1994.
8. Herbsleb, J.D. and Goldenson, D.R. A systematic survey of CMM experience and results. In *Proceedings of ICSE '96* (Berlin, Mar. 25–30).
9. Humphrey, W.S., Snyder, T.R., and Willis, R.R. Software process improvement at Hughes Aircraft. *IEEE Soft.* 8,4 (July 1991) 11–23.
10. Krishnan, M.S. Cost and Quality Considerations in Software Product Management. Dissertation, Graduate School of Industrial Administration, Carnegie Mellon University, 1996.
11. Lawlis, P.K., Flowe, R.M., and Thordahl, J.B. A correlational study of the CMM and software development performance. *CrossTalk* (Sept. 1995), 21–25.
12. Wohlwend, H and Rosenbaum, S. Schlumberger's software improvement program. *IEEE Trans. Soft. Eng.* 20, 11 (Nov. 1994), 833–839.

JAMES HERBSLEB (herbsleb@research.bell-labs.com) is a member of the technical staff in the Software Production Research Group, Bell Laboratories, Lucent Technologies, Naperville, Ill.

DAVID ZUBROW (dz@sei.cmu.edu) is a member of the technical staff at the Software Engineering Institute, Carnegie Mellon University, Pittsburgh, Pa.

DENNIS GOLDENSON (dg@sei.cmu.edu) is a member of the technical staff at the Software Engineering Institute, Carnegie Mellon University, Pittsburgh, Pa.

WILL HAYES (wh@sei.cmu.edu) is a member of the technical staff at the Software Engineering Institute, Carnegie Mellon University, Pittsburgh, Pa.

MARK PAULK (mcp@sei.cmu.edu) is a member of the technical staff at the Software Engineering Institute, Carnegie Mellon University, Pittsburgh, Pa.

This work is sponsored by the U.S. Department of Defense.

Spice Trials Phase 2

Bob Smith

European Software Institute

The SPICE Project Organisation, established in June 1993, is an international collaborative effort to assist in the development of an emerging ISO Standard for Software Process Assessment and to undertake user Trials to capture early feedback for revision of the Standard.

The project has allowed a fast development route for the Standard. An essential feature of the SPICE Project is the conduct of industrial user trials to validate the prospective Standard against the defined goals and requirements; and to verify the consistency and usability of its component products. The project aims to test the proposed process assessment standard across a representative sample of organisations, for differing scenarios of use, in order to obtain rapid feedback and allow refinement prior to publication as a full international standard. The trials should also determine whether the proposed standard satisfies the needs of its prospective users.

The objectives of the SPICE Trials were stated as [1]:

- to identify shortcomings in the SPICE document set for resolution prior to standardisation, particularly regarding coverage, usability and applicability,

- to seek evidence that the results of SPICE-conformant assessments are valid and repeatable, and

- to initiate the collection of data regarding the benefits resulting from the use of SPICE.

The trials are planned to be conducted over three separate phases each of which have their own detailed objectives and scope which are linked to the increasing maturity of the document set. Phase 1 of the Trials was conducted in 1995. Phase 2 started in September 1996 for a period of one year. Phase 3 will follow and will be aimed at verifying that the significant user feedback which will be collected in Phase 2 and the feedback through the ISO National Body organisations has been adequately incorporated into the Standard. Phase 3 will also provide continuous feedback from the use of the Standard to validate it against its own requirements and to initiate data collection on the benefits of its use.

The purpose of Phase 1 Trials was to test the design decisions for the core parts of the proposed Standard, namely the model for process management, the requirements for rating processes, the guidance on

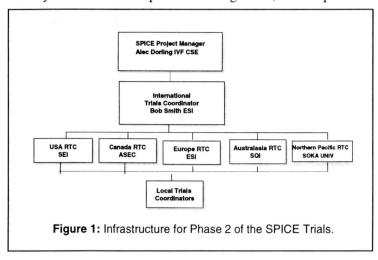

Figure 1: Infrastructure for Phase 2 of the SPICE Trials.

conducting assessments and the requirements and guidance on the construction, selection and use of assessment instruments and tools. In addition preliminary impressions of the benefits of SPICE were collected.

Phase 2 will be concerned with :

- testing product integrity to check consistency across all products, interfaces between all products and the effectiveness of the products as a whole,

- testing the usefulness of SPICE for process improvement and capability determination, and

- beginning to validate that the SPICE products satisfy the project goals and requirements, and in particular that repeatability of assessment results has been achieved.

Phase 3 will be concerned with the complete validation of the project goals and requirements. It will also be aimed at initiating a data collection mechanism to demonstrate the benefits of using the Standard.

SPICE Trials Organisation

A SPICE Trials team was established which is responsible for planning the trials activities which include:

- designing the necessary questionnaires and forms to support the trial assessments;

- developing a trials database to store the results of the assessments; and

- collecting and analysing the data to report the results.

The Trials team is headed by the International Trials Coordinator (ITC) who reports directly to the SPICE Project Manager on all aspects related to the trials (see Figure 1). Currently there are around 18 members in the Trials team from 12 different countries developing the infrastructure necessary to support Phase 2 and for the longer term [2].

The conduct of the trials are managed in the five designated SPICE Technical Centres (TC) of the SPICE Project which are Europe, USA, Canada and Australasia and Northern Pacific. Each Technical Centre has a nominated Regional Trials Coordinator (RTC) who is a member of the trials team. Each RTC is responsible for coordinating all trials activities in their region to ensure all the necessary information is available and that all the trial assessment data is collected and included in the database.

A new feature for the Phase 2 Trials is the introduction of a Local Trials Coordinator (LTC). For Phase 2 a significant increase in the number of trial assessments is expected. The Local Trials Coordinator will work with the RTC to deal with the increased workload in supporting organisations and assessors; to collect and process the trials results; and to ensure that all participants receive quick and efficient responses to questions and solutions to problems. The requirements to become a Local Trials Coordinator are described in the SPICE SPOTLIGHT section of this newsletter by Alec Dorling.

Summary of Phase 1

The Phase 1 Trials were based on the use of indicative case studies, conducted in 4 of the 5 SPICE technical regions to test out the model for process management, the requirements for rating processes, the guidance on conducting assessments and the requirements and guidance on the construction, selection and use of assessment instruments and tools. In addition preliminary impressions of the benefits of SPICE were collected. Each case study assessment was led by an experienced assessor who had been involved in the development of the SPICE document set.

Feedback was collected via trial-specific questionnaires and forms (to gather data for testing the hypotheses) and observation reports, as well as the project-wide problem reporting process.

Phase 1 of the Trials achieved reasonable coverage of the SPICE model for process management in a good cross-section of application domains. The data used in the analysis was collected from a total of 35 trials.

The results from the trials have provided very useful feedback from the user community for the improvement of the SPICE products. A number of conclusions and recommendations have been drawn from the results and experiences of the trials, relating to both the document set and the trials process [3].

The results from these trials are generally positive about SPICE although a number of issues have been highlighted which are being addressed in a revision of the SPICE document set in preparation for Phase 2 Trials.

Following completion of Phase 1 and the ISO review of version 1 of the SPICE document set a number of changes were proposed. In summary the reasons for these changes were:

- the need to simplify the model to address problems identified during Phase 1 trials particularly related to the capability dimension

- the need for much closer alignment to ISO 12207 Software Life-cycle Processes [4]

- the need to make the Standard less prescriptive

- the need to provide a clear route for migration/harmonisation of existing model providers

A key decision in implementing these goals was to establish a Reference Model for Software Process Assessment, based upon the former Part 2 of Version 1, to provide a basis for comparison between assessments conducted using different models and methods.

Phase 2 Trials

The objectives of Phase 2 will be aimed at testing whether these changes have been correctly implemented in the new document set. In particular the objectives of the Phase 2 Trials will be [5]:

- To evaluate the Reference Model as a basis for software process assessment.

- To evaluate the adequacy of the requirements for conducting a software process assessment.

- To evaluate the usefulness of the guidelines for conducting a software process assessment.

- To evaluate the usefulness of the guidelines for software process improvement.

- To evaluate the usefulness of the guidelines for process capability determination.

- To evaluate the Assessment Model as a basis for conducting a software process assessment; to evaluate its compatibility with the Reference Model; and to evaluate it as guidance for the development of assessment models compatible with the Reference Model.

- To evaluate the usefulness of the guidelines for Assessor Qualification and Training.

Requirements for Participation

All Phase 2 Trials participants will be expected to meet the following minimum requirements to participate:

- participate in one of the trial types that will be defined as part of the Phase 2 Studies described below,

- provide the ratings of a trial assessment to the SPICE Trials team for inclusion in the trial database and for analysis,

- answer the Trials questionnaires associated with the trial type,

- each Trial Assessor must demonstrate relevant SPICE knowledge and Assessment experience to conduct the assessment to satisfy the organisational sponsor,

- when an assessment is conducted it must use a model compatible to the SPICE Reference Model. The compatible model contained in Part 5 of the document set may be used or another model such as CMM, Bootstrap, PPA, Trillium where these are shown to be compatible by the model provider, and

- all trials should adhere to the instructions provided for the conduct of the trial.

Phase 2 Studies

To achieve the objectives of Phase 2 a number of trials studies are being designed. These studies will be incorporated into the trial activity with minimal overhead. Some will require special tasks to be performed such as following the guidelines included in the SPICE document set; some will require the Trials Assessor to collect and report the individual assessment of each team member as well as the final assessment report; and others will simply require questionnaires to be completed.

To achieve the defined objectives a number of special requirements are being defined which will ask participants to perform some small tasks in addition to the assessment and to provide a small amount of data for analysis. These additional requirements will support the following types of study.

Repeatability Studies

To test the repeatability of assessment results a number of different types of trials will be designed. These will require assessment ratings to be produced in several different ways which will include the use of different assessment teams; different assessment methods; different assessment models; or different assessment instruments.

Harmonisation Studies

To test whether the Standard provides a clear route for the harmonisation of existing assessment model providers, a study will be designed to enable a trial assessment to be conducted using SPICE-compatible assessment models and associated methods.

Process Capability Determination Studies

These studies will be aimed at testing the specific guidance material developed by the SPICE Project for Process Capability Determination. Participants will be required to test concepts such as:

- setting a target SPICE profile for an Invitation To Tender Document;

- identifying gaps between a target and assessed profile to quantify potential risk; or

- evaluating the guide to Process Capability Determination.

Process Improvement Studies

These studies will be aimed at testing the specific guidance material developed by the SPICE Project for Software Process Improvement. Participants will be required to test concepts such as :

- developing a Process Improvement Plan to meet a required assessment profile;
- using the proposed measurement framework as a roadmap for Process Improvement; or
- evaluating the proposed Process Improvement methodology.

Applicability Studies

These studies will be aimed at analysing the applicability of the process assessment standard to different domains such as business sector, application type, organisation size and international region.

Phase 2 Trial Types

Participation in the trials will involve an organisation selecting one of the defined trial types. Both the organisational sponsor and the trials assessor will be required to complete a small set of questionnaires associated with the trial type to provide the essential feedback on the use of the Standard. Currently it is planned to have the following types of trials:

- an assessment using the assessment model contained in Part 5 of the document set,
- an assessment using a SPICE-compatible assessment model,
- Capability Determination trial using the guidelines contained in Part 8 of the document set. This does not necessarily involve the conduct of an assessment, and
- Process Improvement trial using the guidelines contained in Part 7 of the document set. This does not necessarily involve the conduct of an assessment.

As Phase 2 trials get underway further trial types may be defined.

Further information on how to participate and what the different trial types mean will be available from the Regional and Local Trial Co-ordinators.

Phase 2 Call For Participation

The SPICE Trials Phase 2 Call For Participation [6] was first issued in January 1996 and an updated Call For Participation released in November 1996. It explains the purpose of the trials; the pre-requisites and conditions of participation which include confidentiality, training and support of the trials studies; and it asks for potential trial participants to register their interest by completing an initial background questionnaire. The Call is aimed at organisations who would like to learn more about SPICE and can support an assessment either by funding an external assessor or through the use of an internal assessment team. It is also aimed at Assessors who are planning assessments and are able to submit them to the Trials activity with the agreement of the organisation being assessed.

Phase 1 of the Trials was restricted to those already involved in the SPICE project due to the evolving nature of the documents which were being developed and the restricted access to them. However, Phase 2 of the Trials has been opened up to all of the software community. Because of this major change and because of the specific objectives of Phase 2 some introductory training or awareness will be essential for those who participate. These training and awareness events will be organised locally within each Technical Centre Region by the Regional Trials Coordinator.

Phase 2 of the SPICE Trials will be conducted in the period September 1996 - September 1997. An interim trials report is scheduled for March 1997 with the final report at the end of Phase 2. Registration for Participation will be accepted at any time before September 1997 although early registration is encouraged to aid the planning activities of the Regional Trials Coordinators.

All data provided by trial participants to the SPICE Trials team will be treated with confidentiality in accordance with the SPICE Trials Data Management Policy which will be provided to all trial participants. The data shall be stored in the database such that it will not be possible to identify the organisation which contributed it. Access to the trials database shall be strictly controlled in accordance with the SPICE data management policy.

The current level of interest in participation in phase 2 of the trials is very encouraging. In Europe over 50 organisations have already responded to the Call For Participation to register their interest. These include organisations from Holland, Belgium, France, Italy, Sweden, Finland, Portugal, Scotland, England, Germany, Switzerland and Hungary. Trials are also being conducted, through the European Regional Trials Centre, in South Africa which has around 12 trials planned and in India which has around 20 trials planned. In the Australasia region over 30 organisations have registered which includes organisations in Australia, Hong Kong, and Singapore. In the US the SEI, as Regional Trials Coordinator, have already committed to a number of trials using the CMM and a number of US organisations have also indicated interest in conducting trials. In Canada 21 trials are currently being planned by the regional trials coordinator at ASEC and will include trials conducted in Mexico, Brazil, Argentina and Chile. In the Northern Pacific Region which has its Regional Trials Coordinator in Japan there are currently 20 trials planned. If this level of interest is maintained and can be converted into actual trials then the total number of trials in Phase 2 could reach 250. This would be a significant effort and produce critical feedback for the completion of the Standard.

Further Information and a Call For Participation package can be obtained from your Regional Trials Coordinator shown below or from the World Wide Web at the following addresses:

http://www.esi.es/Projects/SPICE.html

http://www-sqi.cit.gu.edu.au/spice/

Regional Trials Coordinators

fujino@t.soka.ac.jp	Kiichi Fujino	Northern Pacific
F.Suraweera@cit.gu.edu.au	Francis Suraweera	Australasia
lguerrer@crim.ca	Luciano Guerrero	Canada
smm@sei.cmu.edu	Steve Masters	USA
bob.smith@esi.es	Bob Smith	Europe

References

[1] The SPICE Project. "SPICE Overall Trials Plan".

[2] The SPICE Project. " SPICE Phase 2 Trials Plan".

[3] The SPICE Project. "SPICE Trials Phase 1 Trials Report".

[4] ISO/IEC 12207: 1995, "Software life cycle processes".

[5] The SPICE Project. " SPICE Trials Phase 2 Requirements Document".

[6] The SPICE Project. "SPICE Trials Phase 2 Call For Participation".

Spice Trials Assessment Profile

Robin Hunter
University of Strathclyde

This paper summarises the demographic information concerning the data collected in conjunction with Phase 2 of the SPICE Trials 1[1] up until 15th December 1997. Further information about the SPICE Trials and the version of the emerging ISO/IEC 15504 international standard that was evaluated during these trials can be obtained from [1]. We first describe the main demographic factors for which a significant amount of data was collected. Then we summarise the trials in terms of process coverage, summarise the ratings and capability levels observed, present some initial analyses on the impact of criticality on process capability, and then present a summary and conclusions.

Summary of Assessments and Projects

A large amount of demographic information concerning the trials was collected (much more than for Phase 1). Some of this data concerned the Organisational Units (OUs) that were assessed and some concerned the projects that were assessed within the OUs. In this section we summarise this information.

OU Data

The Organisational Unit data (OU data) included the SPICE region in which the OU was situated, the industrial sector in which the OU operated, the target sector for which the OU produced software, the total number of staff in the OU, and the number of IT staff in the OU .

From Figure 1 it is seen that the assessments were split roughly equally between two of the five SPICE regions, with 16 in Europe and 14 in the Southern Asia Pacific region, giving a total of 30 assessments for which we have data.

The distribution shown in Figure 2 shows that, out of the 30 assessments, 90% (27/30) used the Part 5 assessment model. The remaining 10% used the Process Professional assessment model. Figure 3 shows the distribution of tools used. Most of the assessments (67%) did not use an assessment tool. Of those that used a tool, 23% (7/30) used the SEAL tool from South Africa (available in [1]), and the remaining 10% (3/30) used the Process Professional assessment tool.

Since more than one assessment may have occurred in a particular OU (for example, multiple assessments, each one looking at a different set of processes), we can see in Figure 4 that organisations involved in the assessments were split with 15 in Europe and eight in the Southern Asia Pacific region, giving a total of 23 different organisations. Figure 5 shows that 11 of the OUs were concerned with the production of software or other IT products or services . Figure 6 shows the target sectors (one or more) in which each of the OUs were involved.

---

[1] The interim Trials Report is available publicly and can be obtained from <http://iese.fhg.de/SPICE> (go to the Trials page) or <http:www.sqi.gu.edu.au/spice/trials.shtml>

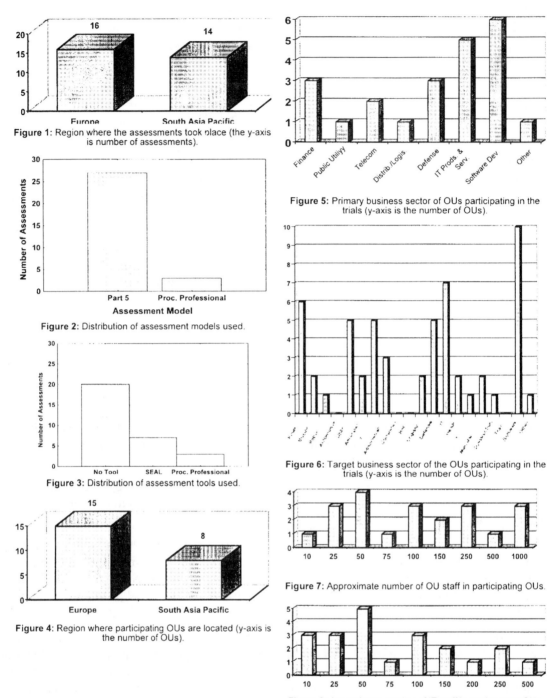

Figure 1: Region where the assessments took place (the y-axis is number of assessments).

Figure 2: Distribution of assessment models used.

Figure 3: Distribution of assessment tools used.

Figure 4: Region where participating OUs are located (y-axis is the number of OUs).

Figure 5: Primary business sector of OUs participating in the trials (y-axis is the number of OUs).

Figure 6: Target business sector of the OUs participating in the trials (y-axis is the number of OUs).

Figure 7: Approximate number of OU staff in participating OUs.

Figure 8: Approximate number of IT staff in participating OUs.

The data for the approximate number of staff and the approximate number of IT staff in the OUs are shown in Figure 7 and Figure 8 for 21 of the 23 OUs. The questions corresponding to these data both asked for approximate numbers of staff, rounded to a suitable number, 'such as' those shown . It would have been perfectly possible for a number greater than 1000 (in the case of Figure 7) and greater than 500

432

(in the case of Figure 8 to have been returned, and the database allowed for this. However, no such numbers were returned from the trials.

As can be seen from this data, there was good variation in the sizes (both small and large) of the OUs that participated in the trials thus far. However, the same cannot be said for the business sectors. No organisations in the following primary business sectors participated in the trials (see Figure 5): business

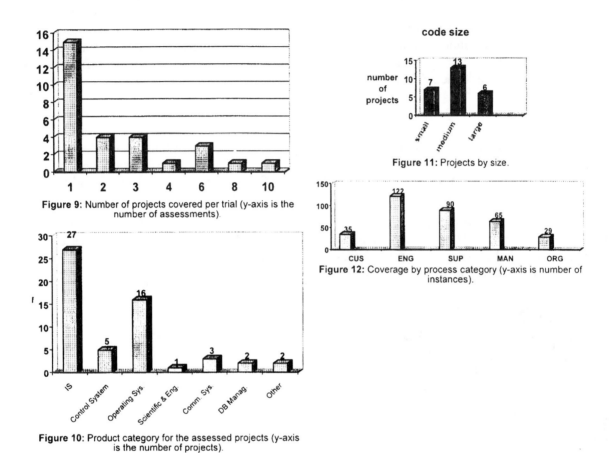

Figure 9: Number of projects covered per trial (y-axis is the number of assessments).

Figure 10: Product category for the assessed projects (y-axis is the number of projects).

Figure 11: Projects by size.

Figure 12: Coverage by process category (y-axis is number of instances).

services, petroleum, automotive, aerospace, public administration, consumer goods, retail, health and pharmaceuticals, leisure and tourism, manufacturing, construction, and travel.

Project Data

More than one project may be assessed in a single assessment. Project specific data we collected included the criticality of the product produced, the perceived importance of the product quality characteristics defined by ISO/IEC 9126, and the category to which the product belonged.

We had data from the 76 projects involved in the trials . Approximately 80% of these were software development projects, approximately 4% were non-software development projects, and approximately 13% were continuous processes within the organisation not associated with a single project .

The number of projects per trial is shown in Figure 9. It is evident that most assessments involved only one project. However, some covered up to 10 projects in a single assessment.

433

The product categories for these projects are shown in Figure 10. We had data from only 56 of these projects. As can be seen, almost half of the projects involved the development of information systems of one sort or another. Of the information system category, two projects were non-software development. Of the operating system category, three were continuous organisational processes. Of the database management category, one was a continuous organisational process.

The distribution of the projects according to code size is shown in Figure 11, where small means less than 10 KLOC, medium, 10-100 KLOC, and large more than 100 KLOC for a software system implemented in 3GL. The data was available for 26 of the 76 projects. Although it is highly dubious to collect line of code data across organisations internationally in such a manner, it still gives a rough indication of project sizes. Perhaps most interesting is the extent of inability of organizations to provide size data on their project (note that size in Function Points was also requested, but there even less data was collected).

Process Coverage

The process instances assessed during the trials (341 in all) were distributed over the five process categories defined by the ISO/IEC 15504 model (CUS, ENG, SUP, MAN, ORG) as in Figure 12. As can be seen, all the process categories were covered by a significant number of assessments although not to the same extent.

The number of process instances per trial is shown in Figure 13. As can be seen, there is a peak at six process instances per trial and the maximum number is 30. The box and whisker plot in Figure 14 shows the variation and the median of seven process instances per trial. Another interesting statistic is the number of process instances assessed per project, ranging from one to 29, with an average of 4.5.

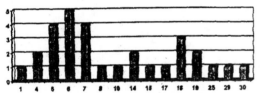

Figure 13: Process instances per trial (y-axis is the number of assessments).

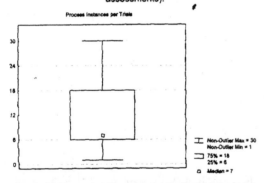

Figure 14: Box and whisker plot showing the variation in the number of process instances rated per trial.

Rating and Profile Analysis

For each of the 341 individual process instances assessed, the ratings were recorded for each of the attributes. The attributes corresponding to the various capability levels are summarised in Table 1.

The total numbers of process instances over all the trial assessments which were rated at each capability level are shown in Figure 15. For clarity, Figure 15 only shows the fully (F), largely (L), and partially (P) values. Process instances not achieved (N) or not assessed (X) are not shown in this figure.

Notice that, as expected, the attributes corresponding to the higher capability levels less often receive the higher ratings than those corresponding to the lower levels. Less obvious, but worth noting, is that of the two attributes at level 2 (pm and wpm), pm is more often highly rated than wpm and of the two attributes at level 3 (pd and pr), pr is more often highly rated than pd. At levels 4 and 5 the difference between the ratings for the two attributes seems less significant.

The pie charts shown in Figure 16 provide an alternative view for some of the same data and distinguish between attributes which were not achieved (N) and those which were not assessed (X).

The ratings of the attributes associated with a process instance may be used to compute the capability of a process. The capability of a process is defined to be the highest capability level for which the process attributes for that level are either rated largely or fully and the attributes for all lower levels are rated fully. A summary of this scheme is provided in Table 2.

When the data in the database is analysed the number of process instances found to be at each of the capability levels is as shown in Figure 17.

A comment on the definition of process capability may be appropriate here. Clearly there are two ways in which a process instance may fail to be rated at a particular capability level:

- The attributes at that level may not be rated fully or largely.

- The attributes at the next lower level may not be rated fully.

The 65 process instances at level 2 were analysed to see which would have been rated at level 3 if this did not require the level 2 attributes to be rated fully rather than largely. The result was that 24 process instances would have been rated at level 3 (37%). Thus in a significant number of cases, process instances fail to achieve a particular capability level because of inadequacies at the previous level, rather than at the level in question.

When performing the above analysis, one anomaly was noticed, namely a process which did not fully satisfy the level 2 attributes and yet fully satisfied the level 3 attributes. The rest of the data suggested that this was an isolated case!

The numbers of process instances at each capability level may also be shown for each process category as in Figure 18, which shows the percentage of process instances in each category achieving at least a particular capability level. Notice that the process instances at level 0 tend to be in the SUP and MAN categories, while the level 4 process instances tend to be in the SUP category.

Criticality

Clearly, as can be seen from the previous sections, there is considerable scope for correlating demographic variables with process ratings. As an example of this, an analysis was performed of how the criticality factors concerning safety, economic loss, security, and environmental impact (as defined in ISO/IEC 14598) affected the process ratings. The capability levels of those process instances associated with projects that the OU considered to be critical with respect to one of the factors (a subset containing 88 of the 341 process instances considered above) are summarised in Figure 19. Most notable are the smaller percentage of level 0 process instances and the larger percentage of level 4 process instances in this set compared with the data relating to all the assessments shown in Figure 17.

Clearly many other such analyses are possible. Further analysis of this type are planned.

Capability Levels	Process Attributes
Level 1	process performance (pp)
Level 2	performance management (pm)
	work product management (wpm)
Level 3	process definition (pd)
	process resource (pr)
Level 4	process measurement (pme)
	process control (pco)
Level 5	process change (pch)
	continuous improvement (ci)

Table 1: The attributes at each capability level (and their acronyms).

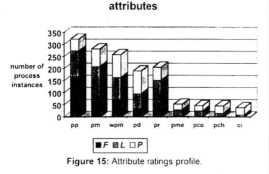

Figure 15: Attribute ratings profile.

Capability Levels	Process Attributes	Rating
Level 1	Process Performance	Largely or Fully
Level 2	Process Performance	Fully
	Performance Management	Largely or Fully
	Work Product Management	Largely or Fully
Level 3	Process Performance	Fully
	Performance Management	Fully
	Work Product Management	Fully
	Process Definition	Largely or Fully
	Process Resource	Largely or Fully
Level 4	Process Performance	Fully
	Performance Management	Fully
	Work Product Management	Fully
	Process Definition	Fully
	Process Resource	Fully
	Process Measurement	Largely or Fully
	Process Control	Largely or Fully
Level 5	Process Performance	Fully
	Performance Management	Fully
	Work Product Management	Fully
	Process Definition	Fully
	Process Resource	Fully
	Process Measurement	Fully
	Process Control	Fully
	Process Change	Largely or Fully
	Continuous Improvement	Largely or Fully

Table 2: Scheme for determining the capability level rating for the first three levels.

Conclusions about Assessments and Ratings

The major findings from the analysis presented in this paper are:

1 Only two regions have participated in the trials by providing data thus far (i.e., December 1997): Europe and South Asia Pacific[22] .

2 We have data from 30 assessments conducted in 23 different organisations in these two regions.

3 There was a good distribution in terms of Organisational Unit size (both large and small). However, there was no participation for OUs whose primary business sector was: business services, petroleum, automotive, aerospace, public administration, consumer goods, retail, health and pharmaceuticals, leisure and tourism, manufacturing, construction, and travel. 4 Most assessments involved only one project in the OU.

5 All processes in the version of the ISO/IEC 15504 Reference Model that was eveluated were covered.

6 The median number of process instances per assessment is seven.

7 In general, we found that the attributes corresponding to the higher capability levels less often receive the higher ratings than those corresponding to the lower capability levels.

---

[2] Since we performed this analysis, data has been collected from Canada and Latin America, USA, and the Northern Asia Pacific.

8 In a significant number of cases, process instances fail to achieve a particular capability level because of inadequacies at the previous level, rather than at the level in question.

9 Approximately 19% of the process instances were at level 0, 50% at level 1, and 19% at level 2.

These findings pertain to the data that has been collected thus far, and of course may be affected when more data is collected before the end of the Phase 2 Trials.

Acknowledgements

The earlier work of Ian Woodman [2] is acknowledged as is the assistance of Khaled El Emam for providing the box and whisker plot in Figure 14 and to John Wilson for discussions on the database issues involved in the above analyses.

References

[1] K. El Emam, J-N Drouin, and W. Melo (eds.): *SPICE: The Theory and Practice of Software Process Improvement and Capability Determinatio*n. IEEE CS Press, 1998.

[2] I. Woodman and R. Hunter: iuAnalysis of assessment data from phase one of the SPICE trialsle. In IEEE TCSE Software Process Newsletter, No. 6, Spring 1996.

Robin Hunter can be reached at: Department of Computer Science, University of Strathclyde, Richmond Street, GLASGOW G1 1XH, UK; Email: rbh@cs.strath.ac.uk

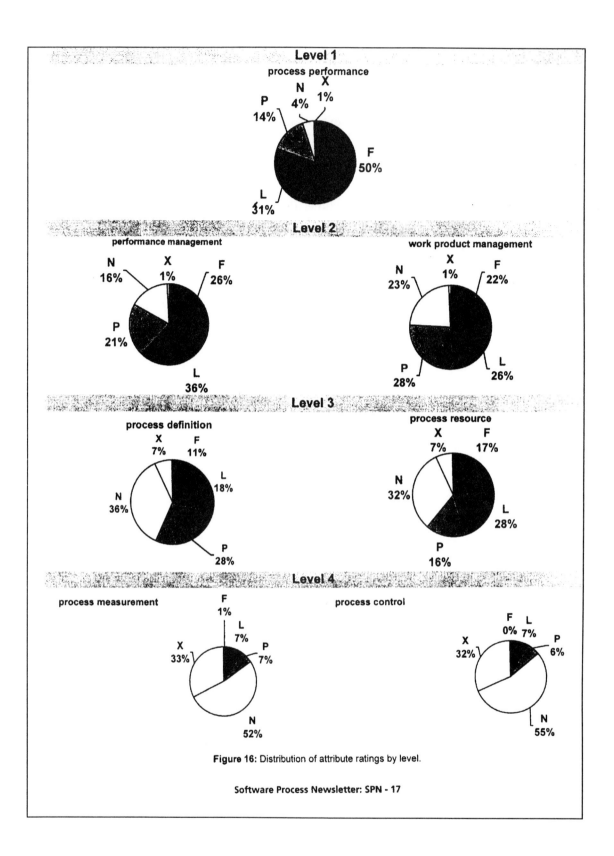

Figure 16: Distribution of attribute ratings by level.

Level 5

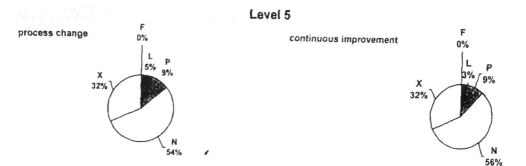

process change

F 0%
L 5%
P 9%
X 32%
N 54%

continuous improvement

F 0%
L 3%
P 9%
X 32%
N 56%

Figure 16: Distribution of attribute ratings by level (contd.).

process capability levels

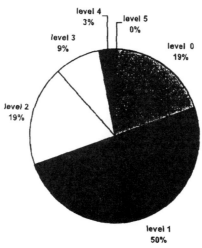

level 4 3%
level 5 0%
level 3 9%
level 0 19%
level 2 19%
level 1 50%

Figure 17: Distribution of capability levels across all process instances.

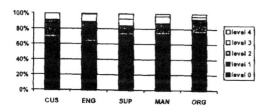

☐ level 4
☐ level 3
☐ level 2
■ level 1
■ level 0

CUS ENG SUP MAN ORG

Figure 18: Profile of process capability across all process instances per process category.

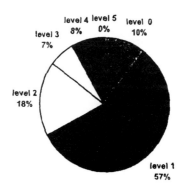

level 4 8%
level 5 0%
level 0 10%
level 3 7%
level 2 18%
level 1 57%

Figure 19: Process capability levels for high criticality products

The Reliability of ISO/IEC PDTR 15504 Assessments

Standards Section

Jean-Martin Simon[1], Khaled El Emam[2]*, Sonia
Rousseau[3], Eric Jacquet[4] and Frederic Babey[5]
[1]A.Q.T., 19, place de la Ferrandière, 69003 Lyon, France
[2]Fraunhofer Institute for Experimental Software Engineering,
Sauerwiesen 6, D-67661 Kaiserslautern, Germany
[3]SANOFI Recherche
[4]SANOFI Pharma, 9, rue du Président S. Allende, 94256 Gentilly,
France
[5]AFNOR, Unité Conseil, Tour Europe, 92049 Paris La Défense,
Cedex - France

During phase two of the SPICE trials, the Preliminary Draft Technical Report (PDTR) version of ISO/IEC 15504 is being empirically evaluated. This document set is intended to become an international standard for software process assessment. One thread of evaluations being conducted during these trials is the extent of reliability of assessments based on ISO/IEC PDTR 15504. In this paper we present the first evaluation of the reliability of assessments based on the PDTR version of the emerging international standard. In particular, we evaluate the interrater agreement of assessments. Our results indicate that interrater agreement is considerably high, both for individual ratings at the capability attribute level, and for the aggregated capability levels. In general, these results are consistent with those obtained using the previous version of the software process assessment document set (known as SPICE version 1.0), where capability ratings were also found to have generally high interrater agreement. Furthermore, it was found that the current 4-point scale cannot be improved substantially by reducing it to a 3-point or to a 2-point scale. © 1997 John Wiley & Sons, Ltd.

Softw. Process Improve. Pract., **3**, 177–188 (1997)

KEY WORDS: software process assessment; reliability of measurement; SPICE

1. INTRODUCTION

The international SPICE (Software Process Improvement and Capability dEtermination) Project developed a set of documents describing a model for software process assessment. These documents, known as SPICE version 1.0, were handed over to the ISO/IEC JTC1/SC7 Working Group 10 to evolve them to an international standard. Under the auspices of ISO/IEC, the documents are known by their number 15504. The 15504 documents have to go through a series of ballots by national bodies before they become an International Standard. Subsequent to each ballot, the documents may be changed to address the ballot comments. The most recent balloting stages for 15504 are as follows:

- A *Preliminary Draft Technical Report* (PDTR) ballot.

* Correspondence to: Khaled El Emam, Fraunhofer Institute for Experimental Software Engineering, Sauerwiesen 6, D-67661 Kaiserslautern, Germany
Contract/grant sponsor: ELF Innovation
CCC 1077-4866/97/030177-12$17.50
© 1997 John Wiley & Sons, Ltd.

- A *Draft Technical Report* (DTR) ballot.

Following a successful DTR ballot, the 15504 documents will become a Technical Report Type 2 (TR-2). This is a designation given to a standard under trial. A TR-2 is expected to be revised within two to three years after its publication, with the intention of making it a full International Standard. A more detailed review of the standardization process for 15504 may be found in El Emam *et al.* (1998).

Since the beginning of the effort to develop an international standard for software process assessment, the importance of empirical evaluation of the evolving document set has been recognized. This recognition is manifested through the SPICE trials, which are conducted by the SPICE Project (Maclennan and Ostrolenk 1995). The first phase of the trials empirically evaluated the SPICE version 1.0 documents, and was completed in calendar year 1995. The second phase of the trials is now under way, and is expected to terminate in the summer of 1998. This second phase is empirically evaluating the ISO/IEC *PDTR* 15504 document set.

One of the issues studied in the SPICE trials is the reliability of assessments (7El Emam and Goldenson 1995). In general, reliability is concerned with the extent of random measurement error in the assessment scores. There are different types of reliability that can be evaluated. For example, one type is the internal consistency of instruments (El Emam and Goldenson 1995, El Emam and Madhavji 1995, Fusaro *et al.* in press). This type of reliability accounts for ambiguity and inconsistency amongst indicators or subsets of indicators in an assessment instrument as sources of error. In addition, in the context of the first phase of the SPICE trials, a survey of assessor perceptions of the repeatability of assessments was recently conducted (El Emam and Goldenson 1996).

Interrater agreement is another type of reliability. It is concerned with the extent of agreement in the ratings given by independent assessors to the same software engineering practices. As with many other process assessment methods in existence today (e.g. TRILLIUM-based assessments (Coallier 1995) and the CBA - IPI developed at the SEI (Dunaway and Masters 1996), those based on 15504 rely on the judgement of experienced assessors in assigning ratings to software engineering practices. This means that there is an element of subjectivity in their ratings. Ideally, if different assessors satisfy the requirements of the 15504 framework and are presented with the same evidence, they will produce exactly the same ratings (i.e. there will be perfect agreement amongst independent assessors). In practice, however, the subjectivity in ratings will make it most unlikely that there is perfect agreement. The extent to which interrater agreement is imperfect is an empirical question.

High interrater agreement is desirable to give credibility to assessment results, for example, in the context of using assessment scores in contract award decisions. If agreement is low, then this would indicate that the scores are too dependent on the individuals who have conducted the assessments. In addition, higher interrater agreement is expected to be associated with lower cost assessments since a consensus-building stage of the assessment method amongst the assessors would consume less time.

During the first phase of the SPICE trials, a number of interrater agreement studies have been conducted (El Emam *et al.* 1996, El Emam *et al.* 1997b, El Emam *et al.* 1997c, El Emam and Marshall 1998). The general conclusion from these studies was that considerable variation in interrater agreement was witnessed, and so models were developed to explain this variation (as in El Emam *et al.* (1997b)).

The most relevant previous study in the current context is that reported in Fusaro *et al.* (1997), where elements of the capability dimension were the unit of analysis (as opposed to process instances or processes being the unit of analysis). That study found that interrater agreement is generally high. In this paper we present the first *evaluation* of the interrater agreement of process capability ratings done according to the ISO/IEC PDTR 15504 document set. This evaluation was conducted within the second phase of the SPICE trials.

Briefly, our results indicate that the capability ratings at each of the first three levels of the ISO/IEC PDTR 15504 capability dimension are highly reliable, and that the computed capability levels assigned to these processes are also highly reliable. Furthermore, we found that the current 4-point scale cannot be substantially improved by combining categories to form 3- or 2-point scales. These results are encouraging for current and potential users since they indicate that assessments using the emerging International Standard maintain high reliability levels after the evolution to the PDTR version.

The next section of the paper provides an overview of the ISO/IEC PDTR 15504 practices rating scheme used during this study. Section 3 presents the research method that was followed for data collection and for evaluating interrater agreement. In Section 4 we present the interrater agreement analysis results. We conclude the paper in Section 5 with a summary and directions for future work.

2. OVERVIEW OF ISO/IEC PDTR 15504

2.1. The ISO/IEC PDTR 15504 Document Set

The ISO/IEC PDTR 15504 document set comprises nine parts. Figure 1 shows the nine parts of the document set and indicates the relationships between them (see El Emam *et al.* (1998) for further details). The most important parts for this paper are Part 2 and Part 5.

Part 2: A Reference Model for Processes and Process Capability defines a two-dimensional reference model for describing the outcomes of process assessment. The reference model defines a set of processes, defined in terms of their purpose, and a framework for evaluating the capability of the processes through the assessment of process attributes, structured into capability levels. Requirements for establishing the compatibility of different assessment models with the reference model are defined. This part is a normative part of the standard.

Part 5: An Assessment Model and Indicator Guidance provides an exemplar model for performing process assessments that is based upon, and is directly compatible with, the reference model in Part 2. The assessment model extends the reference model through the inclusion of a comprehensive set of indicators of process performance and capability.

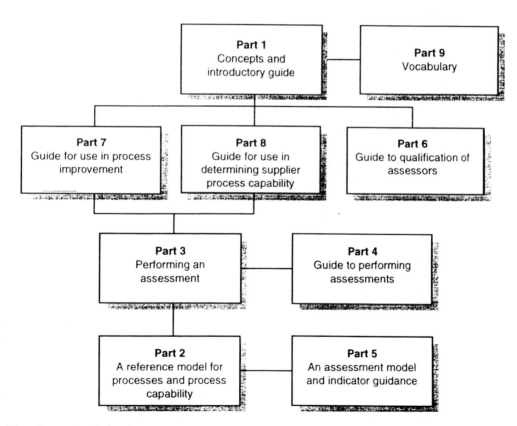

Figure 1. The nine parts of the document set

2.2. The Capability Rating Scheme in ISO/IEC PDTR 15504

As alluded to above, the ISO/IEC PDTR 15504 architecture is two-dimensional. Each dimension represents a different perspective on software process management. The first is the process dimension, and the second is the capability dimension.

The process dimension is divided up into five process categories. Within each category is a set of processes. Each process is characterized by a process purpose. Satisfying the purpose statement of a process represents the first step in building process capability (capability level 1). The process categories are summarized in Table 1, and their associated processes are summarized in Table 2.

The capability dimension consists of six capability levels. Within levels 1 to 5 there exists one or two attributes that can be used for evaluating achievement of that level. The levels and their associated attributes are summarized in Table 3. A 4-point achievement scale can be used to rate the attributes during an assessment. These are designated as F, L, P, N, and are summarized in Table 4. It is also possible to convert the F, L, P, N ratings of attributes into a single number that characterizes the capability of a process instance. The scheme for doing so for the first three levels is summarized in Table 5.

Within the context of an ISO/IEC PDTR 15504 assessment, the scope of an assessment is an organizational unit (OU) (El Emam *et al.* 1998). This is defined as all or part of an organization with a coherent sphere of activity and a coherent set of business goals. The characteristics that determine the coherent scope of activity – the process context – include the application domain, the size, the criticality, the complexity, and the quality characteristics of its products or services.

Ratings during an assessment are of process instances (El Emam 1998). A process instance is a singular instantiation of a process that is uniquely identifiable and about which information can be gathered in a repeatable manner.

3. RESEARCH METHOD

3.1 Data Collection

For conducting interrater agreement studies, we divide the assessment team into two groups. In

Table 1. Description of the process categories

Process category	Description
Customer-supplier	The *Customer–Supplier* process category consists of processes that directly impact the customer, support development and transition of the software to the customer, and provide for its correct operation and use.
Engineering	The *Engineering* process category consists of processes that directly specify, implement, or maintain a system and software product and its user documentation. In circumstances where the system is composed totally of software, the Engineering process deals only with the construction and maintenance of such software.
Management	The *Management* process category consists of processes which contain practices of a generic nature which may be used by anyone who manages any sort of project or process within a software life cycle.
Support	The *Support* process category consists of processes which may be employed by any of the other processes (including other supporting processes) at various points in the software life cycle.
Organization	The *Organization* process category consists of processes which establish the business goals of the organization and develop process, product, and resource assets which, when used by the projects in the organization, will help the organization achieve its business goals. Although organizational operations in general have a much broader scope than that of software process, software processes are implemented in a business context, and to be effective, require an appropriate organizational environment.

the current study, each of these groups had one assessor. Ideally both assessors should be equally competent in making attribute achievement ratings. In practice, both assessors need only meet minimal competence requirements since this is more congruent with the manner in which the 15504 documents would be applied. Each assessor would be provided with the same information (e.g. all would be present in the same interviews and provided with the same documentation to inspect),[1] and then

---

[1] Under this requirement, one assessor may obtain information that was elicited by the other assessor, which s/he would have not asked for. The alternative to this requirement is that the

Table 2. The processes and process categories

Process category		Process	
ID	Title	ID	Title
CUS	Customer Supplier process category		
		CUS.1	Acquire software
		CUS.2	Manage customer needs
		CUS.3	Supply software
		CUS.4	Operate software
		CUS.5	Provide customer service
ENG	Engineering process category		
		ENG.1	Develop system requirements and design
		ENG.2	Develop software requirements
		ENG.3	Develop software design
		ENG.4	Implement software design
		ENG.5	Integrate and test software
		ENG.6	Integrate and test system
		ENG.7	Maintain system and software
SUP	Support process category		
		SUP.1	Develop documentation
		SUP.2	Perform configuration management
		SUP.3	Perform quality assurance
		SUP.4	Perform work product verification
		SUP.5	Perform work product validation
		SUP.6	Perform joint reviews
		SUP.7	Perform audits
		SUP.8	Perform problem resolution
MAN	Management process category		
		MAN.1	Manage the project
		MAN.2	Manage quality
		MAN.3	Manage risks
		MAN.4	Manage subcontractors
ORG	Organization process category		
		ORG.1	Engineer the business
		ORG.2	Define the process
		ORG.3	Improve the process
		ORG.4	Provide skilled human resources
		ORG.5	Provide software engineering infrastructure

Table 3. Overview of the capability levels and attributes

ID	Title
Level 0	Incomplete Process
	There is general failure to attain the purpose of the process. There are no easily identifiable work products or outputs of the process.
Level 1	Performed Process
	The purpose of the process is generally achieved. The achievement may not be rigorously planned and tracked. Individuals within the organization recognize that an action should be performed, and there is general agreement that this action is performed as and when required. There are identifiable work products for the process, and these testify to the achievement of the purpose.
1.1	Process performance attribute
Level 2	Managed Process
	The process delivers work products of acceptable quality within defined timescales. Performance according to specified procedures is planned and tracked. Work products conform to specified standards and requirements. The primary distinction from the Performed Level is that the performance of the process is planned and managed and progressing towards a defined process.
2.1	Performance management attribute
2.2	Work product management attribute
Level 3	Established Process
	The process is performed and managed using a defined process based upon good software engineering principles. Individual implementations of the process use approved, tailored versions of standard, documented processes. The resources necessary to establish the process definition are also in place. The primary distinction from the Managed Level is that the process of the Established Level is planned and managed using a standard process.
3.1	Process definition attribute
3.2	Process resource attribute
Level 4	Predictable Process
	The defined process is performed consistently in practice within defined control limits, to achieve its goals. Detailed measures of performance are collected and analysed. This leads to a quantitative understanding of process capability and an improved ability to predict performance. Performance is objectively managed. The quality of work products is quantitatively known. The primary distinction from the Established Level is that the defined process is quantitatively understood and controlled.
4.1	Process measurement attribute
4.2	Process control attribute
Level 5	Optimizing Process
	Performance of the process is optimized to meet current and future business needs, and the process achieves repeatability in meeting its defined business goals. Quantitative process effectiveness and efficiency goals (targets) for performance are established, based on the business goals of the organization. Continuous process monitoring against these goals is enabled by obtaining quantitative feedback and improvement is achieved by analysis of the results. Optimizing a process involves piloting innovative ideas and technologies and changing non-effective processes to meet defined goals or objectives. The primary distinction from the Predictable Level is that the defined process and the standard process undergo continuous refinement and improvement, based on a quantitative understanding of the impact of changes to these processes.
5.1	Process change attribute
5.2	Continuous improvement attribute

two assessors interview the same people at different times to make sure that they only obtain the information that they ask for. However, this requirement raises the risk that the interviewees 'learn' the right answers to give based on the first interview, or that they volunteer information that was asked by the first assessor but not the second. Furthermore, from a practical perspective, interviewing the same people more than once to ask the same questions would substantially increase the cost of assessments, and thus the cost of conducting the study. It is for this reason that these studies are referred to as 'interrater' agrement since, strictly speaking, they consider the reliability of ratings, rather than the reliability of whole assessments. The study of 'interassessment' agreement would involve accounting for variations in the information that is collected by two different assessors during an assessment.

Table 4. The 4-point attribute rating scale

Rating and Designation	Description
Not achieved, N	There is no evidence of achievement of the defined attribute
Partially achieved, P	There is some achievement of the defined attribute
Largely achieved, L	There is significant achievement of the defined attribute
Fully achieved, F	There is full achievement of the defined attribute

Table 5. Scheme for determining the capability level rating for the first three levels

Scale	Process attributes	Rating
Level 1	Process Performance	Largely or fully
Level 2	Process Performance	Fully
	Performance Management	Largely or fully
	Work Product Management	Largely or fully
Level 3	Process Performance	Fully
	Performance Management	Fully
	Work Product Management	Fully
	Process Definition and Tailoring	Largely or fully
	Process Resource	Largely or fully

Table 6. Guidelines for conducting interrater agreement studies

- For each process, divide the assessment team into two groups with at least one person per group.
- The two groups should be selected so that they both meet the minimal assessor competence requirements with respect to training, background and experience.
- The two groups should use the same evidence (e.g. attend the same interviews, inspect the same documents etc.), assessment method, and tools.
- The first group examining any physical artefacts should leave them as close as possible (organized/marked/sorted) to the state that the assessees delivered them.
- If evidence is judged to be insufficient, gather more evidence and both groups should inspect the new evidence before making ratings.
- The two groups independently rate the same process instances.
- After the independent ratings, the two groups then meet to reach consensus and harmonize their ratings for the final ratings profile.
- There should be no discussion between the two groups about rating judgement prior to the independent ratings.

they would perform their ratings independently. Subsequent to the independent ratings, the two assessors would meet to reach a consensus or final assessment team rating. In the context of the SPICE Project, this overall approach is being considered as part of the trials (El Emam and Goldenson 1995). General guidelines for conducting interrater agreement studies are given in Table 6. The actual phases of the assessment method that was followed are summarized below.

3.1.1. Preparation Phase

As required by the ISO/IEC PDTR 15504, we defined the assessment *input* at the beginning of the assessment. This consists of:

(a) the identity of the sponsor of the assessment and the sponsor's relationship to the organizational unit being assessed;

(b) the assessment purpose including alignment with business goals;

(c) the assessment scope including;

- the processes to be investigated within the organizational unit

- the highest capability level to be investigated
- the organizational unit that deploys these processes
- the process context

(d) the assessment constraints which may include;

- availability of key resources
- the maximum amount of time to be used for the assessment
- specific processes or Organization Units (OUs) to be excluded from the assessment
- the minimum, maximum or specific sample size or coverage that is desired for the assessment
- the ownership of the assessment outputs and any restrictions on their use
- controls on information resulting from a confidentiality agreement.

(e) the identity of the model used within the assessment;

(f) the identity of the assessors, including the competent assessor responsible for the assessment;

(g) the identity of assessees and support staff with specific responsibilities for the assessment;

(h) any additional information to be collected during the assessment to support process improvement or process capability determination.

During the preparation, an important issue is to collect the context of the Organizational Unit since the result of the assessment is context dependent. Being 'context dependent' can best be explained through an example.

In our example, we can consider two organizations: the first is developing a software package with 2000 users on a worldwide basis; the second is a production department which provides a specific MIS application to 20 users who are in the same building. The way those two organizations should organize their Help Desk in order to provide the best 'customer service' (CUS.5, see Table 2) is completely different. For example:

(a) The first one established a service level agreement with dedicated resources and formal procedures to handle any request and to manage interviews and questionnaires to appraise user satisfaction.

(b) The second one mandated its project leader to log any request and to meet on a regular basis the users to appreciate their level of satisfaction.

In the first case, the actions taken are congruent with the complexity and the magnitude of the requirements. However, the same actions seem exaggerated for the second organization. The assessors therefore have the responsibility to tune their judgement about the capability attributes for the relevant process according to the context.

The context tackles the following parameters:

(a) the size of the organization being assessed;
(b) the number of Organizational Units involved in the assessment;
(c) the demographics of the Organizational Unit;
(d) the application domain of the products or services of the Organizational Unit;
(e) the level of organizational participation in performing the assessment (collecting the information, demonstrating conformance);
(f) the maturity of the supplier–sponsor relationship (the level of trust between the organization and sponsor);
(g) the needs of the sponsor.

(h) the size, criticality and complexity of the products or services;
(i) the characteristics of the project for which the processes are evaluated.

3.1.2. Data Collection Phase

To conduct the assessment, we used the interview technique based on the assessment model described in Part 5 of ISO/IEC PDTR 15504 (see El Emam et al. (1998)), plus documents examination.

If necessary, we provided some additional base practices to the model of Part 5 for some processes where we deem the Part 5 is too vague. For example, for the CUS.3 Process, we added the following base practices to the CUS.3.7 Deliver and install software:

(a) CUS.3.7.0 Identify requirements for replication, packaging, storage, handling before delivery.
(b) CUS.3.7.1 Identify Infrastructure Environment for delivery.
(c) CUS.3.7.2 Identify training requirements for the client for delivery.
(d) CUS.3.7.3 Identify duties from the customer or the client for delivery.
(e) CUS.3.7.4 Check delivery before installation.
(f) CUS.3.7.5 Perform the installation of the software.
(g) CUS.3.7.6 Validate the installation.

For all of the processes within the scope of the assessment, only capability levels 1 to 3 were covered.

3.1.3. Ratings Phase

Each assessor collected his own assessment record during the interview. At the end of the day, each assessor took some time to review his own record and to make the process attributes ratings. Therefore, a specific meeting is dedicated to consolidate the assessment record and to establish a consensus between the two assessors when some divergence arises for one or several attribute ratings. This aspect is very important since one of the assessors may have missed or misunderstood some information. In the case that both assessors have missed some information, the sponsor (or the interviewee(s)) is contacted to obtain the missing information.

447

3.1.4. Debriefing

At the end of the assessment week (the number of days may depend on the number of assessed processes), the two assessors present to the interviewees the main results of the assessment. The objectives of this presentation are:

(a) to remind them about the concepts of ISO/IEC PDTR 15504;

(b) to ensure the understanding of the meaning of the attributes by the interviewees;

(c) to consolidate with the interviewees the results of the assessment.

During this meeting, the interviewees have the opportunity to 'negotiate' the results by, for example, presenting further evidence. At this time, the results are only presented using a graphical approach.

3.1.5. Reporting

We performed the final assessment report where we synthesized the results (weaknesses and strengths) per process at the OU level. This global analysis is completed with the detailed analysis result for every assessed process for the considered projects. This report is sent to the sponsor for approval.

3.2. Description of Organization and Projects

In our study, we used data from two assessments that were conducted in France during Phase 2 of the SPICE trials. In these assessments, the ISO/IEC PDTR 15504 documents were used. The company where the assessments were conducted is called Sanofi.

The Sanofi company belongs to the ELF Group. Its activities focus on drug research and production. All pharmaceutical molecules must undergo six to twelve long years of development from the moment of their discovery to the time they are given product licence approval. Sanofi R&D has 2500 employees, in nine units in six countries (France, UK, Italy, Hungary, Spain and USA). From the research stage on the compound, to international commercialization, Sanofi R&D controls each phase to test scientifically both the indications for and the effects of the compounds.

The IS (Information Systems) department interact with all of these activities as a support service. Computerized systems are necessary for several domains: discovery; preclinical studies; clinical investigation, and support. Development methods are either conventional (V model) or prototype based. Software packages are largely used. The architecture is still 'mainframe' for some systems, but mostly 'Client-Server'. The IS department manages the computerized systems life cycle from the initialization of the system to retirement. They are used to working closely with users and with the support of the Research Quality Assurance.

Two OUs within this company were assessed. A combination of organizational and project level processes were assessed in each OU. Three projects were assessed in the first OU and two projects in the second OU. The characteristics of these five projects are summarized in Table 7. The processes that were assessed and the number of instances in each are summarized in Table 8.

Table 7. Characteristics of assessed projects

	X1	X2	X3	Y1	Y2
Size of project in terms of effort	3 man-years	2,5 man-year	1 man-year	2 man-years	1 man-year
Programming language	C, Visual Basic + off-the-shelf software	Third generation language	specific SQL	C, Visual Basic + off-the-shelf software	specific SQL
Development or maintenance projects	maintenance	maintenance	validation	maintenance	maintenance
Application domain	Electronic document management	data processing: collection, processing, visualization	database, Client-server	Electronic document management	database, Client-server

Table 8. Number of instances of each process assessed

Process	Number of Instances
ORG.1	2
ORG.2	2
ORG.3	2
ORG.4	2
ORG.5	2
CUS.3	5
CUS.4	4
CUS.5	5
ENG.7	4
SUP.1	4
SUP.2	4
MAN.1	4
Total	40 process instances

3.3. Description of Assessors

The same two assessors conducted both assessments. Both assessors met the minimal requirements stipulated in the ISO/IEC PDTR 15504 documents. In terms of experience and background, this is summarized in Table 9.

Both assessors who took part in our study were external. A previous study (El Emam *et al.* 1997c) identified potential systematic biases between an external and an internal assessor (i.e. one assessor would systematically rate higher or lower than the other). Having only external assessors removes the possibility of this particular bias.

3.4. Evaluating Interrater Agreement

To evaluate interrater agreement, we can treat the ISO/IEC PDTR 15504 achievement ratings as being on a nominal scale. Cohen (1960) defined coefficient kappa (κ) as an index of agreement that takes into account agreement that could have occurred by chance. The value of kappa is the ratio of observed excess over chance agreement to the maximum possible excess over chance agreement. See Fleiss (1981) for the details of calculating kappa.

If there is complete agreement, then $\kappa = 1$. If observed agreement is greater than chance, then $\kappa > 0$. If observed agreement is less than would be expected by chance, then $\kappa < 0$. The minimum value of κ depends upon the marginal proportions. However, since we are interested in evaluating agreement, the lower limit of κ is not of interest.

The variance of a sample kappa has been derived by Fleiss *et al.* (1969). This would allow testing the null hypothesis that $\kappa = 0$ against the alternative hypothesis $\kappa \neq 0$. If we use a one-tailed test, then we can test against the alternative hypothesis $\kappa > 0$, which is more useful. This means we test whether a value of kappa bigger than zero as large as the value obtained could have occurred by chance.

The standard version of the kappa coefficient assumes that all disagreements are equally serious. We used a weighted version of kappa that allows different levels of seriousness to be attached to different levels of disagreement. This has been defined in Cohen (1968). The weighted version of kappa was used in previous studies on the reliability of process assessments (El Emam *et al.* 1996, Fusaro *et al*, 1997). We also use the same weighting scheme as applied in previous studies in the SPICE trials (El Emam *et al.* 1996, Fusaro *et al.* 1997). This assigns greater seriousness to disagreements on non-adjacent categories on the 4-point achievement scale, and hence essentially treats it as an ordered scale.

Table 9. Experience and background of assessors

	Assessor A	Assessor B
Years in the software industry	14	3
Years in process assessment and improvement	7 (including software quality improvement)	2
Assessment methods and models they have experience with	ISO 9001, SPICE V1, and ISO/IEC PDTR 15504	ISO 9001, Bootstrap, and ISO/IEC PDTR 15504
Number of SPICE-based assessments done in the past	6 (approximately 150 process instances)	3 (approximately 90 process instances)
Internal versus external to the organization	external	external

3.5. Interpreting Interrater Agreement

After calculating the value of kappa, the next question is 'how do we interpret it?' A commonly used set of guidelines in previous interrater agreement studies (e.g. see El Emam *et al.* (1996), Fusaro *et al.* (1997)) are these of Landis and Koch (1977) (see Table 10).

In addition, we can determine whether the obtained value of kappa meets a minimal requirement (following the procedure in Fleiss (1981)). The logic for a *minimal* requirement is that it should act as a good discriminator between assessments conducted with a reasonable amount of rigour and precision, and those where there was much misunderstanding and confusion about how to rate practices. It was thus deemed reasonable to require that agreement be at least moderate (i.e. kappa > 0.4). This minimal requirement on interrater agreement has been used in previous studies in the SPICE trials that evaluate the reliability of process capability ratings (Fusaro *et al.* 1997).

We evaluate whether interrater agreement using weighted kappa is greater than moderate agreement for each of the five attributes in levels 1 to 3 of the capability dimension. When performing so many statistical tests, the probability of incorrectly rejecting one of these null hypotheses (type 1 error) is approximately 0.4. This means that there is reasonably high probability that at least one significant result would be found by chance alone. We therefore use a Bonferroni adjusted alpha level for hypothesis tests on the five attributes in our study (see Rice (1987) for an overview of the Bonferroni procedure).

4. RESULTS

The results of evaluating interrater agreement for the five capability attributes are shown in Table

Table 10. The interpretation of the values of kappa

Kappa statistic	Strength of agreement
< 0.00	Poor
0.00–0.20	Slight
0.21–0.40	Fair
0.41–0.60	Moderate
0.61–0.80	Substantial
0.81–1.00	Almost perfect

11. As can be seen, ratings on all five attributes have at least moderate agreement at an experimentwise alpha value of 0.1. These results concur in general with evaluations of interrater agreement of capability ratings for the previous version of the document set (known as SPICE Version 1.0) (Fusaro *et al.* 1997.

For the interrater agreement of capability level ratings for each of the processes, the results also indicate statistical significance at an alpha level of 0.1 (see Table 11). Agreement was also found to be consistently higher than 'moderate agreement'.

The combination of these results indicates that whether one uses the attribute ratings or the capability ratings, their reliability is higher than moderate agreement. If it is accepted that **moderate agreement is a minimum for practical usage**, then these results are encouraging for users of ISO/IEC PDTR 15504.

In order to investigate possible sources of disagreement on the 4-point scale, we calculated the weighted kappa coefficient for the following two cases:

1. Combining the two middle categories of the achievement scale (L and P). If there is confusion between these two categories, then it would be expected that agreement would increase when these two categories are combined. This results in a three category scale (F,[L,P],N).

2. Combining the categories at the ends of the scale (F and L, and P and N). If there is confusion between the F and L categories and the P and N categories, then it would be expected that agreement would increase when these categories are combined. This results in a two category scale ([F,L],[P,N]).

The results of this analysis are shown in Table 12. As can be seen, in most cases the 4-point scale provides the highest kappa values when compared with the 3- or 2-category scales. The zero value for Attribute 2.2 is due to the data set exhibiting very little variation when reduced to a 2-point scale, and this tends to attenuate the values of kappa. The conclusion from this table is that the 4-point scale cannot be improved in terms of reliability by reducing it to a 3- or a 2-point scale.

It should be noted that these results have limitations in terms of their generalizability. First, further research is necessary to determine whether

Table 11. Interrater agreement evaluation results (* indicates statistical significance)

Attribute number	Description of attribute	Weighted kappa value	Interpretation
1.1	*Process performance attribute* The extent to which the execution of the process uses a set of practices that are initiated and followed using identifiable input work products to produce identifiable output work products that are adequate to satisfy the purpose of the process	0.78*	Substantial
2.1	*Performance management attribute* The extent to which the execution of the process is managed to produce work products within stated time and resource requirements	0.64*	Substantial
2.2	*Work product management attribute* The extent to which the execution of the process is managed to produce work products that are documented and controlled and that meet their functional and non-functional requirements, in line with the work product quality goals of the process	0.60*	Moderate
3.1	*Process definition attribute* The extent to which the execution of the process uses a process definition based upon a standard process, that enables the process to contribute to the defined business goals of the organization	0.64*	Substantial
3.2	*Process resource attribute* The extent to which the execution of the process uses suitable skilled human resources and process infrastructure effectively to contribute to the defined business goals of the organization	0.86*	Almost perfect
Capability level	Process capability calculated according to scheme in Table 5	0.70*	Substantial

Table 12. Comparing achievement scales with different numbers of response categories

Attribute number	4-category	3-category	2-category
1.1	0.78	0.59	0.78
2.1	0.64	0.42	0.56
2.2	0.60	0.64	0
3.1	0.64	0.52	0.63
3.2	0.86	0.84	0.79

similar results would be obtained for a different pair of assessors. While both assessors who took part in this study met the requirements for qualified assessors as stipulated in the ISO/IEC PDTR 15504 documents, further empirical investigation is necessary to ascertain whether *any* assessors that meet these requirements can attain such interrater agreement results. Second, the assessments from which our data were collected were conducted using a particular assessment method. This method is similar to the method used in previous interrater agreement studies (Fusaro *et al.*, 1997). However,

it remains to be investigated whether the usage of different methods will produce similar results.

5. CONCLUSIONS

In this paper we have presented the method and results of a study to evaluate the interrater agreement of the ISO/IEC PDTR 15504 emerging international standard for software process assessment. The study was based on two assessments conducted in France during the second phase of the SPICE trials. The results of the study indicate that the interrater agreement of these assessments was high, raising confidence in the usage of this version of the 15504 document set for process assessments. In addition, we found that the interrater agreement cannot be improved by reducing the scale to a 3-point nor to a 2-point scale.

Further studies of interrater agreement are planned during the second phase of the SPICE trials. As well as evaluations, we plan to develop models to explain the variation in the reliability of assessments in order to provide guidelines for increasing reliability.

ACKNOWLEDGEMENTS

This study is supported by ELF *Innovation* to promote software process assessment as a new technique for software quality management.

REFERENCES

Coallier, F. 1995. TRILLIUM: a model for the assessment of Telecom product development and support capability. *IEEE TCSE Software Process Newsletter*, 2, 3–8.

Cohen, J. 1960. A coefficient of agreement for nominal scales. *Educational and Psychological Measurement*, XX(1), 37–46.

Cohen, J. 1968. Weighted kappa: nominal scale agreement with provision for scaled disagreement or partial credit. *Psychological Bulletin*, 70(4), 213–220.

Dunaway, D. and S. Masters. 1996. CMM-Based Appraisal for Internal Process Improvement (CBA IPI): Method Description. Technical Report CMU/SEI-96-TR-7, Software Engineering Institute.

El Emam, K. and D. R. Goldenson. 1995. SPICE: an empiricist's perspective. *Proceedings of the Second IEEE International Software Engineering Standards Symposium*, 84–97.

El Emam, K. and N. H. Madhavji. 1995. The reliability of measuring organizational maturity. *Software Process Improvement and Practice*, 1(1), 3–25.

El Emam, K., D. R. Goldenson, L. Briand and P. Marshall. 1996. Interrater agreement in SPICE based assessments: some preliminary results. *Proceedings of the Fourth International Conference on the Software Process*, 149–156.

El Emam, K. and D. R. Goldenson. 1996. An empirical evaluation of the prospective International SPICE standard. *Software Process Improvement and Practice*, 2(2), 123–148.

El Emam, K., R. Smith and P. Fusaro. 1997b. Modelling the reliability of SPICE based assessments. *Proceedings of the International Symposium on Software Engineering Standards*, 69–82.

El Emam, K., J-N. Drouin and W. Melo (eds). 1998. *SPICE: The Theory and Practice of Software Process Improvement and Capability Determination*. IEEE CS Press.

El Emam, K., L. Briand and R. Smith. 1997c. Assessor agreement in rating SPICE processes. *Software Process Improvement and Practice* 2(4), 291–306.

El Emam, K. and P. Marshall. 1998. Interrater agreement in assessment ratings. In K. El Emam, J-N Drouin and W. Melo (eds). *SPICE: The Theory and Practice of Software Process Improvement and Capability Determination*. IEEE CS Press.

Fleiss, J. 1981. *Statistical Methods for Rates and Proportions*. Wiley.

Fleiss, J., J. Cohen and B. Everitt. 1969. Large sample standard errors of kappa and weighted kappa. *Psychological Bulletin*, 72(5), 323–327.

Fusaro, P., K. El Emam and B. Smith. 1997. Evaluating the interrater agreement of process capability ratings. *Proceedings of the Fourth International Software Metrics Symposium*, 2–11.

Fusaro, P., K. El Emam and B. Smith. In press. The Internal Consistencies of the 1987 SEI Maturity Questionnaire and the SPICE Capability Dimension. *Empirical Software Engineering: An International Journal*, Kluwer Academic Publishers.

Landis, J. and G. Koch. The measurement of observer agreement for categorical data. *Biometrics*, 33, 159–174.

Maclennan, F. and G. Ostrolenk. 1995. The SPICE trials: validating the framework. *Software Process Improvement and Practice*, 1, 47–55.

Rice, J. 1987. *Mathematical Statistics and Data Analysis*. Duxbury Press.

European Experiences with Software Process Improvement

Fran O'Hara
Insight Consulting Ltd.
114 Granitefield
Dun Laoghaire
Co. Dublin, Ireland
Ph: +353-1-2854510
fran.ohara@insight.ie
http://www.insight.ie

ABSTRACT

This paper/presentation will provide a brief overview of the status of Software Process Improvement (SPI) in Europe – its history, current situation and future direction.

Four case studies will then be presented covering a diverse range of business domains, organisational sizes and approaches to SPI.

The author has worked closely with each of the organisations involved in support of their SPI programmes. The case studies will show the starting position of each company, the approach taken, results achieved and lessons learnt. A number of themes such as assessment approach used, cultural/people issues, etc. will be used to explore the experiences of the various companies. The four case studies are

- NewWorld Commerce (formerly Cunav Technologies),

- Motorola Cork,

- Silicon and Software Systems and

- Allied Irish Bank.

Assessment models used include SPICE (ISO/IEC TR 15504) [1] and Software Engineering Institute's CMM[1] [2] (one organisation also achieved ISO9001 certification).

Keywords

Software Process Improvement, CMM, SPICE

[1] Capability Maturity Model is a service mark of Carnegie Mellon University and CMM is registered in the U.S. patent and trademark office.

1 SPI – THE EUROPEAN PERSPECTIVE

In Europe there has been quite a significant interest in and uptake of Software Process Improvement. Historically, the quality management system approach using ISO9001 certification was the approach of choice for man companies in Europe. Schemes such as the UK TickIT scheme provided additional software emphasis to the certification. However, there was a growing interest in incremental software process improvement based at least in part on the significant uptake of the Capability Maturity Model [2] in the U.S.

Unlike the U.S. strategy of providing funding for the development of tools to support SPI (i.e. the CMM and associated deliverables from the SEI), the European Commission chose a different strategy to stimulate a support the adoption of SPI. They provided funding directly to companies under the European Software Systems Initiative (ESSI) scheme. ESSI funded man programmes including, for example,

- awareness and training actions,

- direct funding to over 200 SMEs (small and medium enterprises) to support Process Improvement Experiments (PIEs – see [3] for the PIE case study repository).

- dissemination actions

The focus was on subsidising organisations to adopt best practices with the hope that this would stimulate further improvements in those organisations and more widely in the software industry. However, the current status of SPI in Europe is that although the ESSI initiative achieved a great deal and SPI is coming more into the mainstream, the breadth of uptake of SPI across organisations is still somewhat fragmented. Local content at European SPI conferences (e.g. European SEPG, EuroSPI) is now of a very high quality but SPI has not yet become ingrained into the culture of the software industry in the manner that it now is in the U.S.

Awareness of the SEI CMM is however high in Europe and there are many organisations who use it as a 'toolbox' for improvement rather than using it as the basis for a formal process improvement programme with the associated formal CMM assessment. Indeed, there are a number of factors that may indicate an increasing widespread adoption of CMM...

- availability of experienced SPI personnel from larger CMM-based organisations moving to other organisations and facilitating effective practical improvements using the CMM

- increasing availability of CMM lead assessors (both in the SEI's assessment method, CBA-IPI, and also in the SEI-accredited assessment method from Compita Ltd., PPA for CMM)

- more experience and data on benefits achieved from CMM improvement programmes resulting in a market driven CMM emphasis based on expected competitive advantage on one hand and it being a required supplier certification on the other

SPICE (15504) is expected to become an ISO standard and should be of interest to those who want to either focus on a few processes to improve or those who want to widen the scope of their improvement program beyond software development (which is the focus of CMM). However, the simple benchmarking levels in the CMM will remain attractive to management in many organisations. ISO9000:2000 will contain added focus on process improvement which may help address the somewhat declining interest in the standard.

2   CASE STUDIES – BACKGROUND

The intent here is not to provide an exhaustive treatment of the experiences of the four organisations. Instead a number of interesting themes of software process improvement will be discussed by using the experiences of one or more of the organisations involved.

NewWorld Commerce (formerly Cunav Technologies):

This is a software systems development and consulting company, which provides IT resources and solutions to customers operating in a variety of application areas, with a focus on web-based development. NewWorld Commerce had approximately 20 staff when they participated in the EU funded SPIRE project [4] that supported focused process improvement projects in small organisations. This case study relates to their experience with SPIRE in 1998 and their experiences since that date.

Motorola Cork

Motorola established the software centre in Cork in 1990 to develop analog switching software and GSM telecommunication systems. There are now well over 400 staff involved in software development. The organisation

has had a strong software process improvement programme in place since 1993 (see [5]).

Silicon and Software Systems:

Silicon & Software Systems (S3) have been providing design services in silicon, software and hardware design since it was established in 1986. Within the software division of approximately 100 software engineers (now 150 software engineers), application areas include telecommunications, consumer electronics, Internet and digital broadcasting. The company embarked on an improvement program in 1994 (see [6]).

AIB Ban I.T. Department:

Allied Irish Bank (AIB) has an IT department comprising about 300 personnel providing IT systems and services to the rest of the bank. They embarked on an improvement programme in 1998.

3   STARTING   POSITION   AND   BUSINESS DRIVERS

NewWorld Commerce performed a review of previous project post-mortems and found some difficulties with managing customer expectations on some projects and excessive amounts of rework due to misunderstanding of initial requirements. Meeting real customer needs and improving project estimates and visibility with the customer were to be the key drivers for the software process improvements. As a small organisation, improvements needed to minimise impact on resources and yet maximise the return on any investments by aligning them with the key business drivers.

Motorola develop systems with high reliability and availability requirements. Given the system requirements and the competitive marketplace, errors and downtime must be kept to a minimum. The telecommunications technology area is constantly evolving, with new products and services continually offered. Time to market is also therefore a key consideration. Motorola's development process is explicitly documented and is evolving as the company follows its program for continuous improvement, which it expects will ultimately lead to an improved CMM rating (Motorola places much emphasis on satisfying the concepts of the CMM).

S3 had a large amount of documentation in their quality management system that required streamlining and a re-evaluation as to the extent that this actually helped people do their jobs. From a business point of view S3 initiall stated time to market as the key business driver for the SPI programme. However, it became apparent that the first goal should really be to measure their time to market. This change coincided with an evolving change in mindset re using measurement to guide their improvements. It could also of course not be ignored that achieving a level on the CMM has clear commercial/marketing value for S3 especially since customers were asking for their CMM rating. However, it was made clear that improvement was the goal, not certification to a level on the CMM for its own sake. This distinction proved to be highly significant and beneficial to the entire improvement program.

AIB recognised the importance of managing all changes (including IT changes) as business changes. IT and the business personnel identified a number of ke principles/drivers that were to shape the improvement effort:

- IT and the Business were to work together in partnership

- The quality of the product needed to be built-in during development

- Speed to market is a key business driver but it must not compromise the quality of the product and the ability to change into the future

These were combined with specific goals and concerns from the various stakeholders of the improvement programme (including IT staff themselves) to provide direction and focus for the improvement efforts.

4   THE ROLE OF THE SPONSOR

The role of the sponsor was of course crucial in each organisation. Without management commitment to the SPI programme the chances of failure are high. Commitment does not simply mean giving approval. It means providing direction, having a good understanding of what is being undertaken and why, providing visible active support and encouragement.

Motorola's management commitment and involvement was demonstrated very well to me on one occasion when we had improved the inspection process with the involvement of a significant number of engineering staff. A key concern raised by the group was whether inspectors would have sufficient time to check adequately for faults given the pressures of project deadlines. The department managers responded by e-mailing all staff that they should notify the managers personally if they found themselves in an inspection where this occurred.

Interestingly AIB's improvement team initially underestimated the real extent of management commitment that existed. The lesson they learnt was to test the level of commitment early. That way when the commitment is forthcoming it 'kick-starts' the improvement programme with the knowledge that it will be supported b management if/when difficulties arise. (In this case the commitment was very strong. However, if the commitment is not forthcoming it raises the issue early so it can be dealt with as appropriate i.e. halt the programme or work on gaining the commitment!). Similarly maintaining a strong

level of management commit ent throughout the improvement programme is crucial to its success.

5   ASSESSMENT APPROACH

NewWorld Commerce participated in the EU funded SPIRE project that provided nominal funding for a focused six month process improvement pilot. An SPI mentor was provided to support the organisation during the pilot. The first task of the mentor was to help identify the process area to improve based on business drivers and the results of a facilitated SPICE self-assessment. This facilitated self-assessment involved using an assessment tool to gather data on their processes based on round table discussions with key personnel. It also involved an SPI questionnaire to gather, from a wider group, the attitude towards SPI before and after the improvement pilot. The self-assessment took one day and had minimal impact on resources. It was by means comprehensive but gave a reasonable indication of strengths and weaknesses for the purpose of the pilot.

Motorola used SEI CMM assessments and its own extension of the assessment approach accredited by the SEI. Between these external assessments, they also performed internal (local) assessments. Interestingly, these local assessments involved comparing the results from the local team's assessment with the results determined by each process area team's assessment of their own process area. This helped ensure a consistent understanding of CMM requirements.

S3 initially achieved ISO9001certification and then used two approaches to CMM assessment. The initial approach used on two occasions was effectively a facilitated self-assessment. This 'interim maturity evaluation' used a questionnaire and consisted of discussions based on the questionnaire and guided by an external consultant. The training value of these sessions was also described as excellent. An external assessment based on the Process Professional Assessor for CMM assessment method was then performed (this is similar to the SEI's CBA-IPI assessment method)

AIB performed a business review of IT competencies which was a high level assessment of the IT department as a whole rather than a process focused assessment. It then held a number of internal workshops to identify process and organisational issues/problems as perceived by IT staff. Each workshop had a process-related theme or area for discussion that had been identified as a 'hot spot' - this served to direct the discussions. The idea was to identify the 'pain' from the bottom up and correlate this with the key business drivers as identified by the business review. Additionally, the CMM was used as a toolbox or reference point to raise questions on the strategy that was planned for improvements. However, this improvement program did not follow a formal assessment approach or improvement model.

6 IMPROVEMENT STRATEGY

AIB are have been so successful in moving new projects to a Rapid Application Development approach (i.e. using a customised DSDM framework) that they are now using the principles of DSDM on their own improvement project and finding it very useful. These include timeboxing improvement activities (typically one month timeboxes), prioritising SPI requirements and actions within each timebox, using facilitation techniques for SPI workshops, etc.

7 PROGRAMME MANAGEMENT

All four companies followed some form of improvement lifecycle based on a Plan, Do, Check, Act cycle.

Motorola used a variation on the IDEAL[2] improvement model from the SEI. This is a recommended set of steps to be followed in any improvement programme.

8 INFRASTRUCTURE

S3 managed to reduce their average time to evaluate and introduce a process change from 533 days prior to the SPI project down to 112 days now using managed pilot projects. A significant factor contributing to this improvement was an infrastructure change (see figure 1.)

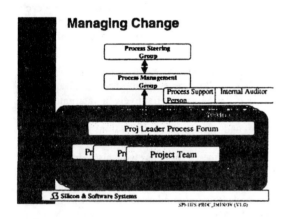

Figure 1. S3's Software Process Improvement Infrastructure

The Process Management Group consisted of the SPI programme manager, project leaders and key process area team leaders (called task forces in S3 – not depicted in figure 1). The infrastructure change was in response to roll-out difficulties (slow, dissemination of process changes not effective enough, etc.). The key addition was a division-specific project leader process forum. These were key people who are more likely to realise the effect on their

---

[2] IDEAL is a service mark of Carnegie Mellon University

projects of any process changes. Improvements that they decided to run with were injected directly into *their* projects where they could assess and monitor the effect of the changes.

9 TRAINING

S3 used a practical approach to training. Initially a oneday overview of the updated quality system was provided which also covered the rationale for changes. This involved a lot of discussion and improvement suggestions were fed back into the system. Process mentors were assigned to each project to support the introduction of new processes. A series of software project management workshops were held that proved highly effective – so much so that it is now done for every new project with a facilitator from the process group. Two project teams participated in each workshop. An introduction to the project was given by the project leader. This was followed by an introduction from the process mentor on the processes that needed to be used/planned (i.e. CMM level 2 processes such as requirements management, project planning itself, configuration management, etc.). Each team then spent the majority of the workshop developing the project plan based on this information. Roles such as project leader were allocated and rotated. This approach introduced people to the quality system, gave the team an understanding of the project leader role and how they could support him/her, was useful as a team building exercise and new projects were doing real work by planning their project!

In terms of external support, S3 used three different consultants during the project that proved useful in providing different perspectives.

Motorola recognise the importance of training and development of a capable workforce. This also helps attract and retain staff in the current climate of high attrition rates. There is a policy of having 40 hours training for each member of staff in Motorola. Motorola made good use of customised training workshops covering a range of topics from CMM overviews to testing and inspections and addressing best practice and the relationship to in-house processes. A key element was the use of in-house projects and documentation for exercises and practicals during training to ensure the training material was related to each participant's own situation.

AIB also used customised training (including AIB's flavour of DSDM, facilitation, Test Management, Peer reviews, etc.) and often held follow-up sessions with the trainer three months after the initial workshop to follow-up on the implementation of the training material thereby enhancing the effectiveness of training.

10 CULTURAL/PEOPLE ISSUES

Winning the hearts and minds of people is crucial to a successful process improvement programme. S3 noted the value of informal communication, especially early in the SPI project, in achieving this – i.e. selling SPI at an individual level. The SPI programme manager coined a key approach used for this... TSDM – the Tea Station Dissemination Mechanism! The key issue, though, in S3's change management and winning people over was having a driving philosophy of achieving real improvement and helping people do their jobs better rather than seeking compliance to a model. Involvement is another key issue – about 70-80% of staff were involved in some manner in the SPI project (e.g. from active involvement in a task force to just acting as a reviewer of proposed changes)

AIB have found that having a strong project focus with direct hands-on support and mentoring of projects by the improvement team has been very effective at enabling effective change. Providing improvement personnel to act as facilitators and mentors on the projects has been the key to this partnership and to viewing process improvement and best practices as a supportive force for the project team. Another key issue has been driving improvements, as least in part, from a bottom up approach whereby improvements are addressing the issues and pain of staff at all levels. At the same time identifying all the stakeholders in the improvement project and ensuring everyone achieves some benefit and has their key needs met greatly increases your chances of success.

One lesson learnt from earlier improvement actions in AIB is the importance of feedback – the loop needs to be closed with people who helped initiate improvements so they see the fruit of their work and have visibility on progress.

Motorola experience is that process ownership and development are best placed with those closest to the process. Empowering staff to define and tailor processes is key to achieving ownership. An example of this was the approach adopted to improving their inspection process [7]. The improvements were defined and agreed in a one-day workshop involving about 35 senior engineers from all departments. This resulted in a great deal of buy-in for the changes.

11 RESULTS OBTAINED

NewWorld Commerce firstly achieved immediate benefits from the pilot projects with the requirements process improvements. This was indicated from data they collected for requirements-related rework and time/budget estimates. However, customers also provided direct feedback on how impressed they were with improved ability to deliver what they wanted. Similarly, the improvements in the project planning and tracking processes (especially in relation to risk management and estimation) resulted in a significant high risk project being delivered successfully.

Motorola achieved level 4 on the CMM scale in 1997. This contributed to the investment in the Cork development group and to its ability to perform highly despite significant and rapid growth.

S3 achieved level 2 on the CMM scale (with a number of level 3 Key Process Areas also satisfied) in 1999. A number of customers (including a CMM level 4 organisation) have performed audits/evaluations on S3 recently and the results have been very positive and have validated the internal improvements undertaken. S3 have even found themselves in the position of being asked b customers to provide advice to them on key process areas that have been seen to be highly effective! From an internal point of view, a significant change in attitude towards SPI has resulted in S3 staff raising numerous improvement requests – they now see what is possible and realise they have the power to make change and improvement happen.

AIB have performed a number of benchmarking exercises including determining productivity (function points/week), delivery rates (time taken from initial request to delivery to production/function point) and quality (defects/function point). In the words of the SPI programme manager ' there has been a huge improvement in each of these three measures'. As significant is the improved way in which people are working together and co-operating.

12 LESSONS LEARNT

S3 believe that the philosophy they adopted in relation to SPI was crucial to their success. They stressed improvement not CMM compliance. The SPI programme manager is convinced they would not have achieved level 2 (and done so well at level 3) if the goal had been level 2 compliance! Indeed although CMM is a good model, it is just a model and its scope may not be wide enough for a given organisation's purpose. Another key lesson was the importance of transitioning improvements through a division/department-specific project leader forum to accelerate the rollout of improvements.

Motorola are providing greater emphasis now on using SPI more directly to support the business objectives. In this way even greater gains can be achieved from the use of SPI and leveraging off the progress made in attaining CMM level 4 certification. In terms of improving visibility and tracking progress one must view process improvement as a project – this means applying more structured planning and tracking mechanisms to the SPI project itself in a manner similar to product development projects. Another lesson learnt was the importance of goal-driven metrics and aligning this to business goals.

ACKNOWLEDGEMENTS
The author would like to acknowledge the kind support of each of the organisations involved in the case studies. The contributions of the following for their help in the

preparation of this paper are particularly noted: Bill Culleton from S3, Hugh Ivory from AIB, Tom O'Kane from Motorola and John McEvoy from NewWorld Commerce. Thanks also to a number of people who contributed to the European perspective on SPI: Colin Tully of European Software Process Improvement foundation (ESPI), Tony Elkington of ESPI and Robert Cochran of the Centre for Software Engineering.

REFERENCES

1. Rout, 'SPICE: A framework for Software Process Assessment, Software Process Improvement and Practice' August 1995, pp 56-66, ISSN:1077-4866

2. Paulk et. al., 'Capability Maturity Model for Software, Version 1.1', Report CMU/SEI-93-TR-24, Software Engineering Institute, Pittsburg, 1991.

3. VASIE Best Practice Repository, The European Comission, DG III Industry, EPSRIT progra <http://www.esi.es/VASIE> This contains ESSI programme results i.e. information on improvement experiments performed in the European software industry, the results achieved and lessons learnt.

4. SPIRE project and handbook, The European Commission, ESPRIT/ESSI 23873, http://www.cse.dcu.ie/spire

5. Fitzgerald and O'Kane, A longitudinal study o Software Process Improvement, IEEE Software, May/June 1999, pp 37-45

6. Kelly and Culleton, Process Improvement for Small Organisations, IEEE Computer, October 1999, pp 41-47

7. O'Hara, O'Kane and Smith, 'Contradictions within an evolving inspection process', EuroSTAR conference, Barcelona, 1999

Chapter 10

Software Process Improvement for Small Organizations

Introduction to Chapter

Considerable attention has been paid to the issues concerned with software process improvement in the context of small organizations and small software projects. In the case of small organizations this has arisen for two reasons:

- the relatively large overhead associated with software process assessment and improvement;

- the different ways in which small organizations operate compared with large ones.

An example of the latter, according to Kuvaja, et al., [5], is the fact that small organizations cannot afford to maintain substantial expertise concerning software improvement internally , but have to buy it in as required. Other relevant features of small organizations are:

- production, management and quality assurance roles often overlap;

- development personnel may have to divide their time between several projects;

- the loss of a key member of staff may be crucial;

- a flat management structure;

- short schedules;

- good communication.

While some of these features, such as the overlapping roles held by some personnel, may tend to inhibit process improvement, other features, such as ease of communication, may actively support process improvement.

It is sometimes suggested that the SW-CMM has been developed largely in the context of large organizations, and the SEI statistics show that some organizations assessed have around 2000 IT staff [3]. However, there have been a large number of publications, for example at the SEPG conferences, that have been devoted to the application of SW-CMM to small organizations. Examples include works by Brinkman, et al.[1], Johnson, et al.[4], and Rabideau, et al [7].

One of the aims of the SPICE project was to develop an international standard for software process assessment and improvement which could be used across a wide range of organizations irrespective of their geographical location, size, etc. Taking the definition of small software organization used by the SPIRE project [8] as one having fewer than 50 software development staff, it is interesting to see (in Figure 1) how phase 2 of the SPICE trials has been spread over organizations of various sizes (see paper by Hunter in Chapter 9 of this tutorial). The number of IT staff peak at about 50, so there are clearly a reasonable number of organizations with 50 or fewer IT staff.

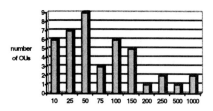

Figure 1 – Approximate numbers of IT staff in the organization

Also in the context of the SPICE trials data, it has been shown by Hunter and Jung [2] that the size of the organization is not normally correlated with the cost, in terms of assessor effort, of an assessment. This means that assessments are disproportionately expensive for small organizations, and this fact has led to the development of rapid methods of process assessment like the one described by Rout, et al., in Chapter 8 of this tutorial.

In Europe, the SPIRE project [8] was set up to lower the barriers inhibiting small software development organizations from undertaking successful software process improvement projects. Its experiences are documented in [8] as well as forming the basis of the third of the papers included in this chapter.

2. Description of Articles

The first paper in this chapter is by Karlheinz Kautz, Henrik Westergaard Hansen, and Kim Thaysen; and is entitled "Applying and Adjusting a Software Process Model in Practice: The Use of the IDEAL Model in a Small Software Enterprise."

The IDEAL model was developed at the SEI as a framework for implementing SW-CMM-based software process improvement, as described by Paulk, et al. [6]. The acronym spells out the five stages of the software process improvement cycle:

- Initiating,

- Diagnosing,

- Evaluating,

- Acting,

- Leveraging/Learning.

While the model does not make any assumptions about the size of the organization to which it is applied, the fact that it was developed at the SEI might suggest that it was intended for large software systems and large organizations, so there could be doubts about how suitable it would be in the context of small software systems and small organizations. The paper investigates the suitability of using the IDEAL model for process improvement in a small Danish software company.

The paper concludes that the IDEAL framework worked reasonably well for the organization in question, and that it is flexible enough so that it can be tailored to the needs of a small organization.

The second paper in this chapter is by Elif Demirörs, Onur Demirörs, Oğuz Dikenelli, and Billur Keskin; and is entitled "Process Improvement Towards ISO 9001 Certification in a Small Software Organization." In it the authors describe a model for process improvement based on the key process areas of the SW-CMM and the requirements of ISO 9001 and ISO 9000-3. The model has three stages:

- Preparation,

- Control,

- Stability.

The preparation phase involves seeking the support of top management, assessing the current state of the organization's process, and lasts about three months. The other two phases should take about nine months each, and are concerned with controlling costs and change control; and product engineering, respectively.

The authors identify some of the challenges involved in applying ISO 9001 to a small organization, and suggest how some of these challenges may be overcome. They also identify features of companies that tend to inhibit software process improvement as well as features that tend to support it. They suggest that their experiences are of particular value in Europe where software development organizations are often quite small and ISO 9001 is widely used.

The third paper in this chapter is by Marty Sanders; and is entitled "Software Process Improvement in Small Organizations." In it Sanders describes some of the work of the SPIRE project [8] as well as including some personal thoughts of her own on the topic.

The paper is addressed to the software process improvement champion in a small organization, and virtually all aspects of software process improvement are covered, including:

- The reasons for improvement;

- Cost/benefit analysis;

- Encouraging business leadership;

- Getting support from the rest of the organization;

- Making the improvements.

The paper concludes by stating that the single biggest benefit of SPI is that it causes organizations to think about what they are doing and why they are doing it; while the biggest single difficulty may be lack of management commitment.

References

[1] S. Brinkman, T. Lawrence, "Implementing CMM Levels 2 and 3 in a Small Project Environment," *SEPG* 1998.

[2] R. B. Hunter, H.-W. Jung; "Some Experiences and Results from the SPICE Trials," *SPICE 2000,* Dublin, 2000.

[3] R. B. Hunter, H.-W. Jung; "The Regional Factor in Software Process Assessment", *Second World Congress for Software Quality,* Yokohama, 2000.

[4] D. L. Johnson, J. G. Brodman; "Applying the CMM to Small Organizations and Small Projects," *SEPG,* 1998.

[5] P. KuvajaJ. Palo, and A. Bicego , "TAPISTRY – A Software Process Improvement Approach Tailored for Small Enterprizes," *Software Quality Journal,* volume 8, number 2, 1999.

[6] M. C. Paulk, C. V. Weber, B. Curtis, M. B. Chrissis; *The Capability Maturity Model: Guidelines for Improving the Software Process,* Addison Wesley, 1995.

[7] M. F. Rabideau, S. Stilley, M. Alfred, A. M. Bishop;"Implementing and Assessing CMM-Based Improvements in a Small Organization," *SEPG,* 1998.

[8] SPIRE Project Team, *The SPIRE Handbook,* Centre for Software Engineering, Dublin, 1998.

Applying and Adjusting
a Software Process Improvement Model in Practice:
The Use of the IDEAL Model in a Small Software Enterprise

Karlheinz Kautz
Copenhagen Business School
Department of Informatics
Howitzvej 60
DK-2000 Frederiksberg
Denmark
Karl.Kautz@cbs.dk

Henrik Westergaard Hansen
Mindpass as
Vardevej 1
DK-9220 Aalborg
Denmark
hwh@mindpass.dk

Kim Thaysen
Mindpass as
Vardevej 1
DK-9220 Aalborg
Denmark
kth@mindpass.dk

ABSTRACT
Software process improvement is a demanding and complex undertaking. To support the constitution and implementation of software process improvement schemes the Software Engineering Institute (SEI) proposes a framework, the so-called IDEAL model. This model is based on experiences from large organizations. The aim of the research described here was to investigate the suitabilit of the model for small software enterprises. It has therefore been deployed and adjusted for successful use in a small Danish software company. The course of the project and the application of the model are presented and the case is reflected on the background of current knowledge about managing software process improvement as organizational change.

Keywords
Software process improvement, improvement models

1 INTRODUCTION
Software process improvement is a demanding and complex undertaking. To support the constitution and implementation of software process improvement schemes and projects, the Software Engineering Institute (SEI) proposes a framework, the so-called IDEAL model, which consists of five phases and which provides a structured approach for continuous improvement.

This model is based on the SEI's experiences with their governmental and industry customers in the US. These are usually very large organizations. However, most software enterprises, even in the US, but more so in Europe and other parts of the world, belong to the category of small and very small software enterprises. Yet, although vital for both academics and practitioners in the field, insights about software process improvement in general and the use of such a model as IDEAL in minor organizations is still scarce (as exceptions, see for example [1], [2]).

The work presented in this article wants to contribute to that body of knowledge. We have therefore investigated the suitability of the IDEAL model for small software enterprises and report our experiences of deploying the approach in a young and small Danish software company. The approach was tailored to meet the organization's needs and this resulted in the successful completion of a first improvement cycle.

The aim of the undertaking was to change the practices in the involved organization, thus the research approach applied falls into the category of action research [3]. The authors participated, each to a different extent, actively in the process as change agents and mentors for the intended alterations. In addition to the involvement in the project, observations, informal conversations, formal interviews, official meetings and document studies were used as methods for collection of the data, on which this article is based.

The article is structured as follows. In the next section the IDEAL model is explained in more detail. Then, the course of the project and the application of the model are presented. Finally, the alignment process and the content of the adjustments and their impact on the improvement project as a whole are discussed and the case is reflected on the background of current knowledge about managing software process improvement as organizational change.

2 THE IDEAL MODEL

The IDEAL model has been developed by the SEI [4]. The objective of the model is to provide a path of actions that constitute a software process improvement program. The model defines five phases: the Initiating phase, the Diagnosing phase, the Establishing phase, the Acting phase, and the Leveraging phase. Each phase consists of up to 10 tasks and some tasks comprise 5 or 6 subtasks. The main activities in each phase are as follows:

achievement are developed.

In the Acting phase solutions, which address the areas of improvement discovered during the Diagnosing phase are created, piloted, and deployed throughout the organization. In the Leveraging phase the information collected in the earlier phases, lessons learned, and metrics on performances, are evaluated to make the next pass through the IDEAL model more effective. By doing this, adjustments of the strategy, the methods and the

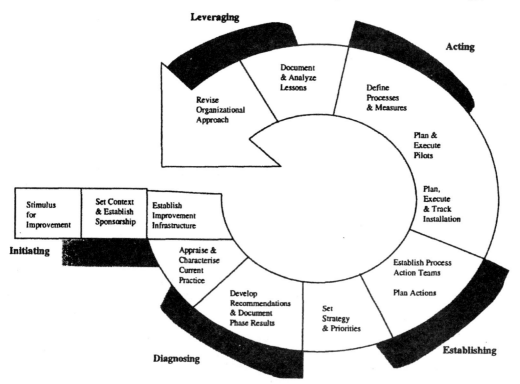

Figure 1: The Ideal Model

In the Initiating phase an improvement infrastructure is established, the roles and responsibilities are initially defined and initial resources are assigned. The general goals of the initiative based on business needs are defined and a management steering group and a software engineering process group are typically established. In addition, an initial improvement plan to guide the organization through the next two phases is created.

In the Diagnosing phase appraisal activities are performed to establish a baseline of the organization's current state. The results and recommendations from the appraisals are included in a first version of an improvement action plan.

In the Establishing phase, the issues that the organization has decided to address are prioritized and strategies for pursuing the solutions are formed. The action plan draft is completed and measurable goals and metrics to control goal

infrastructure used in the SPI program can be performed.

This description, which is a very brief summary of a 220-pages long, very detailed document, the above included graphical representation of the phases, and the tasks' presentations in process flow charts as a series of activities in the user's guide, suggest a sequential course through all phases and tasks.

Such a sequential pass is indeed recommended as a best case scenario. However, it is acknowledged that "real-life events prevent organizations from following a set sequence" – a formulation that seems to convey an attitude, where deviations from a model are seen as a problem rather than an opportunity. Therefore, it is expected that organizations will, respectively must tailor the steps to their particular situation and it is affirmed that the boundaries between the phases are not as clearly defined as shown in the graphical representation of the model. Furthermore it is indicated that many activities can be pursued in a parallel fashion.

Little advice is however given of how to tailor the approach and which factors and their interdependencies have to be taken into account other than that the adjusted methodolog has to fit an organization's vision, business objectives and resources.

The model is based on the SEI's experiences with their governmental and industry customers, which are usually very large organizations. However, most software companies belong to the category of small and very small enterprises. Therefore, insight about the use of such model as IDEAL in minor organizations is vital, but still scarce.

The work presented here wants to contribute to that body of knowledge. We have investigated the suitability of the IDEAL model for small software enterprises and report our experiences of deploying the approach in a small Danish software company.

3. THE CASE

The company NP was founded in early 1997 by 2 persons, with a business and an IT background, respectively. The company's business idea is to pursue a solution for the problem of how to present 20000 warehouse items on a 14'' screen through a slow network in a fast and structured way.

At the start of the investigation in early 1998 it had 25 employees of whom 15 were directly involved in software development and the rest in business administration, marketing, and sales. The two founders function as management. Software development is roughly divided in 2 divisions of the same size: A production division, which delivers standard intra- and internet solutions. This division generates the company's income for the time being. It consists besides software developers also of operational - network administration - staff and art designers.

The other part of the organization's operation is largely financed by public money and takes place in the other division, which is called research and development. It deals with *the* future product of the organization.

It is this division, which is in the main focus of our investigation. During the period of time, which is described here, the first version of the product was still under development, though some of its modules underwent internal integration tests already.

The work in this division is rather project-oriented. Two project leaders function as coordinators for a varying number of subprojects where the employees, in groups of 4 – 5, perform all sorts of development tasks. These project groups often only exist for a short period of time and are dissolved when the problem, which led to the establishment of the subproject, is solved. To solve these problems quite

regularly also members, especially the art designers, of the production group are involved.

From the start, the organization showed an originative interest in quality and quality management matters. In addition, the company's economical foundation is for a limited period largely based on EU support for the development of new businesses. In its business plan, which functions as a contract with the sponsor, the organization has committed itself to create a quality assurance group or division and it is determined that some of the support actually has to be used for this objective.

Management therefore, continuously explores the market both with respect to improve the product and to improve its business processes and took contact with the university[1] as they had heard about research there concerning software process improvement.

This set the stage for the first period of an ongoing improvement project. Here we report our experience with the deployment of the IDEAL model during a 10 weeks period in 1998: one week initiating, three weeks diagnosing, and six weeks establishing and acting in parallel. Leveraging, respectively learning, took place throughout the whole period.

The improvement project is still going on and is subject of a longitudinal study

3.1 The Initiating Phase

As a consequence of the initial contact, a start-up meeting between company management and university personal took place. On that meeting management stated their vision for their organization as a company known for high qualit products based on professional craftsmanship. Therefore they wanted to have all basic work practices established and kept under control as soon as possible, especially with regard to the expected increase of personal. The researchers explained how an improvement project could look like.

As a result, it was determined that two researchers should be hired as full time consultants for an initial 10 weeks project with options for extension to start a process improvement initiative. One project leader was directl assigned half time to the project.

The consultants' first tasks were to prepare a contract and to draft a general improvement plan to be discussed at an introductory meeting 2 days later. The contract comprised the mutual commitments between management and consultants, in particular resources, which the organization was willing to use. It was for example determined that each

---

[1] At the time of performing the study, all three authors were members of the Department of Computer Science at Aalborg University, Denmark.

employee was granted at least 90 minutes interview time for an appraisal. The first version of the improvement plan, which served as a project plan contained preliminary descriptions of the objectives for the project, of possible approaches and of a time schedule. The plan was inspired by the known Plan-Do-Check-Act cycle and as a more concrete refinement of this approach the course of the work was oriented tentatively at the IDEAL model.

At the introductory meeting management and both project leaders participated and the documents were discussed. The consultants gave a short introduction into software process improvement in general and – due to the organization's earlier stated interest in the US marked - specifically into CMM-based improvement[2].

The overall objectives as stated by management gave the initiative a long-term perspective. To establish a short-term perspective as well, these were refined on that meeting. Whereas management was most attracted by a quantitative profile of the organization with regard to CMM level 2 and general project and quality management practices, the project leaders were most interested in concrete project planning and estimation techniques. Also at the meeting expectations concerning the effort could be clarified and adjusted. Management had hoped that getting the practices in place would only take some weeks and had a hard time understanding that this would take at least a year.

After the meeting, the need and conditions for and the benefits of process improvement were clear for management and project leaders. They were therefore well equipped to inform the other employees why such a project was relevant for all of them. The improvement plan was refined and contained now a goal description based on the CMM level 2 processes, and a concise schedule for an appraisal and the resulting establishment and enactment of the actual improvement activities during the 10 weeks period. The plan also included a proposal for the establishment of a small software engineering process group (SEPG) to define, monitor and track the course of the project. This group was formally approved and from the on consisted of the project leader and the two consultants. A first SEPG meeting was held directly after the introductory meeting to prepare an orientation meeting for all employees.

At that meeting all employees were informed about the project, management communicated the objectives and their origin and introduced the consultants who gave a presentation on software development, its problems and possible solutions.

The developers could identify themselves with many of the

[2] In the context of this article it is assumed that the reader is familiar with the basic concepts of the Capability Maturity Model (CMM).

problems described. There was a consensus among the developers that something should be done to improve the work practices and they were looking forward to the initiative to be implemented. The whole initiating phase took a total of one week.

3.2 The Diagnosing phase

In the diagnosing phase a tailored CMM-inspired approach [5] was chosen to perform a development process specific appraisal and a more general organizational analysis. The two project leaders filled in a questionnaire especially designed for CMM level 2 assessments and 6 people were interviewed before and after the questionnaire sessions, in all 7 out of 11 employees involved in R & D tasks were directly involved in these activities. In addition, documents were reviewed and observations were made.

The questionnaires, which were filled in while the consultants were present for necessary clarifications, delivered the basic material for the requested, quantified profiles. The answers from the questionnaires were then supplemented and substantiated by the interview results.

Concerning the interviews it is important to know that we asked the employees what they experienced as problems and not what a model like the CMM defined as a potential problem area. This approach uncovered problems, which were outside the direct scope of the CMM, but invaluable for a professional, improvement-oriented organization. An example here was the meeting culture. Many meetings were hold, but resulting information was not communicated to all relevant persons. There was a lack of structure and documentation rules. Other results were the lack of an overall life cycle model, of project estimation routines and of code documentation. It has to be mentioned that during the interviews the employees did not only describe the status quo, but also made significant proposals for improvement. Finally, the interviews had the effect that the consultants and employees got to know each other, which facilitated the further cooperation.

The document reviews either delivered further evidence or uncovered other problems. An example was that both questionnaires and interviews postulated that detailed time schedules were produced as part of the planning. The documents showed however that no data was kept after revision of plans about the old plans and the reasons for the change. Another example was the above-mentioned meeting culture. The document review revealed that no minutes of the decisions were taken.

The general organizational analysis unveiled as described above a project-oriented organization in which a creative, dynamic, energetic and at times hectic atmosphere prevailed. Project groups emerged frequently on an ad-hoc basis and were determined by the situations.

The company can be characterized as a simple structure where the directors determine the overall scope and frame, take the strategic business and product related decisions, negotiate deadlines with account officers and the project leaders, and control and co-ordinate that commitments and contracts are kept. They expect that everyone takes responsibility, can see the company's aim and works for a common interest. They decide what has to be done, but not how it has to be done. The management style is management-by-walking. The project leaders keep overview over the technical tasks and achievements and the developers have a relatively large liberty and right of self-determination. They have technical responsibility and decisions concerning detailed technical problems as well as the purchase of tools are taken autonomously by them They show commitment and motivation and often work overtime.

An open office landscape mirrors the organization's wish for an open and relaxing atmosphere where the employee can develop a feeling of community and security, and which supports internal communication and in a natural way a co-ordination mechanism of mutual adjustment. Finally, to support this culture, the organization employs to a great extent young, newly graduated staff with an education both in information systems or computer science, who have no 'bad' habits and who are open for innovations.

The initial assessment with interviews and questionnaires itself took one week, while writing the full report based on additional collection of evidence through the documents reviews and observations took another 2 weeks.

The assessment report [6] concluded that NP was a typical level 1 organization with relative strengths in project tracking and oversight and in project planning, and some control over requirement management. Weaknesses were found for configuration management and quality assurance. This however was partly related to the fact that the organization only worked on the first version of its product and had not reached the test phase yet. Besides the CMM related findings, the report contained the identified problems from outside the model and a list of recommendations for both areas as well as a slightly refined plan for action.

Finally, the outcome of the investigation was presented to the organization on two meetings. Initially, the report was exposed to management in a 2 hours session and after they had accepted and approved the document, the results were introduced to all employees. On that meeting first the overall maturity profile was shown. Then, the most acute and concrete problems, whose solution was judged by the SEPG to be a precondition for any CMM-related improvements and whose settlement was considered to have a direct effect on the organization, were presented.

All improvement proposals were without further prioritization discussed by placing them in a concrete life-

cycle model. The spiral model was used for this purpose and showed to be most appropriate for the organization's situation.

This approach illustrated that fast progress was possible and made the relationship between the individual findings and recommendations visible. It supported a holistic understanding of the situation and the necessary actions, and provided an overall structure for all development and improvement activities.

Although three weeks without any action seem to be a long time, the consultants - as they were present every day in the organization - could keep the momentum going. This was manifested in the next two phases.

3.3 The Establishing Phase

The transition between this phase and the preceding one was somehow blurred. The presentation of the diagnosis results went, as described above, beyond a mere account of possible improvements: it contained the distinction between acute problems and principle – process-centered - problems and utilized a particular model to explain their relationship and their effect. These were both used again during the performance of the three main tasks the SEPG worked upon in this phase, namely a further refinement of the improvement proposals, a prioritization of the proposals and the development and documentation of the final plan for action.

The leading principle for the subsequent processing of the improvement proposals was to avoid too much bureaucracy in the form of extensive documentation and of numerous inspections, reviews and audits, but to still keep in the range of the CMM.

The governing parameters for the prioritization were to delimit extra economical resources and to delimit the additional workload for the employees. Through placement in the now known life cycle model for the product development it had become clear which improvement proposals fitted best to which development activities. Thus, due to the fact that the next actual life cycle activity in the development project was testing the first version of the product, quality assurance which had been judged weak got the highest priority together with the actual introduction of the life cycle model. As a result the CMM-related, process-centered improvements and those problem-centered improvements, which fitted into the life cycle, were planned such that they followed the organization's life cycle for (the) product development.

As a result of this phase a report including a detailed improvement and action plan was produced and delivered at the end of the 10 weeks period. The establishment phase took a total of six weeks. Many of the subtasks were performed in accordance with the IDEAL model. Yet, explicit reviews of the organization's vision and business plan were judged to be not necessary as these had been discussed only a few weeks earlier. In addition, the report did not comprise a concrete metrics program. This wa considered too early given the fact that the organization first should establish some basic processes. Instead a proposal for the establishment of routines to gather both qualitative and quantitative knowledge was included. In contrast to the IDEAL model where a distinction between problem-centered and process-centered improvement is first introduced for the acting phase, such a differentiation took already place here and was helpful in constituting the improvement plan.

The work tasks in this phase were also influenced by the fact that the SEPG and the participants of the meeting where the diagnosis results were presented judged two of the acute problems as so important that they immediately after the meeting founded two technical working groups with the approval of management to solve these problems. This concerned the lack of meeting structure and meeting guidelines and the lack of code documentation routines. Thus no proper prioritization and long-term plans for these activities were developed.

As a consequence an unforeseen, direct transition from the diagnosis phase to the acting phase to deal with these issues took place and in parallel work was performed in both phases.

3.4 The Acting Phase
The first activity in the acting phase, which can also be considered as an establishing activity was the founding of the two working groups (TWGs – Technical Working Groups in terms of the model) which should work with two of the acute problem areas.

In accordance with the organization's work routines, all meeting participants, thus all employees of the R & D department were in line with their own preferences assigned to one of the two temporary project groups. The SEPG members scheduled dates for first group meetings and appointed one person as responsible for the preparation of that meeting. The SEPG members also participated in the first meeting of each group. The 'meeting' group needed two more sessions to develop a solution, whereas the 'code documentation' group only met once more.

Finally, on a common meeting the two groups informed each other and accepted the prepared proposals. The whole process took one week and the remaining time was used to pilot and to implement the new routines. No special action had to be taken for these tasks as all employees had been involved in the definition process.

At the end of the period two new groups, a 'life cycle' group and a 'quality assurance and test' group, were established who documented their work in two short reports. However at the end of the 10-week period none of the routines, and thus no process-centered and CMM-related improvement had been implemented. This has

however happened afterwards and a life cycle model, quality assurance, configuration management, project planning and measurement routines are now in use [7].

3.5 The Leveraging Phase
A distinct leveraging phase in the sense of the IDEAL model did not take place as part of the first 10 weeks period. Learning happened of course during the whole project and the lessons learned were already collected during each phase.

After the original project period however, the two process improvement specialists evaluated the whole process and produced an additional report [8]. The report stated that the only improvement, which really had been institutionalized were the meeting performance rules as all meetings now had an agenda and minutes. In the beginning everyone followed the code documentation guidelines, but after a while some employees stopped using them. According to one project leader this was due to time pressure and lack of control. In general, management liked things as little bureaucratic as possible, whereas the developers themselves would have liked a little more formalism.

Nevertheless both groups considered the project a success and the lessons learned, together with a refined action plan have been used to continue the improvement effort of the organization and to introduce the new, above mentioned processes and procedures. More then a year after the initial project, the two process improvement specialists are still full-time employed by the company and work there as process improvement specialists.

4. DISCUSSION AND CONCLUSION
In the preceding sections we have presented a successful software process improvement endeavor. To perform the project activities the IDEAL model has been applied and adjusted. The IDEAL model guide [4] itself recommends tailoring the approach to fit the organization's resources, their visions and their business objectives. In the following we want to revisit the case and discuss in more detail which adjustments were made, which criteria guided that process and in which environment this took place. In doing so, we want to emphasize what lessons other, especially small organizations can learn from the case.

The first lesson for small organizations, which wish to perform improvement activities, is that it makes sense to use a structured model to organize the process. The second lesson is that is makes sense to adjust the model to the particular conditions of the organization; and the third lesson is that it makes sense to perform the improvement activities as a project with clearly assigned and documented roles, responsibilities and resources.

The IDEAL model stresses these features. It is suitable for tailoring and the case demonstrates how such tailoring can look like in a concrete situation.

Resource assignment was taken seriously at NP and was performed according to the organization's objectives and capabilities and thus was no major problem. Two process improvement specialists were hired full-time, one project leader was assigned half time to the SEPG and all developers were granted time to participate in the project. Resources were scarce in terms of time, the organization wished first results in a short time period, and thus the whole first improvement cycle was determined to be 10 weeks. For the actual implementation of some of the improvement proposals, resources were more critical. Therefore, they were planned in such a way to cause as little additional work for staff as possible.

Instead of the organization's vision and business objectives, more concrete structural and cultural elements were the shaping forces. Structurally, the fact that the organization was comparably small with a relatively flat hierarchical configuration and short communication ways, and culturally that it was open, energetic, dynamic, fast reacting, action-oriented enterprise geared towards fast results played a major role.

In this respect two adjustments were most significant. The IDEAL model proposes to first distinguish between problem-centered – easily identifiable, fast fixable, short term effective – and process-centered – key process area related, long-term effective – issues in the acting phase. In contrast at NP this distinction was already introduced at the end of the diagnosing phase. It was used to present all findings in a meaningful way and to rapidly prepare potent actions.

This lead to the second adjustment. For the problem-centered issues, no separate establishing phase other tha forming the TWGs was necessary and the establishing phase for the process-centered issues was run in parallel to the acting phase of the problem-centered issues.

Concerning the use of the model within the individual phases, the tasks' and subtasks' lists were taken as guidelines and checklists to secure that all important questions had been taken into account rather than procedures which had to be followed sequentially and full as the IDEAL document recommends for a perfect course of activities.

As mentioned earlier, due to the short time interval between the initiating phase and the establishing phase, some of the review tasks of the latter phase were judged unnecessary by the improvement specialists. Another example can the found in the initiating phase itself where a separate Management Steering Group was found dispensable as the required information was exchanged through the daily contact between management and all projects, and most wanted meetings could easily be arranged without an additional organizational structure. The model's request for education in this phase was also adjusted. As the employee

were well educated with university degrees, only two theoretical lectures to familiarize them with the basic concepts of software process improvement were needed.

This reinforces that the project took place in an environment characterized by openness and a high level of education, which was well suited for innovation, change and improvement [9]. Beyond the adjustment of general models, Kautz [10] points out the significance of factors like management support and commitment, project planning and organization, education and training, assessment, monitoring and evaluation, staff involvement, support and knowledge transfer by external consultants, usability and validity of the introduced changes and cultural feasibility for process improvement in software organizations.

Taking these factors adequately into account, is another lesson to be learned by small organizations.

Many of the factors can be found in the organization independently from the IDEAL model; some of them like management commitment and teamwork were strengthened; others like project planning and staff involvement were made explicit and thus supported by the model; whereas yet others would not specifically be fostered by the model. IDEAL, for example, recommends to assess the climate for software process improvement and suggests as a consequence to develop strategies to reduce barriers, to manage resistance, and to increase the organization's capacity for change, but leaves open how this could be done.

This brings the discussion finally to the wider context of the IDEAL model as part of an organizational change strategy. Borum [10], f. ex., distinguishes between a technical-rational and a humanistic change strategy and describes their main dimensions.

In the technical-rational strategy, the objective of change is effectiveness and efficiency and organizations are seen as production systems. To achieve the aim, the change agents, namely management and analysts, apply re-design a rationalization methods which are often imposed on production units to accomplish better output in quantitative terms.

In contrast, in the humanistic strategy, the aim is to adjust the work milieu and to adopt novelties and innovation in organizations, which are seen as hierarchical, diverse, but nevertheless open, social systems. The change agents, primarily management and process consultants, appl reflection and learning processes and modify interaction and communication channels. The targets are groups, which, to accept changes in behavior, norms and artifacts, are informed, involved and trained.

The IDEAL model can definitely be used within both strategies. Due to the characteristics of the organization, in the case of NP, the application of the humanistic change strategy seemed most adequate. One might speculate whether embedding the IDEAL model in a less fitting strategy would have lead to the same positive results.

However, applied in the right context with the appropriate adjustments, it showed to be apt and fairly flexible for the organization of a software process improvement endeavor in a small enterprise; it supported the project and provided a framework for a smooth performance of all respective activities.

As such it provided further insights about software process improvement in small organizations and might serve as an inspiration for other companies.

REFERENCES

1. Brodman, J. D., D. L. Johnson (1994). What Small Businesses and Small Organizations say about the CMM. In Proceedings of the 16 th International Conference on Software Engineering, IEEE Computer Society, pp. 331-340, May 1994.

2. Kautz, K. (1999). Making Sense of Measurements for Small Organizations. IEEE Software, Vol. 16, No.2, pp. 14-20.

3. Argyris, C., D. A. Schoen (1991). Participator Action Research and Action Science Compared. In Whyte, W. F. (ed.), Participatory Action Research. Sage, Newbury Park, Ca., USA.

4. McFeeley, B. (1996). IDEAL^{SM} : A User's Guide for Software Process Improvement. Handbook CMU/SEI-96-HB-001. Software Engineering Institute, Carnegie Mellon University, Pittsburgh, PE, USA.

5. Iversen, J., J. Johansen, P.A. Nielsen, and J. Pries-Heje (1998). Combining Quantitative and Qualitative Assessment Methods in Software Process Improvement. In Baets (ed.), Proceedings of the 6th European Conference on Information Systems (ECIS), Aix-en-Provence, France, pp. 451-466, June 4-6, 1998.

6. Westergaard Hansen, H. , K. Thaysen (1998a). NP - Assessment Process Report (in Danish). University of Aalborg, Institute for Electronic Systems, Department of Computer Science, Denmark.

7. Westergaard Hansen, H., K. Thaysen (1998b). Process Improvement in a Small Danish Software Company (in Danish). MSC Thesis, University of Aalborg, Institute for Electronic Systems, Department of Computer Science, Denmark.

8. Kautz, K., K. Thaysen (2000). Knowledge, learning and IT Support in a Small Software Company, in Proceedings of BPRC CONFERENCE on 'Knowledge Management: Concepts and Controversies' 10-11, February, 2000: University of Warwick, Coventry, UK.

9. Rogers, E. M. (1983). Diffusion of Innovations (3rd edition). The Free Press, New York.

10. Kautz, K. (1999). Software Process Improvement in very Small Enterprises: Does it pay off? In Journal of the Software Process – Improvement and Practice, Special Issue on Organizational Change with Software Process Improvement, Vol. 5.

11. Borum, F. (1995). Strategies for Organizational Change (in Danish). CBS Publishing Company. Copenhagen, Denmark.

Process Improvement Towards ISO 9001 Certification in a Small Software Organization

Elif Demirörs
Assistant Professor
Dept. of Computer Eng.
Dokuz Eylul University
Izmir TURKEY
+90-232- 388 0373
elif@cs.deu.edu.tr

Onur Demirörs
Associate Professor
Dept. of Computer Eng.
Dokuz Eylul University
Izmir TURKEY
+90-232- 388 0373
onur@cs.deu.edu.tr

Oğuz Dikenelli
Assistant Professor
Dept. of Computer Eng.
Ege University
Izmir TURKEY
+90-232- 445 9852
dikenelli@ege.edu.tr

Billur Keskin
Product Manager
Software Dev. Unit
A1 Software House
Izmir TURKEY
+90-232-388 7221
billur.keskin@a1.com.tr

ABSTRACT

Software process improvement in small organizations is a challenging task where the "smallness" brings a number of unique problems. In this paper, we report the status of our work on creating ISO 9001 compliant quality system in a small software organization.

Keywords

Software process improvement. ISO 9001, software quality

1 INTRODUCTION

Since 1980s a large number of software process improvement efforts have been initiated world wide to increase quality and productivity while decreasing cost. Different models are being used depending on the market goals of the organizations. Capability Maturity Model (CMM) [Paulk et al., 1993] is popular among the companies that target the US market. On the other hand, for European market certification to ISO 9001 [Ibanez et al., 1996] is the most commonly accepted quality initiative.

Experience with both CMM and ISO 9001 has shown that small software organizations with 15 or less developers have some difficulties in applying these models [Grunbacher, 1997]. The fundamental problem is the models' inherent assumptions on the organization size. The quality practices that need to be installed require several groups working in parallel on different issues. In small companies, the same group of people has to overtake these responsibilities thus overloading the employees. On the other hand, both ISO 9001 and CMM fail to benefit from the "smallness" which usually means flexibility, fast

reaction time, and enhanced communication. In spite of these difficulties, the number of small organizations initiating process improvement is increasing since the return of investment comes in the form of a larger market. To satisfy the needs of such organizations, different studies addressing the "smallness" issue have been launched [Chroust et al., 1997]. However there is still no model that has been applied to real life projects.

In this paper, we report the status of our work on installing ISO 9001 compliant quality system in a small software organization. The smallness and current process state of the organization (Level 1) have raised a number of unique issues. To address these issues we have defined a model for process improvement based on the key process areas defined in CMM and on the requirements and suggestions of ISO 9001 and ISO 9000-3. The model is now being implemented and experiences of team members are promising. We believe that it will provide the much needed assistance to small software organizations in their work towards process improvement.

2 ORGANIZATIONAL BACKGROUND

A1 Software House is a small software organization offering solutions for a specific business domain since 1987. It has 39 employees, eight of them working in software development. The main product is an integrated system of several applications offering a complete solution for the product distribution sector. The system is fully customizable to address the needs of small as well as multinational companies. The product consists of 600+ programs totaling to 400000+ lines of code. The implementation language is C supported with the Btrieve file management system.

In 1991, A1 decided to reengineer the product and a new version incorporating the new architecture was scheduled for 1993. However the project was still ongoing in 1995 and under customer pressure, the software was marketed before thoroughly tested. Because of its unique properties, the product received attention in the market. However offering the software with many bugs increased the maintenance work tremendously. The work load has reached to its peek in the last quarter of 1996 after A1 got a contract of a large multi-national company. The chaotic process within A1 became a major obstacle in satisfying the customer demand. The software development department took all the blame of late deliveries, and unsatisfied customers.

In early 1997, the CEO of the company initiated a major restructuring project with the goal of preparing the company for the international market. Increasing product reliability and structuring the organization were the tasks with highest priorities. Among the other targets of this initiative were a wider customer base, better software development practices, support for multiple platforms and transformation to object technology. All the departments responded well to these restructuring efforts excluding the software people. The serious problems of software department and their past difficulties in restructuring efforts forced the company to seek external consultancy.

3 A MODEL FOR SOFTWARE PROCESS IMPROVEMENT

Installing an ISO 9001 compliant quality system in a small software organization has a number of challanges that can be listed as:

- Lack of guidance: The ISO 9001 standard explains the quality system elements that should exist but fail to provide any guidance on where to start and how to install these elements. ISO 9000-3 document and TickIt studies which include domain specific information does not provide the adequate assistance to software organizations as well.
- Lack of action knowledge: The interpretation of ISO 9001 quality standard for a software organization requires an understanding of underlying process improvement principles. Such expertise is often missing in small software organizations. On the other hand companies offering ISO 9001 consultancy often lack experience in software domain thus fail to provide the much needed suggestions for action.
- Lack of maturity: With respect to CMM framework an organization should be Level 3 with some Level 4 activities to satisfy ISO 9001 requirements. In practice reaching to this maturity will probably take 4 to 6 years for a Level 1 organization. For most small organizations such a long term commitment is not possible.
- Lack of quality personel: In a small sofware organization it is usually not possible to form a dedicated process improvement group. Instead process improvement has to be a part time job for senior technical personnel who are usually less motivated for change.

In order to guide software process improvement efforts within A1, we have developed a work plan which addresses the above problems. A generalization of this work plan can

be viewed as a model of process improvement for small software development organizations. The model divides the project into three phases namely preparation, control and stability phases. The preparation phase takes about three months while other phases are expected to take about nine months each.

During the preparation phase, the organization prepares for the process improvement initiative. Key activities to be performed include:
- Establishing commitment of top management and demonstration of this commitment.
- Assesment of the current state of organization's process
- Organizational restructuring.

During the control phase, the organization establishes rigorous management of commitments, costs, schedules and changes. Key activities to be performed include:
- Establishing project management and tracking processes.
- Establishing configuration management and change management processes.
- Product reverse engineering to create the stepping stones for quality phase activities including requirements management, quality assurance, testing and product engineering.
- Establishing procedures not directly related to software development.

During the stability phase, product engineering is rigorously applied throughout the organization and processes for process and product quality are established. Key activities include:
- Establishing requirements management process
- Establishing formal testing and review process
- Establishing quality assurance process
- Establishing product engineering process
- Establishing maintenance guideliness

So far we have implemented the first two phases of this project succesfully and we are developing the action plan for the third phase. Details of the implementations are given in the following sections.

4 IMPLEMENTATION OF PREPARATION PHASE

Our first step was to perform an assessment in order to understand the current software development process in the organization. We formed a set of questions that investigate the existing software practices with respect to the key process areas defined for a CMM Level 2 company. We then performed face-to-face, free style interviews structured around these questions. We also observed organizational culture to identify the potential obstacles as well as enablers of an improvement initiative. The small size of the company allowed us to meet with everyone related to software development as depicted in Table 1.

Table 1. Summary of interviews

Focus	People Interviewed	Issues explored
Top Management	CEO	The top management's view of software development; company policies; long term plans; commitment
Software Management	Product manager and chief programmer	Managerial problems; responsibilities of the management; plans of software department; history of the department; relations with other departments
Software development process	Software development unit	Practices used for project, configuration, requirements management, product engineering, testing; team's view of current process, problems, expectations.
Customer support	Customer support unit	Practices used for customer support; the role of customer feedback; satisfaction of customers; problems and expectations.

The interviews revealed several characteristics of the organization some of which have the potential to prohibit process improvement efforts. These are:
- Low self-esteem of software development team
- Over loaded software team (burned-out members)
- Inadequate knowledge on software engineering techniques, and tools
- Conflicts among expectations of different groups
- Major organizational learning problem
- Undefined responsibilities
- Unclear product sale and pricing policies; impossible to perform a long-term analysis
- Relaxed attitude towards blown schedules and plans
- No feedback (positive or negative).

On the other hand, we observed a number of properties from which an improvement initiative will benefit. These are:
- Commitment of top management
- Everyone agrees that they have an exceptional product that can be improved
- Everyone agrees that the company has a software management problem
- Software team is aware of the problems
- Everyone is willing to work towards higher quality; better planning;

The assessment results have shown that A1 is a Level 1 company. Guidelines for software development and management were undefined, and projects had been managed based on daily facts and personal decisions. In order to establish a quality model within the company a major cultural change was needed. Detailed findings of the assessment with respect to the key process areas of CMM are not included but can be requested from the authors.

5 IMPLEMENTATION OF THE CONTROL PHASE

Software process improvement initiative has been started based on the work plan developed at the end of the preparation phase. For each process area of the plan a study group is formed including a consultant and 1-2 people from the company. Each group then pursued the following activities independently:

- Workshop: Work in each process area started with a short course on the concepts, techniques and tools. These courses were attended by the whole software team as well as other related people from the company.
- Tool selection: Based on the knowledge established during the workshop, each study group had investigated available tools. For tool evaluation, besides the standard requirements of each process area, properties considered were: easy to learn, inexpensive, wide availability, and easy integration to the current environment.
- ISO procedures: Based on the discussions held during the workshop and on the properties of the tools selected, each study group decided on the activities to be carried out in its specific process area. These activities were then written in the form of ISO procedures. Initially we defined four procedures namely configuration management, change management, project planning, and life-cycle procedures.
- Integration: In order to resolve conflicts between the procedures several meetings were held with the participation of all groups. These meetings gave us a chance to further simplify the procedures, and to minimize the number of documents to be created.
- Pilot project: ISO procedures were tried in a pilot project in order to identify practical problems and/or inefficiencies. Since most of these activities were new to the software team, several problems were encountered which were resolved in weekly tracking meetings.

After the completion of the control phase of software process improvement efforts, status of the organization can be summarized as follows :
- Software team is highly motivated
- A common vision has been established within the company based on software teams point of view.
- Software team has become a respectable unit within the company.
- The product is under a rigorous configuration management.

- Project management is established and recent projects were on time within budget.
- The workflow of the software department is formally defined.
- A production planning group is formed with representatives from all functional units of the organization. The goal was to create consensus among different functional groups.

A1's next target is to implement the stability phase and then to apply for a formal ISO 9001 assessment. An analogous work plan developed for the control phase will be used for the stability phase.

6 ADDRESSING THE SMALLNESS ISSUE

During our studies, the small size of the software unit has introduced a number of issues which were addressed as follows:

Conjoining different roles: Different roles are combined into one, such as the role of configuration control board is given to production planning group. Also some roles such as configuration manager, are eliminated and their responsibilities are assigned to the owners of consecutive actions, in this case to the unit inspector.

Shorter development cycles: Projects are developed in several builds. In each build complete development cycle is covered. In this way early builds can be marketed earlier when needed.

Enhancing early communication: Initial planning and early phases of software development are performed as a team. As a result, better communication among team members has been achieved in the early phases. Early communication is very valuable to surface inherent assumptions of team members that might create difficult to resolve conflicts later in the development process.

Simplifying procedures: ISO procedures are simplified in most cases by combining them into a single procedure. For example, change management is treated as an extension of the life-cycle procedure. Most procedures benefit from the smallness of the organization by substituting direct communication to paperwork whenever written records are not required.

Minimizing paperwork: To decrease the time that is considered overhead, the paperwork suggested by ISO 9001 is minimized. In most cases a single form is defined to collect all related information and for eliminating duplication.

7 CONCLUSIONS

Creating quality systems in small software organizations has primary importance, specifically, for software industry in Europe and developing countries where majority of software organizations are small. Application of widely used process improvement models such as ISO 9001 and CMM has inherent difficulties for small organizations. These models do not provide the much needed guidance and fail to emphasize benefits of the smallness.

We have developed and implemented a work plan to create a ISO 9001 compliant quality system in a small software organization. A generalization of this plan is presented as a process improvement model for small companies. The model introduces three phases, each of which incorporates the activities that need to be followed. The results of implementation of the model are promising indicating that it provides guidance for process improvement initiatives in small software organizations.

ACKNOWLEDGMENTS

We would like to thank all members of A1 for a truly enjoyable project as well as for a wonderful environment to work. We also acknowledge the suggestions of Mr. Selcuk Aytimur, the director of Bureau Veritas Izmir Branch, on ISO 9001.

REFERENCES

1. G. Chroust, P. Grunbacher, and E. Schoistsch. To SPIRE or not to SPIRE. In *Proceedings of EUROMICRO 97*, Budapest, Hungary, September 1997. IEEE Computer Society Press.

2. P. Grunbacher. A software assessment process for small software enterprises. In *Proceedings of EUROMICRO 97*, Budapest, Hungary, September 1997. IEEE Computer Society Press.

3. M. Ibanez, H.J. Kugler, and S. Rementeria. Has Europe learnt enough?. *Journal of system architecture*, 42(8): 583-590, (December 1996).

4. M.C. Paulk, B.Curtis, M.B. Chrissis, and C.V. Weber. Capability maturity model version 1.1. *IEEE Software*, 10(4): 18-27, (July 1993).

Software Process Improvement in Small Organizations

Marty Sanders

Sanders Enterprises

Introduction

By definition, small[1] organizations are nearly always limited in resources and usually limited in time and money, too. Therefore, they do not always see that efficient processes can be the key to their cost-effective creation of the desired products. To address this, the SPIRE (Software Process Improvement in Regions of Europe) project was sponsored by the European Commission under contract ESPRIT/ESSI 23873 and managed by the Centre for Software Engineering (CSE), located at Dublin City University. SPIRE was designed to help small organizations improve their ability to develop and/or maintain software by using a mentor to assist with the following:

- Refinement of business goals as they relate to software;

- Assessment of current software practices, using a SPICE-based assessment tool;

- Evaluation of staff attitudes toward management of software;

- Development of a focused plan for improvements in areas highlighted by the assessment process as needing more work to help meet the business goals;

- Implementation of the plan with stated goals for improvement; and

- Evaluation of the improvement process and results so a successful methodology can be reused for future improvements in other areas.

This worked very well in SPIRE and may be a good model for other small businesses to follow in making improvements.

The SPIRE Handbook—Better, Faster, Cheaper Software Development in Small Organizations (Bicego *et al.,* 1998) provides extensive instructions for making software process improvements in small organizations, using the results of SPICE self-assessments for guidance. This cannot be replicated in a tutorial of this nature, although some material is extracted and adapted here, complemented by additional original material from the author. Additional information that might be useful to you is the collection of SPIRE case studies available through the CSE Web site, http://www.cse.dcu.ie/spire.

Other parts of this tutorial address the SPICE standard (ISO/IEC 15504) and the assessment process that uses it. This section describes the practical aspects and pitfalls of making improvements in small organizations that probably do not think any changes are needed in the first place, or at least not software process improvement (SPI) changes.

---

[1] *Small* means as large as 500 employees to the European Commission. For SPIRE, we generally meant much smaller, less than 100 perhaps. A better definition of *small* is probably related to only a few projects and the potential to involve nearly everyone in the process improvement activities because communication is relatively easy and the key players in SPI can interact with the whole organization.

The writing is slanted toward someone who has to actively make things happen to improve an organization's software process, although all types of readers are, of course, welcome. Making things happen requires both sales and education. Consequently, we look at the job of selling SPI to people and the kinds of problems that are likely to be encountered when doing so, as well as the management of the improvement process. You should be able to adapt this material to develop (1) a convincing proposal for change to present to your manager or a prospective customer, (2) a training session for other employees, or (3) a checklist to see if you are covering the necessary topics with the right people.

Why Don't We Do It Right to Begin With?

Every organization starts somewhere, developing software with a particular style. Why isn't this always the most efficient and effective way to work from the very first day? Let's look at some reasons:

1. *The whole is sometimes less than the sum of its parts.* While each individual may develop software in a way that works for them individually, these ways are seldom the same and frequently are not compatible. In small organizations in particular, where each individual must look and seem productive, the organization may not take steps to see that the *entire group* is productive if this is likely to look like it sets back the individuals even temporarily. Thus, time and resources are not allowed for:

- Assessment of current practices and how functional and appropriate they are,

- Development of new processes that everyone can use,

- Training in how to use these processes,

- Review of how well the processes are being used, and

- Evaluation of results that may lead to some repeat of the cycle of improvement.

Notice in the last paragraph phrases like "must *look and seem* productive" and "to *look like* it sets back the individuals." The truth is that what *looks* productive is not always productive. If Jane develops module A efficiently and effectively (in isolation) and Bill does the same with module B, they both look and seem productive. But if modules A and B do not interface cleanly and both Jane and Bill have to redesign and rewrite to get the interface correct, was it so productive?

2. *A problem is not always visible until it is well established.* Consider this scenario: one or two people start a company, adding a few more individuals every now and again. This expansion, whether rapid or slow, usually takes place in an environment of crisis, which is what forced the hiring in the first place. As we might expect, only mature organizations have the insight to recognize that each individual has to be trained to work in a way that improves the whole organization. So problems develop as each individual continues to work in the way that worked before, even though it may be creating a small, hidden catastrophe in the new work environment.

3. *It is difficult to isolate the individual problems once they are entrenched in the system.* We need an assessment of the software processes currently implemented to know where to begin to make improvements. Visualize your own organization: are a number of people each developing software in his or her own individual way, perhaps coming together sometimes for meetings or tests? Can you say right now what is causing the late deliveries or dissatisfied customers? If you can, can you also define what corrections to make, implement these corrections successfully, and prevent reoccurrence of the problem(s)? If you can do these things, stop reading this and go make those changes. If you cannot, perhaps the rest of this article will help you.

Before you try to get people to change *what* they are doing, you need to understand *why* they are doing it. Open your eyes and look around you. Listen to what people say about their work environment. Observe what is working and what fails. This will give you a sound basis to start promoting SPI in the organization.

Reasons for Improvement

Software is everywhere and unfortunately its strength is its weakness. Because it is so easy to develop software, it is just as easy to make mistakes. In a hardware manufacturing environment the discipline of strictly followed processes is self-reinforcing because you cannot make 1,000 balls all exactly alike unless you follow one automated process strictly 1,000 times. In most software environments, 10 programmers might be following 10 different processes to create hundreds of different programs or modules and when they all come together to create a system, all we can do is hope they mesh. This simply is not good enough, but we seem to accept it for some reason.

Your business is driven by market requirements for higher quality products, more timely delivery, and/or lower cost. This is true whether you create off-the-shelf products for sale at the local store or develop custom software as a subcontractor. It is increasingly true for in-house management software developers and government departments—managers have realized they might be able to buy a package rather than go through the pain of having custom software developed. Nobody can afford to ignore the forces that are driving their customers, regardless of who those customers are.

To improve your business you have to improve what you and your people do daily:

- Think about what you are doing and why you are doing it this way.

- Reduce or eliminate wasted time and resources.

- Take advantage of synergies so the organization is more productive.

This means you need to start thinking about the processes your people follow in developing software. Are they inefficient? Do they overlap and repeat tasks? Is too much time spent fixing bugs (which the customer probably is not paying for) and too little time on future projects that will ensure the growth of the company?

Software development/maintenance is no different from any other aspect of the organization. It needs to be managed to ensure the highest return on investment. That investment should include the provision of appropriate time and resources to assess the quality of your software processes and the products they are used to create, then make improvements based on what you find out.

Cost–Benefit Analysis

The benefits of SPI are varied, the first benefit being that you have to start thinking about what you are doing and why. Some figures quoted by the Software Engineering Institute (SEI) are that waste amounts to 20 to 50 percent of an organization's annual net income, with an average of around 40 percent (Rozum, 1193). So for every 1,000 units of profit earned, 400 may not be realized. Process improvement takes place to help capture that unrealized 400 units. Almost everyone can see the value in doing so!

Look around your own place to find the waste and excess—it will not be difficult to find. Table 1 shows some ways in which SPI might benefit an organization; these benefits are likely to ultimately translate to cash in the bank (Software Productivity Consortium, 1993).

Reduced	Improved
• Development costs because of less repetition and greater reuse	• Teamwork and more effective communication
• Rework because you identify and eliminate problems early rather than later	• Project staff start-up time because training is on defined processes
• Reliance on testing to ensure quality	• Predictability of budgets and schedules
	• Tool usage to complement the processes used
	• Project start-up time because of documented history of past projects

Table 1. Potential Benefits of SPI

The manager is likely to have some questions about improvement, such as "How much does it cost?" and "What is the payback and when will I see it?" Being honest, it is difficult to answer this type of question directly; data on process improvement that are obviously applicable to your organization may be hard to find for the following reasons:

- Companies that need process improvement may not be disciplined enough to keep data before the improvement. Without that pre-improvement data it is difficult to assess data after the improvement.

- We have no standard way to measure either cost or benefits. Work is in progress at the level of international standards to rectify this, but right now, we have no universally accepted method of measurement.

- Sustainable improvement of any type takes time—usually much longer than we think it does. Very often organizations will embark on process improvement, see no good results, and abandon the project when the real improvements are just starting to take place.

However, we do have some figures from the SEI (Herbsleb *et al.,* 1994). Data were collected over time from 13 organizations that represented various size and maturity levels. The goal was to show any gains in productivity, early defect detection, time to market, and quality.

These results are summarized in Table 2 and show the kinds of gains possible in a favorable environment.

Category	Range	Median
Total yearly cost of SPI activities	$49,000–$1,202,000	$245,000
Years engaged in SPI	1–9	3.5
Cost of SPI per software engineer	$490–$2,004	$1,375
Productivity gain per year	9–67%	35%
Early detection gain per year (defects discovered pretest)	6–25%	22%
Year reduction in time to market	15–23%	19%
Yearly reduction in postrelease defect reports	10–94%	39%
Business value of investment in SPI (value returned on each dollar invested)	4.0–8.8	5.0

Table 2. Summary of Overall Results of SEI survey

From the results shown in Table 2, the companies who are represented have some good advice for all of us:

- As the champion (the SEI term for someone who is in charge of SPI in an organization), do not be afraid to fail—keep working on it until you get it right.

- Share that concept with others—let them know they also have the right to fail and try again with SPI.

- Take the long view, expecting cultural shifts and changes.

- Recognize that benefits take many guises and some are important but difficult to measure objectively.

- Do not wait for the "ideal"—work with the resources you have.

- Be prepared for ups and downs and the occasional plateau.

You can work with your managers and other employees to develop your own process for determining the cost and savings of your software process improvement program. One example of how to do this is shown in Figure 1; each company needs to determine what makes sense for it.

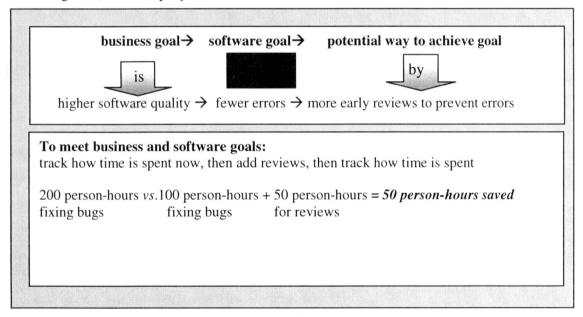

Figure 1. Determining the costs and savings of SPI.

This tutorial is not the place for a detailed discussion of the cost and benefits of SPI. As something to get you started in thinking about it, the following process is one you can use to determine the activities that apply to your organization (Rozum, 1993):

- *Translate your organization's goals and objectives into characteristics of your software products.* This goes with better (less than x errors per MLOC), faster (software delivery within x months of requirements agreement), and cheaper (reuse of $x\%$ of software). These are some examples—think of the ones that make sense for your organization.

- *Consider what process improvement activities will help create these characteristics.* What can help create fewer errors (more reviews? better requirements?), faster delivery (rapid application development processes?), or cheaper software (development of modular software?)?

- *Establish a cost baseline for the current software process.* This is the most difficult task and is nearly impossible to do unless you keep track of how people spend their time, such as time spent in fixing bugs or documenting software.

- *Determine the cost of improvement activities undertaken.* Again this requires documenting how people are spending their time, particularly on new activities for improvement.

- *Compare and track the cost of the improvement activities versus the savings that result from the changes.* In the Figure 1 example, if a company used to experience an average of 200 person-hours/month spent fixing bugs on a project, and that decreases to 100 person-hours/month because the company spent 50 person- hours/month on reviews, this is a savings of 50 person-hours/month that can be used to do something more profitable.

Differences in costs or savings are usually the result of reduced rework, less effort to produce something, increased productivity, or reduced maintenance costs.

Costs of the improvement activities are either nonrecurring or recurring. Nonrecurring costs are those used to establish a process or purchase an asset such as training or consultant expertise. Recurring costs are everything else associated with the improvement. If you start doing design reviews, for example, a nonrecurring cost is developing the format for the review comments. Recurring costs include evaluating documents in advance, attending the reviews, and writing review reports. SPI cost = the sum of nonrecurring costs + the sum of recurring costs.

Savings can be measured by putting a value on the following items:

- Increased productivity, usually measured by lines of documented tested code/units of resource to create it;

- Early error detection and correction, estimating the time to fix if found later;

- Elimination of errors, measured by keeping track of defects;

- Decreased maintenance work, measured by simply keeping track of time spent in maintenance work; and

- Eliminating extra steps, measured by keeping track of time spent on all software activities and seeing decreases on specific tasks.

SPI savings = the sum of savings from finding errors earlier + making fewer errors + making the process more efficient and/or effective + decreasing warranty cost and/or maintenance + increasing productivity.

SPI benefit index = SPI savings/SPI cost

A basic set of data to collect so you can develop your figures for return on investment includes these items:

- How person-hours are spent,

- Error data (when the error was introduced and when it was found), and

- Size information about the software being created or maintained.

Encouraging Business Leadership

Some organizational factors seem to be closely related to SPI success (Goldenson and Herbsleb, 1995; SPICE, 1998):

1. *SPI goals are well understood.* This means the vision of success can be communicated along with what will be different for employees once that vision is accomplished. You might start by getting the leaders and managers to develop a few important points about what they would like the organization to be. Give them lists of adjectives or descriptive phrases that might appear in the newspaper if the organization is profiled. Using this, work with the software people to determine how this might translate into better software management. Keep the goals visible and active for guidance on where improvements need to be made.

2. *Technical staff are involved in SPI.* If you, as champion, are the only one involved in SPI, it will never become an integral part of the "way we do business." Look at where people are having problems—late deliveries, version control, and so on—and work with them to identify process improvements that will solve *their* problems. Recast the technical problems into the management problems that result from them or cause them. Get the managers interested in SPI solutions that might help solve their problems. Once they start realizing the benefits of SPI, they will help others make it work.

3. *Senior management monitors SPI.* Try to develop some strategies to make SPI visible and interesting for everyone, including senior management. Creating a big schedule where everyone can see improvement happening or stagnation starting is one way. Ask to be at senior staff meetings and present material in a way the participants will care about—shortened schedules, higher quality products, increased customer interest, and so forth. Senior management will not monitor SPI activities unless they are meaningful in some way. It is your job as SPI champion to help make that happen.

4. *SPI responsibilities are compensated as well as other technical tasks.* You will not get compensated properly unless you can show your value, just like every other employee. You must start collecting data, documenting even small improvements, and translating those improvements into something that is important enough to get paid for.

5. *SPI people are well respected in the organization.* This is partly dependent on who is assigned the job, but it is very dependent on your actions. You will create the job in your own image and have to earn respect for it and yourself, even if you are already valued for other reasons.

6. *Staff time and resources are dedicated to process improvement.* This will not happen unless you can show value for the time already being spent. Pick small, visible improvements to start with. Manage them well. Keep data on what is happening and what benefits result. Be able to project value for more SPI effort, and show limitations if it is not spent. Look for ways to spend the time you have most effectively.

Here are some ways organizations in SPIRE and other improvement programs have used to make time for SPI:

- One organization spends a half day every week on new SPI work and the rest of the week incorporating it into their software development activities.

- In another, every software engineer has a subject for which he or she is responsible for suggesting improvements. These suggestions are reviewed frequently and regularly by senior management for selection and implementation of the best.

- A third company decided to have a well-trained full-time champion who could train others in small groups and help get individual SPI projects going.

There is no right way or wrong way to work in your company. Find the way that works for you and the rest of the group, then do it.

Figure 2 shows a few of the personal views of managers that can inhibit the improvement process, as well as a few ideas you might use to counter these.

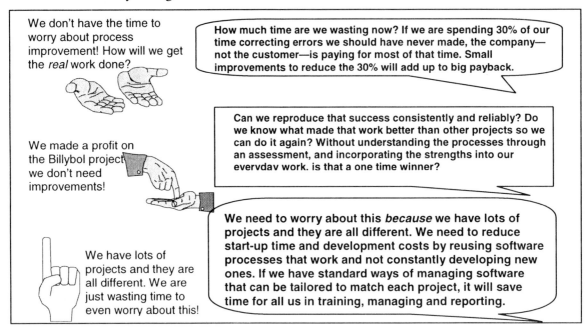

Figure 2. Countering a typical manager's response to SPI.

Champions are often in the difficult position of having responsibility with no authority to make it happen. Rather than complain about it, try the following:

- Understand the total current environment; whatever you are trying to do is a small part of the overall picture and has to be seen in context.

- Try to understand what will make SPI a winning proposition for others, selling them on the benefits to them as individuals as well as to the organization as a whole.

- Relate the benefits to the language of the business, not the language of SPI.

- Before you ask for something, think about what you can give in return.

- Learn to think like other people and see things through their eyes.

Getting Support from the Rest of the Organization

This is difficult but not impossible. Most champions carry on about SPI, using words that are not even understood, let alone agreed with. Here is another approach:

- *Get people to start thinking like the customers,* asking themselves things like, "Would I buy my own software?" You had to climb out from behind your computer to be a champion—encourage others to expand their horizons too. When people start to recognize there may be room for improvement, be ready to help them think about that improvement and what form it should take.

- *Involve everyone in the improvement process*, encouraging them to look at improvements that would make their own work more effective. You, too. Make sure your own work can be seen to be beneficial to the organization and that you are setting a good example.

- *Emphasize process improvement as part of everyone's job*, in the same way testing and documentation are. Looking for the better way to do things should become commonplace (including for you too, of course).

- *Establish an environment of open communication*, where people are not pointing the finger, but looking for the better way together. Be prepared to take criticism yourself and use it constructively to improve the process of process improvement. Be honest and open in your own dealings with others, helping them get what they need.

- *Objectively measure process performance* and be prepared to offer improvement suggestions based on what the data tell you. Measure the process improvement process, too, and be prepared to make changes as needed.

Making the Improvements

Figure 3 shows the cycle of improvement as a more detailed version of the general SPICE software process improvement steps. It includes some features of the SPIRE improvement process, such as the evaluation of staff attitudes, and some specific details and examples for your improvement plan. The SPICE improvement process is a continuing cycle within which this focused improvement fits. For overall improvements, you will have many of these focused improvements, leading to a higher organizational capability to manage software development and maintenance.

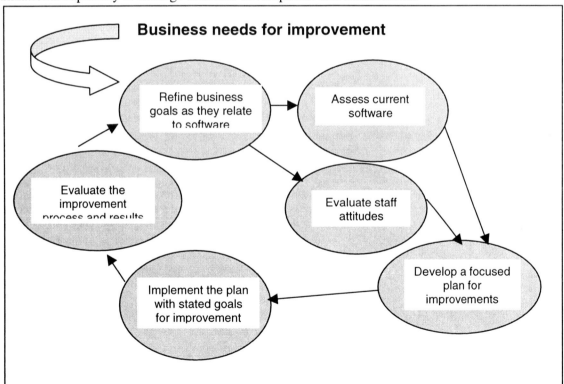

Figure 3. Focused process improvement cycle.

Step 1: Refining Business Goals as They Relate to Software

Well-defined business goals are not as common as we might expect. Most companies are focused on better quality, faster delivery, lower costs, or some combination of these. You must understand which of these is the principal driver for the organization's management in order to understand what is required from your software development processes. Even the areas that need to be assessed might be different, depending on your business needs for quality, speed, or budget. Any manager will tell you that all three are needed (and they are), but one is nearly always prominent. Some examples:

Janeyre Software specializes in development of very precise interface software for manufacturing systems. Janeyre's engineers work as suppliers of a small set of well-defined interfaces, or they develop custom software for larger system developers of manufacturing systems. They never see the end user on the assembly line. In fact, most end users are robots. Clearly, if the software is not error-free, problems will occur. Also, they have to be able to make the schedules of their customers and the price has to be right or their products will not be bought. However, a good case can be made that quality is their highest priority. Once their software is embedded in the larger system, any corrections are exceedingly difficult and one small problem in the original software is multiplied hundreds of times on the assembly line. Also, these are very specialized interfaces that do a few things precisely and well instead of many things with varying degrees of perfection. Product quality is not important here—it is essential.

BigBears develops game software. As long as errors have an easy recovery, product quality probably is not as important as speed of product (to keep an interested player), speed of production (to make the Christmas market), and cost of development (to keep the product price right). Note that although quality probably is not the primary driver, better quality software is likely to automatically lead to shorter schedule and lower costs because of less rework.

Your own business drivers need to be understood to make sure that both assessment and improvement plans address the factors that are most likely to affect the success of your organization in meeting its goals.

Make sure everyone understands these goals and how they relate to each individual. If a business goal is to create high-quality products, a software goal might be for x percent defect reduction quarterly, and each individual should understand how to help meet this goal.

Step 2: Assessing Current Software Practices

The technical steps of doing the assessment are covered elsewhere in this book. Figure 4 shows how people react to software process assessments. The first response—spoken or not—is fear. You can probably think of some other responses based on your personal experience.

Figure 4. Reactions to software process assessments.

Once you consider the assessment process at all, in every discussion, every document you must make it clear that the group as a whole is being assessed. Processes, not people, are under the microscope. Only then are you likely to get honest contributions from less nervous people, which leads us to step 3.

Step 3: Evaluating Staff Attitudes

A staff attitude survey is not part of every process assessment but in the SPIRE project we included it because the biggest stumbling blocks to improvement are nearly always personal, not technical. The survey is another form of assessment with the same rules: set goals, do a survey, make improvements, do another survey, evaluate results of improvement actions against the goals.

If you wish to create your own staff survey, you might ask questions such as these:

- Do you understand what the words *software process* mean?

- Do you understand what the words *software process improvement* mean?

- Do you believe that if we improve our software processes, we will be able to deliver software better, faster, or cheaper?

- Do you believe that if we improve our software processes, it will affect you in any way at all?

- Do you believe that if we improve our software processes your life will be better?

One thing we found out in doing the SPIRE surveys was that the level of understanding of the terms *software process* and *software process improvement* varies extremely widely, even among staff with higher education degrees in computer science. *Never* assume that the jargon of SPI is understood by the people in your group. For several of our clients, the SPIRE survey was as much a tool for education as it was for assessment of personal viewpoints. You may find the same if you decide to do a survey.

One purpose of the survey and follow-on discussions should be to find out where people believe they have problems. Initially, at least, these will undoubtedly have been caused by somebody else or the managers or the company—it is a brave person who stands up early in the improvement process and says, "I have this problem and I created it myself." Over time people will start to take ownership of problems as well as processes but it usually takes a while for that to happen.

Think about how people are likely to view SPI from their own position in the company. If you are a hero who is recognized as the best programmer, will you embrace a program that is likely to spread your hero status around through communally used processes?

Step 4: Developing a Focused Plan for Improvement

You have gathered a lot of data—business goals, results of the process assessment, knowledge of how people in the organization view the SPI process. Now you have to do something with it. First and foremost: try to get the greatest results for the least effort.

Look for the small improvements that will give the most payback. In SPIRE we used tables that matched business needs with the processes that supported those needs. This was then compared to the results of the SPICE assessment to determine the relevance of various improvements to meeting the business needs. For example, if the organization has a need for high-quality products and the assessment shows a low capability in quality assurance and requirements management, these are two areas from which you might select the improvement project. If you also have difficulty with your customer in maintaining requirements for the product you are developing, better requirements management might help. So requirements management might be the best area for improvement to give you relief in two areas.

Requirements management might be a general area for improvement, but you now have to select a specific subject for an improvement project, large enough to make a difference and small enough to be manageable. Then you need a project plan that describes what you are going to do and how. Here are some sections you should include in your plan:

- Company commitment to completion and success, with expected business benefits;

- Cost–benefit analysis;

- Project summary, with overview and objectives;

- Project detailed objectives, related to the results of the assessment;

- Project resource plan, a summary of the work packages and the resources for each;

- Project schedule;

- Project methods and tools;

- Project standards and measures;

- Project budget, with justification of costs;

- Project deliverables; and

- Work plan, with each work package described, including the approach to implementation of the work package, key issues/risks/dependencies, and deliverables.

The work packages (WP) themselves might look something like this:

WP 1: Project Management

Deliverable 1-1 SPI project plan

Deliverable 1-2 Monthly progress reports

Deliverable 1-3 SPI project results and recommendations

WP 2: Create Software Requirements Specification (SRS) Template

Deliverable 2-1 Criteria for definition and evaluation of requirements

Deliverable 2-2 SRS template

WP 3: Develop Customer Approval Process

Deliverable 3-1 Requirements approval process

Deliverable 3-2 Template for customer sign-off sheets

WP 4   Dissemination of Results throughout Organization

Deliverable 4-1 Presentation of requirements specification and approval process

Deliverable 4-2 Set of articles for monthly newsletter

This is project management, just like any other project. SPI has to be planned and executed with the same care you would give to building a ship. It does not just happen. You, as the SPI project manager, should have the same access to resources and the same achievement and reporting requirements as any other project managers in your organization.

Step 5: Implementing the Plan with Stated Goals for Improvement

The single most neglected aspect of implementation—yet one of the most important—is maintaining visibility of the improvement project. You have a good plan, you have developed the goals for improvement, all the preliminary work is finished, some implementation work starts, then real life intervenes and that is the end of it. Or at least, that sometimes happens. One of the biggest causes of failure, especially at the early stages, is lack of visibility and therefore seeming lack of importance. To keep this from happening, try the following:

- Keep goals firmly in mind and clearly documented in all task descriptions, meeting agendas, reports, and so on. Do not forget and do not let others forget why you are doing what you are doing. If meetings go off in tangents, see if this is helping you meet your SPI goals. If not, bring attention to this and get back to business.

- Post a big schedule where everyone can see it often and document the improvement results as they happen. Champions frequently think they do not have time to do this, but make time. A passive schedule on the computer that people can look at if they want to is not the same. You need a schedule that is visible and actively being updated, monitored, and evaluated, especially by senior management. Do the work. It will get the attention it deserves.

- Ask to be put on the agenda of staff meetings and other gatherings. If you do not treat the SPI project as one of importance for the business, neither will anyone else.

- Report on progress and results, not just activities. For example,

  "Four project managers and six software engineers met with us Monday to discuss the SPI project planning. We agreed on a schedule of six months, at the completion of which the following will have been accomplished. [Hand out list of deliverables and schedule.] We estimate that we are spending a minimum of $xxxxx annually on rework because of unclear and changing requirements, so while $xxx is allocated for the SPI project, we should save at least x times that by using the new process."

  This is a much more informative report than "We had a meeting on Monday and discussed SPI."

  This assumes of course that you have done your homework and have some idea of where these figures come from and how valid they are. You do not necessarily need precision in your estimates. You might ask the software engineers to keep track for 2 to 3 weeks of how much time they are spending on rework because of unclear or incorrect requirements. Use this to establish some minimum figures for how much time is probably being spent on each project and how much it is costing the company. The very fact that they are keeping track of this data and analyzing how much time is spent on rework for this reason puts you way ahead of where you were—they are now thinking about the process instead of just doing it.

Step 6: Evaluating the Improvement Process and Results

The final report should contain these items:

- A summary of the outcome. This includes not only a discussion of goals being met (or not), but ancillary benefits like training provided or communications and interfaces improved. The initial parameters under which the SPI project was established have probably changed—show these changes and how they affected the project. Anything you accomplished is a benefit, even if it is to show what not to do the next time.

- The collection of data that enables you to show goals met or other useful information. In the example, you might be tracking number of requirements, number of added or changed requirements, and other data of this type.

- Lessons learned in the improvement project itself and in the process of making the improvements. Some things we relearn on nearly every project: things always take longer than we think they will, it is hard to keep people focused on SPI when the customer is demanding something else, employee turnover adds to the problems of SPI projects just like other types of projects, and so on. But analysis of each project will probably show you a better way to do things next time.

- Recommendations for further improvement, either related to this SPI project or in a new area.

- Final cost statement, including any cost reductions. In our example, you might have software engineers tracking how much time they are spending on rework because of defective requirements (which should now be less than before) plus how much time is spent on getting the requirements right—documenting requirements in the SRS, meeting with customer representatives, reviewing changes, and so forth. At best, less time is spent to arrive at a set of requirements that correctly defines the product. At worst, the same or more time is spent to get a better set of requirements. Either way, the company is better off.

Summary

The single biggest benefit of any SPI project is that it causes people to think about what they are doing and why. People and organizations develop a way of working that sometimes seems to have simply grown with the times. It probably did. As a champion of SPI, you are in a unique position to help people look at themselves and the way they work, evaluating potential improvements and discarding what no longer makes sense.

It is a tough job but if you stay focused, you can do it. The most common complaint we hear is about lack of management commitment. It is part of your job to get and keep that commitment. Someone had an idea that SPI was important or you would not be in the job in the first place. It is now up to you to justify that original thought and sustain it. Do not get caught up in improvement for the sake of improvement. Always be able to connect improvements with customer needs and the (sometimes long-term) bottom line. If you do that, you will succeed and the entire organization—including you—will be better off.

References

Bicego, A., G. Chroust, C. Morrison, M. Sanders, and H. Wickberg (1998), *The SPIRE Handbook—Better, Faster, Cheaper Software Development in Small Organizations,* M. Sanders, ed., Centre for Software Engineering Ltd. (CSE), Dublin City University campus, Dublin 9, Ireland, +353-1-704-5750, ISBN 1-874303-02-9, http://www.cse.dcu.ie.

Goldenson, D., and J. Herbsleb (1995), *After the Appraisal: A Systematic Survey of process Improvement, Its Benefits, and Factors that Influence Success,* DCMU/SEI-95-TR-009, Software Engineering Institute, Carnegie Mellon University, Pittsburgh, PA.

Herbsleb, J., A. Carleton, J. Rozum, J. Siegel, and D. Zubrow (1994), *Benefits of CMM-Based Software Process Improvement: Initial Results,* CMU/SEI-94-TR-13, Software Engineering Institute, Carnegie Mellon University, Pittsburgh, PA.

Rozum, J. (1993), *Concepts on Measuring the Benefits of Software Process Improvements,* SEI-93-TR-009, Software Engineering Institute, Carnegie Mellon University, Pittsburgh, PA.

Software Productivity Consortium (1993), *Managing Process Improvement A Guidebook for Implementing Change,* SPC-93105-CMC, SPC Building, 2214 Rock Hill Road, Herndon, VA, 22070.

SPICE Phase 2 Trials Interim Report, Version 1.00, March 24, European Software Institute, 1998.

Chapter 11

Benefits of Software Process Improvement

1. Introduction to Chapter

Software Process Improvement was originally, and to some extent remains, an act of faith based on Humphrey's premise:

The quality of a software system is governed by the quality of the process used to develop and maintain it [2].

However, data is now becoming available that makes it possible to investigate the premise in an objective manner. Benefits that have been claimed for software process improvement include:

- improved control, predictability and effectiveness of the process;

- increased product quality;

- increased productivity;

- increased staff morale;

- increased customer satisfaction;

- increased ability to meet budget.

The first of the benefits is predicted by Paulk, et al. [3], and the others are supported by a survey described by Herbsleb, et al. [1]. In addition, 74% of those questioned in this survey agreed that the (CMM) assessment was worth the money and effort expended on it.

491

While such statistics are reassuring, it should also be noted that process improvement efforts are not always successful, especially if all the circumstances are not correct. Full justification for a software process assessment initiative should be (and increasingly has to be) made on a return on investment (ROI) argument. In other words, for software improvement to be justified, the financial benefits which will accrue from it must exceed the cost of implementing it.

The costs of software process improvement are not too difficult to itemize and quantify. They include, for example:

- Staff training costs;

- Costs of regular process assessments;

- Cost of staff responsible for the process;

- Costs of data collection for process monitoring.

Clearly, the lower these costs are kept, the greater the opportunity there is for recouping them from the benefits of software process improvement.

The financial benefits of software process improvement initiatives are harder to measure and predict than the costs. Some of the benefits are more qualitative than quantitative and can only be estimated from appropriate indicators. For example, *increased staff morale* can be indicated by lower staff turnover, and the consequent savings measured in terms of lower staff training costs and avoidance of additional project costs following from lack of staff continuity. In a similar way, *increased customer satisfaction* can be inferred from increased repeat orders, and quantified in terms of the value of these orders.

Increased maturity of the process should lead to fewer faults appearing in the software due to human error, and hence reduce the rework required. This is just one of the reasons why productivity should increase as the software process is improved.

We can see, therefore, that over a period of time it is possible, based on some reasonable assumptions, to measure the effects of software process improvement and to estimate the return on investment over the period. What would be even more useful would be to be able to predict in advance the financial benefits that would be expected to accrue through a software process improvement program. While this may be barely feasible at present, research based on the data already available should ultimately lead to useful predictions in this area. Of course, it will still be important for organizations to ensure that all the parameters are favorable for their process improvement program, if the anticipated benefits are to be realized. As in most things, success is not guaranteed and will only come to those who get it right.

2. Description of Articles

The first paper in this chapter, entitled "Journey to a Mature Software Process," is by C. Billings, J. Clifton, B. Kolkhorst, E. Lee and W. B. Wingert. It is concerned with the highly successful software developed for the space shuttle. The organization that produced the software was part of IBM Federal Systems, but has since been sold off to the Loral Corporation, now part of the Lockheed Martin Corporation.

In 1989 the project was part of a SW-CMM assessment and was rated at level 5, making the site one of the first (and few) to be rated at this level. Consistent with this, the space shuttle software has been found to be highly reliable and virtually fault-free.

In their paper, the authors confirm much of the accepted wisdom about what makes a successful software project, including:

- Attention to requirements;

- Attention to configuration management;

- Importance of design and code reviews;

- Understanding of the application domain;

- Good customer relations;

- Use of coding standards;

- Quality culture;

- Collection of fault data;

- Independent verification;

- Customer-driven review board structure;

- Incremental development and prototyping.

The authors describe how the software process was successively improved over several decades. The process underwent a number of assessments, the first as early as 1984, when it was assessed against criteria which would eventually form part of the SW-CMM. At this stage the process was rated 3.25 (on average). Four areas were suggested for improvement, and when these improvements were performed the process was reassessed in 1989 and found to be at level 5. The paper makes good reading and provides what might be described as a textbook account of software process improvement.

The second paper in this chapter, entitled "Schlumberger's Software Process Improvement Program," also makes good reading. It is by Harvey Wohlwend and Susan Rosenbaum and describes Schlumberger's experiences based on a corporate-wide software process improvement effort. The program was led by the Schlumberger Laboratory for Computer Science, which performed assessment "studies" throughout the Schlumberger organization. Similar issues were highlighted throughout the organization and clear benefits identified from the ensuing improvements. For example, attention to each of the SW-CMM level 2 key process areas produced identifiable benefits as follows:

- Attention to requirements reduced time to market;

- Attention to project planning helped projects to keep to schedule;

- Attention to software quality assurance improved customer relations.

The authors go on to describe some of the difficulties of software process assessment and draw some conclusions from their work, some, but not all, of which have been documented elsewhere.

The third paper in this chapter, entitled "Accumulating the Body of Evidence for the Payoff of Software Process Improvement - 1997," is by Herb Krasner. In it, after summarizing the characteristics of a mature software organization and the requirements for a successful software process improvement program, the author goes on to look at the evidence for successful ROI in software process improvement. A number of case histories of SPI payoff are described, including the SPI programs at:

- NASA/Software Engineering Laboratory;

- Loral (formerly IBM and now part of the Lockheed Martin Corporation);

- Hewlett Packard Corporation;

- Raytheon Equipment Division;

- Motorola India Electronics Department.

In order to assess payoff in terms of ROI, Krasner suggests measures for process quality, product quality, and project predictability. In terms of ROI he claims that benefits of between 5 to 1 and 9 to 1 are being reported over a two year period. He concludes with the view that software organizations that have yet to embark on software process improvement activities had better do so before the competition gets too far ahead. The extensive references at the end of the paper include descriptions of many SPI programs and the payoffs achieved by them.

References

[1] J. Herbsleb, D. Goldenson; A Systematic Survey of CMM Experience and Results, *International Conference on Software Engineering*, ICSE-18, 1996.

[2] W. S. Humphrey; "Software Process Program," *SEI Affiliate Symposium*, Pittsburgh, 1987.

[3] M. C. Paulk, C. V. Weber, B. Curtis, M. B. Chrissis, *The Capability Maturity Model: Guidelines for improving the Software Process*, Addison Wesley, 1995.

Journey to a mature software process

by C. Billings
J. Clifton
B. Kolkhorst
E. Lee
W. B. Wingert

Development process maturity is strongly linked to the success or failure of software projects. As the word "maturity" implies, time and effort are necessary to gain it. The Space Shuttle Onboard Software project has been in existence for nearly 20 years. In 1989 the project was rated at the highest level of the Software Engineering Institute's Capability Maturity Model. The high-quality software produced by the project is directly linked to its maturity. This paper focuses on the experiences of the Space Shuttle Onboard Software project in the journey to process maturity and the factors that have made it successful.

There is currently much discussion in the software industry and in the literature about software process maturity and the correlation of process maturity to software quality. At its site in Houston, Texas, the IBM Federal Systems Company (FSC) develops highly reliable software for the federal government. One job, the Onboard Shuttle project, has been evaluated at the highest level on the Software Process Capability Maturity Model[1] of the Software Engineering Institute at Carnegie Mellon University. The FSC software development organization in Houston consistently produces high-quality software and receives accolades from auditing organizations across the nation. This organization was the first contractor to receive the prestigious NASA Excellence Award and is the only contractor to receive this award twice. The Houston site was twice named the IBM Best Software Lab and was twice awarded the Silver Level in an IBM internal assessment matched against the Malcolm Baldrige National Quality Award criteria. It might be assumed with such a consistent record of success, that Houston has discovered the "silver bullet" for software development. Of course, this is not so. Indeed, Houston was only enacting process principles that were known as early as 1960.[2] Sound program management techniques, software engineering principles, employee empowerment, and a culture dedicated to quality are the basis of this software development process. Houston's success is the result of following these processes with discipline and control. This discipline and control evolved over a period of 25 years of service to the federal government and prime contractors. Attention to customer requirements and extensive interaction with the customer are also crucial to the evolution of this mature software process.

Background of the Onboard Shuttle project

Focusing on project management, FSC developed a comprehensive set of software development standards in the early 1980s. Configuration management was rigorously practiced even before automated tools supported this activity. Configura-

"Journey to a Mature Software Process" by C. Billings, et al., from *IBM Systems Journal*, Volume 33, number 1, pp. 46-61, IBM, 1994. Reprinted by permission.

tion management of requirements is absolutely essential for the development of large, complex software systems. In the 1970s Houston maintained detailed manual lists of software requirements changes and their impact on software development and testing.

A unique cultural heritage developed, fueled by focusing on "doing things right," accountability to the customer, and the determination of the National Aeronautics and Space Administration (NASA) to develop a space program that is safe for manned missions. Manned flight awareness was a part of every programmer's and engineer's training and a daily emphasis of the management team. Historically, employees were empowered to stop the "software assembly line," if quality issues arose. High visibility and national awareness of manned space flights contributed to this focus on quality.

Building on experience with the early space systems, Houston pioneered the development of the Space Shuttle Onboard Data Processing System. IBM and NASA, the customer, developed a strong relationship based on trust and a common mission. The IBM and customer team consistently produced software that was highly reliable and almost error-free. Houston was ultimately accountable for the operational performance of the entire system. A description of the Space Shuttle Onboard project is the key to understanding how this software development process matured.[3]

Houston's software development process produces highly reliable software for both the Shuttle Onboard project and support systems. Improvements to the development processes made during this project built on development practices already in place in Houston. Disciplined application of program management techniques, use of team reviews, audits, systematic data collection, and independent testing during the 1970s prepared the project for more process advancements in the 1980s.

The 1970s

The space shuttle program built the Primary Avionics Software System from the ground up in the 1970s. All efforts were directed toward developing an architecture and design for the Onboard Primary Avionics System. Major system deliver-

ies were required for approach and landing tests and the orbital flight test software. Critical functions combined in the two systems provided the capability to fly the space shuttle ballistically into orbit, support the orbiter while in space, and fly

---

The IBM and customer team consistently produced software that was highly reliable and almost error-free.

---

it through re-entry to a safe landing on a dry lake bed at Edwards Air Force Base in California. Delivering major capabilities such as these while preparing for an operational flight environment presented serious challenges. According to plans at that time, when the space shuttle became operational, numerous software systems were to be managed simultaneously to meet the needs of the envisioned 30 flights a year. Strong software management[4] through program management and configuration control techniques was established early and designed with an eye to the future needs of the program.

A special focus on requirements used engineers dedicated to requirements analysis. Engineers serving as requirements analysts interpreted the requirements. Each analyst worked closely with the NASA engineering community. Requirements analysts understood the intent of the requirements, helped to select the best implementation option, and made certain that the intent was communicated in the approved version of the requirements document. The analysts became the IBM experts on the requirements throughout the development of the software. Requirements analysis was recognized as an essential part of the software development life cycle.

With many parallel development activities underway, establishing and adhering to a system architecture was a fundamental problem. Houston formed a software architecture review board to address this issue. Chaired by a senior engineer, the board included representatives from each development area of the project. The board established operating procedures, and the project followed these procedures whenever development affected the systems architecture. For example, when a new program module was created, its execution priority had to be approved by the board. This procedure assured a priority consistent with the critical nature of the function. The board published standards for coding certain operations to ensure correct synchronization of the multiple computer environment. Any deviation from these standards had to be approved by the board after analysis had verified that the change could be made without system degradation.

Manual processes that implemented the procedures of the board had no checks and balances to ensure that procedures were followed. Engineers and programmers understood the criticality of the software being produced and did not want to make a mistake in implementation. Review by the board helped share the serious responsibility that each engineer and programmer felt for the safe execution of the final product. The developers' acceptance of team review led to the use of reviews as the technique of choice for ensuring product quality. In addition, the enforcement of discipline in following the process set the stage for future success.

During the 1970s the project used measurements to track schedules and costs but had only begun to consider quality metrics. Houston monitored the total numbers of open problem reports but only as a program management indication of the progress toward delivery. Although quality measurement techniques were not advanced, a valuable activity was underway: data collection. Because of the necessity of total accountability on product problems to NASA, data were collected on all software problems for the project. Houston systematically collected and retained data about each problem. Every problem had to be explained to NASA. NASA asked probing questions, such as why was a mistake made, were there any other similar problems in the software, and what actions would be taken to prevent the same type of error in the future.

Gaining information on each software problem required insight that could only be provided by the software development team. The systematic analysis of each problem did more than strengthen processes. Developers were key members of the analysis team and felt accountable for each error. The focus was always placed on the error and never on the individual who made the error. Nonetheless, professional pride made pro-

---

Gaining information on each software problem required insight that could only be provided by the software development team.

---

grammers feel responsible. From each problem the developers learned to avoid that error in the future. Each oversight reinforced the need to rely on process to remove errors.

Systematic data collection on problems became well-established with information retained in a database, both electronically and on paper. This repository made it possible to do trend analysis as soon as a formal measurement program was established in 1982. Database information became the basis for sophisticated reliability estimates and for research on software complexity metrics.

Data collection paid off quickly. Late additions to requirements were disruptive to development activities. Pressure to satisfy the customer's needs for software capabilities subverted project planning and development processes. Analysis of problem data from released software revealed that an out-of-control requirements management process was the primary cause. Use of the data convinced IBM management and the customer's requirements approval board to put more control on the requirements approval process, eliminating over-commitment as a cause of problems.

Finding answers to customer questions also required an audit of the software product. Once a problem was fully understood, the development organization designed an audit to find similar instances in the code, if they existed. Each instance identified was analyzed to determine whether it was also in error. The audit results allowed customer questions to be answered with confidence. Any new problems found by the audit could be corrected before they caused the software to fail. The audit, in addition to the error causal analysis done for each problem, provided a basis for formal defect prevention initiatives.

Design and code reviews were conducted during those early days. Review participants included the development programmer, the requirements analyst for the area under review, and peer programmers. Reviews lacked a formal moderator, rigorous documentation and follow-up on issues identified, and a checklist of items to inspect. The developer was the one who decided whether a re-review was necessary. Configuration control was informally tied to the reviews, since the basis for the review was the approved requirements. Most software products were reviewed during this era. However, since a documented process was lacking, the teams did not have a consistent approach. Despite the lack of rigor, developers shared the responsibility for the product under review. This review method continued to reinforce the culture of team oversight and procedural discipline. Developers became accountable for each product error and were inspired to share responsibility for the quality of their software.

In time, project processes formalized the cultural acceptance of the need for procedural discipline. This was demonstrated dramatically during the flight of the Space Shuttle STS-49. Astronauts struggled to capture a malfunctioning satellite. NASA requested a change to the Remote Manipulator Arm (RMS) software to improve astronaut control of the RMS. This software update had to work the first time and had to be delivered in a matter of hours. With the astronauts waiting in orbit, programmers developed and tested the software change. They executed all required process steps, including inspections of requirements, design, and code before the update was released to NASA. The STS-49 astronauts successfully used the update with several other methods before the satellite was finally captured. In a crisis, a mature process is relied upon to produce the needed results, not ignored out of expediency.

During this era, an independent test organization verified the software before delivery. Testing was conducted with extensive use of simulation to model the operating environment of the software.

Execution of the code was initially done on a simulated flight computer. When the Flight Electronic Interface Device became available, testing was conducted on actual flight hardware.

The combination of error causal analysis, an evolving focus on measurements, and a growing formalization of processes brought about a gradual decline in product errors. As shown in Figure 1, the software development process continued to mature throughout the 1980s and into the 1990s, based on the firm foundations that had been established in the 1970s. A culture of shared responsibility through team review, procedural discipline, data collection and analysis, product audits, independent testing, and controlled system architecture was in place.

The 1980s

Project management. The shuttle program went through first flight and became operational in the 1980s. Moving to an operational environment with an increasing flight rate tested Houston's resolve to stick to its processes, but strong project management led to higher quality, reduced costs, and increased productivity.

In the 1980s, project management strove to balance control and responsiveness. A system of boards evolved to ensure configuration control of the software, communication flow within the project, and a single interface to NASA. These boards dealt with all aspects of development and continue to be critical to the success and discipline of the project.

The original structure, illustrated in Figure 2, had two main boards: the Project Control Board (IBM) and the Customer Configuration Control Board. Additionally, Houston established three key subboards: the Discrepancy Report Board, the Requirements Review Board, and the Support Software Board. The Project Control Board, Discrepancy Report Board, and the Requirements Review Board controlled the three most important aspects of the process.

The Project Control Board had a key role as the clearinghouse for all project status and major decisions. All boards were subordinate to the Project Control Board. This board maintained the configuration of the software and established

Figure 1 Product quality improvement based on process focus

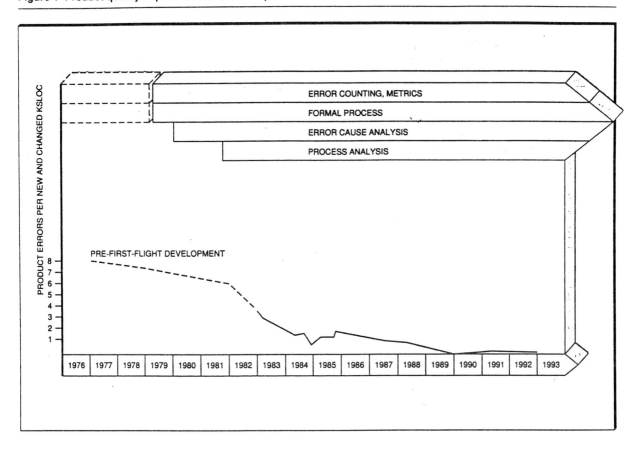

IBM's position on proposed changes. During the 1980s, this board became the primary point of contact with the customer. This board determined all schedules and milestones. Again, representatives of each major function had a voice in the decision.

The Discrepancy Report Board dealt with how Houston would respond to a problem found in the software. Problem reports came from internal sources or from one of over 200 external NASA user groups and external contractors. The board met weekly or on demand to discuss current discrepancies and their effect on the flight software. The Discrepancy Report Board determined Houston's recommendation to fix or not fix a software problem. A board representative presented this recommendation to the NASA Configuration Control Board where a final decision was made. A single point of customer contact was provided

by the board. Additionally, the board provided an open forum for engineers to state their position on a software problem in a nonthreatening environment, fostering an atmosphere of trust.

In determining how and when to implement a fix, the Discrepancy Report Board coordinated inputs from many sources. A fix, for example, could be applied to an incremental release or to one or more specific flights. These decisions were based on fix criticality and current schedules. A representative of each stage of the development process had a voice prior to the final IBM position being determined.

The Requirements Review Board ensured that project resources were fully utilized and schedules could be met. This board closely coordinated changes required with the resources available and kept the customer informed. Changes to the soft-

Figure 2 Onboard Shuttle control boards

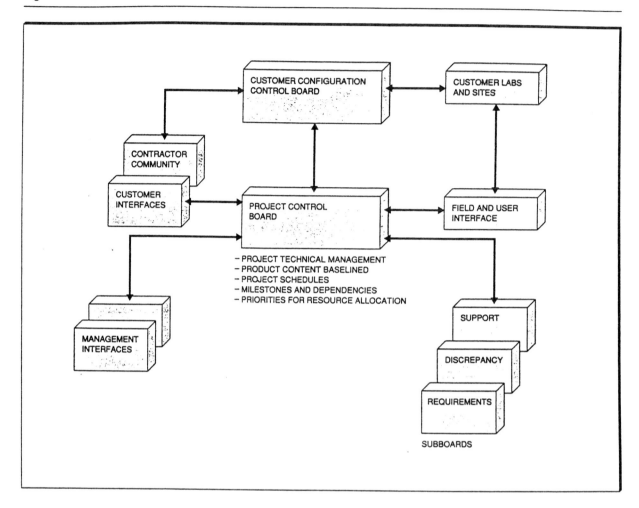

ware could not be approved by the customer without inputs from this board. This was a key step in eliminating errors early in the process that were caused by poor requirements or over-commitment of resources. Inputs to the board included the readiness of the requirements for implementation, the interactions with other changes in process, and the development and verification costs associated with the change. This board provided project management with the costs and risks associated with each change to the flight software. This information allowed schedules to be developed, tracked, and coordinated with other project activities. Costs to the customer were reduced, since the earlier in a process that defects are removed, the less expensive they are

to fix. For example, an error caught during the requirements phase is fixed once and cheaply, whereas the same error detected after delivery may have to be fixed on several released systems, escalating maintenance costs.

Key areas of the software project were brought together regularly by these boards. Each board provided an open forum to express concerns and provide status. The board chairpersons were part of an independent staff department, helping the boards to keep the customer's interests in focus.

Houston established other boards that dealt with specific aspects of the development process as shown in Figure 2. Parallel boards were established for the ground support software. A board to track the development of user tools was established to foster communication and reuse of software among the various project elements.

Houston found that a strong customer-driven board structure was a key item for maintaining quality, delivering on schedule, and staying within budget. Houston's board structure mirrored the customer's organization. This structure provided each key customer process with a single point of contact with the analogous function in the development organization. All boards were staffed and chaired by experienced nonmanagement technical personnel who worked in the program for years, some since its inception. This method of project management has had quantifiable successful results:

- High-quality software
- An extremely satisfied customer (excellent customer evaluations)
- No significant budget overruns

The board structure is in place to ensure that this success continues.

Incremental release strategy. An incremental release strategy grew out of a need to isolate the development process from the day-to-day operations of the space shuttle program. For the first six flights of the shuttle, the flight software consisted of the software for the previous flight plus new capabilities. For example, the ability to abort a shuttle mission to Africa or Spain did not exist on the third flight but was added for the fourth flight. As the flight rate increased, this method would prove less manageable.

NASA and IBM decided to support multiple flights with one release of software called an operational increment, or OI. An OI would be reconfigured prior to each flight to account for the mission-specific parameters such as payload, orbit, time-of-year, etc. This approach allowed the development cycle to operate somewhat independently of the flight operations.[5]

Operational increment testing focused on new software capabilities rather than flight-specific testing. A new level of testing was created to address the flight-specific verification. The latter dealt with mission or flight operations and the former with the longer-term development items and

maintenance. This strategy reduced the potential for resource conflicts and allowed optimization of each process to meet its particular customer's requirements. Today, a typical release of software is used for one year as shown in Figure 3.

This approach is more flexible than a traditional waterfall process. It allows for new requirements and other changes to the software at multiple points along the way. This flexibility is demon-

---

An incremental release strategy grew out of a need to isolate the development process from the day-to-day operations.

---

strated by the fact that the software that has flown shuttle missions has undergone more than 3000 requirements changes. Since the late 1970s, the software required more than 382 000 source lines of code to be added, modified, or deleted. These changes were implemented via more than 900 software builds and 175 patches. IBM has provided these evolutionary software versions to NASA through 260 separate software releases. Even though a typical development cycle is one year, Houston's incremental release process responds to the short-term needs of the customer as well.

An incremental strategy was used as well to produce prototype versions of the flight software. Houston's prototypes involved setting up a "mock" incremental release and following the existing process in an expedited fashion. This technique dramatically improved final product quality. The development organization identified additional requirements errors (5 percent) and design or coding errors (23 percent). If these errors were discovered later, they would have been more costly to fix.

It is important to note that when NASA approved the final requirements, the prototype was retired, and the defined process was followed for the real implementation. This is a key step, since the pro-

501

Figure 3   Generic Onboard Shuttle operational increment

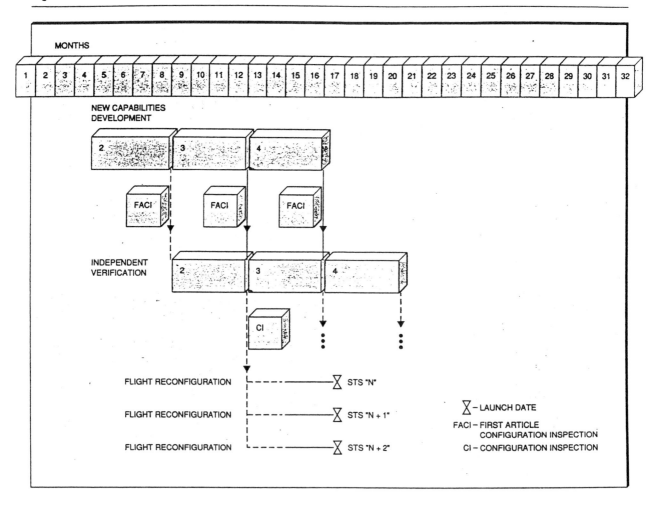

cess is sound and should not be bypassed. The advantages of prototyping are not lost, resulting in less rework and maintenance costs.

Requirements planning. With the introduction of the incremental release strategy, NASA began taking a longer-term look at software development. NASA focused on determining the strategic priority of candidate changes to the flight software. IBM provided guidance as to what could be accomplished with the skills available. Together, NASA and IBM planned the development of several releases to be done in the future. NASA approved all software changes affecting related areas together to simplify both the development and the verification process.

At any given time, NASA planned two to four years in advance. With this approach, all affected areas could plan their activities, such as training, with advance information. Of course, not all changes could be anticipated, but software was treated as a subsystem that could be improved and upgraded much like hardware components and often as a result of hardware upgrades.

Life-cycle changes—Independent verification. In the 1970s, Houston established an independent verification function as a separate line organization without managerial or personnel ties to the development organizations. Independent verification analysts maintained a healthy adversarial

Figure 4 Onboard Shuttle test levels

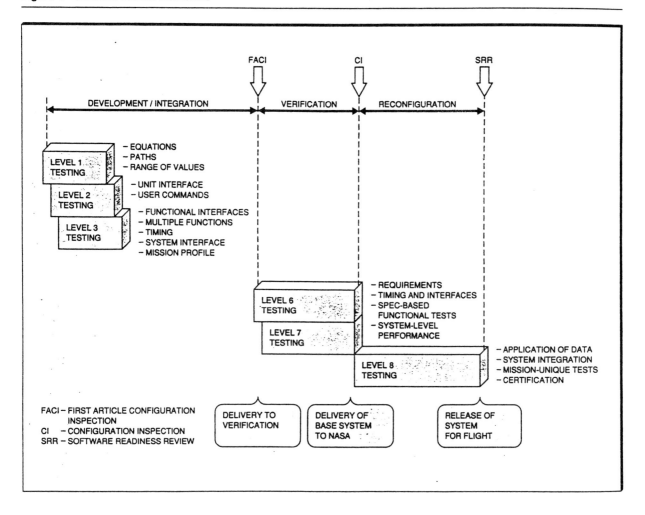

relationship with the software developers. Multiple test phases were defined (Figure 4), and the independent tests were based on an assumption that the software was untested by the development programmers. Verification analysts developed independent test plans for requirements-based testing, independent functional testing, and independent code desk checks and audits. Verification analysts were responsible for a system-level test phase that emphasized customer-oriented testing and shuttle community involvement in test planning and in analysis of test results.

Verification staffing nearly equaled the development levels, and verification personnel had requirements analysis, software development, and onboard systems experience. Configuration control of test products was a key element of test quality and test documentation and analysis. Results were controlled and archived with the incremental release software under test. This archive supplied reusable test components for regression testing and retest of changed software.

During the early 1980s, Houston changed the software process to improve early detection of software errors. Resource allocation was shifted to the front end of the software development life cycle to support formalized inspections. These inspections included mandatory involvement of independent verification personnel in software design and code inspections. This requirement was initially resisted by verifiers, who felt it would compromise their independence. A modification in the inspection process to separate inspections of the software from inspections of unit and functional test plans and test cases satisfied this concern. The result of this process change was a dramatic increase in detection of software errors during inspections. The decrease in rework due to the early detection of errors more than paid for the shift of resources, thus increasing overall productivity.

Secondary benefits from the involvement of the verification group in software inspections include:

- Verification analysts were more knowledgeable of the implementation.
- Team fellowship and product ownership were fostered.

The independence of the verification group was not compromised for two reasons. First, verification analysts did not have knowledge of development testing and could continue to consider the software untested. Second, the verification analysts inspected the software from a different perspective than developers. Verification analysts considered inspections a "first test" and reviewed design and code for weak spots, constraints, data anomalies, and other characteristics that would typically be represented in test strategies. Verifiers uniquely find approximately 20 percent of inspection errors—errors that might otherwise have to be found through dynamic testing.[6]

When the Onboard Shuttle flight system became operational, the detail verification group adopted a delta test strategy to concentrate testing activity on only affected code statements and logic in new or changed code. This strategy required detailed tracking of software changes to test plans and cases developed to test that software. Configuration control and test documentation improved, resulting in even tighter control over test products.

A process team was formed to improve performance verification quality and effectiveness. The system performance verification process began to take shape in the early 1980s when performance testing was designed and a review process was established to improve the quality of the test products. A system performance testing board reviewed and approved (1) preliminary verification assessments (considerations on whether or not to explicitly test a changed requirement, how much to test, etc.); (2) test specifications (how to test, what conditions will be tested, etc.); and (3) test reports (actual results vs expected results, analysis of discrepancies, etc.). This board resolved most technical disagreements and was the forerunner of the process teams, discussed in the next section.

Process assessments. Throughout the 1980s, FSC Houston sought out independent evaluations of its processes. Applying for the NASA Excellence Awards, Malcolm Baldrige Award, and internal IBM quality awards, as well as internal IBM assessments, provided measurements against widely accepted (and consistent) criteria. Houston used these evaluations as a means to identify process "weak spots."

For example, in early 1984, a team working under Watts Humphrey rated the two largest projects in FSC Houston against a set of criteria that were to become the Process Capability Maturity Model of the Software Engineering Institute at Carnegie Mellon University. A one-week independent review of each project was conducted, concentrating on software development processes for each life-cycle phase, as well as processes spanning the life cycle: performance, information development, quality assurance, and change control. Process attributes were evaluated against 5 levels (with 5 as the highest rating). The Onboard Shuttle project average across the 11 areas was 3.15, and the system test phase scored 4.

The following areas were suggested for improvement:

- Data collection, analysis, and feedback were insufficient at the process level.
- Proven methodologies were not being consistently used in inspections.
- Test process consistency, configuration management, and coverage measurement could be improved.
- Documentation preparation was largely done manually.

On the basis of the assessment recommendations, a continuous focus on these items brought about process and product improvement. In 1989, the Onboard Shuttle project was evaluated by a NASA team using the Software Engineering Institute (SEI) Capability Maturity Model. The shuttle project scored a "5," the highest possible rating. A review of these results by Humphrey confirmed the NASA findings.[7]

Process improvements. Measurements and inspections were important in improving the process.

Process and product measurements. To understand processes and the effects of change, an organization must be able to measure its processes. During the 1980s the Onboard Shuttle project went from the "primitive" project measurements of the 1970s to precise measurements of software quality and the development process. Major project measurements are:

- Software quality measurements monitored as a group

Early detection percent

$$= \frac{\text{major inspection errors} \times 100}{\text{total errors}}$$

Process error rate

$$= \frac{\text{valid errors pre-delivery}}{\text{thousand source lines of code (KSLOC)}}$$

Product error rate

$$= \frac{\text{valid errors post-delivery}}{\text{thousand source lines of code (KSLOC)}}$$

- Process measurement

Total inserted error rate

$$= \frac{\text{major inspection errors} + \text{all valid errors}}{\text{thousand source lines of code (KSLOC)}}$$

Collecting measurements is not enough. It is necessary to properly analyze and understand the information. Trends in process errors, for example, must be examined in conjunction with the trends in early detection and product errors. If early detection trends increase and both process and product error trends decrease, the trends are favorable. If, in contrast, process errors decrease and product errors increase, the software development process must be examined to find the weaknesses that allow errors to be delivered to the customer.

Measurements of the subprocesses gauge their effectiveness and the effect of process changes. For example, concentration on the early detection measurement resulted in improvements to the design and code inspection process discussed

---

> **To understand processes and the effects of change, an organization must be able to measure its processes.**

---

in the next subsection. Measurements demonstrated the increased effectiveness of the process. As seen in Figure 5, process analysis through measurement has demonstrated improved processes that have resulted in improved software products.

Inspections. In 1981, a mandatory inspection process was formalized. This led to a significant increase in early error detection. The formal inspection process required checklists for design and code inspections, a formally trained moderator team, and participation by the requirements analysts and verification analysts. Later improvements included assignment of specific responsibilities for each inspection participant and further refined procedures.

Checklist item responsibilities were assigned to individual team members, but the team goal was to detect all errors in the design and code. The primary reason for conducting a meeting in addition to individual inspection activity is the synergy created through face-to-face interaction. The moderator is a formally trained chairperson of the inspection meeting and has overall responsibility for the inspection activities.

Procedures were refined to define the contents of the inspection packages; scheduling algorithms

Figure 5 Quality improvement in the 1980s

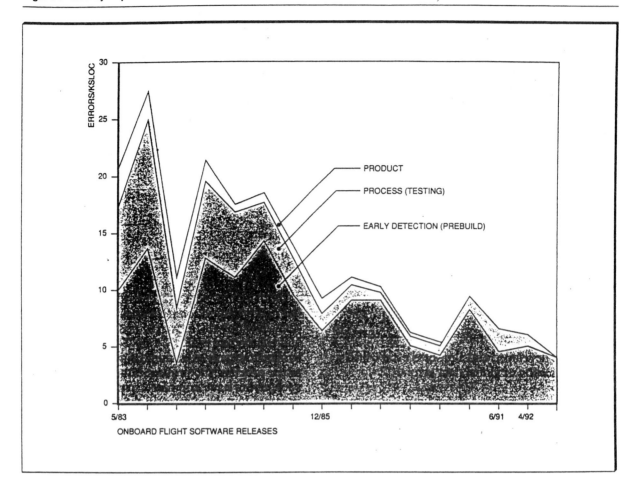

ERRORS/KSLOC

PRODUCT

PROCESS (TESTING)

EARLY DETECTION (PREBUILD)

ONBOARD FLIGHT SOFTWARE RELEASES

were designed to allow adequate preparation time for all participants; formal documentation of action items were required; and waiver mechanisms for process deviations were initiated.

The results were dramatic. Early detection improved from the 50 percent levels of the 1970s to above 80 percent in the 1980s.

This success caused the inspection process to be propagated to requirements and test products. The inspection process was modified for each development stage. For example, the customer was included in the requirements and test inspections but excluded from the design and code inspections. Formal inspections dramatically improved the quality of requirements, significantly reduced

verification test resource usage, and increased test effectiveness.

Defect prevention process. The Onboard Shuttle project defect prevention process is based on audits and analyses. In the 1970s errors were classified and, if a particular error was severe, audits were performed to detect other instances of that error class. In one case, a critical error was detected in multipass data usage. The symptoms and characteristics of this error class were identified, and an intensive analysis effort was conducted by the development and verification organizations to find other instances. Global variables were another area of concern due to the complexity of global data usage and computer synchronization.

Figure 6　Four-step defect prevention process

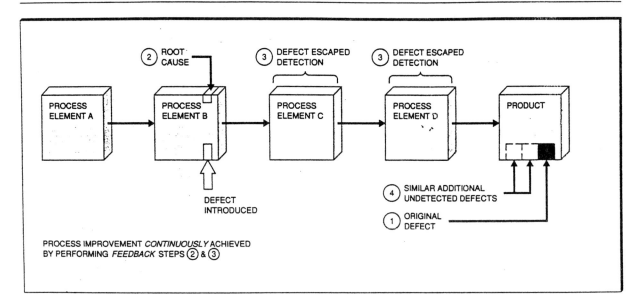

PROCESS IMPROVEMENT *CONTINUOUSLY* ACHIEVED
BY PERFORMING *FEEDBACK* STEPS ② & ③

Tools were developed and a process established to prevent insertion of global data errors.

The causal analysis and defect prevention process consists of identifying classes of errors, searching for their causes, and modifying the processes to prevent the occurrence of those errors in the future. Special teams investigate every error. These teams are composed of members from all software development phases and are responsible for determining how an error escaped detection and for finding any similar errors.[8]

The teams use the following rigorous four-step approach shown in Figure 6:

1. Find the error and fix it.
2. Find and eliminate the cause of the error.
3. Fix other faults in the process that allowed the error to go undetected through the process.
4. Look for similar, as-yet-undetected, errors and eliminate them too.

In addition to the four-step process, a periodic analysis of error trends is conducted. If as a result of this analysis it is concluded that the process needs to be changed, changes are designed and implemented. In this disciplined approach, both improving the quality of the product through a systematic error search and improving the quality of the processes to prevent future occurrences of such errors have combined to produce the near-zero product error rates in the software.

Applying the shuttle process. The Houston process has been successfully tailored for use in other projects. Tailoring reduces or modifies activities that are not appropriate for the new application. For example, without the requirement to have a system able to support human life, the large investment in independent testing can be reduced. Although most Houston processes relate well to other projects, requirements analysis is particularly applicable. In any development project, understanding the customer's requirements and documenting them correctly will reduce errors more than any other single step. Houston applied the requirements process to a small engineering lab upgrade. The resulting set of requirements provided a clear picture of what was needed to satisfy the users. Although the customers and developers were frustrated at first by slow progress, the actual implementation proceeded smoothly, and the end result clearly benefited from the requirements effort.

Additionally, Houston transferred the code inspection and requirements analysis process to its ground support software project during the 1980s. The result has been a drop in product error rates from 0.72 errors per 1000 lines of code in 1986 to 0.30 in 1993.[9]

Even on small software teams, most or all of the process can be used effectively. A team can decide the level of rigor they will impose on themselves based on the criticality of their application. Aspects of the shuttle process are used today on the space station program, the air traffic control system, and others.

Reliability. During the 1980s, the shuttle project began to use a large historical database to predict the reliability of software. This gave Houston the ability to redirect resources to reduce errors before the software was released. Using models, Houston is able to predict when and how many errors are likely to be found.[10] The analysis of the data found several key points. First (and central to Houston's approach to defect elimination) is that all software errors cannot be found by testing. In fact, less than 10 percent are found in shuttle testing today (Figure 7). This outcome is due to the emphasis placed on removing errors prior to the test phase. Second, about half the errors that escape the inspection process are found by testing. The remaining errors are found by static analysis (code audits, desk checks, etc.). Lastly, reliability model data are used to decide when to stop testing as opposed to waiting for time or money to run out. Reliability measurements require access to historical data to be accurate. These historical data, combined with the knowledge of the planned software changes, allow reliability to be estimated.

The 1990s

The 1990s brought the need to be more competitive through increased productivity, while maintaining the software quality that the customer has come to expect. Houston pursued a strategy of selective insertion of new technology into the software development process in combination with actions to optimize the existing process. Commercial off-the-shelf hardware and software are used to enact the process. Process ownership teams work to optimize the development processes.

Enactment of the software development process. Houston learned from experience and through

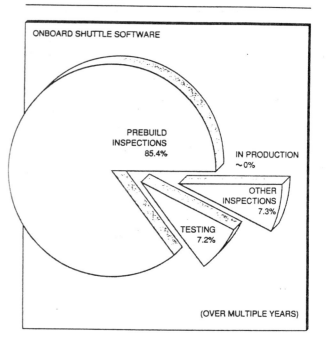

Figure 7 Where errors are found in the space shuttle software

benchmarking with other companies that computer-assisted software engineering (CASE) tools are, at best, only a partial answer to productivity improvement.[11] Since the shuttle software is written in unique programming languages, a lack of commercial products increases the challenge of technology insertion. Rather than focus on the use of technology to design and code software, the Onboard Shuttle project has focused on enabling the formal processes that govern the production of the software. The objective is to free the software developers from administering the process and to focus their technical skills on producing software.

Process ownership teams applied. In 1990 it was recognized that technical management of the software development process needed to reside with people who performed the processes. They knew better than anyone what worked and what could be improved. If the process could be optimized, the development teams had the insight to make the changes.

Following the model of the successful design and code inspection teams, ownership teams were assigned to each of the processes: requirements evaluation, development design and code, development test, and independent test. Each team monitored and controlled its process. The team's responsibilities were to:

- Document the process
- Collect process metrics
- Benchmark the process
- Analyze process metrics and optimize the process
- Provide education to process users

Teams were encouraged to find new means of improving process efficiency. They often included both vendors and customers as part of their process improvement activities. The team approach has been ingrained in the Houston culture and is considered to be a normal business routine.

One of the first successes involved the development test team. Soon after they formed, the team identified the inability of unit test to discover errors. Inspection of the requirements, design, and code left virtually no errors in the software detectable by traditional unit testing. The few errors that remained consisted of interface problems and errors in rare execution scenarios that fell outside the scope of unit testing. The team responsible for the development testing process changed their testing philosophy from that of unit and functional test to scenario testing. Early results of this process change are encouraging, with increased error detection in this development stage. Detection of errors has been moved so that it is earlier in the development life cycle, reducing the cost of rework.

Leaders of the process teams are members of a Process Evaluation Team. The Process Evaluation Team meets regularly to discuss cross-functional process issues and to evaluate each process.[12] Improved communications has spread process concepts from one process to another. Ownership teams are accelerating the evolutionary optimization of the Houston processes.

Conclusion

Sophisticated processes to develop the space shuttle software evolved over many years. Several factors influenced the overall success of the project. Maturity grew out of practical experience and innovative ideas from industry and academia, as well as through trial and error. Disciplined application of the resulting processes has produced software systems that have been virtually error-free. Although these processes were developed for a complex aerospace application, many are fundamental for any type of software development. Strong program management, adherence to the process even during times of pressure, and procedural discipline have a significant positive influence on project results. None requires sophisticated technology. They are organizational, procedural, and cultural and can be implemented by managers and software professionals who have the desire to improve their development environment.

Houston demonstrated that disciplined use of program management, team inspections, independent testing, incremental development, requirements management, and measurement programs result in predictable product quality delivered on time and within budget. Additional important factors in attaining extremely low error rates were the use of product audits when process weaknesses were discovered, using independent testers as inspectors in requirements, design, and code inspections, and process evolution driven by problem causal analysis.

The software development life cycle is an integration of all the processes necessary to produce the software products. Process maturity comes from focusing on each of these processes and ensuring that all the steps are necessary, that the process is followed, and that the door is open to better ways of completing the activity. Maturity develops in both the processes and in the attitudes of those who must execute the processes.

Cited references and note

1. *Capability Maturity Model for Software*, CMU/SEI-91-TR-24, Software Engineering Institute, Carnegie Mellon University, Pittsburgh, PA 15213 (August 1991).
2. N. H. Madhavji, K. Toubache, and E. Lynch, *The IBM-McGill Project on Software Process*, Technical Report 74-077, Centre for Advanced Studies, IBM Canada Ltd., Toronto (October 1991).
3. J. F. Hanaway and R. W. Moorehead, *Space Shuttle Avionics System*, National Aeronautics and Space Administration Office of Management, Scientific and Technical Information Division, Washington, DC.
4. C. P. Lecht, *The Management of Computer Programming Projects*, American Management Association, New York (1967).
5. W. Madden and K. Rone, "Shuttle Operational Increments: Design and Development of the Space Shuttle Pri-

mary Flight Software System," Houston Technical Direction, IBM Federal Systems Company (1979).

6. E. Lee, "Using Testing Resources for Defect Prevention," *5th International Software Quality Week*, Software Research, Inc., San Francisco (May 1992).
7. W. S. Humphrey, Director, Software Process Program, Software Engineering Institute, Carnegie Mellon University, Pittsburgh, PA, stated, "We were delighted with the degree to which your experiences reinforce the SEI maturity framework and particularly by the way the continuous improvement culture seems to pervade your organization. . . . Four-step process for defect prevention was particularly impressive and represents a step beyond what we had been considering." (July 1990).
8. R. G. Mays, C. L. Jones, G. J. Holloway, and D. P. Studinski, "Experiences with Defect Prevention," *IBM Systems Journal* **29**, No. 1, 4–32 (1990).
9. "Use of Testing Resources for Early Defect Elimination," E. Lee, *Software Management News* **11**, No. 6 (November/December 1993).
10. N. F. Schniedewind and T. W. Keller, "Applying Reliability Models to the Space Shuttle," *IEEE Software* **9**, No. 4, 28–32 (July 1992).
11. F. P. Brooks, "No Silver Bullets ... The Essence and Accidents of Software Engineering," *Computer* **20**, No. 4, 10 (April 1987).
12. E. Lee, "Process Evaluation Teams," *8th Annual NASA/Contractors Conference and 1991 Symposium on Quality and Productivity*, ISSN 1049-667X, NASA (April 1992), Sec. 8.1.4, p. 127.

Accepted for publication September 8, 1993.

Note: At the time of publication, Federal Systems Company, now a unit of Loral Corporation, was an IBM-owned company. Addresses for authors may still be considered valid.

Cyndy Billings *IBM Federal Systems Company, 3700 Bay Area Boulevard, Houston, Texas 77058-1199.* Ms. Billings is a consultant with the IBM Federal Application Development Consulting Practice, specializing in test process and methodology for high-quality software. She has over a decade of experience in the testing and verification of complex embedded software systems, with five years of management experience in space station and Onboard Shuttle Software testing.

Jeanie Clifton *IBM Federal Systems Company, 3700 Bay Area Boulevard, Houston, Texas 77058-1199.* Ms. Clifton began her career with IBM in 1981 in Tucson, Arizona, working in a product reliability, availability, and serviceability group. She later worked in the Tucson Customer Support Center, the first of its kind within IBM, solving customer computing problems and instructing them in the use of many IBM software and hardware products. Following the Space Shuttle Challenger accident in 1986, Ms. Clifton transferred to IBM's Federal Sector Division and played a key role in revalidating the Onboard Shuttle Software. She has been a technical lead within the Onboard Shuttle Software project, being the chairperson of the Development and Inspection Process group. This process is recognized around the world as the key to developing the "zero defect" shuttle software. She is currently a member of the IBM Federal Application Development Consulting Practice, helping software development laboratories both internal and external to IBM.

Barbara Kolkhorst *IBM Federal Systems Company, 3700 Bay Area Boulevard, Houston, Texas 77058-1199.* Ms. Kolkhorst is a senior systems engineer with the IBM Federal Application Development Consulting Practice. Her work has focused on evaluating and improving the software development process to produce affordable, highly reliable software systems. Ms. Kolkhorst has extensive experience as both a software development manager and a technical leader in the development of software products for NASA's space shuttle program. She has over 30 years experience in all phases of the software development life cycle, developing highly reliable software for applications supporting manned space flight, nuclear energy, and modeling for business economics.

Earl Lee *IBM Federal Systems Company, 3700 Bay Area Boulevard, Houston, Texas 77058-1199.* Mr. Lee has 27 years of experience on large, complex, data processing systems. These have included the semi-automation of the FAA's Nation Air Space Enroute Air Traffic Control System and the Space Shuttle Onboard Data Processing System. He has been involved in software development for 18 years in both technical and management roles, and his experience spans the entire software development life cycle. As a manager, he led the establishment of software process evaluation methods on the space shuttle project. Mr. Lee is currently a member of the IBM Consulting Group.

William Bret Wingert *IBM Federal Systems Company, 3700 Bay Area Boulevard, Houston, Texas 77058-1199.* Mr. Wingert joined IBM as an aerospace engineer in 1982 where he worked in the Space Shuttle Onboard Flight Software Guidance, Navigation, and Control (GN&C) Requirements Analysis and Performance Verification organization until 1988. In 1989, he worked on various upgrade strategies for onboard avionics and ground systems. He also investigated ways to reuse shuttle software technology on other manned and unmanned launch systems. In 1991, he began managing the Space Shuttle Onboard Flight Software GN&C organization. He currently acts as a consultant to various internal and external organizations on testing and requirements analysis.

Reprint Order No. G321-5532.

Schlumberger's Software Improvement Program

Harvey Wohlwend and Susan Rosenbaum

Abstract— A corporate-wide software process improvement effort has been ongoing at Schlumberger for several years. Through the motivation efforts of a small group, productive changes have occurred across the company. We see improvements in many development areas, including project planning and requirements management. The catalysts behind these advances include capability assessments, training, and collaboration.

Index Terms— Process improvement, SEI, software process management, software engineering.

I. INTRODUCTION

SCHLUMBERGER IS AN international company located in 100 countries, employing over 53 000 people representing 75 nationalities. Schlumberger's businesses include well-site exploration and production services for the petroleum industry; testing and electronic transaction products; and metering products, which are sold to public utilities, governments, laboratories, and industrial plants worldwide. Ten years ago, software was a key component in only a small percentage of Schlumberger's products. Now, it is responsible for 50–100% of many of the products' engineering investment. Due to this, senior management in all of the businesses has initiated software improvement efforts.

The Schlumberger Laboratory for Computer Science (SLCS) was formed in 1989 as a corporate-wide resource to enhance the quality and creativity of software products within Schlumberger and to improve the productivity of software development. Part of SLCS's charter is to help the company's software engineers improve both software development productivity and software product quality.

Evaluating and suggesting software improvements is a challenge due to the scope of the activity as well as the geographically dispersed engineering population and product range with which we are working. Engineering groups in Schlumberger range in size from 5 to 180 people, working on products that vary from 4-bit microprocessors to massively-parallel supercomputers. Schlumberger's products primarily fall into two types: data acquisition and data interpretation. Most of the software systems are either embedded real time products or scientific applications. The primary language used is C. Some groups co-develop products with organizations that may be located around the world; others work independently on products that are developed solely in one location.

Manuscript received October 1992; revised September 1994. Recommended for acceptance by R. A. De Millo.

H. Wohlwend is with Sematech, Austin, TX USA; e-mail: harvey.wohlwend@sematech.org.

S. Rosenbaum is with Schlumberger, Austin, TX 78726 USA; e-mail: rosenbaum@austin.asc.slb.com.

IEEE Log Number 9406479.

Because of this wide range of needs, we had to decide which techniques SLCS's small software improvement team could use most effectively. This paper will describe the choices that we made and the effectiveness of those choices in our work with Schlumberger's engineering organizations. In particular, we found that a small active group can be effective as a stimulus for change.

What is particularly unique about this paper is that it is one of the earliest to document the use of tailored assessments. A major contribution of this paper is the total approach to software improvement: assessment, training, measurement, technology, consulting, and communication.

In the same manner as Daskalantonakis' paper on a practical view of software measurements at Motorola [2], we describe a practical view of the software improvement program at Schlumberger. Section II describes the different improvement methods we considered; Sections III and IV go into detail about our assessment choice and how we introduced software improvement to the corporation. Section V provides an overview of all of the improvement activities that have been undertaken. Sections VI and VII discuss the results of this work. The remaining sections provide additional insights into the model we used to bring about change.

II. IMPROVEMENT EFFORT CHOICES

Many Schlumberger business units, particularly those in Europe and Japan, have participated in quality initiatives and improvement efforts such as NATO's Allied Quality Assurance Publication [1] and ISO9000 [8]. A few divisions of Schlumberger had been participating in a TQM program.

While these efforts are useful, they are not sufficient. The difference between these quality initiatives and the improvement activities we help motivate is our focus on software. The software-related industry certification, such as the ISO9000-3 portion of ISO9000, is just now being included in audits of Schlumberger centers. We based our approach on the technique developed by the Software Engineering Institute (SEI) at Carnegie Mellon University [4]. The technique is a multiphase approach used to stimulate improvement initiatives. We have found it to be quite successful.

The SEI view of process and process management has led to the creation of a process maturity model. This maturity model characterizes an organization's software development capabilities by establishing five maturity levels, identifying characteristics of organizations at each of the levels, and identifying key problem areas commonly associated with each level. The model also specifies how to advance to the next higher level by satisfying key requirements. Once the maturity level is known, the actions needed to move to the next level are defined.

III. OUR MODIFIED ASSESSMENT PROCESS

Assessment efforts using the techniques of the SEI have been described in recent publications [3], [6]. This technique is fast becoming an industry standard for judging the capabilities of software development groups. The focus on software process is based on the premises that (1) the quality of a software product is largely governed by the quality of the process used to create and maintain it, and (2) the process of producing and evolving software products can be defined, managed, measured, and progressively improved.

Schlumberger has been using the SEI assessment technique since late in 1989 as a way both to measure the current maturity level of a software organization and to motivate future improvements of the organization. The assessment technique as formally taught by the SEI requires that a team of 5 to 8 trained software professionals spend an intense week with each software organization, identifying observations and relaying findings back to the respondents in such a way that the organization agrees with the outcome.

Given our limited resources, we use a modified approach for the first visit to an organization that we call a "study" rather than an "assessment." The initial step of our SEI-based study is to identify participating software organizations in the company with which to work, based on size or reputation, and to request those organizations to identify projects to participate in the study. Knowing the product line of the organization, we help focus the project selection by requesting representative projects. Normally two to five projects are selected as being indicative of the process used in the entire organization. These participating projects complete the SEI questionnaire. We analyze the responses and then visit the site for one or two days of follow-up interviews, which are conducted by one member of the SLCS staff. The on-site interviews include members of both the technical staff and management. The interviews are used to improve our understanding of each organization's software practices and to validate the responses to the questionnaire. The interview questions strive to be open-ended, encouraging the local personnel to discuss topics that are of particular interest and concern to them. At the end of the interview sessions, we develop a set of eight to 10 findings that we believe are most beneficial for improvement efforts. We base these findings on common observations that we see in each of the projects studied. At the end of each visit, we present these findings to the site senior management. We have found that use of our "study" technique has not diminished the improvement impetus resulting from the findings. Continuing contacts serve as a basis for organizational buy-in to the assessment results. Our findings correlate closely with those presented in SEI's 1992 Process Assessment Results Analysis [9]. The organization invariably agrees with our list of findings and begins planning steps to rectify the problems.

As an interesting note, several organizations have borrowed the study technique and perform "self-studies" at regular intervals throughout the year as a way of assessing progress towards improvement.

IV. INITIAL EVALUATION ACTIVITIES

We began our initial studies by identifying the software organizations in the company. During the course of the initial studies, 76 organizations were identified as developing product software. We visited 20 through early 1990. The total number of software developers in the 76 organizations is approximately 2000; 10% of the developers were interviewed during these studies. The 20 organizations represent about 70% of the Schlumberger software developers. Since 1990, we have extended our studies and site visits to over 30 sites.

As we expected, the initial studies found that most organizations needed improvement in the same areas. These areas included project management, process definition and control, and project planning and control. Our initial recommendations to most of the organizations were to begin improvement efforts immediately (if they had not already done so) and to focus on the following additional areas: (a) tracking the deliverable size and effort on current projects; (b) gathering data about code and testing errors; (c) investing in resources to support improvement activities; and (d) reviewing how project commitments are made. We presented these findings at each site and promised to come back and perform an assessment of the organization at a later date.

We began follow-up assessments in late 1991 with a changed format. We now perform a more in-depth analysis on the return assessment and include the participating organization on the assessment team. Therefore, we organize the assessments in a slightly different fashion than that used for the initial studies and more closely follow the SEI model. We schedule three days to spend with the engineering center and use a four-person assessment team of selected Schlumberger employees. Usually the four-person team consists of two members of SLCS, one person from the site under assessment, and one person from an organization that develops products similar to that of the assessment site.

We are able to condense the normal five-day SEI assessment into a three-day period by reducing the number of feedback meetings and by reviewing and analyzing answers to the questionnaire prior to the visit. In addition, our ongoing contact with these centers between the initial study and the return assessment helps us focus more quickly on the most serious problem areas. Even with the reduced time frame, we have been satisfied with the quality and motivational benefits of the assessments. One of the most valuable things we have learned is to hold a postmortem with the assessment team members at the very end of the assessment and to generate a list of activities that went well and things that could have been done better over the three-day period. We use this feedback as input to the next assessment.

V. CONTINUING IMPROVEMENT ACTIVITIES

While the initial SEI studies and assessments were a catalyst for many improvement activities, particularly with regard to raising an organization's SEI level, we realize that periodic evaluation of an organization is not enough to effect long-lasting change. We observe that three key components drive all improvements in software development productivity: process,

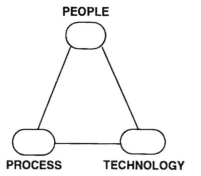

PEOPLE

PROCESS   **TECHNOLOGY**

Fig. 1. Key components of software development.

people, and technology; we concentrate on encouraging continuous improvement in each of these areas.

A. Process

Our initial process involvement included participation in the development of software process documents, trying to capture on paper the good points of their current process and suggesting changes that should be adopted. IEEE standards [7] were often used as the starting point for this activity. During the course of the involvement, we have seen major changes occur; most of the large centers and many of the smaller ones now have a written process document that is followed for software development. Documents that have been produced include not only process descriptions, but also guidelines to be used for requirements, planning, testing, etc.

We encourage the use of improvement teams to foster specific improvement activities in an organization. Many of the Schlumberger sites have formed either full-time budgeted improvement teams or part-time volunteer improvement teams. We support these teams both electronically and by frequent visits to participate in improvement meetings all over the world. Our active involvement with so many improvement efforts enables us to alert engineers to similar work occurring in other parts of the company, thereby leveraging one another's experiences and results.

In the early stages, no two engineering centers followed the same development process. Through the improvement teams and our multigroup interactions, we have fostered the sharing of process descriptions across geographically diverse organizations. Groups with similar product lifecycles are now sharing the same software process and making changes only as required by the differences in their business cycles. For example, two separate business units with locations around the world have each formed software committees consisting of one to two representatives from each participating site. Committee members' collaborations include developing common standards and guidelines for process, configuration management, defect tracking techniques, etc. The meetings, alternating between North America and Europe, encourage the sharing of design and implementation information. Groups are now sharing product components rather than developing their own, as was true in the past.

B. People

We analyzed the results of our studies and found we could make a major contribution in the area of people improvement by providing training. We consequently focus on developing and teaching courses that are particularly relevant to the ongoing improvement work. The major training effort is in software project management and peer technical reviews. Since Schlumberger hires engineers from a variety of disciplines, including geophysics, electrical engineering, and mechanical engineering, we find that software engineering training is vital to aid in software product development.

One major decision that we had to make was whether to develop classes ourselves or to contract with established training institutions. For several reasons, we decided to develop and teach the software project management and peer technical review classes in-house, rather than to send people to outside classes. We customize material in the classes to be Schlumberger-specific, using actual product development histories as sources of case studies, exercises, and "war stories." In addition, we want to effect change in organizations in a fairly quick manner. When people attended classes in the past, it had usually been only as a one- or two-person contingent from an organization. After returning to work, they found it difficult to have enough critical mass and enthusiasm to effect a cultural change in their organization. By offering in-house classes, we find that large numbers of people from one site will either take the class together or in close proximity to each other. When they return to work, the ideas that were developed in class can be shared much more easily, because many people have been exposed to the same educational and motivational material. As trainers, we use the information we learn during the class as the basis for site-specific collaborative activities. We use senior people in the organization as trainers so that they can provide insight based on past experiences and interact knowledgeably on later collaborations.

We see an additional training benefit that parallels the work on software process: people from different groups attending the same class often discover an unexpected commonality either in the products on which they are working, the tools they are using, or the software process they are following. This synergy enables them to stay in contact with each other long after the class period ends.

C. Technology

Technology, or the tools used to develop software, is the third component of improving software development. SLCS performs technology watches on commercial software development tools that are important to the software engineering centers. These tools include user interface prototyping tools, "upper" CASE tools, C++ environments, and requirements tools. All the evaluations are in-depth, based on collaborative projects with Schlumberger development organizations. At the completion of an evaluation, we either publish a company-internal technical report describing our findings or post a finding summary to a company-internal software engineering bulletin board. This ensures that the information is instantly available globally. Initially, we posted most of the summaries;

now, we find that at least 95% of the postings are coming from engineers in other Schlumberger organizations. The fact that Schlumberger has an electronic network that reaches even the most remote business sites greatly aids in this disbursement of information.

We also act as industry contacts in looking for improvement activities in companies outside of Schlumberger and periodically update engineers on the current status and trends of similar organizations. Contacts at several U.S. and European universities also help keep us abreast of important changes in the field of software engineering.

D. Collaboration

The primary emphasis of our improvement activities is collaboration. Collaborative projects have included involvement in technical reviews of project plans, usability studies on existing products, and object-oriented design consulting on future products. We have collaborated on exploring techniques and products in the areas such as configuration management and defect tracking.

We encourage close collaboration with the business units to provide a natural feedback loop, which enhances our program members' understanding and knowledge and consequently improves the quality of our courses and collaborative activities. Our emphasis on involvement with business units is to aid in areas in which they would not be working themselves, particularly in the areas of software engineering methodology and tools.

VI. RESULTS-POSITIVE

After several years of improvement activities, it is interesting to step back and see how well the improvement goals are being met. Overall, we find many positive benefits. All of the organizations that set improvement goals have moved up the SEI maturity scale. Not surprisingly, some of the organizations are motivated towards improvements due not only to the assessments, but also because other related organizations are working towards improvements, and none wants to get left behind. This friendly interorganizational competition is helpful and healthy. We have found that a community formed among all of the groups working on software process improvement. Individuals across the company who previously did not know one another are now interacting on a regular basis.

Traditionally, some groups within the company either share code or provide code for a jointly-built system. In the past, there has been a great deal of friction between the groups when software was received on an unknown schedule with unexpected or incomplete functionality. One of the "receiving" engineering organizations had told us several times in the past about the delivery problems they were having with a sister organization. This year, the same engineering group told us (with some amazement) that the software they were shipped was: (a) on time; (b) correct; and (c) well-documented. The sister organization's improvement efforts helped not only with products delivered to its external customers, but also with those delivered internally.

Additional benefits are also obvious. We see better project and product communication both between engineering centers and within departments of the same center, and customer reports on recently released products mention that the quality of the products has improved.

We are finding other positive, quantifiable results. The metrics reported in this paper focus on the measurements taken at the beginning of the improvement activities with those taken after. We can view samples of these results in light of the Key Process Areas (KPA's) of SEI Level 2. The KPA's are part of the new assessment methodology [10] being developed by the SEI based on the experience with the original SEI questionnaire [4]. In the new technique, the specific organizational capabilities in the SEI model are described in terms of a "capability maturity model (CMM)," a set of criteria that describes expected characteristics of mature software organizations. The CMM is composed of the five maturity levels as initially described by the SEI [5], but these levels have been detailed by listing the key process areas within each level. KPA's are the pieces that together establish the development process maturity of an organization; each KPA defines a set of related activities and products that together define the KPA's attainment.

The key process areas for level 2 are:

- Requirements management
- Software project planning
- Software project tracking and oversight
- Software subcontractor management
- Software quality assurance
- Software configuration management

These areas were selected based on the goal of level 2: attaining a repeatable process that can ensure product schedule and quality. Mechanisms for each of these key areas are required for an organization to be able to reliably repeat earlier successes in product development. Examples of the improvements found in the groups with which we work for each of these KPA's include:

- Requirements Management—An engineering group that works on complex, embedded real-time systems found a vast improvement in its time-to-market once requirements were managed both at the start and during product development. A product completed prior to the introduction of requirements management took 34 validation cycles (code/test/re-code) before the product met the customer's requirements. Post introduction of requirements management, the next product on a similar system took only 15 validation cycles. An additional benefit of better requirements management was the increase in productivity. Average productivity measured in noncommented source statements (NCSS)/person month more than doubled in the later product as measured against the earlier product. The improvement in requirements handling helped reduce the amount of code that had to be written during successive cycles. The primary change in requirements management was the formation of a "core team," a multifunctional team of people from different disciplines who are organized to work on a specific project. The

514

core team had the ultimate responsibility for achieving the product goals.

- Software Project Planning—One engineering group that began concentrating on process improvements in mid-1990 found that 94% of their engineering projects were completed on schedule in 1992, compared with 89% in 1991 and only 51% on-schedule deliverables in 1990. The group points to an improvement in initial project planning in making this change. Whereas project planning in the past had been a fairly ad hoc activity, it is now a set of actions and validation steps that help ensure that adequate preparation has been done.

- Software Project Tracking and Oversight—Two and a half years ago, one site found that projects normally finished in twice the estimated elapsed time (see Fig. 2). A site-wide improvement team helped put project status reporting and regular project reviews into place. Due both to better project tracking and improved initial project planning, by the middle of 1991, projects were being completed with a cumulative progress rate (schedule adherence) of 87%; rather than completing 50% late as before, there was an average slip of only 13% against the original planned schedule. By the end of 1992, projects finished on average at a rate of 99% as measured against the original schedule; there is only a 1% slip against the original plan. During the same time period, the quality of all of the group's products improved, even as the product sizes increased. At the start of the improvement work, the total line count for the products was almost 400 000 lines of NCSS with an average defect rate of 0.22/KNCSS. Today, the same group has developed over 700 000 lines of NCSS with an average defect rate of 0.13/KNCSS.

- Software Subcontractor Management—A Schlumberger engineering organization had an experience with a large subcontracting contract that taught them the importance of good subcontractor management. At the end of the relationship with the software subcontractor, the Schlumberger group received over 1 000 000 lines of undocumented, nonworking code. Procedures are now being put into place to properly manage the next one. We are working with the group to use the SEI assessment technique on future subcontractors.

- Software Quality Assurance—One group's SQA department set specific quality goals for their products. Formerly, there had been a problem with poor quality products being delivered to the customer. The SQA group was formed in early 1990 with a goal of improving customer satisfaction by reducing the number of customer-discovered post release defects. In 1989, 25% of total product defects were post release defects discovered by the customer. SQA set a release goal of having no more than 10% of the total number of product defects found by the customer. At the end of 1990, 18% of the defects in the product release were customer-reported; by the December 1991 product release, the goal of 10% post release customer-reported defects had been achieved.

- Software Configuration Management-Software configuration management became a large issue in a group

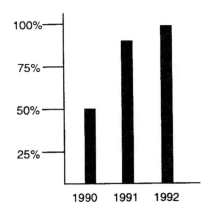

Fig. 2. Schedule adherence improvements.

after the organization had grown by a factor of 4. Once the developers had overwritten each other's files several times, the group put a configuration management system into place.

Many of the European sites that are ISO9001-certified feel they are in a stronger position for current and future ISO audits because of our SEI process improvements. In the past, they felt unsure during each ISO audit about their state of readiness. Now the groups have more materials to show the ISO auditors and sense that they will already satisfy any changes that may be imminent in ISO requirements. Our process improvement efforts have prepared them for their next ISO audits.

The resource investments for software improvements varies among groups. The larger engineering centers (120 to 180 engineers) have from one to five full-time staff people devoted to process improvements. Slightly smaller sites (50 to 120 engineers) have up to three full-time people working on improvements. Smaller engineering centers work with volunteer committees. In one organization, all of the engineers (20 people) are active on the software improvement team and involved in monthly meetings; in another organization, three task groups were formed to focus on process, metrics, and architecture.

VII. RESULTS–DISAPPOINTMENTS

All has not been perfect in the improvement efforts. As we perform assessments, we find groups who are almost "too ready" for the evaluation. The engineers are so well-coached as to the correct responses to our inquiries, it is extremely difficult to discover the true picture of the organization's practices. We find that the assessments now take a lot more time and energy than had been true during the first round of discussions; we have to take much more time in scripting questions prior to the assessment to ensure that we understand the true status and can develop meaningful findings. During the initial studies, we easily uncovered typical software development problems; now as groups have improved and become more sophisticated, we have to work harder to discover the software issues in an organization.

All organizations have not been motivated by our efforts. It is disappointing that a crisis is needed before an improvement initiative can take hold.

Another problem we see and cannot explain at this time is the turnover in the permanent staff that works on improvement activities. We wonder if the position of software improvement leader has enough prestige to act as a career catalyst (or at least not a career negative). Unless engineers see the value in the position and view it as career enhancing, we are afraid that highly career-motivated individuals may begin to shy away from the assignment.

VIII. STEPS REQUIRED FOR MEASURABLE IMPROVEMENT

It is difficult to assess the exact time and resource requirements needed for the improvements. We see durations from 12 to 18 months before significant improvement occurs and the changes become part of the organization's normal operation. A good deal depends on the readiness of the site. If the site is already ISO- or AQAP-certified, as is true for many of Schlumberger's European organizations, then it is likely that the process under which the organization is managed already contains many of the necessary activities. If the need exists to define and implement a totally new development procedure, the change process will take more time. Introducing new improvement activities where none previously existed requires a cultural change in the way product development occurs.

In our assessments and collaborations, we help each group focus on the improvement areas they should first address, but do not push any particular solution to the way changes should be made. This provides a significant advantage for organizational buy-in, in that the information we are transferring to the business groups is done through a joint decision process. Although it may take more time to have group ownership of the improvement initiatives occur, we believe in the long run that this is vital if the change is going to remain.

We have organized Software Improvement Team workshops for each of the past two years. Attendees at the workshops are the software improvement champions from each of the organizations. The attendees talk in-depth about changes that have been made at their organization, citing both the changes that were successful and those that were unsuccessful. Twenty-eight organizations participated in the most recent workshop. Participants have stayed in touch between the workshops through a very active e-mail attendee distribution list.

In all of these instances, the key behind the success of the improvement effort lies with the management of the organization; if upper management is behind the improvement effort, then the improvement moves ahead. When it is obvious that upper management does not support the improvement activities, little progress is made. However, time may still be spent in improvement meetings and other process activities. It is also true that in some organizations, senior management is much more in favor of the improvement efforts than some of the middle management team. In these cases, we fear that as senior management moves to other Schlumberger positions, unless an equally strong improvement proponent is brought in, all improvement will be lost. With the current strong support of the chief executive officer of the company, the improvement effort should continue to be quite strong.

IX. WHAT WE WOULD DO DIFFERENTLY

In looking back over the activities of the last years, it is interesting to think about what we have learned. In their paper regarding lessons learned from software assessments [11], Mark Paulk *et al.*, asked, "since most organizations typically know the problems in their development methodologies, why aren't they fixing them?" Problems continue to persist because when a group perceives a large number of problems, they have difficulty selecting which to concentrate on first. We help with this concentration effort, but sometimes feel that we need to stay more involved to maintain the improvement momentum in the group. Our perception is that when groups do not hear of positive progress there is an assumption that nothing is happening. Consequently our saying is *No News is Bad News*.

Generally, senior management and the engineers support the improvement efforts; this is less true for the middle-level managers. There are several reasons for this. Senior managers often dictate that an improvement change be made without completely realizing the time and effort (resources) required for the change. They assume that the change will occur without modification of other commitments. The middle managers, however, find themselves caught in the middle of a difficult situation, trying to modify the way in which their team works without affecting preexisting milestones and deadlines. To improve this situation, we need to spend more time working with middle managers before presenting findings to senior management so that we can discuss not only the specific findings but also time and resource estimates.

We also find that it is not enough to spend time improving software development; the improvement activities must involve the other parts of the business with which software interacts, namely marketing, hardware development, sales, manufacturing, etc. When we visit an organization and exclusively work with the software engineers, they have a difficult time causing a cultural change that will spread throughout the business. It is one thing to develop software following a written process; it is another thing to develop software following a written process when the process is not coordinated with hardware and marketing activities. If we were starting from scratch at this point, we would make sure that the entire organization received information describing the work that we were doing and the goals that we had in helping motivate organizational changes. We are now encouraging all parts of an organization to participate in improvement initiatives.

X. WHAT WE PLAN TO DO NEXT

We have found major benefits in the work that we have undertaken and will continue to concentrate on improvement motivation and collaboration.

The assessment results provided by SLCS have motivated improvement initiatives throughout Schlumberger. We believe that the demand for assessments will exceed our team's resources. Therefore, we plan to train and qualify additional assessors within the company to conduct assessments. Once trained, rotating assessment teams will be organized to provide evaluations of the business units, with a member of SLCS acting as lead assessor on the team. We will ensure that each team will be consistent in its approach to an assessment, thereby ensuring comparable findings.

We plan to expand the audience of the training program, as appropriate, to management, marketing, and other parts of the organization, to ensure that all parts of the business are learning the same information. We will emphasize the overall product development process in the training.

The primary emphasis of our work will continue to be in-depth collaborations with the engineering centers. We find that assessments and training serve to "introduce" us and our ideas to an organization. We then find that close contact with the engineers and management of a site helps cause the culture to actually change.

XI. CONCLUSION

In summary, we draw the following conclusions from our work. Many of these echo the lessons learned at Hughes [6].

- Strong sponsorship by the chief executive officer is critical
- Assessments are useful for motivating software process improvements in organizations.
- Assessments can be successfully done by small assessment teams (two–four people).
- Assessments must be followed by active efforts to encourage formation of software improvement initiatives.
- A central, experienced team should participate in software improvement initiatives.
- In-house groups should be trained together to effect a cultural change.
- To encourage process transfer, one should train across organizations with engineers from different sites.
- A significant lesson we learned was that we were primarily acting as change agents and secondarily as software technologists.
- It is important to provide technical analyses and distribute them effectively. (The Internet is a useful distribution channel.)
- Groups must choose their own method of improvement so that "ownership" occurs.
- Other parts of the organization must participate in the improvement process.
- Communicate constantly.
- Last, but not least, keep the pressure on.

REFERENCES

[1] *NATO Software Quality Control System Requirements*, Allied Quality Assurance Publication, Aug. 1981.
[2] Daskalantonakis and K. Michael, "A practical view of software measurement and implementation experiences within Motorola," *IEEE Trans. Software Eng.*, Nov. 1992.
[3] Dion and Raymond, "Elements of a process-improvement program," *IEEE Software*, July 1992.
[4] W. S. Humphrey, *et al.*, "A method for assessing the software engineering capability of contractors," Software Eng. Inst., Tech. Rep. CMU/SEI-87-TR-23, Sept. 1987.
[5] W. S. Humphrey, D. H. Kitson, and T. C. Kasse, "The state of software engineering practice: A preliminary report," in *Proc. 11th Int. Conf. Software Eng.*, May 1989.
[6] W. S. Humphrey, R. T. Synder, and R. R. Willis, "Software process improvement at Hughes Aircraft," *IEEE Software*, July 1991.
[7] "IEEE Software Engineering Standards Collection," IEEE, Spring 1991.
[8] "Quality management and quality assurance standards," Int. Org. for Standardization, 1987.
[9] D. H. Kitson, and S. Masters, "An analysis of SEI software process assessment results: 1987–1991," Software Eng. Inst., Tech. Rep. CMU/SEI-92-TR-24, July 1992.
[10] M. C. Paulk, B. Curtis, and M. B. Chrissis, "Capability maturity model for software," Software Eng. Inst., Tech. Rep. CMU/SEI-91-TR-24, , Aug. 1991.
[11] M. C. Paulk, W. S. Humphrey, and G. J. Pandelios, "Software process assessments: Issues and Lessons Learned," Soft. Eng. Inst., Tech. Rep., to be published.

Harvey Wohlwend has been Project Manager of the SEMATECH Software Process Improvement Project since August 1994. The project's goal is to improve software that supplier companies deliver to semiconductor manufacturers. In 1989, as Program Leader for the Software Practices Program, he initiated the corporate-wide software improvement program at Schlumberger described in this paper. As a result of his varied software experiences, he became interested in the combined application of both software process and software tool technologies.

Susan Rosenbaum received the B.A. degree in mathematics from the University of Texas at Austin, and the M.S. degree in computer science from the University of Texas at Arlington.

She has worked in the computer science field for over 16 years. Prior to joining Schlumberger, she managed a variety of software product development efforts. In 1990, she joined the Software Practices group in the Schlumberger Laboratory for Computer Science where she collaborated with Schlumberger engineering centers on software project management and software engineering improvements. She is now working in Schlumberger Austin Systems Center as the manager of the Common Software & Tools group.

Accumulating the Body of Evidence for the Payoff of Software Process Improvement—1997

Herb Krasner

President, Krasner Consulting

1. What Is Software Process Improvement?

Improvements in the software process have been going on for several decades. Under the rubric of software engineering, the primary thrust has been better discipline, methods and automated technology to support software development. Software Process Improvement (SPI) guided by organizational process maturity principles has emerged in the United States in the last 12 years, the charge being led by the Software Engineering Institute (SEI) (Humphrey, 1989), and now internationally by the emerging International Organization for Standardization (ISO) SPICE initiative.

Achieving a mature process establishes a project management and engineering foundation for quantitative control of the software process, which becomes the basis for continuous process improvement. An organization with a mature process will take full responsibility for executing its planned commitments.

In a fully mature software organization, the following holds:
- Quality is defined and therefore predictable.
- Costs and schedules are predictable and normally met.
- Processes are defined and under statistical control.
- Roles and responsibilities are clear - interdisciplinary communications are good.
- Software measurement discipline is practiced.
- Success rides on organizational capability, and individual talent flourishes within that.
- Technology that supports the process is used effectively.
- Staff development practices for software talent growth are established and effective.
- Corporate success factors recognize "core competency" of software as important and software strategy is aligned with the business strategy.
- Management and staff are committed to total quality and continuous improvement, and results are obvious.

The primary mechanism for achieving maturity and bottom line results in a specific organization is a focused, structured, and institutionalized program of continuous software process improvement. This requires the cyclic application of a model-based improvement method. In addition to a well-defined set of improvement objectives, such a method may use one or more of several popular goal-oriented models for guiding the improvement program.

A successful systematic SPI program requires:
- Well-defined objectives, some of which are measurable and measured;
- A method for catalyzing and institutionalizing the improvement program in an organizational setting;
- One or more goal/maturity models for guidance;

• Best practice examples and benchmarks from which to draw;

• An organizational commitment to action in the form of an improvement road map that is defined, resourced and followed;

• Expertise in process diagnosis, culture change tactics, process problem solving, and so forth; and

• A set of champions/change agents that can sponsor, commit to, and effectively implement a planned improvement program.

An SPI road map will focus on targeted organizational improvement areas at all organizational levels. It is assumed that some type of projects is being done, where a project could be anything from a one-person custom product variation effort to a large multi-team contract systems development. It is simply a matter of defining the scope of work to be managed as a project unit.

The following areas are typically addressed: within projects focusing on better project planning and control, across projects focusing on cross project coordination/learning, and at the business unit/company level focusing on TQM issues. A foundation software measurement program supports all areas.

1. Better project planning and execution. The basic benefits of improvements in this area are better predictability and control of projects, and the improved ability to recognize off-track or out-of-control projects earlier. Typical improvements made include these:

• A rigorous planning and tracking framework is established for projects.

• Changes to requirements and associated objects are identified and managed.

• Responsibility is taken for planned commitments (individual, team, project).

2. Better cross-project learning and coordination. The basic benefits of improvements in this area are improved people portability and better organizational communication, learning, and efficiencies. Typical improvements include these:

• A common process framework is defined and reused.,

• Educational vehicles deliver common training needs.

• Teamwork is enhanced via structured techniques.

• Focused responsibility for process improvement is established.

• Process-based technology usage is facilitated,.

• Lessons learned, and planning data are collected and passed from old to new projects.

• Common standards and system architectures are created to facilitate reuse.

3. Foundation software measurement program. The benefit of improvement in this area is the creation of a factual basis for dealing with issues in the other three areas. Measurement provides quantitative feedback that reinforces and even accelerates improvements. Typical improvements include these:

• Customer satisfaction, software quality, software resource consumption, and schedule delivery performance are all measured.

• Software rework, cost of conformance to requirements, and problem resolution effectiveness are all measured.

• Team effectiveness is measured.

• The effectiveness of implemented improvements is measured.

4. Focus on total quality and continuous improvement. The basic benefits of improvements in this area are common values, context, and lexicon and a culture that encourages constant improvements and values staff and the results of previous developments as assets to the organization. Typical improvements include these:

- Customer satisfaction feedback is aligned with internal directions.
- People are treated as assets—hiring and career development is aligned with core competency requirements and project needs.
- Leadership and empowerment are facilitated by the establishment of a quality oriented culture.
- A multidisciplinary systems design process is integrated with the software process (in those organizations that deliver more than software).
- A continuous improvement culture is established.

Specific improvement objectives and a fully elaborated road map will point to specific processes to be improved within a given organization. The highest leverage areas for improvement are best identified by the results of rigorous empirical evaluation of recurring software problems (e.g., Curtis, Krasner, and Iscoe, 1988).

2. What Is Payoff and Why the Need for Data?

By *payoff* we mean the reward/result/benefits for doing SPI, usually in quantitative terms (e.g., dollars). In some cases, the nonquantifiable payoffs (e.g., pride in work, company reputation) may be even more important. If the costs of doing SPI are viewed as an investment, then the payoff is expressed in a temporally shifted, return-on-investment (ROI) model. The observable payoff is delayed in time, sometimes by as much as several years, due to the complexities of deployment, institutionalization and culture change. This delay can stress the attention span of short-term, delivery-oriented, crisis-driven, middle managers whose support is necessary for SPI to flourish.

The payoff that will be of most interest to a specific organization will depend on that organization's business objectives for doing SPI.

Payoff data are needed for at least three reasons:

1. Data from external sources are needed to justify the beginnings of an SPI program until significant internal results can be demonstrated.

2. Data from internal sources are needed to close the feedback loop on the impact of internal improvements, which then helps to sustain the program.

3. To validate process maturity based approaches that may have started on good faith but are now being squeezed by financial conditions.

The latter will continue to be true until the pursuit of SEI Maturity Level X becomes less of a process hygiene factor and more of a certification requirement for doing business (as in the ISO community).

The costs of SPI are usually more obvious, since they consume identifiable resources. These costs can be easily measured if flexible effort collection mechanisms are already in place, and if SPI work can be separated from business-as-usual activities. The magnitude of typical costs for SPI depends on organizational size, type and the scope of changes made. A guideline cited by the SEI states that SPI costs should be 3% to 5% of an organization's total software development costs. Sometimes, these costs are deployed throughout an organization, and not necessarily concentrated within a software engineering process group (SEPG). In an organization that has SPI embedded in its culture, the distinction between improvements and normal discipline may be blurred. Since this paper is primarily about payoff, the discussion of the costs of SPI will be treated in the context of overall ROI analysis.

3. Previous Reports of SPI Payoffs

Prior to the crystallization of the process maturity movement by the SEI in the late 1980s, quantitative payoffs for specific process improvements were reported in a haphazard fashion in a wide variety of places. For example, the payoff for using a formal inspection technique within a business unit setting has been reported in several different conference proceedings, in books, in refereed journals, and in various newsletters. The same is true for various software engineering methods and tools.

The earliest report of the potential payoff from a holistic maturity-based process improvement program came when Krasner (1990) reported on the results of a set of formal SEI assessments in five major divisions of Lockheed (these assessments included a snapshot of 28 large projects). Data collected showed that projects at higher levels of maturity were 3 to 5 times more productive than Level 1 projects. A tentative correlation was hypothesized between Capability Maturity Model (CMM) levels and other key project performance factors (quality, cycle time, effort, etc.). This early report received considerable attention until 1991–1992, when reports of the Hughes, Raytheon and HP programs were published.

At about the same time, the NASA SEL (McGarry, 1993) and the IBM Houston shuttle program (Rhone, 1990) started to publish reports of the payoffs resulting from their improvement programs.

In 1993–1996, along with the case studies presented here, numerous other reports of the results of systematic SPI programs were published, including reports from Schlumberger, IBM Toronto, Litton Data Systems, Rockwell, Oklahoma Air Logistics Center, and the TI Systems Group. These are all summarized in Table 1 and are included in the reference section at the end of this paper. In each report, the notion of payoff is defined and measured differently, and typically reflects improvement in at least one dimension of the software development project challenge model shown in Figure 1.

In this model, the challenge of software development is represented as the "push–pull" attempt to control and manage the four major project outcome factors—cost, schedule, scope, and quality—and one internal factor, the process. The outcome factors are viewed as "springs" that are dynamically compressed or decompressed during the life of a project. The process is viewed as the rubber band holding those springs together and whose shape must change as changes occur in the manipulation of each factor.

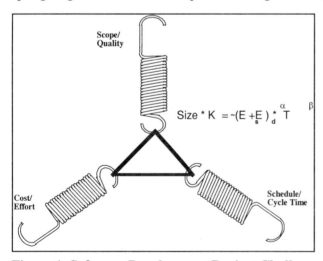

Figure 1. Software Development Project Challenge Model

The payoff metrics that have been reported in published sources include the following:
- Cost metrics such as ratio of actual versus planned cost of work performed, engineering hours saved, productivity increases, nonconformance/rework cost reduction, and reuse increases;

• Quality metrics such as defect density or rate reduction, percent defects discovered by customer reduced, early defect detection rate improvements, complexity/size growth control, and operational reliability improvements;

• Time-based metrics such as cycle time reduction, on-time delivery rates improved, schedule slippage rates reduced, and requirements validation cycle time decreased; and

• Process metrics such as process maturity level increases, and improvements in defect removal effectiveness.

Summary Reports of Industry-Wide Payoff

In mid-1993, Broadman and Johnson (1994) undertook a research project for the U.S. Air Force to investigate the existence of ROI data for SEI CMM-based SPI initiatives. The study included an analysis of 20 questionnaires, 22 interviews, and a literature search that turned up 100 sources. They found that even though many definitions of ROI existed, numerous reports of quantified results existed in areas such as productivity, quality, cost, schedule, and effort. They also noted that the number of metrics collected increased with maturity level; for example, twice the number of metrics on average were collected by Level 3 organizations over Level 1 organizations. ROI data were empirically linked to the CMM in the areas of productivity, quality and schedule.

In early 1994, the Empirical Methods Project at the SEI began a study to investigate the results of CMM-based software process improvement efforts. Survey data were collected from 13 leading organizations representing Department of Defense (DoD) contractors, commercial companies, and government organizations, including Bellcore, Bull, GTE, HP, Hughes, Loral FSD, Lockheed, Motorola, Northrup, TI, Siemens, and Tinker AFB. The study attempted to identify SPI impact in the areas of cost, productivity, schedule, quality, and ROI. Sparse data were reported in each area, but the data generally showed substantial gains in productivity, time to market, quality, reduced rework, and ROI (Herbsleb, 1994). Herbsleb and Zubrow (1994) described their study results of the 13 leading SPI organizations surveyed. Their summarized results indicated that the following:

1. Average number of years engaged in their SPI program was 3.5,

2. Average cost of SPI per software professional per year was $1,375.

3. Annual productivity gain was 37 percent (based on four reports).

4. Annual reduction in time to market was 19 percent (based on two reports).,

5. Annual reduction in post delivery defect reports was 45 percent (based on five reports).

6. Average ROI for SPI was 5.7 to 1 (based on four reports).

In future studies, the SEI may attempt to empirically validate the CMM. Programs based on models other than the CMM have not received the attention the SEI approach has. Results are therefore sparsely found in the open literature.

Even though SPI payoff data are being reported, these reports have not generally included results in the areas of better cross-project learning, organizational coordination, and total quality improvement. Such payoff reports might eventually include such things as reputation for excellence, competitiveness, timeliness to market, organizational learning efficiency, process architecture effectiveness, and customer satisfaction rates. The current lack of such payoff information may be due to the fact that there are not many high-maturity organizations, and those that do exist either do not have such data yet, or will not report on it.

4. Case Histories of SPI Payoff

Demand for data on successful SPI programs continues as the SPI movement proliferates to new sectors and companies. Therefore, several short case studies of successful SPI programs serve as valuable examples.

A number of successful organizational SPI programs have reported the payoffs from their efforts in the open literature. In the following section, we highlight a representative set of programs, so that the potential for payoff in specific situations can be seen. These organizations may be considered as SPI benchmarks for the industry—they were chosen because their payoffs have been reasonably well documented. We briefly describe the SPI programs of the following organizations:

1. NASA SEL,

2. IBM (now Loral) Federal Systems- Space Shuttle Program,

3. Hewlett Packard Corporation,

4. Raytheon Equipment Division, and

5. Motorola India Electronics Laboratory.

These organizations have had SPI initiatives for at least 5 to 10 years. In these cases, the payoffs took several years to become observable through measurements.

NASA SEL

The NASA Software Engineering Laboratory (SEL) represents a consortium involving NASA Goddard Space Flight Dynamics Division, the Computer Science Department of the University of Maryland, and Computer Sciences Corporation's Software Engineering Operation. This lab houses software developed and maintained for flight dynamics (e.g., orbit, mission analysis) that is characterized as scientific/mathematical with tight delivery constraints imposed by launch schedules. They have had an ongoing SPI program for 18 years, during which many experiments, case studies and trials have been performed. Their SPI approach is characterized as domain specific, product based, and quality improvement paradigm (QIP) based. They have been evaluating changes and fine-tuning life cycle processes, evaluating significant changes to technology/methods (e.g. Cleanroom), and providing support to the development organizations to help them with process definition, modeling, and so on.

The results they have achieved are within the context of a dynamic environment in which the complexity of systems doubled, the number of requirements doubled, and the code size tripled. In spite of that, they report the following payoffs:

- Development error rates were reduced by 75 percent (from 4.5 to 1/KSLOC).
- The cost per SLOC decreased.
- Predictability of cost, schedule, and quality improved.
- Reuse went from 20 percent to 79 percent on similar systems.
- Overall reduction of 55 percent in total software costs was realized.

See Heller and Page (1993), McGarry (1993), Basili and Green (1994), and Krasner, (1995) for more information. In 1994, the NASA SEL organization was awarded the first IEEE Computer Society Award for Software Process Achievement. A presentation on their accomplishments was given by Frank McGarry at the August 1994 SEI Software Engineering Symposium, and has been described in a technical report from the SEI (McGarry et al., 1994).

IBM Federal Systems Company (then Loral and now Lockheed Martin)—Space Shuttle Program

This organization has been developing on-board and ground support software for NASA shuttle missions for almost 18 years. Approximately 300 software professionals work in this organization, which has produced a base system of almost 10 MSLOC. The current version of the system has 0.5 MSLOC on-board software, and about 1.7 MSLOC of ground support software. In response to an almost continuous flight schedule, they delivered a new release every 4 to 8 months (every 12 months during the last few years), with each new version consisting of from 10 to 53 KSLOC new code. The program's quality goal is to produce error-free software. Their SPI program consists of performing assessments, defining their process (using ETVX), formal process training, adopting advanced software engineering methods (waterfall + spiral), conducting rigorous in-process inspections, performing defect cause analysis and prevention, and utilizing specialized testing methods and tools. The following payoffs from their program have been cited:

- They have the ability to predict costs within 10 percent.
- Only one deadline has been missed in 15 years.
- They learned the relative cost of fixing defects ranged from 1x during inspection to 13x during system test and 92x during operation,
- Productivity 180–200 SLOC/MM; maintenance cost of ~ $20/SLOC (1/2 of the maintenance costs of other IBM software shops),
- Early error detection went from 48 to 95 percent from 1982 to 1993,
- Reconfiguration time (weeks) went from 11 to 5 weeks from 1982 to 1985,
- Product error rate (defects/KSLOC) went from 2.0 to .01 from 1982 to 1993.

In 1989 they were evaluated by a NASA-led, SEI-trained team which determined that they had many Level 5 characteristics—the first organization to be recognized as such. For more information see Krasner (1994), Paulk, et. al. (1995), Humphrey (1991); Gomez (1994); and Billings et al.(1994).

Hewlett Packard Corporation

Hewlett Packard is in many businesses ranging from printers to medical systems to computer workstations. In the mid-1980s, they established a corporate software quality goal of achieving a 10x reduction in software defects. Even though software size and complexity were growing exponentially, in many product lines they have achieved significant results. Their program focused on improvements in process, systems definition and design, configuration management, inspections, maintenance, and reuse. The payoffs from their program have been cited as follows:

- Corporate aggregate defects rate went from 1/KSLOC to 0.1/KSLOC from 1988 to 1993 (10x objective achieved).
- Inspections in widespread use are saving 5 hours per inspection on average (saved $20 million in last year alone due to inspections).
- Average time to fix a defect was cut in half in one business unit.
- Time to market was reduced by 5x over a 5 year period in another business unit.

All of these were achieved in spite of large growth in software size and complexity.

For more information see Platt (1993), Grady (1992) and Grady and Van Slack (1994).

Raytheon Equipment Division—Software Systems Laboratory (now RES)

The Raytheon Equipment Division Software Systems Laboratory (SSL) began their SPI initiative in earnest in August 1988 after an extensive planning phase that began in 1987. This report discusses the results from 1988 until 1994 when their organization was merged with two others into the newly created Raytheon Electronic Systems (RES) Software Engineering Laboratory. The SSL had about 600 software engineers working on defense electronics systems for government customers during the span of the period reported here.

Their SPI goals included the improved predictability of software development, for which they wanted quantitative measures of improvements made. To address this challenge, they selected an approach for measuring ROI based on the business goal of reducing the amount of rework involved in developing software. This cost of software quality approach was adapted from Crosby (1984). They later supplemented this approach with the analysis of productivity on projects and also cost at completion as compared to original budget (CAC/budget) to measure predictability of project performance. Defect density analysis was used to measure overall software product quality. They continue to use these four basic measures on their projects today—cost of quality, productivity, predictability, and product quality—to monitor the impact of their SPI initiative.

Using a tailored CMM-based approach, SSL (and subsequently RES) have made steady process maturity progress. They cite the following achievements:
- SSL made SEI level 3 in late 1991.
- All new projects are required to operate at Level 4, which they reached in 1995
- A cost–benefit demonstration and full institutionalization of level 4 behavior is being pursued.
- A goal to achieve Level 5 has been set.
- Their defined process has been institutionalized, and subsequently transferred to other Raytheon organizations in the United States and beyond.
- In 1995, they received the IEEE Computer Society Software Process Achievement Award— only the second organization in the United States to do so.

The annual investment into the SPI initiative was at a level of about $1 million per year. Because there were about 600 software engineers in the SSL, this amounted to about $1,666 per software engineer per year invested into SPI efforts. Over the lifetime of the initiative (1988–1994), the following effects were measured:
- Rework was reduced from 40 percent of development costs down to about 10 percent.
- Productivity of the development staff increased by a factor of 170 percent
- Predictability of project budget and schedule has been reduced from about 1.41 (40 percent overrun on average) to a range of ± 3 percent.
- Product quality (defect density) went from about 17 to 4 TRs/KDSI (TRs are software trouble reports, KDSI means thousands of delivered source instructions).

In 1990 the ROI was 7.7 to 1. This is based on a total savings of $4.48 million utilizing a total investment of $0.58 million that year. The savings came from reduced rework measured on projects. By 1994, 18 completed projects were represented in their ROI database. In addition (not included in the ROI), in 1991 they received a $9.6 million schedule incentive award for bringing one of their major projects in 6 percent under budget. That award alone more than paid for the SPI initiative (1 million x 7 years = 7 million).

They cite the following primary reasons for their successful SPI initiative:
- Vision and active commitment from management,
- Sponsorship and support,
- Improvements that clearly and continually demonstrated business benefits to projects,

- Careful consideration of the culture and how to change it, and
- Running the program from within the ranks of the software organization led to ownership and empowerment.

Specific leverage points were identified as the major contributors to their sustained SPI growth

- System and requirements definition practices,
- Inspections,
- Integration and qualification testing,
- Development planning and management controls,
- Training, and
- Pathfinding.

For more detailed information about the SSL SPI program see Haley et al. (1995).

Motorola India Electronics Laboratory, Ltd. (MIEL)

MIEL was established as a wholly owned subsidiary of Motorola in Bangalore, India, in 1991 with 22 staff members in order to develop software for internal Motorola engineering use in a variety of application domains. This was part of a company initiative to create effective, off-shore software factories. MIEL had the opportunity to create their process from a clean sheet a paper based on software factory principles using the CMM as a guideline. Therefore Motorola created MIEL with the intent of initially being a Level 3 organization with a well-defined process and a firm commitment to institutionalized common practices. They recruited staff who were willing to follow their process, and with a relatively high turnover rate, this was critical to long-term success. This approach served as a model for other Motorola international software factories. By 1995, MIEL had grown to about 250 software engineers working in several major product lines.

Process innovation was not their SPI objective, with most of their practices based on commonly accepted standards (e.g., IEEE Software Engineering Standards Collection). Their processes are highly integrated. They did create and follow their process religiously, keeping all 18 CMM KPAs in their vision as they evolved. Their biggest hurdle was in going from level 1 to level 2. The rest of their growth was deemed (by them) to be a logical conclusion of the initial transformation. They were assessed (by trained Motorola assessors) to be at SEI Level 5 in December 1993. Subsequent visits to MIEL by SEI luminaries acknowledged the existence of high process maturity characteristics.

These improvement results were achieved over the 1991–1994 period:
- Delivered about 2 million LOC over this period.
- Produced more than 43 non-comment lines of code (NCLOCs) per staff-day.
- Productivity increased about 3.5x as they went from Level 3 to Level 5.
- Post-release quality better than 2 defects per 930 KLOCs (50 percent with no known defects).
- In-process quality less than 1.1 defects per KNLOC.
- Less than 3.75 percent rework was required due to in-process faults.
- Cost of error detection and correction less than 17 percent of total costs.
- Estimation accuracy on project schedule and effort better than 90%, and
- Cycle time was reduced by 40 percent in a 12-month period.

These quantitative results are based on 42 data elements that MIEL regularly collects from their projects. Their causal analysis showed that most defects resulted from process noncompliance. They encourage process improvement changes but insist that all changes be justified with data and be controlled (piloted first, then deployed after success is demonstrated).

The CMM aspects that had the most early impact on their overall results were, in order of priority:

- Product engineering,
- Peer reviews, and
- Configuration management.

Regarding peer reviews, inspection was one of the biggest contributors to quality, and was a strong support technique for the Cleanroom approach. Inspection was also an excellent technique for collecting software metrics. If a review becomes formal, it is an excellent point for data collection. They also maintain a risk repository for all identified risks and make decisions based on overall risk levels. They define quality as compliance with implicit and explicit requirements of the customer. Recognizing that changing of requirements is the prerogative of the customer and will happen, the plans must change accordingly.

MIEL's approach to implementing SPI was as follows:

1. Develop a first draft of the development process.

2. Ensure that the organization structure is "in synch" with the actual process as practiced (not just to satisfy the CMM).

3. Assign key persons to all key process areas (Note: they did not address only one level at a time).

4. Select pioneers.

5. Conduct integrated induction training (42 hours of training of which process, tools, and techniques were taught by the managers of the organization).

6. Require total compliance with process.

7. Demonstrate the benefits early.

8. Improve the process based on experience.

9. Grow capabilities incrementally by iterating on this approach

As a result of their process development, MIEL believes the following are some of their "best practices":

1. Integrated induction training;

2. Career development plan in which each engineer works in each of the functional areas (e.g., engineering, QA, systems, test, CM, project management) before they can attain their highest job rank;

3. Cost of quality measurement system (which supports the claim that it costs less to detect and correct a defect in the stage in which it is created than at a later stage) and its use to evaluate piloted changes;

4. Phase and project post mortems;

5. Ruse;

6. Data modeling, including the number of hours of testing necessary to reachSix Sigma given test time and an estimate of latent defect density;

7. Estimation techniques;

8. Senior management reviews which include managers and software professionals; and

9. Senior management review of all customer commitments.

For more information about MIEL's SPI program see page 92 of the March 1992 issue of IEEE Software, Srikant Inamdar (1994), and Curtis and Statz (1996).

Summary of Case Histories

These common themes have been observed in successful SPI programs:

1. They are all in SPI for the long term.

2. They focus on software quality and related project performance issues.

3. They all have intensive measurement programs.

4. They all focus on the improvement of processes that lead to measured improvement toward business-based objectives.

5. They all exhibit the sustained commitment needed to institute the changes.

Tables 1, 2, and 3 contain brief summaries of other known cases of reported SPI payoff that were not highlighted in the above section. The reader interested in becoming an expert may wish to acquire and read the cited references.

Table 1 - Summary of US Organizational SPI Payoffs - pre 1996

Organization	Payoff Summary	References
Hughes	predictability improved as measured by cost performance index which went from .94 to .97 in 3 years, $2 Million annual reduction in cost overruns	Humphrey, W., Snyder, T. and Willis, R. (1991)
Lockheed	Assessment project survey concluded that CMM Level 3 projects are 3-5 times more productive than Level 1 projects	Krasner, H. (1990); McConnell, S. (1993) (unattributed)
SEMATECH Equipment Supplier	Operational software reliability of process tool improved by 48X	Krasner, H. And Ziehe, T. (1995)
Litton Data Systems	76% less defects encountered in integration - inspections benefit	Dixon, S. (1994)
USAF Oklahoma City Air Logistics Center	SPI ROI of 6.35X	Lipke, W. and Butler, K. (1992)
IBM Toronto Lab	10X reduction in delivered defect rates, productivity up by 240%, rework reduced by 80%	Schwarz, J. (1993)
Rockwell	for 2 major projects: 625% improvement in post release defect reports, 97% pre-release defects detected, improvements in cost/schedule/quality performance indicies, and award fees up to 93%	Selfridge, W. (1994)
Schlumberger	4X reduction in betatest bugs, ISO certification, early deliveries of products, open defect rate dropping as size and complexity increases	Wohlwend, H. and Rosenbaum, S. (1993); Lloyd, P. (1994)
Texas Instruments - Systems Group	60% productivity improvement over 2 years, 10X reduction in delivered defect rate over 3 years, 12% annual cycle time reduction	Hudec, J. and Suddarth, G. (1996)
Procase Corporation	cycle time reduction of 4.3X over 18 month period	Sudlow, B. (1994)
Computer Sciences Corp.	predictability improved, error rates reduced by 65%, cost per SLOC reduced slightly in spite of dramatic increases in size and complexity required	Heller, G. and Page, G.(1993)
USAF survey	positive corrolation was determined between increasing CMM levels (1-3) and cost and schedule performance on 13 previous large USAF ASC/ESC contracts	Lawlis, P., Flowe, R. and Thordahl, J. (1995)

Table 2 - recently reported payoff summaries in the US - 1996-97

Organization	Payoff Summary	References
Boeing Info. Systems	project estimates within 20% using historical data, CPK 38% better, defect containment effectiveness at 80%, cycle time improved 36%, staff support needs down 62%, staff size reduced 31%, customer satisfaction score up 10%, $5.5 M saved in 1996 alone (1992-1996 results)	Vu, J., 1997
Boeing STS	customer satisfaction rated excellent, pre-release defect containment effectiveness at 99%, 31% reduction in rework-inspections benefit, employee satisfaction level from mean of 5.7 to 8.3, operational systems performance close to bullseye, level 5 process injected into new programs	Yamamura, G. and Wigle, G., 1997
Bellcore	defects 10X lower than industry average, customer satisfaction rates improved from 60 to 91% over 4 years, acheived 9 hr. cutover to add 888 to 800 system with no reported defects	Bellcore Press Release, Feb. 5, 1997
HP SESD	3X3 SPI program, 1 year benefits include: cycle time reduced by 33%, major open defects reduced from 4.6 to 1.6, fewer missed deadlines, ROI - 9:1	Lowe and Cox, 1996
Harris ISD DPL	2.5X productivity gain over norm, 90% defect rate reduction, cycle time down to 6-9 months	Robeson, D., Davidson, S. and Bearden, L., 1997
Motorola	3X productivity improvement, 3X cycle time reduction, 7X quality improvement, results from '92-'96 representing 85% of all products & released software, 75% of product development orgs. are >= level 3	Major, J., 1996
Motorola GED	On 34 current programs compared to baseline - each CMM level increases quality by 2X, significant decreases in cycle time as higher levels reached (2-7X), productivity increases of 2-3X at highest levels of maturity, 6.77X SPI ROI	Diaz, M. and Sligo, J., 1997
SAIC Health Tech.	50% improvement in customer satisfaction, 71% reduction in error rate, 12% annual improvement in developer productivity, production rate up 30%	Lane, J. and Zubrow, D., 1997

Table 3 - International payoff summaries - 1997

Organization	Payoff Summary	References
Siemens	cycle time cut in half in OEN & EWSD projects, 90% reduction in released defects, new process acceptance rate of 94%	Mobrin, J. and Wasterlid, 1997
Ericsson	product faults reduced in all phases, 60% reduction in operational faults over 4 years since 1993, delivery delays significantly reduced	Volker, A. and Wackerbarth, G., 1997
Thomson-CSF	CPI improved 17% in 2 years, SPI improved drastically, 12% cost reduction, reduced the cost of pre-test defect correction 4X, ROI of 3.6:1	des Rochettes, G.,1997

5. Measuring Payoff

Payoff that can be quantified in dollars is relatively easy to show if you collect certain data and are patient enough to observe the long-term trends as improvements become institutionalized.

A simple model of payoff that can be used is:

Payoff (t+i) = [old costs (t) - new costs (t+i)] - cost of improvements (i-t),

C/B ratio(t+i) = [old costs (t) - new costs (t+i)] /cost of improvements (i-t),

where: *t* is a point in time when performance costs were baselined over a selected set of projects,

t+i is a new point in time when performance costs are remeasured on a current selected set of projects,

i-t is the interval of time in which improvement costs were spent and new practices were learned.

This model can be used at the SPI program level or at the specific improvement level to yield a first-order approximation for payoff. This assumes that the benefits of SPI will show up in reduced costs of performance.

This simple model also neglects the time shifting of the widespread impact of the improvements from the point at which the new behaviors are introduced, which could be as much as up to 2 years in a large organization. A standard pro forma analysis can determine the break-even point for the SPI program.

Many issues are routinely faced when building an organization-specific cost–benefit argument for justifying an SPI program. A standard SPI ROI method would be useful, but does not currently exist. Guidance is needed on how to create an ROI argument using an ROI model and case examples for gaining support and commitment from management for the initiation of an SPI program that requires up-front investment capital, and a multiyear time frame prior to seeing the benefits. Gathering and analyzing of data are stressed on the cost of sub-par performance aspects such as terminated projects, missed deliveries, schedule overruns, defect fixing, rework, customer complaints, growth and complexity trends. Presenting the case to management is done in terms of current performance results, improvement opportunities, benchmarks from other companies, SPI action plans, and measurement approaches for evaluating SPI impact. This helps to establish a quantitative basis for making the SPI decision within an organization that likely has not had any meaningful data on software project performance in the past. Cost–benefit determination requires establishing a baseline level of performance to compare against. Deciding what projects go into the baseline(s) and how often to rebaseline are key choices to be made, and should be done in conjunction with the assessment–improvement cycle in mind. Improvement results indicators need to be intelligently interpreted because periodic baseline figures are developed from a set of projects that may have different scopes, time frames, domains, levels of complexity, and organizational teams. In small organizations, a major project failure may skew the overall improvement results when normalized.

SPI costs are sometimes straightforward to compute, especially when resources are consumed or effort is spent on doing something differently than before. A simple metric is the additional dollars spent per software staff member on SPI. However, in some cultures, improvement is a natural part of doing the work and can be difficult to compute separately. Benefits can be much harder to compute, but can be made visible if the measurement program is well defined. To the extent that all benefits can somehow be computed in dollars, we can show an overall cost–benefit ratio. Aspects such as improved job satisfaction are not easily quantified in dollars (except in turnover statistics and the cost of expertise replacement, which is very seldom measured).

Improvements in average project performance relative to an established baseline that can be precisely measured and are relevant to the improvement objective that was established will be the most compelling and easiest to demonstrate.

Example ROI models that have been used to date often include measurements on:

1. Cost of software quality (Dion, 1991),

2. Cost of high reliability (Keller, 1992),

3. Delivered defect rate trends (Keller, 1992),

4. Cost and schedule performance indices (Lawlis et al, 1995),

5. Productivity growth trends, and

6. Cycle time reduction trends.

Measuring performance costs can get quite complicated. Dion (1993) makes use of one possible cost model for collecting this kind of information. Curtis and Statz (1996) provided needed advice on the construction of specific cost–benefit models for SPI programs. In my opinion, to determine a true reflection of SPI payoff, improvements in at least process and product quality should be measured. Other measurements will depend on the SPI program's specific goals (e.g., cycle time reduction, predictability improvements, etc.).

Process Quality

One way that process quality can be directly measured is by examining the amount of rework that occurs on projects. Rework percentages for immature organizations have been reported to be in the range of 40 to 60 percent of total software effort. Because rework takes away resources from new functionality development, it can be directly tied to business measures such as customer needs or requirements satisfaction.

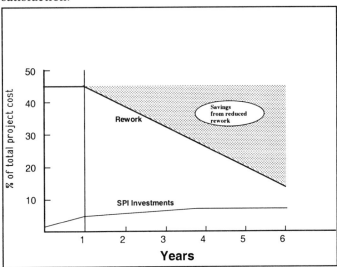

Figure 2. Process Quality Measurement

If project and improvement costs are collected and analyzed in typical work breakdown structure categories with rework and SPI investments added, then rework percent can be plotted over time as in Figure 2. A payoff is indicated by computing the savings accrued from reduced rework over time, less the cost of the improvement investments. An excellent example of this can be found in Dion (1993).

Measurements of process quality can be directly tied to specific process improvement implementations.

Product Quality

Process improvement for the sake of process improvement alone will not be sustainable in the long run. The changes must show up as improvements in the products or systems being developed. One simple measure of product quality that is frequently used is delivered defect density. The average trend over a number of projects within an organization tells us much about whether institutionalized process improvements are paying off over time.

Figure 3 is an extrapolation based on the experiences of IBM, HP, and Motorola. It shows how average defect density can be tracked over a multiyear SPI program, once it is baselined. An excellent example of this can be found in Platt (1993).

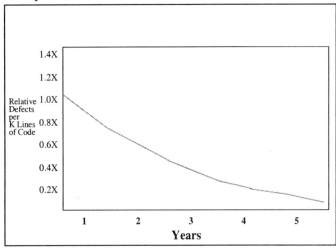

Figure 3. Product Quality Trends

Underlying this simple chart is an organization-wide data collection and analysis scheme. This scheme precisely defines for that organization the meaning of the terms *software defect* and *line of code*. Analysis procedures describe legal variations and how data are combined to form overall results. In some cases, an organization-wide defect database and tracking system are in place that facilitate uniformity. Product quality measures can be directly tied to customer and requirements satisfaction results, thus making SPI a part of achieving business objectives.

Project Predictability

Project predictability can be measured in several ways by examining the trends in actual versus planned progress, on-time delivery rates, and schedule slippage rate. Figure 4 shows an example of the improvement in the percentage of projects that deliver their software products on time over a 5-year period. An average of actual costs versus budgeted cost of work performed can be similarly plotted. As an organization's ability to more accurately plan their work gets better, these metrics get better. See Humphrey et al. (1991) and Wohlwend and Rosenbaum (1993) for good examples of this.

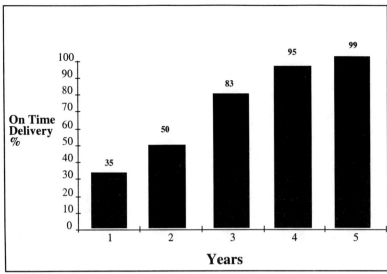

Figure 4. On time product delivery trends

Other Measures of Payoff

Other important areas of payoff have not yet been reported, and there are numerous qualitative benefits of SPI that are recognizable but not yet measurable. Training and other human resource development efforts create skill depth and breadth. We have not yet seen reports of SPI payoff in this area. Customer satisfaction is measurable, and is often measured for fielded products, yet we have not seen reports of SPI payoff in this area.

6. Conclusions

Many companies in many different business sectors are reporting successful SPI programs. They report ROI figures between 5 to 1 and 9 to 1, with approximately a 2-year lag between the investments and the observable benefits—but these ROI figures have different underlying measures. The amount of lag usually depends on organization size, type, and scope of improvements attempted.

Several notable systematic SPI programs have emerged that may serve as models for the remainder of the U.S. software industry. These have been summarized here. However, many formal SPI programs that attempted to start in the late 1980s faltered soon after a formal assessment was performed (⅔ reportedly died), are now in decline, or perhaps will soon fail. This may be happening because of a flawed strategy, a lack of commitment, lack of follow-through, not measuring improvements, or lack of crisp SPI objectives that may not have been tied to business objectives. Newer SPI programs may be more likely to succeed because they can learn from the mistakes of the pioneers, and explicitly represent that process maturity is a means to an end. For example, Krasner and Ziehe (1995) describe the results of the SEMATECH SPI initiative, which has caused improved operational reliability of the software embedded in semiconductor manufacturing equipment, using CMM-based SPI methods.

A defined SPI payoff function must tie business, engineering/development and personnel improvement objectives together in a meaningful way. SPI works best when payoff is demonstrated in all three of these areas simultaneously (Win, Win, Win). A payoff function that demonstrates the pursuit of higher quality software seems to do that. The following high-level payoff impact areas should be considered when setting SPI program objectives:

- Improving profitability, market share, time to market, competitiveness, productivity, competence, and so forth;

- Delivering ever-improving software quality to customers/users;
- Maximizing the overall predictability, productivity, and effectiveness of the software development process;
- Reducing the amount of crisis-driven chaos by managing growth and change in scope, size, and complexity,;
- Increasing the pride in workmanship, use of new skills learned, and personal empowerment in decision making.

Management indicators within this payoff function would include measures of: product quality, process quality (rework, productivity), project predictability, skill base growth, and customer satisfaction.

Some of the biggest payoffs of SPI are expressible in human terms, not dollars,and could involve better job satisfaction, pride in work, an increased ability to attract, retain and grow experts that will innovate, company reputation for excellence, and so forth.

For organizations that are not fully mature yet, the existing data suggest that there is no reason not to start a well-focused, well-designed SPI program. Crisp SPI objectives should be tied to corporate business success factors. Executive sponsorship and demonstrated commitment by management will help motivate the program. Measurement discipline is a key to success—quantitative baselines must be established and then measured against. A focus on improved software quality seems to accelerate an SPI program and should be targeted. Starting quickly with specific improvements that demonstrate early results raises the level of confidence in the program. Periodic reappraisals and process audits reinforce and stimulate the program. Remember to be patient, because payoff measures resulting from culture changes may not be visible for years. Setting realistic expectations of upper management are important if the SPI program is to be perceived as credible. This article is intended to be useful for that purpose, but not to suggest what specific improvements should be undertaken by any specific organization.

The question of how to get started with an SPI program is often asked. The advice usually given is to start small, demonstrate a success and then build momentum. Improving the basic understanding of software phenomena in small, low-maturity organizations is achievable within a few months (Krasner, 1994c). A formal systematic SPI program should then be pursued in expanding cycles that consist of establishing sponsorship for the program; baselining project performance, process maturity ,and current "as is" process definition,; setting improvement goals; formulating and executing an improvement road map; measuring progress; adjusting the program as needed; and continuing until a "world class" software shop is achieved.

But by any means—get going—the competition may be getting ahead.

The preponderance of data from companies that are successful at SPI suggests the possibility of an underlying theory that relates level of organizational process maturity and expected level of project performance (reflected in delivered quality, timeliness, cost, productivity, and/or rework). A speculative causal model has been developed that attempts to explain the relationship between the key factors that induce organizational change that then shows up in measurable organizational indicators (Krasner, 1994b).

7. References

Basili, V., and Green, S. (1994), "Software Process Evolution at the SEL", *IEEE Software*, Vol. 11, No. 4, July.

Bellcore (1997)Press Release, February 5, and SEPG97 BOF.

Billings, C., Clifton, J., Kolkhorst, B., Lee, E., and Wingert, W. (1994), "Journey to a Mature Software Process", *IBM Systems Journal*, Vol 33, No. 1, pp. 46–61.

Broadman, J., and Johnson, D. (1994), "Measurement Programs: Does One Size Fit All", presented at the 8th Annual Conference on Improving Productivity in System Development, Scottsdale, AZ, February.

CMM: Two publications that document the Capability Maturity Model for software are Paulk, M., Curtis, B., Chrissis, M., and Weber, C., *Capability Maturity Model for Software, Version 1.1*, CMU/SEI-93-TR-024, Software Engineering Institute, Pittsburgh, PA; and Paulk, M., Weber, C., Garcia, S., M., and Bush, M, *Key Practices of the Capability Maturity Model, Version 1.1*, , CMU/SEI-93-TR-025, Software Engineering Institute, Pittsburgh, PA.

Curtis, B., and Statz, J. (1996) "Building the Cost–Benefit Case for SPI", presented at 1996 National SEPG Conference Tutorial, Atlantic City, NJ, May 23.

Curtis, B., Krasner, H., and Iscoe, N. (1988), "A Field Study of the Software Design Process for Large Systems", *Communications of the ACM*, Vol. 31, No. 11, pp. 1268–1287.

des Rochettes, G. (1997) "Five Years Experience in SPI: Lessons Learned", presented at 2nd European SEPG Conference, June.

Diaz, M., and Sligo, J. "How SPI Helped Motorola", *IEEE Software*, Vol. 15, No. 5, September, pp. 75–81.

10. Dion, R. (1991) "Elements of a Software Process Improvement Program", *IEEE Software*, July (originally reported at the 2nd SEPG Workshop, November 1990).

11. Dion, R. (1993), "Process Improvement and the Corporate Balance Sheet", *IEEE Software*, Vol. 10, No. 4, July pp. 28–35.

Dixon, S. (1994), "Software Process Improvement Lessons Learned at Litton Data Systems", presented at the 6th National SEPG Conference, Dallas, TX, April.

Gomez, E. (1994), "Lessons Learned and Observations of a Level 5 Organization: The Space Shuttle Project", presented at the Austin SPIN, Austin, TX February 17.Summarized in *Software Quality Matters*, Vol. 2, No. 2, Summer 1994, newsletter of the UT Software Quality Institute, Austin, TX.

Grady, R. (1992), *Practical Software Metrics for Project Management and Process Improvement*, Prentice Hall, Englewood Cliffs, NJ.

Grady, R., and Van Slack, T. (1994), "Key Lessons in Achieving Widespread Inspection Use", *IEEE Software*, Vol. 11, No. 4, July.

Haley, T., Ireland, B., Wojtaszek, E., Nash, D., and Dion, R. (1995), *Raytheon Electronic Systems Experience in Software Process Improvement*, CMU/SEI-95-TR-017, Carnegie Mellon University, SEI, Pittsburgh, PA, November

Heller, G., and Page, G. (1993). "Impact of a Process Improvement Program in a Production Software Environment: Are We Any Better?", in *Society for Software Quality Journal*, November, pp. 1–8, (previously presented at the NASA SEL Workshop, November 1990).

Herbsleb, J. (1994), "Results of Software Process Improvement Efforts: Work in Progress", presented at the 6th National SEPG Meeting, Dallas, TX, April.

Herbsleb, J., and Zubrow, D. (1994), "Software Process Improvement: An Analysis of Assessment Data and Outcomes", *Proc. of the SEI Software Engineering Symp.*; also Technical Report CMU/SEI 94-TR-13, Software Engineering Institute, Pittsburgh, PA, August 1994.

Hudec, J. and Suddarth, G. (1996), "Experiences in Implementing Quantitative Process Management", *Proc. 1996 National SEPG Conf.*, Atlantic City, NJ, May.

Humphrey, W. (1989), *Managing the Software Process*, Addison-Wesley, Reading, MA.

Humphrey, W. (1991), "Hardware and Software", in *Texas Instruments Technical Journal*, Vol. 8, No. 3, May-June, pp. 5–12.

Humphrey, W., Snyder, T., and Willis, R. (1991), "Software Process Improvement at Hughes Aircraft", *IEEE Software*, Vol. 8, No. 4, July, pp. 11–23.

Krasner, H. (1990), "The Payoff of Software Process Maturity", presented at the 2nd National SEPG Conference, Washington, DC, November 1990; also republished (unattributed) in (a) Pietrasanta, A. (1991), "A Strategy for Software Process Improvement", at the 9th Pacific Northwest Software Quality Conference, October 1991, and (b) McConnell, S., in *Software Development Magazine*, Vol. 1, No. 1, July, 1993, pp. 51–57.

Krasner, H. (1994), A Case History of the Space Shuttle Onboard Systems Project, SEMATECH Technology Transfer #94092551A-TR, October 31.

Krasner, H. (1994a), "Better Living Through Software Quality and Process Improvement", *Proc. Achieving Quality Software IV Conf.*, San Diego, CA, January, pp. 198–206.

Krasner, H. (1994b), "The State of the Union of Software Quality in the U.S.", keynote speech at ASQC 4th International Conference on Software Quality, Tyson's Corner, VA, October 3.

Krasner, H. (1994c), *SPI Improvement Report to SEMATECH*, KC TR-ST-94.4.

26. Krasner, H. (1995), A Case History of Software Process Improvements at the NASA Software Engineering Laboratory, SEMATECH Technology Transfer #94122662A-TR, January 31, 1995

Krasner, H., and Ziehe, T. (1995), "Lessons Learned From The Semiconductor Industry Initiative for Improving Software Process, Quality, and Reliability", *Proc. of the 1st World Congress for Software Quality*, San Francisco, CA, June.

Lane, J. and Zubrow, D. (1997), "Integrating Measurement with Improvement", *Proc. .19th ICSE*, May.

Lawlis, P., Flowe, R., and Thordahl, J. (1995), "A Correlational Study of the CMM and Software Development Performance", *Crosstalk*, Vol. 8, No. 9, September, pp. 21–25.

Lipke, W. and Butler, K. (1992), "Software Process Improvement: A Success Story", *Crosstalk*, No. 38, pp. 29–39 (published by the U.S.A.F. Software Technology Support Center, Hill AFB, UT, November 1992).

Lloyd, P. (1994), "ROI from Continuous SPI in an International Company", *Proc. 5th Int'l Conf. on Software Quality*, Austin, TX, October.

Lowe and Cox (1996), "Implementing the CMM for Software Development", *HP Journal*, August.

Major, J. (1996), "The Software Challenge: The Next Imperative", keynote speech at the National SEPG Conference, Atlantic City, NJ, May 22.

Major, J. (1994), "Driving for Software Excellence: On the Road with Motorola", keynote speech at the 6th National SEPG Conference, Dallas, TX, April.

McGarry, F. (1993), presented at the NASA SEL Workshop, NASA Goddard Space Flight Center, Greenbelt, MD, December.

McGarry, F., *et al.* (1994), *Software Process Improvement at the NASA SEL*, CMU/SEI 94-TR-22, Software Engineering Institute, Pittsburgh, PA, December.

Mobrin, J. and Wasterlid, A. (1997), "The Improvement Engine of the ESSI", presented at the 2nd European SEPG Conference, June.

NASA SEL (1976-1993), P*roc. NASA/SEL Software Engineering Workshop*, NASA GSFC, Greenbelt, MD.

Paulk, M., Weber, C., Curtis, B., and Chrissis, M. (1995), "The Capability Maturity Model: Guidelines for Improving the Software Process", SEI Series on Software Engineering, Addison Wesley, Reading, MA.

Platt, L. (1993), keynote address at the SEI Software Engineering Symposium, Pittsburgh, PA, August 24.

Rhone, K. (1990), "The IBM Space Shuttle Program", presented at the 2nd National SEPG Conference, Washington, DC, November.

Robeson, D., Davidson, S. and Bearden, L. (1997), "Evolution of a Software Engineering Factory", *Crosstalk*, September.

Schwarz, J. (1993), presentation at the 10th IEEE Conference on Software Maintenance, Montreal, Canada, September (reported by Hicks, M., and Card, D., in *IEEE Software*, Vol. 11, No. 1, January 1994, pp. 114–115).

Selfridge, W. (1994), "Process Improvement at Rockwell—Experiences, SEPG Process, PAL, Recognition of ROI", presented at the 6th National SEPG Conference, Dallas, TX, April.

Srikant Inamdar (1994), "The SEI Certification Process at Motorola India Electronics Ltd. (MIEL)", published paper in the National Seminar on Software Quality Assurance, Bangalore, India, August 4–6, Institution of Electronics and Telecommunications Engineers (IETE).

Sudlow, B. (1994), *Software Development Magazine*, December, pp. 37–40.

Volker, A. and Wackerbarth, G. (1997), "Competence in Software and Engineering", presented at 2nd European SEPG Conference, June.

Vu, J., "Software Process Improvement Journey", presented at 2nd European SEPG Conference, June.

Wohlwend, H. and Rosenbaum, S. (1993), "Software Improvements in an International Company", Proc. *15th Int'l Conf. on Software Engineering*, Washington, DC.

Yamamura, G., and Wigle, G., "SEI CMM Level 5: For the Right Reasons", *Crosstalk*, August (and related articles in September and October issues).

Chapter 12

Software Process

1. Introduction to Chapter

So far we have only considered the software process in the context of software process assessment and software process improvement. However, the software process has been extensively studied and modeled in other contexts as well. Models of the software process have been used for a wide variety of purposes, such as:

- to design software development environments;

- to study software evolution and maintenance;

- to simplify (and hence improve) the software process;

- to identify critical parts (bottlenecks) of the software process;

- to design tools to support the software process.

What constitutes a good process model depends on the purpose for which it is to be used. It is important that the model should capture most of the aspects of the process that are relevant to the purpose for which the model is being used. Process models may be relatively informal and be described in natural language such as English, possibly augmented by a few

diagrams; or may be more formal, based on petri nets or statecharts [2]. Process models may use a single representation for the process or may use orthogonal representations to represent different aspects of the process such as control flow, data flow and structure. Process models may also be fine grained or course grained.

At the ninth International Conference in Software Engineering held in 1987 (ICSE '87), Leon Osterweil's seminal paper *Software Processes are software too* [4] introduced the idea of Software Process Programming. In it, Osterweil proposed the use of programming languages to represent software process descriptions, which are static, and which he distinguished from software processes, which are dynamic. In his paper he used a Pascal-like language to show how the loops and conditional statements in the language could be readily be used to describe aspects of the software process. He also pointed out that rule-based features of programming languages had a role to play in describing software processes, and proposed research to identify the language paradigm most suited to process description. In later work Osterweil himself uses a variation of Ada to describe software processes.

Osterweil advocated process programming for the following reasons:

- it allows process re-use, since the process can be represented in an unambiguous manner;

- programming languages, unlike other representations for software processes such as Pert charts, tend to be general enough to capture *all* aspects of the software process;

- software professionals should be comfortable using process programs, which should be readily understandable to them;

- process programs may be compiled to check aspects of consistency, and executed in part by humans and in part by computers.

Osterweil saw applications of software process programming in the areas of software environments, software metrics, and software reuse.

Osterweil's enthusiasm for software process programming was not entirely shared by Manny Lehman, who responded to Osterweil's keynote address at the ninth ICSE. In his response, entitled *Process Models, Process Programs, Programming Support* [3], Lehman maintained that algorithmic descriptions were not appropriate for processes since they cannot be fully described algorithmically. He claimed that the ideas of process programming would be inclined to divert attention from the real issues concerning the software process, and could never be used to described creative activities.

According to Lehman, the types of process models which were required were those which contributed to the understanding of software development and evolution, and not those based on process programming that assumed that these matters were already understood.

And there the matter might have rested, had not both the protagonists been invited to update their views at the 19th ICSE held ten years later.

2. Description of Articles

The first paper in this chapter is an update on Leon Osterweil's ICSE 9 paper, (presented at ICSE 19) and is entitled *Software Processes are Software Too, Revisited; An Invited Talk on the Most Influential paper of ICSE 9*. In it, Osterweil attempts to clarify some of the misconceptions that arose from his original paper and summarizes the research in the area that has taken place over the previous ten years. He also suggests some future research directions.

Osterweil notes the considerable interest in process evaluation, largely based on the CMM, which has developed over the last ten years. He suggests that process evaluation based on process outputs is analogous to software testing, and suggests that CMM type process assessment models are equivalent to test plans for software. The conventional wisdom that it is better to build quality into software (and other engineering artefacts) than to test it in to them suggests that software processes should also have quality built into them.

Osterweil also points out that software processes usually have well defined requirements (business aims), and these requirement have much in common with software requirements but are rarely treated as such. For example, software processes nearly always have performance requirements such as deadlines, and robustness requirements concerned with minimizing the effect of things going wrong, such as the loss of key personnel. These types of requirements can be met by replication, redundancy and backup, as they would be for application software.

If software processes can be considered as software, Osterweil asks whether other types of processes may be thought of as software, too. If so, he claims, it suggests that the technology applied to develop application software may be used to help support the development, definition, and evolution of all kinds of processes.

Osterweil sees the continuing debate about whether software processes are software too as useful in itself, not that the matter may ever be resolved on way or the other, but that it may lead to a better understanding of the nature of software and software processes.

It was appropriate that Osterweil's paper at the nineteenth ICSE should be followed again by a contribution from Manny Lehman entitled *Process Modeling - Where Next?*, a slightly updated version of which is the second paper in this chapter. For the main part, Lehman's views on process programming have changed little (he remains sceptical) but he suggests that thinking about the software process has moved on a lot in the previous ten years, and illustrates the changes in the contexts of:

- Software process improvement;
- Feedback in the software process;
- Business process improvement.

Lehman argues that process programming has little to offer in the area of software process improvement since it is not concerned with organizational issues, which become increasingly significant as an organization moves up through the levels of the SW-CMM.

The real issue that needs to be addressed, according to Lehman, is that of feedback in the software process, and none of the current methods of process modeling address this adequately.

Lehman also sees the Software Process as merely a part of the business process, and argues that it is the total business process that needs to be modeled and improved. This is a much more general process than the software process on its own, and requires new insights and methods of modeling.

The papers of Osterweil and Lehman are not so much contradictory as complementary, and read together provide valuable insights into the ongoing issues concerning the software process.

The third paper in this chapter is by Alfonso Fugetta; and is entitled "Software Process : A Roadmap." It was originally presented at ICSE 2000 and subsequently included in a text book edited by Anthony Finkelstein, entitled *The Future of Software Engineering 2000* [1].

In the paper, the author summarizes the work performed in the software process area since it began in the 1980's. One aspect of this is the development of process assessment and improvement through models such as the SW-CMM, ISO 9001, and ISO/IEC 15504/SPICE. The author believes that software processes are less special than is often thought and that process assessment models must bear in mind that software production is a human-centered process, as are many other engineering and design processes in our society. His final conclusion is

The scope of software improvement methods and models should be widened in order to consider all the different factors affecting software development activities. We should reuse the experiences gained on other business domains and in organizational behaviour research.

References

[1] A. Finkelstein (editor), *The Future of Software Engineering*, ACM, 2000.

[2] D. Harel, H. Lachover, A. Naamad, A. Pnueli, M. Politi, R. Sherman, A. Shtull-Trauring, M. B. Trakhtenbrot; 'STATEMATE: A Working Environment for the Development of Complex Reactive Systems,' *IEEE Transactions on Software Engineering,* vol. 16, pp. 403-414, 1990.

[3]M. M. Lehman; 'Process Models, Process Programs, Programming Support,' *International Conference on Software Engineering (ICSE 9),* 1987.

[4] L. J. Osterweil; 'Software Processes are software too,' *International Conference on Software Engineering (ICSE 9),* 1987.

Software Processes Are Software Too, Revisited:
An Invited Talk on the Most Influential Paper of ICSE 9 *

Leon J. Osterweil
University of Massachusetts
Dept. of Computer Science
Amherst, MA 01003
USA
+1 413 545 2186
ljo@cs.umass.edu

ABSTRACT

The ICSE 9 paper, "Software Processes are Software Too," suggests that software processes are themselves a form of software and that there are considerable benefits that will derive from basing a discipline of software process development on the more traditional discipline of application software development. This paper attempts to clarify some misconceptions about this original ICSE 9 suggestion and summarizes some research carried out over the past ten years that seems to confirm the original suggestion. The paper then goes on to map out some future research directions that seem indicated. The paper closes with some ruminations about the significance of the controversy that has continued to surround this work.

Introduction

"Software Processes are Software Too." How many times I have heard that phrase quoted back to me in the past ten years! And how many times it has been (sometimes amusingly) misquoted too. Often I have been flattered to have had the ICSE9 paper [15] and its catchy title referred to as being "classic" and "seminal". But often I have also been asked, "what does that really mean?" The idea is, alas, still misunderstood and misconstrued in some quarters. But amazingly, and gratifyingly, the phrase is still used, and the discussion of the idea still continues, even after ten years.

The suggestion that software, and the processes that deal with it, might somehow be conceptually similar remains a powerfully appealing one that seems to have

*This work was supported in part by the Air Force Materiel Command, Rome Laboratory, and the Defense Advanced Research Projects Agency under Contract F30602-94-C-0137.

led to a considerable body of investigation. The suggestion was immediately controversial, and continues to be argued. Subsequently I discuss why I believe this discussion indicates a pattern of behavior typical of traditional scientific inquiry, and therefore seems to me to do credit to the software engineering community.

But what of the (in)famous assertion itself? What does it really mean, and is it really valid? The assertion grew out of ruminations about the importance of orderly and systematic processes as the basis for assuring the quality of products and improving productivity in developing them. Applying the discipline of orderly process to software was not original with me. Lehman [13] and others [18] had suggested this long before. But I was troubled because I had started to see the development of a whole new discipline and technology around the idea of software process, and to notice the emergence of many notions and tools that seemed eerily familiar. I was starting to see the creation of a software process universe parallel to the universe of notions and tools surrounding application software development. The more I looked, the more similarities I saw. Processes and applications are both executed, they both address requirements that need to be understood, both benefit from being modelled by a variety of sorts of models, both must evolve guided by measurement, and so forth. Thus it seemed important to suggest that software process technology might not need to be invented from scratch (or reinvented), but that much of it might be borrowed from application software technology.

I have often been reminded that application software technology is still badly underdeveloped and that using it as a model for software process technology might be of dubious value. This, however, overlooks clear evidence that, while we have not mastered application software technology, we have, nevertheless, created a powerful assortment of tools, principles, and techniques in this domain. Thus, there is much to be gained from using obvious parallels to hasten the maturation of software process technology. It seemed important to suggest that the community should look to the more traditional and better-developed disciplines of application development to see what might be borrowed or adapted. It seemed clear that there were strong similarities, but likely that there were differences as well. Investigation of the extent of each seemed to be in order. The ICSE 9 talk invited community investigation of how processes and application software are the same and how they differ, so that relevant findings, approaches, and tools of one could be of use to the other. It has been gratifying to see that this invitation has been taken up and that these explorations are still ongoing.

Conversely it has been disappointing to see the way in which the suggestion has continued to be misconstrued in some quarters. Subsequent sections will deal with these misconceptions in more detail, but the following brief summary seems in order here.

Software is not simply code. Neither are software processes. Application software generally contains code. This suggests that software processes might also contain code. Coding software processes thus seems to be an interesting possibility. Research has borne this out.

Programming is not the same as coding, it entails the many diverse steps of software development. Software process programming should, likewise, not simply be coding, but seemed to entail the many non-coding steps usually associated with application development. Process modelling, testing, and evolution research seems to have borne that out.

There are many examples of application code that are not inordinately prescriptive, authoritarian, or intolerable to humans (eg. operating systems). Thus, there should be no presumption that process code must be overly prescriptive, authoritarian, or intolerable either. Process programs need not treat humans like robots—unless that is the intention of the process programmer. Process modelling and coding languages demonstrate this.

Finally, good software code is written at all levels of detail. Code contains fine scale details, but they emerge at lower levels, after high level code addresses larger issues. Similarly process code contains details that are nested below higher abstract levels. Process code, like application code, can demonstrate that precise implementation of broader notions in terms of lower level engineering details. Contemporary process coding languages demonstrate this too.

The following section summarizes some research that suggests continued and broadened research into these issues.

Parallels Between Software Processes and Application Software

Much work seems to demonstrate the existence of significant parallels between software processes and application software, although not all of this work was intended to do so. This section briefly surveys what has been learned.

Process Modelling

There has been a great deal of study of how well various application software modelling formalisms model software processes. For example, Petri Nets [1], [5], Finite State Machines [6], [11], and data flow diagrams [19] have been used to model software processes. These activities have clearly demonstrated that application software modelling approaches can be strong aids in conceptualizing processes, in helping people to communicate about processes and collaborate in their execution, and in raising intuition about processes.

As with application software modelling, different types of process models are good for different things. Petri Net models, for example, are quite useful in elucidating parallelism and concurrency, but are less useful in modelling artifacts. Petri Nets process models seem to have very similar properties. They help to identify parallelism in processes, but have generally required augmentation in order to effectively elucidate the flow of software artifacts through processes. Other similar examples could readily be pointed out.

In general, models, by their nature, abstract away details in order to focus on specific narrow issues, which are thereby made correspondingly clearer and more vivid. Thus, Petri Net models depict parallelism clearly in part because depictions of other less relevant details are specifically omitted. Thus, any particular model should be expected to be useful in some contexts, but less helpful in others. To support understanding of various aspects of a software product different models are generally needed. Thus, a number of modelling systems (eg. [6]) support the development and coordination of multiple models of application software. Experience in the software process domain has been similar. Statemate was used as a process modelling tool [11], and its support for multiple models was useful precisely because the different models supported understanding and reasoning from a variety of aspects. In the application software domain there is a growing understanding of which modelling tools and formalisms best elucidating which issues. We expect similar understandings to emerge in the software process domain.

But, as with application software modelling, it has also become clear in process modelling that there are reasons why models, even multiple models, are sometimes inadequate. The very lack of certain types of details in models means that models inevitably lack specifics that can be very important. In addition, many modelling formalisms (eg. graphical models) are based upon weak and shallow semantics. Because of this it is usually impossible or unsafe to reason about such models. Models expressed in a formalism with a weak semantic base may convey an intuitive impression, but they usually cannot support precise, reliable reasoning. For example, many modeling notations (especially graphical notations) can indicate parallel activities, but offer no semantics for defining the precise nature of the parallelism. This lack of semantics leaves human interpreters free to suppose whatever form of parallelism they like. Inevitably this leads different interpreters to different conclusions about what the model represents. The result is often miscommunication and misunderstanding. Where the intent of the model was presumably clarity, the effect will have been quite the opposite. Even where the semantics of such constructs as parallelism are incorporated in the modelling formalism, it is unusual for there to be much variety in the sorts of parallelism. This semantic sparseness usually causes such formalisms to be inadequate to depict the full range of parallel constructs needed to represent the full range of parallelism that process modelling seems to require. Thus, there seems to be a growing understanding that models of processes meet some needs (eg. raising one's intuition about processes), but that there are more needs that are unlikely to be met by single process models, or even combinations of process models.

Process Coding

While there is good evidence that processes need to be represented by executable code, as well as by models, as in the case of application code, it is difficult to draw a sharp distinction between coding languages and modelling languages. Certain coding languages are imprecise about the execution semantics of certain constructs, and certain modelling languages have very precise execution semantics. There are often disputes about whether particular application languages should be considered to be coding or modelling languages. The process community has experienced similar disputes and disagreements about process languages during the past years.

Such disputes are unproductive. The important distinctions among these languages are the nature, depth, and scope of the semantic details that they provide. As noted in the previous sections, modelling formalisms tend to offer relatively weak, shallow, or narrow semantics. Thus, while a strong modelling formalism may support deep and reliable reasoning about a narrow aspect of the software it models, such formalisms are at best helpful only in narrow contexts. When broad categories of powerful precise, reliable reasoning is required

stronger, broader semantics and greater detail are essential. In reasoning, for example, about the presence or absence of deadlocks and race conditions in processes it is essential for the process to be defined in a formalism that supports precise definition of parallelism and shared access to data and resources. The semantics needed to support such reasoning must be quite precise and powerful, and are generally consistent with semantics found in full coding languages, rather than in modelling languages. Processes, like applications, at times benefit from the existence of codelike representations that offer a wide range of semantic power and definition detail. At some times the detail will be undesirable, interfering with clarity and intuition. But at other times it will be essential as the basis for effective reasoning and actual execution.

There are other reasons why it is important to reduce software to code. Application developers know that, until software has been coded, it is unknown whether the possibly myriad models that have preceded it can actually be reduced to practice. Similarly a set of software process models may depict an enticing view, but can still leave open to question just how a process consistent with all of those views will actually work. It is the interplay of all of the details, both present and absent, from all of the models that characterizes and defines the actual application or process. Only a language that can specify and interrelate all of these details can support definitive demonstrations of the realizability of the desired product. In short, real code provides real assurances; models mostly provide enticements.

The original ICSE 9 paper emphasized yet another reason for defining processes in coding languages. That paper suggested that processes should be viewed as prescriptions for the synergistic coordination of the efforts of humans, computers, and software tools. Process code was suggested as the vehicle for specifying the precise details of this coordination. Because coding languages have executable semantics, the paper suggested that computers could execute such code and could, in doing so, supervise the integration of the efforts of people, machines and tools.

This point has been the subject of much unfortunate misinterpretation and caricature. Careless reading of this point has taken it to suggest that all processes could, or should, be reduced to computer executable instructions. This was neither the intent nor the proposal of the original paper. Indeed, the paper stated that software development processes should refrain from elaborating the details of how humans should carry out their tasks. Human tasks should be represented as functions or procedures for which the definition is omitted, thereby leaving the human free to execute the task as he or she sees fit. The level to which any human task is elaborated by the process code is the choice of the process coder, who, in doing so, specifies the extent to which the process is authoritarian and prescriptive, or permissive and relaxed.

The vehicle of process code is thus not a device for dictating what a human must do, but rather a vehicle for specifying the degree to which human activities are to be circumscribed by the defined process. The act of defining the process by executable code does not necessarily unduly restrict the human, although the nature of the code may do so. Indeed, the JIL [23] language, is an example of a process coding language that supports considerable latitude in the degree of specificity of process definition.

Here too, experience suggests that a wide range of process coding languages and coding styles seem to be of value. Less detailed process code is preferable, for example when the process is to be performed by seasoned experts who can exercise good judgement in devising sequences of process steps to carry out a task. More detailed and precise process code is of value in other circumstances, for example in restricting and regulating the work of software developers who are novices, or whose actions may eventually be subject to careful scrutiny (as, for example in the case where an organization wishes to provide protection against possible subsequent legal claims of carelessness in software development).

As suggested above, detailed process code specifications are also of particular importance in specifying how tools and automated procedures are to be integrated into processes, and how the activities of humans are to be coordinated with them. This requires precise specifications of how various software artifacts are to be fed into tools and extracted from their outputs, precise specification of how such artifacts are to be made available to the right humans at the right time, and how human development artifacts are to be channeled to the right colleagues and tools. All of this requires a great deal of precise specification that is consistent with the levels of detail and precision found in the executable semantics of coding languages.

Experimental research of the past few years seems to confirm that coding languages are particularly adept at expressing the specifics of the interactions of process steps and software artifact operands, while modelling languages tend to be particularly ineffective at this. Modelling languages tend to focus on either activity or artifact modelling, thereby failing to support the choreography of artifacts through tools and humans. Coding languages tend to be superior in this regard.

Thus there seems to be considerable evidence that software processes require and benefit from both modelling

and coding for very much the same reasons that software applications benefit from both of these activities.

Process Evaluation

There is also considerable evidence that software processes are amenable to evaluation using approaches that bear important similarities to the approaches used in evaluating application software. Indeed, the past ten years have witnessed explosive growth in work on the evaluation of software processes. Most of this work has grown out of the proposal of Humphrey and his colleagues at the Software Engineering Institute, of the Capability Maturity Model (CMM) [7] [16]. The aim of the CMM is to provide an evaluation vehicle for determining the quality of an organization's software development processes. Organizational software process evaluation is done by a variety of means, but is usually based upon questionnaire-based surveying, and by examination of the artifacts produced by past software development projects.

Although the CMM does not take the explicit position of viewing software processes as software, it seems useful for us to do so. Taking the position that an organization has a process that it executes in order to develop its products leads to the conclusion that such products are reasonably viewed as the outputs of the execution of that process. If the quality of the process is evaluated through examination of such outputs, then doing so is essentially a testing activity. This leads us to conclude that the CMM establishes the structure for a process testing regimen, and that such instruments as the CMM-based questionnaires function as process test plans.

These observations demonstrate that testing and evaluation of software processes has been a prevalent activity over the past several years, even despite the fact that explicit process representations may not have been available. The lack of explicit process definitions forces the process evaluator to examine output artifacts, and to take a testing-like approach to process evaluation. From our perspective of viewing processes as software, we suggest that this is analogous to testing quality into the software process. Experience in such fields as manufacturing suggests that it is preferable to build quality in, rather than test it in. Building quality into processes seems to require the explicit representation and definition of the processes. We view this as yet another key reason why processes should be precisely defined using formalisms with strong semantics.

Indeed, going one step further, we observe that carrying out a CMM-based evaluation or assessment is in fact the execution of a process-testing process. As such, this sort of process too should be amenable to specification by process formalisms. Such formally specified process-testing processes are examples of higher-order processes that should be developed for the evaluation of processes and the feeding back of such evaluations as part of larger process improvement processes. Formal specifications of such higher-order processes should facilitate more precise and sure reasoning about these key processes. These ideas are developed more fully in [14].

Process Requirements

The observed parallels between modelling, coding, and evaluating application software and software processes might suggest that similar parallels have been demonstrated between application requirements specification and process requirements specifications. It is startling to note that such parallels have not been demonstrated yet due to an apparent lack of interest in studying software process requirements.

Especially in view of the intense interest in supporting the modelling, coding, and evaluation of processes, it seems almost bizarre that there has been virtually no work in supporting the specification of process requirements. Indeed early suggestions that more attention be focussed on process requirements sometimes brought disbelief in the very existence of process requirements. The enterprise of process modelling should instantly raise in trained software engineers important questions about the validation of such models. That, in turn should suggest that the models are there in large measure to demonstrate that a particular process approach is effective in addressing certain process problems, as enunciated in a set of requirements.

Software processes generally have clear (albeit unstated) performance requirements, (eg. deadlines for completion of the entire process or various of its steps). Further, these requirements function very much in the way that application software requirements do, often influencing important choices about what steps to parallelize, in which way, and to what degree. Similarly processes often have robustness requirements, specifying how processes must react to such adverse situations as the loss of key personnel or artifacts. Replication, redundancy, and backups are the standard application software approaches to addressing these requirements, and they are also process architecture approaches to similar process requirements. Processes also have functional requirements, for example specifications of the range of software artifacts to be produced as the final output of the process, and the nature of the required demonstrations of internal consistency.

Despite these rather obvious types of process requirements, and the fact that they should function as essential baselines against which to measure both process models and process test plans, there has been virtually no interest in developing and using process requirement

formalisms. Thus, although the parallelism between application software requirements and software process requirements seems apparent, there has been scant research to demonstrate it. This seems to be an area that is very much in need of considerably more investigation.

Looking Ahead

It seems increasingly clear that the weight of evidence is supporting the hypothesis that software processes are indeed very much like application software in many important ways. That being the case, we should expect to be able to exploit the similarities in a number of ways. The previous section has suggested some of these ways. In this section we suggest some others.

Programming Key Processes

It seems clear that it is time to get on with the important work of developing models and code of key software development processes. There are important benefits to be gained from this. Software engineering (indeed any sort of engineering) has as two of its key objectives the reduction of costs and the improvement of the quality of products. Processes play a key role in both of these. As software costs derive almost exclusively from the cost of human labor, cost reduction must come from reduction in labor. Explicit software process representations can be analyzed to identify needless and unproductive human labor, and to identify process steps that might be performed by automated devices. Both then lead to reductions in labor costs. Further, as noted above, quality is generally understood to be built into products through periodic careful testing and analysis of the product as it evolves through the development process. Here too, explicit process representations should be effective bases for identifying where and how to carry out these periodic tests and analyses.

Thus, the development, demonstration, and reuse of demonstrably superior software processes still remains the goal that it was as enunciated in the original ICSE 9 paper. However, now, ten years later, we should have greater assurance that this goal is achievable, and a weight of experimentation suggesting how to proceed. We have demonstrated a variety of modelling formalisms (largely borrowed from application software technology). We have also begun to understand the demanding requirements of process coding languages. But, here application software coding languages have proven less useful. Experimentation has demonstrated the value of various programming paradigms, such as the procedural programming paradigm (eg. with the APPL/A language [22]), the rule based programming paradigm (eg. with MSL, the Marvel Specification Language [8]), and real-time programming approaches (eg. with Adele [2]). But this experimentation has also shown the inadequacy of each of these by itself. Experience has shown that representing in a clear and straightforward way all of the details and complexities of software processes by means of a language with executable semantics is far more difficult and challenging than was expected ten years ago. Second generation languages such as JIL [23], which enable the blending of the benefits of various programming language paradigms, seem to hold promise. More experimentation and evaluation of such languages is clearly indicated.

In order for the cost and quality improvements mentioned above to be realized, execution engines for such languages will have to be developed. Recent research is leading to understandings that such engines must have highly flexible distributed architectures. The Amber project [9], and the Endeavors project [3] offer good examples of such architectures. These projects should provide encouragement to believe that the superior process code to be written in the new generation of process coding languages will be effectively executable to provide the sort of strong support needed to reduce costs and improve quality in developed software.

Once these languages and execution engines are in place the development of exemplary software processes should begin. Some examples of processes that should greatly benefit from such encodings are: processes for collaborative design, processes for integrated testing and analysis, processes for configuration management, processes for tracking bug fixing, and processes for effecting successful reuse. Indeed, the last ten years has seen a growing awareness of the broad range of processes that are executed in the course of developing software. As these processes have been more clearly identified, they have become increasingly important targets for understanding and improvement. Detailed encodings should support reliable analyses and detailed dynamic monitoring of these processes that should then lead to the kinds of deep understandings that are needed in order to effect improvements reliably.

Creating a practice of software process engineering that will lead to reliable techniques for systematic improvements to processes through engineering of process program artifacts is clearly some distance off. But the progress of the past ten years seems to indicate that it is still a worthy goal, and to justify greater belief in assertions that it is definitely achievable than could have been justified ten years ago.

Scientific Classification and Comparison of Software Processes

While most of the process technology research of the past ten years has focussed on supporting the synthesis of new processes, there has also been an important demonstration of the use of process technology to support the analysis of existing processes. As noted above, there has been a growing recognition of the number and diversity of processes in use to support software development. Thus, designing, debugging, requirements specification, and configuration management have come to be recognized as key software development processes. In some of these areas, for example software design, there has been a long history of suggested approaches to performing the process. These suggestions have all too often taken the form of imprecise and/or incomplete prose articles, courses, and books, often consisting largely of examples. Attempts to compare and contrast these suggested software design approaches have been reduced to similarly informal, often anecdotal, treatments of the various approaches. The lack of definitive, precise characterizations and comparisons of these design approaches frustrates practitioners who must choose from among them, and impedes progress towards the establishment of a scientific discipline of software engineering.

Regarding software design as a process that can be expressed in precise modelling and coding formalisms seems to help considerably. This perspective suggests that the writings about various software design approaches might be considered to be specifications of requirements and/or architectures of contrasting software design processes. It further suggests that detailed models and encodings of these processes, using formalisms that are based on precise and deep semantics, can be bases for correspondingly precise characterizations, classifications, and comparisons.

A series of papers published over the past five years demonstrates the viability of this approach [20, 21, 17]. In these papers popular software design methods (SDM's) are modelled using popular software process modelling formalisms (eg. HFSP [10] and Slang [1]). Comparison frameworks are hypothesized to guide classification of SDM features. A carefully defined SDM comparison process is executed to extract comparison results from the classifications of the models of the SDM's. The papers demonstrate that this approach can be used to produce classification and comparison results that agree with and extend classifications and comparisons arrived at based on informal models and comparison techniques. The precision and specificity of both the models and the comparison process itself (it is a process programmed in process modelling and coding languages) suggest that these classification and comparison results are reproducible by different human comparators.

Work in this area is just now beginning to proliferate, and it seems that this kind of work could be most critical to fostering the maturation of software engineering. If software engineering is to mature into an orderly discipline it seems that it must develop a core set of well-understood, well-supported standard processes, and a cadre of practitioners who understand what the processes are and how to use them. Certainly the older, better established engineering disciplines, such as Chemical Engineering and Industrial Engineering, exemplify this sort of use of process. In order for such a core set of standard processes to emerge there must be a considerable amount of differentiation and sorting out of the processes that are currently in existence, and an orderly way of dealing with the steady flow of new process proposals, especially in such active areas as software design.

The work just described seems particularly promising because it suggests that structures and processes can be put in place that will serve to support standardized comparisons and evaluations of the processes that must form the core of disciplined software engineering practice. It is unfortunate that debates about the relative merits of different approaches to such key activities as software design are currently argued in the advertising pages of *IEEE Software*, rather than in the scholarly works of *IEEE Transactions on Software Engineering* or *ACM Transactions on Software Engineering Methods*. If our discipline is to mature satisfactorily that must change. The frameworks and processes suggested in the papers referred to above are suggested initial starting points, and it can only be hoped that the community will take them as such and work collaboratively to develop them into agreed upon standards. With such standards in place it should then be possible for objective evaluators to produce specifications and descriptions that characterize clearly and understandably the merits of competing methods. Such evaluations should also then be usable in estimating the costs and results of applying these methods.

This suggests a line of experimental research that focuses on performing software engineering process classifications and comparisons, but with an eye towards evaluating the standard classification frameworks, the standard process modelling formalisms, and the standard comparison process. Evolution of all of the above is to be an expected outcome of this experimentation. A steadily growing and improving stream of classifications, characterizations, and comparisons should also result. This line of research seems to be converging interestingly with research being done by the Method Engineering community (see, eg. [4]).

Beyond Software Engineering
In examining the hypothesis that software processes are software, there seems to be nothing particularly special about *software* processes. This suggests a hypothesis that processes in general are also software. Confirmation of that hypothesis would be of particular interest as it would suggest that application software technology can also help support the development and evolution of all kinds of processes. In particular it suggests that software engineers might have something of par-

ticular value to offer those who engineer manufacturing systems, management systems, classical engineering systems, and so forth. A variety of private conversations and preliminary investigations seem to confirm that these systems often have (or should have) architectures, that they are intended to satisfy understood requirements, and that their implementations are generally on virtual machines consisting of people, devices, and computers. In addition, these systems are usually continuously being evaluated and evolved. All of this suggests that they are software in the same sense in which we believe that software processes are software. That being the case, it suggests that software process researchers ought to widen their sights and study the applicability of the emerging software process technology to manufacturing, management, and allied disciplines.

Conclusions
The foregoing sections of this paper have been intended to suggest that there are numerous technological benefits from considering software processes to be software, and that examining them should lead to a considerable amount of worthwhile research. But there is yet another aspect of this work that seems worth remarking upon, and that is its contribution to the scientific underpinnings of software engineering. It was clear from the moment I concluded the original talk at ICSE 9 that the suggestion that software processes might be software had initiated a type of discussion that was different from other discussions following other papers that I had given. The substance of the discussions and debates that have followed has rarely been at the level of technical details, but rather at more philosophical levels. There were debates about whether it was seemly or possible to use the rigorous semantics of programming languages to describe what people did or should do. There were debates about whether processes were a subtype of application software, or vice versa. There were debates about whether processes have a different character than applications.

The distinguishing characteristic of most of these debates has been the fact that there did not, and still does not, seem to be much possibility that these debates and questions can be resolved definitively. One reason is that there is no agreed upon definition of what software is. Likewise there is no firm agreement on what programming is, or what a process is for that matter. Thus, the debates and discussions that have swirled around the original suggestion have been largely philosophical, and the opinions expressed have been based largely upon personal aesthetics. The suggestion that software and processes are made out of basically the same stuff sets well with some people, and not so well with others. The suggestion implies that what we know and can learn about one transfers to some extent over to the other. This suggestion has obvious importance for the technologies in these two areas, but this has been met with skepticism and reticence in some quarters.

Skepticism, reserve, and the impossibility of definitive adjudication of these questions, however, should not be allowed to obscure what seems to be the most significant implication of the suggestion, namely its potential to shed some light on the nature of software itself. If it is shown that software is highly akin to something else about which we can have a variety of new and different insights, then those insights illuminate the nature of software. Thus, in the debates about the relationship between process and software I see the reflections of a broader debate about the nature of software. In that software engineering purports to be a discipline devoted to the effective development of software, it seems essential that we as a community have a shared view of what software is. Debates such as these, that help lead to that shared view, are critically important.

In his renowned book, *The Structure of Scientific Revolutions* [12], the historian of science, Thomas S. Kuhn, suggests that progress in a scientific discipline is discontinuous, progressing incrementally within the bounds circumscribed by the current paradigms, but then lurching forward occasionally when a new paradigm is agreed to account better than the old paradigm for natural phenomena or to provide more assistance in solving practical engineering problems. Kuhn argues that the old and new paradigms are generally mutually incompatible and that, therefore, it is impossible to use either to prove the falsity of the other. Thus shifts from an older paradigm to a newer paradigm generally take place over a period of time during which there is considerable intellectual ferment and philosophical dispute. If the new paradigm is to supplant the older paradigm it will happen only after careful research has demonstrated that the new paradigm is more robust and successful than the old paradigm. After the shift has occurred, the shape of the science, its view of its problems, and the manner of its approaches and explanations will have been substantively changed. Most practitioners will accept the paradigm shift, but adherents to the old paradigm may persist.

It seems just possible that what we have been witnessing is a slow paradigm shift to a view of software and software development that is rooted in the centrality of the notion of process as a first-class entity whose properties are very much like those of software itself. The nature of the debates that we have been witnessing are consistent with what would be expected if this were the case, being essentially discussions that are based more on aesthetics than upon the ability to perform definitive demonstrations. As the accretion of evidence of the power of a process-centered view of software grows it

seems conceivable that we are seeing the establishment of a new paradigm. The preceding discussions in this paper do seem to suggest that grasping the importance of process, and exploiting its relation to software, does help deal more effectively with important technological and conceptual issues. Pursuing the research agenda outlined in the previous section should go a long way towards confirming this suggestion or to demonstrating its inadequacy. In either case it seems most encouraging to observe that the intense debates and discussions of the premise that "software processes are software too," seems to be quite consistent with the behavior of a responsible community of scientists doing real science. Ultimately this affirmation of our growing maturity as a scientific community may be the most important outcome of the proposal and ensuing discussions.

Acknowledgments

My ideas and work on software processes has been greatly helped and influenced by many people, indeed too many to mention here. The earliest impetus for the ideas of process programming arose out of meetings and conversations with Watts Humphrey and his team at IBM in the early 1980's. The specific proposal of the notion of process programming was honed and sharpened through many conversations with Manny Lehman at Imperial College and John Buxton at Kings College, London in 1985 and 1986. Confidence in the idea was built through intense conversations with many people, but most notably with Dennis Heimbigner. Over the past ten years I have been fortunate to have been able to collaborate with Stan Sutton and Dennis Heimbigner on process programming language design and implementation and Xiping Song on software method comparison formalization. Numerous conversations with Dick Taylor, Bob Balzer, Gail Kaiser, Alex Wolf, Dewayne Perry, Mark Dowson, Barry Boehm, Wilhelm Schafer, Carlo Ghezzi, and Alfonso Fuggetta have also shaped this work in important ways. I would also like to thank the (Defense) Advanced Research Projects Agency for its support of this work, and particularly Bill Scherlis, Steve Squires, and John Salasin for their support, even while these ideas were formative and while they continue to be controversial.

REFERENCES

[1] S. Bandinelli, A. Fuggetta, and S. Grigolli. Process modeling in-the-large with SLANG. In *Proc. of the Second International Conference on the Software Process*, pages 75 – 83, 1993.

[2] N. Belkhatir, J. Estublier, and Walcelio L. Melo. Adele 2: A support to large software development process. In *Proc. of the First International Conference on the Software Process*, pages 159 – 170, 1991.

[3] G. A. Bolcer and R. N. Taylor. Endeavors: A process system integration infrastructure. In *Proc. of the Fourth International Conference on the Software Process*, pages 76 – 85, Dec. 1996.

[4] S. Brinkkemper, K. Lyytinen, and R. J. Welke. *Method Engineering*. Chapman & Hall, New York, 1996.

[5] V. Gruhn and R. Jegelka. An evaluation of FUN-SOFT nets. In *Proc. of the Second Eurpoean Workshop on Software Process Technology*, Sept. 1992.

[6] D. Harel, H. Lachover, A. Naamad, A. Pnueli, M. Politi, R. Sherman, A. Shtull-Trauring, and M. Trakhtenbrot. STATEMATE: A working environment for the development of complex reactive systems. *IEEE Trans. on Software Engineering*, 16(4):403 – 414, Apr. 1990.

[7] W. S. Humphrey. *Managing the Software Process*. Reading, MA:Addison-Wesley, 1989.

[8] G. E. Kaiser, N. S. Barghouti, and M. H. Sokolsky. Experience with process modeling in the MARVEL software development environment kernel. In B. Shriver, editor, *23rd Annual Hawaii International Conference on System Sciences*, volume II, pages 131 – 140, Kona HI, Jan. 1990.

[9] G. E. Kaiser, I. Z. Ben-Shaul, S. S. Popovich, and S. E. Dossick. A metalinguistic approach to process enactment extensibility. In 4TH INTERNATIONAL CONFERENCE ON THE SOFTWARE PROCESS *(to appear)*, Dec. 1996.

[10] T. Katayama. A hierarchical and functional software process description and its enaction. In *Proc. of the 11th International Conference on Software Engineering*, pages 343 – 353, 1989.

[11] M. I. Kellner. Software process modeling support for management planning and control. In *Proc. of the First International Conference on the Software Process*, pages 8 – 28, 1991.

[12] T. S. Kuhn. *The Structure of Scientific Revolutions*. University of Chicago Press [Chicago], 1962.

[13] M. M. Lehman. The Programming Process. In *IBM Res. Rep. RC 2722*, IBM Res. Center, Yorktown Heights, NY 10594, Sept. 1969.

[14] Leon J. Osterweil. Improving the quality of software quality determination processes. In R. Boisvert, editor, *The Quality of Numerical Software: Assessment and Enhancement*. Chapman & Hall, London, 1997.

[15] L. J. Osterweil. Software Processes are Software Too. In *Proceedings of the Ninth International Conference of Software Engineering*, pages 2–13, Monterey CA, March 1987.

[16] M. C. Paulk, B. Curtis, and M. B. Chrisis. Capability maturity model for software, version 1.1. Technical Report CMU/SEI-93-TR, Carnegie Mellon University, Software Engineering Institute, Feb. 1993.

[17] R. M. Podorozhny and L. J. Osterweil. The Criticality of Modeling Formalisms in Software Design Method Comparison,. Technical Report TR–96–049, University of Massachusetts, Computer Science Department, Amherst, MA, Aug. 1996.

[18] Potts C. (ed). Proc. of the softw. process worksh. In *IEEE cat. n. 84CH2044-6, Comp. Soc.*, Washington D. C., Feb. 1984. order n. 587, 27 – 35.

[19] Richard J. Mayer et al. IDEF family of methods for concurrent engineering and business re-engineering applications. Technical report, Knowledge Based Systems, Inc., 1992.

[20] X. Song and L. Osterweil. Toward Objective, Systematic Design-Method Comparisons. *IEEE Software*, pages 43 – 53, May 1992.

[21] X. Song and L. J. Osterweil. Experience with an approach to comparing software design methodologies. *IEEE Trans. on Software Engineering*, 20(5):364 – 384, May 1994.

[22] S. M. Sutton, Jr., D. Heimbigner, and L. J. Osterweil. APPL/A: A language for software-process programming. *ACM Trans. on Software Engineering and Methodology*, 4(3):221 – 286, July 1995.

[23] S. M. Sutton, Jr. and L. J. Osterweil. The design of a next-generation process language. Technical Report CMPSCI Technical Report 96–30, University of Massachusetts at Amherst, Computer Science Department, Amherst, Massachusetts 01003, May 1996. Revised January, 1997.

Process Modelling - Where Next

M M Lehman
Department of Computing
Imperial College of Science. Technology and Medicine
180 Queen's Gate, London SW7 2BZ, UK
+44 (0171) 594 8214
mml @doc.ic.ac.uk

ABSTRACT
After limited interest prior to the 1980s, the software process attracted the attention of a small group of researchers and practitioners as evidenced by a series of International Process Workshops commencing with the first in 1984. General interest had, however, to wait until Osterweil's now classic paper being honoured today and the present author's response were delivered at ICSE 87. This brief paper seeks to move forward from the positions presented then to introduce three process related issues, software process improvement, feedback in the software process and business process improvement. The first is, currently the principal focus of the software process community. The second, it is believed, should be. The third is equally relevant. Individually and collectively these issues appear, to this author at least, to make the majority view of the current focus of process modelling in general and process programming in particular largely irrelevant.

Keywords
Process: modelling, process programming, process improvement, feedback, feedback systems system dynamics

PROCESS MODELLING AND PROGRAMMING
The ICSE 97 program committee will not have found it difficult to select Lee Osterweil's classic paper *Software Processes are Software Too* [1] as the most influential paper of ICSE 87. As evidenced by a number of earlier publications [2, 3, 4, 5] and the first three of the now regular International Process Workshops [6, 7, 8] this paper did not pioneer the concept of process studies and process modelling. But, as predicted, his fresh approach and the underlying philosophy captured and retained the imagination and fascination of individual and groups of researchers in unparalleled fashion. Whether the resulting R & D effort produced major new insight, understanding, and progress in planning, designing, controlling and improving the process is a matter for debate. But this in no way detracts from the originality of Osterweil's thinking or the influence, for better or worse, that his paper has had on the directions that software engineering research has taken in the last decade.

As is well known, I was a doubter from the start. I must express my special appreciation to the program committee of ICSE 97 for, nevertheless, associating me with this award.

In the short time available to me today I am not able to reopen the earlier debate. That is recorded in the ICSE 87 proceedings [1, 9] and there is little in what I said then that I would wish to change; though something could be added. I restrict myself to a brief outline of three developments that have surfaced in recent years. Individually and collectively they imply a change of direction for software process modelling and relegate the original concept of process programming to an interesting technique with conceptual implications but one that cannot be expected to have major impact on future development.

SOFTWARE PROCESS IMPROVEMENT
Following on the pioneering work of the SEI [10], model based software process improvement has become a major research and applied software engineering activity in both academia and industry. In the application of process modelling to process improvement, as with the SEI CMM models for example, a wide range of activities at many levels are considered. Process programming based modelling, on the other hand, focuses, primarily, on technical development, definition, control, direction and sequencing of activities. It concentrates on individual and small group activity where individual actions can be well specified, rather than on organisational activity. As discussed below, this aspect of process plays only a limited role in process improvement, except at low levels of process achievement. In primitive processes the introduction of a new method or tool has more than a local impact; the introduction of a method or tool, for example, can yield visible improvement in some aspect of the overall process. Once these have been introduced at these levels and a degree of maturity achieved, further improvement requires attention to a whole gamut of issues, managerial, organisational and high level technical (eg the addition of additional process steps, the use of metrics). Improvement of individual steps, better development methods, improved support tools, whatever their local effect, have little impact at the global level [11].

One is forced to conclude that once one has advanced beyond primitive processes, CMM levels one and two for example, the principal current procedural process modelling approaches have little, if anything, to contribute to the search for process improvement. What is required in any particular context is high level understanding and representation of the needs of the business and of relevant organisational processes in that context. One must achieve thorough insight into the manner in which these act and interact. One must learn how to design, control and modify individual and joint action to produce the desired global output and impact. One must assess the effectiveness of the process as experienced and evaluated by the world outside the development, marketing and support organisations.

Detailed design of constituent steps in general, and technical steps in particular, is not the most critical issue in seeking to achieve the desired overall processes or their improvement. Local fine tuning cannot be expected to make a major contribution to global effectiveness. It is a well known property of complex systems that local optimisation usually causes global sub-optimisation. And even without this effect the impact is small. After all, a fifty per cent efficiency improvement in an activity that represents, say, five per cent of the activity or resource required to produce the product from start to finish, makes at best a two and a half percent impact, often very much less. The essential lesson to be derived from current improvement approaches is that one must develop a global view and comprehensive insight as to how, through their processes, organisations achieve and maintain quality products. This goal demands models of the processes and techniques to achieve and exploit them that are quite different to the majority of those current in the process modelling community at large.

FEEDBACK IN THE SOFTWARE PROCESS

A second major development that signals a change in direction for process modelling arises from the realisation that the software process is a complex, multi-loop, multi-level feedback system [11]. This was first recognised following a 1969 study of the IBM programming process [3, 12] which led eventually to a study of the evolution of OS/360 and to the conclusion that the system's growth was regulated by a self stabilising feedback process [13]. From this it followed that understanding and improving the process required it to be treated as a feedback system [14]. Moreover, in these systems, intrinsically, humans play a major controlling role. This greatly complicates disciplined analysis of such systems.

Some years ago, in asking why the global industrial process still leaves so much to be desired despite the many advances in software technology, these observations were recalled. Now, an intrinsic property of systems that include negative feedback loops and mechanisms, however controlled, is that the impact of changes to individual forward path mechanisms outside the loop is attenuated in proportion to the amplification in the loop. This phenomenon is not simple to interpret in the software process context. Nevertheless, it may explain why global characteristics of software development processes are not responsive to changes in individual forward path steps or to the introduction of new ones except in primitive processes where negative feedback control is weak or absent. Where negative feedback is present it is likely to constrain forward path improvements such as the use of high level languages, structured programming, new development paradigms,

formal methods, disciplined requirements analysis and specification, CASE support and so on to explain why all these are limited in their global impact. It leads to the paradoxical situation that the more advanced a process, the more technical, management, organisational and user derived feedback control is applied the less benefit will accrue from local *technological* change *unless feedback controls are adapted to the circumstance created by such change*. Processes not employing feedback control can yield significant improvement as a consequence of technological advances alone. Mature processes are likely to respond to localised improvements only if feedback mechanisms are also adjusted. Adjusting only the latter may, in fact, itself yield significant improvement to global process characteristics.

This observation and its implications were expressed in a hypothesis, the FEAST hypothesis, as follows, [11, 15]: *As complex feedback systems, E-type [13, 16] software processes evolve strong system dynamics and with it the global stability characteristics of other feedback systems. Consequent stabilisation effects are likely to constrain efforts at process improvement.* It was restated in a project proposal [17] as:- *As for other complex feedback systems, the dynamics of real world software development and evolution processes will possess a degree of autonomy and exhibit a degree of global stability.* The resultant FEAST/1 project in the Department of Computing at Imperial College is now investigating this hypothesis.

This short presentation is not the place for a detailed review of the project or to present our results to date. It is, however, appropriate to remark that early results [18, 19] are encouraging. So far the analysis has concentrated on the evolution of the Logica plc FW financial transaction system now in its tenth release. The data indicates that the evolution of this system has characteristics similar to those of OS/360 [16]. The growth trend ripple as in figure 1, for example, is reminiscent of that of OS/360 as in figure 2. It was, of course, this ripple that first suggested the presence of feedback control. Moreover, the laws of software evolution as previously stated [14, 16, 20, 21] are upheld [22], or rather, not negated, by the data. There is also strong evidence [18], that a controlling internal dynamics develops over the early releases, as in figure 3. The "E" parameter of that figure is the constant of Turski's inverse square growth model [18]. The plot shows that data from the first six releases suffice to determine the value of E. Thereafter, the internal dynamics dominates further growth and the model provides a growth trend predictor accurate to better than 5%. This is a remarkable result [18] that greatly increases confidence in the validity of the FEAST hypothesis.

That all but the most primitive *E*-type software processes constitute a feedback system is indisputable. This, by itself implies that they cannot be satisfactorily modelled using the techniques widely in vogue in the process modelling community. The R&D challenge is, therefore, to discover and develop more appropriate techniques. As a first step, the FEAST/1 project, which involves also four major industrial collaborators, is using black box analysis of real industrial processes. Figures 1 and 3 represent early results

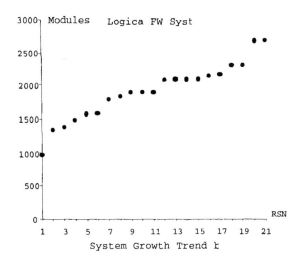

Fig. 1. 1990s System - Logica FW

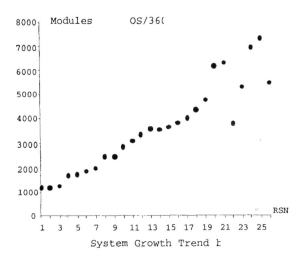

Fig. 2. 1970s System - OS/360

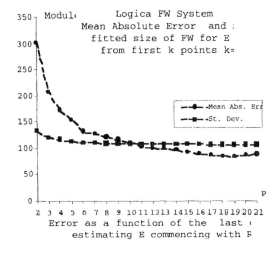

Fig. 3. - Development of the Logica FW System Dynamics

from that analysis whose aim is to demonstrate feed-back-like behaviour and the presence of system dynamics effects. White box studies based on systems dynamics modelling [24, 25] will then seek to identify actual feedback control mechanisms, assess their impact on the global process and on the impact of changes to them, and identify, implement and measure or otherwise evaluate potential improvements [17]. Multi agent modelling techniques will also be explored in this context.

BUSINESS PROCESS IMPROVEMENT

One further brief observation must be made. In general, *E*-type software systems are not developed for their own sake. They are required to address, in the most effective manner, a need in some domain. In seeking to use computers in the late fifties and early sixties US banks and insurance companies for example, the first business organisations to attempt major, if not total, automation, soon recognised that it was not effective to simply install computers as electronic clerk- replacements. In introducing them one must ask the question *"How shall our business be conducted now that computers are available?"*. Only recently has this awareness spread more widely; have organisations begun the search for overall *business process* improvement as a disciplined and integrated activity that also includes computer supported processes. In addressing this question it was soon discovered that for businesses operating *legacy* computer systems the freedom to change is severely constrained unless the computer software is reliably, responsively and economically adaptable. Modelling and improving a software process, a process including *ab initio* development, fault fixing, adaptation and extension (ie. software evolution), or modifying and extending its products must be done in the context of the total business including its clients, not as a self contained exercise. And this is also true for the software industry where software evolution is, basically, just another business process. There is, therefore, little point in modelling the technical software development process in ever greater detail. The *total* process must be modelled in its business environment to include all relevant activities and their feedback mechanisms. This requires that the latter are identified and understood, and that appropriate techniques are available.

CONCLUSIONS

This very brief analysis indicates why many of the current approaches to process modelling and the objectives they have been directed at have largely outlived their usefulness. More appropriate approaches and techniques must now be identified, explored, developed and applied. I believe that feedback control dominates the software process both in its technological aspects and in its organisational context. Mastery of feedback mechanisms demands adequate quantitative models individually calibrated against real world software evolution environments. Eventually it may be possible to develop generic models but that lies in the distant future. A widespread concerted effort at global software process modelling is required, one that takes into account the facts as outlined. Current modelling approaches and techniques will need to be augmented by others that promise hope of success in domains that are significantly wider and more complex than those currently considered.

ACKNOWLEDGEMENTS

As the FEAST core group, Dr Dewayne Perry and Professors Vic Stenning and Wlad Turski have played a major role in developing and exploring the concepts and results presented here [26]. More recently Dr Paul Wernick and Juan F Ramil have joined the FEAST/1 team and have also made significant contributions. It is also appropriate to mention the many participants in the three International FEAST Workshops (1994/5) who in their critical appraisal and creative criticism of the work of the core group helped ensure FEAST/1 funding, launch and further progress. Acknowledgement is also due to the EPSRC for grants numbers GR/K86008 supporting FEAST/1 and and GR/LO7437 that permits the continuing involvement of Professor Turski and Dr Perry.

REFERENCES

1. Osterweil L, Software Processes are Software Too, *Proc. 9th Int. Conf. on Softw. Eng., Monterey, CA, 30 March - 2 Apr. 1987, IEEE Comp. Soc. Pub. n. 767, IEEE Cat. n. 87CH2432-3*, 2 - 13

2. Bennington H D, Production of Large Computer Programs, *Proc. Symp. on Advanced Computer Programs for Digital Computers, sponsored by ONR*, June 1956, Republished in *Annals of the History of Computing*, Oct. 1983, 350 - 361

3. Lehman M M, The Programming Process, *IBM Res. Rep. RC 2722, IBM Res. Centre, Yorktown Heights, NY 10594*, Sept. 1969. Also. in [13], 39 - 83

4. Royce W W, Managing the Development of Large Software Systems, *IEEE Wescon*, Aug. 1970, 1 - 9

5. Boehm B W, Software Engineering, *IEEE Trans. on Comp., v. C-5, n. 12*, Dec. 1976, 1226-1241

6. Potts C (ed), *Proc. of the Softw. Process Worksh.*, Egham, Surrey, UK, Feb. 1984. *IEEE cat. n. 84CH2044-6, Comp. Soc.*, Washington D.C., *order n. 587*, 27 -35

7. Wileden J C and Dowson M (eds), *SE Notes, Special Issue on The 2nd International Workshop on the Software Process and Software Environments*, Coto de Caza, Cal., 27-29 March 1985, *Softw. Eng. Notes, v. 11, n. 4*, Aug. 1986

8. Dowson M (ed), Iteration in the Software Process, Proc. *3rd Int. Proc. Worksh., IEEE Comp. Soc. Press*, March 1987

9. Lehman M M. Process Models, Process Programs, Programming Support - Invited Response to a Keynote Address by Lee Osterweil, *Proc. 9th Int. Conf. on Softw. Eng., Monterey, CA*, 30 March 2 - Apr. 1987, *IEEE Comp. Soc. pub. n. 767, IEEE Cat. n. 87CH2432-3*, 14 - 16

10. Paulk M C, Curtis B and Chrisi M B, Capability Maturity Model for Software, Version 1.1, *Softw. Eng. Tech. Rep., CMU/SEI-93-TR*, Feb. 24 1993

11. Preprints of the (first) FEAST Workshop, M M Lehman (ed), *Dept. of Comp., ICSTM*, June 1994

12. Lehman M M and Belady L A, Program Evolution, - Processes of Software Change, *Academic Press*, London, 1985, 538 p.

13. Belady L A and Lehman M M, An Introduction to Growth Dynamics, *Proc. Conference on Statistical Computer Performance Evaluation*, Brown U. 1971, *Academic Press*, 1972, W Freiberger (ed.), 503 - 511

14. Lehman M M, Laws of Program Evolution - Rules and Tools for Programming Management, *Proc. Infotech State of the Art Conf., Why Software Projects Fail*, - April 9 - 11 1978, 11/1 - 11/25

15. Lehman M M, *Feedback, Evolution And Software Technology, Pos.* Paper - *ISPW9, Proc. 9th Int. Softw. Process Workshop*, 5 - 7 Oct. 1994, publ. by *IEEE Comp. Soc.*, 1995

16. Lehman M M, Programs, Life Cycles and Laws of Software Evolution, *Proc. IEEE Special Issue on Softw. Eng., v. 68, n. 9*, Sept. 1980, 1060 - 1076

17. Lehman M M and Stenning V, FEAST/1 - Feedback, Evolution And Software Technology; Case for Support, *EPSRC Research Proposal, Dept. of Comp., ICSTM., London SW7 2BZ*, Nov. 1995/March 1996, 11 p.

18. W M Turski, A Reference Model for the Smooth Growth of Software Systems, U. of Warsaw, March 1996, *IEEE Trans. Softw. Eng., v. 22, n. 8*, Aug. 1996, 599 - 600

19. Lehman M M, Process improvement - The Way Forward, Invited Keynote Address, *Proc. Brazilian Softw. Eng. Conf.*, 14 - 18 Oct. 1996, 23 - 35

20. Lehman M M, Programs, Cities, Students, Limits to Growth?, Inaug. Lect., May 1974. Publ. in *Imp. Col of Sc. Tech. Inaugural Lect. Ser., vol 9, 1970, 1974*, 211 - 229. Also in *Programming Methodology*, (D Gries ed.), *Springer Verlag*, 1978, 42 - 62

21. Lehman M M, On Understanding Laws, Evolution and Conservation in the Large Program Life Cycle, *J. of Sys. and Softw., v. 1, n. 3*, 1980, 213 - 221

23. Lehman M M, Laws of Software Evolution Revisited, Pos. Paper, *EWSPT96, Oct. 1996, to be published by Springer Verlag*

24. Abdel-Hamid T and Madnick S E, Software Project Dynamics: An Integrated Approach, *Prentice Hall, Englewood Cliffs*, 1991, NJ 07632, 264 p.

25. Madachy R J, System Dynamics Modelling of an Inspection Process, *Proc. ICSE 18*, Berlin, 25 - 29 Mar. 1996, *IEEE Comp. Soc. ord. n. PR07246, IEEE Cat. n. 96CB35918*, 376 - 386

26. Lehman M M, Perry D E and Turski W M, Why is it so hard to find Feedback Control in Software Processes?, Invited Talk, *Proc. of the 19th Australasian Comp. Sc. Conf.*, Melbourne, Australia, 31 Jan - Feb 2 1996. 107-115.

Software Process: A Roadmap

Alfonso Fuggetta
Politecnico di Milano
Dipartimento di Elettronica e Informazione
P.za Leonardo da Vinci, 32
20133 Milano (Italy)
Tel. +39-0223993623
Alfonso.Fuggetta@polimi.it

ABSTRACT

Software process research deals with the methods and technologies used to assess, support, and improve software development activities. The field has grown up during the 80s to address the increasing complexity and criticality of software development activities. This paper aims to briefly present the history and achievements of software process research, some critical evaluation of the results produced so far, and possible directions for future work.

1 INTRODUCTION

During the past 20 years, software has conquered an essential and critical role in our society. We increasingly depend on the features and services offered through computerized systems. Any modern product or service embeds and/or exploits some piece of software. As an example, companies sell (or plan to sell in the near future) systems to automate building operations and to embed Internet-features into home appliances.

Unfortunately, software applications are complex products that are difficult to develop and test. Very often, software exhibits unexpected and undesired behaviors that may even cause severe problems and damages. Every issue of the *ACM Software Engineering Notes*, a newsletter published by the ACM SIGSOFT interest group, contains a section that presents a comprehensive (and also frightening) report of the problems and accidents caused by software systems faults. For these reasons, researchers and practitioners have been paying increasing attention to understanding and improving the quality of the software being developed. This is accomplished through a number of approaches and techniques. One of the main directions pursued by researchers and practitioners is centered on the study and improvement of the process through which software is

developed. The underlying assumption is that there is a direct correlation between the quality of the process and the quality of the developed software. The research area that deals with these issues is referred to using the term *software process*.

As an autonomous discipline, the software process area was started in the 80s, through a series of workshops and events (in particular, the *International Software Process Workshop*). Along the years, new events and journals on the subject have been started, such as the *European Workshop on Software Process Technology* and the *Software Process – Improvement and Practice* journal. Important institutions have been created in the USA and in Europe to study software processes: the *Software Engineering Institute* (SEI, Pittsburgh, USA) and the *European Software Institute* (ESI, Bilbao, Spain). Even standardization organizations have started important efforts centered on software processes. For example, ISO has created two important standards such as the ISO 12207 (software lifecycle activities) and 15504 (software process capability determination).

This paper aims to critically present and discuss the main results that the software process research area has achieved in the past decades. This is accomplished by evaluating both technological and methodological aspects. Indeed, there are other publications that offer a comprehensive overview of the results achieved so far in software process research (see for example [1], [2], and [3]). For this reason, the focus of this paper is on offering *a critical evaluation of the attitude and modes of the research work conducted so far*. Accordingly, the paper is structured in three sections.

- Section 2 presents a quick overview of the history and achievements of the software process research areas.

- Section 3 presents a critical evaluation of the work accomplished so far.

- Section 4 summarizes some possible directions for future work.

- Finally, Section 5 draws some conclusions.

2 A BRIEF OVERVIEW OF SOFTWARE PROCESS RESEARCH HISTORY AND ACHIEVEMENTS

The notion of process

The first important contribution of the software process research area has been the increasing awareness that *developing software is a* complex *process*. Researchers and practitioners have realized that developing software is not just a matter of creating effective programming languages and tools. Software development is a collective, complex, and creative effort. As such, the quality of a software product heavily depends on the people, organization, and procedures used to create and deliver it.

This vision has its roots in the work accomplished in the 60s and 70s. In those two decades, researchers and practitioners focused their activity on three main goals:

- Development of structured programming languages (e.g., Algol, Pascal, and C).
- Development of design methods and principles (e.g., information hiding, top-down refinement, functional decomposition).
- Definition of software lifecycles (e.g., waterfall, incremental development, prototype-based).

The third topic mentioned above (lifecycles) is directly related with the notion of software process. A software lifecycle defines the different stages in the lifetime of a software product. Typically, they are requirements analysis and specification, design, development, verification and validation, deployment, operation, maintenance, and retirement. Moreover, a software lifecycle defines the principles and guidelines according to which these different stages have to be carried out. For instance, the waterfall model suggests that a specific phase should be started only when the deliverables of the previous one have been completed. Conversely, the spiral model considers software development as the systematic iteration of a number of activities driven by risk analysis. In general, a software lifecycle defines the *skeleton* and *philosophy* according to which the software process has to be carried out. However, it does not prescribe a precise course of actions, an organization, tools and operating procedures, development policies and constraints. Thus a lifecycle is certainly an important starting point to define how software should be developed. Still, adopting a specific lifecycle is not enough to practically guide and control a software project.

The notion of software process builds on the notion of lifecycle and provides a broad and comprehensive concept to frame and organize the different factors and issues related to software development activities. *A software process can be defined as the coherent set of policies, organizational structures, technologies, procedures, and artifacts that are needed to conceive, develop, deploy, and maintain a software product*. Thus, a software process exploits a number of contributions and concepts:

1. *Software development technology: technological support used in the process*. Certainly, to accomplish software development activities we need tools, infrastructures, and environments. We need the proper technology that makes it possible and economically feasible to create the complex software products our society needs.

2. *Software development methods and techniques: guidelines on how to use technology and accomplish software development activities*. The methodological support is essential to exploit technology effectively.

3. *Organizational behavior: the science of organizations and people*. In general, software development is carried out by teams of people that have to be coordinated and managed within an effective organizational structure.

4. *Marketing and economy*. Software development is not a self-contained endeavor. As any other product, software must address real customers' needs in specific market settings. Thus different stages of software development (e.g., requirements specification and development/deployment) must be shaped in such a way to properly take into account the context where software is supposed to be sold and used.

Viewing software development as a process has significantly helped identify the different dimensions of software development and the problems that need to be addressed in order to establish effective practices. Indeed, addressing the problems and issues of software development is not just a matter of introducing some effective tool and environment. It is not sufficient to select a reasonable lifecycle strategy either. Rather, we must pay attention to the *complex interrelation of a number of organizational, cultural, technological, and economic factors*.

Process modeling and support

The emphasis placed on the notion of software process has motivated a number of research initiatives. A first area of investigation is related to the techniques and methods to model software processes and to support their execution (or enactment). Because software processes are complex entities, researchers have created a number of languages and modeling formalisms (often called Process Modeling Languages or PMLs) that make it possible to represent in a precise and comprehensive way a number of software process features and facets:

- Activities that have to be accomplished to achieve the process objectives (e.g., develop and test a module).

- Roles of the people in the process (e.g., software analyst and project manager).
- Structure and nature of the artifacts to be created and maintained (e.g., requirements specification documents, code modules, and test cases).
- Tools to be used (e.g., CASE tools and compilers).

There are many different types of PMLs. For a detailed discussion of the existing approaches, the reader is invited to refer to a number of surveys published in the past years ([1], [2], [4]). In general, existing PMLs are based on a number of linguistic paradigms that are extended in order to increase their expressive power. For instance, several approaches exploit Petri nets (SPADE, FUNSOFT nets), while others are centered on logical languages (Sentinel/Latin). Lee Osterweil has adopted a somewhat different approach with the notion of process programming. This approach is based on the idea that processes can be described using the same kind of languages that are exploited to create conventional software. This view has been initially pursued with the development of a language based on Ada (called APPL/A) and recently of a new language (called JIL) that incorporates constructs and concepts typical of different programming languages.

PMLs can be used for different purposes:

- Process understanding. A PML can be used to represent in a precise way how a process is structured and organized [5]. This can be instrumental to eliminate inconsistencies in the process specification (i.e., the company quality manual).
- Process design. Proactively, a PML can be used to design a new process, by describing its structure and organization.
- Training and education. A precise description of the process can be useful to teach company procedures and operations to newly hired personnel.
- Process simulation and optimization. A process description can be simulated to evaluate possible problems, bottlenecks, and opportunities for improvement.
- Process support. A precise description of the process can be interpreted and used to provide different levels of support to the people operating in the process [6].

An environment that supports the creation and exploitation of software process models is often called Process-centered Software Engineering Environment (PSEE).

Process improvement
As any other human-centered endeavor, software processes can exhibit unexpected or undesired performance and behaviors. The experiences of the past years have emphasized a wide range of situations where this phenomenon can be observed. Let's consider some typical examples:

- Delivered products do not exhibit the desired quality profile in terms of reliability, functionality, or performance.
- A specific sequencing of process operations introduces unnecessary delay and overhead that can be eliminated or at least reduced by allowing a redistribution of responsibilities and work assignments.
- It is difficult to keep track of the changes and variations of the software products generated by different members of the developed team.

The above situations are meant to be just examples and do not represent the entire range of problems faced by software engineers. In general, researchers and practitioners have realized that processes cannot be defined and "frozen" once for all. Processes need to continuously undergo changes and refinements to increase their ability to deal with the requirements and expectations of the market and of the company stakeholders. Hence, *process need to be continuously assessed and improved*.

These observations have motivated a range of projects devoted to the creation of *quality models* and *improvement methods* for *software process improvement*. A quality model (such as the SEI Capability Maturity Model – CMM – and the ISO 9001 standard [7]) defines the requirements of an ideal company, i.e., a reference model to be used in order to assess the state of a company and the degree of improvement achieved or to be achieved. An improvement method (i.e., SPICE and IDEAL) suggests the steps to be accomplished in order to improve the quality of a software process. Basically, improvement methods indicate how to carry out the "process of improving a process".

An important part of process improvement is *process assessment*, i.e., the determination of the degree of maturity of a process with respect to a quality model. Indeed, some of the most important contributions in process improvement have been originally started with the goal of creating assessment models and methods (e.g., CMM).

Metrics and empirical studies
The techniques and methods discussed in the previous two sections (process modeling and support, and process improvement) need to be based on reliable and effective practices. PMLs and support environments may certainly be useful, but we need to know how to structure and organize the process to be described and supported using PMLs/PSEEs. Similarly, to improve we need to identify the techniques and tools that are really instrumental to enhancing the performance of a specific process. Basically, we need answers to a number of questions such as the following ones:

- What are the indicators that can tell us something about the quality of a process?

- What techniques are more effective to improve a specific process?
- What is the cost and expected impact of a tool on the performance of software processes?

In general, researchers and practitioners have realized that there is an increasing need for a systematic evaluation of the quality of a process, of its constituents (tools, procedures, ...), and of the resulting products. This evaluation is essential to support the implementation of improvement strategies and of any other decision-making activity related to software development. For this reason, in the past decade there has been a significant development of techniques and methods related to *software metrics and empirical studies*. In this context, there are three main kinds of contributions:

- *Definition of (new) metrics*. We need indicators that are able to quantify in a coherent and simple way the properties of the entities involved in software development [8]. For instance, how can we evaluate the size and complexity of a Java program? Or also, what is the productivity of a Java programmer?
- *Empirical methods*. Defining (new) metrics is not enough. We also need experimental approaches to guide the evaluation of a specific process [9]. In order to derive meaningful insights, we must be confident that the approach followed in studying the process is appropriate and sound.
- *Empirical results*. Metrics and empirical methods are the means that we use to study a phenomenon. Once defined, we apply these means to understand and assess specific problems and settings, in order to learn something on the nature of software development processes. These lessons learned (i.e., *empirical results* such as "technique X is not effective in context Y") increase our ability to successfully manage software development projects. The quality of empirical results has to be proved with respect to two different kinds of validity criteria [10]. We need to be sure that the study has been designed correctly (*internal validity*). Moreover, we need to understand if and under what circumstances the results of the study can be applied in different settings (*external validity*).

Processes, eventually!

The consolidated experiences of researchers and practitioners have been instrumental to define and consolidate successful processes. It is worthwhile to mention here two well-known examples: the Personal Software Process [11] and the Unified Software Development Process [12].

- The Personal Software Process (or PSP) is a collection of practices and techniques that are meant to guide the work of a software engineer. PSP has been defined by Watts Humphrey on the basis of his experiences and observations of real software development organizations.

- The Unified Software Development Process has been recently created by Jacobson, Booch, and Rambough. The Unified process is a set of guidelines and process steps that should be followed to apply UML in the different stages of software development.

Summing up

This section has provided a very quick and high-level overview of the activities that are often qualified as software process research. Clearly, the presentation is not intended to be exhaustive and technically complete. Rather, the goal was just to frame the different contributions and activities in order to give an overall picture of the work that has been carried out in the previous decade. Notice also that some of the topics that have been qualified as software process research, such as software metrics and empirical studies, can be considered autonomous research areas. Indeed, other papers in this volume discuss these topics. Still, I think it is important to mention here specific research activities on metrics and empirical studies whose subject of study is the software process.

As a general comment, it is possible to observe that there are a number of important achievements that have increased the quality and effectiveness of software development processes. Nowadays, we are able to conceive, create, and deploy software systems whose complexity is orders of magnitude larger than 15 years ago. Still, despite the large amount of results produced so far, software process research is undergoing a crisis that is visible through a number of symptoms:

- Most technologies developed by the software process community have not been transferred into industrial use.
- The number of papers on the software process modeling and technology presented at conferences and published in journals is decreasing.
- There is an increasing feeling that the community is stuck and unable to produce innovative and effective contributions.

This might be a pessimistic view. Still, as in any other area of software engineering [13], we need to rethink the way we are carrying out the research activity. This is instrumental to identify new directions and approaches to research. Consequently, the next section will present some considerations and observations on the work done so far and propose some criteria to guide future research activities.

3 CRITICAL ISSUES IN SOFTWARE PROCESS RESEARCH

The critical issues and problems in software process research can be summarized by four position statements (see also [14]).

Software processes are processes too

I took the liberty to rephrase one of the most successful and well-known mottos of the past decade. Created by Lee Osterweil for his invited talk at ICSE 87, the expression "Software processes are software too" has driven the work of many researchers and practitioners (including myself). The variation of Osterweil's motto proposed here is meant to be provocative and to stimulate a reflection on the attitude and approach of most software process research. We have often considered software processes as a "special" and "unique" form of processes. Consequently, we have basically assumed that it was inappropriate and even impossible to reuse the approaches and results produced by other communities (e.g., workflow and CSCW). Indeed, this attitude has caused a major problem. The software process community has redone some of the work accomplished by other communities, without taking advantage of the existing experiences. This insufficient willingness to analyze the results and contributions of other areas has slowed down the rate of innovation. Moreover, we have not taken the opportunity to learn from other researchers' mistakes. We should heavily invest in finding and evaluating commonalities and similarities [15], rather than identify differences that often appear to be quite artificial.

The purpose and nature of PMLs/PSEEs must be rethought

As discussed in Section 2, one of the key topics of software process research has been the development of PMLs and related PSEEs. As a matter of fact, after more than 10 years of research on the topic, few (if any) of the proposed approaches have been transferred into industrial practice.

If we consider process modeling, we realize that practitioners do not use the PMLs we have defined. Indeed, practitioners' most important need is to describe processes with the purpose of understanding and communicating them. Consequently, PMLs must be easy to use, intuitive, and "tolerant", i.e., their formality should not become a burden for the modeler. Conversely, existing PMLs are complex, extremely sophisticated, strongly oriented towards detailed modeling of processes. This is justified by the desire to be precise and to provide enough and coherent information to enable "process enactment", i.e., the execution and, often, the "automation" of the process. Moreover, this attitude is often exacerbated by the desire of most software process researchers to model "too much of a process", i.e., all the details concerning software development (e.g., steps and procedures of a design method). Unfortunately, this creates significant barriers to entry and, consequently, limits the possibility for PMLs to be adopted in practice.

The problems with existing PMLs are reflected into PSEEs. Very often, PSEEs are complex and intrusive. In order to pursue even simple operations such as editing and compiling a program, the initial effort needed to setup a PSEE is often very high. Moreover, the attitude towards modeling all the details of a process tends to make PSEEs rigid and inflexible. If we look at the market, we may observe that successful environments are characterized by a somewhat different philosophy. For instance, several researchers believe that Configuration Management (CM) environments (e.g., Continuus and CCC) are "the" real process-centered environments. Even if the effort needed to setup a CM environment is significant, the activities (i.e., process fragments) automated by this class of products are very complex and, at the same time, extremely boring and repetitive. For instance, managing the checkout of a software release can be automated, relieving software engineers from a lot of highly repetitive work, reducing the chances of mistakes, and shortening delivery time significantly. CM environments have become so important to software engineers that no large-scale development initiative can be launched without setting up an appropriate CM environment. *The motivation for this success is that CM environments automate in a very effective way only those process fragments that are reasonable to automate.* This should be considered an important lesson for software process researchers. Can we claim the same for existing PSEEs? Aren't we trying to model and automate something that intrinsically can't be modeled and automated? Isn't the failure of PSEEs due to an inappropriate and unrealistic definition of the goals?

Empirical studies are a means, not an end

In the past years, research in empirical software engineering has increased at a very fast pace. New events and journals have been created and the number of submissions on the subject to conferences is dramatically increasing. The motivation for this growing interest in empirical studies is the legitimate desire to increase our understanding of the principles and nature of software development. In other scientific domains, empirical scientists have made a substantial contribution to the development of our knowledge. Therefore, it is reasonable and appropriate to apply the methods and approaches of empirical sciences to software engineering.

The results of the empirical studies conducted so far, however, have produced mixed feelings. There are two major problems that several researchers have raised on the subject:

- *Significance.* The results of most empirical studies appear to be not very significant. Even if it is certainly true that most empirical studies have the purpose of providing a formal and credible foundation for practitioners and researchers' beliefs, often the added value of these experiments is limited. For instance, a paper that has been recently accepted for publication in a major journal spends about 50 pages of data and statistics to state that there is some evidence that the adoption of requirement engineering techniques is often positively correlated to improved software process performance. What is the reader supposed to learn from this study? Shouldn't researchers' energy be directed at studying more promising questions?

- *External validity.* Many empirical studies carried out so far tend to be characterized by a very limited external validity. Namely, it is difficult to generalize the conclusions of the study outside the context where the study was carried out. There is an increasing sense of dismay in reading papers whose results are difficult to reuse. Certainly, an important added value of an experiment is its design and structure, since it can be reused in different contexts. But this does not remove the sensation that the reuse of these empirical results is limited and problematic.

In general, as any other scientific domain, we should keep in mind that *empirical studies are a means, not an end.* Thus, we should pay more attention to their significance and contribution, and not just to the quality of the experiment design or, worse, to the amount of statistical curve fitting. Moreover, we should not automatically disqualify as "non" scientific those efforts that are not based on statistical evidence and controlled experiments. In a landmark paper [16], Lee states that "… the natural science model does not involve, as objectives, the utilization of any of the following … : laboratory control, statistical controls, mathematical propositions, and replicable observations. Instead, each of these happens to be a means to an objective in scientific research rather the objective itself. *MIS case studies are capable of achieving the same scientific objectives through different means*". [1]
Some of the most important contributions in computer science were not based on empirical studies (as we define them today) and statistical evidence. Did Parnas statistically verify that the adoption of information hiding is positively correlated to the quality of the developed software (and vice versa)? Certainly, Parnas made his assertion on the basis of a deep and mature experience. But the relevance of his intuition was illustrated by qualitative observations. As a provocation, I claim that by today's evaluation criteria, his work would probably not be considered scientifically valid. Nowadays, would we accept Parnas's paper "On the criteria to be used to decompose systems into modules" for publication in IEEE TSE or ACM TOSEM or ICSE?

---

[1] The executive overview of the paper reads as follows: "The classical research requirements cannot be met in a case study. Confounding variables typically make it exceedingly difficult to sort out causal relationships. The imposition of classical experimental controls and rigor, aimed at overcoming these problems, may require such an artificial environment that the validity of the results is called into question."

Software process improvement is process improvement too
I have once again "stolen" Osterweil's paper title to assert that software process improvement should take much more into account what other disciplines and researchers have discovered about process quality and process improvement. As in the case of software process technology, we often consider software processes as special and different from any other engineering and design process. Therefore, we derive that software process deserves specific improvement methods. Unfortunately, often these new and specific methods ignore or overlook the contributions of organizational scientists [17], [18]. Thus the risk is to reinvent the wheel and ignore important issues that may play a critical role in any improvement initiative. For instance, most of the indications suggested by the CMM focus on engineering aspects only. Unfortunately, the successful implementation of these indications often requires a deep reconsideration of the organization carrying out the development activity. This kind of implications is inadequately addressed by most software process improvement methods [19]. Certainly, software development is characterized by specific issues and problems. Still, we cannot forget that software development is carried out by teams of people involved in a highly creative activity. *It is, indeed, a human-centered process as many others engineering and design processes in our society.*

4 LOOKING FOR RESEARCH DIRECTIONS
Constructively, the observations and comments presented in this paper can be used to propose the following directions for future research:

- PMLs must be tolerant and allow for incomplete, informal, and partial specification. The goal should be to ease the adoption of PMLs. Practitioners should be able to incrementally build their process models, being informal and incomplete during the early stages of the modeling activity when it is impossible or inconvenient to be precise and exhaustive. If needed, the model should be incrementally enriched and made formal to address specific issues such as enactment and simulation.

- PSEEs must be non-intrusive, i.e., they should smoothly integrate and complement a "traditional" development environment. Moreover, it must be possible to deploy them incrementally so that the transition to the new technology is facilitated and risks are reduced.

- PSEEs must tolerate and manage inconsistencies and deviations. This requirement reflects the nature of a creative activity such as software development, where consistency is the exception and not the rule [20].

- PSEEs must provide the software engineer with a clear state of the software development process (from many different viewpoints).

- The scope of software improvement methods and models should be widened in order to consider all the different factors affecting software development activities. We should reuse the experiences gained in other business domain and in organizational behavior research.

5 CONCLUSIONS

Software development is a critical activity of our society, as we increasingly depend on software in most modern products and services. Therefore, software process research has an important role to play in the future of the software engineering research and practice. To face this challenge effectively, however, we as software process researchers should frankly and openly evaluate the errors and mistakes of the past, in order to avoid them in the future and to increase the effectiveness of the solutions we are going to propose. In this paper, I have presented four propositions that summarize some of the concerns raised in the community in the past years. In general, software process researchers and practitioners should reuse the experiences and achievements of other areas and disciplines. Moreover, we should rethink the approach we have adopted in studying and supporting software processes. These observations might appear as quite obvious and even trivial. Still, I do believe that they are the underlying motivations for the partial lack of results we observe in the discipline.

ACKNOWLEDGEMENTS

The author wishes to thank Anthony Finkelstein, Carlo Ghezzi, Mehdi Jazayeri, Dino Mandrioli, David Rosenblum, and Alex Wolf for their comments and suggestions.

REFERENCES

[1] V. Ambriola, R. Conradi, and A. Fuggetta, "Assessing process-centered software engineering environments," *ACM Transactions on Software Engineering and Methodology*, vol. 6, 1997.

[2] G. Cugola and C. Ghezzi, "Software processes: a retrospective and a path to the future," *Software process - Improvement and practice*, vol. 4, pp. 101-123, 1998.

[3] A. Fuggetta and A. Wolf, "Trends in Software Processes," in *Trends in Software*, B. Khrisnamurthy, Ed.: John Wiley, 1995.

[4] P. Garg and M. Jazayeri, "Process-centered Software Engineering Environments," : IEEE Computer Society Press, 1996.

[5] S. Bandinelli, A. Fuggetta, L. Lavazza, M. Loi, and G. P. Picco, "Modeling and improving an industrial software process," *IEEE Transactions on Software Engineering*, 1995.

[6] S. Bandinelli, E. Di Nitto, and A. Fuggetta, "Supporting cooperation in the SPADE-1 Environment," *IEEE Transactions on Software Engineering*, vol. 22, 1996.

[7] M. O. Tingey, *Comparing ISO 9000, Malcolm Baldrige, and the SEI CMM for Software*: Prentice Hall, 1997.

[8] N. Fenton, "Software measurement: a necessary scientific basis," *IEEE Transactions on Software Engineering*, vol. 20, pp. 199-206, 1994.

[9] C. M. Judd, E. R. Smith, and L. H. Kidder, *Research methods in social relations*, Sixth ed. Fort Worth, TX (USA): Holt, Rinehart and Winston, Inc., 1991.

[10] L. Votta, A. Porter, and D. Perry, "Experimental Software Engineering: a report on the state of the art," presented at 17th International Conference on Software Engineering (ICSE 17), Seattle (WA), 1995.

[11] W. S. Humphrey, *A discipline for Software Engineering*: Addison-Wesley Publishing Company, 1995.

[12] I. Jacobson, G. Booch, and J. Rumbaugh, *The Unified Software Development Process*. Reading, Massachusetts 01867: Addison Wesley Longman, Inc., 1999.

[13] A. Fuggetta, "Rethinking the modes of software engineering research," *The Journal of Systems and Software*, vol. 47, pp. 133-138, 1999.

[14] R. Conradi, A. Fuggetta, and M. L. Jaccheri, "Six theses on software process research," presented at 6th European Workshop on Software Process Technology (EWSPT '98), Weybridge (UK), 1998.

[15] G. A. Bolcer and R. N. Taylor, "Advanced workflow management technologies," *Software process - Improvement and practice*, vol. 4, pp. 125-171, 1998.

[16] A. S. Lee, "A scientific methodology for MIS case studies," *MIS Quarterly*, vol. 13, pp. 33-50, 1989.

[17] F. Cattaneo, A. Fuggetta, and L. Lavazza, "An experience in process assessment," presented at ICSE 17 - 17th International Conference on Software Engineering, Seattle (USA), 1995.

[18] P. Carlson, "Information technology and organizational change," presented at Seventeenth annual International Conference on Computer documentation, New Orleans (LA), 1999.

[19] F. Cattaneo, A. Fuggetta, and D. Sciuto, "Pursuing coherence in software process assessment and improvement," CEFRIEL, Milano, Technical Report September 1998.

[20] B. Balzer, "Tolerating inconsistencies," presented at International Conference on Software Engineering (ICSE 13), Austin (TX), 1991.

Software Process Improvement Glossary

Richard H. Thayer
Mildred C. Thayer

Scope

This glossary defines the terms used in the field of *software process improvement* and supporting disciplines. These definitions have their roots in several management and technical domains: system and hardware engineering, general (mainstream) management, and project management. In addition, there are new definitions and old terms with new meanings, so read the definitions carefully.

The domain of the definition should be understood or identified in the first sentence of the definition. When the definition was taken from another source and the domain of definition was not obvious, the domain was added.

Glossary Structure

Entries in the glossary are arranged alphabetically. An entry may consist of a single word, such as *process*; a phrase, such as *process maturity*; or an acronym such as *CMM*. Phrases are given in their natural order *(process improvement)* rather than reversed *(improvement, process)*.

The singular version of nouns is always used except in those rare occasions when a singular version of a noun does not exist. Proper names are always capitalized; nonproper nouns are not capitalized.

Blanks *are* taken into account in alphabetizing. They precede all other characters. For example, *test report* precedes *testability*. Hyphens and slashes follow blanks. For example, *software work products* precedes *software-related group*. Alternative spellings are shown as separate glossary entries with cross-references to the preferred spelling.

No distinction is made between acronyms and abbreviations. Where appropriate, a term that has a common acronym or abbreviation contains the acronym or abbreviation in parentheses following the term. The abbreviation or acronym might also be a separate entry. The definition is placed with the term or abbreviation, depending on which one has the most usage; the other is cross-referenced. For example, *CMM*, an acronym for capability maturity model, is defined under *capability maturity model (CMM)*. In contrast, *SPICE*, an acronym for *Software Process Improvement and Capability dEtermination,* is defined under *SPICE*.

If a term has more than one definition, the definitions are listed with numerical prefixes. This ordering does not imply preference. Where necessary, examples and notes have been added to clarify the definitions.

The following cross-references are used to show a term's relationship to other terms in the glossary:

- *See* refers to a preferred term or to a term whose definition serves to define the term that has been looked up.

- *See also* refers to a related term.

- *Synonymous with* refers to a term that is always or nearly always synonymous with the defined term.

- *Sometimes synonymous with* refers to a term that may or may not be synonymous with the defined term, that is, it is a nonstandard usage.

- *Contrast with* refers to a term with an opposite or substantially different meaning.

In a few cases, nonstandard cross-references are used to clarify a particular definition.

Sources

In those cases in which a definition is taken or paraphrased from another source or paper, the source is designated in brackets following the definition, for example [Smith, 1998] or [ANSI/IEEE Std 610.12-1990]. The use of a source reference does not imply an exact quote, but is an acknowledgment of the source of the definition. A list of all sources used in this glossary is provided at the end of the glossary.

Glossary

ability to perform — In a capability maturity model, the precondition is the condition that must exist in the project or organization prior to implementing the software process competently. Ability to perform typically involves resources, organizational structures, and training. *See also common feature.* [CMU/SEI-93-TR-25]

acceptance criteria — The criteria that a system or component must satisfy in order to be accepted by a user, customer, or other authorized entity. [ANSI/IEEE Std 610.12-1990]

acceptance testing — Formal testing conducted to determine whether or not a system satisfies its acceptance criteria and to enable the customer to determine whether or not to accept the system. [ANSI/IEEE Std 610.12-1990]

accreditation — Procedure by which an authoritative body gives formal recognition that a body or person is competent to carry out specific tasks. [ISO/IEC Std Guide 2:1996]

acquirer — An organization that acquires or procures a system, software product, or software service from a supplier. The acquirer could be one of the following: buyer, customer, owner, user, or purchaser. [IEEE/EIA Std 12207.2-1997]

acquisition — The process of obtaining a system, software product, or software service. [IEEE/EIA Std 12207.2-1997]

action item — (1) A unit in a list that has been assigned to an individual or group for disposition. (2) An action proposal that has been accepted. [CMU/SEI-93-TR-25]

action plan — In management, a work plan detailing measurable steps that focus on achieving a specific goal; or alternatively, one of several work plans that are required to accomplish a single goal.

action proposal — A documented suggestion for change to a process or process-related item that will prevent the future occurrence of defects identified as a result of defect prevention activities. *See also software process improvement proposal.* [CMU/SEI-93-TR-25]

activity — Any step taken or function performed, both mental and physical, toward achieving some objective. In project management, the activities include all of the work the managers and technical staff do to perform the tasks of the project and organization. *Contrast with task.* [CMU/SEI-93-TR-25]

activity performed — In a capability maturity model, this is a description of the roles and procedures necessary to implement a key process area. Activities performed typically involve establishing plans and procedures, performing the work, tracking it, and taking corrective actions as necessary. *See also common feature.* [CMU/SEI-93-TR-25]

agreement — The definition of terms and conditions under which a working relationship will be conducted. [IEEE/EIA Std 12207.2-1997]

allocated requirement — *See system requirements allocated to software.* [CMU/SEI-93-TR-25]

application domain — A bounded set of related systems (i.e., systems that address a particular type of problem). Development and maintenance in an application domain usually requires special skills and/or resources. Examples include payroll and personnel systems, command and control systems, compilers, and expert systems. [CMU/SEI-93-TR-25]

ASSESPRO — A Brazilian software product evaluation scheme that awards prizes for the "best" software product in separate categories.

assessed capability — In software process assessment, the output of one or more recent, relevant process assessments conducted in accordance with the provisions of ISO/IEC Standard TR 15504. [ISO/IEC Std TR 15504-9:1998]

assessment — In software, the process of comparing measurements of product, process, or service characteristics against specifications of those characteristics. [SCOPE, 1989–1993] *See also software process assessment.* [CMU/SEI-93-TR-25]

assessment approach — In an ISO/IEC compatible assessment, the assessment approach is one of (1) self-assessment or (2) independent assessment. [ISO/IEC Std TR 15504-4:1998]

assessment constraint — In software process assessment, the restrictions placed on the freedom of choice of the assessment team regarding the conduct of the assessment and the use of the assessment outputs. [ISO/IEC Std TR 15504-9:1998]

assessment indicator — In software process assessment, an objective attribute, or characteristic of a practice or work product that is necessary to support the judgment of the performance or capability of an implemented process. [ISO/IEC Std TR 15504-9:1998]

assessment input — In software process assessment, the collection of information required before a process assessment can commence. [ISO/IEC Std TR 15504-9:1998]

assessment instrument — In software process assessment, a tool, or set of tools, that is used throughout an assessment to assist the assessor in evaluating the performance or capability of processes and in handling assessment data and recording the assessment results. [ISO/IEC Std TR 15504-9:1998]

assessment model — A comprehensive set of indicators of process performance and process capability used to make judgments about the capability of an organization's processes. [ISO/IEC TR 15502-4:1998]

assessment output — In software process assessment, all of the tangible results from an assessment. *See also assessment record.* [ISO/IEC Std TR 15504-9:1998]

assessment participant — In software process assessment, it is an individual who has responsibilities within the scope of the assessment. Some examples are the sponsor, assessor, and organizational unit members. [ISO/IEC Std TR 15504-9:1998]

assessment purpose — In software process assessment, a statement, provided as part of the assessment input that defines the reason for performing the assessment. [ISO/IEC Std TR 15504-9:1998]

assessment record — In software process assessment, an orderly, documented collection of that information that is pertinent to the assessment and adds to the understanding and verification of the process profiles generated by the assessment. [ISO/IEC Std TR 15504-9:1998]

assessment scope — In software process assessment, a definition of the boundaries of the assessment, provided as part of the assessment input, encompassing the organizational limits of the assessment, the processes to be included, and the context within which the processes operate. *See also process context.* [ISO/IEC Std TR 15504-9:1998]

assessment sponsor — In software process assessment, the individual, internal or external to the organization being assessed, who requires the assessment to be performed, and provides financial or other resources to carry it out. *See also assessment participant.* [ISO/IEC Std TR 15504-9:1998]

assessor — In software process assessment, an individual or organization who has responsibilities within the scope of the assessment for performing the assessment. Within the SPICE framework, two types of assessors are appointed to conduct an assessment with the roles of leader and support assessor. The team leader prepares the plan of the assessment, while the support assessor records any relevant discussion.

assignable cause variation — Variations that arise from events that are not part of a normal process. They represent sudden or persistent abnormal changes to one or more of the process components.

attribute — A measurable physical or abstract property of an entity. Note that attributes can be internal or external. [ISO/IEC Std 14598-1-1998]

audit — An independent examination of a work product or set of work products to assess compliance with specifications, standards, contractual agreements, or other criteria. It can be conducted by an authorized person for the purpose of providing an independent assessment of software products and processes in order to assess compliance with requirements. [ANSI/IEEE Std 610.12-1990]

Australian Software Quality Institute (SQI) — Part of Griffith University in Brisbane, Australia; a leading organization concerned with the SPICE trials.

base practice — A software engineering or management activity that directly addresses the purpose of a particular process and contributes to the creation of its output. A base practice is an essential activity of a particular process. [El Emam, Drouin, and Melo, 1998]

baseline — A formally approved version of a configuration item, regardless of media, formally designated and fixed at a specific time during the configuration item's life cycle. [IEEE/EIA Std 12207.2-1997]

baseline configuration management — The establishment of baselines that are formally reviewed and agreed on and serve as the basis for further development. Some software work products, for example, the software design and the code, should have baselines established at predetermined points, and a rigorous change control process should be applied these items. These baselines provide control and stability when interacting with the customer. *See also baseline management.* [CMU/SEI-93-TR-25]

baseline management — In configuration management, the application of technical and administrative direction to designate the documents and changes to those documents that formally identify and establish baselines at specific times during the life cycle of a configuration item. [ANSI/IEEE Std 610.12-1990]

Bell Laboratories — Bell Laboratories (Bell Labs) is the R&D arm of Lucent Technologies, the systems and technology company formed by AT&T as part of AT&T's restructuring. At the beginning of 1996, Bell Labs had some 25,000 R&D employees in eight states of the United States and 22 other countries. Bell Labs is known for its work in the three key sciences of the Information Age — microelectronics, photonics, and software — and for engineering these sciences into the basic technologies of networked computing, wireless, messaging, visual communications, and voice and audio processing. [Bell Labs Web page]

benchmark — A standard against which measurements or comparisons can be made. [ANSI/IEEE Std 610.12-1990]

bidder — An individual, partnership, corporation, or association that has submitted a proposal and is a candidate for award of a contract to design, develop, and/or manufacture one or more products. [CMU/SEI-93-TR-25]

Bootstrap — An assessment model developed in Europe in the early 1990s by the European ESPRIT project. The original SEI CMM approach was adopted in the methodology, and extended with features based on the guidelines from ISO 9000 quality standards and European Space Agency (ESA) process model standards.

BS 5750 – A U.K. predecessor to the ISO 9000 series of standards.

business aim — A requirement of the business process [British usage]. *Also called business goal.*

business driver — Those elements of a business that are most likely to affect the success of your organization in meeting its goal.

business process improvement — *See process improvement.*

callgraph — In software, a callgraph is a graph representing a program's calling structure. [SCOPE, 1989–1993]

capability determination (CD) — the process of comparing the capability of an organization with a set of criteria in order to identify, analyze, and quantify strengths, weaknesses, and particularly risks in undertaking a specific project. [Zahran, 1998]

capability determination sponsor — The organization or person initiating a process capability determination. [ISO/IEC Std TR 15504-9:1998]

capability dimension — In software process assessment, the set of process attributes comprising the capability aspects of the reference model of processes and process capability. These attributes are organized into capability levels, comprising an ordinal scale of process capability. [ISO/IEC Std TR 15504-9:1998]

capability level — A well-defined evolutionary plateau toward achieving a mature software process. The five maturity levels in the SEI's capability maturity model are *initial, repeatable, defined, managed,* and *optimizing.* [CMU/SEI-93-TR-25]

capability maturity model (CMM) — A description of the stages through which software organizations evolve as they define, implement, measure, control, and improve their software processes. This model was developed by the SEI in the early 1990s. It provides a guide for selecting process improvement strategies by facilitating the determination of current process capabilities and the identification of the issues most critical to software quality and process improvement. *Also known as capability maturity model for software (SW-CMM).* [CMU/SEI-93-TR-25]

Capability Maturity Model for Software (SW-CMM) — *See capability maturity model (CMM).*

capability maturity model version 1.1 — The February 1993 version of the capability maturity model. [CMU/SEI-93-TR-24] *See also capability maturity model (CMM).*

case study — A documented illustration or example of the application of a technique or methodology to a real-world problem.

causal analysis — The analysis of defects to determine their underlying root cause. [CMU/SEI-93-TR-25]

causal analysis meeting — A meeting, conducted after completing a specific task, to analyze defects uncovered during the performance of that task. [CMU/SEI-93-TR-25]

CCB — *See software configuration control board (CCB).*

CD — The acronym for capability determination.

Centre de recherche informatique de Montréal (CRIM) — An Applied Software Engineering Center that has a cooperative partnership with the SEI for the distribution of SEI products and services.

certificate of conformity — Document issued under the rules of a certification system, indicating that adequate confidence is provided that a duly identified product, process, or service is in conformity with a specific standard or other normative document. [ISO/IEC Std Guide 2:1996]

certification — Procedure by which a third party gives written assurance that a product, process, or service conforms to specified characteristics. [SCOPE, 1989–1993]

certification body — A body that conducts certification of conformity. [ISO/IEC Std Guide 2:1996]

certification scheme — As related to specified products, processes, or services to which the same particular standards and rules, and the same procedures, apply. [ISO/IEC Std Guide 2:1996]

certification system – A system that has its own rules of procedure and management for carrying out certification of conformity. [ISO/IEC Std Guide 2:1996]

CMM — Acronym for capability maturity model. [CMU/SEI-93-TR-25]

CMM-Integration (CMMI) — A SEI project conceived in 1998 to produce a new CMM based on the integration of the SE-CMM, IPD-CMM, and SE-CMM.

commitment — A pact that is freely assumed, visible, and is expected to be kept by all parties. [CMU/SEI-93-TR-25]

commitment to perform — In a capability maturity model, the actions the organization must take to ensure that the process is established and will endure. Commitment to perform typically involves establishing organizational policies and senior management sponsorship. *See also common feature.* [CMU/SEI-93-TR-25]

committee draft — A stage on the normal route toward international standardization. A committee draft is the first stage at which the standard documents are subjected to formal ballot.

common cause (of a defect) — A cause of a defect that is inherently part of a process or system. Common causes affect every outcome of the process and everyone working in the process. *Contrast with special cause.* [CMU/SEI-93-TR-25]

common cause variation — A variation in process performance due to normal or inherent interaction among process components characterized by a stable and consistent pattern over time.

common feature — The subdivision categories of the CMM key process areas. The common features are attributes that indicate whether the implementation and institutionalization of a key process area are effective, repeatable, and lasting. See also ability to perform, activity performed, commitment to perform, measurement and analysis, verifying implementation. [CMU/SEI-93-TR-25]

compatible assessment model — An operational model, used for performing assessments, that meets the defined requirements (for model purpose, scope, elements and indicators, mapping to the reference model, and translation of results) for conformance to the reference model. [ISO/IEC Std TR 15504-9:1998] An example would be the CMM.

competent assessor — A person who has demonstrated the necessary skills, competencies, and experience for performing process assessments. [ISO/IEC Std TR 15504-9:1998]

complexity — (1) The degree to which a system or component has a design or implementation that is difficult to understand and verify. (2) Pertaining to any of a set of structure-based metrics that measure the attribute in (1). [ANSI/IEEE Std 610.12-1990]

component process — In ISO/IEC TR 15504, the lowest level of refinement in the process dimension.

conceptual model — In system/software system engineering, a requirements model of the system/software system to be developed, its internal components, and the behavior of both the system and its environment. [Roman, 1985]

configuration — In configuration management, the functional and physical characteristics of hardware or software as set forth in technical documentation or achieved in a product. [ANSI/IEEE Std 610.12-1990]

configuration control — An element of configuration management, consisting of the evaluation, coordination, approval or disapproval, and implementation of changes to configuration items after formal establishment of their configuration identification. [ANSI/IEEE Std 610.12-1990]

configuration identification — An element of configuration management, consisting of selecting the configuration items for a system and recording their functional and physical characteristics in technical documentation. [ANSI/IEEE Std 610.12-1990]

configuration item — In configuration management, (1) an aggregation of hardware, software, or both that is designated for configuration management and treated as a single entity in the configuration management process. [ANSI/IEEE Std 610.12-1990] (2) An entity within a configuration that satisfies an end use function and that can be uniquely identified at a given reference point. [IEEE/EIA Std 12207.2-1997]

configuration management — A discipline applying technical and administrative direction and surveillance to identify and document the functional and physical characteristics of a configuration item, control changes to those characteristics, record and report change processing and implementation status, and verify compliance with specified requirements. [ANSI/IEEE Std 610.12-1990]

configuration management library system — The tools and procedures used to access the contents of the software baseline library. [CMU/SEI-93-TR-25]

configuration unit — In configuration management, the lowest level entity of a configuration item or component that can be placed into, and retrieved from, a configuration management library system. [CMU/SEI-93-TR-25]

conformity — Fulfillment by a product, process, or service of specified requirements. [ISO/IEC Std Guide 2:1996]

consistency — The degree of uniformity, standardization, and freedom from contradiction among the documents or parts of a system or component. [ANSI/IEEE Std 610.12-1990]

constructed capability — A capability constructed from process profiles of elements of organizational units or of different organizations that are assembled for the purposes of achieving a particular specified requirement. [ISO/IEC Std TR 15504-9:1998]

contingency factor — An adjustment (increase) of a size, cost, or schedule plan to account for likely underestimates of these parameters due to incomplete specification, inexperience in estimating the application domain, etc. [CMU/SEI-93-TR-25]

contract — A binding agreement between two parties, especially enforceable by law, or a similar internal agreement wholly within an organization, for the supply of software service or for the supply, development, production, operation, or maintenance of a software product. [IEEE/EIA Std 12207.2-1997]

contract terms and conditions — The stated legal, financial, and administrative aspects of a contract. [CMU/SEI-93-TR-25]

control chart — A diagrammatic representation of process outputs that allows variations in these outputs due to normal process variations and/or process anomalies to be identified.

correctness — (1) The degree to which a system or component is free from faults in its specification, design, and implementation. (2) The degree to which software, documentation, or other items meet specified requirements. (3) The degree to which software, documentation, or other items meet user needs and expectations, whether specified or not. [ANSI/IEEE Std 610.12-1990]

CRIM — Acronym for Centre de recherche informatique de Montréal.

criteria — In a project management system, the standard or metric on which a decision will be made.

critical computer resource — The parameters of the computing resources deemed to be a source of risk to the project because the potential need for those resources may exceed the amount that is available. Examples include target computer memory and host computer disk space. [CMU/SEI-93-TR-25]

critical path — A series of dependent tasks for a project that must be completed as planned to keep the entire project on schedule. [CMU/SEI-93-TR-25]

critical software — Software whose failure could have an impact on safety or could cause large financial or social loss. [IEEE Std 1012-1986]

customer — The individual or organization that is responsible for accepting the product and authorizing payment to the developing organization. [CMU/SEI-93-TR-25]

defect — (1) A flaw in a system or system component that causes the system or component to fail to perform its required function. (2) An unintentional condition in a hardware/software system that, when encountered, may cause the system to fail to perform its intended function.

defect density — The number of defects identified in a product divided by the size of the product component (expressed in standard measurement terms for that product). [CMU/SEI-93-TR-25]

defect prevention — The activities involved in identifying defects or potential defects and preventing them from being introduced into a product. [CMU/SEI-93-TR-25]

defect root cause — The underlying reason (e.g., process deficiency) that allows a defect to be introduced. [CMU/SEI-93-TR-25]

defined level — *See Maturity Level 3.* [CMU/SEI-93-TR-25]

defined maturity level — *See Maturity Level 3.*

defined process — The operational definition of a set of activities for achieving a specific purpose. *Note* that a defined process may be characterized by standards, procedures, training, tools, and methods. [ISO/IEC Std TR 15504-9:1998]

dependency item — A product, action, piece of information, etc., that must be provided by one individual or group to a second individual or group so that the second individual or group can perform a planned task. [CMU/SEI-93-TR-25]

developer — An organization that performs development activities (including requirements analysis, design, and testing through acceptance) during the software life cycle process. [IEEE/EIA Std 12207.2-1997]

developmental configuration management — In configuration management, the application of technical and administrative direction to designate and control the software and associated technical documentation that define the evolving configuration of a software work product during development. Developmental configuration management is under the direct control of the developer. [CMU/SEI-93-TR-25]

deviation — A noticeable or marked departure from the appropriate norm, plan, standard, procedure, or variable being reviewed. [CMU/SEI-93-TR-25]

DIN 66285 — A German standard on quality requirements and testing standards. The ISO/IEC standard 12119 was based on this standard.

direct measure — A measure of an attribute that does not depend on a measure of any other attribute. [ISO/IEC 14598-1-1998]

direct measurement — Measurement of an attribute that does not depend on the measurement of any other attribute. *Contrast with indirect measurement.* [Fenton, 1991]

dissemination activity — The act of making information available to the general public. An example would be to use the Web to "publish" technical reports and other technical information.

documented procedure — *See procedure.* [CMU/SEI-93-TR-25]

draft international standard — A stage on the normal route toward international standardization. This is the final stage before an international standard is produced by formal balloting.

draft technical report — A stage on the technical report route toward international standardization. This is the final stage before a technical report is produced.

dynamic analysis — The process of evaluating a system or component based on its behavior during execution. *Contrast with static analysis. See also testing.* [ANSI/IEEE Std 610.12-1990]

effective process — A process that can be characterized as practiced, documented, enforced, trained, measured, and able to improve. *See also well-defined process.* [CMU/SEI-93-TR-25]

efficiency — In software, a set of attributes that bears on the relationship between the level of performance of the software and the amount of resources used, under stated conditions. [ISO/IEC Std 9126:1991]

embedded computer system — A computer system integral to a larger system whose primary purpose is not computational; for example, a computer system in a weapon, aircraft, automobile, communication network, intelligent point-of-sales system, automatic teller machine, and talking spelling checker for children.

embedded software — Software for an embedded computer system. *See also embedded computer system.*

EN 29001 — The European version of the ISO 9001 standard.

EN 29004-2:1993 — *See BS 5750.*

end user — The end user is the individual or group who will use the system for its intended operational use when it is deployed in its environment. [CMU/SEI-93-TR-25]

end user representative — One of a selected sample of end users who represent the total population of end users. [CMU/SEI-93-TR-25]

engineering group — A collection of individuals (both managers and technical staff) representing an engineering discipline. Examples of engineering disciplines include systems engineering, hardware engineering, system test, software engineering, software configuration management, and software quality assurance. [CMU/SEI-93-TR-25]

enhanced capability — A capability greater than currently assessed capability, justified by a credible process improvement program. [ISO/IEC Std TR 15504-9:1998]

enterprise resource planning (ERP) — Configurable information system packages that integrate information and information-based processes within and across functional areas in an organization. The current generation of ERP systems also provides reference models or process templates that claim to embody the current best business practices. [Kumar and Hillegersberg, 2000]

ESSI (European Systems and Software Initiative) — In Europe, a program that has funded experiments and activities in software process improvement, as well as dissemination of the results of these activities and experiments.

European Software Institute (ESI) — A European institute, based in Bilbao, Spain, whose mission is to support its members and European industry in general to improve competitiveness by promoting and disseminating best practices in software development and maintenance. [ESI Web site]

European Space Agency (ESA) — An international organization devoted to enhancing humans' presence in space. Born out of two earlier groups — the European Space Research Organization and the European Launcher Development Organization — the ESA is 15 nations strong. The work of the agency is in the areas of earth-monitoring and telecommunications satellites, as well as piloted space flight programs. [ESA Web site]

European Systems and Software Initiative (ESSI) — *See ESSI (European Systems and Software Initiative).*

evaluation — A systematic determination of the extent to which an entity meets its specified criteria. *See also software capability evaluation.* [IEEE/EIA Std 12207.2-1997]

evaluation level — Depth or thoroughness of an evaluation with respect to the set of evaluation techniques to be applied and the fulfillment of evaluation objectives.

evaluation module — A package of evaluation technology for a specific software quality characteristic or subcharacteristic. The package includes evaluation methods and techniques, inputs to be evaluated, data to be measured and collected, and supporting procedures and tools. [ISO/IEC Std 14598-1:1998]

event-driven review/activity — A review or activity that is performed based on the occurrence of an event within the project (e.g., a formal review or the completion of a life cycle stage). *Contrast with periodic review/activity.* [CMU/SEI-93-TR-25]

exemplar assessment model — In the context of ISO/IEC 15504, an example of an assessment model that meets the requirements of ISO/IEC 15504 and that supports the performance of an assessment by providing indicators for guidance on the interpretation of the process purposes and process attributes defined in ISO/IEC 15504. [ISO/IEC 15504-5]

external attribute — Attributes of a product, process, or resource that can only be measured with respect to how the product, process, or resource relates to its environment. *Contrast with internal attributes.* [Fenton, 1991]

external measure — An indirect measure of a product derived from measures of the behavior of the system of which it is a part. [ISO/IEC Std 14598-1:1998]

external metric — This metric uses measures of a software product derived from measures of the behavior of the system of which it is a part. *Contrast with internal metrics.* [ISO/IEC Std 9126:1991]

external quality — The extent to which a product satisfies stated and implied needs when used under specified conditions. [ISO/IEC Std 14598-1:1998]

failure — The inability of a system or component to perform its required functions within specified performance requirements. *Special note:* The fault tolerance discipline distinguishes between a human action (a mistake), its manifestation (a hardware or software fault), the result of the fault (a failure), and the amount by which the result is incorrect (the error). [ANSI/IEEE Std 610.12-1990]

failure analysis — In software engineering, (1) the process of investigating an observed software fault to identify the cause of the fault, the phase of the development process during which the fault was introduced, methods by which the fault could have been prevented or detected earlier, and the method by which the fault was detected. (2) The process of investigating software errors, failures, and faults to determine quantitative rates and trends.

fast track — A quick, sometimes shortcut, method or approach to accomplishing a task or obtaining approval for an action. It is usually an approved process for use under special circumstances. SPICE uses a fast-track route to standardization via a series of technical reports.

fault — (1) A defect in a hardware device or component, for example, a short circuit or broken wire. (2) An incorrect step, process, or data definition in a computer program. [ANSI/IEEE Std 610.12-1990]

fault elimination — The correction or elimination of a fault type through fault analysis.

finding — The conclusions of an assessment, evaluation, audit, or review that identify the most important issues, problems, or opportunities within the area of investigation. [CMU/SEI-93-TR-25]

firmware — The combination of a hardware device and computer instructions or computer data that reside as read-only software on the hardware device. The software cannot be readily modified under program control. [IEEE/EIA Std 12207.2-1997]

first-line software manager — A manager who has direct management responsibility (including providing technical direction and administering the personnel and salary functions) for the staffing and activities of a single organizational unit (e.g., a department or project team) of software engineers and other related staff. [CMU/SEI-93-TR-25]

fitness for purpose — Ability of a product, process, or service to serve a defined purpose under specific conditions. [ISO/IEC Std Guide 2:1996]

flow graph — In software, a directed graph representing a program's flow of control. [SCOPE, 1989–1993]

formal review — A formal meeting at which a product is presented to the end user, customer, or other interested parties for comment and approval. It can also be a review of the management and technical activities and of the progress of the project. [CMU/SEI-93-TR-25]

frameworks quagmire — A negative term used by organizations who wish to remain competitive and to comply with all positive contractor evaluation criteria while at the same time questioning the many different and sometime contradicting frameworks.

Fraunhofer Institut Experimentelles Software Engineering (Institute for Experimental Software Engineering) (IESE) — The IESE focuses on bridging the gap between research and industry, and performs applied research within software engineering. The Fraunhofer IESE helps to change industrial development practices from craftsmanship to engineering. As a competence provider, mentor, and coach, the Fraunhofer IESE supports industry to continuously improve their software competence. [Fraunhofer IESE Web site]

function — A set of related actions, undertaken by individuals or tools that are specifically assigned or fitted for their roles, to accomplish a set purpose or end. [CMU/SEI-93-TR-25]

functionality — In software, a set of attributes that bears on the existence of a set of functions and their specified properties. The functions are those that satisfy stated or implied needs. [ISO/IEC Std 9126:1991]

goal — In a CMM, a summary of the key practices of a key process area that can be used to determine whether an organization or project has effectively implemented the key process area. The goals signify the scope, boundaries, and intent of each key process area. [CMU/SEI-93-TR-25]

group — The collection of departments, managers, and individuals who have responsibility for a set of tasks or activities. A group could vary from a single individual assigned part-time, to several part-time individuals assigned from different departments, to several individuals dedicated full-time. [CMU/SEI-93-TR-25]

Gütegemeinschaft Scheme — An association founded in Germany in the mid-1980s with the aim to define quality criteria for software products and to organize a software quality certification scheme. This resulted in the 1990 publication of the German standard DIN 62285. This was again published in 1998 as ISO/IEC Standard 12119.

host computer — A computer used to develop software. *Contrast with target computer.* [CMU/SEI-93-TR-25]

ICSE — Acronym for International Conference on Software Engineering.

IDEAL model – IDEAL (initiating, diagnosing, evaluating, acting, leveraging — repeating 2–5 as often as necessary) is a model to support the construction and implementation of software process improvement schemes. The SEI has proposed an IDEAL middle framework.

IEC — Acronym for International Electrotechnical Commission.

IEE — Acronym for Institution of Electrical Engineers.

IEEE — Acronym for Institute of Electrical and Electronics Engineers.

IEEE Std 1002-1987 — *IEEE Standard Taxonomy for Software Engineering Standards* (IEEE Std 1002-1987 was revised in 1992 and later withdrawn).

IEEE Std 1012-1986 — *IEEE Standard for Software Verification and Validation* (IEEE Std 1012-1986 was superseded by IEEE Std 1012-1998).

IEEE Std 829-1983 — *IEEE Standard for Software Test Documentation* (IEEE Std 829-1983 was superseded by IEEE Std 829-1998).

implied need — A need that may not have been stated but is an actual need when the entity is used under particular conditions. Sometimes implied needs are real needs that may not have been documented. [ISO/IEC Std 14598-1:1998]

ImproveIT — A U.K. project, sponsored by the Defence Evaluation Research Agency, to investigate methods of selecting competent suppliers of software-intensive products.

independent assessment — An assessment conducted by assessors who are independent of the organizational unit being assessed. [ISO/IEC Std TR 15504-4:1998]

indicator — A measure that can be used to estimate or predict another measure. [ISO/IEC Std 14598-1:1998]

indirect measurement — Measurement of an attribute that involves the measurement of one or more other attributes. *Contrast with direct measurement.* [Fenton, 1991]

infrastructure — The underlying foundation or basic framework of a system or organization.

initial level — *See Maturity Level 1.* [CMU/SEI-93-TR-25]

initial maturity level — *See Maturity Level 1.*

inspection — (1) A static analysis technique that relies on visual examination of development products to detect errors, violations of development standards, and other problems. Types include code inspection and design inspection. [ANSI/IEEE Std 610.12-1990] (2) A semiformal to formal evaluation technique in which software requirements, design, or code are examined in detail by a person or group other than the originator to detect faults, violations of development standards, and other problems. The review members are peers (equals) of the designer or programmer. Traditional error data are collected during inspections for later analysis and to assist in future inspections. *Sometimes called a walkthrough or peer review.*

inspection process — *See inspection.*

institutionalization — The building of and infrastructure and corporate culture that support methods, practices, and procedures so that they are the ongoing way of doing business, even after those who originally defined them are gone. [CMU/SEI-93-TR-25]

instrumentation — Devices or instructions installed or inserted into hardware or software to monitor the operation of a system or component. [ANSI/IEEE STD 610.12-1990]

Integrated Product Development CMM — A maturity model (analogous to the SW-CMM and developed by the same team) for Integrated Product Development (IPD). IPD is a systematic approach to product development that achieves a timely collaboration of necessary disciplines throughout the product life cycle to better satisfy customer needs. It typically involves a teaming of the functional disciplines to integrate and concurrently apply all necessary processes to produce an effective and efficient product that satisfies the customer's needs. [SEI Web site]

integrated software management — The unification and integration of the software engineering and management activities into a coherent defined software process based on the organization's standard software process and related process assets. [CMU/SEI-93-TR-25]

integration — *See software integration.* [CMU/SEI-93-TR-25]

intermediate software product — A product of the software development process that is used as input to another stage of the software development process. [ISO/IEC Std 14598-1:1998]

internal attribute — An attribute of a product, process, or resource that can be measured purely in terms of the product, process or resource itself. *Contrast with external attributes.* [Fenton, 1991]

internal measure — A measure of the product itself, either direct or indirect. For example, the number of lines of code, complexity measures, the number of faults found in a walkthrough, and the Fog Index are all internal measures made of the product itself. [ISO/IEC 14598-1-1998]

internal metric — This metric measures internal attributes or indicates external attributes by analysis of the static properties of the intermediate or deliverable software products. *Contrast with external metric.* [ISO/IEC Std 9126:1991]

internal quality — The totality of attributes of a product that determine its ability to satisfy stated and implied needs when used under specified conditions. *See also quality.* [ISO/IEC Std 12207:1995]

International Organization for Standardization (ISO) — ISO is the International Organization for Standardization, founded in 1946 to (1) promote the development of international standards and related activities, including conformity assessment, and (2) to facilitate the exchange of goods and services worldwide. ISO is composed of member bodies from more than 90 countries, the U.S. member body being the American National Standards Institute (ANSI). ISO's work covers all areas except those related to electrical and electronic engineering, which are covered by the International Electrotechnical Commission (IEC). The results of ISO's technical work are published as international standards or guides.

international standard — A standard that is developed or used in a multinational environment, for example, ISO standards and IEEE software engineering standards. *See also International Organization for Standardization (ISO).*

interrater agreement — In software process assessment, the degree of agreement between different process assessors.

IPD CMM (Integrated Product Development CMM) — *See Integrated Product Development CMM.*

ISO — This is the short title for the International Organization for Standardization. It is not an acronym. "ISO" is a word, derived from the Greek *isos* meaning "equal," that is the root of the prefix "iso-," which occurs in a host of terms, such as "isometric" (of equal measure or dimensions) and "isonomy" (equality of laws, or of people before the law).

The name ISO is used around the world to denote the organization, thus avoiding the plethora of acronyms resulting from the translation of "International Organization for Standardization" into the different national languages of members, for example, "IOS" in English, "OIN" in French (from *Organisation internationale de normalisation*). Whatever the country, the short form of the Organization's name is always ISO.

ISO Standard 9000-1:1994 — *Quality Management and Quality Assurance Standards — Part 1: Guidelines for Selection and Use.*

ISO Standard 9000-2:1997 — *Quality Management and Quality Assurance S— Part 2: Generic Guidelines for the Application of ISO 9001, ISO 9002, and ISO 9003.*

ISO Standard 9000-3:1997 — *Quality Management and Quality Assurance Standards — Part 3: Guidelines for the Application of ISO Standard 9001:1994 to the Development, Supply, Installation and Maintenance of Computer Software.*

ISO Standard 9001: 1994 — *Quality Systems — Model for Quality Assurance in Design, Development, Production, Installation, and Servicing.*

ISO Standard 9004-2:1991 — *See BS 5750.*

ISO/IEC JTC1/SC7 — Joint Technical Committee One Information Technology/SC 7 Subcommittee on Software Engineering (a combined ISO and IEC committee).

ISO/IEC Standard 12119:1994 — *ISO/EIA Standard on Information Technology — Software Packages — Quality Requirements and Testing.*

ISO/IEC Standard 12207:1995 — *Information Technology — Software Life Cycle Processes.*

ISO/IEC Standard 14598-1:1999 — *Information Technology — Software Product Evaluation — Part 1: General Overview.*

ISO/IEC Standard 14598-2:2000 — *Software Engineering — Product Evaluation — Part 2: Planning and Management.*

ISO/IEC Standard 14598-3:2000 — *Software Engineering — Product Evaluation — Part 3: Process for Developers.*

ISO/IEC Standard 14598-4:1999 — *Software Engineering — Product Evaluation — Part 4: Process for Acquirers.*

ISO/IEC Standard 14598-5:1998 — *Information Technology — Software Product Evaluation — Part 5: Process for Evaluators.*

ISO/IEC Standard 9126:1991 — *Information Technology; Software Product Evaluation; Quality Characteristics and Guidelines for Their Use.*

ISO/IEC Standard Guide 2:1996 — *General Terms and Their Definitions Concerning Standardization and Related Activities, 1996*

ISO/IEC Standard TR 15504-1:1998 — *Information Technology — Software Process Assessment — Part 1: Concepts and Introductory Guide.*

ISO/IEC Standard TR 15504-2:1998 — *Information Technology — Software Process Assessment — Part 2: A Reference Model for Processes and Process Capability.*

ISO/IEC Standard TR 15504-3:1998 — *Information Technology — Software Process Assessment — Part 3: Performing an Assessment.*

ISO/IEC Standard TR 15504-4:1998 — *Information Technology — Software Process Assessment — Part 4: Guide to Performing Assessments.*

ISO/IEC Standard TR 15504-5:1999 — *Information Technology — Software Process Assessment — Part 5: An Assessment Model and Indicator Guidance.*

ISO/IEC Standard TR 15504-6:1998 — *Information Technology — Software Process Assessment — Part 6: Guide to Competency of Assessors.*

ISO/IEC Standard TR 15504-7:1998 — *Information Technology — Software Process Assessment — Part 7: Guide for Use in Process Improvement.*

ISO/IEC Standard TR 15504-8:1998 — *Information Technology — Software Process Assessment — Part 8: Guide for Use In Determining Supplier Process Capability.*

ISO/IEC Standard TR 15504-9:1998 — *Information Technology — Software Process Assessment — Part 9: Vocabulary.*

IUSware — This is a methodology designed to evaluate software products in a formal and rigorous way.

key practices — In the capability maturity model, the infrastructures, and activities that contribute most to the effective implementation and institutionalization of a key process area. [CMU/SEI-93-TR-25]

key process area — In a capability maturity model, a cluster of related activities that, when performed collectively, achieve a set of goals considered important for establishing process capability. The key process areas have been defined to reside at a single maturity level. They are the areas identified by the

SEI to be the principal building blocks to help determine the software process capability of an organization and understand the improvements needed to advance to higher maturity levels.

- The Level 2 key process areas in the CMM are requirements management, software project planning, software project tracking and oversight, software subcontract management, software quality assurance, and software configuration management.

- The Level 3 key process areas in the CMM are organization process focus, organization process definition, training program, integrated software management, software product engineering, intergroup coordination, and peer reviews.

- The Level 4 key process areas are quantitative process management and software quality management.

- The Level 5 key process areas are defect prevention, technology change management, and process change management. [CMU/SEI-93-TR-25]

language — A systematic means of communicating ideas by the use of conventionalized signs, sounds, gestures, or marks as well as rules for the formation of admissible expressions. *See also programming language.* [ANSI/IEEE Standard 729-1983]

lead assessor — *See assessor.*

life cycle — *See software life cycle.*

life cycle model — A framework containing the processes, activities, and tasks involved in the development, operation, and maintenance of a software product, spanning the life of the system from the definition of its requirements to the termination of its use. [IEEE/EIA Std 12207.2-1997]

maintainability — In software, a set of attributes that bears on the effect needed to make specified modifications. [ISO/IEC Std 9126:1991]

maintainer — An organization that performs maintenance activities. [IEEE/EIA Std 12207.2-1997]

maintenance — The process of modifying a software system or component after delivery to correct faults, improve performance or other attributes, or adapt to a changed environment. [ANSI/IEEE Std 610.12-1990] [CMU/SEI-93-TR-25]

managed and controlled — The process of identifying and defining software work products that are not part of a baseline and, therefore, are not placed under configuration management but that must be controlled for the project to proceed in a disciplined manner. "Managed and controlled" implies that the version of the work product in use at a given time (past or present) is known (i.e., version control), and changes are incorporated in a controlled manner (i.e., change control). [CMU/SEI-93-TR-25]

managed level — *See Maturity Level 4.* [CMU/SEI-93-TR-25]

managed maturity level — *See Maturity Level 4.*

manager — A role that encompasses providing technical and administrative direction and control to individuals performing tasks or activities within the manager's area of responsibility. The traditional functions of a manager include planning, staffing, organizing, directing, and controlling work within an area of responsibility.

mark of conformity — In certification, a protected mark, applied or issued under the rules of a certification system, indicating that adequate confidence is provided that the relevant product, process, or service is in conformity with a specified standard or other normative document. [ISO/IEC Std Guide 2:1996]

mature software organization — In a capability maturity model, a mature software organization is a software development organization that is highly rated [usually at Level 3 or higher].

maturity — (1) The degree of experience, capability, seasoning, level headedness, judgment, and responsibility exercised by an individual or organization. 2. In a capability maturity model, the level of software maturity. *See also mature software organization.*

maturity level — A well-defined evolutionary plateau toward achieving a mature software process. The five maturity levels in the SEI's capability maturity model are *initial, repeatable, defined, managed,* and *optimizing.* [CMU/SEI-93-TR-25]

Maturity Level 1 — In the capability maturity model (CMM), Maturity Level 1 is the initial level. At the initial level, the organization typically does not provide a stable environment for developing and maintaining software. When an organization lacks sound management practices, the benefits of good software engineering practices are undermined by ineffective planning and reaction-driven commitment systems. [CMU/SEI-93-TR-25]

Maturity Level 2 — In the capability maturity model, Maturity Level 2 is the repeatable level. At the repeatable level, policies for managing a software project and procedures to implement those policies are established. Planning and managing new projects is based on experience with similar projects. An objective in achieving Maturity Level 2 is to institutionalize effective management processes for software projects, which allow organizations to repeat successful practices developed on earlier projects, although the specific processes implemented by the projects may differ. [CMU/SEI-93-TR-25]

Maturity Level 3 — In the capability maturity model, Maturity Level 3 is the defined level. At the defined level, the standard process for developing and maintaining software across the organization is documented, including both software engineering and management processes, and these processes are integrated into a coherent whole. This standard process is referred to throughout the CMM as the organization's standard software process. [CMU/SEI-93-TR-25]

Maturity Level 4 — In the capability maturity model, Maturity Level 4 is the managed level. At the managed level, the organization sets quantitative quality goals for both software products and processes. Productivity and quality are measured for important software process activities across all projects as part of an organizational measurement program. An organization-wide software process database is used to collect and analyze the data available from the projects. [CMU/SEI-93-TR-25]

Maturity Level 5 — In the capability maturity model, Maturity Level 5 is the optimizing level. At the optimizing level, the entire organization is focused on continuous process improvement. The organization has the means to identify weaknesses and strengthen the process proactively, with the goal of preventing the occurrence of defects. Data on the effectiveness of the software process are used to perform cost–benefit analyses of new technologies and proposed changes to the organization's software process. Innovations that exploit the best software engineering practices are identified and transferred throughout the organization. [CMU/SEI-93-TR-25]

maturity model — A model of an organization that can represent various stages of process maturity. *See also capability maturity model, mature software organization, maturity, software process maturity.*

maturity profile — A profile of national and international software development organizations reflecting their process maturity. As an example, the August 1999 summary of SEI results showed that 43% of organizations assessed were at the initial level, 34% at the repeatable level, 17% at the defined level, 4% at the managed level, and 1% at the optimizing level of the SW-CMM.

maturity questionnaire — A set of questions about the software process that sample the key practices in each key process area of the CMM. The maturity questionnaire is used as a springboard to appraise the capability of an organization or project to execute a software process reliably. [CMU/SEI-93-TR-25] In the first public version of CMM, the maturity questionnaire was concerned with the maturity of the software process (principally how well it was defined and controlled). *Contrast with technology questionnaire.*

mean time between failures (MTBF) — The expected or observed time between consecutive failures in a system component. [ANSI/IEEE Std 610.12-1990]

mean time to repair (MTTR) — The expected or observed time required to repair a system or component and return it to normal operation. [ANSI/IEEE Std 610.12-1990]

measure (noun) — The number or category assigned to an attribute of an entity by making a measurement of, for example, source lines of code or document pages of design. [ISO/IEC Standard 14598-1:1998]

measure (verb) — To make a measurement. [ISO/IEC Standard 14598-1:1998]

measurement — The dimension, capacity, quantity, or amount of something (e.g., 300 source lines of code or 7 document pages of design). [CMU/SEI-93-TR-25]

measurement and analysis — In a capability maturity model, the description of the need to measure the process and analyze the measurements. Measurement and analysis typically include examples of the measurements that could be taken to determine the status and effectiveness of the activities performed. *See also common feature.* [CMU/SEI-93-TR-25]

method — A reasonably complete set of rules and criteria that establish a precise and repeatable way of performing a task and arriving at a desired result. [CMU/SEI-93-TR-25]

methodology — A collection of methods, procedures, and standards that defines an integrated synthesis of engineering approaches to the development of a product. [CMU/SEI-93-TR-25]

metric — The defined measurement method and the measurement scale. [ISO/IEC 14598-1:1998]

MicroScope — MicroScope is a commercial software quality evaluation method. This approach was introduced by DELTA Software Engineering in 1991. MicroScope is based on the results of the SCOPE project and follows ICE/IEC 9126 and ISO./IEC 14598-5. The MicroScope evaluations are being used to state the conformance to a specified external standard or regulation and to validate that the level of documentation and safety for a software product is satisfactory. [Bøegh, 1999]

milestone — A scheduled event for which some individual is accountable and that is used to measure progress. [CMU/SEI-93-TR-25]

moderator — An individual specifically trained and qualified to plan, organize, and lead a peer review. [CMU/SEI-93-TR-25]

monitoring — An examination of the status of the activities of a supplier and of their results by the acquirer or a third party. [IEEE/EIA Std 12207.2-1997]

MTBF — *See mean time between failures.*

MTTR — *See mean time to repair.*

mutation testing — A testing methodology in which two or more program mutations are executed using the same test cases to evaluate the ability of the test cases to detect differences in the mutations. [ANSI/IEEE Std 610.12-1990]

NACCB (National Accreditation Council for Certification Bodies) — Now known as UKAS (United Kingdom Accreditation Service) — *see entry for UKAS.*

National Accreditation Council for Certification Bodies — *See NACCB (National Accreditation Council for Certification Bodies).*

new work item — A proposal for a new standardization project to be created. The proposal has to be accepted by formal ballot and at least six countries must be prepared to participate in the new project for the project to go ahead.

nondeliverable item — Hardware or software product that is not required to be delivered under the contract but may be employed in the development of a software product. [IEEE/EIA Std 12207.2-1997]

nontechnical requirement — Agreements, conditions, and/or contractual terms that affect and determine the management activities of a software project. [CMU/SEI-93-TR-25]

objective evidence — Qualitative or quantitative information, records, or statements of fact pertaining to the characteristics of an item or service or to the existence and implementation of a process element, that is based on observation, measurement, or testing and that can be verified. [ISO/IEC Standard TR 15504-9:1998]

object-oriented approach to software development — *See object-oriented development.*

object-oriented development — A software engineering methodology in which the system is viewed as a collection of objects, attributes of objects, operations on the objects, and messages that are passed from object to object.

off-the-shelf — *See off-the-shelf product.*

off-the-shelf product — Product that is already developed and available, usable either "as is" or with modification. [IEEE/EIA Std 12207.2-1997]

operational software — The software that is intended to be used and operated in a system when it is delivered to its customer and deployed in its intended environment. [CMU/SEI-93-TR-25]

operator — An individual, group, or organization that operates a system. [IEEE/EIA Std 12207.2-1997]

optimizing — In software process improvement, continuous process improvement is enabled by quantitative feedback from the process and from piloting innovative ideas and technologies. [CMU/SEI-93-TR-25]

optimizing level — *See Maturity Level 5.* [CMU/SEI-93-TR-25]

optimizing maturity level — *See Maturity Level 5.*

ordinal scale — In scales of measurement, subjects are grouped into separate categories according to some order of value. *See also scale.*

organization — A unit within a company or other entity (e.g., government agency or branch of service) within which many projects are managed as a whole. All projects within an organization share a common top-level manager and common policies. [CMU/SEI-93-TR-25]

organization's measurement program — The set of related elements for addressing an organization's measurement needs. It includes the definition of organization-wide measurements, methods, and practices for collecting organizational measurement data, methods, and practices for analyzing organizational measurement data, and measurement goals for the organization. [CMU/SEI-93-TR-25]

organization's software process assets — A collection of entities, maintained by an organization, for use by projects in developing, tailoring, maintaining, and implementing their software processes. These software process assets typically include:

- The organization's standard software process,

- Descriptions of the software life cycles approved for use,

- The guidelines and criteria for tailoring the organization's standard software process,

- The organization's software process database, and

- A library of software process-related documentation.

Any entity that the organization considers useful in performing the activities of process definition and maintenance could be included as a process asset. [CMU/SEI-93-TR-25]

organization's software process database — A database established to collect and make available data on the software processes and resulting software work products of an organization, particularly as they relate to the organization's standard software process. The database contains or references both the actual measurement data and the related information needed to understand the measurement data and assess it for reasonableness and applicability. Examples of process and work product data include estimates of software size, effort, and cost; actual data on software size, effort, and cost; productivity data; peer review coverage and efficiency; and number and severity of defects found in the software code. [CMU/SEI-93-TR-25]

organization's standard software process — The operational definition of the basic process that guides the establishment of a common software process across the software projects in an organization. It describes the fundamental software process elements that each software project is expected to incorporate into its defined software process. It also describes the relationships (e.g., ordering and interfaces) between these software process elements. [CMU/SEI-93-TR-25]

orientation — An overview or introduction to a topic for those overseeing or interfacing with the individuals responsible for performing in the topic area. *Contrast with training.* [CMU/SEI-93-TR-25]

Pareto analysis — The analysis of defects by ranking causes from most significant to least significant. Pareto analysis is based on the principle, named after the 19th-century economist Vilfredo Pareto, that most effects come from relatively few causes, that is, 80% of the effects come from 20% of the possible causes. [CMU/SEI-93-TR-25]

pass/fail criteria — Decision rules used to determine whether a software item or a software feature passes or fails a test. [IEEE Std 829-1983]

P–CMM (People CMM) — *See People CMM (P-CMM).*

peer review — A review of a software work product, following defined procedures, by peers of the producers of the product for the purpose of identifying defects and improvements; examples are walkthroughs or inspections. *See also inspection, walkthrough.* [CMU/SEI-93-TR-25]

peer review leader — *See moderator.*

People CMM (P-CMM) — The P-CMM is a maturity framework that describes the key elements of managing and developing the workforce of an organization. It describes an evolutionary improvement path from an ad hoc approach to managing the workforce, to a mature, disciplined development of the knowledge, skills, and motivation of the people that fuels enhanced business performance. [SEI Web page]

people issue — Software development and maintenance issues that are particularly affected by humans; for example, creative aspects of development and maintenance.

periodic review/activity — A review or activity that occurs at specified regular time intervals. *Contrast with event-driven review/activity.* [CMU/SEI-93-TR-25]

personal process — *See personal software process (PSP).*

personal software process (PSP) — A software development process developed by Watts Humphrey at the SEI that is designed to help software engineers organize and plan their work, track their performance, manage software quality, and analyze and improve their personal process. The PSP has a well-defined process supported by process scripts, forms, data collection, and analysis techniques and tools.

PERT (Program Evaluation and Review Technique) — An activity network used in project management. A variation of the critical path method in which minimum, maximum, and most likely times are used to estimate the mean and standard deviation of each activity item. These values are used to compute estimated path times and to find the critical path, and the critical path values are used to find the standard deviation of the completion time for the whole project. PERT was developed by the U.S. Navy for managing the Polaris Fleet Ballistic Missile Program. Development began in 1957 and was completed in 1960.

PERT chart — *See PERT (Program Evaluation and Review Technique).*

Petri net — (1) An abstract, formal model of information flow, showing static and dynamic properties of a system. A Petri net is usually represented as a graph having two types of nodes (called places and transitions) connected by arcs, and markings (called tokens) indicating dynamic properties. [ANSI/IEEE Standard 729-1983] (1) A software engineering methodology used to analyze and represent real-time applications.

Phase of the SPICE trial — The SPICE trials were conducted in three phases, each with its own timescale and objectives.

Plan–Do–Check–Act cycle — A software quality improvement process developed by Shewhart in the 1930s. [Shewhart, 1931]

policy — A guiding principle, typically established by senior management that is adopted by an organization or project to influence and determine decisions. [CMU/SEI-93-TR-25]

portability — In software, a set of attributes that bears on the ability of the software to be transferred from one environment to another. [ISO/IEC Std 9126:1991]

practice — A software engineering or management activity that contributes to the creation of the output (work products) of a process or enhances the capability of a process. [ISO/IEC Std TR 15504-9:1998]

prime contractor — An individual, partnership, corporation, or association that administers a subcontract to design, develop, and/or manufacture one or more products. [CMU/SEI-93-TR-25]

procedure — A written description of a course of action to be taken to perform a given task. [ANSI/IEEE Std 610.12-1990]

process — (1) A sequence of steps performed for a given purpose; for example, the software development process. [ANSI/IEEE Std 610.12-1990] (2) A set of interrelated activities that transforms inputs into outputs. "Activities" can sometimes use resources. [IEEE/EIA Std 12207.2-1997]

process assessment — A disciplined evaluation of an organization's software processes against a model compatible with the ISO/IEC 15504 reference model. *See also software process assessment.* [ISO/IEC Std TR 15504-9:1998]

process assessment method — The stages through which software organizations evolve as they define, implement, measure, control, and improve their software processes. The CMM was the first process assessment method to be widely used and is still arguably the best-known model in use.

process attribute — A measurable characteristic of process capability applicable to any process. [ISO/IEC Std TR 15504-9:1998]

process attribute rating — A judgment of the level of achievement of the defined capability of the process attribute for the assessed process. [ISO/IEC Std TR 15504-9:1998]

process capability — (1) The ability of a process to achieve a required goal. [ISO/IEC Std TR 15504-9:1998] (2) The range of expected results that can be achieved by following a process. *Contrast with process performance.* [CMU/SEI-93-TR-25]

process capability baseline — A documented characterization of the range of expected results that would normally be achieved by following a specific process under typical circumstances. A process capability baseline is typically established at an organizational level. *Contrast with process performance baseline.* [CMU/SEI-93-TR-25]

process capability determination — A systematic assessment and analysis of selected software processes within an organization against a target capability, carried out with the aim of identifying the strengths, weaknesses, and risks associated with deploying the processes to meet a particular specified requirement [ISO/IEC Std TR 15504-9:1998]

process capability determination sponsor — The organization, part of an organization, or person initiating a process capability determination. [ISO/IEC Std TR 15504-9:1998]

process capability level — A point on the six-point (in the case of ISO/IEC 15504) ordinal scale (of process capability) that represents the increasing capability of the performed process; each level builds on the capability of the level below. [ISO/IEC Std TR 15504-9:1998]

process capability level rating — A representation of the achieved process capability level derived from the process attribute ratings for an assessed process. [ISO/IEC Std TR 15504-9:1998]

process category — A set of processes addressing the same general area of activity. The process categories, defined in ISO/IEC 15504, address five general areas of activity: customer-supplier, engineering, support, management, and organization. [ISO/IEC Std TR 15504-9:1998]

process context — In software process assessment, the set of factors, documented in the assessment input, that influences the judgment, comprehension, and comparability of process attribute ratings. [ISO/IEC Std TR 15504-9:1998]

process database — *See organization's software process database.*

process description — The operational definition of the major components of a process. Process description documentation specifies, in a complete, precise, verifiable manner, the requirements, design, behavior, or other characteristics of a process. It may also include the procedures for determining whether these provisions have been satisfied. Process descriptions may be found at the task, project, or organizational level. [CMU/SEI-93-TR-25]

process development — The act of defining and describing a process. It may include planning, architecture, design, implementation, and validation. [CMU/SEI-93-TR-25]

process dimension — The set of processes comprising the functional aspects of the reference model of processes and process capability. *Note* that the processes are grouped into categories of related activities. *See also process category.* [ISO/IEC Std TR 15504-9:1998]

process evaluation — A method that measures the performance of a process and investigates methods by which that performance can be improved. [ANSI/IEEE Std 610.12-1990]

process implementation workshop — A workshop whose aim is to provide training in the software process, software risk assessment, identification of critical aspects of the implementation program, and analysis of the gap between the existing and the standard software process. [McGill, 2001]

process improvement — Action taken to change an organization's processes so that they meet the organization's business needs and achieve its business goals more effectively. [ISO/IEC Std TR 15504-9:1998]

process improvement action — An action planned and executed to improve all or part of the software process. *Note* that a process improvement action can contribute to the achievement of more than one process goal. [ISO/IEC Std TR 15504-9:1998]

Process Improvement Experiment (PIE) — The PIE consists of European industrial experiments in the area of software process improvement, supported by ESSI.

process improvement program — All the strategies, policies, goals, responsibilities, and activities concerned with the achievement of specified improvement goals. *Note* that a process improvement program can span more than one complete cycle of process improvement. [ISO/IEC Std TR 15504-9:1998]

process improvement project — Any subset of the process improvement program that forms a coherent set of actions to achieve a specific improvement. [ISO/IEC Std TR 15504-9:1998]

process instance — A single instantiation of a process, where its purpose is fulfilled in terms of taking process inputs, performing a set of practices, and producing a set of process outputs. [El Emam, Drouin, and Melo, 1998]

process management — The direction, control, and coordination of work performed to develop a product or perform a service. An example is quality assurance. [IEEE Std 1002-1987]

process maturity — The extent to which a specific process is explicitly defined, managed, measured, controlled, and effective. [SEI Web site]

process maturity level — *See maturity level.*

process measurement — The set of definitions, methods, and activities used to take measurements of a process and its resulting products for the purpose of characterizing and understanding the process. [CMU/SEI-93-TR-25]

process model — A model (or simplification) of a process, which may be descriptive or mathematical, that provides insights into the nature of the process and is useful for defining, describing, or analyzing the process.

process outcome — An observable result of the successful implementation of a process. *Note* that a list of the principal process outcomes forms part of the description of each process in the reference model. [ISO/IEC Std TR 15504-9:1998]

process performance — A measure of the actual results achieved by following a process. *Contrast with process capability.* [CMU/SEI-93-TR-25]

process performance attribute — In ISO/IEC 15504, an attribute that is a measure of process capability at Level 1.

process performance baseline — A documented characterization of the actual results achieved by following a process that is used as a benchmark for comparing actual process performance against expected process performance. A process performance baseline is typically established at the project level, although the initial process performance baseline will usually be derived from the process capability baseline. *Contrast with process capability baseline.* [CMU/SEI-93-TR-25]

process profile — The set of process attribute ratings for an assessed process. [ISO/IEC Std TR 15504-9:1998]

process program — The Software Process Program led by Watts Humphrey was responsible for developing the Capability Maturity Model for Software (SW-CMM). This SW-CMM was developed in the mid-1980s by the Software Engineering Institute. The purpose was to provide leadership in advancing the state-of-the-practice of software engineering to improve the quality of systems that depend on software.

process purpose — The high-level measurable objectives of performing the process and the likely outcomes of effective implementation of the process. [ISO/IEC Std TR 15504-9:1998]

process quality — The degree to which the process possesses a desired combination of attributes that describe the degree to which the software will meet the expectations of the developer.

process resource attribute — In ISO/IEC 15504, an attribute that is a measure of process capability at Level 3.

process standard — Standard that specifies requirements to be fulfilled by a process, to establish its fitness for purpose. [ISO/IEC Std Guide 2:1996]

process tailoring — The activity of creating a process description by elaborating, adapting, and/or completing the details of process elements or other incomplete specifications of a process. Specific business needs for a project will usually be addressed during process tailoring. [CMU/SEI-93-TR-25]

process variation — The total effect of common cause variation and assignable cause variation. [Florac and Carleton, 1999]

product — The result of activities or processes. [ISO Std 8402:1986]

product certification — Certification that a product conforms to specified product characteristics. [SCOPE, 1989–1993]

product improvement — Software product improvement is concerned with finding ways to produce better products efficiently and effectively.

product management — The definition, coordination, and control of the characteristics of a product during its development cycle. An example is configuration management. [IEEE Std 1002-1987]

product quality — *See software product quality.*

product specification — (1) A document that specifies the design that production copies of a system or component must implement. *Note:* For software, this document describes the as-built version of the software. (2) A document that describes the characteristics of a planned or existing product for consideration by potential customers or users. [ANSI/IEEE Std 610.12]

product standard — A standard that specifies requirements to be fulfilled by a product or a group of products to establish its fitness for purpose. [ISO/IEC Std Guide 2:1996]

profile — A comparison, usually in graphic form, of plans or projections versus actuals, typically charted over a period of time. [CMU/SEI-93-TR-25]

programming language — In computer science, a computer language that allows a human to communicate with a computer. *See also language.*

project — An undertaking requiring concerted effort that is focused on developing and/or maintaining a specific product. The product may include hardware, software, and other components. Typically, a project has its own funding, cost accounting, and delivery schedule. [CMU/SEI-93-TR-25] *Note:* A project can include process improvement projects.

project manager — The role with total business responsibility for an entire project; the individual who directs, controls, administers, and regulates a project building a software or hardware/software system. The project manager is the individual ultimately responsible to the customer. [CMU/SEI-93-TR-25]

project software manager — The role with total responsibility for all the software activities for a project. The project software manager is the individual the project manager deals with in terms of software commitments and who controls all the software resources for a project. [CMU/SEI-93-TR-25]

project's defined software process — The operational definition of the software process used by a project. The project's defined software process is a well characterized and understood software process, described in terms of software standards, procedures, tools, and methods. It is developed by tailoring the organization's standard software process to fit the specific characteristics of the project. *See also organization's standard software process, effective process, and well-defined process.* [CMU/SEI-93-TR-25]

proof of correctness — (1) A formal technique used to prove mathematically that a computer program satisfies its specified requirements. (2) A proof that results from applying the technique in (1). [ANSI/IEEE Std 610.12-1990]

proposed capability — The process capability that the organization proposes to bring to bear in meeting the specified requirement. For core process capability determination, the proposed capability is the organization's current assessed capability, whereas for extended process capability determination, the proposed capability is either an enhanced capability or a constructed capability. [ISO/IEC Std TR 15504-9:1998]

proposed draft technical report — A stage in the development of an ISO technical report.

provisional assessor — A person who has the skills and competencies required to carry out assessments under the guidance and supervision of a competent assessor. [ISO/IEC Std TR 15504-9:1998]

PSP — *See personal software process (PSP).*

purpose built software — Software that has been designed and developed to meet a specific need [British usage]. *Contrast with software package.*

qualification — The process of determining whether a system or component is suitable for operational use. [ANSI/IEEE Std 610.12-1990]

qualification requirement — A set of criteria or conditions that have to be met in order to qualify a software product as complying with its specifications and being ready for use in its target environment. [IEEE/EIA Std 12207.2-1997]

qualification testing — Testing, conducted by the developer and witnessed by the acquirer (as appropriate), to demonstrate that the software product meets its specifications and is ready for use in its target environment. [IEEE/EIA Std 12207.2-1997]

quality — (1) The degree to which a system, component, or process meets specified requirements. (2) The degree to which a system, component, or process meets customer or user needs or expectations. [ANSI/IEEE Std 610.12-1990]

quality assurance — *See software quality assurance.*

quality attribute — A feature or characteristic that affects an item's quality. *Note:* In a hierarchy of quality attributes, higher-level attributes may be called "quality factors" and lower level attributes called "quality attributes." *See also internal and external attributes.* [ANSI/IEEE Std 610.12-1990]

quality carrying attribute — *See quality attribute.*

quality defect — An unintentional condition in a hardware/software system that, when encountered, may cause the system to have reduced quality factors. *See also quality, defect.*

quality evaluation — In software, the process that comprises validation, verification, measurement, and assessment of software. [SCOPE, 1989–1993]

quality factor — *See quality attribute.*

quality in use — The extent to which a product used by specified users meets their needs to achieve specified goals with effectiveness, productivity, and satisfaction in specified contexts of use. The term *usability* refers to the software quality characteristic described in ISO/IEC Std 9126:1991. [ISO/IEC Std 14598-1:1998]

quality management — All activities of the overall management function that determine the quality policy, objectives, and responsibilities and implement them by means such as quality planning, quality control, quality assurance, and quality improvement, within the quality system. [ISO Std 8402:1986]

quality metric — (1) A quantitative measure of the degree to which an item possesses a given quality attribute. (2) A function whose inputs are software data and whose output is a single numerical value that can be interpreted as the degree to which the software possesses a given quality attribute. [ANSI/IEEE Std 610.12-1990]

quality model — The set of characteristics and the relationships between them that provide the basis for specifying quality requirements and evaluating quality. [ISO/IEC Std 14598-1:1998]

quality modeling — The mapping of high-level quality characteristics onto low-level quality criteria and/or metrics. [SCOPE, 1989–1993]

quality system — The organizational structure, responsibilities, procedures, processes, and resources needed to implement quality management. [ISO Std 8402:1986]

quality-in-use metric — A measure of the extent to which a product meets the needs of specific users to achieve specified goals with effectiveness, productivity, safety, and satisfaction in a specified context of use. [ISO 14598-1:1998]

quantitative control — Any quantitative or statistically based technique appropriate for analyzing a software process, identifying special causes of variations in the performance of the software process, and bringing the performance of the software process within well-defined limits. [CMU/SEI-93-TR-25]

rating — The action of mapping the measured value to the appropriate rating level. Used to determine the rating level associated with the software for a specific quality characteristic. [ISO/IEC Std 14598-1:1998]

rating level — A scale point on an ordinal scale that is used to categorize a measurement scale. [ISO/IEC Std 14598-1:1998]

reference model — In standards development, a framework within which every other standard will be formulated. [Hall, 1989]

release — A particular version of a configuration item that is made available for a specific purpose (for example, test release). [IEEE/EIA Std 12207.2-1997]

reliability — In software, a set of attributes that bears on the capability of software to maintain its level of performance under stated conditions for a stated period of time. [ISO/IEC Std 9126:1991]

reliability growth — The improvement in reliability that results from correction of faults. [ANSI/IEEE Std 610.12-1990]

repeatable — In CMM, basic project management processes are established to track cost, schedule, and functionality. The necessary process discipline is in place to repeat earlier successes on projects with similar applications. [CMU/SEI-93-TR-25]

repeatable level — *See Maturity Level 2.*

repeatable maturity level — *See Maturity Level 2.*

request for proposal — A document used by the acquirer as the means to announce its intention to potential bidders to acquire a specified system, software product, or software service. *See also request for tender.* [IEEE/EIA Std 12207.2-1997]

request for tender — *Synonymous with request for proposal* [British usage]

required training — Training designated by an organization as required for performance of a specific role. [CMU/SEI-93-TR-25]

requirements management — In system/software system engineering, the process of controlling the identification, allocation, and flowdown of requirements from the system level to the module or part level, including interfaces, verification, modifications, and status monitoring.

retirement — (1) Withdrawal of active support by the operation and maintenance organization. (2) Partial or total replacement by a new system, or installation of an upgraded system. [IEEE/EIA Std 12207.2-1997]

return on investment (ROI) — In the context of process improvement, ROI is defined as the difference between the financial benefits from process improvement and the original investment in process improvement.

review process — In system/software system engineering, a formal meeting at which a product or document is presented to the user, customer, or other interested parties for comment and approval. It can be a review of the management and technical progress of the hardware/software development project.

risk — The possibility of suffering loss. [CMU/SEI-93-TR-25]

risk management — An approach to problem analysis that weighs risk in a situation by using risk probabilities to give a more accurate understanding of the risks involved. Risk management includes risk identification, analysis, prioritization, and control. [CMU/SEI-93-TR-25]

risk management plan — The collection of plans that describe the risk management activities to be performed on a project. [CMU/SEI-93-TR-25]

roadmap — A device used by the Trillium model that leads from one level to another, as distinct from the key process areas emphasized in the CMM.

ROI — *See return on investment (ROI).*

role — A unit of defined responsibilities that may be assumed by one or more individuals. [CMU/SEI-93-TR-25]

root cause analysis — Analysis of the original or basic cause of a software error, fault, or failure.

S4S — Acronym for "SPICE for Space." This is a method that aims to encourage the production of the best possible software products and services within the European space industry.

SA-CMM (Software Acquisition CMM) — *See Software Acquisition CMM (SA-CMM).*

scale — A set of values with defined properties. Examples of types of scales are a nominal scale, which corresponds to a set of categories; an ordinal scale, which corresponds to an ordered set of scale points; an interval scale, which corresponds to an ordered scale with equidistant scale points; and a ratio scale, which not only has equidistant scale points but also possesses an absolute zero. Metrics using nominal or ordinal scales produce qualitative data, and metrics using interval and ratio scales produce quantitative data. [ISO/IEC 14598-1-1998]

SCE — Acronym for software capability evaluation.

SCM — Acronym for software configuration management.

SCOPE — Acronym for Software Certification Programme for Europe, ESPRIT Programme.

SDCE (Software Development Capability Evaluation) — The SDCE is a structured methodology for assessing an organization's ability to develop software for mission-critical computer resources. The primary purpose of the SDCE is to reduce acquisition risk for software-intensive systems. The SDCE is conducted as an integral part of the source selection process and addresses each offerer's ability to develop the software required by a specific request for proposal (RFP). The evaluation covers the total software development process, including systems and software engineering, management, quality, product control, organizational support, tools, facilities, and personnel experience and qualifications. Reduction of risk to the government is achieved by increasing the probability of selecting a fully capable offerer with the capacity to develop software consistent with the RFP requirements and program baselines, by early and comprehensive visibility into the offerer's proposed capabilities, and by ensuring contractual commitment by the offerer to use the processes proposed. [Software Productivity Consortium Web site]

SE-CMM — *See Systems Engineering CMM (SE-CMM).*

security — The protection of information and data so that unauthorized persons or systems cannot read or modify them and authorized persons or systems are not denied access to them. [IEEE/EIA Std 12207.2-1997]

SEI — *See Software Engineering Institute (SEI).*

SEL — *See Software Engineering Laboratory (SEL).*

self-assessment — An assessment carried out by an organization to assess the capability of its own software process. [ISO/IEC Std TR 15504-4:1998]

senior manager — A management role at a high enough level in an organization that the primary focus is the long-term vitality of the organization, rather than short-term project and contractual concerns and pressures. In general, a senior manager for engineering would have responsibility for multiple projects. [CMU/SEI-93-TR-25]

SEPG — *See software engineering process group (SEPG).*

service — The results generated by activities at the interface between the supplier and the customer, and by supplier internal activities to meet the customer needs. [ISO Std 8402:1986]

Six Sigma — An approach to process improvement developed at Motorola. In a normal distribution of defects, a six-sigma deviation from the norm is interpreted to mean 3.4 defects per million opportunities. As applied at corporations like Motorola, it is interpreted to mean that the system being built has, for all practical purposes, no errors.

small software organization — A small software organization can be defined in terms of its staff size or in terms of the number of projects it has at one time. Typically, a small software organization would have fewer than 50 (or 100) staff and be working on no more than one or two projects. [Sanders, 2001].

software — (1) All or part of the programs, procedures, rules, and associated documentation of an information processing system. *Note:* Software is an intellectual creation that is independent of the medium on which it is recorded. [ISO/IEC 2382-1-1993] (2) Computer programs, procedures, and possibly associated documentation and data pertaining to the operation of a computer system. [ANSI/IEEE Std 610.12-1990]

Software Acquisition CMM (SA-CMM) — The SA-CMM is a capability maturity model for organizations that acquire or procure software-intensive systems. It is used to assess their maturity and help them improve the systems acquisition process for software intensive systems. The SA-CMM provides acquisition organizations with guidance on how to gain control of their software acquisition processes and helps them to:

- Enhance understanding of software life cycle activities in relation to system acquisitions,

- Benchmark the maturity level of the organization's acquisition process through assessment,

- Improve the acquisition processes for software intensive systems,

- Set senior management goals for improvement, and

- Enable prediction of potential acquisition process performance. [SEI Web site]

software architecture — The organizational structure of the software or module. [ANSI/IEEE Std 610.12-1990] [CMU/SEI-93-TR-25]

software baseline audit — An examination of the structure, contents, and facilities of the software baseline library to verify that baselines conform to the documentation that describes the baselines. [CMU/SEI-93-TR-25]

software baseline library — The contents of a repository for storing configuration items and the associated records. [CMU/SEI-93-TR-25]

software build — An operational version of a software system or component that incorporates a specified subset of the capabilities that the final software system or component will provide. [ANSI/IEEE Std 610.12-1990]

software capability evaluation — An appraisal by a trained team of professionals, using a method such as the SEI software capability evaluation method, to identify contractors who are qualified to perform the software work, or monitor the state of the software process used on an existing software effort. *See also software process assessment.* [CMU/SEI-93-TR-25]

software configuration control board (CCB) — A group responsible for evaluating and approving or disapproving proposed changes to configuration items and for ensuring implementation of approved changes. [CMU/SEI-93-TR-25]

software configuration management (SCM) — In software engineering, the discipline of identifying the configuration of a software system at discrete points in time with the purpose of systematically controlling changes to the software configuration and maintaining the integrity and traceability of the configuration throughout the system life cycle.

software development — The process by which user needs are translated into software requirements, software requirements are translated into design, the design is implemented in code, and the code is tested, documented, and certified for operational use. *See also software engineering.* [Dorfman, 1990]

software development environment — In software engineering, a coordinated collection of software tools, techniques, and methods organized to support some approach to software development or conform to some software process model.

software development plan — The collection of plans that describe the activities to be performed for the software project. It governs the management of the activities performed by the software engineering group for a software project. It is not limited to the scope of any particular planning standard, such as IEEE/EIA Std 12207 and IEEE Std1058, which may use similar terminology. [CMU/SEI-93-TR-25]

software development process — The process by which user needs are translated into a software product. The process involves translating user needs into software requirements, transforming the software requirements into design, implementing the design in code, testing the code, and, sometimes, installing and checking out the software for operational use. *Note:* These activities may overlap or be performed iteratively. [ANSI/IEEE Std 610.12-1990]

Software Diagnostic — The Software Diagnostic is a software process improvement system that was developed for use by "small" software development organizations in Scotland. The development of the Software Diagnostic was originally sponsored by the Scottish Development Agency, a U.K. government body concerned with economic development in Scotland. It has been extensively applied by Compita, a private company based near Edinburgh in Scotland.

software engineering — (1) The practical application of computer science, management, and other sciences to the analysis, design, construction, and maintenance of software and its associated documentation. (2) An engineering science that applies the concept of analysis, design, coding, testing, documentation, and management to the successful completion of large, custom-built computer programs. (3) The systematic application of methods, tools, and techniques to achieve a stated requirement or objective for an effective and efficient software system.

software engineering group — The collection of individuals (both managers and technical staff) who have responsibility for software development and maintenance activities (i.e., requirements analysis, design, code, and test) for a project. Groups performing software-related work, such as the software quality assurance group, the software configuration management group, and the software engineering process group, are not included in the software engineering group. [CMU/SEI-93-TR-25]

Software Engineering Institute (SEI) — A federally funded research and development center established in 1984 by the U.S. Department of Defense with a broad charter to address the transition of software engineering technology. The SEI is an integral component of Carnegie Mellon University and is sponsored by the Office of the Under Secretary of Defense for Acquisition, Technology, and Logistics.

Software Engineering Laboratory (SEL) — The Software Engineering Laboratory consists of a consortium including the University of Maryland, NASA's Goddard Space Flight Center, and Computer Sciences Corporation. The SEL's approach to software process improvement is heavily project based and is concerned with collecting data from ongoing projects (each viewed as an experiment) in order to assess the effectiveness of the software process used, and to identify process improvements to be applied to the processes used in connection with ongoing and follow-on projects. The SEL approach for process assessment/improvement is sometimes referred to as a bottom-up approach as distinct from the SEI's top-down approach.

software engineering process group (SEPG) — A group of specialists who facilitate the definition, maintenance, and improvement of the software process used by the organization. In the key practices, this group is generically referred to as "the group responsible for the organization's software process activities." [CMU/SEI-93-TR-25]

software engineering staff — The software technical people (e.g., analysts, programmers, and engineers), including software task leaders, who perform the software development and maintenance activities for the project, but who are not managers. [CMU/SEI-93-TR-25]

software engineering standard — Mandatory requirements employed and enforced to prescribe a disciplined uniform approach to software development.

software failure analysis — *See failure analysis.*

software integration — A process of putting together selected software components to provide the set or specified subset of the capabilities the final software system will provide. [CMU/SEI-93-TR-25]

software intensive system — A software intensive system is one in which the software portion is extensive enough that it defines the total system capability and represents the technical challenge to the developer. Examples typically include control hardware, computer hardware, communications, as well as software. Software may constitute either a minor or a major portion of the system.

software life cycle — The period of time that begins when a software product is conceived and ends when the software is no longer available for use. The software life cycle typically includes a concept phase, requirements phase, design phase, implementation phase, test phase, installation and checkout phase, operation and maintenance phase, and, sometimes, a retirement phase. [ANSI/IEEE Std 610.12-1990]

software manager — Any manager, at a project or organizational level, who has direct responsibility for software development and/or maintenance. [CMU/SEI-93-TR-25]

software plan — The collection of plans, both formal and informal, used to express how software development and/or maintenance activities will be performed. Such a collection could include a software development plan, software quality assurance plan, software configuration management plan, software test plan, risk management plan, and process improvement plan. [CMU/SEI-93-TR-25]

software process — A set of activities, methods, practices, and transformations that people use to develop and maintain software and the associated products (e.g., project plans, design documents, code, test cases, and user manuals). [CMU/SEI-93-TR-25]

software process assessment — An appraisal by a trained team of software professionals to assess the state of an organization's current software process, determine the high-priority software process-related issues facing an organization, and obtain the organizational support for software process improvement. [CMU/SEI-93-TR-25]

software process capability — *See process capability.* [CMU/SEI-93-TR-25]

software process description — The operational definition of a major software process component identified in the project's defined software process or the organization's standard software process. It documents, in a complete, precise, and verifiable manner the requirements, design, behavior, or other characteristics of a software process. *See also process description.* [CMU/SEI-93-TR-25]

software process element — A constituent element of a software process description. Each process element covers a well-defined, bounded, closely related set of tasks (e.g., software estimating element, software design element, coding element, and peer review element). The descriptions of the process elements may be templates to be filled in, fragments to be completed, abstractions to be refined, or complete descriptions to be modified or used unmodified. [CMU/SEI-93-TR-25]

software process framework — A software process framework provides a variety of methods, tools, procedures, document templates, and so forth for enacting the various work processes used in developing a software system.

software process improvement (SPI) — Action taken to change an organization's software processes so that they meet the organization's business needs and help it to achieve its business goals more effectively. [ISO/IEC Std TR 15504-9:1998]

Software Process Improvement and Capability dEtermination (SPICE) — *See SPICE.*

Software Process Improvement Network — *See SPIN (Software Process Improvement Network).*

software process improvement plan — A plan derived from the recommendations of a software process assessment that identifies the specific actions that will be taken to improve the software process and outlines the plans for implementing those actions. Sometimes referred to as an action plan. [CMU/SEI-93-TR-25]

software process improvement proposal — A documented suggestion for change to a process or process-related item that will improve software process capability and performance. *See also action proposal.* [CMU/SEI-93-TR-25]

software process maturity — The extent to which a specific process is explicitly defined, managed, measured, controlled, and effective. Maturity implies a potential for growth in capability and indicates both the richness of an organization's software process and the consistency with which it is applied in projects throughout the organization. [CMU/SEI-93-TR-25]

software process performance — *See process performance.*

software process programming — The use of a programming language to represent software process descriptions, which are static, and that can be distinguished from software processes, which are dynamic.

At the *Ninth International Conference in Software Engineering* held in 1987 (ICSE'87), Leon Osterweil's seminal paper "Software Processes Are Software Too," introduced the idea of software process programming. In his paper he used a Pascal-like language to show how the loops and conditional statements in the language could be readily be used to describe aspects of the software process. He also pointed out that the rule-based features of programming languages had a role to play in describing software processes, and proposed research to identify the language paradigm most suited to process description. [Osterweil, 1987]

software process-related documentation – Examples include documents and document fragments that are expected to be of use to future projects when they are tailoring the organization's standard software process. The examples may cover subjects such as a project's defined software process, standards, procedures, software development plans, measurement plans, and process training materials. [CMU/SEI-93-TR-25]

software product — The complete set, or any of the individual items of the set, of computer programs, procedures, and associated documentation and data designated for delivery to a customer or end user. *Contrast with software work product.* [ANSI/IEEE Std 610.12-1990]

software product quality — The totality of characteristics of the product that bear on its ability to satisfy stated and implied needs. [ISO/IEC 14598-1:1998]

software production — *See software development.*

Software Productivity Consortium (SPC) — An organization chartered by the aerospace companies that own it (called "member companies") to improve the productivity of software developers in those companies. Member companies include many of the top U.S. Department of Defense contractors, which have a combined income of more than US$100 billion and are responsible for major U.S. defense programs.

software project — An undertaking requiring concerted effort that is focused on analyzing, specifying, designing, developing, testing, and/or maintaining the software components and associated documentation of a system. A software project may be part of a project building a hardware/software system. [CMU/SEI-93-TR-25]

software proposal — In system/software engineering, a plan for accomplishing an engineering objective as proposed by a company or a development organization. It can be (1) in response to a formal request for proposal (RFP) where the RFP specifies the needs of a potential customer, (2) in response to informal, often verbal statements by a potential customer, or (3) unsolicited, in which a proposal is sent to a prospective customer by a software developer.

software quality — *See software product quality.*

software quality assurance — All the planned and systematic activities implemented within the quality system, and demonstrated as needed, to provide adequate confidence that an entity will fulfill requirements for quality. [IEEE/EIA Std 12207.2-1997]

software quality characteristic — A set of attributes of a software product by which its quality is described and evaluated. A software quality characteristic may be refined into multiple levels of subcharacteristics. [ISO/IEC Std 9126:1991]

software quality goal — Quantitative quality objectives defined for a software work product. [CMU/SEI-93-TR-25]

software quality management — The process of defining quality goals for a software product, establishing plans to achieve these goals, and monitoring and adjusting the software plans, work products, activities, and quality goals to satisfy the needs and desires of the customer and end users. [CMU/SEI-93-TR-25]

software requirement — A condition or capability that must be met by software needed by a user to solve a problem or achieve an objective. [ANSI/IEEE Std 610.12-1990]

software requirements specification — Documentation of the essential requirements (functions, performance, design constraints, and attributes) of the software and its external interfaces. [ANSI/IEEE 610.12]

software service — Performance of activities, work, or duties connected with a software product, such as its development, maintenance, and operation. [IEEE/EIA Std 12207.2-1997]

software system — A system consisting solely of software and possibly the computer equipment on which the software operates.

software tender — *Tender* is a British word that is synonymous with *proposal. See software proposal.*

software tool — A computer used in the development, testing, analysis, or maintenance of a program or its documentation. Examples include comparator, cross-reference generator, decompiler, driver, editor, flow charter, monitor, test case generator, and timing analyzer. [ANSI/IEEE Std 610.12-1990]

software unit — A separately compilable piece of code. [IEEE/EIA Std 12207.2-1997]

software work product — Any artifact created as part of defining, maintaining, or using a software process, including process descriptions, plans, procedures, computer programs, and associated documentation. It may or may not be intended for delivery to a customer or end user. *Contrast with software product.* [CMU/SEI-93-TR-25]

software-related group — A collection of individuals (both managers and technical staff) representing a software engineering discipline that supports, but is not directly responsible for, software development and/or maintenance. Examples of software engineering disciplines include software quality assurance and software configuration management. [CMU/SEI-93-TR-25]

SPA — Acronym for software process assessment. [CMU/SEI-93-TR-25]

special cause (of a defect) — A cause of a defect that is specific to some transient circumstance and not an inherent part of a process. Special causes provide random variation (noise) in process performance. *Contrast with common cause.* [CMU/SEI-93-TR-25]

specification — A document that specifies, in a complete, precise, and verifiable manner, the requirements, design, behavior, or other characteristics of a system or component, and, often, the procedures for determining whether these provisions have been satisfied. [ANSI/IEEE Std 610.12-1990]

SPI — *See software process improvement (SPI).*

SPICE — SPICE is a major international initiative to support the development of an International Standard for Software Process Assessment [ISO/IEC Std 15504]. The project has three principal goals:

- To develop a working draft for a standard for software process assessment,

- To conduct industry trials of the emerging standard, and

- To promote the technology transfer of software process assessment into the software industry worldwide. [SPICE Web site]

SPICE conformant assessment — An assessment using an assessment model that conforms to the ISO/IEC 15504 reference model.

SPICE for Space — *See S4S.*

SPICE trial — A trial software process assessment that uses a version of the ISO/IEC 15504 documents.

SPIN (Software Process Improvement Network) — SPIN groups have been set up throughout the world. These groups exist to allow the sharing of successful and unsuccessful experiences of software process improvement projects.

SPIRE handbook — A handbook written and edited by the European SPIRE project team to support software process improvement in small software organizations.

sponsor — *See assessment sponsor and process capability determination sponsor.* [ISO/IEC Std TR 15504-9:1998]

SQA — Acronym for software quality assurance. [CMU/SEI-93-TR-25]

SQUID — A European-supported project in the area of developing quality software. The SQUID method provides a means of modeling, measuring, and evaluating software quality during the development process. The SQUID toolset assists in quality specifications, quality planning, quality control, and quality evaluation. [Bøegh, 1999]

staff — The individuals, including task leaders, who are responsible for accomplishing an assigned function, such as software development or software configuration management, but who are not managers. [CMU/SEI-93-TR-25]

stage — A partition of the software effort that is of a manageable size and that represents a meaningful and measurable set of related tasks, which are performed by the project. A stage is usually considered a subdivision of a software life cycle and is often ended with a formal review prior to the onset of the following stage. [CMU/SEI-93-TR-25]

standard — *See software engineering standard.*

standard process — The operational definition of the basic process that guides the establishment of a common process in an organization. *Note* that a standard process describes the fundamental process elements that are expected to be incorporated into any defined process. It also describes the relationships (e.g., ordering and interfaces) between these process elements. *See also defined process.* [ISO/IEC Std TR 15504-9:1998]

standard software process — *See organization's standard software process.* [CMU/SEI-93-TR-25]

standards working group — An organization that has been chartered to develop a standard, normally under the sponsorship of a professional organization, a company or firm, a government agency, or a standards development organization.

statechart — A diagrammatic method of showing control flow in a process that is hierarchical and allows parallelism (and broadcasting).

statement of work — A document used by the acquirer as the means to describe and specify the tasks to be performed under the contract. [IEEE/EIA Std 12207.2-1997]

static analysis — The process of evaluating a system or component based on its form, structure, content, or documentation. *Contrast with dynamic analysis. See also inspection, walkthrough.* [ANSI/IEEE Std 610.12-1990]

statistical process control (SPC) — A process is under statistical process control if its future performance is predictable within established statistical limits. [Humphrey, 1989]

structured analysis (SA) — In software engineering (methodology), a state-of-the-art software analysis technique that uses dataflow diagrams (DFDs), data dictionaries, and processes descriptions to analyze and represent a software requirement.

structured analysis and design — *See structured analysis. See structured design.*

structured design — (1) In software engineering, a design technique that involves hierarchical partitioning of a modular structure in a top-down fashion, with emphasis on reduced coupling and strong cohesion. [DeMarco, 1979] (2) A disciplined approach to software design that adheres to a specified set of rules based on principles such as top-down design, stepwise refinement, and dataflow analysis. [ANSI/IEEE Standard 729-1983]

study period — In international standardization development, a period of study used to prepare a new work item proposal.

subcharacteristic — A refinement of a characteristic.

subcontract manager — A manager in the prime contractor's organization who has direct responsibility for administering and managing one or more subcontracts. [CMU/SEI-93-TR-25]

subcontractor — An individual, partnership, corporation, or association that contracts with an organization (i.e., the prime contractor) to design, develop, and/or manufacture one or more products. [CMU/SEI-93-TR-25]

supplier — (1) An organization that provides a product to the customer [ISO/IEC Std TR 15504-9:1998] (2) An organization that enters into a contract with the acquirer for the supply of a system, software product, or software service under the terms of the contract. [ISO/IEC Std 12207-1995]

SW-CMM model — *See capability maturity model (CMM).*

symbolic execution — A software analysis technique in which program execution is simulated using symbols, such as variable names, rather than actual values for input data, and program outputs are expressed as logical or mathematical expressions involving these symbols. [ANSI/IEEE Std 610.12-1990]

system — (1) A collection of components organized to accomplish a specific function or set of functions. [ANSI/IEEE Std 610.12-1990] (2) An integrated composite that consists of one or more of the processes, hardware, software, facilities, and people, and that provides the ability to satisfy a stated need or objective. [IEEE/EIA Std 12207.2-1997] (3) A collection of related elements related in such a way that allows the accomplishment of some tangible objective. [Pressman, 1982]

system engineering group — The collection of individuals (both managers and technical staff) who have responsibility for specifying the system requirements; allocating the system requirements to the hardware, software, and other components; specifying the interfaces between the hardware, software, and other components; and monitoring the design and development of these components to ensure conformance with their specifications. [CMU/SEI-93-TR-25]

system requirement — A condition or capability that must be met or possessed by a system or system component to satisfy a condition or capability needed by a user to solve a problem. [ANSI/IEEE Std 610.12-1990]

system requirements allocated to software — The subset of the system requirements that are to be implemented in the software components of the system. The allocated requirements are a primary input to the software development plan. Software requirements analysis elaborates and refines the allocated requirements and results in software requirements, which are documented. [CMU/SEI-93-TR-25]

Systems Engineering CMM (SE-CMM) — The SE-CMM describes the characteristics exhibited by a good systems engineering process. It is not a process, but a set of characteristics or requirements on systems engineering processes. These characteristics can be used as guidance in developing, improving, or self-appraising an organization's process.

SE-CMM was instituted in August 1993, in response to industry requests for assistance in coordinating and publishing a model analogous to the CMM for the systems engineering community.

The development effort was a collaboration among several organizations, including the SEI. [SEI Web site]

tailor — To modify a process, standard, or procedure to better match process or product requirements. [CMU/SEI-93-TR-25]

target capability — That process capability that the process capability determination sponsor judges will represent an acceptable process risk to the successful implementation of the specified requirement. [ISO/IEC Std TR 15504-9:1998]

target computer — The computer on which delivered software is intended to operate. *Contrast with host computer.* [CMU/SEI-93-TR-25]

task — (1) A sequence of instructions treated as a basic unit of work. [ANSI/IEEE Std 610.12-1990] (2) A well-defined unit of work in the software process that provides management with a visible checkpoint into the status of the project. Tasks have readiness criteria (preconditions) and completion criteria (postconditions). *Contrast with activity.* [CMU/SEI-93-TR-25]

task kick-off meeting — A meeting held at the beginning of a task of a project for the purpose of preparing the individuals involved to perform the activities of that task effectively. [CMU/SEI-93-TR-25]

task leader — The leader of a technical team for a specific task who has technical responsibility and provides technical direction to the staff working on the task. [CMU/SEI-93-TR-25]

team — A collection of people, often drawn from diverse but related groups, assigned to perform a well-defined function for an organization or a project. Team members may be part-time participants of the team and have other primary responsibilities. [CMU/SEI-93-TR-25]

team software process (TSP) — The TSP, developed by Watts Humphrey, is a software life cycle process based on the PSP that helps software engineering teams learn how to work effectively when developing a software product. The TSP has a well-defined process supported by process scripts, forms, and data collection and analysis techniques and tools.

technical report (type 2) or a TR-2 — A stage on the technical report route toward international standardization. An international standard is expected to be produced within 2 or 3 years of the production of a TR-2.

technical report route (toward international standardization) — A "fast track" method of producing an international standard. A technical report (type 2) is produced prior to a full international standard.

technical requirement — Those requirements that describe what the software must do and its operational constraints. Examples of technical requirements include functional, performance, interface, and quality requirements. [CMU/SEI-93-TR-25]

technology — The application of science and/or engineering in accomplishing some particular result. [CMU/SEI-93-TR-25]

technology questionnaire — In the first public version of CMM, the technology questionnaire was concerned with the extent to which advanced technology was used in the process. *Contrast with maturity questionnaire.*

test — Technical operation that consists of the determination of one or more characteristics of a given product, process, or service according to a specified procedure. [ISO/IEC Std Guide 2:1996]

test coverage — The extent to which the test cases test the requirements for the system or software product. [IEEE/EIA Std 12207.2-1997]

test criteria — The criteria that a system or component must meet in order to pass a given test. [ANSI/IEEE Std 610.12-1990]

test method — Specified technical procedure for performing a test. [ISO/IEC Std Guide 2:1996]

test report — Document that presents test results and other information relevant to a test. [ISO/IEC Std Guide 2:1996]

testability — (1) The degree to which a system or component facilitates the establishment of test criteria and the performance of tests to determine whether those criteria have been met. (2) The degree to which a requirement is stated in terms that permit establishment of test criteria and performance of tests to determine whether those criteria have been met. [ANSI/IEEE Std 610.12-1990]

testing — The process of operating a system or component under specified conditions, observing or recording the results, and making an evaluation of some aspect of the system or component. [ANSI/IEEE 610.12]

testing laboratory — A laboratory that performs tests. [ISO/IEC Std Guide 2:1996]

TickIT certification — A certification of compliance by a software organization with ISO/EIC Standard 9001 by accredited TickIT auditors.

tool — An instrument or device used to improve the effectiveness or efficiency of an action or task. In software engineering, a means of improving the intellectual capacity and capability of a software engineer in developing a software system. A software engineering tool can be either manual or automated. Examples of software engineering tools are structured analysis methods, FORTRAN compiler, and Microsoft Word.

traceability — The degree to which a relationship can be established between two or more products of the development process, especially products having a predecessor–successor or master–subordinate relationship with one another. [ANSI/IEEE Std 610.12-1990]

train — To make proficient with specialized instruction and practice. *See also orientation.* [CMU/SEI-93-TR-25]

training — In management (staffing), the process of developing knowledge on how to use, operate, or make something. Training is typically used to satisfy a short-term requirement for skilled personnel on a particular activity or task. *Contrast with orientation.*

training group — The collection of individuals (both managers and staff) who are responsible for coordinating and arranging the training activities for an organization. This group typically prepares and conducts most of the training courses and coordinates use of other training vehicles. [CMU/SEI-93-TR-25]

training program — The set of related elements that focuses on addressing an organization's training needs. It includes an organization's training plan, training materials, development of training, conduct of training, training facilities, evaluation of training, and maintenance of training records. [CMU/SEI-93-TR-25]

training waiver — A written approval exempting an individual from training that has been designated as required for a specific role. The exemption is granted because it has been objectively determined that the individual already possesses the needed skills to perform the role. [CMU/SEI-93-TR-25]

Trillium — A software process improvement scheme developed in 1991 by a partnership between Northern Telecom and Bell Northern Research, which was inspired by the SEI's CMM. Trillium is used for two purposes: (1) to assess a supplier's development process and (2) to make internal process improvements.

TSP — *See team software process (TSP).*

UKAS (United Kingdom Accreditation Service) — The sole national body recognized by the U.K. government for the accreditation of testing and calibration laboratories, certification, and inspection bodies. A not-for-profit company, limited by guarantee, UKAS operates under a memorandum of understanding with the government through the Department of Trade and Industry. [UKAS Web site]

unit — (1) A separately testable element specified in the design of a computer software component. (2) A logically separable part of a computer program. (3) A software component that is not subdivided into other components. [ANSI/IEEE Std 610.12-1990]

usability — In software, a set of attributes that bears on the effort needed for use and on the individual assessment of such use by a stated or implied set of users. [ISO/IEC Std 9126:1991]

user — An individual or organization that uses the operational system to perform a specific function. *Note:* The user may perform other roles such as acquirer, developer, or maintainer. *See also end user.* [IEEE/EIA Std 12207.2-1997]

validation — In verification and validation, a process for determining whether the requirements and the final, as-built system or software product fulfills its specific intended use. [IEEE/EIA Std 12207.2-1997, Para 6.5]

Value Added Software Information for Europe (VASIE) — *See VASIE (Value Added Software Information for Europe).*

VASIE (Value Added Software Information for Europe) — A dissemination activity evolving from process improvement experiments. VASIE uses the ESI Web site to make reports available to the public. VASIE's aim is to provide value-added information for the European software best practice repository and to permanently disseminate the validated Process Improvement Experiment results. All improvement projects are reviewed, categorized, and added continuously to the repository for dissemination.

verification — In verification and validation, a process for determining whether the software products of an activity fulfill the requirements or conditions imposed on them in the previous activities. [IEEE/EIA Std 12207.2-1997, Para 6.4]

verification and validation (V&V) — The process of determining whether the requirements for a system or components are complete and correct, the products of each development phase fulfill the requirements or conditions imposed by the previous phase, and the final system or component complies with specified requirements. [ANSI/IEEE Std 610.12-1990]

verifying implementation — In a capability maturity model, the steps to ensure that the activities are performed in compliance with the process that has been established. Verification typically encompasses reviews and audits by management and software quality assurance. *See also common feature.* [CMU/SEI-93-TR-25]

version — An identified instance of an item. Modification to a version of a software product, resulting in a new version, requires configuration management action. [IEEE/EIA Std 12207.2-1997]

waiver — *See training waiver.* [CMU/SEI-93-TR-25]

walkthrough — A static analysis technique in which a designer or programmer leads members of the development team and other interested parties through a segment of documentation or code, and the participants ask questions and make comments about possible errors, violation of development standards, and other problems. [ANSI/IEEE Std 610.12-1990]

well-defined process — A process that includes readiness criteria, inputs, standards, and procedures for performing the work, verification mechanisms (such as peer reviews), outputs, and completion criteria. *See also effective process.* [CMU/SEI-93-TR-25]

WG 10 — The working group of Subcommittee 7 of Joint Technical Committee 1 (JTC1) of ISO and IEC, responsible for software process assessment.

work product — An artifact associated with the execution of a process. *Note* that a work product might be used, produced, or changed by a process. [ISO/IEC Std TR 15504-9:1998]

work product management attribute — This is a Level 2 attribute of the SPICE software process improvement scheme.

working draft — A stage on the normal route toward international standardization. Normally the first complete set of standard documents is regarded as a working draft, and there is usually several working draft versions produced before the next stage (a committee draft) is produced. Working drafts are reviewed within the working group.

References

ANSI/IEEE Std 610.12-1990, *IEEE Standard Glossary of Software Engineering Terminology*, IEEE, New York, 1990.

ANSI/IEEE Std 729-1983, *IEEE Standard Glossary of Software Engineering Terminology,* IEEE, New York, 1983.

Bøegh, Jorgen, "Quality Evaluation of Software Products," *Software Quality Professional,* Vol. 1, 1999, pp. 26–37.

CMU/SEI-93-TR-24, Paulk, Mark C., Bill Curtis, Marybeth Chrissis, and Charles V. Weber, *Capability Maturity Model for Software, Version 1.1,* Software Engineering Institute, Carnegie Mellon University, Pittsburgh, PA 15213, February 1993.

CMU/SEI-93-TR-25, Mark C. Paulk, Charles V. Weber, Suzanne M. Garcia, Marybeth Chrissis, and Marilyn Bush, *Key Practices of the Capability Maturity Model, Version 1.1,* Software Engineering Institute, Carnegie Mellon University, Pittsburgh, PA 15213, February 1993.

DeMarco, T., *Structured Analysis and System Specification*, Prentice-Hall, Upper Saddle River, NJ, 1979.

Dorfman, M., "System and Software Requirements Engineering," in *System and Software Requirements Engineering*, R. H. Thayer and M. Dorfman (eds.), IEEE Computer Society Press, Los Alamitos, CA, 1990.

El Emam, K., J.-N. Drouin, and W. Melo, *SPICE: The Theory and Practice of Software Process Improvement and Capability Determination*, IEEE Computer Society Press, Los Alamitos, CA, 1999.

Fenton, N.E., *Software Metrics — A Rigorous Approach,* Chapman and Hall, London, 1991.

Florac, W.A., and A.D. Carleton, *Measuring the Software Process*, Addison-Wesley, Reading, MA, 1999.

Hall, P.A.V., "Software Development Standards," *Software Engineering Journal*, Vol. 4, No. 5, May 1989, pp. 143–147.

Humphrey, W.S., *Managing the Software Process*, Addison-Wesley, Reading, MA, 1989.

IEEE Std 1002-1987, *IEEE Standard Taxonomy for Software Engineering Standards*, IEEE, New York, 1987. (IEEE Std 1002-1987 was revised in 1992 and later withdrawn.)

IEEE Std 1012-1986, *IEEE Standard for Software Verification and Validation*, IEEE, New York, 1986. (IEEE Std 1012-1986 was superseded by IEEE Std 1012-1998.)

IEEE Std 829-1983, *IEEE Standard for Software Test Documentation*, IEEE, New York, 1983. (IEEE Std 829-1983 was superseded by IEEE Std 829-1998.)

IEEE/EIA Std 12207.2-1997 — *Guide for ISO/IEC 12207 lifecycle processes Implementation considerations,* IEEE, New York, 1997.

ISO Std 8402:1986, *Quality — Vocabulary,* ISO, Geneva, 1986. (a.k.a. BS 4778)

[ISO/IEC Std 2382-1:1993] *Information technology — Vocabulary — Part 1: Fundamental terms*

ISO/IEC Std 12207:1995 — *Information Technology — Software Life Cycle Processes.*

ISO/IEC Std 14598-1:1999, *Information Technology — Software Product Evaluation — Part 1: General Overview,* ISO/IEC, Geneva, 1999.

ISO/IEC Std 9126:1991, *Information Technology — Software Product Evaluation — Quality Characteristics and Guidelines for Their Use,* ISO/IEC, Geneva, 1991.

ISO/IEC Std Guide 2:1996: *General Terms and Their Definitions Concerning Standardization,* ISO/IEC, Geneva, 1996.

ISO/IEC Std TR 15504-2:1998 — *Information Technology — Software Process Assessment — Part 2: A Reference Model for Processes and Process Capability.*

ISO/IEC Std TR 15504-4:1998 — *Information Technology — Software Process Assessment — Part 4: Guide to Performing Assessments.*

ISO/IEC Std TR 15504-9:1998, *Information Technology — Software Process Assessment — Part 9: Vocabulary,* ISO/IEC, Geneva, 1998.

Kumar, K., and Jos Van Hillegersberg (eds.), "ERP Experiences and Evolution," *Communications of the ACM*, Vol. 43, No. 4, April 2000.

McGill, Sandra G., "Overcoming Resistance to Standard Processes or ... 'Herding Cats'," in *Software Process Improvem*ent, Robin B. Hunter and Richard H. Thayer (eds.), IEEE Computer Society Press, Los Alamitos, CA, 2001.

Osterweil, L.J., "Software Processes Are Software Too," presented at Ninth International Conference on Software Engineering, 1987.

Pressman, R.S., *Software Engineering: A Practitioner's Approach*, McGraw-Hill, New York,1982.

Roman, G.-C., "A Taxonomy of Current Issues in Requirements Engineering," *IEEE Computer*, Vol. 18, No. 5, April 1985, pp. 14-22.

Rout, Terence P., "The SPICE Approach to Software Process Improvement," in *Software Process Improvem*ent, Robin B. Hunter and Richard H. Thayer (eds.), IEEE Computer Society Press, Los Alamitos, CA, 2001.

Sanders, M., "SPICE for Small Companies," in *Software Process Improvement,* Robin B. Hunter and Richard H. Thayer (eds.), IEEE Computer Society Press, Los Alamitos, CA, 2001.

SCOPE: Software Certification Programme for Europe, ESPRIT programme, CEC, Brussels, 1989–1993.

Shewhart; W., *Economic Control of Quality of Manufactured Product*, Van Nostrand, New York, 1931.

Spire Project Team, *The SPIRE Handbook,* Centre for Software Engineering, Dublin, 1998.

Zahran, S., *Software Process Improvement*, Addison-Wesley, Reading, MA, 1998.

Robin B. Hunter, PhD

Robin B Hunter is a senior lecturer in the Computer Science Department in the University of Strathclyde in Glasgow, Scotland. He has been in this department for over thirty years, having previously been on the teaching staffs of the University of Glasgow and the University of Newcastle upon Tyne. He has B.Sc. and Ph. D. degrees, both from the University of Glasgow, and is a member of the IEEE Computer Society.

His principal interest is in software quality and he has researched and undertaken consultancy in both product and process aspects of software quality. He was a grant holder for the European union project SCOPE on the certification of software product quality based on the ISO/IEC 9126 quality factors. He also served as an adviser to a Brazilian government funded project concerned with software product and process quality, and was involved in a Royal Society funded joint project with a Russian colleague concerned with the definition of software product metrics. He has also advised on the setting up of a national software product certification scheme.

He has been involved in the SPICE (Software Process Improvement and Capability dEtermination) project which is supporting the development of the international standard ISO/IEC 15504 on software assessment, capability determination and process improvement. The SPICE project has been organizing extensive world wide trials of the emerging standard and Dr Hunter has been involved in the analysis of data collected from the SPICE trials. This work is ongoing (at the time of writing - 2001) and will continue until ISO/IEC 15504 is a full international standard.

He has published extensively on product and process aspects of software quality as well as in the area of language compilers, another of his areas of interest in which he has authored a number of text books. He is a member of the editorial board of the Software Quality Journal and has served on the program committee of a number of international conferences.

Richard H. Thayer, Ph.D.

Richard H. Thayer, Ph.D., is consultant in the field of software engineering and project management. Prior to this he was a Professor of Software Engineering at California State University, Sacramento, California, United States of America. Dr. Thayer travels widely where he consults and lectures on software engineering, project management, software engineering standards, software requirements engineering, and software quality assurance. He is a Visiting Researcher and Lecturer at the University of Strathclyde, Glasgow, Scotland. His technical interests lay in software project management and software engineering standards

Prior to this, he served over 20 years in the U.S. Air Force as a Senior Officer. His experience includes a variety of positions associated with engineering, computer programming, research, teaching, and management in computer science and data processing. His numerous positions include six years as a supervisor and technical leader of scientific programming groups, four years directing the U.S. Air Force R&D program in computer science, and six years of managing large data processing organizations.

Dr. Thayer is a Fellow of the IEEE, a member of the IEEE Computer Society, and the IEEE Software Engineering Standards Committee. He is a principle author for a Standard for a Concept of Operations (ConOps) document (IEEE std 1362-1998) and a principle author of the Standard for Software Project Management Plans (IEEE std 1058-1998)

He is also an Associate Fellow of the American Institute of Aeronautics and Astronautics (AIAA) where he served on the AIAA Technical Committee on Computer Systems, and he is a member of the Association for Computing Machinery (ACM). He is also a registered professional engineer.

He holds a BSEE degree and an MS degree from the University of Illinois at Urbana (1962) and a Ph.D. from the University of California at Santa Barbara (1979) each in Electrical Engineering.

He has edited and/or co-edited numerous tutorials for the IEEE Computer Society Press: Software Engineering Project Management (1997), Software Engineering (1997), Software Requirements Engineering (1997), and Software engineering -- A European Prospective (1992). He is the author of over 40 technical papers and reports on software project management, software engineering, and software engineering standards and is invited to speak at many national and international software engineering conferences and workshops.